S0-BBU-333

A General Introduction to the Bible

Revised and Expanded

A General Introduction to the Bible
Revised and Expanded

NORMAN L. GEISLER
and
WILLIAM E. NIX

MOODY PRESS
CHICAGO

The use of selected references from various versions of the Bible in this publication does not necessarily imply publisher endorsement of the versions in their entirety.

Library of Congress Cataloging in Publication Data

Geisler, Norman L.
A general introduction to the Bible.

Bibliography: p.
Includes indexes.
1. Bible—Introductions. I. Nix, William E.
II. Title.
BS475.2.G39 1986 220.6'1 86-5171
ISBN 0-8024-2916-5

4 5 6 7 Printing/RR/Year 91 90 89

Printed in the United States of America

To our wives,
BARBARA and EULAINE,
who have been
constant sources of encouragement
and assistance

Contents

Part Three:
Transmission of the Bible

Part Four:
Translation of the Bible

Photographs

Charts

Foreword to the Revised Edition

This book is a lifetime investment. It is one of the top fifteen books that ought to be in every Christian's library. For nearly two decades and twenty printings this work has been the standard in the field. It has had a significant influence in my own life, as well as the lives of scores of thousands who have purchased the book. What is now even better is that *General Introduction* has been thoroughly revised, expanded, and updated.

There is really no book like this one on the market that covers the whole gamut of topics in bibliology, including inspiration, Apocrypha, the process of copying, and the multitude of Bible translations. If you want to know how we got our Bible, how we know which books belong in it, how we can be sure it was copied accurately, and the history of modern translations of the Bible, then this book is a must.

Norman L. Geisler and William E. Nix combine their academic backgrounds and a generation of teaching in Bible, history, and apologetics to put together a most comprehensive treatment of the Bible "from God to us." It is simply and clearly written, with numerous illustrations and charts, glossary of terms, Scripture, author and topical indexes, a comprehensive bibliography, and a helpful appendix listing more than 1,100 English translations of the Bible.

This revised edition of *General Introduction* promises to be a useful book for years to come. It is a pleasure to commend it to all who seek to know more about the nature, background, and history of the greatest book ever written, the infallible and inerrant Word of God.

JOSH MCDOWELL

Foreword to the First Edition

This general introduction to the Bible is timely and significant. Numerous are the questions currently being asked concerning the origin and transmission of the Bible. It is to these inquiries and related problems that the authors of this volume devote their research and scholarship in the following pages.

Never before has any generation had available so many versions of the Scriptures. Faced with a variation of translations the average reader of the Bible rightfully raises questions concerning the origin, authority, and canonicity of the books that constitute the Bible as well as the accuracy with which they have been transmitted throughout the centuries.

What distinguishes the Bible from other ancient literature? If the books of the Bible were produced only by the initiative and ability of the authors, then their writings would be primarily human productions. If these books were dictated by God—and I know of no biblical scholar who maintains this view—then they would be primarily divine products. A recognition of both the human and divine aspects in the writing of the Scriptures is essential for regarding the Bible as unique in being a human-divine product.

When were the books of the Bible recognized as authoritative, and by whom? Did the Israelites and the Christian church declare the books of the Bible authoritative, or did they recognize them as divinely inspired and on that basis regard them as valuable and authoritative?

How were the books of the Bible transmitted? Did scribes correct and change the Scriptures, or did they transmit them with care and accuracy? How reliable are our present versions when compared with the oldest manuscripts of the Scriptures available to modern scholarship?

Why do some Bibles include the Apocrypha and others omit them? On what basis do the limits of the canon vary?

The authors of this book are to be commended for their consideration of these questions so frequently discussed in regard to the Bible. Refreshingly significant is the attitude reflected throughout these pages expressed in the assertion that "Christ is the key to canonicity." Modern scholarship that gives serious consideration to the attitude and teaching of Jesus concerning these problems related to the Bible deserves commendation.

SAMUEL J. SCHULTZ

Preface to the Revised Edition

Since the first edition of *A General Introduction to the Bible* (1968), significant developments have necessitated a more thorough treatment of the questions about the inspiration, authority, and inerrancy of Scripture. The discoveries at Ebla and Nag Hamadi have occasioned additional discussion relating to the canon and text of Scripture.

This revised and expanded edition of *General Introduction* has been reorganized into four sections: inspiration, canonization, transmission, and translation. In addition to revising and updating all of the chapters, some completely new chapters have been added (chaps. 8 and 9). Several chapters have been substantially enlarged (chaps. 1, 2, 3, 7, 10, 11, 12, 16, 17, 21, 22, 25, 26, 28, 30, 31, 32). Numerous charts have been revised or added. Of special interest are the new charts on the New Testament (chap. 1), on various theories of inspiration (chap. 10), on the reliability of the New Testament documents (chap. 11), on the genealogy of the English Bible (chap. 16), on the history of the Old Testament text (chap. 21), on the history of the New Testament text (chap. 22), and on the language families (chap. 30). The new Appendix, "A Short-Title Checklist of English Bible Translations," contains more than 1,100 entries. The emergence of the debate among proponents of various textual traditions that incorporate the "majority" text and "eclectic" text methodologies is an important new topic of analysis in this edition as well.

Since the first edition, numerous new translations of the Bible have been produced, including those from almost every major private group and religious body. Hence, the section on Bible translations has been separated and significantly expanded.

In all the various areas of general introduction to the Bible, efforts have been made to offer a comprehensive survey and critical evaluation of representative positions. The result of more than thirty years of study in this area has deepened our conviction that the committee translations of the English Bible are careful renditions of the Hebrew and Greek texts that accurately transmit the infallible and inerrant Word of God.

Preface to the First Edition

This book on general biblical introduction covers the three main areas of the general field: inspiration, canonization, and transmission of the biblical text. It is not concerned as such with the problems of authorship, date, and purpose of the individual books of the Bible, as these are the subjects of special biblical introduction. This work is designed to give a general survey of the process of the transmission of the Bible from God to man. It expounds the claim that God inspired the biblical books, that men of God wrote them, and that the Fathers (Hebrew and Christian) collected and transmitted them to future generations. The bulk of the material considered here deals with the transmission of the Bible from the earliest centuries to the present time. It attempts to answer in the affirmative the all-important question: Is the Bible used today (and the Hebrew and Greek texts upon which it is based) a faithful representation of the text as originally written by the authors of the Old and New Testaments?

Part One

INSPIRATION OF THE BIBLE

1

The Structure and Divisions of the Bible

The Bible and Its Testaments: Definitions

Meaning of "Bible"

The word *Bible* can rightfully claim to be the great-grandson of the Greek word *biblos,* which was the name given to the outer coat of a papyrus reed in Egypt during the eleventh century B.C. The plural form of *biblos* is *biblia,* and by the second century A.D. Christians were using this latter word to describe their writings. *Biblia* gave birth to the Latin word of the same spelling, *biblia,* which was in turn transliterated into the Old French *biblia* by the same process. The modern English word *Bible* is derived from the Old French, with the Anglicized ending. The word is thus the product of four stages of transliteration and transmission. The term Bible is often used synonymously with "Scripture" or "Word of God" (see chap. 3).

Meaning of "Testament"

Next to the fact that the Bible is a biblos, or one book, the most obvious fact is that it is divided into two parts called Testaments. The Hebrew word for testament is *berith,* meaning "covenant, or compact, or arrangement between two parties." The Greek word *diathēkē* is often translated "testament" in the King James Version.[1] This is a poor translation and is one of the corrections made in newer versions of the Bible that regularly translate it as

1. Thirteen of the thirty-three times *diathēkē* occurs in the New Testament it is translated "testament" in the King James Version (*Englishman's Greek Concordance,* p. 144). Technically, however, the English term "testament" requires action on the part of one person only (the one making the testament or will). The heir's agreement is not necessary to the disposition of the testament. That is not true of a covenant.

"covenant."[2] The Greek version of the Old Testament, the Septuagint (LXX), translates the Hebrew word *berith* as *diathēkē*, thus showing the derivation of the Greek term. The Old Testament was first called *the* covenant in Moses' day (Ex. 24:8). Later, Jeremiah announced that God would make a "new covenant" with His people (Jer. 31:31-34), which Jesus claimed to do at the Last Supper (Matt. 26:28, cf. 1 Cor. 11:23-25; Heb. 8:6-8). Hence, it is for Christians that the former part of the Bible is called the *Old* Covenant (Testament), and the latter is called the *New* Covenant.[3]

The relationship between the two covenants is well summarized by the famous statement of St. Augustine: "... the Old Testament revealed in the New, the New veiled in the Old ...."[4] Or, as another has put it, "The New is in the Old contained, and the Old is in the New explained."[5] For the Christian, Christ is the theme of both covenants (cf. Heb. 10:7; Luke 24:27, 44; John 5:39), as may be seen from the accompanying chart.

In the Old Testament Christ is:	In the New Testament Christ is:
in shadow	in substance
in pictures	in person
in type	in truth
in ritual	in reality
latent	patent
prophesied	present
implicitly revealed	explicitly revealed

The Bible and Its Ancient Forms

Hebrew Form

Probably the earliest division of the Hebrew Bible was twofold: the Law and the Prophets.[6] This is the most common distinction in the New Testament and is confirmed as well by Jewish usage and the Dead Sea Scrolls.[7] However, from less ancient times the Jewish Bible was arranged in three sections totaling twenty-four books (twenty-two books if Ruth is listed with Judges

2. Except in Heb. 9:16-7, where the context indicates that the wider sense of *diathēkē* is demanded, namely, "will," or "testament." See Preface, *The Holy Bible, American Standard Version* (1901).
3. Cf. Heb. 8:13: "When He said, 'A new covenant,' He has made the first obsolete."
4. Augustine *Expositions on the Book of Psalms,* Ps. 106:31 in Philip Schaff, ed., *Nicene and Post-Nicene Fathers,* 2d series, vol. 8.
5. W. Graham Scroggie, *Know Your Bible,* 1:12.
6. See discussion in chap. 14.
7. R. Laird Harris, *Inspiration and Canonicity of the Bible,* pp. 146ff.

and Lamentations is listed with Jeremiah).[8] This Old Testament contains all thirty-nine of the books of the Protestant Old Testament in English. The basic difference is that the books are grouped differently (see discussion in chap. 15).

THE HEBREW OLD TESTAMENT ARRANGEMENT*		
The Law (Torah)	The Prophets (Nevi'im)	The Writings (Kethuvim)
1. Genesis 2. Exodus 3. Leviticus 4. Numbers 5. Deuteronomy	A. Former Prophets 1. Joshua 2. Judges 3. Samuel 4. Kings B. Latter Prophets 1. Isaiah 2. Jeremiah 3. Ezekiel 4. The Twelve	A. Poetical Books 1. Psalms 2. Job 3. Proverbs B. Five Rolls (Megilloth) 1. Ruth 2. Song of Songs 3. Ecclesiastes 4. Lamentations 5. Esther C. Historical Books: 1. Daniel 2. Ezra-Nehemiah 3. Chronicles

*This is the arrangement in the New Jewish Version of the Old Testament based on the Masoretic Text (MT). See *TANAKH: A New Translation of THE HOLY SCRIPTURES According to the Traditional Hebrew Text;* Rudolf Kittel and Paul E. Kahle, eds., *Biblia Hebraica;* and K. Elliger and W. Rudolph, eds., *Biblia Hebraica Stuttgartensia*. This is not the arrangement as it appears in Alfred Rahlfs, ed., *Septuaginta: Id est Vetus Testamentum graece iuxta LXX interpretes*.

Some believe a threefold classification may be implied in the words of Jesus in Luke 24:44: "All the things which are written about Me in the law of Moses and the Prophets and the Psalms must be fulfilled."[9] Philo, the Jewish philosopher at Alexandria, alluded to a threefold classification of the Old

8. According to Roger Beckwith, *The Old Testament Canon of the New Testament Church and Its Background in Early Judaism,* p. 256, "The numeration 22 arose not from a smaller canon but from the number of letters in the Hebrew alphabet. It is to that extent artificial, while the numeration 24 is more straightforward....If so, the numeration 24 must be older not younger than the numeration 22, and must likewise go back at least to the first century BC." Also see the discussion in Sid Z. Leiman, *The Canonization of Hebrew Scripture: The Talmudic and Midrashic Evidence,* especially pp. 53-56.
9. Psalms was the first and largest book in this portion of the Hebrew Scriptures and may have become the unofficial nomenclature for the entire section; hence, it could be used here as a reference to the section as a whole.

Testament, and Flavius Josephus arranged the twenty-two books of the Hebrew Scriptures into three sections, saying that the twenty-two books "contain the records of all the past; . . . five belong to Moses, . . . the prophets, who were after Moses, wrote down what was done in their times in thirteen books. The remaining four books contain hymns to God, and precepts for the conduct of human life."[10]

Perhaps the earliest testimony to a threefold classification, however, comes from the prologue to Ecclesiasticus, which reads, ". . . my grandfather Jesus, after devoting himself especially to the reading of the law and the prophets and the other books of our fathers. . . ."[11] The modern threefold classification, with eleven books in the Writings, stems from the Mishnah (Baba Bathra tractate), which in its present form dates from the fifth century A.D.

Some have suggested that this threefold classification is based on the official status of the writers in a descending order: Moses the lawgiver appeared first, with his five books; next came the prophets, with their eight books; finally, the nonprophets, or wise men, kings, and princes, appear with their books. Others have pointed to a chronological arrangement of books with the third section placing the books in descending order of size, which originated with Judas Maccabaeus in the mid-second century B.C.[12]

Greek Form

The Hebrew Scriptures were translated into Greek at Alexandria, Egypt (c. 250-150 B.C.). This translation, known as the Septuagint (LXX), introduced some basic changes in the format of the books: some of the books were reclassified, others regrouped, and some were renamed (see the chart at the end of this chapter). The Alexandrian tradition arranged the Old Testament according to subject matter, which is the basis of the modern classification of five books of Law, twelve books of History, five books of Poetry, and seventeen books of Prophecy.

The order of these books varies in the early canonical lists, but the grouping of the books remains the same throughout.[13] The accompanying chart illustrates this arrangement, which contains the same content but a different total than its Hebrew counterpart.

10. Josephus *Against Apion* 1.8, William Whiston, trans.
11. "The Prologue of the Wisdom of Jesus the Son of Sirach," in *Apocrypha* (RSV), p. 110.
12. Roger Beckwith, p. 316.
13. For example, the Gospels were sometimes placed in other sequences, and on some occasions the General Epistles appeared before the Pauline. Cf. Brooke Foss Westcott, *A General Survey of the History of the Canon of the New Testament;* also see his *The Bible in the Church,* Appendix B, pp. 302-11.

The Law (Pentateuch)—5 books	Poetry—5 books
1. Genesis 2. Exodus 3. Leviticus 4. Numbers 5. Deuteronomy	1. Job 2. Psalms 3. Proverbs 4. Ecclesiastes 5. Song of Solomon

History—12 books	Prophets—17 books	
1. Joshua 2. Judges 3. Ruth 4. 1 Samuel 5. 2 Samuel 6. 1 Kings 7. 2 Kings 8. 1 Chronicles 9. 2 Chronicles 10. Ezra 11. Nehemiah 12. Esther	A. Major 1. Isaiah 2. Jeremiah 3. Lamentations 4. Ezekiel 5. Daniel	B. Minor 1. Hosea 2. Joel 3. Amos 4. Obadiah 5. Jonah 6. Micah 7. Nahum 8. Habakkuk 9. Zephaniah 10. Haggai 11. Zechariah 12. Malachi

To that arrangement the early Christian Fathers added the books of the New Testament, which were classified in four groups: Gospels (four books), History (one book), Epistles (twenty-one books), and Prophecy (one book). Further, the twenty-one Epistles were subdivided into the Pauline (thirteen)[14] and the General (eight).

GOSPELS—4 books	HISTORY—1 book
1. Matthew 2. Mark 3. Luke 4. John	1. Acts

14. In the Eastern church the tendency was to classify them as fourteen Pauline Epistles (including Hebrews) and seven General; the Western church tended to follow the classification as presented above.

EPISTLES—21 books	
A. Pauline—13 books	B. General—8 books
1. Romans	1. Hebrews
2. 1 Corinthians	2. James
3. 2 Corinthians	3. 1 Peter
4. Galatians	4. 2 Peter
5. Ephesians	5. 1 John
6. Philippians	6. 2 John
7. Colossians	7. 3 John
8. 1 Thessalonians	8. Jude
9. 2 Thessalonians	
10. 1 Timothy	
11. 2 Timothy	
12. Titus	
13. Philemon	

PROPHECY—1 book
1. Revelation

Latin Form

The grouping of books in the Latin Bible (the Vulgate) follows that of the Septuagint (LXX), or Greek version. Jerome, who translated the Latin Vulgate (c. 383-405), was familiar with the Hebrew division, but Christendom had come to favor (or be associated with) the Greek version; thus it was only natural for him to adopt its fourfold classification. In fact, any other classification would no doubt have been unacceptable to Latin Christians.[15]

The Bible in Its Modern Form

The Historical Reason for the Structure of the English Bible

After the Vulgate had reigned for a thousand years as the standard Bible of Christendom, it is to be expected that Wycliffe's first English Bible would follow the timeworn divisions of its Latin precursor. As a matter of fact, the fourfold division of the Old Testament and the similar division of the New

15. For a brief discussion of the acceptance of the LXX by Christians and the rejection of it by Jews see chaps. 27 and 28; F.F. Bruce, *The Books and the Parchments*, pp. 150-52.

Testament have been the standard ever since. As a result, the divisions of the modern English Bible follow a *topical* rather than a *chronological* order, in contrast to the Hebrew Bible. Yet, within that overall topical structure, there is a semichronological listing of the books from Genesis through Revelation.

The Topical Reason for the Structure of the English Bible

Because the present structure of the English Bible has been subject to several historical variations, it would be too much to assume that it is God-given. The order as we have it is not, however, purely arbitrary. In fact, the order shows evidence of being purposefully directed, at least insofar as it falls into meaningful categories, because it presents the historical unfolding of the drama of redemptive revelation.

Since redemption and revelation center about the Person of Jesus Christ, it may be observed that the several sections of Scriptures form a Christocentric structure (Luke 24:27, 44; John 5:39; Heb. 10:7). That is, Christ is not only the theme of both Testaments of the Bible, as mentioned above, but He may also be seen as the subject in the sequence of each of the eight sections of the Scriptures.[16]

Section	Name	Christocentric Aspect	Viewpoint
1	Law	Foundation for Christ	Downward Look
2	History	Preparation for Christ	Outward Look
3	Poetry	Aspiration for Christ	Upward Look
4	Prophecy	Expectation of Christ	Forward Look
5	Gospels	Manifestation of Christ	Downward Look
6	Acts	Propagation of Christ	Outward Look
7	Epistles	Interpretation and Application of Christ	Upward Look
8	Revelation	Consummation in Christ	Forward Look

Structure and Divisions of the Bible

In the Old Testament, the books of the law lay the foundation for Christ in that they reveal how God chose (Genesis), redeemed (Exodus), sanctified (Leviticus), guided (Numbers), and instructed (Deuteronomy) the Hebrew nation, through whom He was to bless all nations (Gen. 12:1-3). The historical books illustrate how the nation was being prepared to carry out its redemptive

16. A similar Christocentric structure has been presented in many works, e.g., Norman L. Geisler, *Christ: The Theme of the Bible;* W. Graham Scroggie, *Know Your Bible*.

mission. In order for the chosen nation to be fully prepared for the task, it had to conquer its land (Joshua—Ruth), to be established under its first king, Saul (1 Samuel), and later to expand its empire under David and Solomon (2 Samuel—1 Kings 10). After Solomon's reign, the kingdom was divided (1 Kings 11 ff.) and later deported to Assyria (721 B.C.) and Babylonia (586 B.C., 2 Kings). However, redemptive hopes were not lost, for God protected and preserved His people (Esther) so He could cause them to return (Ezra) and their holy city to be rebuilt (Nehemiah).

In the law the foundation is laid for Christ; in the historical books the nation takes root in preparation for Christ; in the poetical books the people look up in aspiration for Christ; in the prophetical books they look forward in expectation of Christ. The law views the moral life of Israel, history records their national life, poetry reveals their spiritual life, and prophecy depicts their prophetical or messianic life and expectations.

The Gospels of the New Testament bring that prophetic expectation to a historical manifestation in Christ. There the promised Savior becomes present; the concealed becomes revealed; the Logos enters the cosmos (John 1:1, 14) as Christ is made manifest in the flesh. The gospels give a fourfold manifestation of Christ: He is seen in His sovereignty (Matthew), ministry (Mark), humanity (Luke), and deity (John). The manifestation was limited in Jesus' day, for the most part, "to the lost sheep of the house of Israel" (Matt. 10:6). After Christ died and rose again, the disciples were commissioned to carry the account of His manifestation "to the end of the earth" (NKJV) as told in the book of Acts. Here is recorded propagation of faith in Christ as He had commanded: "And you shall be My witnesses both in Jerusalem and in all Judea and Samaria, and even to the remotest part of the earth" (Acts 1:8).

The Gospels give the manifestation of Christ, Acts the propagation of faith in Him, and the epistles the interpretation of His person and work. The Gospels and Acts record the deeds of Christ and His disciples, but the Epistles reveal His doctrine as it was taught by the apostles. The former give the historic foundation for New Testament Christianity; the latter give the didactic interpretation and application of it.

The climactic chapter of Christocentric revelation comes in the final book of the New Testament, Revelation, where all things are brought to a consummation in Christ. The "Paradise Lost" of Genesis becomes the "Paradise Regained" of Revelation. Whereas the gate to the tree of life is closed in Genesis, it is opened forevermore in Revelation. All things are to be summed up in Him (Col. 2:9), for all things were made by Him, redemption was accomplished through Him, and it is only fitting that all things should be consummated in Him (Eph. 1:10).

Summary and Conclusion

The Bible is a *biblos,* a single book. It has two Testaments, better called covenants or agreements between God and His people. Those two parts of the Bible are inseparably related: the New Testament is in the Old concealed, and the Old is in the New revealed.

Down through the centuries the Bible has been subdivided into sections and has had several different arrangements of its books. The Hebrew Bible came to have a threefold division (Law, Prophets, and Writings), so categorized according to the official position of the writer. However, beginning with the Septuagint and continuing in the Latin and modern English translations, the Old Testament has been given a fourfold topical structure. The New Testament was also given a fourfold topical arrangement of Gospels, Acts, Epistles, and Revelation.

When viewed carefully, those sections of the Bible are obviously not arbitrarily put together. Instead, they form a meaningful and purposeful whole, as they convey the progressive unfolding of the theme of the Bible in the person of Christ. The law gives the *foundation* for Christ, history shows the *preparation* for Him. In poetry there is an *aspiration* for Christ and in prophecy an *expectation* of Him. The Gospels of the New Testament record the historical *manifestation* of Christ, the Acts relate the *propagation* of Christ, the Epistles give the *interpretation* of Him, and in Revelation is found the *consummation* of all things in Christ.

A Comparative Chart of the Names of Bible Books
Old Testament

Hebrew (with Translation)	Greek	Latin	English
B^{e}r'ēshîth (In [the] beginning)	Genesis	Genesis	Genesis
Sh^{e}mōth (Names)	Exodos	Exodus	Exodus
Wayyigrā (And he called)	Leuitikos	Leviticus	Leviticus
B^{e}mīdbar (In the wilderness)	Arithmoi	Numeri	Numbers
D^{e}vārîm (Words); 'Elleh ha-Dêbārīm (These are the words)	Deuteronomion Touto	Deuteronomium	Deuteronomy
Y^{e}hôshūa' (Joshua)	Iesous Neue	Iosua	Joshua
Shōphêtīm (Judges)	Kritai	Iudicum	Judges
Rūt (Ruth)	Routh	Ruth	Ruth
Sh^{e}mû-'ēl A (Asked [heard] of God)	Basileion A	Regum I	1 Samuel
Sh^{e}mû-'ēl B (Asked [heard] of God)	Basileion B	Regum II	2 Samuel
M^{e}lchīm A (Kings; kingdoms)	Basileion G	Regum III	1 Kings
M^{e}lchīm B (Kings; kingdoms)	Basileion D	Regum IV	2 Kings
Dibrê hayyāmîm A (The affairs [words] of the days)	Paraleipomenon A	Paralipomenom I	1 Chronicles
Dibrê hayyāmîm B (The affairs [words] of the days)	Paraleipomenon B	Paralipomenom II	2 Chronicles
Edsra (Ezra)	Esdras	Esdras I	Ezra
Nêh^{e}mīah (Nehemiah)	Neemias	Esdras II	Nehemiah
Hadassah (Myrtle)	Esther	Esther	Esther
'Iyyôb (Job)	Iob	Iob	Job
T^{e}hillîm (Praises)	Psâlterion	Psalmi	Psalms
Mish^{e}lê (Proverbs; parables)	Paroimia	Proverbia	Proverbs
Qōhelet (One who assembles)	Ekklesiastes	Ecclesiastes	Ecclesiastes
Shîr hash-shîrîm (Song of songs)	Asma	Canticum Canticorum	Song of Solomon
Y^{e}sha'-yāhû (Jehovah is salvation)	Esaias	Iēsaias	Isaiah
Yirm^{e}yāhû (Jehovah will raise or lift up)	Ieremias	Ieremias	Jeremiah
'êkâ (Ah, how! Alas!)	Threnoi	Threnorum	Lamentations
Y^{e}hezqēl (God strengthens)	Iesekiel	Ezechiel	Ezekiel
Daniēl (God is my judge)	Daniel	Daniel	Daniel
Hosh^{e}a (Salvation)	'Osee	'Osee	Hosea
Yô'ēl (Jehovah is God)	Ioel	Ioel	Joel
Amos (Burden)	Amos	Amos	Amos
'ôbedyâ (Servant [worshiper] of Jehovah)	Obdiou	Abdias	Obadiah
Yônah (Dove)	Ionas	Ionas	Jonah
Mîkāyāhû (Who is like Jehovah?)	Michaias	Michaeas	Micah
Nāhûm (Consolation; consoler)	Naoum	Nahum	Nahum
H^{a}bâkûk (Embrace; embracer)	Ambakoum	Habacuc	Habakkuk
S^{e}panyâ (Jehovah hides; Jehovah has hidden)	Sophonias	Sophonias	Zephaniah
Hâggaī (Festive; festal)	Aggaios	Aggeus	Haggai
Z^{e}chârīah (God remembers)	Zecharias	Zacharias	Zechariah
Malachiah (The messenger of Jehovah)	Malachias	Malachias	Malachi

A Comparative Chart of the Names of Bible Books
New Testament

Greek	Latin	English
Ta Euangelia	Evangelia	The Gospels
Kata Maththaion	Secundum Mathaeum	According to Matthew
Kata Markon	Secundum Marcum	According to Mark
Kata Loukan	Secundum Lucam	According to Luke
Kata Ioannen	Secundum Ioannem	According to John
Praxeis	Acti	Acts
Praxeis Apostolon	Actus Apostolorum	Acts of the Apostles
Hai Epistolai	Epistolae	Epistles
Pros Romaious	Ad Romanos	Romans
Pros Korinthious A	[I] Ad Corinthios	1 Corinthians
Pros Korinthious B	[II] Ad Corinthios	2 Corinthians
Pros Galatas	Ad Galatas	Galatians
Pros Ephesious	Ad Ephesios	Ephesians
Pros Philippesious	Ad Philippenses	Philippians
Pros Kolossaeis	Ad Colossenses	Colossians
Pros Thessalonikeis A	[I] Thessalonicenses	1 Thessalonians
Pros Thessalonikeis B	[II] Thessalonicenses	2 Thessalonians
Pros Timotheon A	[I] Ad Timotheum	1 Timothy
Pros Timotheon B	[II] Ad Timotheum	2 Timothy
Pros Titon	Ad Titum	Titus
Pros Philemona	Ad Philemonem	Philemon
Pros Hebraious	Ad Hebraeos	Hebrews
Iakobou	Iacobi Apostoli	James
Petrou A	[I] Petri Apostoli	1 Peter
Petrou B	[II] Petri Apostoli	2 Peter
Ioannou A	[I] Ioannis Apostoli	1 John
Ioannou B	[II] Ioannis Apostoli	2 John
Ioannou G	[III] Ioannis Apostoli	3 John
Iouda	Iudae Apostoli	Jude
Apokalypsie	Apocalypsis	Revelation
Apokalypsie Ioannou	Apocalypsis Ioannis Apostoli	Revelation of John

2

Definitions of Revelation and Inspiration

The most basic question about the nature of the Bible centers in its claim to be "inspired" or to be the "Word of God." Just what is meant by and what is included in that claim is the subject of the first link and, in that sense, the most important link in the chain of communication "from God to us."

Inspiration Defined

The starting point in the discussion of inspiration is the claim of the Scriptures themselves. It is only proper that the Bible should be permitted to witness about its own nature. Once the claim is understood clearly, the character and credentials should be checked carefully; but the Scriptures should not be denied the opportunity to testify on their own behalf.[1] The starting point for such an examination, then, is the claim of inspiration as it is asserted by the Bible, and the procedure will be to study that claim in the light of the phenomena of Scripture.

Biblical Description of Inspiration

The Biblical Terminology. There is some confusion over the doctrine of inspiration that is due to the very term itself. In order to clarify this possible confusion three terms need to be distinguished. First, "inspiration," derived from *inspirare* (Latin), means "to breathe upon or into something." According to the *Oxford English Dictionary* (OED)[2] this notion is used as early as the

1. It is sometimes thought that this is *petitio principii*, or arguing in a circle. Actually it is not, because we first ask only what the Bible claims about itself and then whether or not it is true. The latter is properly a question of apologetics and not of biblical introduction; nevertheless, it will be treated briefly in chapter 11.
2. James Augustus Henry Strong et al., eds., *A New English Dictionary on Historical Principles*, known generally as the *Oxford Dictionary, Oxford English Dictionary,* or the *New English Dictionary*. Also see *The Compact Edition of the Oxford English Dictionary: Complete Text Reproduced Micrographically.*

time of Geoffrey Chaucer (c. 1386) and by others thereafter. By extension the term is used of analogous mental phenomena; hence a sudden spontaneous idea is called an "inspiration." Theologically, "inspiration" is often used for the condition of being directly under divine influence and it is viewed as the equivalent of the Greek term *theopneustia,* or its adjective *theopneustos* (cf. 2 Tim. 3:16).

A second important term is "enthusiasm," which is derived from the Greek *enthusiasmos (en + theos),* to signify the first century A.D. notion of "being possessed by a god." The authoritative *Oxford English Dictionary* (OED) indicates that the earliest usage of "enthusiasm" in English appeared in 1579. It came into prominence in the post-Reformation era when possession by a divine spirit (*pneuma*) was regarded as necessarily accompanied by the intense stimulation of the emotions.[3] In turn this notion of immanence contributed to the rise of modern religious subjectivism. The nearest approach to this typically Greek idea of inspiration as "a complete surrender of the mind and will to the overpowering Holy Spirit" is in 2 Peter 1:21.[4]

The third important term dealing with the biblical definition of inspiration is *theopneustia,* "God-breathed" (from *theopheustos*), which is translated "inspired by God" in its only New Testament usage (2 Tim. 3:16). The term does not imply a particular mode of inspiration, such as some form of divine dictation. Nor does it imply the suspension of the normal cognative faculties of the human authors. On the other hand, it does imply something quite different from poetic inspiration. It is an error to omit the divine element from the term implied by *theopneustos* as is done in rendering the phrase "every inspired Scripture" or "every Scripture inspired" in the *American Standard Version* (ASV) of 1901, and the *New English Bible* (NEB) of 1970.[5] The New Testament usage clearly does not imply that some canonical Scriptures are inspired while others are not. The sacred Scriptures are all expressive of the mind of God. The sacred Scriptures are the "God-breathed" revelation of God which result in their practical outworking in life (2 Tim. 3:16-17).

The Biblical Data. This brings the subject to the biblical teaching itself.[6] Some prominent New Testament passages set the stage for for the discussion of inspiration.

1. In 2 Timothy 3:16-17 the apostle Paul declares that "all Scripture is inspired by God and profitable for teaching, for reproof, for correction,

3. See H.D. McDonald, *Theories of Revelation: An Historical Study, 1700-1960,* 1:63-64; 2:70.
4. Colin Brown, ed., *The New International Dictionary of New Testament Theology,* s.v., "Spirit," 3:689-709. Also see Gerhard Kittel, ed., *Theological Dictionary of the New Testament,* 6:453-455.
5. See discussion in chapter 31.
6. This discussion follows William E. Nix, "Inerrancy: Theological Watershed Issue of the Hour?" Winnipeg Theological Seminary Lectureship Series, Otterbourne, Manitoba, January 1980.

for training in righteousness; that the man of God may be adequate, equipped for every good work." There are four key terms crucial to a proper exegesis of this passage. The first term is "all" (*pasa*). This term can be translated "every" or "all." It is not essential that one term is better than the other because both refer to the entire canon of the Old Testament, which Timothy had known from his youth (cf. v. 15). The second term is "scripture" (*graphē*). This means a "writing" or "written document." It is clear from the usage of this term that the locus of inspiration is in the written record rather than in the ideas or concepts or even oral expressions of the writer. Although the word *graphē* itself can have a more general usage than a canonical writing, nevertheless, the context clearly indicates that the entire Old Testament is in view (see also Rom. 15:4; 2 Pet. 3:15-16). Third, since there is no verb stated in the text, the word "inspired" (*theopneustos*) is the critical term in the passage. The term *theopneustos* is an adjective that belongs to a special class called "verbal adjectives." As such, it may be viewed either as a predicate adjective (the implied verb "is" precedes the adjective) or an attributive adjective (the implied verb "is" follows the adjective). It does not mean, as the English word "inspire" might imply, that God *breathed in* the word but rather that the very words were *breathed out* (see above definitions). A parallel is found in the words of Jesus who referred to what is written as "every word that proceeds out of the mouth of God" (Matt. 4:4).

What is of central importance in this passage is the relationship of *theopneustos* to *graphē*. It is grammatically possible to take *theopneustos* as descriptive of *graphē;* all inspired scripture is of God (attributive adjective). Nevertheless, there are several reasons for rejecting this possibility in favor of the much better substantiated "all Scripture is inspired of God" (predicate adjective). Several reasons support this conclusion.

a. 2 Timothy 3:16 has an identical structure to 1 Timothy 4:4, where the two adjectives are predicate.

b. The usual position of the attributive adjective construction would be *theopneustos graphē* instead of *graphē theopneustos*.

c. The absence of a verb suggests that *theopneustos* (God-breathed) and *ophelimos* (profitable) are to be viewed in the same manner, for they are both the same and *ophelimos* cannot be translated attributively without leaving the sentence without a predicate.

d. Words joined by *kai* (and) are usually understood as being joined by the conjunction "and." If *ophelimos* and *theopneustos* were attributive, the *kai* would be pointless.

e. The use of *theopneustos* as an attributive adjective would stress the *usefulness* of Scripture rather than its inspiration.

f. The use of *theopneustos* as an attributive would leave open the possibility of some "uninspired *graphē*," which is contrary to the meaning of "all scripture" (as discussed above).

Fourth, grammatically the word "profitable" (*ophelimos*) can either mean the Scriptures are inspired because they are profitable (attributive) or the Scriptures are profitable because they are inspired (predicate). The context, however, would confirm the conclusion that the Scriptures are profitable because they are inspired. Thus, they are useful because of what they are: their intrinsic quality produces results. Hence the translation "All Scripture is inspired" shows that *because* they are God-breathed, they are therefore useful (*ophelimos*) for the work of the ministry, *not the reverse*.

Some implications of this translation of 2 Timothy 3:16 may be drawn.

a. Inspiration deals with the objective text of Scripture, not the subjective intention of the writer.

b. The doctrine of Scripture applies to *all* or *every* Scripture, that is, the Bible in part or in whole is the Word of God.

c. The Scriptures *are* the very spirated (breathed out) Word of God. The *form and content* of Scripture are the very words of God. This does not mean that each individual word is inspired *as such* but only *as part of a whole* sentence or unit of meaning. There is no implication in Scripture of an *atomistic* inspiration of each word but only of a *holistic* inspiration of all words used. Just as an individual word has no meaning apart from its use in a given context, so individual words of Scripture are not inspired apart from their use in a whole sentence.

2. In 2 Peter 1:19-21 what the apostle Peter asserts is more than the divine origin of Scripture (compare 2 Tim. 3:16-17). Here he adds to the understanding of *how* God produced the Scriptures. This was accomplished through the instrumentality of men who "spoke from God." More specifically, these spokesmen were "moved along by the Holy Spirit" (cf. Acts 27:15). In the context of this passage, Peter has assured his readers that what he was making known to them was not by "cleverly devised tales (*mythos*)" (v. 16) nor even personal experience (v. 18). Instead, it was "the prophetic word *made* more sure" (v. 19). Here is an implicit affirmation of the authority (certainty) of the "prophetic word" presented by eyewitnesses (Peter, James, John) of the Lord (Matt. 17:1-13). "No prophecy was ever made by an act of human will, but men moved by the Holy Spirit spoke from God" (2 Peter 1:21). So, in biblical terminology, inspiration is the process by which Spirit-moved writers recorded God-breathed writings. Hence, when inspiration is extended to the total process, it includes both the writer and the writings; but when it is limited to its biblical

usage (as in 2 Tim. 3:16), it relates only to the written product (*graphē*). That is well summarized in Hebrews 1:1: "God . . . spoke long ago to the Fathers *in the prophets*," to which 2 Timothy 3:16 would add the thought *in their writings*.

3. John 10:34-35. This passage is important because in it Jesus uses the expressions "Scriptures," "Torah" (Law), "it is written," "word of God," and "cannot be broken" interchangeably. Thus He affirmed that the written Old Testament Scriptures are the unbreakable law and Word of God. The phrase "cannot be broken" (*outhenai*) means cannot be destroyed, abolished, or done away with (cf. John 7:23). Thus the Scriptures are viewed as the indestructible Word of God.

The Biblical Process. The whole process of communication "from God to us" begins with the matter of divine revelation.

1. First, God spoke *to* the prophets. This was done "in many and various ways" (Heb. 1:1).

   a. God sometimes spoke to the prophets by angels, as He did to Abraham in Genesis 18 and to Lot in Genesis 19.

   b. God also spoke to the prophets in dreams (Dan. 7:1; cf. Num. 12:6).

   c. Sometimes God used visions, as He did with Isaiah and Ezekiel (Isa. 1:1; Ezek. 1:1; 8:3; 11:24; 43:3; cf. Hos. 12:10).

   d. On occasion God used miracles to speak to the prophets, for instance, Moses and the burning bush (Ex. 3:2); Gideon's enterprise (Judg. 6:37); and Jonah's experiences (Jonah 1:1; 4:6 ff.).

   e. Even nature was used to speak to the psalmist (Ps. 19:1).

   f. Sometimes God spoke in an audible voice (1 Sam. 3:4).

   g. No doubt the most common method God used was the inner voice of the individual's conscience and communion with God. That is probably what is most often meant when the prophets write, "And the word of the Lord came unto me saying. . . ."

   h. The priests discovered the will of God by means of the Urim and Thummim (Ex. 28:30; Num. 27:21).

   i. Even casting lots was designated as a means by which God indicated His will (Prov. 16:33).

   j. Finally, some of the prophets received divine communication from the study of other prophetic writings (Dan. 9:1-2).

2. God not only spoke *to* the prophets in various ways, but He spoke *in* their words whether written or oral (Heb. 1:1). That is, the prophets' messages were God's message; their voices were God's voice. God was saying what they were saying; or, to put it more precisely, they were saying what God wanted said.

   a. This is verified in a general way by 2 Peter 1:21 and Hebrews 1:1, which indicate that the oral message of the prophets came from God; it was God's word given through the prophets' mouths. It is what David said in 2 Samuel 23:2: "The Spirit of the LORD spoke by me, and His word was on my tongue." Jeremiah also cites God as saying, "Behold, I have put My words in your mouth" (Jer. 1:9).

b. This is borne out in particular by the prophetic formulas, as each prophet introduced his oral message by statements such as "Thus says the LORD," "The word of the LORD," "The LORD spoke" (see chaps. 4-6).

THEOLOGICAL DEFINITION OF INSPIRATION

From the biblical description of the process of inspiration, the necessary constituents of a theological definition of inspiration may be derived. There are three:

1. *Divine causality.* The prime mover in inspiration is God: "No prophecy was ever made by an act of human will, but men moved by the Holy Spirit spoke from God" (2 Peter 1:21). In other words, God *moved*, and the prophet *mouthed* the truths; God *revealed*, and man *recorded* His word. The Bible is God's word in the sense that it originates with Him and is authorized by Him, even though it is articulated by men. God speaks *in* their written records.

2. *Prophetic agency.* The prophets played an important role in the overall process of inspiration; they were the means by which God spoke. The word of God was written by men of God. God used persons to convey His propositions. In other words, as J.I. Packer perceptively observes, there God exercised "*concursive operation* in, with and through the free working of man's own mind."[7] He amplifies the concept further, saying,

> We are to think of the Spirit's inspiring activity, and, for that matter, of all His regular operations in and upon human personality, as (to use an old but valuable technical term) *concursive;* that is, as exercised in, through and by means of the writers' own activity, in such a way that their thinking and writing was *both* free and spontaneous on their part *and* divinely elicited and controlled, and what they wrote was not only their own work but also God's work.[8]

God prepared the prophets by training, experience, gifts of grace, and, if need be, by direct revelation to utter His word. "By it [inspiration], the Spirit of God, flowing confluently with the providentially and graciously

7. James I. Packer, *"Fundamentalism" and the Word of God,* p. 82; J.I. Packer, *God Has Spoken,* esp. pp. 45-124. Also see I. Howard Marshall, *Biblical Inspiration,* pp. 40-43.
8. Packer, *"Fundamentalism,"* p. 80.

determined work of men, spontaneously producing under the Divine directions the writings appointed them, gives the product a Divine quality unattainable by human powers alone."[9] In inspiration, then, God is the primary cause, and the prophets are the secondary causes. Thus the divine influence did not restrict human activity but rather enabled the human authors to communicate the divine message accurately.

3. *Scriptural authority* is the final product of God's causality and the prophetic agency. Hence, the Bible is a divinely authoritative book. God moved the prophets in such a way as to breathe out (literally, "spirate") their writings. In other words, God spoke to the prophets and is speaking in their writings. Although some might argue that the prophetic model of inspiration is inadequate,[10] thereby shifting the basis of the believer's authority from Scripture to some other locus, Carl F. H. Henry rightly observes that "the church is neither the locus of divine revelation, nor the source of divine inspiration, nor the seat of infallibility. Rather, the church has the task of transmitting, translating, and expounding the prophetic-apostolic Scriptures."[11] The cause of inspiration is God, the means is the men of God, and the end result is the word of God in the language of men.

Therefore, this definition of inspiration is suggested: *Inspiration is that mysterious process by which the divine causality worked through the human prophets without destroying their individual personalities and styles to produce divinely authoritative and inerrant writings.*

Inspiration Distinguished from Revelation and Interpretation

Revelation Concerns the Origin and Giving of Truth (1 Cor. 2:10)[12]

Still another concept must be distinguished in the process of divine communication. It is interpretation (hermeneutics). The Hebrew word for revelation, *galah,* "to uncover," and the Greek word *apocalyptein,* "to unveil,"

9. Benjamin B. Warfield, *The Inspiration and Authority of the Bible,* pp. 154-60.
10. Paul J. Achtemeier, *The Inspiration of Scripture: Problems and Proposals,* pp. 29-31, 74-75, 99-100, 122-23, and elsewhere. Clark Pinnock, *The Scripture Principle,* uncritically accepts this notion, stating, "The Bible is more than prophecy, and although direct divine speech is part of the record, there are many other kinds of communication as well, some of them more indirect and ambiguous" (p. 63), and indicating that "Paul J. Achtemeier has called attention to the inadequacy of the prophetic model for representing the biblical category of inspiration in its fulness" (p. 234 n. 8).
11. Carl F. H. Henry, *God, Revelation and Authority,* vol. 2: *God Who Speaks and Shows: Fifteen Theses, Part One,* pp. 13-15.
12. Cf. Merril F. Unger, *Introductory Guide to the Old Testament,* 2d ed., pp. 22-25.

are roughly identical in meaning. Along with their synonyms in the Old and New Testaments, these terms convey the idea of "the removal of obstacles to perception," or "the stripping away of that which keeps one from seeing an object as it is." This notion was contained in the Latin *revelare* (to reveal), from which the English word *revelation* is derived.[13] In other words, revelation involves "disclosure" rather than "discovery." As it relates to Scripture, all these terms refer to a *divine disclosure*. Sometimes it may be a disclosure of a person (as in Christ, the Living Word of God, Gal. 1:16), while at other times it may be of *propositions* (as in Scripture, the *written* Word of God,[14] John 10:35). In the ultimate sense, God gives the revelation or disclosure of truth; man can have an interpretation or discovery of that truth. Some scholars, such as John Macquarrie and Leon Morris, have attempted to extend revelation to the experiences of believers in subsequent generations, calling it "repetitive revelation" as opposed to "primordial," "classical," or "formative" revelation in the Scriptures.[15] However, such a view not only confuses revelation and interpretation, but it also broadens the locus of revelation from the Scriptures alone to the ongoing experiences of the Christian community.

Inspiration Relates to the Reception and Recording of Truth (2 Peter 1:20-21)

God revealed truth to men who received and recorded it. Inspiration is the means God used to achieve His revelation in the Bible. Inspiration involves man in an active sense, whereas revelation is solely the activity of God. In inspiration, the prophet received from God what he in turn related to others. Inspiration as a total process includes both the prophet and the product of his pen.

Interpretation Focuses on the Apprehension and Understanding of Truth (1 Cor. 2:14-16)

The Greek term *hermeneuein* (to interpret) is applied to the interpretation of Scripture in the study of hermeneutics.[16] Whereas revelation is an objective disclosure of God, and inspiration includes the process and product God used

13. See Colin Brown et al., "Revelation," in *The New International Dictionary of New Testament Theology,* 3:309-340. Also see Gerhard Kittel, ed., *Theological Dictionary of the New Testament,* 3:556-592.
14. *Revelation* is often used of written (or spoken) words. See Rom. 16:25; 1 Cor. 14:6, 26; Eph. 3:3.
15. See John Macquarrie, *Principles of Christian Theology,* and the discussion of his position in Leon Morris, *I Believe in Revelation,* pp. 68-89.
16. The Greek term came into English by way of New Latin *hermeneutica* from the masculine noun *hermeneutikos* (interpretation). For a treatment of the theological issues involved in the interpretation of the Bible, see Earl D. Radmacher and Robert D. Preus, eds., *Hermeneutics, Inerrancy, and the Bible*.

in communicating, interpretation emphasizes the apprehension and understanding of God's revelation to man. In revelation God unveils truth; by interpretation man understands that truth. Even though the three concepts are interrelated in the total process of God's communication, they are quite distinguishable. They form three necessary links in the chain "from God to us": (1) revelation is the fact of divine communication, (2) inspiration is the means of divine communication, and (3) interpretation is the process of understanding that divine communication.[17]

Inspiration Discussed

What Is Inspired, the Writer or His Writings?

Although the biblical concept of inspiration has been outlined in general, several important questions must be discussed about inspiration in particular. Is it the writers, their ideas, their writings, or a combination of these which is inspired? As was mentioned above, inspiration certainly includes the man and his ideas, but it must not exclude his writings. James Orr believes that "inspiration belongs primarily to the person and to the book only as it is the product of the inspired person."[18] Other theologians would reverse that opinion, asserting, "Properly speaking, inspiration pertains to the holy Scriptures themselves. It may be said, however, that the writers too were inspired by God."[19] Regardless of which position is primary, it must be held that the person as well as his pen is under the direction of the Holy Spirit in the total process of inspiration. Nevertheless, the New Testament reserves the word "inspiration" only for the product of that process, that is, the writings, or *graphē* (2 Tim. 3:16).[20] Failure to make that distinction leads some scholars, such as Paul J. Achtemeier and William J. Abraham, to the erroneous conclusion that the inspiration is the totality of the process of gathering traditions, proclamations, writing, and editing on an ongoing basis. Although God is actively involved throughout the total process of producing the Scriptures (2 Peter 1:20-21), the inspiration (*theopneustos*) and subsequent authority of those Scriptures is reserved for the written Scriptures themselves (2 Tim. 3:16-17), which are illuminated by the Holy Spirit (1 Cor. 2:14-16). As I. Howard Marshall aptly observes, "There is a gap between the process of inspiration and the text of the Bible which causes some disquiet, particularly when we

17. Illumination as described in Scripture (1 Cor. 2:14-16; Eph. 1:18) does not refer so much to the *understanding* of the *meaning* of a passage but to the *application* of the *significance* of its truth to one's life. See the helpful statement on hermeneutics in Radmacher and Preus, eds., *Hermeneutics, Inerrancy, and the Bible,* pp. 881-904.
18. James Orr, *Revelation and Inspiration,* p. 162.
19. Robert Preus, *Inspiration of Scripture,* p. 22.
20. Benjamin B. Warfield, *International Standard Bible Encyclopaedia,* s.v. "Inspiration."

remember that according to 2 Timothy it is the Scriptures which are inspired rather than the process of composition."[21]

That inspiration of necessity involves the very words of Scripture may be seen for two reasons: (1) Linguistically, words are necessary for the adequate expression of thought.[22] If God in any meaningful sense expressed Himself to the prophets, He had to use words. Words are the "clothes of ideas," and a naked thought is a very nebulous entity at best. The desire for clarity in revelation would scarcely be consonant with the ambiguity of unsymbolized ideas. In fact, an idea without a symbol to express it is an unexpressed idea, and an unexpressed idea is scarcely a revelation or communication. (2) Biblically, it is the repeated claim that "words" are God-given. Observe how many times Jesus and the apostles used the phrase "it is written" or similar expressions (see chap. 5). The Bible literally abounds with the assertions that God gave the *very words* of the prophets (see chap. 6). Moses was told, "I will be with your mouth, and teach you what you are to say" (Ex. 4:12). God charged Ezekiel, saying, "You shall speak My words to them" (Ezek. 2:7). Of the Decalogue it is said, "And God spoke all these words" (Ex. 20:1). Paul claimed to speak "in words ... taught by the Spirit" (1 Cor.2:13). Those references illustrate that the very words of the Bible were God-given.

What Is Inspired, the Autographs[23] or the Copies?

If every word of the Bible is inspired, does every copy, translation, or version of the Scriptures necessarily have to be inspired too? There are some who think so. But, here again, two extremes must be avoided.

"Every translation is inspired in the same sense as the original." This extreme position was held by the Jewish philosopher Philo in the first century of the present era. He said of the Greek translation of the Hebrew Old Testament, known as the Septuagint, that the translators "under inspiration, wrote, not each several scribe something different, but the same word for word, as though dictated to each by an invisible prompter."

Dewey M. Beegle reflects a similar view when he writes, "There is no evidence to show that the apostles denied the inspiration of the LXX .... The correct inference, therefore, is that in spite of some mistakes, all reasonably accurate translations of Scripture are inspired."[24] This position, as can be seen, necessitates the recognition of errors (errancy) in inspiration, because

21. Marshall, p. 38.
22. An autograph is usually an original, or author's, manuscript. It may have been written by either the author himself (2 Cor. 13:10; Gal. 6:11) or a secretary (1 Pet. 5:12).
23. Philo *Life of Moses* 2.37, F. H. Colson, trans.
24. Dewey M. Beegle, *The Inspiration of Scripture*, pp. 38-40.

some errors of copyists have obviously crept into the text.[25] If this be so, one is forced to the absurd conclusion that there are divinely inspired errors in the Bible.

"Only the autographs are inspired, not the translations." If only the errorless autographs were God-breathed, and the translators were not preserved from error, how can there be certainty about any passage of Scripture? Perhaps the very passage that comes under question is a mistaken transcription or copy. The scholarly procedure of textual criticism (see chap. 26) treats this problem by showing the accuracy of the copies of the originals. To borrow this conclusion in advance, the copies are known to be accurate and sufficient in all matters except minor details. The resultant situation, then, exists that although only the autographs are inspired, it may be said nevertheless that all good copies or translations are *adequate*.

Some have objected to what they consider a retreat to "inerrant autographs" from errant copies, as if the doctrine of inspiration were created to protect the inerrancy of the Bible. To argue, as does Ernest R. Sandeen,[26] that the belief in inerrant originals emerges from the apologetic purposes of the Princeton tradition of Charles Hodge and B.B. Warfield to defend the Bible against charges of error, are misdirected. The distinction between inerrant autographs and errant copies can be found in much earlier writers, including John Calvin (1509-64) and even Augustine (A.D. 354-430). They chide that no one in modern times has ever seen these "infallible originals." Although no one in modern times has ever seen an infallible original, it is also true that no one has ever seen a fallible one. In light of this situation, it is well to note that the pursuit of the original renderings is at least an objective science (textual criticism) rather than a subjective guess at recovering the actual text of the inerrant autographs.

Just why God did not see fit to preserve the autographs is unknown, although man's tendency to worship religious relics is certainly a possible determining factor (2 Kings 18:4). Others have noted that God could have avoided the worship of the originals by simply preserving a perfect copy.[27] But He has not seen fit to do even this. It seems more likely that God did not

25. For example, 2 Kings 8:26 gives 22 as the age of Ahaziah, whereas 2 Chron. 22:2 gives 42. The latter cannot be correct, or he would have been older than his father. Nevertheless, the best available *copies* of the originals render 2 Chron. 22:2 as "42 years." According to 2 Chron. 9:25, Solomon had 4,000 horses, but 1 Kings 4:26 says 40,000; some copyists must have made a mistake in the Kings passage. See discussion in chap. 26; William E. Nix, "1 Chronicles," and "2 Chronicles," in W.A. Criswell, ed., *The Criswell Study Bible;* J. Barton Payne, "The Validity of Numbers in Chronicles," *Bulletin of the Near East Archaeological Society,* new series II (1978):5-58.
26. Ernest R. Sandeen, *The Roots of Fundamentalism: British and American Millenarianism, 1800-1930*.
27. See Greg L. Bahnsen, "The Inerrancy of the Autographa," in Norman L. Geisler, *Inerrancy,* pp. 172-73.

preserve the originals so no one could tamper with them. It is practically impossible for anyone to make changes in thousands of existing copies. The net result, however, has proved to be profitable insofar as it has occasioned the very worthwhile study of textual criticism. Another valuable side effect of not preserving all the copies from error is that it serves as a warning to biblical scholars not to esteem paleographic, numeric, or other trivia over the essential message of the Scriptures.[28]

"Only the autographs were actually inspired; good copies are accurate." In seeking to avoid the two extremes of either an unattainable original or a fallible one, it must be asserted that a good copy or translation of the autographs is *for all practical purposes* the inspired Word of God. It may not completely satisfy the scholar who, for technical purposes of theological precision, wants both the correct text and the exact term in the original language, but it certainly does suit the preacher and layman who desire to know "what says the Lord" in matters of faith and practice. Even when the accuracy of a reading in the original *text* cannot be known with 100 percent accuracy, it is possible to be 100 percent certain of the *truth* preserved in the texts that survive. It is only in minor details that any uncertainty about the textual rendering exists, and no major doctrine rests on any one minor detail. A good translation will not fail to capture the overall teaching of the original. In this sense, then, a good translation will have doctrinal authority, although actual inspiration is reserved for the autographs.

How Much of the Bible Is Inspired?

Another question to be asked concerns the degree of inspiration. Are all sections of the Bible equally inspired, or are some parts of Scripture more inspired than others? The question itself confuses the issue and fails to distinguish between the nature of truth and the importance of that truth. Certainly the biblical truth that Christ died for our sins is more important than the truth that the pool of Bethesda had five porticoes (John 5:2). However, both statements are equally the truth. Truth does not come in degrees. A statement is either true or false. Just because a given passage, at certain times and under stated circumstances, is more "inspiring" to a particular person does not thereby mean that it is more inspired than other passages. Inspiration merely vouches for the truth of the record, no matter how valuable that particular record may be to the individual's edification or even to the overall picture of redemption.

The record is either true or false; inspired or not inspired; of God or not of God. If the various passages are true, they are equally true, and not more or

28. Cf. John W. Haley, *An Examination of the Alleged Discrepancies of the Bible*, pp. 30-40.

less true. Although it may not be the "whole" truth from the vantage point of the full and ultimate revelation, it is nonetheless a true record of that which God wanted to reveal at that particular time in His progressive revelation of the whole truth. Certainly all statements of truth must be understood in their context. For "a text out of its context is a pretext." Everything should be understood as the author meant it. But what is meant does not come in degrees of truth, even though different truths may vary in degrees of importance.

How Does Inspiration Operate?

A final question concerns the means, or process, of inspiration. What means did God's causality employ to produce scriptural authority without interfering with the personality, freedom, and individuality of the prophetic agents? Or, how did God produce an infallible book through fallible men? A frank and forthright answer, yet one often very reluctantly given by biblical scholars, is "We don't know." It must be asserted *that* God inspired the Scriptures even if we cannot ascertain exactly *how* He did it. Just because man does not know how God created the world from nothing does not mean it is unreasonable to believe that He did so (cf. Heb. 11:3). Likewise, ignorance of the means used by the Holy Spirit to produce an infant in the virgin's womb does not mean that the biblical teaching about the virgin birth of Christ (Luke 1:26-38) must be rejected.

Some attempted explanation. Several solutions have been suggested for this problem, all of which have their own inherent difficulties.

1. One suggestion is that God dictated the words to the prophets, who acted as recording secretaries (see chap. 10). Although this may explain how every word was inspired, it would not explain how or why so many distinctly individual traits of the various human writers are so apparent in the Scriptures or why the biblical writers themselves claimed to have used human sources for some of their information (see chap. 3). Mechanical word-for-word dictation may account for some of Scripture (e.g., the Ten Commandments or some prophecies), but it certainly does not account for *all* of it.

2. Another view is that God produced much of the truth of Scripture by His providential control over natural processes and that He could have produced it all in this manner. Kenneth Kantzer writes,

> No theist who believes in God's providential control of the universe can possibly use this objection [viz., that "divine inspiration must necessarily negate the freedom and humanity of the Biblical writers"] against the inspiration of the Bible. The God of Romans 8:28, who works all things together for good, including the sinful acts of wicked men, could certainly have

> worked through the will and personality of His prophets to secure the divine Word which He wished to convey through them.[29]
>
> Although it may not be disputed that God could have secured the truth of the inspired record through providence, it must not be supposed that He operated in that manner exclusively. The truth of the matter is that it is not always known how Providence works. As Kantzer admits, "The mechanics of inspiration are left unexplained."[30]

The nature of the problem. The problem of the means of inspiration falls within the category of a theological "mystery." Two sides of the overall picture are given to man in the Bible, and it is asserted that they are both true. No one can show that they are contradictory, nor can anyone show exactly how they are complementary. They are not contrary to reason, but they are beyond finite reasoning. The reason both sides of inspiration are given is that man may have the "whole" truth, and not just one "part" or side of it. It is like a two-sided coin which an infinite God may comprehend completely at once, but which a finite man must apprehend partially, one side at a time. If it be admitted that the words of the Bible are truly God's, yet distinctly man's, there would seem to be no way of denying that the process is a mystery without eventuating in one of the two extremities.

Two extremes to avoid. If the human nature of the Bible is emphasized on the one hand, the divine may be compromised on the other. If the divine is emphasized, the human is in danger of being relegated to the hypothetical. In one case the divine nature is taken seriously and the human is viewed only incidentally. In the other extreme, the human is so prominent that the divine is obscured. The difficulty is not with the revelation of both sides of the truth, it is with their reconciliation. In that connection it is well to remember that man's inability to understand a mystery does not render ineffective God's ability to accomplish one. Thus, it would seem that, by the activity of the Holy Spirit and through the instrumentality of the prophets, the infallibility of the Scriptures was effected (John 10:35), even though this is admittedly a great mystery.

A close parallel. The inspiration of the Bible is not the only mystery in Scripture. The incarnation of Christ affords an excellent illustration of the divine and human sides of Scripture. Both the Savior and the Scriptures have heavenly and earthly natures. And both are united in a common medium of expression, one personal and the other propositional. Christ is a theanthropic Person, and the Bible is a theanthropic Book. In both the human side is perfect, as is the divine. Just as it is unorthodox to try to explain away the

29. Merrill C. Tenney, ed., *The Word for This Century,* p. 46.
30. Ibid.

divine nature of Christ in order to *understand* His human nature (as did the Arians),[31] or to sacrifice His true human nature in order to *explain* His divine nature (as did the Docetics),[32] so it is wrong to deny that the words of Scripture are *both* divine and human in their nature. The mistake is in trying to explain the inexplicable and in trying to fathom the unfathomable.

In the whole question of the *modus operandi* (mode of operation) of inspiration, a balance must be sought between the two extremes of divine dictation and human fallibility. Such a balance must guarantee the final product (the words of the Bible) and still guard the freedom and humanity of the authors. Just as one's salvation is both divinely determined (Rom. 8:29) and yet is freely chosen (John 1:12), so God working through the free expression of the human authors of Scripture produced the exact words He had infallibly predetermined.[33]

Summary and Conclusion

Inspiration encompasses the mysterious process by which divine causality on the prophetic agency resulted in scriptural authority, the Bible. Revelation is the *fact* of divine communication, inspiration is the *means* by which that communication is brought to the written record, and interpretation is the *understanding* of that communication. The total process of inspiration includes both the writer and the writing, although the product of inspiration is the authoritative writing and not the man. It is only the autographs (original writings) that are actually inspired, although accurate copies or translations are doctrinally authoritative, inasmuch as they correctly reproduce the original. There are no degrees of inspiration; all the Bible is equally inspired, that is, equally authoritative and true. The means or process of inspiration is a mystery of the providence of God, but the result of this process is a *verbal* (the words), *plenary* (extending to all parts equally), *inerrant* (errorless), and *authoritative* record.

31. Their error led to a call for the Council of Nicea (I), A.D. 325, where Arianism was condemned.
32. Their argument was that Christ did not actually die on the cross, but that He only "appeared" to die or "seemed" (Gk., *dokein*) to die on the cross.
33. See N.L. Geisler, "Inerrancy and Free Will," pp. 349-53.

3
Scriptural Claims for Inspiration in General

The Claim for Inspiration

In order to understand what is meant by inspiration as a whole, the biblical claim must be examined and compared with the character and contents of the Bible. The fact of inspiration as claimed in the Bible must be understood in the phenomena of inspiration. What the Bible says about itself should be understood in light of what the Bible shows in itself. In order to demonstrate the divine authority of the Scriptures, it must be shown that the Bible has a divine *claim* corroborated by a divine *character* and supported by divine *credentials*. For the present, however, discussion is limited to the general claim and character of inspiration (see chaps. 11 and 13).

Some Biblical Declarations and Implications About Inspiration

It is sometimes objected that it is a "circular argument" to refer to biblical passages in support of biblical claims. But that objection is unfounded for several reasons. (1) *Practically,* there is no better place to begin than with what is self-claimed. (2) *Legally,* a man can testify in his own behalf in a court of law. Why should not the Bible be permitted to witness in its own behalf? (3) *Logically,* the claim is not being used to *support* itself, but as a point of departure to *study* itself. The claim for inspiration within the Bible itself includes several pertinent characteristics.

It is verbal. The classical text for inspiration in the Bible (2 Tim. 3:16) affirms that the *writings* are inspired. Inspiration extends to the very *words* of Scripture. "Moses *wrote* down all the *words* of the LORD" (Ex. 24:4). Isaiah was told to "take for yourself a large tablet and *write*" (Isa. 8:1) and to "inscribe it on a *scroll,* that it may serve in the time to come as a witness forever" (30:8).[1] The distinct claim of the New Testament is that what had

1. See chap. 2 for additional references.

been written by the prophets is God's word; for example, the gospel of Mark introduces the prophet's word by the statement "It is written."[2]

Some have denied that the Bible actually claims to be verbally inspired by saying, "We need to remind ourselves that the verbal plenary formulation is, after all, only a doctrine—a nonbiblical doctrine at that."[3] However, in the light of the repeated general and specific claims that the *words* of the prophets are God's words, it would be a more consistent view simply to admit that the Bible does claim "verbal inspiration" for itself, whether or not that claim is accepted. The evidence that *the very words* of the Bible are God-given may be summarized briefly as follows:

1. It is the claim of the classical text that the *writings* are inspired (2 Tim. 3:16).
2. It is the emphatic testimony of Paul that he spoke in "*words* ... taught by the Spirit" (1 Cor. 2:13).
3. It is evident from the repeated formula "It is *written*" (e.g., Matt. 4:4, 7, 10).
4. Jesus said that that which was *written* in the whole Old Testament spoke of Him (Luke 24:27, 44; John 5:39; Heb. 10:7).
5. The New Testament constantly equates the Word of God with the *Scripture (writings)* of the Old Testament (cf. Matt. 21:42; Rom. 15:4; 2 Pet. 3:16).
6. Jesus indicated that not even the smallest part of a *Hebrew word* or *letter* could be broken (Matt. 5:18).
7. The New Testament refers to the *written record* as the "oracles of God" (Heb. 5:12).
8. Occasionally the writers were even told to "not omit *a word*" (Jer. 26:2), and John even pronounced an anathema upon all who would add to or subtract from the "*words* of the book of this prophecy" (Rev. 22:18-19).
9. The *very words* uttered by men in the Old Testament were considered to be God's words by the New Testament writers. It may be an academic option to deny that the Bible claims "verbal inspiration" for itself, but it is clearly not a biblical possibility.
10. *It is identified* with God's words. The words of the writers of Scripture are used interchangeably with what "God said." This gives rise to the

2. See chap. 5 for elaboration of this point.
3. Dewey M. Beegle, *The Inspiration of Scripture*, p. 187.

expression "What Scripture says, God says." Sometimes the Old Testament gives what the human author said, and the New Testament quotes the statement as what "God said." At other times the Old Testament records what "God says" and the New Testament quotes that text as what the human author says. Thus, what the author says and what God says are used interchangebly, as the following chart illustrates.

What Scripture Says, God Says	
GOD SAYS ...	SCRIPTURE SAYS ...
Gen. 12:3 Ex. 9:16	Gal. 3:8 Rom. 9:17
SCRIPTURE SAYS ...	GOD SAYS ...
Gen. 2:24 Ps. 2:1 Ps. 2:7 Ps. 16:10 Ps. 95:7 Ps. 97:7 Ps. 104:4 Isa. 55:3	Matt. 19:4-5 Acts 4:24-25 Heb. 1:5 Acts 13:35 Heb. 3:7 Heb. 1:6 Heb. 1:7 Acts 13:34

It is unbreakable. Another biblical claim for inspiration is that the written word is unbreakable, or *infallible*. Jesus said to the Jews, to whom He had quoted from Psalm 82, "Scripture cannot be broken" (John 10:35). Edward J. Young has put it,

> The force of his argument is very clear, and it may be paraphrased as follows: "what is stated in this verse from the psalms is true because this verse belongs to that body of writings known as Scripture, and the Scripture possesses an authority so absolute in character that *it cannot be broken*." When Christ here employs the word Scripture, he has in mind, therefore, not a particular verse in the psalms, but rather the entire group of writings of which this one verse is a part.[4]

For Jesus, then, inspiration meant a divinely authoritative and *unbreakable writing*.

It is irrevocable. Another claim for inspired writings is that their message is irrevocable. The Bible states, "For truly I say to you, until heaven and earth pass away, not the smallest letter or stroke shall pass away from the Law, until

4. Edward J. Young, "The Authority of the Old Testament," in *The Infallible Word*, by Ned B. Stonehouse and Paul Woolley, p. 55.

all is accomplished" (Matt. 5:18). Again, "But it is easier for heaven and earth to pass away than for one stroke of a letter of the Law to fail" (Luke 16:17). The claim is unequivocal; the message of the written word, including the smallest letters, must be fulfilled. In a similar claim, Jesus included the whole Old Testament, section by section, as He said, "All the things that are written about Me in the Law of Moses and the Prophets and the Psalms *must be fulfilled*" (Luke 24:44). Peter added these words: "Brethren, the Scripture had to be fulfilled, which the Holy Spirit foretold" (Acts 1:16).

It has final authority. The biblical writers and Jesus Himself claim that the written word is the *final arbitrator* in matters of faith and practice. Jesus quoted the Old Testament Scriptures with finality when resisting the tempter (Matt. 4:4, 7, 10). He used the Old Testament decisively to settle the question about the resurrection in His answer to the Pharisees (Matt. 21:42) and in vindicating His authority to cleanse the Temple (Mark 11:17). Paul used the Scriptures as the basis for his *arguments* with the Jews (Acts 17:2). Peter declared that "the untaught and unstable distort [Scriptures] ... to their own destruction" (2 Pet. 3:16). In fact, the finality that is based on the verbal inerrancy of the Old Testament as the word of God "is demonstrated by New Testament arguments which rest on a small historical detail (Heb 7:4-10), a word or phrase (Acts 15:13-17), or even the difference between the singular and the plural (Gal. 3:16)."[5]

It is plenary (full, complete, extending to every part). It is the claim of 2 Timothy 3:16 that *all* of Scripture (i.e., the whole Old Testament) is inspired, and not just part of it. That inspiration extends universally to all of Scripture is borne out by the use of the inclusive phrases "it is written," "the Scriptures," "the law and the prophets," "the word of God" (cf. Mark 7:13; see chap. 5 for a more complete elaboration of this point). Jesus referred to all sections of the Hebrew canon as predictive of Himself (Luke 24:27, 44), and Peter considered the Old Testament as a whole to be "prophetic writing" (2 Pet. 1:20-21) given by the "Spirit of Christ" (1 Pet. 1:10-11).

In light of these numerous claims concerning the divinely authoritative nature of Scripture, it is difficult to understand why James Barr asserts that the Bible does not teach its own inspiration and inerrancy. Carl Henry's "Introduction" discusses this very issue to the contrary of Barr's thesis, and he expounds it throughout fifteen theses in four volumes entitled *God, Revelation and Authority.*[6]

It has complete inerrancy. The Bible is wholly true and without error. Jesus said, "Thy Word is truth" (John 17:17). To those who denied the truth of

5. John A. Witmer, "The Biblical Evidence for the Verbal-Plenary Inspiration of the Bible," *Bibliotheca Sacra* 121, no. 483 (1964), p. 250.
6. James Barr, *Fundamentalism,* pp. 78-84 and elsewhere. Henry, *God, Revelation and Authority,* see especially pp. 7-16, where he introduces the issue of the nature of God's objective revelation in the authoritatively inerrant Scriptures.

Scripture He said, "You are mistaken, not understanding the Scriptures" (Matt. 22:29). The psalmist said, "The law of the Lord is perfect," and, "The sum of Thy word is truth" (Pss. 19:7; 119:160). The Bible is God's Word, and God cannot err (Heb 6:18; Titus 1:2). Scriptures are the utterances of the Holy Spirit (2 Tim. 3:16), and the Spirit of Truth cannot err. "To err is human," but the Bible is not a mere human book. It is divinely inspired, and a divinely inspired error is a contradiction in terms.[7]

Some Conclusions About Inspiration

Although it must be recognized that much of what has been claimed refers *explicitly* only to the Old Testament Scriptures, nevertheless, logically and *implicitly* the New Testament is included within this same claim of inspiration.

1. *The New Testament is "Scripture."* Stated in logical or syllogistic form, this argument is as follows:

> All "Scripture" is inspired (2 Tim. 3:16).
> The New Testament is also "Scripture" (1 Tim. 5:18; 2 Pet. 3:16).
> Therefore, the New Testament is inspired.

The use of the word *Scripture* has a distinct and technical sense in the New Testament, as may be readily seen by its specialized application. The term is reserved in its definitive and articular sense for only the authoritative and canonical books of Holy Writ. For the devout although converted Jews who wrote the books of the New Testament to describe any other books by this technical word amounts to claiming inspiration for them. As a matter of fact, that is precisely what Peter does claim for Paul's epistles when he writes, "Our beloved brother Paul . . . wrote to you . . . as also in all his letters . . . which the untaught and unstable distort, as they do also the rest of the *Scriptures*" (2 Pet. 3:15-16). Here Paul's writings are considered Scripture in the same sense as the Old Testament writings referred to earlier in the same passage (cf. 2 Pet. 3:5, 7-8). Although this passage does not claim that all the New Testament books are Scripture, it does include many of them. In 1 Timothy 5:18 the apostle Paul quotes from Luke, placing it on the same level with the rest of Scripture, using the introduction "for the Scripture says" (with reference to Luke 10:7). Certainly if Paul's and Luke's writings were considered Scripture, then the epistles of the apostles of Jesus, and particularly those of the "inner circle" (Peter and John), which traditionally make up most of the remainder of the New Testament, cannot logically be excluded from the category of inspired Scripture.

7. Stephen T. Davis holds this view. See his *The Debate About the Bible: Inerrancy Versus Infallibility*, pp. 118-19.

2. *The New Testament is "prophetic writing."* Another logical deduction about inspiration substantiates the foregoing. According to 2 Peter 1:20-21, no prophetic utterances (and writings) ever come by any other means than the moving of the Holy Spirit. Because the New Testament writings are considered to be "prophetic writings" too, it would follow that they must be included within the group of Spirit-moved utterances. Jesus promised to give His disciples a Spirit-directed ministry (John 14:26; 16:13), and the New Testament church claimed that prophetic gift (Eph. 4:11; 1 Cor. 14:31-32). Like their Old Testament counterparts, the New Testament prophets exercised their ministry both orally (Agabus, Acts 11:28) and in writing. John, the author of the book of Revelation, classified himself with his "brethren the [Old Testament] prophets" (Rev. 22:9). By direct inference, therefore, his writing claimed to be a prophetic writing. Indeed, that is what John himself said when he wrote, "I testify to everyone who hears the *words of the prophecy of this book:* if anyone adds to them, God shall add to him the plagues which are written in this book" (Rev. 22:18). Paul also considered his writings to be prophetic. In Ephesians 3:3-5 he speaks of his revelation and mystery "which in other generations was not made known to the sons of men, as it has now [in Paul's time] been revealed to His holy apostles and prophets[8] in the Spirit." Apostles and prophets are classed together, as are their revelations and writings, as Paul declared: "By revelation there wrote before in brief. And by referring to this, when you read you can understand my insight into the mystery of Christ."

To summarize, then, it is suggested that:

All "prophetic writings" are inspired (2 Pet. 1:20-21).
The New Testament is a "prophetic writing" (Rev. 22:18; Eph. 3:5).
Therefore, the New Testament is inspired.

3. *The New Testament is the "Word of God."* A further implication is that *both* the Old and New Testaments are the Word of God. The Old Testament is called "the Word of God" by Jesus (Matt. 15:6; John 10:35). Likewise, the New Testament writers considered it to be "the Word of God" alongside

8. In fact, the very prophets spoken of here may be New Testament prophets, upon whose teaching the foundation of the New Testament church is built (cf. Eph. 2:20; Acts 2:42). Commenting on the "prophets" of Eph. 2:20, Charles J. Ellicott wrote, "In spite of much ancient and valuable authority, it seems impossible to take the 'prophets' of this verse to be the prophets of the Old Testament. The order of the two words and the comparison of chaps. 3:5 and 4:11, appear to be decisive— to say nothing of the emphasis on the present, in contrast with the past, which runs through the whole chapter." See *Ellicott's Commentary,* 7:30. The same conclusion is stated by S.D.F. Salmond in *The Expositor's Greek Testament,* ed. W. Robertson Nicoll, 3:299. He comments, "Hence the *prophetai* are to be understood as *Christian* prophets, of whom large mention is made in the book of Acts and the Epistles—the N.T. prophets who in this same Epistle (3:5) are designated as *Christ's* prophets and are named (4:11) among the gifts of the ascended Lord to His Church."

the Old Testament (cf. 2 Cor. 4:2; Heb. 4:12; Rev. 1:2). Hence the argument may be summarized as follows:

> The Word of God is inspired (John 10:35).
> The New Testament is the Word of God (Heb. 4:12).
> Therefore, the New Testament is inspired.

The Character and Content of Inspiration

The Nature of Inspiration

The inspiration of Scripture includes its inerrancy, for the Bible is the Word of God (see chap. 5) and God cannot err (Heb. 6:18; Titus 1:12). To deny the inerrancy of Scripture is to impugn either the integrity of God or the identity of the Bible as the Word of God. This argument may be stated as follows:

> The Bible is the Word of God.
> God cannot err (Heb. 6:18; Titus 1:2).
> Therefore, the Bible cannot err.

It becomes apparent that what the Bible *means* by what it *says* about itself is what is manifest by the phenomena. That is, the claim for inspiration must be understood in light of the phenomena of Scripture (see chap. 2). Hence, attention must be centered on the *practical manifestations* of the *theological declaration* of inspiration. Such an examination reveals that whatever is meant by inspiration, it certainly *does not exclude* the following factors.

The use of variety of expression. Because God said the same thing in different ways, or at least from different viewpoints, at different times, inspiration cannot be meant to exclude a diversity of expression. The four Gospels relate the same story in different ways to different groups of people and sometimes even quote Christ as saying the same thing with different words. Compare, for example, Peter's famous confession at Caesarea Philippi:

Matthew records it:	"Thou art the Christ, the Son of the living God" (16:16).
Mark records it:	"Thou art the Christ" (8:29).
Luke records it:	"The Christ of God" (9:20).

Even the Decalogue, "written by the finger of God" (Deut. 9:10), is stated with variations the second time that God gave it (cf. Ex. 20:8-11 with Deut. 5:12-15).[9] There are many variations between the books of Kings and Chroni-

9. For example, Exodus gives creation as the reason for rest on the Sabbath, and Deuteronomy gives redemption as the reason.

cles in their description of identical events, yet there is no contradiction in the story they tell.[10]

If such important utterances as Peter's confession of Christ and the inscription on the cross (cf. Matt. 27:37; Mark 15:26; Luke 23:38; John 19:19) and such permanent and special laws as the one "written with the finger of God" can be stated in different ways, then there should be no problem in extending to the rest of Scripture a diversity of expression within the concept of a verbal inspiration.

The use of individuality and personalities. Inspiration does not exclude the use of different personalities, with their own literary styles and idiosyncrasies, in recording the written word of God. To observe this, one need only compare the powerful style of Isaiah with the mournful tone of Jeremiah in the Old Testament. In the New Testament, Luke manifests a marked medical interest,[11] James is distinctly practical, Paul is theological and polemical, and John has an obvious simplicity. God has communicated through a multiplicity of human personalities with their respective literary characteristics. The traditional biblical authors include a lawgiver (Moses), a general (Joshua), prophets (Samuel, Isaiah, et al.), kings (David and Solomon), a musician (Asaph), a herdsman (Amos), a prince and statesman (Daniel), a priest (Ezra), a tax collector (Matthew), a physician (Luke), a scholar (Paul), and fishermen (Peter and John). With such a variety of occupations represented by biblical writers, it is only natural that their personal interests and differences should be reflected in their writings.

The use of nonbiblical documents. Undoubtedly the doctrine of inspiration does not mean to exclude the use of human documents as a source of divine truth, because the use of such is exactly what the Bible does claim. Luke's gospel may have been based on the research he had done in the written sources of his day (cf. Luke 1:1-4). The writer of Joshua used the Book of Jasher for his famous quotation about the sun's standing still (Joshua 10:13).[12] The apostle Paul quoted unhesitatingly from a heathen poet (Acts 17:28) in his well-known Mars Hill address. Jude cited a noncanonical saying about the prophecy of Enoch (v. 14). The use of nonbiblical sources should not be thought incongruous with inspiration because it is to be remembered that "all truth is God's truth." The God "who said, 'Light shall shine out of darkness' " (2 Cor. 4:6) is able to speak truth through a pagan prophet (Num. 24:17), an unwitting high priest (John 11:50), and even a stubborn donkey (Num. 22:28).

10. See Gleason L. Archer, *Encyclopedia of Bible Difficulties,* pp. 191-92. Also see Nix, "1 Chronicles," and "2 Chronicles," in *The Criswell Study Bible,* pp. 428-519, 520-61; Payne, "The Validity of Numbers in Chronicles," pp. 5-58.
11. Cf. W. M. Ramsay, *St. Paul the Traveller and the Roman Citizen,* 3d ed. (Grand Rapids: Baker, 1949), pp. 38-39.
12. See Nix, "Joshua," in *The Criswell Study Bible,* pp. 267-96.

The use of nonscientific language. Inspiration certainly does not necessitate the use of scholarly, technical, or scientific language. The Bible is written for the common men of every generation, and it therefore uses their common, everyday language. The use of observational, nonscientific language is not *un*scientific, it is merely *pre*scientific. The Scriptures were recorded in *ancient* times by ancient standards, and it would be anachronistic to superimpose *modern* scientific standards upon them. It is no more unscientific to speak of the sun standing still (Joshua 10:12) than it is to refer to the sun rising (Joshua 1:16).[13] Contemporary meteorologists still speak daily of the times of "sunrise" and "sunset." The Scriptures say that the Queen of Sheba "came from the ends of the earth" (Matt. 12:42). Since "the ends of the earth" was only several hundred miles away, in Arabia,[14] it is apparent that this is another example of the use of observational language. In like manner, on the Day of Pentecost there were people "from every nation under heaven" (Acts 2:5). These nations are identified in Acts 2:9-11, and they do not include all the world literally (e.g., North and South America are excluded). Thus, universal language is used in a *geographical*[15] sense and is to be taken generally to mean "the then-known world."[16] The Bible was written to a nonscientific people in a prescientific age, and it is not reasonable for one to say the Bible is scientifically *incorrect*; it is merely scientifically *imprecise* by modern standards. But, in sacrificing scientific precision, the Bible has gained a perfection by its universality and simplicity of style.

The Bible also uses round numbers (e.g., 1 Chron. 19:18; 21:5). It may be imprecise from the standpoint of a contemporary technological society to speak of 3.14159265... as three, but it is not incorrect for an ancient nontechnological people. Three and fourteen hundredths can be rounded off to three. That is sufficient for a "cast *metal* sea" (2 Chron. 4:2) in an ancient Hebrew temple, even though it would not suffice for a computer in a rocket. But one should not expect scientific precision in a prescientific age. The Bible speaks correctly in the language of its day in the mode of understanding of the people of that day. The Bible must be judged by the very nature of the divine revelation. The revelation came from God through men speaking human language and living in a cultural context. To be meaningful it had to come in the language of the prophets and apostles and employ the cultural background of figures, illustrations, analogies, and other things generally associated with linguistic communication. No artificial or abstract theory of inerrancy that imposes modern scientific or technical precision upon the Scriptures is warranted.

13. Ibid.
14. Emil G. Kraeling, *Rand McNally Bible Atlas,* p. 231, map IV; Yohanan Aharoni and Michael Avi-Yonah, *The Macmillan Bible Atlas,* rev. ed., p. 21, map 15.
15. Universal language used in a *generic* sense, as in Rom. 3:23, is different. Language used generically includes all who participate in the common nature or name.
16. Cf. Bernard Ramm, *Protestant Biblical Interpretation,* rev. ed., pp. 134 ff.

The use of a variety of literary devices. Finally, it should not be thought that an "inspired" book must have been written in one, and only one, literary mold. Man is not limited in his modes of expression, and there is no reason to suppose that God can utilize only one style or literary genre in His communication to man. The Bible reveals a number of literary devices. Several whole books are written in *poetic* style (e.g., Job, Psalms, Proverbs). The synoptic gospels are filled with *parables*. In Galatians 4, Paul uses an example of an *allegory*. The New Testament abounds with *metaphors* (e.g., 2 Cor. 3:2-3; James 3:6) and *similes* (cf. Matt. 20:1; James 1:6); *hyperboles* may also be found (e.g., Col. 1:23; John 21:25; 2 Cor. 3:2). And Jesus Himself used the device of *satire* (Matt. 19:24 with 23:24). In a word, then, the claim for inspiration, as understood in the light of the character of the inspired record itself, reveals that "inspiration" must not be viewed as a mechanical or wooden process. It is, rather, a dynamic and personal process that results in a divinely authoritative and inerrant product—the written Word of God.

The Extent of Inspiration

Some have suggested that the Bible is true as a whole but not necessarily in every part (see chap. 2 discussion). They argue that Scripture can always be trusted on moral matters, but is not always correct on historical matters. They say the Bible can always be relied on in the spiritual domain, but not always in the scientific area. They came to this conclusion because they believe that "it is the intention of the Holy Spirit to teach us how one goes to heaven, and not how the heavens go."[17] This position is inadequate for several reasons.

Inspiration includes everything the Bible teaches.

1. The Bible teaches only *truth* (John 17:17), but it contains some *lies*, for example, Satan's lie (Gen. 3:4; cf. John 8:44) and Rahab's lie (Josh. 2:4). Inspiration covers the Bible fully and completely in the sense that it records accurately and truthfully even the lies and errors of sinful beings. The truth of Scripture is to be found in what the Bible *reveals* not in everything it *records*. Unless this distinction is held, it may be incorrectly concluded that the Bible teaches immorality because it narrates David's sin (2 Sam. 11:4), that it promotes polygamy because it records Solomon's (1 Kings 11:3), or that it asserts atheism because it quotes the fool as saying "there is no God " (Ps. 14:1). In each case the interpreter of Scripture must seek the *commitment of the writer* of the particular passage in question. The important thing for the interpreter to keep in mind is not what the writer *seems* to say, not what he refers to, nor even whom he quotes, but what he *really affirms* in the text.

17. *"Cio e l'intenzione dello Spirito Santo essere d'insegnarci come si vadia al cielo, e non come vadia il cielo,"* "Lettera a Madama Cristina di Lorena Granduchessa di Toscana (1615)" *Le Opere Di Galileo Galilei,* 5:307-48.

2. The scientific (factual) and spiritual truths of Scripture are often inseparable. (*a*) For example, one cannot separate the spiritual truth of Christ's resurrection from the physical fact that His body permanently vacated the tomb (Matt. 28:6; 1 Cor. 15:13-19). The resurrection of Christ is more than a physical event (Rom. 4:25)—it is also a spiritual victory (1 Cor. 15:50-58)—but it is not less than a physical event. Thus, if one does not accept the truth of the physical resurrection, then there is no basis for spiritual salvation. As Paul put it, "If Christ has not been raised, your faith is worthless; you are still in your sins" (1 Cor. 15:17). (*b*) Likewise, the virgin birth of Christ cannot be merely a spiritual truth. If Christ were not born of an actual virgin, then He is not the sinless Son of God He claimed to be. Although the virgin birth did not cause His deity, it was an indication of it. It was not the source of Christ's divinity, but it was a symbol of it (Matt. 1:23). For if He were not virgin-born then He is no different from the rest of the human race, on whom the stigma of Adam's sin rests (Rom. 5:12). Here again the physical and the spiritual dimensions of the truth go hand-in-hand so that to deny the biological reality is to deny the spiritual truth. (*c*) The same is true of Christ's crucifixion. It is not merely physical blood that saves, but "without the shedding of [physical] blood there is no forgiveness" (Heb. 9:22). Likewise, Adam's existence and fall cannot be a myth. If there were no literal Adam and actual fall, then the spiritual teaching about inherited sin and eventual or physical death (Rom. 5:12) are wrong. The historical reality and the theological doctrine stand or fall together. The inseparable relation between the physical and the spiritual is evident in the nature of man, who is made up of soul and body. Man is made in the image of God, but an attack upon the body (murder) is considered an attack on the image of God and worthy of capital punishment in the Old Testament (Gen. 9:6) There, too, one cannot negate the physical dimension of man without also rejecting the spiritual aspect.

3. Moral truths of Scripture are often based on or are inseparably connected with scientific or factual truths. *(a)* The depravity of man and his consequent physical death is based on the truth of a literal Adam (Rom. 5:12). *(b)* The doctrine of the incarnation is inseparable from the historical truth about Jesus of Nazareth (John 1:1, 14). *(c)* Jesus' moral teaching about marriage was based on His teaching about God's joining a literal Adam and Eve together in marriage (Matt. 19:4-5). In each of those cases the moral or theological teaching is devoid of its intended meaning apart from the historical or factual space-time event. If one denies that the literal space-time event occurred, then there is no basis for believing the scriptural doctrine built upon it.

4. Jesus often made a direct comparison between important spiritual truths and Old Testament events He presented as historically true. For instance,

using a strong comparison Jesus said, "*Just as* Jonah was three days and three nights in the belly of the sea monster, *so shall* the Son of Man be three days and three nights in the heart of the earth" (Matt. 12:40). Both the occasion and the manner of that comparison make it clear that Jesus was affirming the historicity of Jonah in connection with the truth about His death and resurrection. He certainly was not saying, "Just as you believe that mythology about Jonah, so I would like to tell you about the historicity of My death and resurrection." In the same way that Jesus closely associated the literal truth about Himself with that of Jonah, He also connected the truth of His literal second coming (cf. Acts 1:10, 11) to the literal truth about Noah's flood. He said, "The coming of the Son of Man will be *just like* the days of Noah" (Matt. 24:37). Both the content and emphasis of these comparisons reveal that Jesus believed in the historicity of those Old Testament events.

5. Jesus asserted that if He could not be trusted in historical matters, then He should not be trusted in heavenly matters either. Just after speaking to Nicodemus about physical birth and winds, Jesus said to him, "If I told you earthly things and you do not believe, how shall you believe if I tell you heavenly things?" (John 3:12). In short, if the Bible cannot be trusted when it speaks about temporal things that we can see, how can it be trusted when it discusses eternal things that cannot be seen (2 Cor. 4:18)? So if the Bible does not speak truthfully about the physical world, it cannot be trusted when it speaks about the spiritual world. The two are intimately related.

Inspiration includes everything the Bible touches. Not only does inspiration include all the Bible explicitly *teaches* but it also includes everything the Bible *touches*. For instance, probably nowhere is the central idea of a biblical passage to teach explicitly about angels or demons. They are virtually always brought in incidentally. Yet everything the Bible says about them incidentally is still absolutely true. For the incidental teachings of Scripture are no less true than the essential teachings. Whatever the Bible declares is true, whether it be a major point or a minor point. The Bible is God's Word, and God cannot err in any point. All the parts are as true as the whole that they comprise.

Some have suggested that only the main purpose of the Bible is true, but not every minor point. They say the meaning of Scripture is to be understood in the light of its saving purpose. And because the central purpose of Scripture is to get men saved (2 Tim. 3:16),[18] then whatever is not essential to that central purpose does not really matter.[19] This position is both inadequate and unbiblical for several reasons.

18. See exposition of 2 Timothy 3:16-17 in chap. 2.
19. Jack B. Rogers and Donald K. McKim, *The Authority and Interpretation of the Bible: An Historical Approach*, pp. 313, 389-90, 401. For a refutation of this view see John D. Woodbridge, *Biblical Authority: A Critique of the Rogers/McKim Proposal*, esp. chaps. 8 and 9, pp. 141-56.

1. Purpose does not determine meaning. Meaning is *what* is said; purpose is *why* it is said. But why something is said does not determine the meaning of what is said. The meaning of many passages of Scripture is understood apart from knowing why they were uttered in the first place. Consider the following: "You are not to boil a kid in the milk of its mother" (Ex. 23:19). "You shall not wear a material mixed of wool and linen together" (Deut. 22:11). Everyone who knows the words of those sentences knows exactly what they mean, even if they do not have the foggiest idea about the author's intended purpose. The command not to boil a kid in its mother's milk would have the same meaning if it appeared in a cookbook, although the significance of the passage is obviously enhanced by its being in God's Book. Likewise, the meaning of the exhortation not to mix wool and linen would mean the same thing in a home economics or textiles book, even though it would have no religious significance in that setting.[20]

2. It is not the *purposes* of the biblical authors that are inspired; the *propositions* of Scripture are inspired. The locus of inspiration is in the written text (2 Tim. 3:16), not in the author's mind behind the text. It is the words that are inspired (1 Cor. 2:13), not merely the ideas behind them. Just as beauty is in the painting and not behind it, even so meaning is expressed in the words of Scripture and not behind them. Hence, it is both wrong and inappropriate to look for the purpose(s) of authors behind their words. Their purposes are expressed in their propositions. It is incorrect to seek the intention of biblical writers beyond their writings; their intentions can be found in their written affirmations. Their meaning is expressed in their written message.

Is there "occasional inspiration"? First Kings 13:11-32 relates a story of an "old prophet" who lied, claiming that God had spoken to him when He had not (v. 18). This raises the question of whether one can be a true prophet on one occasion and a false one at another time. That is, could there be occasional inspiration (really, revelation)? If so, then how could one know when to trust a prophet and when not to trust him? There are two possible responses. First, one can deny "occasional inspiration" and point out that 1 Kings 13 does not say the old prophet was a true prophet or that he ever gave a genuine prophecy from God. In that connection it could be noted that his prophecy was not given publicly, nor was it confirmed by any signs as a genuine prophecy by a true prophet (see 1 Kings 13:3). The other alternative is to argue that all prophets give revelation only on certain occasions. Whenever there is doubt about the divine origin of a message, it is confirmed by miracles. That is illustrated by God's confirmation of Moses over Korah (Num. 16:1-50), and Elijah over the prophets of Baal (1 Kings 18:15-40). True prophets are confirmed by God, and false ones are condemned by Him. Either

20. Norman L. Geisler, "Meaning and Purpose: The Cart and the Horse."

explanation is consistent with the orthodox view of inspiration and canonization. The crucial question is not whether there were other occasions when biblical writers wrote uninspired books. All that is necessary is that the ones they wrote, which are in the Bible, be possessed of divine inspiration.[21]

Accommodation or adaptation? Some have asserted that in the process of communicating their message, the biblical writers accommodated their teaching to some erroneous beliefs of their day. Some even believe that that kind of accommodation is a necessary part of conveying infinite truth in finite terms.[22] Several things render those conclusions false. First of all, they confuse *accommodation* to human error with *adaptation* to human finitude. Just because God condescends to man's level to communicate His truth to them does not mean He has to compromise His truth in doing so. Adaptation to human limitations does not necessitate accommodation to human error. A mother may answer a four-year-old child's question about where babies come from by saying, "Babies come from their mothers' tummies." That is not false, but it is truth adapted to the child's level. A few years later, when the child asks how the baby got there, it would also be true to say, "Daddy placed a seed there and it grew." Neither is this the whole story, but at least it is not the stork story, which is false. God uses anthropomorphisms when speaking to man (*anthropos*), but He does not use myths (2 Peter 1:16). In short, God adapts His truth to limited human understanding, but He never accommodates Himself to human error.

The biblical view of inspiration does not assert that prophets and apostles were infallible, nor that in their own learning they were exempt from limitations imposed by their cultures. What it asserts, rather, is that the writers did not teach the doubtful views of the cultures in which they lived.[23] In fact, there is abundant evidence in the New Testament that Jesus never accommodated Himself to the false beliefs of His day. Some of the following examples will serve to illustrate.

1. Jesus rebuked those who believed "tradition" rather than the Word of God (Matt. 15:1-3).
2. Jesus set His words over against the false beliefs of Jewish teachers six times by using emphatic words: "you have heard . . . but I say to you . . ." (Matt. 5:21, 27, 31, 33, 38, 43).

21. This becomes a question of canonicity (see chap. 12). Chap. 13 has a discussion of the characteristics of a true prophetic writing.
22. Rogers and McKim, pp. 309, 342, 431-33; Gerhard Maier, *The End of the Historical-Critical Method,* esp. pp. 88-92. Harry R. Boer, *Above the Battle? The Bible and Its Critics*, pp. 78-109, has utilized such an approach to devise two types of infallibility: traditional and organic.
23. Carl F. H. Henry, ed., *God, Revelation and Authority,* vol. 4, *God Who Speaks and Shows: Fifteen Theses, Part Three,* p. 152.

3. Jesus rebuked the famous teacher of the Jews, Nicodemus, saying, "Are you the teacher of Israel, and do not understand these things?" (John 3:10).
4. Jesus bluntly declared to the Sadducees, "You are mistaken . . ." (Matt. 22:29).
5. Jesus' severe words of Matthew 23 are scarcely accommodating: "Woe to you, blind guides . . ." (v. 16); "you fools . . ." (v. 17); you serpents, you brood of vipers . . ." (v. 33).
6. When Jesus took a whip and chased the animals of the money changers from the Temple, He was not accommodating to their false beliefs and practices (John 2:15-16).

In short, Jesus never accommodated truth to error. Instead, He rebuked error with the truth. He said, "You shall know the truth, and the truth shall make you free" (John 8:32). Even Jesus' enemies acknowledged His straightforwardness, saying, "Teacher, we know that You are truthful and teach the way of God in truth, and defer to no one" (Matt. 22:16).

Limitation or misunderstanding? An important question arises from the issue of Jesus never accommodating to human error, and it is related to His divine-human nature. The Bible speaks of Christ's "increasing in wisdom" (Luke 2:52), not knowing what was on the fig tree (Matt. 21:19), and not knowing the time of His second coming (Matt. 24:36). If Jesus were limited in His understanding as a man, was it not possible that He made some mistakes in His teaching?

This question is built on a confusion of limitation and misunderstanding. It is one thing to have a limited understanding and quite another to have a wrong understanding. All human understanding is limited. It is limited because man himself is a finite creature. But it does not follow from that that every human understanding is in error.

Further, even if Jesus were limited in what He knew as a man, it does not follow that He was wrong in what He did know. A limited knowledge of truth is not the same as error. In fact, whatever Jesus did know He affirmed with absolute authority, saying, "All authority has been given to Me in heaven and on earth" (Matt. 28:18). Some twenty-five times He introduced His teachings with the formula, "Verily, verily" or "truly, truly" (cf. John 3:3, 5, 11). Jesus placed His words on the very level with God's words (Matt. 7:26-29). He declared, "Heaven and earth will pass away, but My words shall not pass away" (Matt. 24:35). Finally, Jesus said He only taught what the Father gave Him to teach: "I speak these things as the Father taught Me" (John 8:28). He also asserted, "I can do nothing on My own initiative . . . because I do not seek My own will, but the will of Him who sent Me" (John 5:30).

In His great prayer toward the end of His earthly ministry Jesus said, "The words which Thou gavest Me I have given to them" (John 17:8). Again He said, "I have given them Thy word" (John 17:14). What Jesus said is what He received from the Father. Hence, to say Christ was misinformed is to charge God the Father with misunderstanding and error. So although Jesus may have been limited in His human understanding regarding issues about which He did not speak, there was no limitation of His authority on the matters He did address.

Summary and Conclusion

The Bible claims to be the verbal, infallible, and inerrant Word of God. Because divine authority extends to every part of Scripture, this is verbal plenary inspiration. Although the general claims of the New Testament explicitly refer to only the Old Testament, they may be applied to the New Testament as well, because it too is "Scripture" and "prophetic."

The divine nature of Scripture does not rule out the fact that it is also a human book, manifesting the variety of literary styles, figures of speech, and individual personalities of its authors. However, like Christ, the Bible is theanthropic, having both the divine and human elements united in one expression. As a result, God adapted His truth to finite understanding, but He did not accommodate it to human misunderstanding. Therefore, on the authority of Christ, the Scriptures are completely inerrant.

4

Specific Claims of Inspiration in the Old Testament

The discussion to this point has centered on a few major texts that claim inspiration for the Bible. Now attention must be given to the specific claims of each section and book of the Bible individually. Is the specific claim *in* these books the same as the claim *for* them by other books? To answer that question fully, the next several chapters will discuss the claim of inspiration *in* the Old Testament (chap. 4), the claim *for* the Old Testament *in* the New Testament (chap. 5), the claim *in* the New Testament (chap. 6), the claim of inspiration *for* the New Testament *in* the church to the Reformation (chap. 8), the doctrines of inspiration since the Reformation (chap. 9), and divergent views of revelation and inspiration in the modern world (chap. 9). The present chapter is concerned with carefully examining what the Old Testament claims in and for its own inspiration.

The Claim for Inspiration in Each Book of the Old Testament

An Examination of the Claim for Inspiration

A brief examination of each of the books of the Old Testament will help to confirm in detail the thesis that each of the individual sections claims to be divinely authoritative. It should be noted that every book of the Old Testament does not have an explicit claim to divine inspiration. Nevertheless, it can be demonstrated that most of them do have such a distinct claim, and that the remainder have either an implicit claim or a character that serves as an implicit claim to inspiration.

Genesis. In Genesis God spoke to the patriarchs (cf. Gen. 12, 26, 46), and they made records in a permanent "family album" of divine dealings under the title "This is the book [*records*] of the generations of . . ." (5:1; 6:9; 10:1; 11:10; 25:12, 19; 36:1; 37:2).

1. *Michelangelo's "Moses" (Metropolitan Museum of Art)*

Exodus. In Exodus the record reads, "God spoke all these words" (20:1). "And the tablets were God's work, and the writing was God's writing" (32:16). Moses said to the people, "These are the things that the Lord has commanded you to do" (35:1).

Leviticus. The introduction to Leviticus says, "The Lord called to Moses and spoke to him from the tent of meeting, saying . . ." (1:1). "The Lord said to Moses" is found repeatedly (cf. 4:1; 5:14; 6:1, 8).

Numbers. This book repeatedly records, "The Lord spoke to Moses" (1:1; see 2:1; 4:1; 5:1; 6:1; 8:1), and it closes by saying, "These are the commandments and the ordinances which the Lord commanded to the sons of Israel" (36:13).

Deuteronomy. In Deuteronomy, Moses' speeches are regarded as God's word, saying, "You shall not add to the word which I am commanding you, nor take away from it" (4:2); it even sets forth tests of truth for divine utterances: "When a prophet speaks in the name of the Lord, if the thing does not come about or come true, that is the thing which the Lord has not spoken" (18:22).

Joshua. In this book, Joshua relates how "after the death of Moses ... the Lord spoke to Joshua, 'This day I will begin to exalt you in the sight of all Israel, that they may know that just as I was with Moses, I will be with you' " (1:1-3:7). "And Joshua wrote these words in the book of the law of God" (24:26).

Judges. After the death of Joshua, the book of Judges reveals that "the Lord said" (1:2), and again, later, God spoke to Gideon (6:25). The angel of the Lord appeared with a message on several occasions (Judg. 2, 5, 6, 13).

Ruth. This book was possibly appended to the book of Judges in its original position (see discussion in chaps. 1, 12) and, if so, needs no explicit reference to God speaking. However, this book does give a record of divine activity, as it records an important link in the messianic chain, namely, the ancestors of David the king, Boaz and Ruth (4:21; cf. Matt. 1:5-6).

1 and 2 Samuel. The books of 1 and 2 Samuel, which were originally one book, have many references to the voice of God. Through Samuel, the traditional author of the book, these books record, "And the Lord said to Samuel" (1 Sam. 3:11); "Thus the word of Samuel came to all Israel" (4:1). Then 1 Chronicles 29:29 adds, "The acts of King David, from first to last, are written in the chronicles of Samuel the seer, in the chronicles of Nathan the prophet, and in the chronicles of Gad the seer."

1 and 2 Kings. These books have no explicit claim to inspiration. Tradition ascribes them to Jeremiah the prophet (Baba Bathra 15a), which would automatically assume them to be prophetic. The emphasis on the divine ministry of the prophets, and the prophetic viewpoint of the books of Kings, would confirm the traditional view that some prophet wrote these books. Hence, they too would be divinely authoritative.

1 and 2 Chronicles. These books lack an overt claim to inspiration, but they do present an authoritative history of Israel, Judah, and the Temple from the priestly point of view. The books *assume* authority rather than stating or claiming it. And because the books are descriptive rather than didactic, there is no need for an explicit reference to their message as being a "thus *says* the Lord." There is, however, an implicit, yet clear, "thus *does* the Lord," which is even more discernible than in Kings (cf. 2 Chron. 35:20-21).

Ezra-Nehemiah. Continuing the Temple-centered history of Judah, Ezra-Nehemiah declares definitely that God was responsible for the restoration of the deported nation. Although the book makes no explicit claim for its inspiration, there is again the clear assumption that it is a record of God's *deeds,* and such a record is no less authoritative than a record of God's words.

Esther. The book of Esther fits into the same category as Ezra-Nehemiah. Even though the name of God is absent from the book (except in acrostic form),[1] nonetheless, the presence of God is certainly evident as He protects and preserves His people. The book implicitly claims to be a *true record* of God's providence over His people, which is what inspiration means (see chap. 2 discussion).

Job. In Job, not only does the author claim to give a view into the very council chamber of heaven (Job 1-2), but he records the actual words of God spoken out of the whirlwind (38:1 ff.). Between chapters 2 and 38, an accurate record of what Job and his friends said is presented.[2]

Psalms. A book addressed primarily *to* God, Psalms can hardly be expected to say, "God said," or, "Thus says the Lord." There is, however, within the very selection and structure of the Psalms, a divine approval of the theology and truth which is reflected in the varied spiritual experiences of the psalmists. It is apparent that God moved particular men to record their select experiences, with His approbation, for future generations. The last five psalms sum up the divine exhortation "Praise the Lord." This is a book in which *God declares how men should praise Him.* In fact, 2 Samuel 23:1-2 says that David, who wrote many of the psalms, was Spirit-directed in his utterances.

Proverbs. This book is introduced as "The proverbs of Solomon" (1:1). That Solomon claims these words of wisdom to be the Word of God is evident when he writes: "Have not I written to you excellent things of counsels and knowledge, to make you know the certainty of the words of truth, that you may correctly answer to him who sent you?" (22:20-21). It will be remembered that Solomon's wisdom was God-given for that very purpose—to help his people (cf. 1 Kings 3:9 ff.). Proverbs 25 and following are "proverbs of Solomon which . . . Hezekiah, king of Judah, transcribed" (25:1) but are nonetheless Solomon's. Proverbs 30 and 31 each claim in the first verse to be an "oracle," or "utterance" (NKJV) from God (cf. 2 Chron. 9:29).

Ecclesiastes. This book has clear and authoritative exhortations (cf. 11:19; 12:1, 12) which lead to this definite conclusion: "When all has been heard . . . fear God and keep His commandments because this applies to every person" (12:13). That is, the teaching of this book claims to be the word from God on the subject.

Song of Solomon. Although it has no explicit claim for its divine inspiration, this book was thought to be inspired by the Jews on the grounds that it gave a picture of the Lord's love for Israel. Others have suggested that it is God's word about the sanctity of marriage.[3] Whatever the interpretation, the implication is that the book is a revelation from God about the intimacy and purity of love (whether human or divine).

1. W. Graham Scroggie, *Know Your Bible,* 1:96.
2. The New Testament quotes from this section using the formula "It is written." Cf. 1 Cor. 3:19, as it cites Job 5:13.
3. Edward J. Young, *An Introduction to the Old Testament,* p. 355.

The Prophets. The prophetical books may be summarily treated, because the record is replete with distinctive claims as to the divine origin of the individual messages. Isaiah 1:1-2: "The vision of Isaiah ... for the Lord speaks." Jeremiah (to which Lamentations was originally appended) 1:1-2: "The words of Jeremiah ... to whom the word of the Lord came." Ezekiel 1:3: "The word of the Lord came expressly to Ezekiel." Daniel received visions and dreams (e.g., Dan. 7:1) as well as angelic messages from God (e.g., 9:21ff.). Hosea through Malachi were all one book (The Twelve) in the Hebrew Bible (see discussion in chap. 1), but each one has an explicit claim, as Amos 1:3 and the opening verse in each of the following books indicate: Hosea, Joel, Obadiah, Jonah, Micah, Nahum, Habakkuk, Zephaniah, Haggai, Zechariah, Malachi.

Although many of these revelations were given originally in oral delivery, they were eventually preserved in written form. Numerous references to such written utterances from God are provided in Scripture (cf. 2 Chron. 21:12; Isa. 30:8; Jer. 25:13; 29:1; 30:2; 36:2; 51:60; Ezek. 43:11; Dan. 7:1; Hab. 2:2).

An Explanation of Books That Lack Explicit Claim for Inspiration

The vast majority of the books of the Old Testament (about eighteen of twenty-four) explicitly claim that they are God's words to men, but some do not have such clear statements as to their origin. Several reasons may be offered in the clarification of this important matter.

They are all part of a given section. Every book is included within the organic unity of a section (the Law and the Prophets) in which there is distinct and indisputable claim for inspiration, which fact thereby speaks for every book within that section. As a result, each individual book does not need to state its own case; the claim has already been made for it by the claim made for the section as a whole and confirmed by the fact that later biblical books refer to the authority of that particular section as a whole. Of course, it is to be assumed that unless a book had an implicit claim to inspiration of its own it would never have been included in the canon from the beginning. This, however, is a matter of canonization and is considered more fully in chapters 12, 14, and 15.

Another reason may be found in their nature. It is only the historical and poetical books that do not contain direct statements as to their divine origin; all of the didactic books do have an explicit "thus says the Lord." The obvious reason that the historical and poetical books do not is that they present "what God *showed*" (History) rather than "what God *said*" (Law and Prophets). Nonetheless, there is an implicit didactic, "thus says the Lord," even in the historical and poetical books. History is what God said in the concrete events of national life. Poetry is what God said in the hearts and aspirations of individuals within the nation. Both are what God said, just as much so as the explicit record He spoke through the law and the other didactic writings.

Traditional writers of the books were men accredited of God with prophetic ministries. Solomon, who is credited by Jewish tradition with writing Song of Solomon, Proverbs, and Ecclesiastes, had God-given wisdom (1 Kings 4:29). Furthermore, he fulfilled the qualification for a prophet laid down in Numbers 12:6: one to whom God spoke in visions or dreams (cf. 1 Kings 11:9). David is credited with writing nearly half of the psalms. And although the psalms themselves do not lay direct claim to divine inspiration, David's testimony of his own ministry is recorded in 2 Samuel 23:2: "The Spirit of the Lord spoke by me, and His word was on my tongue." Jeremiah, the traditional author of 1 and 2 Kings, has well-known prophetic credentials (cf. Jer. 1:4, 17). Chronicles and Ezra-Nehemiah are attributed to Ezra the priest, who functioned with all the authority of a prophet interpreting the law of Moses and instituting civil and religious reforms thereupon (cf. Jer. 1:10, 13). So then, either the books of the Old Testament testify for themselves, or the men who are believed to have written them, almost without exception,[4] claim them to be the authoritative word of God.

The Claim of Inspiration in the Law and the Prophets

The earliest and most basic division of the Old Testament Scriptures was that of the Law and the Prophets, that is, the five books of Moses and then all of the prophetic writings that came after them. The New Testament refers to this twofold arrangement about a dozen times (cf. Matt. 5:17; 7:12), and only once does it even suggest a possible threefold (Luke 24:44). However, in the same chapter, Jesus refers to "Moses and . . . the prophets" as being "all the Scriptures" (Luke 24:27). Within the Old Testament itself there is a basic, twofold division between the law of Moses and all the prophets who came after him (Neh. 9:14, 26 and Dan. 9:2, 11). The same twofold division is carried on in the period between the Old and New Testaments (2 Macc. 15:9) and in the Qumran community (*Manual of Discipline* 1.3; 8.15; 9.11). A consideration of these two divisions of the Hebrew Old Testament will reveal what each claimed for itself and what one claimed for the other as regards the matter of divine inspiration.[5]

4. The book of Esther does not have an explicit claim to inspiration and its author is unknown. Any book of undetermined authorship raises questions about its authority. Only those who originally recognized it as part of the canon were in a position to know its prophetic source. See the discussion on Esther and these other Old Testament books of questioned authority in chap. 15.
5. See discussion in chaps. 14 and 15.

The Law

The first and most important section of the Old Testament is the Torah, or law of Moses. The claim for inspiration in this section of the Bible is very distinct, as has already been seen from the previous examination of the individual books of the Law.

The claim in the Law for inspiration. The books of Exodus (32:16), Leviticus (1:1), Numbers (1:1), and Deuteronomy (31:26) all make an explicit claim to inspiration. Genesis alone has no such direct claim. However, Genesis too was considered to be part of the "book of Moses" (cf. Neh. 13:1;2 Chron. 35:12) and by virtue of that association has the same divine authority. Whatever holds for one book holds for all of them. In other words, a claim by or for one book in this canonical section is thereby a claim for all of them, since they were all unified under a title such as *the* book of Moses or *the* law of Moses.

The claim for the Law. Throughout the remainder of the Old Testament, in an unbroken succession, the law of Moses was enjoined on the people as the law of God; Moses' voice was heeded as God's. Joshua began his ministry as Moses' successor by saying, "This book of the law shall not depart from your mouth ... that you may be careful to do according to all that is written in it" (Josh. 1:8). In Judges 3:4, God tested the people of Israel to know whether they "would obey the commandments of the Lord, which He had commanded their fathers through Moses." "Then Samuel said to the people, 'It is the Lord who appointed Moses and Aaron and who brought your fathers up from the land of Egypt ... But they forgot the Lord their God' " (1 Sam. 12:6, 9). In Josiah's day, "Hilkiah the priest found the book of the law of the Lord given by Moses" (2 Chron. 34:14). In exile, Daniel recognized Moses' law as God's Word, saying, "The curse has been poured out on us, along with the oath which is written in the law of Moses the servant of God, for we have sinned against Him. Thus He has confirmed His words which He had spoken against us" (Dan. 9:11-12). Even in postexilic times, the revival under Nehemiah came as a result of obedience to Moses' law (cf. Ezra 6:18, Neh. 13:1).

The Prophets

The next section of the Hebrew Scripture was known as "The Prophets." This section literally abounds with claims of its divine inspiration.

The claim in the Prophets. The characteristic "thus says the Lord" and similar expressions are found here and in other parts of the Old Testament hundreds of times.[6] A sample survey finds Isaiah proclaiming, "Listen, O heavens, and hear, O earth; for the Lord speaks" (Isa. 1:2). Jeremiah wrote,

6. See for example, Robert L. Thomas, gen. ed., *New American Standard Exhaustive Concordance of the Bible* (Nashville: Holman, 1981), pp. 1055-65.

"And the word of the Lord came to me, saying . . ." (Jer. 1:11). "The word of the Lord came expressly to Ezekiel" (Ezek. 1:3). Similar statements are found throughout the twelve "minor" prophets (cf. Hos. 1:1-2; Joel 1:1).

The claim for the Prophets. Some references in the later prophets reveal a high regard for the utterances of earlier prophets. God spoke to Daniel through the writings of Jeremiah (cf. Dan. 9:2 with Jer. 25:11). Ezra likewise recognized the divine authority in Jeremiah's writings (Ezra 1:1), as well as in those of Haggai and Zechariah (Ezra 5:1). One of the strongest passages is found in one of the last of the Old Testament prophets, Zechariah. He speaks of "the law and the words which the Lord of hosts had sent by His Spirit through the former prophets" (Zech. 7:12). In a similar passage in the last historical book of the Old Testament, Nehemiah writes, "Thou [God] didst bear with them for many years, and admonished them by Thy Spirit through Thy prophets" (Neh. 9:30). These examples confirm the high regard that the latter prophets had for the writings of their predecessors; they considered them to be the Word of God, given by the Spirit of God for the good of Israel.

The books of the prophets later sectioned off as "Writings"[7] are automatically included in the overall claim for the prophets of which they were a part. Even the book of Psalms (part of the "Writings"), which Jesus singled out for its messianic importance (Luke 24:44), was part of the Law and the Prophets that Jesus said constituted "all the Scriptures" (Luke 24:27). Josephus placed Daniel (which was later in the "Writings") in the "Prophets" section of his day (*Against Apion* 1.8). So whatever alternate (or later) manner of arranging the Old Testament books into three sections may have existed, it is clear that the early arrangement was a twofold division of Law and Prophets (which included the books later to be known as "Writings") from late Old Testament times through the "intertestamental" period and on into the New Testament era.

The Claim for Inspiration in the Old Testament as a Whole

Throughout the foregoing discussion runs the concept that a writing was considered the Word of God if it was written by a prophet of God. In order, therefore, to see that the Old Testament as a whole claims to be the Word of God, it must be determined what is meant by a prophet and a prophetic utterance.

The Function of a Prophet

A prophetic utterance, of course, is that which comes from a prophet in the exercise of his prophetic ministry. Hence, the nature of the prophetic gift becomes crucial in the understanding of the authoritative character of the

7. See R. Laird Harris, *Inspiration and Canonicity of the Bible*, pp. 169ff.

Old Testament Scriptures which were written as a result of this prophetic gift.

Names given to a prophet. First, a brief examination of the names given to a prophet will help to reveal the character and origin of his ministry. He is called:

1. a man of God (1 Kings 12:22), meaning that he was chosen by God
2. a servant of the Lord (1 Kings 14:18), indicating that he was to be faithful to God
3. a messenger of the Lord (Isa. 42:19), showing that he was sent by God
4. a seer (*Ro'eh*), or beholder (*Hozeh*) (Isa. 30:9-10), revealing that his insight was from God
5. a man of the Spirit (Hos. 9:7; cf. Mic. 3:8), telling that he spoke by the Spirit of God
6. a watchman (Ezek. 3:17), relating his alertness for God
7. a prophet (which he is most commonly called), marking him as a spokesman for God

In summary, all of the prophetic titles refer essentially to the same function, that of a man receiving a revelation from God and relating it to others.

Nature of his office. The same conclusion is substantiated by an examination of the nature of the prophetic office. The etymology of the word "prophet" (*nabhi*) is obscure,[8] but the nature of the prophetic office is clearly defined throughout the Old Testament. The prophet was one who felt as Amos, "The Lord God has spoken! Who can but prophesy?" (Amos 3:8) or even as the prophet Balaam, who said, "I could not do anything, either small or great, contrary to the command of the Lord my God" (Num. 22:18).

Not only was a prophet one who felt the constraint to relate faithfully the command of the Lord, but he was indeed the very mouthpiece of God to men. The Lord said to Moses, "See, I make you as God to Pharaoh, and your brother Aaron shall be your prophet" (Ex. 7:1). In accordance with that, Aaron spoke "all the words which the Lord had spoken to Moses" (4:30). In Deuteronomy 18:18 God describes a prophet in these words: "I will put My words in his mouth, and he shall speak to them all that I command him." Moses was told, "You shall not add to the word which I am commanding you, nor take away from it" (Deut. 4:2). Micaiah the prophet confirmed the same: "As the Lord lives, what the Lord says to me, that I will speak" (1 Kings 22:14). The nature of the prophetic ministry, then, was to be the voice of God to men. And that voice had to be heeded; the prophets demanded that the nation give obedience to their message as to God Himself (cf. Isa. 8:5; Jer. 3:6; Ezek. 21:1; Amos 3:1).

8. It is variously derived from root words meaning (1) to bubble forth, (2) to speak, (3) to announce, (4) ecstatic behavior, (5) a speaker, (6) a called one. See Edward J. Young, *My Servants the Prophets*, pp. 56-57.

Thus, the Old Testament concept of a prophet was one who served as a mouthpiece of God. Aaron was to be a "prophet" for Moses, and Moses was told, "He shall be as a mouth for you, and you shall be as God to him" (Ex. 4:16). Edward J. Young summarizes well the nature of the Old Testament prophet when he writes, "We conclude, then, that upon the basis of the Old Testament usage, the *nabhi* was a speaker who declared the word that God had given him."[9]

The Whole Old Testament Is a "Prophetic Utterance"

The prophets were the voice of God not only in what they *said* but in what they *wrote* as well. Moses was commanded, "Write down these words" (Ex. 34:27). The Lord ordered Jeremiah to "take again another scroll and write on it all the former words that were on the first scroll" (Jer. 36:28). Isaiah testified that the Lord said to him: "Take for yourself a large tablet and write on it" (Isa. 8:1). And again God told him: "Go, write it on a tablet before them and inscribe it on a scroll, that it may serve in the time to come as a witness forever" (Isa. 30:8). A similar command was given to Habakkuk: "Record the vision and inscribe it on tablets, that the one who reads it may run" (Hab. 2:2). There can be little doubt, then, that the prophets did write, and what they wrote was the Word of God just as much as what they spoke was the Word of God. That being the case, it remains only to discover whether the Old Testament was the work of the prophets in order to establish it, in its entirety, as the very Word of God.

Besides the fact that the New Testament repeatedly refers to all of the Old Testament as Law and Prophets (cf. Luke 16:31; 24:27), there are several lines of evidence within the Old Testament that all of the books were written by prophets (whether recognized as such by their office or only by their spiritual gift).

1. Moses was a prophet (Deut. 34:10). Moreover, he was a mediator and lawgiver with whom God spoke "face to face" (Ex. 33:11) and "mouth to mouth" (Num. 12:8). Hence, his books are prophetic beyond question.
2. All of the second division of the Old Testament known as Prophets, and divided into "former" and "latter" prophets in the Hebrew Bible, is considered to be written by prophets, as the name of the section suggests (cf. Zech. 7:7, 12; Neh. 9:30).
3. Even if it be argued that the Hebrew canon was originally arranged into three sections—the Law, Prophets, and Writings—the books classed as Writings were prophetic utterances written by men who did not hold the

9. Ibid., p. 60.

prophetic *office* but who possessed a prophetic *gift*.[10] In fact, Daniel, whose book is found in the Writings, is called by Jesus "Daniel the prophet" (Matt. 24:15). Solomon, whose books appear among the Writings, was a prophet by definition, because he had visions from the Lord (Num. 12:6; cf. 1 Kings 11:9). David, who wrote many of the psalms, is called a prophet in Acts 2:30. David's testimony of himself was: "The Spirit of the Lord spoke by me" (2 Sam. 23:2; cf. 1 Chron. 28:19). If there is a distinction between the prophetic office and the prophetic gift, it in no way affects the prophetic function, which was possessed by all of the Old Testament writers.

The Whole Old Testament Is the Word of God

In other words, if the whole Old Testament is a prophetic writing, as it claims to be and the New Testament says it is (cf. 2 Pet. 1:20), and if all "prophetic writing" comes from God, then it follows that the whole Old Testament is the Word of God.

To summarize the foregoing discussion, it may be contended that:

> All "prophetic utterances" are the Word of God.
> All the Old Testament Scriptures are "prophetic utterances."
> Therefore, all the Old Testament is the Word of God.

Summary and Conclusion

An examination of each book of the Old Testament reveals either a direct or an indirect claim to be the Word of God. The claims in the historical and poetical books are usually indirect because they are not primarily a record of what God *said* to Israel but what He *did* in Israel's national life (History) and in their individual lives (Poetry). Further, the Old Testament was originally divided into two sections: the Law and the Prophets. Each of those sections was considered a unit; hence, the claim that holds for the section as a whole holds for every book in that section. On that basis, all of the books, Law and Prophets, are seen to claim divine authority. Finally, the Old Testament as a whole claims to be a "prophetic utterance," even the books that were sometimes classified as "Writings." Because a "prophetic utterance" means an utterance of the Word of God, it follows that the Old Testament as a whole lays claim to be the divinely inspired Word of God, since the whole claims to be a prophetic utterance.

10. Edward J. Young and Merrill F. Unger follow William H. Green, *A General Introduction to the Old Testament: The Canon*, p. 85, in making this distinction as the basis for classification of the third section of the Old Testament, namely, the Writings.

5
Supporting Claims for the Inspiration of the Old Testament

Not only does the Old Testament claim inspiration for itself, but that claim is overwhelmingly supported by the New Testament use of the Old Testament. A careful examination of the New Testament writings reveals that the whole Old Testament is substantiated in its claim to authenticity and authority by New Testament references to sections and books of the Old Testament.

New Testament References to the Old Testament as a Whole

The New Testament has varied descriptions of the Old Testament as a whole. Each declares in its own way the divine origin of the entire canon of Hebrew Scriptures.

"Scripture"

The New Testament uses the term *Scripture* in a technical sense. It occurs some fifty times, and in most cases it refers unmistakably to the Old Testament as a whole. To first-century Christians, the word *Scripture* meant primarily the canon of the Old Testament,[1] which is called "sacred" (2 Tim. 3:15) or "holy" (Rom. 1:2). These they acknowledged to be "inspired" of God (2 Tim. 3:16) and the rule for faith and practice (2 Tim. 3:17; cf. Rom. 15:4). Several New Testament passages may be cited (italics added) to illustrate this point.

1. In Matthew 21:42 Jesus charges the Pharisees saying, "Did you never read in the *Scriptures*?" The question implied that they were ignorant of their own sacred authority, the Old Testament.
2. In Matthew 22:29 Jesus answers the Sadducees in like manner, saying,

1. Even in the first century, however, Christians applied the term *Scripture* to the books of the New Testament as well, the beginning of which may be seen in 2 Pet. 3:16 and 1 Tim. 5:18. See J. D. Douglas, ed., *The New Bible Dictionary,* s.v. "Scripture."

"You are mistaken, not understanding the *Scriptures* or the power of God."

3. On the eve of His betrayal, in Matthew 26:54,56 Jesus refers to the Old Testament *Scriptures* as He says, "But all this has taken place that the *Scriptures* of the prophets may be fulfilled."
4. Luke 24 is a crucial passage in the present discussion, for Jesus not only opened to the disciples "the *Scriptures*" (v.32), but the *Scriptures* are described as everything written about Christ "in the Law of Moses and the Prophets and the Psalms" (v.44). Earlier in this same chapter, while relating Christ's exposition of the Old Testament law and prophets, Luke called these "all the *Scriptures*" (v.27).
5. John 2:22 states that after Jesus was raised from the dead, the disciples "believed the *Scripture*, and the word which Jesus had spoken."
6. In John 5:39 Jesus says of the Jews: "You search the *Scriptures* ... it is these that bear witness to Me."
7. Several times in the gospel of John the word *Scripture* (singular) is used without citing a specific passage from the Old Testament, for example, "As the *Scripture* said" (John 7:38; cf. 7:42; 19:36; 20:9). That statement is somewhat akin to the current expression "The Bible says."
8. In John 10:35, another crucial passage, Jesus asserts that "*Scripture* cannot be broken," showing that He considered the sacred Scriptures to be infallible.
9. In Acts, the words *Scripture* and *Scriptures* are used in the same manner as they were by Jesus. The apostle Paul "reasoned with them [the Jews] from the *Scriptures*" (Acts 17:2). The Bereans "examined the *Scriptures* daily" (Acts 17:11). Apollos, who was called "an elegant man...mighty in the *Scriptures*," ministered to the Jews, "demonstrating by the *Scriptures* that Jesus was the Christ" (Acts 18:24,28).
10. Paul repeatedly used the word *Scripture(s)* to refer to the entire authoritative canon of the Old Testament. In Romans he wrote that God had promised the gospel "through His prophets in the holy *Scriptures*" (Rom. 1:2). The expression "What does the *Scripture* say?" occurs several times in that same epistle (e.g., 4:3; 9:17; 10:11; 11:2). In Romans 15:4 Paul says that whatever was written in former days in the *Scriptures* was for the believer's admonition. He also spoke of "the *Scriptures* of the prophets" (16:26). In his other epistles the apostle Paul said that Christ had died and arisen "according to the *Scriptures*" (1 Cor. 15:3-4); that the "*Scripture*" foresaw that God would justify the Gentiles (Gal. 3:8); that "the *Scripture* has shut up all men under sin" (Gal. 3:22). He also asked, "What does the *Scripture* say?" (Gal. 4:30); made the statement, "The *Scripture* says" (1 Tim. 5:18); and declared that "all *Scripture* is inspired by God" (2 Tim. 3:16).

11. The apostle Peter added to the picture, as he wrote that *"Scripture"* did not come "by an act of human will, but men moved by the Holy Spirit spoke from God" (2 Pet. 1:20-21; see 3:16).
12. In a number of New Testament passages the word *Scripture* (singular) refers to a particular section or quotation from the Old Testament: Luke 4:21; John 13:18; 17:12; 19:24, 28, 37; Acts 1:16; 8:32, 35; James 2:8, 23; 4:5; 1 Peter 2:6.

In summary, Jesus and the New Testament writers referred to the complete Hebrew canon of their day, including the Law and Prophets (or, the Law, Prophets, and Psalms), as inspired, unbreakable, authoritative in disputes, prophetic of Christ, given by the Holy Spirit through the prophets, and, in effect, *the very Word of God.*

"It Is Written"

Other captions closely allied to the word for Scriptures (*graphē*) are forms of the verb "to write" (*graphō*) and "it is written" (*gegraptai*). These expressions occur about ninety-two times in the New Testament in direct reference to the Old Testament.[2] Although the vast majority of the references are to specific passages in the Old Testament, in terms of quotations or paraphrases, some of them are more general in scope, for example, "How *is it written* of the Son of Man that He should suffer many things and be treated with contempt?" (Mark 9:12). Other examples of this usage would include, "For the Son of Man is to go, as *it is written* of Him" (Mark 14:21); "All things *which are written* through the prophets about the Son of Man will be accomplished" (Luke 18:31); and other statements such as those in Luke 21:22; 24:44; John 1:45. Furthermore, all of these passages—whatever specific quotations or general references—imply an authoritative collection of writings. The expression "it is written" either directly implies or specifically refers to the authoritative writings—sacred Scripture—of the Jewish Old Testament. These references actually mean "*It is written* in *the* writings [Scriptures]."

"That It Might Be Fulfilled"

Another expression that either implies or applies to the whole Old Testament is "That it might be fulfilled." This statement is found thirty-three times in the New Testament.[3] Like the clause "It is written," this statement usually refers to a given passage in the Old Testament, but it is sometimes used in a general sense to apply to the entire Hebrew canon. For example, in Matthew 5:17 Jesus says, "I did not come to abolish [the Law and the Prophets], but *to fulfill*." So it is in Luke 24:44, where Jesus says that the Law, Prophets

2. *Englishman's Greek Concordance*, pp. 127-28.
3. Ibid., p. 630.

and Psalms "*must be fulfilled*," and in Luke 21:22 He foretells the time "all things which are written *may be fulfilled*." In specific instances this introduction applies to Old Testament predictions that must come to pass. For example, "Today this Scripture *has been fulfilled* in your hearing" (Luke 4:21). However, there are times when the expression refers to the preparatory nature of the whole Old Testament, which awaited completion in Christ (see Matt. 5:17).[4] In the latter cases, there is a direct acknowledgement of the inspiration of the entire Old Testament, whereas in the former cases there is implicit recognition. In either case, the formula "that it might be fulfilled," as used in reference to the Old Testament, implies a direct acknowledgment of the prophetic nature of those writings; prophetic writings were considered to have been divine and authoritative (cf. 2 Peter 1:20-21).[5]

"The Law"

Although the term *Law* was often reserved for the first five books of the Hebrew canon as a shortened form of the expression "the *law* of Moses," it was sometimes used to refer to the Old Testament as a whole. In fact, the use of the word for other than the Mosaic writings demonstrates that they too were considered to have equal authority with the great lawgiver's writings. Matthew 5:18 uses "*Law*" in parallel reference to "*Law* or the Prophets" (Matt. 5:17). In John 10:34 Jesus says to the Jews, "Has it not been written in your *Law*?" just prior to quoting Psalm 82:6. Similarly, John 12:34 uses "the *Law*"; John 15:25, "their *Law*"; "your *Law*" appears in John 18:31; and Acts 25:8 refers to "the Law of the Jews." Paul's epistles make broad usage of the term, as he applies it to the Gentiles, who "do not have the Law" (Rom. 2:14), speaks of the "works of the Law" (3:20), the "righteousness which is based on the Law; (10:5), and cites Isaiah 28:11-12, after the introduction "In the *Law* it is written" (1 Cor. 14:21). Hebrews 10:28 refers to "the *Law* of Moses." Thus, by extension, the term *Law*, which originally denoted the God-given books of Moses, came to be applied to the remainder of the Old Testament by both the Jews and the New Testament writers. Hence, the whole Old Testament was variously called by the authoritative titles "the *Law*," "the *Law* of the Jews," and even "the *Law* of God" (cf. Rom. 7:22).

"The Law and The Prophets"

Other than the word *Scriptures*, the most common designation of the Old Testament is "the Law and the Prophets." This is what Jesus called the Old

4. See J. Barton Payne, *Encyclopedia of Biblical Prophecy*, p. 477. Also see Robert D. Culver, "The Old Testament as Messianic Prophecy," *Bulletin of the Evangelical Theological Society*, 7:91-97.
5. See also chap. 4.

Testament on two occasions during His Sermon on the Mount (Matt. 5:17; 7:12). Sometimes the parallel "Moses and the Prophets" was used (cf. Luke 16:29, 31; 24:27; Acts 26:22). The canonical breadth of the title is revealed in Luke 16:16, which states, "*The Law and the Prophets* were proclaimed until John." In other words, the Law and Prophets included all God's written revelation to the time of John the Baptist. Further, it was "*the Law and the Prophets*" that were read in the synagogues (Acts 13:15). Paul, in his defense before Felix, asserted that he worshiped "the God of our fathers, believing everything that is in accordance with *the Law*, and that is written in *the Prophets*" (24:14). The apostle's point was that he believed and practiced the whole of God's revelation to Israel up to the time of Christ, and the phrase "the Law and the Prophets" describes the totality of that revelation.

"The Word of God"

Another expression that reflects the totality and authority of the Old Testament Scriptures is "the word of God." It is used several times in the New Testament. In Mark 7:13 Jesus charged that the Pharisees made void "*the word of God*" through their tradition. John 10:35 uses "*the word of God*" as a parallel to the "Scripture," which "cannot be broken." Referring to the Old Testament, Paul says, "It is not as though *the word of God* has failed" (Rom. 9:6). There are numerous other New Testament references to "the word of God," most of which are not positively identifiable with the Old Testament. However, many references may be applied to the present discussion. In 2 Corinthians 4:2 Paul records the Christians' refraining from "adulterating *the word of God*"; the writer of Hebrews states that "*the word of God* is living and active" (4:12); and Revelation 1:2 tells of John "who bore witness to *the word of God* and to the testimony of Jesus."

"The Oracles of God"

Closely allied with the foregoing descriptions of the Old Testament is the expression *the oracles of God*. Romans 3:2 indicates that the Jews were "entrusted with *the oracles of God*." Hebrews 5:12 refers to the Old Testament by this introduction, as it states the need for "someone to teach you the elementary principles of *the oracles of God*" before the readers could go on into maturity in Christ. In these references the Old Testament as a whole is viewed as the voice of God, a divine oration.

"From Abel to Zechariah"

On one occasion Jesus used still another phrase that includes the totality of the Old Testament, when He accused the Jews of the guilt of "all the righteous blood shed on earth, from the blood of righteous Abel to the blood of Zechariah" (Matt. 23:35; cf. Gen. 4:8; 2 Chron. 24:20-22). Because Abel's death was at the beginning of Old Testament history and Zechariah's at the end, the phrase "from Abel to Zechariah" is somewhat akin to the expression "from Genesis to Revelation."[6]

Previous discussion (chap. 1) has indicated that the Hebrew canon contained twenty-two (or twenty-four) books in New Testament times. Jesus and the apostles referred to that collection of books by various titles, all of which are reducible to the simple formula "the inspired Word of God." The terms they used to identify the Old Testament as the authoritative God-given guide for mankind shows that the entire Hebrew canon was held to be for them the very Word of God.

New Testament References to Sections of the Old Testament

As has been previously stated, the Hebrew Old Testament had two sections. A brief survey of the New Testament references to those sections further confirms the authoritative nature of the Old Testament.

References to Both Sections

The whole Old Testament was divided into two basic sections: the Law and the Prophets. The phrase combining them, namely, "the Law and the Prophets" or "Moses and the Prophets," occurs twelve times in the New Testament (see Matt. 5:17; 7:12; 11:13; 22:40; Luke 16:16, 29, 31; 24:27; Acts 13:15; 24:14; 26:22; Rom. 3:21). That these two sections encompass the whole Old Testament is obvious from several passages. In Luke 24:27 Jesus referred to them as "all the *Scriptures*." In Luke 16:16 Jesus said, "*The Law and the Prophets* were proclaimed until John" (cf. Matt. 11:13), which engulfs the entire time span of God's revelation through Old Testament prophets up to New Testament times. Further, the other passages reveal that it was the foundation of moral and religious belief—that final authority to which appeal is made in all such matters. In brief, the two sections were the whole written Word of God for Jesus and the Jews of His day.

References to Individual Sections

There are also numerous separate references to the Law and to the Prophets in the New Testament.

6. For additional discussion of this point see Roger Beckwith, *The Old Testament Canon of the New Testament Church and Its Background in Early Judaism*, pp. 220-22.

The Law. This section of the Old Testament is variously referred to as "the Law" (Matt. 12:5; 22:40); "the Law of Moses" (Acts 13:39; Heb. 10:28); "Moses" (2 Cor. 3:15); "the book of Moses" (Mark 12:26); and "the book of the *law*" (Gal. 3:10). Each reference is a direct appeal to the divine authority of Moses' writings. That the New Testament considered the law of Moses in its entirety to be the inspired Word of God is beyond question.

The Prophets. This section is usually called "the Prophets" (Luke 18:31; John 1:45), but it is also labeled "the Scriptures of the prophets" (Matt. 26:56) and "the book of the prophets" (Acts 7:42). In each case the reference is clearly to the books or writings of the prophets, and the appeal to them is to a group or collection of books that serve as a divine authority in matters moral and theological.

The most common description of the Old Testament is "the Law and the Prophets." Sometimes the New Testament refers to one or the other of these two sections. In any case, whether as a whole or individually, the Old Testament canon, with both of its sections and all of its books known and used by Jesus and the first century church, was considered to be the inspired Word of God.

New Testament References to the Individual Old Testament Books

There are many references to the authority of the Old Testament as a whole, but the particular references to the individual books and events of the Old Testament are even more illuminating in their bearing on both authority and authenticity, because of their specific and definitive nature. As a result, the following discussion will be treated under those two heads.

New Testament References to the Authority of Old Testament Books

Not only does the New Testament lend support to the claim of inspiration of the Old Testament as a whole, and for each of its two sections, but it provides a direct confirmation for the authority of most of the individual books of the Old Testament, as may be seen in the following sample survey.

Genesis. The book of Genesis is authoritatively quoted by Jesus in Matthew 19:4-5 (cf. Gen. 1:27; 2:24) as He says, "Have you not read, that He who created them from the beginning made them male and female, and said, 'For this cause a man shall leave his father and mother, and shall cleave to his wife; and the two shall became one flesh'?" Here the assertion is made that God said what is written in Genesis. Romans 4:3 refers to Genesis 15:6 saying, "For what does the Scripture say?"

Exodus. Jesus quotes Exodus 16:4, 15 in John 6:13: "As it is written, 'He gave them bread out of heaven to eat.' " "Honor your father and mother" is from

Exodus 20:12 and is cited in Ephesians 6:2 as authoritative.

Leviticus. This book was referred to by Jesus when He commanded the cleansed leper, "Go, show yourself to the priest, and present the offering that Moses commanded" (Matt. 8:4; cf. Lev. 14:2). Leviticus 20:9 is cited in Mark 7:10: "He who speaks evil of father or mother, let him be put to death" (the passage is also found in Ex. 21:17).

Numbers. Although not a direct citation, Numbers 12:7 is alluded to authoritatively in Hebrews 3:5: "Now Moses was faithful in all [God's] house." Although this is not a direct quote, it is a clear reference to the teaching of Numbers. Paul in 1 Corinthians 10:5-11 refers to the events of Numbers as things written for the admonition of New Testament believers (see v. 11).

Deuteronomy. This is one of the most often quoted Old Testament books. For example, the three quotations used by Jesus when He resisted the tempter in Matthew 4:4, 7, 10: "Man shall not live on bread alone" (cf. Deut. 8:3); "You shall not put the Lord your God to the test" (cf. Deut. 6:16); "You shall worship the Lord your God, and serve Him only" (cf. Deut. 6:13).

Joshua. Joshua 1:5 is quoted as God's word of promise in Hebrews 13:5: "I will never desert you, nor will I ever forsake you."

Judges. Although this book is not directly cited in the New Testament, several of its personages are authenticated (see Heb. 11:32).

Ruth. Ruth is not directly cited in the New Testament, but it is obviously the authoritative source for the Messianic genealogies in Matthew and Luke (Ruth 4:18-22; cf. Matt. 1:3-6; Luke 3:32-33).

1 and 2 Samuel. These books are referred to in Matthew 12:3-4 when Jesus said to the Pharisees, "Have you not read what David did when he became hungry, he and his companions; how he entered the house of God, and they ate the consecrated bread?" (1 Sam. 21:1-6).

1 and 2 Kings. These are quoted in Romans 11:4: "I have kept for Myself seven thousand men who have not bowed the knee to Baal" (cf. 1 Kings 19:18, where God replies to Elijah).

1 and 2 Chronicles. Although these books are not quoted in the New Testament, events from them are authenticated. Among those events are the slaying of Zechariah (2 Chron. 24:20-22; cf. Matt. 23:35) and Solomon's building the Temple (Acts 7:47-48; cf. 2 Chron. 6:1-3; 1 Kings 8:17-27).

Ezra-Nehemiah. There is one quotation in the New Testament, in John 6:31, from Nehemiah 9:15: "He gave them bread out of heaven to eat" (however, there are similar passages from which that quotation may have been adopted; cf. Ps. 78:24; 105:40).

Esther. This book is not clearly quoted in the New Testament. There is a possible literary dependence on Esther 5:3 in Mark 6:23 in the phrase "up to half of my kingdom." Revelation 11:10 refers to those who "make merry" and "send gifts," as was done in Esther 9:22 during the Feast of Purim. John 5:1, "a feast of the Jews," may have been this same Feast of Purim mentioned in Esther.

Job. Job 5:12 is distinctly quoted in 1 Corinthians 3:19: "For it is written, 'He is the one who catches the wise in their craftiness' " (cf. also James 5:11).

Psalms. This is another book frequently quoted by the New Testament writers. It was one of Jesus' favorite books. Compare Matthew 21:42: "Did you never read in the Scriptures, 'The stone which the builders rejected'?" (Ps. 118:22-23) and Hebrews 1:6: "Let all the angels of God worship Him" (Ps. 97:7).

Proverbs. Proverbs 3:34 is clearly cited in James 4:6: "God is opposed to the proud, but gives grace to the humble" (cf. Proverbs 25:6; Lk. 14:8).

Ecclesiastes. This book is not directly quoted in the New Testament, although there are a number of passages that have a close *doctrinal dependence* on its teachings. The following references illustrate this fact:

What we sow we reap.	Eccles. 11:1, cf. Gal. 6:7 ff.
Avoid lusts of youth.	Eccles. 11:10, cf. 2 Tim. 2:22
Death is divinely appointed.	Eccles. 3:2, cf. Heb. 9:27
Love of money is evil.	Eccles. 5:10, cf. 1 Tim. 6:10
Do not be wordy in prayer.	Eccles. 5:2, cf. Matt. 6:7

If these New Testament passages are doctrinally dependent on the teaching of Ecclesiastes, then the New Testament confirms the inspiration, or authority, of the book.

Song of Solomon. This book is not referred to directly by the New Testament. There is at least one possible example of borrowing a descriptive phrase from this book. In John 4:10 the reference to "living water" indicates possible literary dependence on Song of Solomon 4:15. However, literary dependence alone is not a sufficient argument for the authority of this book, but its Solomonic authorship is (1:1), since God spoke through him.

Isaiah. This book has numerous New Testament quotations. John the Baptist introduced Jesus by citing Isaiah 40:3: "Make ready the way of the Lord" (Matt. 3:3). Paul prefaced his quote of Isaiah 6:9-10 with the words "The Holy Spirit rightly spoke" (Acts 28:25). Jesus read from Isaiah 61:1-2 in His hometown synagogue, saying, "The Spirit of the Lord is upon me" (Luke 4:18-19).

Jeremiah. Jeremiah 31:15 is quoted in Matthew 2:17-18, and the new covenant of Jeremiah 31:31-34 is quoted twice in Hebrews (cf. 8:8-12 and 10:15-17).

Lamentations. Lamentations 3:30 is alluded to in Matthew 27:30: "And they spat upon Him, and took the reed and began to beat Him on the head."

Ezekiel. This book is not clearly cited by the New Testament, but Jesus' question to Nicodemus in John 3:10 implies that Nicodemus should have known about the new birth on the basis of Ezekiel 36:25ff. Further, Paul felt morally bound by Ezekiel's warning (33:8) not to be guilty of the blood of the wicked (Acts 20:26). In addition, there are these possible allusions: John 7:38, "As the Scripture said, 'From his innermost being shall flow rivers of living water,'" is very similar to Ezekiel 47:1, although it may refer to Isaiah 58:11. Ezekiel 18:20, "The person who sins will die," may be reflected in Romans 6:23, "The wages of sin is death." Revelation 4:7 is undoubtedly taken from Ezekiel 1:10.

Daniel. This book is clearly quoted in Matthew 24:15 (cf. Dan. 9:27; 11:31; 12:11): "So when you see the abomination of desolation which was spoken of through Daniel the prophet." Further, Matthew 24:21 and 30 are taken directly from Daniel 12:1 and 7:13 respectively.

The Twelve. Books from the Minor Prophets, or The Twelve, are quoted several times in the New Testament. Habakkuk 2:4, "The righteous will live by his faith" is quoted three times in the New Testament (Rom. 1:17; Gal. 3:11; Heb. 10:38). Hebrews 12:26 is a clear quotation of Haggai 2:6, "I am going to shake the heavens and the earth." Zechariah 13:7 is quoted in Matthew 26:31 as follows: "For it is written, 'I will strike down the shepherd, and the sheep of the flock shall be scattered.'"

In summary, of the twenty-two books of the Hebrew Old Testament, as many as eighteen of them (all but Judges, Chronicles, Esther, and Song of Solomon) are quoted or referred to as authoritative.[7] There are New Testament teachings that are directly dependent upon the teachings of those Old Testament books. It should be pointed out that the absence of reference to a specific Old Testament book does not mean that particular book lacks authority; instead, it indicates that the New Testament writers had no occasion to refer to it. This is not difficult to understand when a person is asked to recall the last time he quoted from Esther or Judges. Some books, by their didactic or devotional nature, lend more readily to quotation and, hence, they are quoted more often; those that lack a didactic nature are not often used in that manner.

New Testament References to the Authenticity of Old Testament Books

Some of the Old Testament books that have no distinct reference to their authority do, however, have clear commitments to their *authenticity*. The

7. Roger Nicole has classified this as 231 quotations, 19 paraphrases, and 45 additional items that have no direct formula (e.g., "It is written"), for a total of 295 citations, about 4.4 percent of the New Testament (approximately one verse of every 22.5). Allusions range from 613 to 4,105, depending on the criteria used. Cf. Carl F. H. Henry, ed., *Revelation and the Bible*, p. 137.

accompanying chart indicates some of the more important people and events of the Old Testament that are verified in the New Testament (which thereby verifies the authenticity of the books that record them).

1. Creation of the universe (Gen. 1)	John 1:3; Col. 1:16
2. Creation of Adam and Eve (Gen. 1-2)	1 Tim. 2:13-14
3. Marriage of Adam and Eve (Gen. 1-2)	1 Tim. 2:13
4. Temptation of the woman (Gen. 3)	1 Tim. 2:14
5. Disobedience and sin of Adam (Gen. 3)	Rom. 5:12; 1 Cor. 15:22
6. Sacrifices of Abel and Cain (Gen. 4)	Heb. 11:4
7. Murder of Abel by Cain (Gen. 4)	1 John 3:12
8. Birth of Seth (Gen. 4)	Luke 3:38
9. Translation of Enoch (Gen. 5)	Heb. 11:5
10. Marriage before the flood (Gen. 6)	Luke 17:27
11. The Flood and destruction of man (Gen. 7)	Matt. 24:39
12. Preservation of Noah and his family (Gen. 8-9)	2 Peter 2:5
13. Genealogy of Shem (Gen. 10)	Luke 3:35-36
14. Birth of Abraham (Gen. 11)	Luke 3:34
15. Call of Abraham (Gen. 12-13)	Heb. 11:8
16. Tithes to Melchizedek (Gen. 14)	Heb. 7:1-3
17. Justification of Abraham (Gen. 15)	Rom. 4:3
18. Ishmael (Gen. 16)	Gal. 4:21-24
19. Promise of Isaac (Gen. 17)	Heb. 11:18
20. Lot and Sodom (Gen. 18-19)	Luke 17:29
21. Birth of Isaac (Gen. 21)	Acts 7:9-10
22. Offering of Isaac (Gen. 22)	Heb. 11:17
23. The burning bush (Ex. 3:6)	Luke 20:32
24. Exodus through the Red Sea (Ex. 14:22)	1 Cor. 10:1-2
25. Provision of water and manna (Ex. 16:4; 17:6)	1 Cor. 10:3-5
26. Lifting up serpent in wilderness (Num. 21:9)	John 3:14
27. Fall of Jericho (Joshua 6:22-25)	Heb. 11:30
28. Miracles of Elijah (1 Kings 17:1; 18:1)	James 5:17
29. Jonah in the great fish (Jonah 2)	Matt. 12:40
30. Three Hebrew youths in furnace (Dan. 3)	Heb. 11:34
31. Daniel in lion's den (Dan. 6)	Heb. 11:33
32. Slaying of Zechariah (2 Chron. 24:20-22)	Matt 23:35

In this sample survey, several things should be noted. (1) Most of the controversial passages of the Old Testament are referred to, for example, the creation, Fall, Flood, miracles of Moses and Elijah, and Jonah in the great fish. Those are not just alluded to, they are *authenticated as historical* events by the New Testament.[8] If these major miraculous events were considered authentic, there is no difficulty in seeing that the New Testament accepted the rest of the events of the Old Testament. (2) Virtually every one of the first twenty-two chapters of Genesis, and each of those prior to Abraham (i.e., chaps. 1-11), has either a person or an event that is confirmed by an authoritative New Testament quotation or reference. If these people and events are authentic, then it may be argued a fortiori that the rest of the Old Testament is authentic. (3) Whereas there are direct quotations or references confirming the *authority* of eighteen of the twenty-two books of the Hebrew Old Testament, events from two of the remaining books have their *authenticity* confirmed by the New Testament. Several of the Judges are referred to in Hebrews 11:32, as are numerous events from Chronicles (cf. Matt. 23:35). Thus, only Esther and Song of Solomon are without any direct confirmation as to their authority or authenticity. Here one must rely on the original and subsequent Jewish community, who knew their prophetic source and that they were a part of the canonical books of the "Prophets" (see discussion in chaps. 13 and 14).

Summary and Conclusion

The claim for inspiration by the Old Testament is supported in three ways in the New Testament. First, there are many terms in the New Testament, such as *Scripture, Word of God, Law,* and *Prophets,* which are used to refer authoritatively to the Old Testament as a whole. Second, both of the sections of the Hebrew canon (Law and Prophets) are viewed as authoritative units by the New Testament. Finally, of the twenty-four (twenty-two)[9] books in the Hebrew canon, eighteen are quoted or referred to by the New Testament, thus confirming their authority. Two others have their authenticity confirmed, which brings the total to twenty of the twenty-four books having their authority and/or authenticity directly affirmed by the New Testament. As a result, at least twenty of the twenty-four books of the Hebrew canon have their claim for inspiration confirmed individually by the New Testament writers, who regard the record of events or teachings therein as authentic and/or divine in origin. The other two books were recognized by the earliest Jewish community as having a divine source and were placed among the "Prophets."

8. The New Testament writers were not accommodating themselves to accepted "myths" of their day (see 1 Tim. 1:4; 4:7; Titus 1:14; 2 Peter 1:16). Cf. chap. 3 for objections to this accommodation theory.
9. See discussion in chap. 1.

6
Specific Claims for the Inspiration of the New Testament

Now that the claim in and for the inspiration of the Old Testament has been examined, a similar examination of the New Testament claim is needed in order to complete the proposition that the Bible as a whole, and the whole Bible, claims to be the authoritative Word of God. The testimony of the New Testament to its own inspiration begins with the words of Christ, the central figure of the New Testament.

The New Testament Writers Were Spirit-Directed

In a real sense, Christ is the key to the inspiration and canonization of the Scriptures. It was He who confirmed the inspiration of the Hebrew canon of the Old Testament; and it was He who promised that the Holy Spirit would direct the apostles into "all truth," the fulfillment resulting in the New Testament.

Jesus Promised That the New Testament Writers Would Be Spirit-Directed

Jesus Himself did not commit His teaching to writing, but on several occasions during His earthly ministry He promised that the apostles would be directed by the Holy Spirit in the utterance and propagation of His teaching. This promise was fulfilled during the life of Christ and extended as well into the postresurrection and post-Pentecostal ministries of the apostles.

Guidance in preaching. First, Jesus promised the guidance of the Holy Spirit in what the apostles would *speak about Him*.

1. When the twelve were first commissioned to preach "the kingdom of heaven" (Matt. 10:7), Jesus promised them, saying, "When they deliver you up, do not become anxious about how or what you will speak; for it shall be given you in that hour what you are to speak. For it is not you

who speak, but it is the Spirit of your Father who speaks in you" (Matt. 10:19-20; cf. Luke 12:11-12).

2. The same promise was also given to the seventy when Jesus authorized them to preach "the kingdom of God" (Luke 10:9), with this added confirmation: "The one who listens to you listens to Me, and the one who rejects you rejects Me; and he who rejects Me rejects the One who sent me" (Luke 10:16).
3. In the Olivet discourse Jesus reiterated the same promise of Spirit-directed utterances for those called on to give an account for their faith in the hour of trial, saying, "And when they arrest you and deliver you up, do not be anxious beforehand about what you are to say, but say whatever is given you in that hour; for it is not you who speak, but it is the Holy Spirit" (Mark 13:11).
4. Later, after the Last Supper, Jesus further elaborated this promise to the eleven, saying, "But the Helper, the Holy Spirit, whom the Father will send in My name, He will teach you all things, and bring to your remembrance all that I said to you" (John 14:26). At that same time He also told them, "When He, the Spirit of truth, comes, He will guide you into all the truth" (John 16:13).
5. The Great Commission of Christ provides the same promise, as it states "that repentance for forgiveness of sins should be proclaimed in His name to all the nations, beginning from Jerusalem. You are witnesses of these things" (Luke 24:47-48). The disciples were further told, "And behold, I am sending forth the promise of My Father upon you; but you are to stay in the city until you are clothed with power from on high" (Luke 24:49). This very commission was recorded by Matthew in the following words, "And lo, I am with you always, even to the end of the age" (Matt. 28:20). Thus, the apostles were again promised the presence of God in and through their preaching and teaching.
6. Just prior to His Ascension, Jesus answered the disciples' inquiry about the future with the promise "But you shall receive power when the Holy Spirit has come upon you; and you shall be My witnesses both in Jerusalem, and in all Judea and Samaria, and even to the remotest part of the earth" (Acts 1:8). That the Holy Spirit would empower them in their *witness* about Christ was their assurance.

Guidance in teaching. Not only were the apostles promised the guidance of the Spirit in their *preaching* about Jesus, but they were also promised that they were to be guided by the Spirit in their *teaching*.

1. According to Matthew's account of the Great Commission, the guidance of the Holy Spirit was to extend to what the disciples taught about Christ, as it stated, "Go therefore and make disciples of all the nations, baptizing them in the name of the Father and the Son and the Holy Spirit, teaching

them to observe all that I commanded you; and lo, I am with you always, to the end of the age" (Matt. 28:19-20).

2. The promise that the Holy Spirit would bring "all things" to their remembrance and lead them into "all the truth" (John 14:26; 16:13) obviously applies to the fullness of apostolic teaching as well as preaching.
3. Further confirmation of this fact is directly implied in the book of Acts, which was the record of what Jesus "began to do and teach" (Acts 1:1-2). Properly speaking, then, Acts is the book of the acts of the Holy Spirit through the works and *words* of the apostles.
4. A very practical manifestation of the teaching ministry of the Holy Spirit through the apostles is that the first church continued in "the apostles' teaching" (Acts 2:42). Apostolic preaching (Acts 2, 4, 10) and teaching (2:42; 6:4) were the foundation stones of the early church. It is in that sense that the church was "built upon the foundation of the apostles and prophets, Christ Jesus Himself being the corner stone" (Eph. 2:20). That is, the church is built upon their teaching, which, as Jesus repeatedly promised, was the result of the ministry of the Holy Spirit through them.

Briefly, Jesus promised that the Spirit of truth (John 15:26) would guide the apostles in the teaching of "all things" (John 14:26), or "all the truth" (obviously meaning all truth necessary for faith and practice; cf. John 20:31; 21:25). There is no more reason to believe that the guidance of the Holy Spirit was limited to their verbal teaching than there is to believe that the Old Testament prophets were Spirit-directed only in what they spoke (see chaps. 4-5). In fact, in direct continuity with the promise of Christ, virtually every New Testament writer claims that his *writing* was divinely authoritative. Furthermore, when knowledge of the apostolic teaching is traced to its original documentary record, the pursuit ends in one, and only one, definite document, that is, the New Testament. Thus, the New Testament is the only primary source for study of the Spirit-directed teaching of the apostles, which teaching was promised by Christ in the gospels. Formally stated, this argument takes the following form:

> Whatever the apostles taught was Spirit-directed.
> The New Testament is what the apostles taught.
> Therefore, the New Testament is Spirit-directed teaching.

The New Testament Writers Claim that They Were Spirit-Directed

In full consciousness and fulfillment of Jesus' oft-repeated promise to guide them unto "all the truth," the apostles claimed divine authority for what they taught orally and in their writings.

New Testament writers compared their message to Old Testament prophets. Remembering how highly esteemed the Old Testament prophets were and how divinely authoritative their writings were considered,[1] the comparison of the New Testament message to the Old Testament Scriptures amounts to a claim for the same *authority and inspiration*. Such is the case in Hebrews 1:1-2, which declares that "God, after He spoke long ago to the fathers in the prophets . . . in these last days has spoken to us in His Son," and adds that after the message "was at the first spoken through the Lord, it was confirmed to us by those who heard" (Heb. 2:3). In other words, the message of Christ as given by His disciples is God's voice today just as much as the message of the prophets was in time past.

New Testament writers claimed their message was the foundation of the church. According to Ephesians 2:20 the church is "built upon the foundation of the apostles and prophets." The word *apostle* should not be limited to only the twelve apostles. Paul was an apostle (Gal. 1; 2 Cor. 12), as was Barnabas (Acts 14:14). James wrote with divine authority (James 1:1), and there were others with prophetic gifts (cf. Agabus in Acts 11:28). The gift of either an apostle or a prophet would qualify one to receive a revelation (cf. Eph. 2:20), and several New Testament writers fit into the "prophet" category (e.g., Mark, Luke, James, Jude). In Acts 2:42 the believers "were continually devoting themselves to the apostles' teaching and to fellowship." The authority of apostolic teaching, then, is seen not only by its equality with the prophets but by its fundamentality to the church. The reasoning may be summarized as follows:

> The New Testament is what the apostles taught.
> What the apostles taught is the authoritative foundation of the church.
> Therefore, the New Testament is the authoritative foundation of the church.

New Testament writers claimed their message was authoritative for the church. Throughout Acts the pronouncements of the apostles were final (Acts 21:11). By their voice the church was born (Acts 2); miracles were performed (Acts 3); rulers were restricted (Acts 4); the disobedient were judged (Acts 5); the Holy Spirit was given to the Samaritans (Acts 8) and the Gentiles (Acts 10). Thus, in accordance with the promise of Jesus that His disciples would be Spirit-directed in what they spoke and taught, the New Testament writers considered their pronouncements and teachings to be equally authoritative with the Old Testament prophets, as well as fundamental to and authoritative for the New Testament church.

1. See chaps. 4-5 for a more detailed comparison.

The New Testament Writings Are Spirit-Directed

The assumption that there is a valid connection between apostolic teaching and the New Testament writings is substantiated abundantly by both general and specific reference in the New Testament.

General Claim that the Whole New Testament Is Spirit-Directed

Outstanding passages. There are two outstanding passages that bear on this point and several others that lend their support. In 2 Peter 1:20-21 it is made clear that all *prophetic Scripture*[2] comes as men are "moved by the Holy Spirit." The reference here is to the Old Testament writings, which have already been seen to be the unbreakable oracles of God (cf. Heb. 5:12). However, because New Testament writers also claimed to be giving prophetic utterances and writings, it follows that they considered their writings to be just as Spirit-directed as the Old Testament writings. Some New Testament writers make a direct claim that their writings are prophetic. In Revelation 22 John is grouped with the Old Testament prophets (v. 9) and he concludes his own message by saying, "I testify to everyone who hears the words of the prophecy of this book" (v. 18). The apostle Paul identifies his revelation of the mystery of Christ as even superior to that of the Old Testament (cf. Eph. 3:5). The writer of Hebrews also identifies his book in line with the revelation through the Old Testament prophets, saying, "God ... spoke long ago to the fathers in the prophets ... in these last days [He] has spoken to us in His Son" (Heb. 1:1), to whose message one must take heed because "it was at the first spoken through the Lord, it was confirmed to us by those who heard [namely, the apostles], God also bearing witness ... by gifts of the Holy Spirit" (Heb. 2:3-4). Hence, the ministry and writings of the New Testament writers are no less prophetic than those of their Old Testament counterparts.

New Testament books considered to be Scripture.[3] Peter refers to Paul's writings as "Scripture" (2 Pet. 3:16), and 1 Timothy 5:18 quotes from Luke 10:7 and Deuteronomy 25:4 under the one phrase "for the Scripture says." If the writings of Luke, who was not an apostle, are quoted as Scripture and Peter, who incidentally was rebuked by Paul (Gal. 2:11), considered Paul's books to be Scripture, then it is not difficult to conceive how the New Testament as a whole would be considered to be Scripture. And, because 2 Timothy 3:16 declares that "all Scripture is inspired by God," it follows that the New Testament as a whole is inspired by God.

Specific claims. There are specific claims of apostolic authority in the New Testament that admit of a wide application. Paul told his sons in the faith to "prescribe" his teachings (1 Tim. 4:11) "with all authority" (Titus 2:15) and

2. See chap. 3, where this point is elaborated.
3. See chap. 3 for discussion.

hinged his authority and even the veracity of the gospel itself on his apostleship (Gal. 1:1, 12). On another occasion Paul wrote, "If anyone does not obey our instruction in this letter, take special note of that man and do not associate with him" (2 Thess. 3:14). Likewise, Peter reminded the believers of apostolic authority, saying, "Remember . . . the commandment of the Lord and Savior spoken by your apostles" (2 Pet. 3:2). In effect, the authority of an apostle was the authority of Christ, and the only credential necessary to commend the authority of any particular writing was its apostolicity.[4]

Books were to be circulated. One final consideration that manifests the high regard for New Testament writings by the first-century church is the fact that the books were commanded to be *circulated, read in the churches, and collected.* It is obvious that Peter had a collection of Paul's books (2 Pet. 3:15-16), and Paul distinctly enjoined the Colossians to read and circulate their epistle (Col. 4:16). The Thessalonians, too, were charged to read their epistle (1 Thess. 5:27). Such regard shows that the books had for them not only a spiritual value but a divine origin (cf. the Jews who read and preserved God's Word, Deut. 31:26).

In general, then, the New Testament writings as a whole claim to be "Scripture," "prophetic writings," authoritative and divine. This is the same as saying they are inspired of God.

Specific Claims that New Testament Books Are Inspired

Not only did Jesus promise divine guidance, and the New Testament as a whole claim to be the product of that guidance, but each individual New Testament book contains a claim to substantiate that position. A brief survey will suffice to support this point.

Matthew. This gospel begins, "The book of the genealogy of Jesus Christ," which, by linking Christ's lineage to the record of the Old Testament, is a tacit acknowledgment that this book is a continuation of messianic truth. In fact, there is implied in the repeated assertion that Christ is the fulfillment of Old Testament prophecy (cf. 5:17-18, 21) that this book is an authoritative account of that fulfillment in Christ. The author closes his book with the command of Christ to teach the truth of Christ to all nations (28:18-20), which by implication is precisely what the book of Matthew is professing to do (cf. 10:7).

Mark. Mark is entitled "The beginning of the gospel of Jesus Christ, the Son of God. As it is written in Isaiah the prophet." Like Matthew, there is no explicit claim to authority; it is merely assumed throughout (cf. 13:11). Because Mark was associated with Peter (1 Pet. 5:13), many take Mark to be Peter's gospel.

Luke. This book has a statement about its own character. In his writing

4. See chap. 16.

Luke claims that it is an authentic "account of the things accomplished [by God through Christ]" that Theophilus "might know the exact truth about the things you have been taught" (1:1, 4). Because Luke was closely associated with Paul, it has an apostolic connection as well.

John. John is likewise clear about the nature of his gospel, saying that it is written "that you may believe that Jesus is the Christ, the Son of God; and that believing you may have life in His name" (20:31). He further adds, "This is the disciple who bears witness of these things, and wrote these things; and we know that his witness is true" (21:24; cf. 14:26, 16:13).

Acts. As a continuation of Luke and of what Jesus "began to do and teach" (1:1), Acts claims to be an authentic record of the teaching (and working) of Christ through the apostles.

Romans. The author of this book claims it to be the work of an apostle of Jesus Christ (1:1). In 9:1 Paul says, "I am telling the truth in Christ, I am not lying, my conscience bearing me witness in the Holy Spirit." The final appeal of the epistle is not to accept any other doctrine than that which they have been taught, which would include, of course, the great teachings of this doctrinal book (16:17).

1 Corinthians. This book contains what "God revealed ... through the Spirit" (2:10; cf. also 7:40). Besides making authoritative pronouncements on morals (5:1-3) and doctrine (15:15), Paul asserts, "The things which I write to you are the Lord's commandment" (14:37).

2 Corinthians. This book is introduced by an apostle of God (1:1), who strongly contests for his own authority (10:8; 12:12) and declares his lofty revelations from God (12:1-4).

Galatians. Galatians states the case for its author's divine authority as strongly as any book in the New Testament: "Paul, an apostle (not sent from men, nor through the agency of man, but through Jesus Christ, and God the Father)" (1:1). "For I neither received it from man, nor was I taught it, but I received it through a revelation of Jesus Christ" (1:12), and "even though we, or an angel from heaven, should preach to you a gospel contrary to that which we have preached to you, let him be accursed" (1:8).

Ephesians. This book, along with the claim to be written by an apostle (1:1), declares itself to be a revelation of the mystery of God, showing "that by revelation there was made known to me [Paul] the mystery" (3:3). Those who read it can gain "insight into the mystery of Christ" (3:4).

Philippians. Philippians not only comes as from an apostle and with the standard greetings "from God our Father and the Lord Jesus Christ" (1:2), but it further enjoins the readers to follow the moral example and spiritual teaching of its author, saying, "Brethren, join in following my example" (3:17). Again it says, "The things you have learned and received and heard and seen in me, practice these things" (4:9).

Colossians. Colossians also comes from "an apostle of Jesus Christ" (1:1), with greetings "from God our Father" (1:2), as an authoritative refutation of heresy (2:4, 8), with a command to be circulated and read in the churches (4:16).

1 Thessalonians. In 5:27, the author charges the church "to have this letter read to all the brethren" and in 4:15 says, "For we say to you by the word of the Lord."

2 Thessalonians. This book adds to its God-given pronouncements a warning about a false letter "as if from" Paul (2:2). It closes by saying, "If anyone does not obey our instruction in this letter, take special note of that man and do not associate with him" (3:14).

1 Timothy. Written by "Paul, an apostle of Christ Jesus according to the commandment of God" (1 Tim 1:1), this epistle speaks with authority, saying, "Prescribe and teach these things" (4:11).

2 Timothy. The author instructed his son in the faith to "retain the standard of sound words which you have heard from me" (1:13), and he charged Timothy "in the presence of God and of Christ Jesus" to "preach the word" (4:1-2).

Titus. Titus also claims to come from Paul "an apostle of Jesus Christ" (1:1), with the injunction to "let these things speak and exhort and reprove with all authority" (2:15). He then adds, "Concerning these things I want you to speak confidently" (3:8).

Philemon. This brief book claims authority from the apostle Paul (v. 1), brings salutation "from God our Father and the Lord Jesus Christ" (v. 3), and asserts apostolic authority (v. 8).

Hebrews. The author of Hebrews introduces his message as the voice of God through Christ "in these last days" (1:2) and concludes his epistle with authoritative exhortations (13:22).

James. James writes as a "servant of God" (1:1) and speaks with authority about doctrine (cf. chap. 2) and practice (chap. 3).

1 Peter. This book is from "an apostle of Jesus Christ" (1:1) and claims to be an exhortation on "the true grace of God" (5:12).

2 Peter. Written by "a bond-servant and apostle of Jesus Christ" (1:1), this epistle gives commandments from the Lord (3:2). The author claims to "have the prophetic word made more sure" (1:19) and gives a prophetic pronouncement about the future (3:10-13).

1 John. This book comes from an eyewitness (1:1) who is proclaiming Christ so that believers' "joy may be made complete" (1:4) and that the reader may be assured of eternal life (5:12).

2 John. In this book John purports to be writing a "commandment" (v. 5), warns against deceivers (v. 7), and claims to possess "the teaching of Christ" (v. 9).

3 John. This is written by one with apostolic authority (v. 9) who claims to have "the truth itself" (v. 12).

Jude. Jude claims to be a record of "our common salvation" and "the faith which was once for all delivered to the saints" (v. 3).

Revelation. The Apocalypse, as its name appears in Greek, begins: "The revelation of Jesus Christ, which God gave" (1:1) through John, who considered himself to be one with the "prophets" (22:9). The book ends with the most severe warning in the Bible for anyone who "adds to" or "takes away from the words of the book of this prophecy" (22:18-19).

So virtually every book in the New Testament contains a claim for its own authority in one manner or another. The cumulative effect of this self-testimony is an overwhelming confirmation that the New Testament writers claimed inspiration.

Sometimes 1 Corinthians 7:10-12 is used to deny this position. In that passage Paul writes, "To the married I give instructions, not I, but the Lord.... To the rest I say, not the Lord." It is argued that Paul is here giving his own opinion and not an authoritative pronouncement. However, it should be observed that Paul probably meant merely to say that Jesus said nothing explicitly about the subject at hand during His earthly ministry. Hence, Paul had to say, "I have no command [*epitagēn*] of the Lord, but I give an opinion" (7:25). His opinion, however, was inspired. Paul said, "I also have the Spirit of God" (7:40). Jesus said to His disciples before His death, "I have many more things to say to you, but you cannot bear them now. But when He, the Spirit of truth, comes, He will guide you into all the truth" (John 16:12-13). The inspired advice of Paul in 1 Corinthians 7 is apparently an example of the fulfillment of that promise. In fact, Paul later said in the same epistle, "The things which I write to you are the Lord's commandment" (1 Cor. 14:37). These things are within the province of the process (2 Pet. 1:20-21) and product (2 Tim. 3:16-17) of inspiration.[5]

Summary and Conclusion

The claim for inspiration in the New Testament is derived from the fact that Jesus promised His disciples that He would guide them into "all the truth" by the Holy Spirit. The New Testament writers claimed the fulfillment of that promise for their oral message and for their writings. They claimed that their oral message was: (1) on the same level as the Old Testament messages of the prophets; (2) the foundation of the New Testament church; (3) authoritative for the church. They also claimed to be directed by the Holy Spirit in their writings, which they held to be: (1) prophetic; (2) sacred Scripture; (3) divinely authoritative; and (4) commanded to be read and circulated in the churches (see Col. 4:16; 1 Thess. 5:27). Furthermore, when a survey is made of all of the books of the New Testament, a claim is found in each individual book for its own divine origin and authority, either directly or indirectly.

5. See discussion in chap. 3.

7

The Continuation of the Doctrine of Inspiration to the Reformation

Just as the Old Testament claim for inspiration finds support in the New Testament, so the New Testament claim for inspiration finds support in the testimony of early Christian writers, the church Fathers. Although the testimony of the Fathers is not authoritative or inspired, it does reveal the orthodox doctrine of inspiration that prevailed throughout the history of the church. Their testimony, with hardly a dissenting voice, reflects the traditional view of the origin and nature of Scripture from apostolic times to the rise of Deism and Rationalism in the seventeenth and eighteenth centuries.

The Early Church (c. a.d. 70-c. 350)

Even as the New Testament writers assumed the inspiration of the Old, the church Fathers assumed the inspiration of the New. This fact is observable in the two major periods of the development of the old Catholic church prior to about a.d. 350.

The Apostolic and Subapostolic Fathers (c. a.d. 70-c. 150)

These writers indicate an early and widespread acceptance of the New Testament claim for inspiration. Several examples should suffice to bear witness to that conclusion.

The Epistle of Pseudo-Barnabas (c. 70-130). So designated because it was falsely ascribed to Paul's first associate, this writing cites the gospel of Matthew (26:31) after stating that it is what "God saith" (5:12). The same writer refers to the gospel of Matthew (22:14) by the New Testament title "Scripture" in 4:14.

Clement of Rome. Clement, a contemporary of the apostles, wrote his epistle *Corinthians* (c. 95-97) after the pattern of the apostle Paul. In it he quotes the synoptic gospels (Matt. 9:13; Mark 2:17; Luke 5:32) after calling them "Scripture" (chap. 2). He urges his readers to "act according to that which is written (for the Holy Spirit saith, 'Let not the wise man glory in his wisdom')" (chap. 1, quoting Jer. 9:23). He further appeals to "the Holy Scriptures, which are true, given by the Holy Spirit" (chap. 45). The New Testament is included as Scripture by the formula "It is written" (chap. 36) and as being written by the apostle Paul "with true inspiration" (chap. 47).

Ignatius of Antioch. Ignatius (d. c. 110) wrote his seven epistles en route to martyrdom in Rome. Although he did not give references to particular citations from the Scriptures, he did make many loose quotations and allusions to them.

Polycarp. The disciple of John, Polycarp referred to the New Testament several times in his *Epistle to the Philippians* (c. 110-135). He introduces Galatians 4:26 as "the word of truth" (chap. 3) and citations of Philippians 2:16 and 2 Timothy 4:10 as "the word of righteousness" (chap. 9). In chapter 12, Polycarp cites numerous Old and New Testament passages as "the Scriptures."

Hermas. The so-called *Shepherd of Hermas* (c. 115-140) follows the pattern of the Apocalypse, although no direct quotations of the New Testament appear in its text.

Didache. Such is the case of the *Didache* or *Teaching of the Twelve* (c. 100-120), as it too makes loose quotations and allusions to the New Testament.

Papias. In about A.D. 130-140 Papias wrote five books entitled *Exposition of the Oracles of the Lord,* which included the New Testament.[1] That is precisely the title ascribed to the Old Testament by the apostle Paul in Romans 3:2.

Epistle to Diognetus. Finally, the so-called *Epistle to Diognetus* (c. 150) makes loose quotations and allusions to the New Testament; however, no direct title is given to them.

The above material illustrates the early (by c. 150) and widespread (West and East) acceptance of the New Testament claim for inspiration. The Fathers looked upon those books with the same regard as the New Testament writers did the Old Testament Scriptures. Where no direct reference is given nor title presented, the loose quotations and allusions lend support to the esteem extended the New Testament writings. That is especially true considering the scarcity of available copies during this early period.

The Ante-Nicene and Nicene Fathers (c. A.D. 150-c. 350)

These writers further support the New Testament claims for inspiration.

Justin Martyr (d. 165). In his first *Apology* (c. 150-155), Justin Martyr

1. Eusebius *Ecclesiastical History* 3.39. Loeb ed., 1.291.

regarded the gospels as the "Voice of God" (chap. 65). He further stated of the Scriptures, "We must not suppose that the language proceeds from men who were inspired, but from the Divine Word which moves them" (*Apology* 1.36). Elsewhere, he went on to say that Moses "wrote the Hebrew character by divine inspiration" and that "the Holy Spirit of prophecy taught us this, telling us by Moses that God spoke thus."[2]

Tatian (c. 110-180). The disciple of Justin, Tatian called John 1:5 "Scripture" in his *Apology* (chap. 13). In this work he made a passionate defense of Christianity and regarded it as so pure that it was incompatible with Greek civilization. He is also noted for his pioneer effort in writing a harmony of the gospels, *Diatessaron* (c. 150-160).

Irenaeus (c. 130-202). As a boy, before he moved to Rome for studies prior to his ordination as a presbyter (elder) and later bishop of Lyons (France), Irenaeus is reported to have actually heard Polycarp. Iranaeus himself was a seminal figure in the development of Christian doctrine in the West, and his role makes him a key individual in understanding the doctrine of Scripture in the early church. In his treatise *Against Heresies* (3.1.1), Irenaeus referred to the authority of the New Testament when he stated,

> For the Lord of all gave the power of the Gospel to his apostles, through whom we have come to know the truth, that is, the teaching of the Son of God .... This Gospel they first preached. Afterwards, by the will of God, they handed it down to us in the Scriptures, to be "the pillar and ground" of our faith.[3]

In fact, he entitled the third book of this treatise "The Faith in Scripture and Tradition," in which he acknowledged the apostles to be "above all falsehood" (3.5.1). He called the Bible "Scriptures of truth," and he was "most properly assured that the Scriptures are indeed perfect, since they are spoken by the Word of God and His Spirit."[4]

Clement of Alexandria (c. 150-215). Clement of Alexandria appeared on the scene about a century later than Clement of Rome. He became head of the Cathechetical School at Alexandria in 190 but was compelled to flee in the face of persecution in 202. Clement held to a rigid doctrine of inspiration but allowed that the Greek poets were inspired by the same God in a lesser sense. In his *Stromata* Clement notes:

> There is no discord between the Law and the Gospel, but harmony, for they both proceed from the same Author, ... differing in name and time to suit the age and culture of their hearers ... by a wise economy, but potentially one, ... since faith in

2. Justin Martyr *Justin's Hortatory Oration to the Greeks*, 8, 12, and 44, as cited in Norman L. Geisler, *Decide for Yourself: How History Views the Bible*, pp. 24-25.
3. Irenaeus *Against Heresies*, in *The Library of Christian Classics*, 3:67.
4. Ibid., 2:28.2; 2.35.4.

> Christ and the knowledge ... of the Gospel is the explanation ... and the fulfillment of the Law.[5]

He does call the gospel "Scripture" in the same sense as the Law and the Prophets, as he writes of "the Scriptures ... in the Law, in the Prophets, and besides by the blessed Gospel ... [which] are valid from their omnipotent authority."[6] Clement of Alexandria went so far as to condemn those who rejected Scripture because "they are not pleased with the divine commands, that is, with the Holy Spirit."[7]

Tertullian (c. 160-220). Tertullian, in "Father of Latin Theology," never wavered in his support of the doctrine of inspiration of both the Old and the New Testaments, neither as a Catholic nor as a Montanist. In fact, he maintained that the four gospels "are reared on the certain basis of Apostolic authority, and so are inspired in a far different sense from the writings of the spiritual Christian; 'all the faithful, it is true, have the Spirit of God, but all are not Apostles.' "[8] For Tertullian,

> apostles have the Holy Spirit properly, who have Him fully, in the operations of prophecy, and the efficacy of [healing] virtues, and the evidences of tongues; not particularly, as all others have. Thus he attached the Holy Spirit's authority to that form [of advice] to which he willed us rather to attend; and forthwith it became not an *advice* of the Holy Spirit, but, in consideration of His majesty, a *precept*.[9]

Hippolytus (c. 170-236). A disciple of Irenaeus, Hippolytus exhibited the same deep sense of the spiritual meaning of Scripture as has already been traced in his immediate teacher and in earlier writers. He writes of the inspiration of the Old Testament, saying,

> The Law and the Prophets were from God, who in giving them compelled his messenger to speak by the Holy Spirit, that receiving the inspiration of the Father's power they may announce the Father's counsel and will. In these men therefore the Word found a fitting abode and spoke of Himself; for even then He came as His own herald, shewing the Word who was about to appear in the world.[10]

Of the New Testament writers, he confidently affirms,

> These blessed men ... having been perfected by the Spirit of Prophecy, and worthily honoured by the Word Himself, were brought to an inner harmony like

5. Brooke Foss Westcott, *An Introduction to the Study of the Gospels,* p. 439. It should be observed, however, that Clement regarded the *Shepherd* as inspired (cf. *Stromata* 5.15, 128).
6. Clement of Alexandria *Stromata* in *The Ante-Nicene Fathers,* 2:408-9.
7. Ibid., 7.21; also see *Stromata* 2.4 and 7.16, which is cited in Geisler, pp. 31-32.
8. Westcott, *Introduction,* p. 434.
9. Tertullian *On Exhortation to Chastity* 4, in *The Ante-Nicene Fathers*.
10. Hippolytus *Contra Noetum* as cited by Westcott, *Introduction,* pp. 431-32.

instruments, and having the Word within them, as it were to strike the notes, by Him they were moved, and announced that which God wished. For they did not speak of their own power (be well assured), nor proclaim that which they wished themselves, but first they were rightly endowed with wisdom by the Word, and afterwards well foretaught of the future by visions, and then, when thus assured, they spake that which was [revealed] to them alone by God.[11]

Novatian (d. c. 251). Novatian, the individual after whom the heretical sect was named, claimed the Old and New Testaments as authoritative Scripture in widespread references in his writings. His "monarchian" views are known largely through the writings of his critics and the schismatic activities of his followers.

Origen (c. 185-c. 254). Origen was successor of Clement at the Catechetical School in Alexandria. Although he deviated from orthodox theology as a result of his allegorical method of interpretation, Origen appears to have held that both *the writer and the writing* were inspired. He believed that God "gave the law, and the prophets, and the Gospels, being also the God of the apostles and of the Old and New Testaments." He wrote, "This Spirit inspired each one of the saints, whether prophets or apostles; and there was not one Spirit in the men of the old dispensation, and another in those who were inspired at the advent of Christ."[12] His view of the authority of the Scriptures is "that the Scriptures were written by the Spirit of God, and have a meaning ... not known to all, but to those only on whom the grace of the Holy Spirit is bestowed in the words of wisdom and knowledge."[13] He went on to assert that there is a supernatural element of thought "throughout all of Scripture even where it is not apparent to the uninstructed."[14]

Cyprian (c. 200-258). Cyprian was bishop of one of the largest cities in the West during the persecution under Decius (A.D. 249-51). In his treatise *The Unity of the Catholic Church,* he appeals to the gospels as authoritative, referring to them as the "commandments of Christ." He also adds the Corinthian letters of Paul to his list of authorities and appeals to Paul's Ephesian letter (4:4-6).

In the same passage, Cyprian reaffirms the inspiration of the New Testament, as he writes, "When the Holy Spirit says, in the person of the Lord." Again, he adds, "The Holy Spirit warns us through the Apostle"[15] as he cites 1 Corinthians 11:19.[16] These and several other examples in his writings lead

11. Hippolytus *De AntiChristo* as cited by Westcott, *Introduction,* p. 432.
12. Origen *De Principiis* in *The Ante-Nicene Fathers,* 4:240.
13. Ibid., p. 241.
14. Ibid., Preface, 4; 4, 1.1, 7, 9, 14, as cited in Geisler, pp. 28-30.
15. Cyprian *The Unity of the Catholic Church,* in *The Library of Christian Classics,* 5:126.
16. Ibid., p. 443.

to the conclusion that Cyprian held that both the Old and New Testaments are "Divine Scriptures."[17]

Eusebius of Caesarea (c. 263 or 265-340). As a church historian, Eusebius spent much time espousing the Old and New Testaments as inspired writings that were commented upon by the successors of the apostles. He also wrote much about the canon of the New Testament in his *Ecclesiastical History.* It was Eusebius of Caesarea who was commissioned to make fifty copies of the Scriptures following the Council of Nicea (325).[18]

Athanasius of Alexandria (c. 295-373). Known by the epithet "Father of Orthodoxy" because of his contributions against Arius at Nicea (325), Athanasius was the first to use the term "canon" in reference to the New Testament books, which he called "the fountains of salvation."[19]

Cyril of Jerusalem (c. 315-86). Cyril adds interesting light to round out the early church period. In his *Catecheses,* he informs his catechumen that he is offering a summary of "the whole doctrine of the Faith" which "has been built up strongly out of all the Scriptures." Then he proceeds to warn others not to change or contradict his teachings because of the Scripture's injunction as found in Galatians 1:8-9.[20] In his treatise *Of the Divine Scriptures,* he speaks of "the divinely-inspired Scriptures of both the Old and the New Testament."[21] He then proceeds to list all of the books of the Hebrew Old Testament (twenty-two) and all of the books of the Christian New Testament except Revelation (twenty-six), saying, "Learn also diligently, and from the Church, what are the books of the Old Testament, and what are those of the New. And, pray, read none of the apocryphal writings." For Cyril the matter was drawn clearly when he wrote, "With regard to the divine and saving mysteries of faith no doctrine, however trivial, may be taught without the backing of the divine Scriptures.... For our saving faith derives its force, not from capricious reasonings, but from what may be proved out of the Bible."[22]

Such evidence, coupled with the other writings of that era of church history, has led many to conclude that *virtually every church Father enthusiastically adhered to the doctrine of the inspiration of the Old and New Testaments* alike. J. N. D. Kelly affirms that position as he writes,

> There is little need to dwell on the absolute authority accorded to the Scripture as a doctrinal norm. It was the Bible, declared Clement of Alexandria about A.D. 200, which as interpreted by the Church, was the source of Christian teaching.

17. Cyprian *Epistle About Cornelius and Novation,* in *The Ante-Nicene Fathers,* 5:328.
18. See chaps. 16 and 24 for discussions about the role of Eusebius in the collection, use, and preservation of the Bible text following the period of empire-wide persecution of the church.
19. Brooke Foss Westcott, *A General Survey of the History of the Canon of the New Testament,* p. 456.
20. Cyril of Jerusalem *Catechetical Lectures,* in *Nicene and Post-Nicene Fathers,* 7:32.
21. Ibid., pp. 26-27.
22. Ibid., 4.17, as cited in J. N. D. Kelly, *Early Christian Doctrines,* p. 42.

> His greater disciple Origen was a thorough-going Biblicist who appealed again and again to Scripture as the decisive criterion of dogma ... "The holy inspired Scriptures," wrote Athanasius a century later, "are fully sufficient for the proclamation of the truth." Later in the same century John Chrysostom bade his congregation seek no other teacher than the oracles of God .... In the West Augustine ... [and] a little while later Vincent of Lerins (†c. 450) took it as an axiom [that] the Scriptural canon was "sufficient, and more sufficient, for all purposes."[23]

In short, the Fathers of the early church believed that both the Old and New Testaments were the inspired writings of the Holy Spirit through the instrumentality of the prophets and apostles. They also believed these Scriptures to be wholly true and without error because they were the very Word of God given for the faith and practice of all believers.

The Established Church (from c. a.d. 350)

The established church period covers a much larger span of time and space, and, as a result, will necessitate an even more cursory treatment of the subject matter. This period extends to the rise of Rationalism, including the medieval church, the Reformation church, and the early modern church in its scope.

The Medieval Church (c. 350-c. 1350)

The medieval church may be represented by several outstanding men who had widespread influence. These individuals represent large and varied segments of Christianity and their collective voices reflect what is known as the traditional teaching on the doctrine of the inspiration and authority of Scripture.

Ambrose of Milan (340-397). Ambrose had the distinctive honor of guiding Augustine in his early Christian experience. The Bishop of Milan also did much work with the Christian Scriptures. His *Letters* gives a clear insight into his view of the New Testament. In his letter to the Emperor Valentinian II, Ambrose cites Matthew 22:21 by using the familiar introductory statement "It is written" (20.19) as he proceeds to quote loosely John 6:15 and 2 Corinthians 12:10 (20.23).[24] He also appeals to "The Divine Scriptures" (10.7) in his letter to the Emperor Gratian, where he presents his disputation with the Arians.[25]

Jerome (c. 340-420). According to H. F. D. Sparks, "Jerome was, next to Origen, the greatest biblical scholar of the early Church."[26] Since he and his

23. Kelly, *Early Christian Doctrines*, pp. 42-43.
24. Ambrose *Letters*, no. 20, as cited in *Library of Christian Classics*, 5:209-17.
25. Ibid., no. 10, pp. 184-89.
26. H. F. D. Sparks, "Jerome as Biblical Scholar," in P. R. Ackroyd and C. F. Evans, eds., *The Cambridge History of the Bible*, vol. 1, *From the Beginnings to Jerome*, p. 510.

work will be discussed at length elsewhere, Jerome needs only to be mentioned in passing. His writings include many references to the "Holy Scriptures" and to their authority.[27] Much of his life work centered around translating the Bible and disputing with others over the canon of the Old Testament. In addition, he assumed the inspiration, canonicity and authority of the New Testament as it has come down to the modern world. According to B. F. Westcott, "The testimony of Jerome may be considered as the testimony of the Roman Church; for not only was he educated at Rome, but his labours on the text of Scripture were undertaken at the request of Damascus bishop of Rome; and later popes republished the canon which he recognised."[28] In a letter to Nepotian in A.D. 394, Jerome set forth a systematic treatise on the duties of the clergy and the rule of life they ought to adopt. In it he writes, "Read the divine scriptures constantly; never indeed, let the sacred volume out of your hand."[29] In the same year he wrote to Paulinus to make diligent study of the Scriptures, and he enumerates the books of the New Testament as he writes,

> I beg you, my dear brother, to live among these books, to meditate upon them, to know nothing else, to seek nothing else. Does not such a life seem to you a foretaste of heaven here on earth? Let not the simplicity of the scripture offend you; for these are due either to faults of translators or else to deliberate purpose: for in this way it is better fitted for instruction.[30]

In his discussion of the difference between righteous ignorance and instructed righteousness, Jerome answers the question, "Why is the apostle Paul called a chosen vessel?" His response is, "Assuredly because he is a repertory of the Law and of the holy scriptures."[31]

The Syrian School at Antioch. John Chrysostom (c. 347-407) and Theodore of Mopsuestia (c. 350-428) are representative exegetes and theologians of the Syrian School at Antioch, where the disciples were first called Christians (Acts 11:26). During the early centuries of the Christain church, Antioch was the chief rival to Alexandria in the struggle for theological leadership in the East. As in the general Antiochene conception of redemption, Theodore and his contemporaries held that the primary author of all Scripture was the Holy Spirit. He viewed the Holy Spirit as providing the content of revelation and the prophet (in cooperation with the Holy Spirit) as giving it the appro-

27. Jerome *Letters,* no. 107, as cited in *Library of Christian Classics,* 5:332-34, will suffice to support this position.
28. Westcott, *A General Survey of the History of the Canon of the New Testament,* p.453.
29. Jerome, Letter 52.7, in *Nicene and Post-Nicene Fathers,* vol. 6, *St. Jerome: Letters and Selected Works,* p. 92.
30. Ibid., Letter 53.10, p. 102.
31. Ibid., Letter 53.3, pp. 97-98.

priate expression and form.[32] Such a notion formed the basis for their literal approach to hermeneutics.

Augustine (354-430). Augustine, the "Medieval Monolith," wholly endorsed the claims of the New Testament for its inspiration. An example of this view may be seen in his *Confessions* (8.29), where the reading of Romans 13:13-14 was sufficient for him to be converted. His monumental work *The City of God* contains much Scripture, and he indicates the authority of Scripture therein in contrast to all other writings (see 11.3; 18.41). All through his letters and other treatises, Augustine asserted the truth, authority, and divine origin of Scripture. In *The City of God* he used such expressions as "Sacred Scripture" (9.5), "the words of God," (10.1), "Infallible Scripture" (11.6), "divine revelation" (13.2), and "Holy Scripture" (15.8). Elsewhere he referred to the Bible as the "oracles of God," "God's word," "divine oracles," and "divine Scripture."[33] With his widespread influence throughout the centuries, such a testimony stood as an outstanding witness to the high regard given to the Scriptures in the church. Speaking of the gospel writers, Augustine said,

> When they write that He has taught and said, it should not be asserted that he did not write it, since the members only put down what they had come to know at the dictation [dictis] of the Head. Therefore, whatever He wanted us to read concerning His words and deeds, He commanded His disciples, His hands, to write. Hence, one cannot but receive what he reads in the Gospels, though written by the disciples, as though it were written by the very hand of the Lord Himself.[34]

Consequently, he added, "I have learned to yield this respect and honour only to the canonical books of Scripture: of these alone do I most firmly believe that the authors were completely free from error."[35]

Gregory I (540-604). Gregory I, "the Great," wrote his *Commentary on Job* in which he refers to Hebrews 12:6 as "Scripture."[36] He, being the first medieval pope, set the tone for the succeeding centuries just as he epitomized the preceding ones. Louis Gaussen summarized the situation very well when he wrote,

> . . . that with the single exception of Theodore of Mopsuestia, (*c.* A.D. 400), that philosophical divine whose numerous writings were condemned for their Nestorianism in the fifth ecumenical council, . . . it has been found impossible to produce, in the long course of the *eight first centuries of Christianity,* a single

32. See M. F. Wiles, "Theodore of Mopsuestia as Representative of the Antiochene School," in P. R. Ackroyd and C.F. Evans, eds., *The Cambridge History of the Bible,* vol. 1, *From the Beginnings to Jerome,* pp. 492-93.
33. Augustine *Expositions on the Book of Psalms* 137.1; 146.12; *Letters* 55.37; *Enchiridion* 1.4; *Harmony of the Gospels* 1.35.54; all in *Nicene and Post-Nicene Fathers,* vol. 8, 2d series.
34. Augustine *Harmony of the Gospels* 1.35.54, as cited in Geisler, *Decide for Yourself,* p. 34.
35. As cited in Geisler, *Decide for Yourself,* p. 40.
36. Gregory the Great *The Commentary of Job,* in *Library of Christian Classics,* 9:189.

doctor who has disowned the plenary inspiration of the Scriptures, unless it be in the bosom of the most violent heresies that have tormented the Christian Church; that is to say, among the Gnostics, the Manicheans, the Anomeans, and the Mahometans.[37]

Anselm of Canterbury (1033-1109). In his famous *Cur Deus Homo?* (chap. 22), Anselm continued to state the orthodox view of inspiration when he wrote, "And the God-man himself originates the New Testament and approves the Old. And, as we must acknowledge him to be true, so no one can dissent from anything contained in these books."[38] As Archbishop of Canterbury, Anselm addressed the question of authority in another treatise, where he said, "Leaving aside what is said in Scripture, which I believe without doubting, of course."[39]

The Victorines. Outstanding men of the Abbey of St. Victor in Paris in the twelfth century followed the historical and literal approach to biblical interpretation in the tradition of the Syrian School at Antioch. Its representatives included Hugh (d. 1142), Richard (d. 1173), and Andrew (d. 1175). They insisted that liberal arts, history, and geography are basic to literal exegesis, which gives rise to doctrine, and that doctrine forms the natural background for allegorization of Scripture. Such literal interpretation they held to be basic to the proper study of the Bible, which they assumed to be the very word of God.[40]

Thomas Aquinas (c. 1225-1274). The foundations for medieval theology were laid by such outstanding scholars as the categorizer Peter Lombard (c. 1100-c. 1160) and the encyclopedist Albert the Great (c. 1193 or 1206-1280). With them the age of medieval Scholasticism emerged. But the chief spokesman of Scholasticism was Thomas Aquinas, the great systematic theologian. Thomas Aquinas clearly held to the orthodox doctrine of inspiration. In his *Summa Theologiae* Aquinas, the Roman Catholic theologian, states that "the Author of Holy Scripture is God."[41] Although he asks the question of "senses" of Scripture, he *assumes* the "inspiration" of both the Old and New Testaments. He concurred with the traditional view that the Scriptures are "divine revelation" (1a. 1,1; 1a. 1,8) and "without error" (2a2ae. 1,6, *In Job* 13.1).

After the time of Aquinas and his critic John Duns Scotus (c. 1265-1308), Scholastic philosophy moved into its period of decline. This trend culminated

37. Louis Gaussen, *Theopneustia*, pp. 139-40.
38. Anselm of Canterbury, *Saint Anselm, Basic Writings: Proslogium, Monologium, Gaunilon's: On Behalf of the Fool, Cur Deus Homo*, trans. S.W. Deane, 2d ed. (LaSalle, Ill.: Open Court, 1962), pp. 287-88.
39. Anselm of Canterbury, *Truth, Freedom, and Evil: Three Philosophical Dialogues*, ed. and trans. Jasper Hopkins and Herbert Richardson, p. 185.
40. Bernard Ramm, *Protestant Biblical Interpretation: A Textbook of Hermeneutics*, p. 51.
41. Thomas Aquinas *Summa Theologiae* 1a. 1, 10. This is an excellent summary of Thomas's view on inspiration.

in the nominalistic skepticism of William of Ockham (c. 1300-1349), and it set the stage for the removal of theology from the untrained during the period between the death of Ockham and the Reformation. Nevertheless, the great scholars, theologians, and doctors of the established church believed, as did the early Fathers, that the whole Bible is the inspired, infallible, and inerrant Word of God written. They accepted it as the divinely authoritative standard for the Christin church without hesitation and without reservation.

The Pre-reformation Church (c. 1350-c. 1500)

In the meantime other movements were making their appearance in Europe and the church. Long before the Reformation era (c. 1500-c. 1650) there was a strong desire among the common people to return to the Scriptures. This desire was evidenced in such movements as the Waldensians, the Lollards, and the Hussites.

Valdes (fl. 1173-1205/1218). Valdes, also known incorrectly as "Peter Waldo," was a rich merchant of Lyons. His followers, the "poor men of Lyons," came to be known as the Waldensians. At the Third Lateran Council (1179) Valdes and his followers sought ecclesiastical recognition and produced vernacular translations of the Bible. They were forbidden to preach except by invitation of the clergy, but they were soon placed under the ban of excommunication (1184). They began to organize themselves increasingly apart from the church, ignore its decrees and sanctions, and appoint their own ministers. Their movement was based on the traditional doctrine of the inspiration and authority of the Scriptures. They tended to doubt the validity of the sacraments administered by unworthy ministers, and they appealed to the Scriptures for support of their opposition to various practices within the church as well as of their right and duty to preach. Soon they spread to Southern France and Spain, and then to Germany, Piedmont, and Lombardy. Their numbers were decimated after the time of Innocent III, the Fourth Lateran Council (1215), and the Inquisition. Although they developed no central leadership or organization, they quickly contacted the Reformers in the sixteenth century.

John Wycliffe (c. 1320-84). Wycliffe marks a turning point in the *transmission* of the Scriptures, but not in the history of the doctrine of the *inspiration* of the Scriptures. From the time of his death onward his name has been associated with the movement for the translation of the Bible into English. The pioneer work of the English reformer and theologian was directed toward the translation and distribution of the Scriptures, which he and his followers, the Lollards, believed to be the very Word of God. Wycliffe felt that the Bible alone in the hands of the people would be sufficient for the Holy Spirit to use among them. So confident of that was he that he advocated the Scriptures as the only law of the church, and he devoted his life and energies to their dissemination. Although Wycliffe and his immediate followers worked within the pale of the church, there was opposition to translations based on several grounds. According to Henry Hargreaves,

> In England, the question of the legality of biblical translations and their use did not come to the fore until the last quarter of the fourteenth century. Old English versions of biblical books seem to have aroused no antagonism, and to judge by the number of manuscripts extant, Rolle's *Psalter* must have had a fair popularity, and possibly therefore official countenance. But the aim of the Wycliffite translators was undoubtedly to set up a new and all-sufficient authority in opposition to the Church. By now the Church sanctioned much that was un-biblical and did not satisfy Wycliffe's criterion for ecclesiastical institutions: that they should conform to the practice of Christ and his followers as recorded in the Scriptures. The Wycliffites therefore appealed to 'Goddis lawe' and 'Christis lawe'—their regular names for the Bible and the New Testament. Moreover, they asserted that these laws were open to the direct understanding of all men on the points most essential to salvation. For such understanding it was necessary that all men should be able to study the Gospels in the tongue in which they might best understand their meaning.[42]

Wycliffe's use of allegory in interpretation was based on his predisposition that the Words of Scripture were utterly reliable.[43] His view of the plenary inspiration of Scripture was the basis for Wycliffe's efforts in Bible translation and theology, which made such an impact on John Hus, Martin Luther, and others that he is known as "The Morning Star of the Reformation."[44]

John Hus (c. 1372-1415). Born of a peasant family at Husinec in Bohemia, John Hus earned his Master's degree at the university in Prague (1396) before being ordained (1400). He became a well-known preacher at Bethlehem Chapel in Prague just as Wycliffe's writings became widespread in Bohemia, and he became a champion of Wycliffe's views. In 1411 a new pope, John XXIII,[45] excommunicated Hus and placed his followers under interdict. Disputations led Hus to publish his chief work, *De Ecclesia* (1413), the first ten chapters of which were taken directly from Wycliffe, and in 1414 Hus left Bohemia for the Council at Constance. He was later arrested and executed at the stake in July 1415. His view of the Scripture was the same as Wycliffe's.

42. Henry Hargreaves, "The Wycliffite Versions," in "The Vernacular Scriptures," G. W. H. Lampe, ed., *The Cambridge History of the Bible, vol. 2, The West from the Fathers to the Reformation,* p. 392.
43. John D. Woodbridge, "Biblical Authority: Towards an Evaluation of the Rogers McKim Proposal," Review Article, *Trinity Journal,* vol. 1, no. 2, New Series (Fall 1980): 177. In a footnote to his discussion, Woodbridge cites a Wycliffe item included in Herbert Winn, ed., *Wyclif—English Sermons* [London: Oxford University Press, 1929], 19. Also see William Mallard, "John Wycliffe and the Tradition of Biblical Authority," *Church History* 30 (1961): 50-60.
44. Hubert Cunliffe-Jones, ed., assisted by Benjamin Drewery, *A History of Christian Doctrine: In Succession to the Earlier Work of G. P. Fisher Published in the International Theological Library Series,* p. 291.
45. Obviously not the same as the more recent pope (1958-63) who took the same name.

In fact, when Martin Luther began his own work of reformation and made his appeal to the Scriptures rather than to the established authorities of the Church, he was frequently chided for following the "error of Hus." The common ground of the Bohemian Hussites (sometimes referred to as Waldenses) and Martin Luther was their appeal to the authority of Scripture.

Summary and Conclusion

When Martin Luther appeared on the scene, he was not entirely original on his point that the Scriptures are the ultimate source of authority for Christians and that the pope is not their sole interpreter. Just as the Old Testament claims for inspiration found support in the New, so the New Testament claims for inspiration found support in the writings of the church Fathers. In the early church the evidence is early and widespread for the acceptance of the New Testament claims for inspiration. In the established church the evidence is consonant with the former period. Throughout the Middle Ages and into the period of the Reformation, church Fathers, scholars, reformers, and others followed the traditional doctrine of the inspiration of Scriptures even when they differed over their interpretation. Roland H. Bainton attested that the Reformers were in this very stream of continuity concerning the inspiration and authority of Scripture. He noted,

> William of Occam had already said that to be saved a Christian is not called upon to belive that which is not contained in Scripture or to be derived from Scripture by manifest and inescapable logic.... The counciliarists appealed to the Bible against the pope.... [and in their Leipzig disputation in 1519] when John Eck told Luther that his teaching betrayed the Bohemian virus, in his reliance 'more on sacred Scripture than on the supreme pontiffs, councils, doctors and universities'.... Luther replied that he did not disdain the opinions of the most illustrious Fathers, but that clear Scripture is to be preferred. The authority of Scripture is beyond all human capacity.[46]

46. Roland H. Bainton, "The Bible in the Reformation," in S. L. Greenslade, ed., *The Cambridge History of the Bible,* vol. 3, *The West from the Reformation to the Present Day,* pp. 2-4.

8

Doctrines of Inspiration Since the Reformation

Introduction

The four centuries between the Reformation and the New Reformation have been characterized as the time of "the making of the modern mind" by John Herman Randall and others.[1] During the period between Martin Luther's *Ninety-Five Theses* (1517) and Karl Barth's *Commentary on Romans* (1919), a growing divergence between the intellectual and theological worlds set a climate of opinion that would enable the emerging scientific method to be used to challenge the authority of the Word of God within the church itself.[2] Critics and supporters alike have come to apply the so-called dialectical method to develop their own doctrines of inspiration and authority of Scripture. However, a correct understanding of the inspiration and authority of Scripture is not properly derived by a dialectical process. The deviations and departures from the historic teaching of the Christian church concerning the nature of Scripture were challenges that caused Christian apologists to respond in defense of the traditional doctrine of Scripture.[3]

The first major deviations from the orthodox doctrine of the inspiration and authority of Scripture emerged after the Reformation of the sixteenth century. As one writer puts it,

1. John Herman Randall, Jr., *The Making of the Modern Mind: A Survey of the Intellectual Background of the Present Age*. Also see standard treatments of the rise of modern thought, such as Crane Brinton, *Ideas and Men: The Story of Western Thought;* Roland N. Stromberg, *An Intellectual History of Modern Europe;* Colin Brown, *Philosophy and the Christian Faith: A Historical Sketch from the Middle Ages to the Present Day.* Also see Herbert Butterfield, *The Origins of Modern Science;* A. R. Hall, *The Scientific Revolution 1500-1800: The Formation of the Modern Scientific Attitude;* Lynn Thorndike, *A History of Magic and Experimental Science*.
2. See H. D. McDonald, *Theories of Revelation: An Historical Study 1700-1960*.
3. See William E. Nix, "The Doctrine of Inspiration Since the Reformation," pp. 443-54, which provides the basis for this discussion of the major traditions within the Christian communion on the doctrine of Scripture.

> Christians early had inherited from the Jews the belief that the biblical writers were somehow possessed by God, who was thus reckoned as the Bible's proper author. Since God could not conceivably be the agent of falsehood, the Bible must be guaranteed free from error. For centuries the doctrine lay dormant, as doctrine: accepted by all, pondered by few. Not until the sixteenth century did inspiration and its corollary, inerrancy, come up for sustained review.[4]

Even then, however, the mainstream of Christian thought continued to adhere to the doctrine of the inspiration and authority of Scripture. Roland H. Bainton suggests that the Reformers dethroned the pope and enthroned the Bible as their ultimate authority; the principle of *sola scriptura* was basic to all Protestants during the Reformation era. At Worms (1521) Martin Luther (1483-1546) affirmed that nothing as to the faith can be asserted that contradicts or goes beyond Scripture or evident reason. Ulrich Zwingli (1494-1551) took his stand on the same ground at the first Zurich disputation before the city council in 1523. John Calvin (1509-64) wrestled with the identical issue; the Anabaptists were the most scriptural of all parties of the Reformation; and the *Thirty-nine Articles* of the Church of England include one article "Of the sufficiency of the Holy Scriptures for salvation."[5] Such a widespread and uniform attitude reflects the general sentiment of the Reformation era that the Bible alone is the complete and sufficient guide in matters of religious faith and practice. Nevertheless, the Reformation period of the sixteenth and seventeenth centuries was an era of creeds and confessions in which each denominational group or sect sought to articulate and to perpetuate its own doctrinal tradition. Although some of those numerous creed-forms tended to become ends in and of themselves, they were generally based on and drawn from Scripture. These more or less formal statements of faith will be reviewed as they emerged in history.

The Anabaptist and Baptist Tradition (c. 1524-c. 1918)

The earliest of these traditions is associated with the Anabaptist and Baptist groups. These noncreedal and nonsacramental bodies tended to use confessions and declarations of faith as descriptions of their doctrinal views rather than as prescriptive formulas to which one gave allegiance through creeds and catechisms. In general they trace their origins to one of three basic traditions: (1) Baptist successionism, (2) Anabaptist-Baptist spiritual kinship, and (3) English separatist dissent. The first two traditions find their teachings reflected in the writings of such individuals and groups as John Wycliffe (c. 1320-1384), John Hus (c. 1372-1415), Balthasar Hubmaier (c. 1480-1528), *The Schleitheim Confession* (1527) of the Swiss Anabaptists,

4. J. T. Burtchaell, *Catholic Theories of Inspiration since 1810,* pp. 1-2.
5. Roland H. Bainton, "The Bible and the Reformation," pp. 1-6.

Martin Bucer (c. 1494-1551), and Menno Simons (1496-1561). Hubmaier opposed Roman Catholicism, the Zwinglians, and the Lutherans in many teachings (especially infant baptism) because they lacked scriptural support. Within his own movement, "An appeal to the Word of God was the method which Hubmaier used to deal with difficulties which threatened the Anabaptist fellowship."[6] It was Hubmaier who "set forth the Reformation principle of obedience to the Bible as his personal conviction."[7] His influence and that principle are clearly seen in one of the earliest doctrinal statements of the Reformation era in which the Anabaptists defined their beliefs, *The Schleth-eim Confession*.[8] In the introduction to his *Treatise Against the Anabaptists*, whom he distinguished from the Libertines and the Spirituals, John Calvin accused them of "many perverse and pernicious errors" but acknowledged that "at least this sect receives the Holy Scripture, as do we."[9]

The influence of Martin Bucer and Menno Simons was directed in other ways during the Reformation era. Bucer's "interpretation of Scripture and the position derived from it was accepted as the official view of the city of Strassburg,"[10] where it exerted influence on John Calvin during the time the Genevan Reformer was in Strassburg. His extensive influence on the leaders and Bible translators of the Reformation era attest to Bucer's view of the inspiration and authority of the Bible.[11] Menno Simons became the leader of the peaceful Anabaptists in the Netherlands.[12] His view of Scripture is clearly set forth in *The Foundation of Christian Doctrine* (1539/40), which took as its text 1 Corinthians 3:11. In it he was concerned with the issues of Christology and the ban, which were common with the views expressed in

6. W. R. Estep, *The Anabaptist Story*, p. 60.
7. Ibid., p. 51. Also See W. R. Estep, "Balthasar Hubmaier: Martyr Without Honor," *Baptist History and Heritage*, no. 2 (April 1978), pp. 5-10.
8. This confessional statement was published at Schleitheim on the Border [Canton Schaffhausen, Switzerland] on February 24, 1527. It has been translated several times and appears in numerous works, such as the translation by John C. Wenger, pp. 247-53.
9. John Calvin, *Treatises Against the Anabaptists and Against the Libertines: Translation, Introduction, and Notes*, ed. and trans. Benjamin Wirt Farley, p. 39.
10. Cornelius J. Dyck, ed., *An Introduction to Mennonite History: A Popular History of the Anabaptists and the Mennonites*, p. 68.
11. Bucer's Latin Psalter (1529) was translated into English and printed at Strassburg in 1530—five years before the first complete English Bible was edited by Miles Coverdale (1535). This Psalter underwent several editions on the Continent, and it was an influence on "Matthew's Bible" (1537) as well as the marginal notes in its Psalter. Several years after Robert Stephanus published it in 1544, this Psalter stirred up controversy when the followers of Jacob Arminius (1560-1609), including Hugo Grotius (1583-1645), accused the Genevan publisher of altering Bucer's doctrinal statements for the sake of Calvinistic interpretation. See discussion in chap. 30. Also see Constantin Hopf, *Martin Bucer and the English Reformation*, pp. 213-17.
12. See especially George Huntston Williams, *The Radical Reformation*, pp. 387-98, and Dyck, *Mennonite History*, pp. 79-88. Also see Menno Simons, *The Complete Writings*, ed. John C. Wenger, trans. Leonard Verduin, which contains "A Brief Biography" by Harold Bender.

The Schleitheim Confession.[13]

The third tradition is consonant with the stance of the Church of England and the so-called "Magisterial Reformation" because it asserts that it arose out of the English spiritual dissent movement.[14] Throughout their history, and well into the twentieth century, Baptists have sought to avoid prescriptive or creedal statements in favor of descriptive or sermonic expressions of their confessional statements, which they enunciate in their particular historical, sociological, and theological setting.[15]

The typical Baptist confessional statement rests firmly on the text and teaching of Scripture, and particularly the New Testament, which are cited profusely at each point in the statements they present. In addition, Baptists have tended to build their confessional statements on earlier models within their particular tradition. Examples of Baptist statements are the *Confession of Faith* (1644) of the seven Baptist churches in London (hence *The London Confession*), published three years prior to the *Westminster Confession of Faith* (1647) of the Church of England. *The London Confession of 1644* was reprinted on numerous occasions before the so-called *Second London Confession* was published (1677). It became the most generally accepted confession of the Regular or Calvinistic Baptists in England, and it was reissued in 1688 and 1689 as *A Confession put forth by the Elders and Brethren of many Congregations of Christians (Baptized upon Profession of Their Faith) in London and the Country.* That statement was a slight modification of the *Westminster Confession* of the Church of England and the *Savoy Declaration* (1658) of the Congregational churches in order to suit the distinctives of Baptist polity and baptism. The *Second London Confession* was "adopted by the Baptist Association met at Philadelphia, Sept. 25, 1742" and called *The Philadelphia Confession*. It followed the model of the *Westminster Confession* by placing the doctrine of Scripture in Article I (paragraphs 1-10), where it states,

> (1) The Holy Scripture is the only sufficient, certain and infallible rule of all-saving knowledge, faith, and obedience .... (4) The authority of the Holy

13. Menno Simons, "On the Ban: Questions and Answers," in George H. Williams and Angel M. Mergal, eds., *Spiritual and Anabaptist Writers: Documents Illustrative of the Radical Reformation*, pp. 261-71. In the introduction to this treatise, the editors state, "Baptism and the ban were the two keys controlling entry to and the exit from the regenerate church of Anabaptism. By [re]baptism one entered the church. By the ban the wayward member was extruded .... The ban was, of course, based on Matt. 18:15-18. With it came to be associated the practice of avoidance or shunning, based on 1 Cor. 5:11" (p. 261).
14. Nix, "Doctrine of Inspiration," pp. 444-45. Williams, *Radical Reformation*, has an outstanding treatment of the distinctions among the various branches of the "Radical Reformation" and their contacts with the "Magisterial Reformation" in its various expressions. Also see William R. Estep, *The Anabaptist Story.*
15. For an excellent and balanced treatment of this point see L. Russ Bush and Tom J. Nettles, *Baptists and the Bible*. Also see Tom J. Nettles, "Baptists and Scripture," in John D. Hannah, ed., *Inerrancy and the Church*, pp. 323-57.

> Scriptures, for which it ought to be believed, dependeth not upon the testimony of any man or church, but wholly upon God (Who is truth itself), the author thereof; therefore it is to be received, because it is the Word of God.[16]

In the area of North Carolina, Separate Baptists joined their efforts with the Sandy Creek Church. In 1758 the Sandy Creek Association was formed, with the Sandy Creek Church as its nucleus. Separate Baptists from Virginia and the Carolinas cooperated in their outreach for more than a dozen years. Article II of its brief doctrinal statement says, "That the Scriptures of the Old and New Testaments are the word of God, and only rule of faith and practice."[17]

During the nineteenth century, Baptists in both the northern and southern United States came to use the shorter and moderately Calvinistic statement, *The New Hampshire Declaration of Faith* (1833). Basically a consensus statement written well after the Calvinistic-Freewill controversies among New England Baptists had ceased following the Great Awakening, it was reprinted in several widely-used Baptist church manuals as the most popular statement of faith for nearly a century throughout the United States. It became the focal point of the theological controversy that occurred in the Northern Baptist Convention after that denomination was organized in 1907. The same statement was adopted, with some additions, deletions, and other changes, as *A Statement of the Baptist Faith and Message* of the Southern Baptist Convention in 1925. *The New Hampshire Declaration* asserts,

> We believe that the Holy Bible was written by men divinely inspired, and is a perfect treasure of heavenly instruction;* that it has God as its author, salvation for its end,* and truth without any mixture of error for its matter;* that it reveals the principles by which God will judge us;* and therefore is, and shall remain to the end of the world, the true center of Christian union,* and the supreme standard by which all human conduct, creeds, and opinions shall be tried.*[18]

This article was adopted verbatim in the *Baptist Faith and Message* (1925), but the Northern Baptists were unable to come to any agreement about a doctrinal statement for their entire constituency because of the impact of the doctrines of modernism and the fundamentalist controversy that ensued. As

16. *The Philadelphia Confession of Faith,* 6th ed., as printed by Benjamin Franklin. See "The London Confession of 1644," pp. 3-8. "The Second London Confession" (1677) is reprinted in William L. Lumpkin, *The Baptist Confessions of Faith,* pp. 241-59; Article I, "Of the Holy Scriptures," is on pp. 248-52. Also see J.E. Carter, "American Baptist Confessions of Faith: A Review of Confessions of Faith Adopted by Major Baptist Bodies in the United States," in William R. Estep, ed., *The Lord's Free People in a Free land: Essays in Baptist History in Honor of Robert A. Baker.* Chapter 5 of this collection presents an overview of the backgrounds, characteristics, etc., of such statements.
17. Lumpkin, *Baptist Confessions,* p. 358.
18. Article "I. Of the Scriptures," *The New Hampshire Declaration of Faith,* as published in the Oklahoma *Baptist Messenger* 58, no. 32 (April 1969), pp. 9-12. There are numerous Scripture citations at each asterisked point in the text of this article, albeit not all issues of the *Declaration* contain the Scripture references as so indicated.

the Northern Baptist Convention went through the throes of the so-called liberal-fundamentalist controversy, groups that moved out of its ranks, as well as independent Baptists and others, adopted *The New Hampshire Declaration* as their own doctrinal expression of faith. In the meantime the Southern Baptist Convention reaffirmed and even strengthened this particular article in its adoption of *The Baptist Faith and Message* (1963).

The Lutheran Tradition (c. 1530-c. 1918)

Martin Luther has often been attacked for not holding to the inspiration of Scripture because of his criticism of certain books of the Bible. James Orr clears the air of this accusation when he writes of Luther's view of the Scriptures, "Luther's views, as his ordinary teaching and use of Scripture show, were scarcely less high; but, applying a subjective standard, his judgments on certain books, as the Epistle of James, Revelation, Esther, even the Epistle to the Hebrews, were rash and arbitrary. These judgments affected canonicity rather than inspiration."[19] In his monumental study *Luther and the Scriptures,* M. Reu traces the development of Luther's attitude toward the inspiration and authority of Scripture. Early in his career, the Reformer had submitted himself to the church and the Fathers. Even before the Diet of Worms in early 1521, Luther began "to divorce himself more and more from these authorities and to advance the notion of *sola scriptura,* the sole authority of the Scriptures.[20]

Luther himself regarded the Bible to be "so much like himself [God], that the Godhead is wholly in it, and he who has the word has the whole Godhead."[21] As for the words of the Bible, Luther writes, "And the Scriptures, although they too are written by men, are neither of men nor from men but from God."[22] Elsewhere he says, "Nothing but God's Word alone should be preached in Christendom."[23]

During the centuries following Luther's *Ninety-five Theses,* the Lutheran churches have espoused nine creeds and confessions of their faith. Those nine statements make up the *Book of Concord,* which was first published in

19. James Orr, *Revelation and Inspiration,* p. 208.
20. Reu's work was reissued with correction to notes in *The Springfielder* (Springfield, Ill.: Concordia Theological Seminary, August 1960). Also see John Warwick Montgomery, "Lessons from Luther on the Inerrancy of Holy Writ," in John Warwick Montgomery, ed., *God's Inerrant Word: An International Symposium on the Trustworthiness of Scripture,* pp. 63-94.
21. Martin Luther, in *Luther's Works,* J. Pelikan and H. T. Lehman, eds., 55 vols., 52:46, as cited by Geisler, *Decide for Yourself,* p. 39.
22. Ibid., 55:153; Geisler, p. 41.
23. Ibid., 30:167; Geisler, p. 42.

1580, although the first authentic Latin edition was not published until 1584.[24] In the "Epitome of the Articles [of Concord]," the first item presented is "Of the Compendious Rule and Norm" touching theological controversies. In three articles concerning the various symbols of the faith, Lutherans "believe, confess, and teach that the only rule and norm, according to which all doctrines ought to be esteemed and judged, is not other than the prophetic and apostolic writings both of the Old and of the New Testament."[25] Although the *Book of Concord* made its appearance in the beginnings of the period of so-called "Protestant Scholasticism," the conclusion of M. Reu is appropriate as it relates the Lutheran position about the Scriptures in the late sixteenth century:

> And, indeed, as long as the divine authority of the Bible is maintained, and as long as it is conceded that it is the product of a unique cooperation of the Holy Spirit and the human writers and, therefore, as a whole and in all its details the Word of God without contradiction and error, so long the question after the mode of inspiration is of an entirely secondary nature, and so long one is in harmony with the best Lutheran theologians from Luther up to the year 1570.[26]

From the time of Martin Luther until well into the twentieth century, Lutherans, and especially those in the United States, in general have held to the position of their founder with regard to the inspiration and authority of Scripture in both their confessions and their catechisms. That may be seen especially in such groups as the American Lutheran Church, the Wisconsin Evangelical Lutheran Synod, and the Lutheran Church-Missouri Synod.[27]

The Evangelical Reformed Tradition (c. 1536-c. 1918)

The reform movements begun under the leadership of Ulrich Zwingli (1484-1531) and John Calvin (1509-1564) laid strong claim to the inspiration and authority of Scripture. Zwingli made constant reference to Scripture during his tenure in Zurich, where he used the Bible in its original languages

24. The Ecumenical Creeds consist of the Apostles', Nicene, and Athanasian creeds. The six Confessions set forth are the *Augsburg Confession* (1530), *Apology of the Augsburg Confession* (1530-31), *Smalcald Articles* (1537), *Luther's Small Catechism* (1529), *Luther's Large Catechism* (1529), and *Formula of Concord* (1576). See *A Short Explanation of Dr. Martin Luther's Small Catechism: A Handbook of Christian Doctrine*, p. 210. See also Philip Schaff, *The Creeds of Christendom*.
25. Schaff, *The Creeds of Christendom*, vol. 3: *The Evangelical Protestant Creeds, with Translations*, pp. 93-94. See also "Articles V-VI," which are concerned with the relationship "of the Law and the Gospel" and "of the Third Use of the Law," pp. 126-35.
26. Reu, *Luther and the Scriptures*, p. 70.
27. Harold Lindsell, *The Bible in the Balance* pp. 44-274, discusses the Lutherans in general before probing into the subject of the Scriptures within the Luthern Church-Missouri Synod. For a discussion of this and related subjects among other denominational groups and institutional settings see Harold Lindsell, *The Battle for the Bible*.

for his pulpit ministry. From his disputations with Luther and Philip Melanchthon at Marburg (1529) it is apparent that Zwingli differed from the other Reformers on some points concerning the *interpretation* of the Scripture, but there was unanimity among them on the *inspiration* and *authority* of Scripture. Even before the Anabaptists were compelled to leave Zurich over differences of scriptural interpretation, Zwingli affirmed his own view of Scripture in the *Sixty-seven Articles* (1523) by writing,

> The articles and opinions below I, Ulrich Zwingli, confess to having preached in the worthy city of Zurich as based upon the Scriptures which are called inspired by God, and I offer to protect and conquer with the said articles, and where I have not now correctly understood said Scriptures I shall allow myself to be taught better, but only from said Scripture.[28]

John Calvin was actually a second-generation Reformer. Having been influenced by Bucer and others, Calvin's impact has been felt by all his successors. As James Orr states, "There is a singular breadth and modernness in Calvin's exegesis; but his faith in the entire inspiration of the Scriptures is profound and uncompromising. The ultimate guarantee of inspiration, as already seen, is found by him in the internal witness of the Holy Spirit. The creeds of the Reformed Church embodied the same conceptions."[29] This observation places Calvin in the historical church tradition on the doctrine of the inspiration and authority of Scripture. Throughout his *Institutes* and his *Commentaries,* Calvin asserted his belief that the Bible is the authoritative, infallible, and unerring norm for the Christian faith. His teaching is treated extensively in the *Institutes* (1.6.1-4; 1.7.1-5, 13; 1.9.1-3). In addition to that doctrinal development, Calvin's *Commentaries* affirm that the Scriptures are "the certain and unerring rule" (Ps. 5:11), and that some of the alleged errors must be attributed to scribal mistakes.[30] Recent treatments confirming Calvin's view of Scripture have been made by John Murray, Kenneth Kantzer, J.I. Packer, and others.[31]

The groups associated with Zwingli and Calvin, or those that arose under their influence, were scattered throughout Europe during the sixteenth and

28. Ulrich Zwingli, *Sixty-seven Articles,* Preface, in Clyde L. Manschreck, ed., *A History of Christianity,* vol. 2, *Readings in the History of the Church from the Reformation to the Present,* pp. 67-70.
29. Orr, *Revelation and Inspiration,* p. 207, where the author makes reference to Calvin's *Institutes of the Christian Religion,* 1.7.4-5.
30. John Calvin, *Commentary on the Harmony of the Evangelists* (Calvin Translation Society), p. 272.
31. John Murray, *Calvin on Scripture and Divine Sovereignty,* 1960, pp. 11-31, reprint articles from *Torch and Trumpet;* Kenneth S. Kantzer, "Calvin and the Holy Scriptures," in John F. Walvoord, ed., *Inspiration and Interpretation,* pp. 115-55; J.I. Packer, "Calvin's View of Scripture," in Montgomery, ed., *God's Inerrant Word,* pp. 95-114. See also, for example, John H. Gerstner, "The View of the Bible Held by the Church: Calvin and the Westminster Divines," in Norman L. Geisler, ed., *Inerrancy,* pp. 383-410, 482-85.

seventeenth centuries. One example of such influence came with John Knox (c. 1513-1572), who arrived to study in Geneva during a period of exile. He took the teachings of Calvin with him when he returned to Scotland. There he established Calvinism as the official religion, including its teaching on the inspiration and authority of Scripture. His disciples in turn trained James VI, later James I (1603-1625) of England, who shared their high regard for Scripture.

In the meantime, Reformed doctrinal expression was preserved and propagated in Switzerland through *The Sixty-seven Articles or Conclusions of Uldrich Zwingli* (1523),[32] *The Ten Conclusions of Berne* (1528),[33] *The First Helvetic Confession* (1536),[34] and *The Second Helvetic Confession* (1566).[35] It was in this tradition that Franz Turretini, or Francis Turretin (1623-1687), and his son Johann Alfons (1671-1737) both taught at Geneva. In France the work of Calvin was perpetuated in the *The Gallican Confession* (1559), which asserts, "We believe that the Word contained in these [canonical] books has proceeded from God, and receives its authority from him alone, and not from men."[36] This Confession was published in a somewhat modified and abridged form and used by the Waldenses as *A Brief Confession of Faith of the Reformed Churches of the Piedmont* (1655).[37]

In the Low Countries the great confessions of the Reformed tradition were set forth in three basic treatises: *The Belgic Confession* (1561),[38] *The Heidelberg (Palatinate) Catechism* (1563),[39] and *The Canons of Dort* (1618-1619).[40]

32. Schaff, *The Creeds of Christendom,* 3:197-207, for the German and Latin texts of these articles first published and defended at Zurich on January 29, 1523.
33. Ibid., 3:208-10, for the German and Latin texts of these, prepared for a large religious conference held in Berne on January 7-26, 1528.
34. Ibid., 3:211-31, for the German and Latin texts of this expression of the faith drawn up for use by all the Reformed cantons of Switzerland in 1536; the earlier confessions were statements with merely local authority.
35. This Confession is a theological treatise rather than a confessional statement as such. Ibid., 3:233-306, for extracts from its contents as well as references concerning translations of the Latin, German, and French editions of Johann Heinrich Bullinger (1504-75) and first published at Zurich in 1566.
36. Prepared by Calvin and his pupil De Chandieu in 1559, this Confession was used among the French Calvinists. It was originally published in French before being translated into German (1562) and Latin (1566). See *Confessio Fidei Gallicana,* in Schaff, *The Creeds of Christendom,* 3:356-82, where Articles II-V, pp. 360-62, concern the Scriptures.
37. Published in French, English, and Latin editions, this confession is still in use among the Waldenses in Italy. Ibid., 3:757-70.
38. Composed in French by Guy de Bres (d. 1567) for the churches in Flanders and the Netherlands in 1561, this confession was adopted by a Reformed synod at Emden (1571) and by the national synod at Dort (1619), following careful revision by comparing French, Latin, and Dutch copies. Ibid., 3:383-436.
39. Ibid., 3:307-55, contains the German text of the third edition along with a new English translation. This catechism was used in the churches and schools of the Electoral Palatinate following its publication in 1563.
40. Ibid., 3:545-97, contains *The Canons of the Synod of Dort,* which are also called the *Five Articles Against the Remonstrants* in response to *The Five Arminian Articles* (1610), ibid., 3:545-49. Also see *Doctrinal Standards of the Christian Reformed Church.*

The Belgic Confession was the basic confessional statement of the Netherlands during the period when Jacob Arminius (1560-1609), a Dutch theologian, promulgated the doctrines now known as Arminianism. His immediate followers were called "the Remonstrants," after their anti-Calvinistic Remonstrance, or "Five Articles," published in 1610. Arminius devoted six of his seventy-nine private disputations to the nature, authority, and adequacy of Scripture. In them he asserted that in the transmission of His Word, God "first employed *oral enunciation* in its delivery, and afterwards, *writing,* as a more certain means against corruption and oblivion ... so that we now have the infallible word of God in no other place than in the Scriptures ... the instrument of religion." He continued his argument by stating that the "authority of the word of God, which is comprised of the Old and New Testament, lies both in the veracity of the whole narration, and of all the declarations, whether they be those about things past, about things present, or about those which are to come, and in the power of the commands and prohibitions, which are contained in the divine word."[41] Representatives at the National Synod at Dort (1618-19) carefully revised *The Belgic Confession* by comparing texts of its French, Dutch, and Latin copies. This confession contains five articles devoted to the Scriptures, including the statement from Article V:

> that this Word of God was not sent nor delivered by the will of man, but that *holy men of God spake as they were moved by the Holy Ghost,* as the apostle Peter saith. And that afterwards God, from a special care which he has for us and for our salvation, commanded his servants, the Prophets and Apostles, to commit his revealed Word to writing; and he himself wrote with his own finger the two tables of the law. Therefore we call such writings holy and divine Scriptures.[42]

Following its presentation of the canonical books and their sufficiency, *The Belgic Confession* ends its statement on Scripture by concluding, "Therefore we reject with all our hearts whatsoever doth not agree with this infallible rule, which the apostles have taught us, saying, *Try the spirits whether they are of God.* Likewise, *If there come any unto you, and bring not this doctrine, receive him not into your house.*"[43] *The Belgic Confession* was adopted as the official doctrinal standard for the Reformed churches following its revision at the Synod at Dort. The Reformed church settled on the Calvinistic position as it pertained to the doctrine of the inspiration and authority of Scripture and held to that position into the twentieth century.

41. Jacobus Arminius, Disputations 5-10, in *The Writings of James Arminius,* 2:14-17.
42. *Confessio Belgica,* Article III, in Schaff, *The Creeds of Christendom,* 3:384-85; also *Doctrinal Standards,* p. 3.
43. *Confessio Belgica,* Article VII, in Schaff, *The Creeds of Christendom,* 3:388-89. See also *Doctrinal Standards,* p. 5.

THE WESTMINSTER TRADITION (c. 1538-c. 1918)

Unlike the Continental Reformation, which was first religious and then political, the English Reformation was first political and then religious.[44] Prior to its separation from Rome the church in England had followed in the train of Wycliffe in its desire to translate the Scriptures into English. William Tyndale (c. 1494-1536), for example, expressed his view that Scripture is inspired through his Bible translation efforts. Showing the influence of Luther and other Reformers on his thought, he appealed to Scripture as his final authority. That in turn led him to oppose papal claims to authority and helped to set the stage for the separation of the Church of England from Rome under Henry VIII (reigned 1509-1547). Once that separation was realized in 1534, the Church of England moved dramatically and sometimes violently from one theological position to another. As a result of the extremes of Edward VI (reigned 1547-1553) and Mary (reigned 1553-1558), Elizabeth I (reigned 1558-1603) sought an outward conformity in matters of religion when she ascended to the throne of her father, Henry VIII. Finally, after numerous previous efforts, *The Thirty-Nine Articles of Religion of the Church of England* became the legal formularies of the Church of England (1571) and Ireland (1615).[45] The *Thirty-Nine Articles* combined features both of the Swiss (or Reformed) and Lutheran confessions. These articles were first published in an *Editio Latina Princeps* in 1561, then in English (1571), and subsequently revised for the Protestant Episcopal church in the United States of America (1801).[46] The Article "Of the Sufficiency of the Holy Scriptures for Salvation" affirms that "Holy Scripture containeth all things necessary to salvation: so that whatsoever is not read therein, nor may be proved thereby, is not to be required of any man, that should be believed as an article of the Faith, *or* be thought requisite or necessary for salvation."[47]

Puritanism arose in England about the time *The Thirty-Nine Articles* were published. It was a movement committed to a "radical purification and reconstruction of Church and State on the sole basis of the Word of God, without regard to the traditions of men. It was a second reformation, as bold and earnest as the first."[48] The Puritans were not a separate organization or sect but an advanced wing within the national church. During the seventeenth century they vied with Anabaptists, Baptists, Congregationalists, Espicopa-

44. W. H. Griffith-Thomas, *The Principles of Theology: Introduction to the Thirty-Nine Articles*, p. xxxiv.
45. Ibid, pp. xxix-xlix, lists among the *Ten Articles* (1536), *Thirteen Articles* (1538), *Six Articles* (1539), *Forty-Two Articles* (1553), and *Thirty-Eight Articles* (1562), as well as other treatises.
46. Schaff, *The Creeds of Christendom,* 3:486-516, places all three texts in parallel columns.
47. Article IV, ibid., 3:489. The American Revision (1801) is here cited.
48. Ibid., 1:703. In a note Schaff indicates that the name *Puritans* (from "pure"), or *Precisians* occurs first in 1564 or 1566. This matter may be pursued by referring to H. W. Clark, *History of English Nonconformity,* and more recent attempts at synthesis by M. M. Knappen, *Tudor Puritanism: A Chapter in the History of Idealism,* and William Haller, *The Rise of Puritanism.*

lians, Presbyterians as well as other Conformist and Nonconformist elements in the struggles for control of the Church of England. Those struggles had a practical and conservative character that operated within the bounds of *The Laws of Ecclesiastical Polity* by Richard Hooker (c. 1554-1600). By "representing the Church as a legislative body which had power to make and unmake institutions and rites not affecting the doctrines of salvation laid down in the Scriptures and ecumenical creeds,"[49] Hooker set the tone for subsequent efforts to steer a course between Romanism on the one hand and Lutheranism and Calvinism on the other. Within her ranks Calvinistic Puritans, Arminian Methodists, liberal Latitudinarians, and Romanizing Tractarians and Ritualists were able to operate by conforming to the official formulas of the Church of England.

The Westminster Assembly of Divines was called in 1642 to legislate for Christian doctrine, worship, and discipline in the state church. Its work stands at the forefront of Protestant councils. The Assembly produced *A Confession of Faith* (1647) and two "Catechisms" that were written in English and used throughout Anglo-Presbyterian churches into the twentieth century.[50] The first article of *The Westminster Confession of Faith* is devoted to the subject "Of the Holy Scripture." Because of the insufficiency of mankind's knowledge of God, His will, and His salvation,

> it pleased the Lord, at sundry times, and in diverse manners, to reveal himself, and to declare that his will unto his Church; and afterwards for the better preserving and propagating of the truth, and for the more sure establishment and comfort of the church against corruption of the flesh, and the malice of Satan and of the world, to commit the same wholly unto writing; which maketh the holy Scripture to be most necessary; those former ways of God's revealing his will unto his people being now ceased.[51]

At a later point the *Confession* adds that

> the authority of Scripture, for which it ought to be believed and obeyed, dependeth not upon the testimony of any man or church, but wholly upon God (who is truth itself), the Author thereof; and therefore it is to be received, because it is the word of God .... yet notwithstanding, our full persuasion and assurance of the

49. Schaff, *The Creeds of Christendom,* 1:607. Four books of the *Laws* were published in 1594, another in 1597, and three more were added after Hooker's death in 1600.
50. The *Westminster Confession of Faith,* completed in 1646, was adopted along with the two *Catechisms* in 1647 and published as *The Humble Advice of the Assembly of Divines, Now by Authority of Parliament, Sitting at Westminster, Concerning a Confession of Faith: With Questions and Texts of Scripture Annexed.* Commonly known as *The Westminster Confession,* it was accompanied by *A Larger Catechism* (1647) and *A Shorter Catechism,* (1647). See Schaff, *The Creeds of Christendom,* 3:598-673; facsimile of title pages of *A Larger Catechism,* 3:674-75; the text of *A Shorter Catechism,* 3:676-704. For the text of *The Westminster Confession,* also see John H. Leith, ed., *Creeds of the Churches,* pp. 292-308.
51. Chapter 1, "Of Holy Scripture, I," in Schaff, *The Creeds of Christendom,* 3:600-601.

infallible truth, and divine authority thereof, is from the inward work of the Holy Spirit, bearing witness by and with the Word in our hearts ....

VI. The whole counsel of God, concerning all things necessary for his own glory, man's salvation, faith, and life, is either expressly set down in Scripture, or by good and necessary consequence may be deduced from Scripture: unto which nothing at any time is to be added, whether by new revelations of the Spirit, or traditions of men ....

IX. The infallible rule and interpretation of Scripture is the Scripture itself ....

X. The Supreme Judge, by which all controversies of religion are to be determined, and all decrees of councils, opinions of ancient writers, doctrines of men, and private spirits, are to be examined, and in whose sentence we are to rest, can be no other but the Holy Spirit speaking in the Scripture.[52]

While the Church of England (and the Protestant Episcopal church in the United States) as well as the Anglo-Presbyterian churches followed these formulas, the Congregationalists modified the *Westminster Confession* to suit their own church polity in *The Savoy Declaration* (1658). One of the key leaders at the Savoy Assembly was the onetime vice-chancellor of Oxford University, Puritan theologian par excellence and leading independent Congregationalist minister John Owen (1616-1683). He has been regarded erroneously by some to be a transitional figure between the "Reformation stance of the Westminster Divines and the Protestant scholasticism of his continental contemporaries." Throughout the volumes that he wrote, Owen "was convinced that in the theological debates with Enthusiasts, Roman Catholics, Rationalists, Socinians, and Arminians the primary issue to be addressed was the question of authority." The year following the Savoy Assembly, he wrote "two especially significant works: *The Divine Original of the Scriptures* and *A Vindication of the Greek and Hebrew Text*. The former presents his distinctive view of authority, and both of them taken together involved him in a controversy regarding the integrity of the available Greek and Hebrew manuscripts."[53] As Congregationalists met in various national councils during the nineteenth century, they continued to address the issue of authority of Scripture. One such expression of their position is seen in *The Oberlin Declaration of the National Congregational Council* (1871) of the United States. In that brief statement the assembled messengers state that they "agree in the belief that the Holy Scriptures are the sufficient and only infallible rule of religious faith and practice; their interpretation thereof being in substantial accordance with the great doctrines of the Christian faith, commonly called

52. Ibid., 3:603-6.
53. Stanley N. Gundry, "John Owen on Authority and Scripture," in John D. Hannah, ed., *Inerrancy and the Church,* pp. 189-221, gives an excellent analysis of Owen's position and the serious misrepresentation of it that has been espoused by Jack Rogers and Donald McKim.

Evangelical, held in our churches from the early times, and sufficiently set forth by former General Councils."[54]

Although John Wesley (1701-1791) desired to remain within the Church of England, his followers in America formed the first Methodist society in New York (1766) among Irish immigrants. After the American Revolution Wesley drew up *The Twenty-Five Articles of Religion,* which were adopted by the American Methodists in 1784. These *Articles* were a liberal and judicious abridgment of *The Thirty-Nine Articles,* with Calvinistic and other features omitted. Nevertheless, in Article II, "The Sufficiency of the Holy Scriptures for Salvation," Wesley set forth that

> the Holy Scriptures contain all things necessary to salvation; so that whatsoever is not read therein, nor may be proved thereby, is not to be required of any man that it should be believed as an article of faith, or be thought requisite or necessary to salvation. In the name of the Holy Scripture we do understand those canonical books of the Old and New Testament of whose authority was never any doubt in the Church.[55]

He frequently affirmed his belief in the inspiration and authority of Scripture as "the oracles of God," written by "men divinely inspired." He attested to their truthfulness by saying, " 'All Scripture is given by inspiration of God,' consequently, all Scripture is infallibly true," and "If there be any mistakes in the Bible, there may as well be a thousand. If there be one falsehood in that book, it did not come from the God of truth."[56]

The early followers of Wesley unanimously continued in the same high view of the inspiration and authority of Scripture. In fact, as Wilber T. Dayton states, "The absolute authority and total reliability of the Bible was taken for granted in early Wesleyanism as emphatically as motherhood has been assumed to be the principle for the survival of the human race. Nothing would have been more repugnant to original Methodism than to cast doubt on the Word of God, the very source of life."[57] The Irish Wesleyan Adam Clarke (c. 1762-1832) frequently affirmed his belief in the plenary inspiration and infallibility of Scripture as "the only complete directory of the faith and practice of man."[58] The first systematic theologian of the Wesleyan movement was Richard Watson (1781-1833), who wrote a two-volume *Theological Institutes* (1823). Watson's understanding of inspiration was that "the sacred writers composed their works under so plenary and immediate an influence

54. Schaff, *The Creeds of Christendom, 3:737*. Also see *The Declaration of the Congregational Union of England and Wales* (1833) and *The Declaration of the Boston National Council* (1865), which speak of the Scriptures as "the testimony of God." 3:730-36.
55. Ibid., 3:808.
56. John Wesley, *The Works of John Wesley,* 5:193, 6:117, 8:45-46; 10:80.
57. Wilber T. Dayton, "Infallibility, Wesley, and British Wesleyanism," in Hannah, ed., *Inerrancy and the Church,* p. 223.
58. Adam Clarke, *Miscellaneous Works,* 12:80, 83, 122. Also see 6:420.

of the Holy Spirit, that God may be said to speak by them to man, and not merely that they spoke to men in the name of God, and by his authority."[59] It was not until the opening years of the twentieth century that Methodism moved from its moorings in this high view of Scripture. Even then, the move was based on tendencies other than the objective and historical record of Scripture. That shift came instead as a result of the impact of subjectivism, secularism, and when the methodology of modern science as the basis of authority in social matters was transferred to theology.

The Roman Catholic Tradition (c. 1545-c. 1918)

The traditional teaching on the doctrine of the inspiration and authority of Scripture had been well established throughout the mainstream of the Christian church long before Luther posted the *Ninety-five Theses* in 1517. The great struggle of the early Reformers was over the issue of the interpretation of the Scriptures. Roland Bainton attests that this "was the main reason why authority had come to be ascribed to the pope in faith and morals. Catholics argued that if there were no infallible interpreter, there could be no infallible revelation."[60] Luther and other Reformers roundly denied that and other claims to such authority. Thus, the great disputations during the sixteenth century revolved around the issue of who would interpret the Scriptures, which were received as God's Word. As a result of those and other controversies the Council of Trent, which held sessions from 1545 to 1563, set down the Roman Catholic position in *The Canons and Dogmatic Decrees of the Council of Trent* (1563). The conservative nature of Roman Catholicism reflected itself during that council, and subsequent events have demonstrated that Catholicism has had less flexibility in the expression of its doctrine of religious authority than have the various communions of the non-Roman traditions.

The church of Rome has continued to perpetuate the view that Scripture and tradition were the dual basis of religious authority, and it set forth that position in the twelve articles of the *Profession of the Tridentine Faith* (1564). In Article III the Council asserted that the faithful must agree to certain admissions, including, "I also admit the Holy Scriptures, according to that sense which our holy mother Church has held and also does hold, to which it belongs to judge of the true sense and interpretation of Scriptures; neither will I ever take and interpret them otherwise than according to the unanimous consent of the Fathers."[61] During the nineteenth century, Pope Pius IX issued *The Papal Syllabus of Errors* (1864) in which he attacked the positions of "Pantheism, Naturalism, and Absolute Rationalism" by listing among their errors the views that "Divine revelation is imperfect, and therefore, subject to

59. Richard Watson, *The Works of Richard Watson,* 6:11.
60. Bainton, "The Bible in the Reformation," p. 1.
61. *Profession of the Tridentine Faith* (1564), in Schaff, *The Creeds of Christendom,* 2:207.

continual and definite progress of human reason.... The prophecies and miracles set forth and narrated in the Sacred Scriptures are fictions of poets ... mythical inventions, and Jesus Christ is himself a mythical fiction."[62] The position of the papacy had not altered concerning the doctrine of the inspiration and authority of Scripture.

The same tradition soon reflected itself again in *The Dogmatic Decrees of the Vatican Council concerning the Catholic Faith and the Church of Christ* (1870) which addressed the question of Scripture as "divine revelation" that can "be known by every one with facility, with firm assurance, and with no mixture of error.... Further, this supernatural revelation, according to the universal belief of the Church, declared by the sacred Synod of Trent, is contained in the written books and unwritten traditions which have come down to us."[63] As James T. Burtchaell has suggested, "The Catholic Church has displayed little spontaneous desire to refine, revise, and improve her doctrinal formulations. Only when she is goaded and provoked from without does she bestir herself to this apparently disagreeable task."[64] Justo L. Gonzalez speaks similarly in referring to the papal response to the development of higher criticism during the late nineteenth and early twentieth centuries. He writes, "When modern forms of critical research were developed, Rome condemned those who tried to relate them to religious questions .... [Which] provides some justification for the commonly held view among Protestants that the Catholic Church was one of the most reactionary forces in the world."[65]

Carl F. H. Henry treats the recent changes in the Roman Catholic position in his discussion of the doctrine of inerrancy among the Reformers. He writes,

> Throughout its long medieval influence, the Roman church therefore promoted the doctrine of scriptural inerrancy and opposed notions of a limited inerrancy restricted to faith and morals. The effort by Henry Holden (1596-1662) in *Divinae Fidei Analysis* to promote limited inerrancy garnered no enthusiasm.
>
> But in the late-nineteenth and early-twentieth century, Roman and Protestant clergy alike shared in the flight from inerrancy. *The New Catholic Encyclopedia* indicates the Roman church's traditional support for inerrancy but then goes on to indicate the contemporary mood: "It is nonetheless obvious that many biblical statements are simply not true when judged according to modern knowledge of science and history ...."

62. *The Papal Syllabus of Errors* (1864), 1.5-7, in Schaff, *The Creeds of Christendom,* 2:214-15.
63. Ibid., 2:240-41.
64. Burtchaell, *Catholic Theories,* p. 1.
65. Justo L. Gonzalez, *The History of Christian Thought,* vol. 3: *From the Protestant Reformation to the Twentieth Century,* p. 373.

> The Vatican II declaration that Scripture teaches "without error that truth which God wanted put into the Sacred Writings for the sake of our salvation" is interpreted descriptively by some priests .... Others interpret it restrictively.[66]

This indicates that the scope of theology in the twentieth century has broadened confessionally to the point that it is no longer possible to consider a Roman Catholic theology in the twentieth century apart from its counterparts in Lutheranism, the Reformed tradition, and so on. Gonzales summarizes the situation as follows:

> The dialogue across denominational lines has become too active and significant for that kind of easy division. Theologians are reading the works of their colleagues in other traditions, not simply as a matter of curiosity or even to refute them, but in order to learn from them and enter into dialogue with them. This was already largely true of Protestantism in the nineteenth century, but the twentieth century has made it true also of Roman Catholics and Eastern Orthodox.[67]

The Eastern Orthodox Tradition (c. 1643-c. 1918)

Although the Eastern church had developed its own separate tradition from the West, its position on Scripture was quite similar to that of Roman Catholicism in maintaining the dual authority of Scripture and tradition. As recently as 1839, for example, *The Longer Catechism of the Orthodox Catholic Eastern Church* contains a lengthy presentation in its "Introduction to the Orthodox Catechism"[68] for use of *The Orthodox Confession of the Eastern Church* (1643).[69] In that introduction the discussion "On Divine Revelation" asks, "Why are not all men capable of receiving a revelation immediately from God?" and answers that it is "owing to their sinful impurity, and weakness both in soul and body." After naming the prophets, our Lord Jesus Christ, and the apostles as the heralds of divine revelation, the Introduction addresses the question, "Can not man, then, have any knowledge of God without a special revelation from him?" and answers by stating that "this knowledge is imperfect and insufficient, and can serve only as a preparation for faith, or as a help towards the knowledge of God from his revelation." In its section "On Holy Tradition and Holy Scripture" the Introduction asks, "How is divine revelation spread among men and preserved in the true Church?" The answer: "By two channels—holy tradition and holy Scripture." The Introduction also says that "the most ancient and original instrument for spreading divine revelation is holy tradition" but that Holy Scripture was given "to this end, that divine

66. Carl F. H. Henry, *God, Revelation and Authority,* vol. 4: *God Who Speaks and Shows: Fifteen Theses, Part 3,* p. 374.
67. Gonzalez, *History of Christian Thought,* 3:391.
68. Schaff, *The Creeds of Christendom,* 2:445-542.
69. Ibid., 2:275-400.

revelation might be preserved more exactly and unchangeably." Question 23 raises the issue of the relationship of the two: "Must we follow holy tradition even when we possess holy Scripture? We must follow that tradition which agrees with the divine revelation and with holy Scripture, as is taught us by holy Scripture itself .... 2 Thess. ii.15."[70]

During the late seventeenth and early eighteenth centuries Russian theology, like that in the Greek world, became subject to a heavy Western influence. During that period the instruction given in Russian seminaries was in Latin rather than either Slavonic or Greek. Two tendencies emerged as both "Latinizers" and "Protestantizers" (mainly Lutheran) extended their influence. It was not until the period 1850-1900 that Russian theology began to come fully into its own. The revolution of 1917 dealt the movement a severe blow within Russia, although the traditions of Russian theology were continued among writers who emigrated.[71] On balance, the history of Eastern Christendom is marked by a deep sense of continuity with the past, and that continuity is apparent in all branches of Byzantine civilization: in literature and philosophy, in political thought and law, and not least in theology. As Kallistos Ware says,

> The "Age of the Fathers" in eastern Christendom does not come to a close with the Council of Chalcedon in the fifth century, nor yet with the last meeting of the last Ecumenical Council in the eighth, but it extends uninterrupted until 1453; and even today—despite heavy borrowings from the Roman Catholic and Protestant west during the seventeenth and following centuries—Eastern Orthodoxy remains basically Patristic in outlook.[72]

Summary and Conclusion

During and after the Reformation era, Christianity entered into an age of creed-forms and confessions as individual groups, denominations, and sects sought to articulate, defend, and perpetuate their own doctrinal traditions. Those more or less official and formal expressions proliferated with the spread of Christianity throughout the world in the various movements. As they are surveyed, they reflect a basic commitment to the doctrines of historic Christianity in general and to the traditional doctrine of the inspiration and authority of Scripture in particular. "The Reformers and Counter-Reformers were disputing whether all revealed truth was in the Scripture alone, and whether it could be interpreted by private or by official scrutiny. Despite a radical disagreement on these issues both groups persevered in receiving the

70. Ibid., Q. 13, 2:447; Q. 15, 2:447-48; Q. 16, 2:448; Q. 21, 2:449; Q. 22, 2:449; Q. 23, 2:449.
71. Kallistos Ware, "A Note on Theology in the Christian East: The Eighteenth to Twentieth Centuries," in Hubert Cunliffe-Jones, ed., assisted by Benjamin Drewery, *A History of Christian Doctrine: In Succession to the Earlier Work of G. P. Fisher Published in the International Theological Library Series*, pp. 455-56.
72. Kallistos Ware, "Christian Theology in the East 600-1453," ibid., pp. 183-84.

Bible as a compendium of inerrant oracles dictated by the Holy spirit."[73] The Eastern Orthodox maintained the same traditional doctrine. When placed into a larger context this limited view may be challenged by some, but the various official statements, creed-forms, and confessions of the mainstream of Christianity during the period from the Reformation to the close of World War I indicate the continued traditional commitment to the traditional doctrine of the inspiration and authority of Scripture. This is reflected in the nonsectarianism of Anabaptists as well as the official statements of the more creedalistic communions. Throughout its broad and diverse ranks, Christians of all major persuasions prior to World War I officially adhered to the belief that the Scriptures are the divinely inspired, authoritative, infallible, and inerrant Word of God.

73. Burtchaell, *Catholic Theories,* pp. 2-3.

9
Divergent Views of Revelation and Inspiration in the Modern World

Introduction

A survey of the more-or-less official and formal expressions of the teachings on the inspiration and authority of Scripture from each of the traditional major Christian traditions as they entered the twentieth century shows the orthodox Christian position on the doctrine of the inspiration and authority of Scripture prevailed.[1] Nevertheless, various challenges to that traditional teaching ultimately led to the bold confrontation of religious authority by proponents of modern science and scientific method. Before 1860 the concern was with specific problems of special revelation; after that time it centered on the serious question of whether there was any revelation at all. The two primary influences that brought these periods into such confrontation were Darwin's *On the Origin of Species* (1859) and the introduction of the so-called historical method.[2]

With that frame of reference, the following discussion will look into the changing climates of opinion as attitudes and methods were developed that affected modern views of revelation, inspiration, and authority of Scripture. Then it will address orthodox responses to those attitudes as well as the development of the methodologies of historical criticism.

1. See chap. 8 discussion as well as William E. Nix, "The Doctrine of Inspiration Since the Reformation," pp. 443-54.
2. H. D. McDonald, *Theories of Revelation: An Historical Study, 1700-1960*, 1:6-16. This is a competent two-volume analysis of the subject with detailed investigation into the writings of leading proponents in the process of deviation that occurred in the 17th-19th centuries. McDonald cites John Dewey's *The Influence of Darwin on Philosophy* to the effect that however true it may be that Darwin's work was the climax of a movement, it certainly is to be marked as the commencement of an era. McDonald also points out that 1859 was the year Karl Marx produced his *Critique of Political Economy*, as concerns about the misery in nature and society brought about a new perception of both after 1860.

Changing Climates of Opinion[3]

It was not until the post-Reformation period that the first major deviations from the traditional doctrine of inspiration of the Scriptures made their appearance. Those deviations were not abrupt challenges to the traditional doctrine of Scripture, but represented a gradual moving away from it.[4] They arose when the authority of the Roman Catholic church had been challenged successfully and dissidents were protected as new ideas and methods of investigation were developed. Early in the period efforts by such men as Nicholas Copernicus (1473-1543), Andreas Vesalius (1514-1564), Tycho Brahe (1546-1601), Francis Bacon (1561-1626), Johannes Kepler (1571-1630), Galileo Galilei (1546-1642), and others forged the modern scientific attitude in the Western world. Their views were often opposed by established religious authorities.[5]

Similar trends occurred in the theological world. Frederick of Saxony protected Martin Luther at Wartburg Castle in 1521-22, and there Luther published a tract on monastic vows and translated the New Testament into German. Elsewhere, the Italian Socinians, Lelio Francesco Maria Sozini (1525-1562) and his nephew Fausto Paolo Sozzini (1539-1604), were able to deny the divinity of Christ as they moved to Poland and joined an active group of Unitarians located there. The *Racovian Catechism* was published there in 1605,[6] before the group was driven from Poland altogether toward the middle of the seventeenth century. In the 1650s John Biddle (1615-62) published the Unitarian tracts that resulted in his being reckoned "the father of Unitarianism." In addition to those episodes, the Christian world experienced other significant changes in the climates of opinion during the seventeenth, eighteenth, and nineteenth centuries.

Pietism (c. 1650-c. 1725)

Pietism arose in Germany under the leadership of Philipp Jakob Spener

3. For a more extended treatment of this topic see William E. Nix, "The Doctrine of Inspiration since the Reformation, Part II: Changing Climates of Opinion," pp. 439-57.
4. John D. Woodbridge, *Biblical Authority: A Critique of the Rogers/McKim Proposal,* has a definitive critique of the unsubstantiated proposal of Jack B. Rogers and Donald K. McKim *(The Authority and Interpretation of the Bible: An Historical Approach)* that the Christian church has often regarded the Scriptures as infallible in matters of faith and conduct but incorrect in matters of historical and scientific detail.
5. For broad background on the intellectual setting of this period see John Herman Randall, Jr., *The Making of the Modern Mind: A Survey of the Intellectual Background of the Present Age;* Crane Brinton, *Ideas and Men: The Story of Western Thought;* Roland N. Stromberg, *An Intellectual History of Modern Europe*. Also see Jean Delumeau, *Catholicism Between Luther and Voltaire: a New View of the Counter-Reformation;* Richard H. Popkin, *The History of Scepticism from Erasmus to Descartes*.
6. Thomas Rees, *The Racovian Catechism, with Notes and Illustrations, translated from the Latin: to which is prefixed A Sketch of the History of Unitarianism in Poland and Adjacent Countries*.

(1635-1705) and his close friend August Hermann Francke (1633-1727). Spener had published the influential *Pia Desideria*[7] (1675) while serving as a pastor in Frankfurt. Later he became a court preacher at Dresden where Francke joined him, but orthodox Lutherans soon reacted against them, and their movement became involved in controversy. By 1694 they were settled at Halle, where they established charitable centers and founded a university. Pietists held to the doctrine of the inspiration of Scripture in the same manner as did the Roman Catholic, Orthodox, Anabaptist, Lutheran, Evangelical Reformed, and Westminster traditions, but the Pietists had a *different emphasis*. They stressed subjective, personal experience rather than biblical doctrines or catechism. As Francke put it, "We may safely assure those who read the word with devotion and simplicity, that they will derive more light and profit from such a practice, and from connecting meditation with it . . . than can ever be acquired from drudging through an infinite variety of unimportant minutiae."[8]

Although Pietists *adhered* to the inspiration of the Bible, they *advocated* the individual feeling as being of primary importance. That may have been an adequate method for avoiding the cold orthodoxy of so-called Protestant Scholasticism, but it opened the door for the equally dangerous enemy of subjective experientialism. First-generation pietists could recall and reflect on their grounding in Scripture while validly advocating the need for individual experience. The second generation would stress the need for individual experience, but often without a proper biblical or catechetical basis. That would leave the third generation to question individual experience without having a biblical or doctrinal standard to serve as an objective criterion. In turn, unanswered questions would demand an authority of some kind. When the Scriptures were neglected, human reason or subjective experience would fill the need as the required standard. Thus, although not causing other movements directly, Pietism gave impetus to Deism, Skepticism, and Rationalism. Those movements were not limited to any particular country prior to the revolutions in America and France, but Deism was most dominant in England and America, Skepticism in France, and Rationalism in Germany.[9]

DEISM (c. 1625-c. 1800)

Deists of the seventeenth and eighteenth centuries adopted what is known as a two-level approach to apologetics and theology. Such an approach utilized philosophy to lay the foundation and then presented the Christian faith

7. See Philipp J. Spener, *Pia Desideria*.
8. See Hermann Francke, *A Guide to the Reading and Study of the Holy Scriptures*, p. 83.
9. Colin Brown, *Philosophy and the Christian Faith: A Historical Sketch from the Middle Ages to the Present Day*, pp. 37-106. Also see Bruce Demarest, "The Bible in the Enlightenment Era," in Gordon R. Lewis and Bruce Demarest, eds., *Challenges to Inerrancy: A Theological Response*, pp. 11-47.

on the strength of the philosophical arguments. Lord Herbert of Cherbury (1583-1648) is usually identified as the father of Deism. His idea was that certain common notions were imprinted upon the human mind by the hand of God independent of particular creeds and revelations, and as such they form the basis of all true religion. These ideas of natural theology were comparable to those of Rene Descartes (1596-1650) and Benedict de Spinoza (1632-1677)[10] except that Lord Herbert attempted to relate them to the Christian experience of revelation. His ideas were also similar to those of a group of influential Platonists who flourished at Cambridge around 1633-88, where Sir Isaac Newton (1642-1727) became the most eminent scientist of his time. Deists had a distaste for both fanaticism and Calvinism, as they extolled the virtues of reason. Their view of God and the universe was quite different from the modern, popular notion that asserts that Deism viewed God as an "absentee landlord" who is too remote to be involved in the day-to-day events of His creation. Nevertheless, their approach to theology did open the door for divergent views about the inspiration and authority of Scripture.

Materialism (c. 1650-present)

While not a materialist himself, Francis Bacon (1561-1626) did set the stage for modern biblical criticism when he systematically expounded the notion that man's power to control nature rests in his own hands and can be achieved if he applies correct methods. In his *Novum Organum* (1620) Bacon claimed that all truth is discovered by induction and known pragmatically.[11] He argued that by making inductions from the simplest facts of experience man could reach forward to discover the fundamental principles, which would issue forth in beneficial practical results—thus making truth and utility the very same things in the world of science. In addition, Bacon completely separated the realm of reason and science from the realm of faith and religion.

Although Bacon made significant contributions, the most prominent materialist philosopher of the post-Reformation period was Thomas Hobbes (1588-1672), who wrote,

> Whatsoever we imagine is finite. Therefore there is no idea or conception of anything we call infinite. No man can have in his mind an image of infinite magnitude, infinite time, or infinite force, or infinite power. When we say anything is infinite, we signify only that we are not able to conceive the ends and

10. *Discourse on Method* (1637) and *Meditations on First Philosophy* (1641) represent Descartes's two chief philosophical works. They and other works have been published together with Benedict de Spinoza's *Ethics* (1677) as vol. 31 of *Great Books of the Western World*, Robert Maynard Hutchins, ed.
11. Francis Bacon, *Advancement of Learning: Novum Organum: New Atlantis*, vol. 30 of *Great Books of the Western World*, pp. 105-95. Also see Norman L. Geisler, "Philosophical Presuppositions of Biblical Inerrancy," in *Inerrancy*, pp. 312-14.

> bounds of the thing named, having no conception of the thing, but our own inability. And therefore the name God is used . . . that we may honour Him.[12]

In view of that, Hobbes concluded:

> The world (I mean not the earth only, that denominates the lovers of it "worldly men," but the universe, that is, the whole mass of all things that are) is corporeal, that is to say, body; and hath the dimensions of magnitude, namely, length, breadth, and depth: also every part of the body is likewise body, and hath the like dimensions; and consequently every part of the universe is body, and that which is not body is no part of the universe: and because the universe is all, that which is no part of it is nothing, and consequently nowhere.[13]

In addition to his materialistic philosophy, Hobbes was one of the first modern writers to engage in explicit higher criticism of Scripture. He states that "the Scriptures by the Spirit of God in man, mean a man's spirit, inclined to Godliness." Hobbes viewed the healing of the demoniac by Jesus as a "parable" when he announced, "I see nothing at all in the Scripture, that requireth a belief, that Demoniacs were any other thing but Mad-men." He understood the miracles of the gospels as parabolical or spiritual but not historical because "Scripture was written to shew unto men the kingdom of God, and to prepare their minds to become his obedient subjects; leaving the world, and the philosophy thereof, to the disputations of men, for the exercising of their natural reason."[14] Hobbes's complete separation of divine revelation (for spiritual truth) from human reason (for cognitive truth) not only anticipates Søren Kierkegaard and Karl Barth, it goes beyond them.

Naturalism (c. 1650-present)

While some Deists had used natural theology to support Christianity, others used it as a rational alternative to what they considered irrational, revealed religion. Benedict de Spinoza, whose philosophical speculation was more explicitly naturalistic than Hobbes, was a rationalist, although "Spinoza has been variously described as a hideous atheist and as God-intoxicated. In fact, he was a pantheist."[15] His rationalistic pantheism was soberly worked out from premises akin to those of Descartes.

12. Thomas Hobbes, *Leviathan, Or Matter, Form, and Power of a Commonwealth Ecclesiastical and Civil,* vol. 23 of *Great Books of the Western World,* p. 54. He also discusses the relation of bodies to the universe, p. 172.
13. Ibid., p. 267. Frederick Copleston, *A History of Philosophy,* vol. 5: *Modern Philosophy: The British Philosophers, Part I, Hobbes to Paley,* pp. 15-16, adds that "Hobbes's philosophy, therefore, is materialistic in the sense that it takes no account of anything but bodies. And in so far as the exclusion of God and all spiritual reality is simply the result of a freely chosen definition, his materialism can be called methodological. Hobbes does not say that there is no God; he says that God is not the subject-matter of philosophy."
14. Ibid., pp. 70-71.
15. Brown, *Philosophy and the Christian Faith,* p. 54.

Spinoza espoused two presuppositions: mathematical deduction and blatant antisupernaturalism. In the former he assumed that *all* truth could be deduced from self-evident axioms (although that assumption itself is far from self-evident). That argumentation led Spinoza to the notion that there is but one substance in the universe, and that that substance can be identified as either God or Nature.[16] His antisupernaturalism caused him to define miracles out of existence because they are based on violations of the inviolable laws of nature. Thus, over two centuries before Emil Brunner would make a similar assertion, Spinoza argued that the Bible does not contain propositional revelation. He said, "I will show wherein the law of God consists, and how it cannot be contained in a certain number of books." For those who might object that "though the law of God is written in the heart, the Bible is nonetheless the Word of God," Spinoza replies, "I fear that such objectors are too dangerous to be pious, and they are in danger of turning religion into superstition, and *worshiping paper and ink* in place of God's Word."[17]

Like Bacon and Hobbes before him, Spinoza relegated the authority of Scripture to purely religious matters. Even though he was steeped in rabbinical tradition, Spinoza concluded that the Bible is fallible. It is clear from his writings, which were so controversial that they were published either anonymously or posthumously, that over a century before Johann Salomo Semler (1725-91) and two centures prior to Julius Wellhausen (1844-1918) Spinoza was engaged in systematic antisupernatural criticism of the Bible. Indeed, virtually all the central emphases in higher critical thought are found in Spinoza.[18]

Similar themes appear in the writings of such Deists as John Toland (1610-1722) and Matthew Tindal (1655-1733), while Anthony Collins (1676-1725) and Thomas Woolston (1670-1733) were among the pioneers of radical biblical criticism.[19] Other prominent transitional figures include the statesman-philosopher John Locke (1632-1707),[20] George Berkeley (c. 1685-1753), and the American naturalist Thomas Jefferson (1743-1826), who composed his

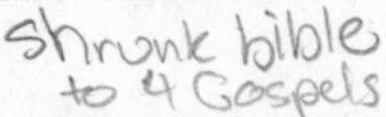

16. Norman L. Geisler, "Inductivism, Materialism, and Rationalism: Bacon, Hobbes, and Spinoza," in Norman L. Geisler, ed., *Biblical Errancy: An Analysis of Its Philosophical Roots*, p. 22.
17. Geisler, "Philosophical Presuppositions," p. 317, cites *The Chief Works of Benedict De Spinoza*, translated with an introduction by R. H. M. Elwes, vol. 1: *Introduction, Tractatus Theologico-Politicus, Tractatus Politicus*, pp. 165-67.
18. Ibid., p. 320. Other themes argued by Spinoza assert that the Bible merely contains the Word of God, the Bible is reliable in religious matters only, a moral criteria for canonicity, the accommodation theory, rationalism, naturalism, and the allegorical interpretation of Scripture.
19. Brown, *Philosophy and the Christian Faith*, pp. 77-78.
20. Woodbridge, *Biblical Authority*, p. 94 and n. 61 (p. 194), p. 98 and n. 97 (p. 198), has a discussion concerning the fact that Locke held to the infallibility of Scripture until 1661 but that those views were troubling him in 1685 when he carefully followed the debate between Richard Simon (1638-1712) and Jean Le Clerc (1657-1736).

own rendition of the Christian Scriptures.[21] They were part of a movement that held to a naturalistic approach to the world and free thought, which came to deny the inspiration of Scripture, teach that God is merely "providentially" involved with the world, and stress such things as the laws of nature and natural rights. In effect they replaced a biblical perspective for a naturalistic one in their reaction against subjectivism and revealed religion. Critics of such naturalism include Thomas Sherlock (1678-1761), Joseph Butler (1692-1752), and William Paley (1743-1805), who attacked it from a rationalistic approach, as well as John Wesley (1703-1791) and his colaborers in the Great Awakening, George Whitefield (1714-1770) and Jonathan Edwards (1703-1758).

Skepticism (c. 1725-present)

Skepticism was an essential ingredient in the attitude of the Enlightenment, as described by Hayden V. White:

> The Enlightenment attitude of mind was complex and internally varied, but it can be characterized roughly as a dedication of human reason, science, and education as the best means of building a stable society for free men on earth. This meant that the Enlightenment was inherently suspicious of religion, hostile to tradition, and resentful of any authority based on custom or faith alone. Ultimately the Enlightenment was nothing if not secular in its orientation; it offered the first program in the history of mankind for the construction of a human community out of natural materials alone.[22]

This outlook was spurred by the revival of Greek skepticism in Western thought following the rediscovery and publication of the writings of Sextus Empiricus (flourished c. late 2d and early 3d centuries A.D.) in 1562.[23] His writings fit into the three major strains of philosophy in the seventeenth century as they became the intellectual orthodoxy of the eighteenth-century

21. Although he did not publish it, Jefferson began work on a religious manuscript, the so-called *Jefferson Bible*, in 1803. He completed the English portion of the work by 1816 and later added Greek, Latin, and French texts in columns side by side. The English portion was printed in 1904. It was edited and republished by Douglas E. Lurton as *The Life and Morals of Jesus of Nazareth*. Jefferson's "Bible" consists of extracts from the gospels from which all miracles and claims of Jesus to His deity have been removed. The closing lines of his work portray Jefferson's views most poignantly: "Now in the place where he was crucified, there was a garden; and in the garden a new sepulchre, wherein was never yet a man laid. There laid they Jesus, and rolled a great stone to the door of the sepulchre, and departed" (p. 158).
22. Hayden V. White, "Editor's Introduction," p. ix, in Robert Anchor, *The Enlightenment Tradition*, which is probably the best brief introduction to this movement. This work has been reprinted more recently with its annotated bibliography updated. Also see Ernst Cassirer, *The Philosophy of the Enlightenment*. Three major works by one of the most distinguished American scholars of the Enlightenment are Peter Gay, *The Enlightenment: An Interpretation; The Party of Humanity: Essays in the French Enlightenment; Voltaire's Politics: The Poet and Realist*.
23. Popkin, *History of Scepticism*, p. 17.

Enlightenment, the distinct turning point in the rise of modern secular thought.

The skepticism of the French Enlightenment moved in a wave that affected the philosophical, theological, and political world of England, America, and Germany. Nevertheless, David Hume (1711-1776) of Scotland was probably the philosopher between Spinoza and Kant to have the greatest adverse effect on views of biblical authority. Antisupernaturalism and an extreme emphasis on empiricism were the two most basic elements of Hume's attempt to undermine the traditional doctrine of Scripture. He rejected the claim that Scripture is inspired or that the Bible is an authoritative revelation of God to humanity. He also denied the deity of Christ and rejected miracles as he sought to make theology the subject of empirical testing.[24] In his essay *An Enquiry Concerning Human Understanding* (1748), Hume argued against the *credibility* of miracles rather than against their *possibility* (as did Spinoza).[25] Nevertheless, Hume's rejection of miracles is emphatic when he says, "A miracle is a violation of the laws of nature; and as a firm and unalterable experience has established these laws, the proof against a miracle, from the very nature of the fact, is as entire as any argument from experience can possibly be imagined."[26]

In Germany, Gotthold Ephraim Lessing (1729-1781), the son of a pastor in Saxony serving as librarian to the Duke of Brunswick after 1770, published a series of *Fragments of an Unknown Writer,* popularly known as the *Wolfenbuttel Fragments* (1774-1778). This document was actually a defense and restatement of skeptical Deism by Hermann Samuel Reimarus (1694-1768), which included a fragment entitled *The Goal of Jesus and His Disciples*. Left unpublished during his own lifetime, this Reimarus fragment claimed to expose the gospel accounts of Jesus as a piece of fraud because of their alleged unfulfilled eschatological predictions. It unreservedly rejected miracles and revelation and cast accusations of conscious fraud, innumerable contradictions, and fanaticism upon the biblical writers. Such a perspective raised a storm of controversy when it was published by Lessing, and it revolutionized the image of Jesus in modern theology. Indeed, it was the point of departure for Albert Schweitzer (1875-1965) in his *The Quest for the Historical Jesus* (1906). Lessing himself wrote an essay in gospel criticism

24. Gary R. Habermas, "Skepticism: Hume," in Geisler, ed., *Biblical Errancy,* pp. 25-49; Geisler, "Philosophical Presuppositions," 320-22.
25. David Hume, *An Enquiry Concerning Human Understanding,* as cited in vol. 35 of *Great Books of the Western World,* p. 491. Hume published his *Treatise on Human Nature* in 1737, his *Essay, Moral, Political* in 1741, and his *Philosophical Essay* in 1748. This last work was later renamed *An Enquiry Concerning Human Understanding*. In 1751 the third book of the *Treatise* was recast and published as *An Enquiry Concerning the Principles of Morals*. Hume's *Four Dissertations,* including one devoted to the *Natural History of Religion,* was published in 1757. He had also completed his *Dialogues concerning Natural Religion,* but on advice of friends its publication was postponed until after his death in 1776.
26. Hume, *An Enquiry Concerning Human Understanding,* edited with an introduction by Charles W. Hendel, p. 122.

entitled *New Hypothesis on the Evangelists considered as merely human historical Writers* (1788), which posited a single Hebrew or Aramaic source behind the gospel narratives and portrayed Jesus as a merely human messiah.

Agnosticism (c. 1750-present)

Immanuel Kant (1724-1804) has been considered by many to be the crossroad thinker of modern philosophy. He fully subscribed to the progressive ideals of the French Enlightenment but saw little hope for those ideals to be realized under the cynical rule of Frederick II, the Great (1712-1786), where he lived in East Prussia. Part of Kant's greatness lay in his ability to synthesize the two dominant but conflicting modes of thought of the Enlightenment, Empiricism and Rationalism, into an intellectual whole.[27] In his creative synthesis, Kant became a philosophical agnostic about reality. He argued that the mind knows only after a construction is made and not before it. For him, only what appears (the *phenomenal*) to one is known, not that which really is (the *noumenal*). In addition, Kant asserted that whenever one attempts to apply the categories of the mind (such as unity or causality) to the noumenal (real) world, hopeless contradictions and antinomies arise.

One consequence of Kant's revolt against reason is his fact/value dichotomy. For him, the "objective" world of fact is the phenomemal world of experience, while the "subjective" world of will cannot be known by pure reason. Instead, the subjective world is known by practical reason, or a morally postulated act of the will. For him, even though it is not possible to *think* that God exists, one must *live* as if God does exist. Thus, Kant philosophically questioned the objectivity and rationality of divine revelation. He placed religion in the realm of the postulated rather than the known. This gave rise to the moral imperative that lies behind Kant's use of "moral reason" as the ground for determining what is essential to true religion. For Kant this reason demanded that he conclude that miracles do not occur.[28] Thus, like Jefferson, he was able to reject the resurrection account at the close of the gospels. In making the moral imperative the criterion for true religion, Kant is the forerunner of Friedrich Daniel Ernst Schleiermacher (1768-1834). Following in the subjective footsteps of Kant and Schleiermacher, Rudolph

27. W. David Beck, "Agnosticism: Kant," in Geisler, ed., *Biblical Errancy,* pp. 53-78; Geisler, "Philosophical Presuppositions," pp. 322-27. The dominant Rationalists were Descartes, Spinoza, and Leibniz; the Empiricists are represented by Locke, Berkely, and Hume. Kant claimed to be awakened from his dogmatic slumbers by reading David Hume. He then wrote *The Critique of Pure Reason* (1781), *The Critique of Practical Reason* (1788), *On Religion Within the Bounds of Reason Alone* (1792), and other works. This last-named work is not published in *The Great Books of the Western World,* vol. 42: *Kant.*
28. Immanuel Kant, *Religion Within the Limits of Reason Alone,* translated with introduction by Theodore M. Greene and Hoyt H. Hudson, pp. 83-84.

Otto (1869-1937) used an irrational basis for his higher criticism of the Bible.[29]

Romanticism (c. 1780-c. 1840)

Nothing seemed more characteristic of the late eighteenth century than the dominance of reason, as unemotional and intellectual questioning swept away ancient superstitions and abuses. Yet a strong opposition arose to that cold, one-sided approach, as the claims of feeling were reasserted. This movement emphasized great men and heroic movements of the past rather than ideas and institutions. The generic term *Romanticism* is generally applied to this complex and elusive movement that radically challenged the older Rationalism. It had advocates in literature, music, painting, and philosophy throughout Europe before running its course in the late 1830s. Its most effective early advocate was Jean Jacques Rousseau (1712-1778), but it became most dominant in Germany, where its participants included Gotthold Lessing (1729-1781), Johan Wolfgang von Goethe (1749-1832), Johan Christoph Friedrich von Schiller (1759-1805), and Johan Christoph Friedrich Holderlin (1770-1843). Romanticism was less a movement in favor of religion than it was an artistic-literary movement that became religious. Its most important theologian was Friedrich Schleiermacher.[30]

Early in the nineteenth century evangelical and pietistic currents appeared that to a considerable extent cut across various confessional and national churches. In the half century following 1810, Roman Catholicism "was washed over by several successive waves of theological revival. After languishing during the darkness of the Enlightenment, theology came alive again in various Catholic centers at different times."[31] Among Protestants in Germany, which was astir with religious and social conflict, Schleiermacher led people to find an experiential basis in the Christian tradition that had been long untapped, while Ernst Wilhem Hengstenberg (1802-1869) led the *Evangelische Kirchenzeitung* during the 1820s and 1830s. Hengstenberg stood firmly for the infallibility of the Bible and the alliance of Christianity with the conservative feudal party in German politics, but he broke away from that movement and became a champion of strict Lutheran orthodoxy about 1840.

In the meantime Schleiermacher, a native of Silesia who had studied and taught at the university in the Pietist center at Halle, developed what is

29. Rudolf Otto, *The Idea of the Holy,* trans. John Harvey, p. 162.
30. Harold O. J. Brown, "Romanticism and the Bible," in Lewis and Demarest, eds., *Challenges to Inerrancy,* pp. 49-65. Also see Brown, *Philosophy and the Christian Faith,* pp. 108-16; Richard V. Pierard, "Romanticism," in Walter A. Elwell, ed., *Evangelical Dictionary of Theology* (Grand Rapids: Baker, 1984), pp. 959-61; W. A. Hoffecker, "Schleiermacher, Friedrich Daniel Ernst," ibid., pp. 981-83.
31. James T. Burtchaell, *Catholic Theories of Biblical Inspiration Since 1810,* p. 3.

sometimes called *positive theology.*[32] Based in personal experience, it was influenced heavily by Romanticism through Friedrich Schlegel (1772-1829) as well as the thought of Spinoza, Leibniz, and Kant. Schleiermacher contended that religion should be based on intuition or feeling (*Anschauung und Gefuhl*), which is independent of all dogma. He redefined "revelation" as he applied the term to every original and new intuition, and he applied "inspiration" to human activity exclusively.[33] As a result, he did not bother with rational proofs for the existence of God. He asserted that the Christian life is the "spontaneous activity in living fellowship with Christ," because religion is the *sense of absolute dependence.*[34] For Schleiermacher, the purest expression of religion is in monotheism, and Christianity is the highest, though not the only true, religion.[35]

Schleiermacher's revision of Christian theology had its most radical impact on the issue of authority, because he argued that no external authority, whether it be Scripture, church, or historic creedal statement, takes precedence over the immediate experience of believers. He also contributed to a more critical approach to the Bible by questioning its inspiration and authority. Further, he rejected doctrines he believed unrelated to the religious experience of redemption: the virgin birth, the Trinity, and the return of Christ. He felt they implied a cognitive and indirect knowledge rather than immediate God-consciousness.

Schleiermacher greatly influenced Christianity through three major achievements. First, he made religion socially acceptable to those who no longer took the Bible and its doctrines seriously by showing its appeal to man's aesthetic tendencies. Second, he attracted to theology countless young men who were interested in religion primarily as an expression of man's imaginative spirit. And third, for a time he changed biblical criticism from historical to literary analysis.[36] His influence, limited to Germany during his lifetime, was enormous on later Protestants because of Albrecht Ritschl (1822-1889), Adolph von Harnack (1851-1930), and Ernst Troeltsch (1865-1923).

32. Brown, *Philosophy and the Christian Faith,* p. 110.
33. Fred H. Klooster, "Revelation and Scripture in Existentialist Theology," in Lewis and Demarest, eds., *Challenges to Inerrancy,* p. 205. In this context, Klooster identifies Schleiermacher as "the father of liberal theology." In the following discussion Albrecht Ritschl is identified as "the founder of theological liberalism." Schleiermacher's role is thus viewed in a broader and more basic context than that of Ritschl.
34. Friedrich D. E. Schleiermacher, *The Christian Faith,* translated by H. R. Mackintosh and J. S. Stewart, pp. 5-12. Brown, *Philosophy and the Christian Faith,* p. 111 n. 1, indicates that the "term *das schlechthinnige Abhangigkeistsgefuhl* is usually translated as *feeling of absolute dependence.* But the word *feeling* is perhaps too strong and positive. What he is trying to analyze often seems to be more a profound awareness or sense of utter dependence."
35. McNeill, *Christian Tradition,* pp. 253-62; Brown, *Philosophy and the Christian Faith,* pp. 108-16.
36. Brown, "Romanticism and the Bible," pp. 60-61.

IDEALISM (c. 1800-PRESENT)

The German idealist movement emerged in the immediate background of the critical philosophy of Immanuel Kant. But unlike Kant, whose primary philosophical questions began in the realm of science, the leading idealists, Johann Gottlieb Fichte (1762-1814), Friedrich Wilhelm Joseph von Schelling (1775-1854), and Georg Wilhelm Friedrich Hegel (1770-1831), all came to philosophy from theology. In seeking to understand the relation between the infinite and the finite, their writings reflect one of the most remarkable flowerings of metaphysical speculation in the history of Western thought.[37]

The most dominant figure of German idealism was Hegel, who is described as "possibly the most stupendous of all nineteenth-century thinkers."[38] His influence has dominated much of philosophical speculation since his unanticipated death from cholera in 1831 while he was at the height of his popularity. Hegel argues that all reality is the outworking of Spirit (*Geist*). To him the Absolute Spirit (God) comes into self-consciousness through a process of struggle. Hence, the sum total of human knowledge is none other than Absolute Spirit thinking out its thoughts through human minds. Although it is customary to describe Hegel's view of the outworking of Spirit as Dialectic (which is simply another word for process or dynamic pattern) of Thesis, Antithesis, and Synthesis, it has been pointed out that such a dialectic is in fact more characteristic of Fichte and others.[39]

Hegel's view that the Absolute Spirit works in such overt manifestations as art, religion, and philosophy has an effect on his view of Scripture, for the Spirit enables man to take religion seriously without his taking the facts of revelation too literally. For Hegel, there are two religious viewpoints—rationalistic skepticism and naive literalism—which demonstrate the poverty of Spirit in the common man. He argues that "one whose understanding of religion is based on Spirit will accept the same beliefs as the naive pietist but will simultaneously be able to interpret them rationally without falling into the skeptic's trap.... The positive and the spiritual are combined." The positive grounding of Christianity is the Bible, but that is not to say that the Bible

37. Frederick Copleston, *A History of Philosophy,* vol. 7, *Modern Philosophy, Part I, Fichte to Hegel*, pp. 15-49, for an excellent overview of this period of post-Kantian idealist systems of thought.
38. R. R. Palmer and Joel Colton, *A History of the Modern World,* p. 434. See also Walter A. Kaufman, *Hegel: A Reinterpretation;* Winfred Corduan, "Hegelian Themes in Contemporary Theology," pp. 351-61. Also see G. W. F. Hegel, *Werke,* Eva Molderhauer and Karl Markus Michel, eds., especially vols. 8-10: *Enzklopadie der philosophischen Wissenschaften;* also see G. W. F. Hegel, *Encyclopedia of Philosophy,* trans. Gustav Emil Mueller.
39. Brown, *Philosophy and the Christian Faith,* p. 121, cites J. N. Findlay, *Hegel: A Re-examination*, p. 70. There is considerable scholarly argumentation against the more popularized notion. See Walter A. Kaufmann, "The Hegel Myth and Its Method," pp. 459-86; Gustav E. Mueller, "The Legend of 'Thesis-Antithesis-Synthesis,'" pp. 411-14; Winfred Corduan, "Transcendentalism: Hegel," in Geisler, ed., *Biblical Errancy,* pp. 81-104.

alone is sufficient for doing Christian theology. "Hegel contends that the 'scientific' theologian will recognize the precedence of Spirit over the Bible.... In the light of Spirit it is then entirely possible to overcome the historical details that may encumber positivistic religion."[40]

After his death Hegel's followers became divided into three main branches. In the center were those Hegelians who held philosophy to be the core of Absolute Spirit; they left room for religion in the system. A second branch contended that Hegel's system must be understood ultimately in theological terms. The third branch effectively destroyed the need for religion in the world of thought. The last group has exercised the most influence on the philosophical conception of the Bible. They are represented by such biblical critics as Bruno Bauer (1809-1882), Ludwig Andreas Feuerbach (1804-1872), David Friedrich Strauss (1808-1874), and Ferdinand Christian Baur (1792-1860). In the meantime, Karl Marx (1818-1883) soon appropriated the so-called "Hegelian dialectic" to new uses. In addition, Hegel's philosophy converged with other currents in Germany to make the study of history more philosophically meaningful than ever before, because history as "the study of time process, seemed to be the very key with which to unlock the true significance of the world."[41]

LIBERALISM (c. 1850-c. 1920)

Although Romanticism had delivered Christianity from near elimination at the hands of Rationalism, it had done so at the terrible cost of depriving it of its relevance to civilization. In particular Romanticism relegated Christianity to the realm of aesthetic feeling and personal morality. That effectively removed it from the realm of history, where nineteenth-century man was convinced middle-class progress could be seen in all its glory.[42] The term *liberalism* specifically refers to the attempt to harmonize the Christian faith with all of human culture, although it is also applied to any Protestant religious movement that questions the basic doctrines of conservative Christianity. Liberalism was a reaction against the alleged monastic or pietistic, introspective Romanticism of Kant and Schleiermacher, and it became virtually a civil religion (*Kulturprostentantismus*) in both its German and American expressions as it took up anew the challenge of the Enlightenment tradition rather than compartmentalizing religion and culture.

Albrecht Ritschl, the founder of theological liberalism, applied the so-called Hegelian dialectic to make theology the interaction of the two focal points of the Christian faith: the concerns of society and civilization as well

40. Corduan, "Transcendentalism: Hegel," pp. 88-89.
41. Palmer and Colton, *History of the Modern World,* p. 435.
42. D. Clair Davis, "Liberalism: The Challenge of Progress," in Lewis and Demarest, eds., *Challenges to Inerrancy,* pp. 67-68.

as those of personal salvation. For him, a proper use of the Bible must correlate with larger concerns as well as to personal salvation. In its cultural setting liberalism accepted the notion that the Bible contains errors and its advocates sought means whereby the newly discovered truths of modern thought could be harmonized with Scripture. The traditional doctrine of verbal inspiration was regarded as a seventeenth-century viewpoint that was understandable in its day but that had become untenable in the modern world. After stating that the Protestant doctrine of inspiration based on its self-interpretation was of little value, Ritschl went on to argue that "the Bible can be employed only for theology and basic morality, but not in the details of life because of the change in the position of Christianity in society."[43] For him the binding elements of Scripture can be recognized by their content rather than by any doctrine of verbal inspiration. That is a basic shift to the view that the Bible merely *contains* the Word of God instead of actually *being* the Word of God.

Ritschl's emphasis was expressed by Wilhelm Herrmann (1846-1922), who served as professor of theology at Marburg and teacher of such men as Karl Barth (1886-1968), Rudolf Bultmann (1884-1976), and J. Gresham Machen (1881-1937), the intellectual leader of American evangelicalism in the early twentieth century. In his most influential book, *The Communion of the Christian with God* (1886), Hermann argued that an individual "does not become a Christian by submitting to some doctrines but by recognizing the great fact of Jesus. Faith in the doctrines about him cannot be demanded as the prerequisite for salvation by Jesus, but rather as the result of that salvation.... The only objective ground for the truth of Christianity is one's moral transformation."[44]

The tenets of liberalism are most clearly stated by the German theologian and church historian Adolf von Harnack (1851-1930). Harnack had made the intellectual sojourn from orthodoxy through the historical-critical approach of the Tübingen School to Ritschlian liberalism before writing *Das Wesen des Christentums* (1900), translated as *What Is Christianity?* (1901), the best-known and most popular expression of the thought of the whole liberal movement. Roman Catholic scholars who were warm to such new ideas, especially as they came from Protestant critics, were informed by Rome in 1910 that they were unwanted, and "a loyalty oath against Modernism was imposed on all clerics whenever they received holy orders, applied for confessional faculties, took papal degrees, began office as religious superiors, or taught in a seminary or pontifically approved faculty."[45]

43. Ibid., pp. 69-70, where Ritschl's *The Doctrine of Justification and Reconciliation* (1882) is cited.
44. Ibid., pp. 73-74.
45. Burtchaell, *Catholic Theories of Inspiration since 1810*, p. 232.

EXISTENTIALISM (c. 1850-PRESENT)

Modern *existentialism* probably goes back to Søren Abby Kierkegaard (1813-1855), whose writings were not widely known outside Denmark prior to 1918. Existentialism grew out of the soil of Kantian agnosticism and is quite diverse in its expression. For some it occupies the place left vacated by idealism as the philosophical basis of Christianity. To others it represents the bankruptcy of Western philosophy. One line of existentialism may be traced through the phenomenalism of Edmund Husserl (1859-1938) and his student Martin Heidegger (1889-1976). The German philosopher and poet Friedrich Wilhelm Nietzsche (1844-1900) and the Russian novelist Feodor Mikhailovich Dostoevsky (1821-1881) also anticipated some ideas that became pronounced in existentialism.

There are some common features between Kierkegaard's thought, existentialism, twentieth-century neo-orthodoxy, and much of neo-evangelicalism. Kierkegaard's primary objective was to attack "the modern gratuitous assumption that truth is impersonal, that it can be attained simply by thinking dispassionately."[46] He did not teach that truth is subjective or that there is no such thing as objective truth, but he dismissed objectivity as a way of knowing ultimate or religious truth.[47] For him, truth, like God, is not paradoxical in itself but only to finite man, who is able to appropriate it by a passionate leap of faith. For Kierkegaard objective or historical truth is not essential to Christianity. He wrote, "If the contemporary generation had nothing behind them but these words: 'We have believed that in such and such a year the God appeared among us in the humble figure of a servant, that he lived and taught in our community, and finally died,' it would be more than enough."[48] Nevertheless, Kierkegaard personally believed in the historicity of the Bible, of Christ, and even of the resurrection.

For Kierkegaard, a personal acceptance of Scripture as inspired need not be supported by objective confirmation. In fact, he deprecated scholarly efforts to defend the inspiration and authority of Scripture.[49] When twentieth-century existential theologians like Rudolph Bultmann, Paul Tillich, John Macquarrie, and others apply the term *revelation* to every original and new intuition and make inspiration an exclusively human activity, they stand in this line of post-Enlightenment thought as John Baillie asserts:

> For the revelation of which the Bible speaks is always such as had place within a personal relationship. It is not the revelation of an object to a subject, but a

46. Brown, *Philosophy and the Christian Faith*, p. 128.
47. Geisler, "Philosophical Presuppositions," p. 327.
48. Johannes Climacus, *Philosophical Fragments: Or a Fragment of Philosophy*, S. Kierkegaard, [ed.]; translation and introduction by David Z. Swenson; translation revised by Howard V. Hong (Princeton: Princeton U., 1936), pp. 53, 130.
49. Søren Kierkegaard, *Concluding Unscientific Postscript*, p. 26.

revelation from a subject to a subject, a revelation of mind to mind. That is the first thing that differentiates the theological meaning of revelation, the revelation that is made to faith, from the sense in which all valid knowledge has been said to be revelation.[50]

Orthodox Views of Inspiration (17th-19th Centuries)

During the seventeenth, eighteenth, and most of the nineteenth centuries the traditional, orthodox doctrine of the inspiration and authority of Scripture remained substantially unchanged in the Christian church.[51] For purposes of illustration four individuals from the Evangelical Reformed and Westminster traditions—Francis Turretin, Jonathan Edwards, Charles Hodge, and Benjamin Breckinridge Warfield—may be cited as leading spokesmen for the continuation of the orthodox doctrine of revelation and inspiration of Scripture.

Francis Turretin (1623-1687)

Francis Turretin and his son Johann Alfons (1671-1737) were leading spokesmen of the Evangelical Reformed tradition in Switzerland. They continued the work of Zwingli and the framers of the Helvetic Confessions as they taught in Geneva. In his *Institutio Theologiae Elenctiae* Turretin asserts that "the question of the authority of Scripture depends upon its origin.... Since it is from God, it cannot be other than genuine (*authenticus*) and divine." As a result, he argues, "it should be assumed without controversy that Scripture is God-breathed and the primary foundation of the faith" and that the authority of Scripture has as its basis "the divine and infallible truth of the books, which have God as author."[52] Thus, he insists, "When the divine quality of Scripture ... has been accepted, its infallibility follows of necessity."[53] For Turretin and the Evangelical Reformed tradition, this meant that the Bible is totally without error because "Scripture is 'God-breathed' " (2 Tim. 3:16).

50. John Baillie, *The Idea of Revelation in Recent Thought,* p. 19. It is interesting to note that although Baillie defines the term *revelation* (p. 19, 59) as a disclosure, he goes on to treat it as a discovery elsewhere. He also mistakenly associates the notion of a propositional revelation with mechanical dictation on p. 40. He prefers to view revelation as anti-propositional personal encounter in his discussions, e.g., pp. 30, 36-38, 40, 75, 121-22.
51. See chap. 8 discussion and bibliographical items covering the entire period from the Reformation to the end of World War I. Also see William E. Nix, "Doctrine of Inspiration since the Reformation," pp. 443-54.
52. Francis Turretin, more accurately Franz Turretini, *The Doctrine of Scripture: Locus 2 of Institutio Theologiae Elencticae,* edited by John W. Beardslee III, pp. 39-40. This translation is based on Francis Turretin, *Institutio Theologiae Elencticae,* 3 vols. which, along with a collection of *Disputationes,* has been frequently reprinted as Turretin's *Opera,* because it was first published in 1688 (Utrecht and Amsterdam: Jacobum a Poolsum, 1701, 1734; Edinburgh, 1847). Also see Leon M. Allison, "The Doctrine of Scripture in the Theology of John Calvin and Francis Turretin," pp. 39-40.
53. Ibid., 57.

The Word of God cannot lie (Ps. 19:8-9; Heb. 6:18), it cannot perish and pass away (Matt. 5:18), it abides forever (1 Pet. 1:25), and it is truth itself (John 17:17)."[54] Furthermore, "whatever contradictions seem to be in Scripture are apparent but not real. [They appear] only with respect to the understanding of us who are not able to perceive and grasp everywhere their harmony."[55] The discrepancies that are difficult to explain "are such because of human ignorance, and not because of the problem itself, so it is better to acknowledge our ignorance than to accept any contradiction."[56]

Turretin was concerned with the form of Scripture as well as its content. He denies, for example, that the Hebrew vowel points "were merely a human innovation made by the Masoretes." He says, "If the points were added at a later date ... it does not follow that they are merely a human device.... so that even if the points were not ... part of the original with regard to their shape, it cannot be denied that they were part of it with regard to sound and value, or power."[57] For Turretin, the Bible is not only perfect in terms of form and content, it is also perfect (complete) in terms of its extent (canon). He argues that the Scriptures "contain perfectly, not absolutely everything, but whatever is necessary for salvation, not explicit and in exact words, but with equal force [to explicit statement] or by valid conclusion (*aequipollenter vel per legitimam consequentiam*), so that there is no need to resort to any unwritten word."[58]

In dealing with the matter of authorship, Turretin also recognized that the Bible is a book written by human authors who "responded to circumstances of time and place." Yet those human authors "could write under the influence of circumstances and at the same time from divine commandment and inspiration" so that "the apostles wrote when God inspired and moved them, although not in a mechanical manner, under coercion."[59]

Jonathan Edwards (1703-1758)

Among the Puritans in America, Jonathan Edwards was a giant. A significant figure in the Great Awakening of the eighteenth century, he believed that "ministers are not to preach those things which their own wisdom or reason suggests, but the things that are already dictated to them by the superior wisdom and knowledge of God."[60] He often spoke of "dictation" and the biblical writers as "penmen" of the Holy Spirit, but Edwards did not

54. Ibid., pp. 59-60.
55. Ibid., p. 61. Brackets supplied by the editor.
56. Ibid., p. 63.
57. Ibid., pp. 131-32.
58. Ibid., p. 169. Brackets supplied by the editor.
59. Ibid., pp. 33-34.
60. Jonathan Edwards, making use of 1 Cor. 2:11-13, "Ordination of Mr. Billing (May 7, 1740)," as cited by John H. Gerstner, "The Nature of Inspiration," p. 27.

believe in what is commonly called "mechanical dictation" of the Scriptures. In reference to Solomon, for example, Edwards wrote, "God's Spirit made use of his loving inclination, joined with his musing philosophical disposition, and so directed and conducted it in this train of imagination as to represent the love that there is between Christ and his spouse. God saw it very needful and exceeding useful that there should be some representation of it."[61] So the "dictation" mentioned by Edwards actually refers to the divinely authoritative product of inspiration and not to the human means by which it was produced. That is affirmed elsewhere by Edwards, who believed that

> Moses was so intimately conversant with God and so continually under the divine conduct, it can't be thought that when he wrote the history of the creation and fall of man, and the history of the church from the creation, that he should not be under the divine direction in such an affair. Doubtless he wrote by God's direction, as we are informed that he wrote the law and the history of the Israelitish Church.[62]

Indeed, "that the prophets after they had once had intercourse with God by immediate revelation from God gained acquaintance with [him] so as afterwards to know him; as it were to know his voice or know what was indeed a revelation from God is confirmed by 1 Sam. 3:7."[63] In brief, for Edwards the Bible is the very Word of God. Thus, "God may reveal things in Scripture, which way he pleases. If by what he there reveals the thing is any was clearly discovered to be the understanding or eye of the mind, 'tis our duty to receive it as his revelation."[64] So, for Edwards as well as for Turretin, whatever the Bible says, God says.

In 1758 Edwards was called to be president of the young Presbyterian college at Princeton. "In theology he was an orthodox Calvinist with a mystical inclination."[65] Death intervened, and Edwards, who with George Whitefield (1714-1770) had been closely associated with the Great Awakening in the American colonies, was unable to assume his post at Princeton. There his successors would establish a conservative bastion when a general seminary for the denomination was established at Princeton in 1812. The first professor in the seminary was Archibald Alexander (1772-1851). He and Charles Hodge (1797-1878), his pupil and colleague, became founders of the Princeton Theology and architects of Reformed confessionalism at the seminary. Sidney Ahlstrom gives an accurate assessment when he states,

61. Edwards, *Miscellanies,* 303, as cited by Gerstner, "The Nature of Inspiration," p. 29.
62. Edwards, *Miscellanies,* 352, as cited in Gerstner, ibid., p. 31.
63. Edwards, *Miscellanies,* 1144 (Andover copy), as cited in Gerstner, ibid., pp. 31-32.
64. Edwards, *Miscellanies,* 1426, as cited in Gerstner, ibid., pp. 31-32.
65. F. L. Cross and E. A. Livingston, eds., *The Oxford Dictionary of the Christian Church,* pp. 446b-447a.

> The Princeton Seminary . . . shaped a new conservatism and created a fortress that held its ground for a century. Regarding the free-ranging intellect of Edwards with suspicion and viewing revivalism as insubstantial, it chose biblical inerrancy and strict confessionalism as its means of defense. To support this strategy Princeton marshaled great dialectical skill, massive theological efforts, and much impressive erudition. It provided shelter whither revivalists and Fundamentalists could flee when the ideas of Darwin or Wellhausen endangered their tents and tabernacles. They taught theological responsibility to anti-intellectuals in many denominations where learning had been held in disrepute.[66]

These men were succeeded in turn by the efforts of Archibald Alexander Hodge (1823-1886), Benjamin Breckinridge Warfield (1851-1921), and J. Gresham Machen (1881-1937), who "maintained the institution's reputation for unbending but erudite conservatism down to 1929-1936, when both the seminary and the denomination were disrupted by conservative secessions."[67]

Charles Hodge (1797-1878)

Hodge's thinking reflects Princetonian theology's central position on the inspiration and authority of Scripture. In fact, his view on Scripture characterizes his system of theology and forms the primary ground for his position in the conservative tradition of American Reformed theology. In his treatment of "The Protestant Rule of Faith," Hodge argues that "all Protestants agree in teaching that 'the word of God, as contained in the Scriptures of the Old and New Testaments, is the only infallible rule of faith and practice.' "[68] He proceeds to cite the *Smalcald Articles* and the *Form of Concord* of the Lutheran tradition and the various symbols of the Reformed churches that "teach the same doctrine" before drawing his conclusion, which asserts,

> From these statements it appears that Protestants hold, (1.) That the Scriptures of the Old and New Testaments are the Word of God, written under the inspiration of the Holy Spirit, and are therefore infallible, and of divine authority in all things pertaining to faith and practice, and consequently free from all error whether of doctrine, fact, or precept. (2.) That they contain all the extant supernatural revelations of God designed to be a rule of faith and practice to his Church. (3.) That they are sufficiently perspicuous to be understood by the people, in the use

66. Sidney E. Ahlstrom, ed., *Theology in America: The Major Protestant Voices from Puritanism to Neo-Orthodoxy,* p. 251. Rogers and McKim, *Authority and Interpretation of the Bible,* pp. 172-88, identify fully-developed Reformed Scholasticism with Francis Turretin and see its method exemplified in his greatest work, *Institutio Theologiae Elencticae,* published in 1674. They trace the institutionalization of Protestant Scholasticism at Princeton through its theologians Archibald Alexander and Charles Hodge. For a discussion of their overdrawn distinction between the views of Calvin and Turretin see Carl F. H. Henry, *God, Revelation and Authority,* vol. 4: *God Who Speaks and Shows,* pp. 378-79.
67. Ahlstrom, *Theology in America,* pp. 45-48. Also see Lefferts A. Loetscher, *The Broadening Church: A Study of Theological Issues in the Presbyterian Church since 1869.*
68. Charles Hodge, *Systematic Theology,* 1:151.

> of ordinary means and by the aid of the Holy Spirit, in all things necessary to faith or practice, without the need of any infallible interpreter.[69]

After a brief treatment of the canon of Scripture, Hodge proceeds with his discussion that "the Scriptures are Infallible, i.e., given by Inspiration of God," where he states that "the infallibility and divine authority of the Scriptures are due to the fact that they are the word of God; and they are the word of God because they were given by inspiration of the Holy Ghost." His first point of discussion concerns "The Nature of Inspiration. Definition," which becomes the basis of his extended treatment of the whole subject. He writes,

> The nature of inspiration is to be learnt from the Scriptures; from their didactic statements, and from their phenomena. There are certain general facts or principles which underlie the Bible, which are assumed in all its teachings, and which therefore must be assumed in its interpretation. We must, for example, assume, (1.) That God is not the unconscious ground of all things; nor an unintelligent force; nor a name for the moral order of the universe; nor mere causality; but a Spirit—a self-conscious, intelligent, voluntary agent, possessing all the attributes of our spirits without limitation, and to an infinite degree. (2.) That He is the creator of the world, and extra-mundane, existing before, and independently of it; not its soul, life, or animating principle; but its maker, preserver, and ruler. (3.) That as a spirit He is everywhere present, and everywhere active, preserving and governing all His creatures and all their actions. (4.) That while both in the external world and in the world of the mind He generally acts according to fixed laws and through secondary causes, He is free to act, and often does act immediately, or without the intervention of such causes, as in creation, regeneration, and miracles. (5.) That the Bible contains a divine, or supernatural revelation. The present question is not, Whether the Bible is what it claims to be; but, What does it teach as to the nature and effects of the influence under which it is written?
>
> On this subject the common doctrine of the Church is, and ever has been, that inspiration was an influence of the Holy Spirit on the minds of certain select men, which rendered them the organs of God for the infallible communication of His mind and will. They were in such a sense the organs of God, and what they said God said.[70]

69. Ibid., 151-152, where Hodge also lists the *Confessio Helvetica, Confessio Gallicana,* the *Thirty-Nine Articles of the Church of England,* and *The Westminster Confession.*
70. Ibid., pp. 153-54. Hodge's extended treatment of the doctrine of inspiration covers pp. 153-72. Following that discussion, he proceeds to treat "Adverse Theories," pp. 172-82, including theists who hold to a mechanical theory of the universe, Deists, and Schleiermacher, those who hold to natural causes under the providential control of God, and several theories of partial inspiration. Edgar Young Mullins, *The Christian Religion in Its Doctrinal Expression,* pp. 137-53, presents a much more descriptive than interpretive approach to this very subject from a Baptist perspective. B. H. Carroll, *The Inspiration of the Bible,* sets forth the position of the founder and first president of Southwestern Baptist Theological Seminary which he taught in lectures during the previous half-century. Carroll held the Bible to be authoritative and without error historically, scientifically, philosophically, and theologically long before the issue of inerrancy arose in the contemporary scene.

Archibald Alexander Hodge (1823-1866) and Benjamin Breckinridge Warfield (1851-1921)

In the ferment of ideas set loose in the controversies following the publication of Darwin's *On the Origin of Species* on November 24, 1859,[71] and the establishment of the higher critical theories following the lead of Karl H. Graf (1815-1869), Abraham Kuenen (1828-1891), and Julius Wellhausen (1844-1918),[72] orthodox Christians found champions for their cause in A.A. Hodge and B.B. Warfield. Their article entitled "Inspiration" became something of a normative statement for most conservative Christians since the time it was first published in 1881.[73] In contrast to those who were beginning to espouse the notion that the Bible *contains* the Word of God, they affirmed that the Bible *is* the Word of God, saying, "The New Testament continually asserts of the Scriptures of the Old Testament, and of the several books which constitute it, that they ARE THE WORD OF GOD. What their writers said God said."[74] For them, it is not merely the thoughts but the very words of Scripture that are infallible, for

> Every element of Scripture, whether doctrine or history, of which God has guaranteed the infallibility, must be infallible in its verbal expression. No matter how in other respects generated, the Scriptures are a product of human thought, and every process of human thought involves language....
>
> Besides this, the Scriptures are a record of divine revelations, and as such consist of words.... Infallible thought must be definite thought, and definite thought implies words.... Whatever discrepancies or other human limitations may attach to the sacred record, *the line* (of inspired or not inspired, of fallible or infallible) *can never rationally be drawn between the thoughts and the words of Scripture*.[75]

71. Charles Darwin, *On the Origin of Species by Means of Natural Selection*. The first edition of 1,250 copies was published November 24, 1859, and was sold out on that very day. It stirred up such controversy that it was reprinted within seven weeks. For an excellent treatment of this period see H. D. McDonald, *Theories of Revelation: An Historical Study, 1700-1960*, 2:198-99.
72. Julius Wellhausen published his *Die Geschichte Israels* in 1878, and it was translated into English in 1883. Its second edition was released as the two-volume *Prolegomena zur Geschichte Israels* in 1883. Continuing to build on the work of others, he published *Die Komposition des Hexateuchs und der historischen Bucher des Alten Testaments* in 1885. According to J. D. Douglas *(The New International Dictionary of the Christian Church*, p. 1033), although Wellhausen spent the remainder of his life working in a similar vein on New Testament studies, his *History of Israel* "gave him a place in biblical studies comparable, it was said, to that of Darwin in biology."
73. Archibald A. Hodge and Benjamin B. Warfield, *Inspiration*. Roger R. Nicole has supplied or written an introduction and several appendixes for this reprint of *Inspiration*, which had been published earlier as an article in *Presbyterian Review* 2 (April 1881): 225-60. It was published again in Robert Howie, ed., *The Westminster Doctrine Anent Holy Scripture: Tractates by A. A. Hodge and Warfield, with Notes on Recent Discussions*. Selections from the reprint edition of this work are cited by Geisler, *Decide for Yourself*, pp. 49-55.
74. Hodge and Warfield, *Inspiration*, p. 29 (emphasis theirs).
75. Ibid., pp. 21-23. Parenthesis and emphasis theirs.

Hodge and Warfield argue that Holy Scripture is "the result of the cooperation, in various ways, of the human agency, both in the histories out of which the Scriptures sprang, and their immediate composition and inscription, is everywhere apparent, and gives substance and form to the entire collection of writings."[76] They go on to assert that they do not wish to "deny an everywhere-present human element in the Scriptures. No mark of the effect of this human element, therefore—in style of thought or wording—can be urged against inspiration unless it can be shown to result in untruth."[77] The obvious humanness of Scripture eliminates any notion of a "mechanical" or "verbal dictation" view of inspiration, because "each sacred writer was by God specially formed, endowed, educated, providentially conditioned, and then supplied with knowledge naturally, supernaturally or spiritually conveyed, so that he, and he alone, could, and freely would, produce his allotted part."[78]

Thus, according to Hodge and Warfield, what biblical writers produced by the inspiration of Scripture is a verbal, plenary, infallible, and inerrant book, the Bible. They indicate as much in their definition of *plenary,* as they write, "the word means simply 'full,' 'complete,' perfectly adequate for the attainment of the end designed, whatever that might have been."[79] And the expression *verbal inspiration* "does not hold that what the sacred writers *do not affirm* is infallibly true, but only that what *they do affirm* is infallibly true."[80] That is accomplished because "throughout the whole of his work the Holy Spirit was present, causing his energies to flow into the spontaneous exercises of the writer's faculties, elevating and directing where need be, and everywhere securing the errorless expression in language of the thought designed by God. This last element is what we call 'Inspiration.' "[81] "Not every copy of Scripture is inerrant, according to Hodge and Warfield; they say, for example, "We do not assert that the common text, but only that the original autographic text, was inspired."[82] "In view of all the facts known to us," they write, "we affirm that a candid inspection of all the ascertained phenomena of the original text of Scripture will leave unmodified the ancient faith of the Church. In all their real affirmations these books are without error."[83]

In response to the rise of negative higher criticism, ushered in by Graf, Kuenen, Wellhausen, and others, Hodge and Warfield write that

> the present writers . . . admit freely that the traditional belief as to the dates and origin of the several books may be brought into question without involving any

76. Ibid., p. 12.
77. Ibid., p. 42.
78. Ibid., pp. 14-15.
79. Ibid., p. 18.
80. Ibid., Appendix 2, "The Truth of Inspiration," p. 80.
81. Ibid., p. 16.
82. Ibid., p. 42.
83. Ibid., p. 27.

> doubt as to their inspiration, yet confidently affirm that any theories of the origin or authorship of any book of either Testament which ascribe to them a purely naturalistic genesis, or dates or authors inconsistent with either their own natural claims or the assertions of other Scripture, are plainly inconsistent with the doctrine of inspiration taught by the Church.[84]

Their position is consistent with the basic orthodox teaching about Scripture that had been held from the first century onward. It is also the position espoused by J. Gresham Machen and others into the present setting. In fact, the position of Hodge and Warfield is essentially the same as that held by leading evangelicals in November 1978 as defined by the International Council on Biblical Inerrancy. That body drafted "A Short Statement," which attests that

> 1. God, who is Himself Truth and speaks the truth only, has inspired Holy Scripture in order thereby to reveal Himself to lost mankind through Jesus Christ as Creator and Lord, redeemer and Judge. Holy Scripture is God's witness to Himself.
>
> 2. Holy Scripture, being God's own Word, written by men prepared and superintended by His Spirit, is of infallible divine authority in all matters upon which it touches: it is to be believed, as God's instruction, in all that it affirms; obeyed, as God's command, in all that it requires; embraced, as God's pledge, in all that it promises.
>
> 3. The Holy Spirit, Scripture's divine Author, both authenticates it to us by His inward witness and opens our minds to understand its meaning.
>
> 4. Being wholly and verbally God-given, Scripture is without error or fault in all its teaching, no less in what it states about God's acts in creation, about events of world history, and about its own literary origins under God, than in its witness to God's saving grace in individual lives.
>
> 5. The authority of Scripture is inescapably impaired if this total divine inerrancy is in any way limited or disregarded, or made relative to a view of truth contrary to the Bible's own; and such lapses bring serious loss to both the individual and the Church.[85]

84. Ibid., p. 39. In his treatment of "Biblical Literalism," Ernest R. Sandeen, *The Roots of Fundamentalism: British and American Millenarianism, 1800-1930*, pp. 103-31, has an extended discussion of the Princeton theology. In that presentation, he argues that the shift to inerrancy came with Warfield rather than his predecessors. That notion is incorrect, as is his "notion that the doctrine of inerrancy 'did not exist in Europe or America prior to its foundation in the last half century' by American Fundamentalists, ... and by Princetonian theologians in particular." See also Ernest Sandeen, *The Origins of Fundamentalism: Toward a Historical Interpretation*, p. 14, and his article, "The Princeton Theology: One Source of Biblical Literalism in American Protestantism," pp. 307-21, both of which are cited in Henry, *God, Revelation and Authority*, vol. 4: *God Who Speaks and Shows: Fifteen Theses, Part Three*, p. 379.
85. *The Chicago Statement on Biblical Inerrancy*. This "Short Statement" is accompanied by a "Preface" as well as nineteen "Articles of Affirmation and Denial" (which are printed in chap. 10).

Thus, the orthodox doctrine that the Bible is the infallible, inerrant Word of God in its original manuscripts has maintained itself from the first century to the present. This position holds that the Bible is without error in everything that it affirms. Indeed, according to the traditional teaching of the Christian church, what the Bible says, God Himself says. That includes all matters of history, science, and any other matter on which it touches. Any results of higher criticism that are contrary to this teaching are incompatible with the traditional doctrine of the inspiration and authority of Scripture as it has been held throughout church history. Being at variance with the traditional teaching of the Christian church in its broadest context, such contrary views of Scripture are actually unorthodox. It is to those unorthodox views of Scripture that we must now turn.

Attempts at Synthesis and the Rise of Higher Criticism

From their cultural and intellectual setting German Rationalists had an unprecedented influence on the doctrines of Christianity. They were not set upon viciously attacking Christianity. In fact, they viewed themselves as champions of the faith. Their approach to the Scriptures was an attempt to answer and counterattack the skepticism that had spread abroad from the French Enlightenment. To their contemporaries, both European and American, they were identified as "Evangelicals."[86] Several of their number may be identified in this regard.

Jean Astruc (1684-1766)

Physician to the court of Louis XIV and professor of medicine at Paris, Astruc was one of the first scholars to bring to prominence the notion that Genesis 1 and 2 were written by two different authors.[87] In 1753 Astruc

86. The term *evangelical* is used in its broadest sense to refer to non-Roman Catholic theologians, especially in the context of Continental Europe.
87. Gleason L. Archer, *Encyclopedia of Bible Difficulties,* p. 66. Astruc was not the first scholar to hold such a view, however. In fact, he looked back at the 1685-1687 controversy between Richard Simon and Jean Le Clerc as one of the decisive encounters in the history of ideas about the Bible. See Woodbridge, *Biblical Authority: A Critique of the Rogers/McKim Proposal,* p. 96. Earlier in his discussion Woodbridge indicates several Continental thinkers who had an influence on the ideas developed by Astruc and others. Among them were Hugo Grotius (1583-1645), Simon, Le Clerc, and Spinoza. LeClerc was a devoted champion of freedom of thought and an opponent of all dogmatism who defended the unlimited rights of reason in the realm of faith. He held altogether advanced critical views on the inspiration of Scripture, and he denied that Job, Proverbs, Ecclesiastes, and the Song of Songs were inspired, while ascribing a late date to portions of the Pentateuch. Simon is called "the originator of biblical criticism" by Jean Delumeau, *Catholicism Between Luther and Voltaire: A New View of the Counter-Reformation,* p. 127. Spinoza is also sometimes referred to as "the father of biblical criticism," but in fact he was a pantheist. Spinoza's was "pantheism-cum-positive rationalism," according to Delumeau (p. 204).

published his *Conjectures,* in which he attempted to reconcile some of the difficulties he found in the Genesis record.[88] As a result, he emphasized the distinctions between such words as "Elohim," "Yahweh Elohim" (or "Jehovah Elohim"), and "El-Elyon" in espousing a view that would become popular among such German Rationalists as Johann G. Eichhorn (1752-1827), Karl H. Graf (1815-1869), Abraham Kuenen (1828-1891), Julius Wellhausen (1844-1918), and others.

JOHANN SEMLER (1729-1791)

Semler is often referred to as the father of German Rationalism because he was the first to advocate the so-called "Accommodation Theory." Such an approach set the stage for the rise of the so-called "historical-critical" method. In his critique of the historical-critical method, Gerhard Maier says, "The general acceptance of Semler's basic concept that the Bible must be treated like any other book has plunged theology into an endless chain of perplexities and inner contradictions."[89] This theory asserts "that Christ accommodated His language to the current opinions of the Jews of His day regarding the Old Testament Scriptures."[90] Semler was reared in Pietism before he became a conservative Rationalist. As a result, "he distinguished between the permanent truths in Scripture and the elements due to the times in which the books were written. He denied the equal value of all parts of Scripture. Revelation, he taught, is in Scripture, but all Scripture is not revelation. The creeds of the church are a growth. Church history is a development."[91]

JOHANN GOTTFRIED EICHHORN (1752-1827)

Johann Eichhorn was a German theologian who seems to have followed the views of Astruc and Joseph Priestly (1733-1804) in preparing the way for others to follow in the beginnings of critical method. The term *higher criticism* had been used as a synonym for historical criticism by Presbyterian

88. Jean Astruc, *Conjectures sur les memoires origineaux dont il paroit que Moyse s'est servi pour composer le livre de la Genese*. Also see Adolphe Lods, "Astruc et la critique biblique de son temps," pp. 123-27. Woodbridge, *Biblical Authority,* p. 196 n. 83, asserts that "Astruc saw himself as advancing Le Clerc and Simon."
89. Gerhard Maier, *The End of the Historical-Critical Method,* p. 11. In the foreword to that work, Eugene F. Klug adds his own opinion "that higher criticism [should] be seen for what it is, an uncritical and unjustified denigration of the Biblical text" (p. 10).
90. This is the accomodationist view as stated in W. Sanday, *The Oracles of God* (1891), as cited in the discussion by McDonald, *Theories of Revelation,* 2:140-50. It is also the view of C. Gore, *The Incarnation of the Son of God* (1891), S. R. Driver, *Introduction to the Literature of the Old Testament* (1891), T. K. Cheyne, *Aids to the Devout Study of Criticism* (1892), R. L. Ottley, *The Doctrine of the Incarnation* (1896), and others. In his Bampton Lectures of 1893, Sanday, *Inspiration: Eight Lectures on the Early History and Origin of the Doctrine of Biblical Inspiration* (London: Longmans, Green, 5th impression, 1903), sought to explain the nature of the restriction of our Lord's knowledge and its relation to biblical criticism.
91. Williston Walker, *A History of the Christian Church,* 3d ed. rev. by Robert T. Handy, p. 483.

minister and scientist Joseph Priestly. Priestly regarded the historical method "to be one of the most satisfactory modes of argumentation" in the preface to his *History of the Corruptions of Christianity* (1782). Eichhorn then used the term *higher criticism* in the preface to his 3-volume *Einleitung in das Alte Testament* (1780-1783).[92] He was one of the first commentators to make a scientific comparison between the biblical books and other Semitic writings. He also divided Genesis into "Jehovist" and "Elohist" sources and distinguished the priestly from the popular law code in the Pentateuch. Although his work was inaccurate, it was popular and did much to encourage biblical study and criticism. Later, higher criticism came to be identified more particularly with literary criticism than with historical method.

Heinrich Eberhard Gottlob Paulus (1761-1851)

In his *The Life of Jesus* (1828),[93] Paulus attempted to reconcile his belief in the substantial accuracy of the gospel narrative with his personal disbelief in miracles and the supernatural. He attempted to turn miracles into ordinary facts and events that had been exaggerated or misconceived, and he treated the gospel writers as sufferers of hallucinations when they intentionally recorded such things as visions and miracles. Paulus applied Eichhorn's principles to the New Testament even though he believed himself to be championing the Bible's cause against rising skepticism. His influence waned in the face of the more radical skepticism of David Friedrich Strauss (1808-1874).

Wilhelm Martin Leberecht De Wette (1790-1849)

Wilhelm De Wette studied at one time under Heinrich Paulus before publishing his own works on biblical criticism from 1806 until 1813, when he turned to theological studies. He was a radical Rationalist early in his career but became more conservative in later years. Although he was a nonsupernaturalist, he continually criticized the theories of Ferdinand Christian Baur (1762-1860) and his disciples at the Tübingen School of New Testament criticism. De Wette was influenced by Friedrich D. E. Schleiermacher and J. F. Fries, and he tried to reconcile the transcendent and finite. He was one of the most respected theologians of the nineteenth century, although he displeased Rationalists with his condemnation of cold reason and

92. McDonald, *Theories of Revelation,* 2:102, indicates that this reference was made in 1787, but *Einleitung in das Alte Testament* was published in 3 volumes in 1780-1783. He also published *Einleitung in die apokryphyischen Bücher das Alte Testament* (1795) and *Einlietung in das Neuen Testament* in two volumes (1804-1812), in which he advocated the so-called "primitive gospel hypothesis," which states that behind the synoptics lay a lost Aramaic gospel record.
93. Heinrich Paulus, *Leben Jesu als Grundlage einer reinen Geschichte des Urchristenthums,* 2 vols. (1828), was supported by his *Exegetisches Handbuch Über die drei ersten Evangelien,* 3 vols. (1830-1833).

offended Pietists by doubting biblical miracles and by reducing the stories of the birth, resurrection, and ascension of Christ to myths. The employment of myths was De Wette's attempt to absolve the bibilical writers from charges of lunacy and imbalance by contending that they prosaically turned metaphor and allegory into fact as they wrote.

David Friedrich Strauss (1808-1874)

David F. Strauss, another German theologian, studied under Baur, Schleiermacher, and Georg F. W. Hegel. In his famous *Leben Jesu* (1835-1836) the "myth theory" was applied to the gospel records. Denying the historical foundation of all supernatural elements in the gospels, Strauss assigned them to an unintentionally created legend ("myth") developed between the death of Christ and the time the gospels were written in the second century. Strauss saw the growth of primitive Christianity in light of the so-called Hegelian dialectic. He essentially negated Christianity in favor of scientific materialism while denying human immortality in his final work, *The Old Faith and the New* (1873). His impact on all subsequent scholarship in German Protestant theology has been profound.[94]

Karl Heinrich Graf (1815-1869), Abraham Kuenen (1828-1891), and Julius Wellhausen (1844-1918)

Graf, Kuenen, and Wellhausen picked up on the notion of Spinoza, who "proposed Ezra as the final composer of the Torah. Although this suggestion was largely ignored by writers during his own generation, it constituted a remarkable anticipation of the final formulation of the documentary hypothesis by Graf, Keunen, and Wellhausen in the latter half of the nineteenth century."[95] The documentary hypothesis had its beginning with Jean Astruc; it moved into its next stage of development with Eichhorn's *Einleitung* (1780-1783); and its third stage was reached with De Wette's *Dissertation* (1805) and *Beiträge zur Einleitung* (1806), with Hermann Hupfeld's epoch-making work *Die Quellen der Genesis* [*The Source of Genesis*] being published in 1853. Graf added to that work with his own efforts to show that the priestly code in the Pentateuch was distinct from and later than Deuteronomy itself (1866). Abraham Keunen refined Graf's work in *De Godsdienst van Israel* [*The Religion of Israel*] (1869).[96] The stage was set for Wellhausen's important contributions, *Die Komposition des Hexateuchs* [*The Composition*

94. Cross and Livingstone, eds. *The Oxford Dictionary of the Christian Church*, pp. 1313-14.
95. Gleason L. Archer, Jr., *A Survey of Old Testament Introduction*, p. 81.
96. Karl H. Graf, *De Godsdienst van Israel tot den Ondergang van den Goodschen Staat*, 2 vols. Published in 1869-70 at Haarlem, it was later translated into English and published as a part of the Hibbert Lectures under the title *National Religions and Universal Religion*, 3 vols. (London, 1882).

of the Hexateuch] (1876), and *Prolegomena zur Geschichte Israels* [*Introduction to the History of Israel*] (1878). Gleason Archer observes that

> Although Wellhausen contributed no innovations to speak of, he restated the documentary theory with great skill and persuasiveness, supporting the JEDP sequence upon an evolutionary basis. This was the age in which Charles Darwin's *Origin of Species* was capturing the allegiance of the scholarly and scientific world, and the theory of development from primitive animism to sophisticated monotheism as set forth by Wellhausen and his followers fitted admirably into Hegelian dialecticism (a prevalent school in contemporary philosophy) and Darwinian evolutionism. The age was ripe for the documentary theory, and Wellhausen's name became attached to it as the classical exponent of it. The impact of his writings soon made itself felt throughout Germany . . . and found increasing acceptance in both Great Britain and America.[97]

Higher Criticism Since Wellhausen (1918-Present)

The publication of Wellhausen's *Introduction to the History of Israel* marks the beginning of the triumph of the *Religionsgeschichte* ("history of religions") approach to Old Testament studies over the next four decades. In England William Robertson Smith, *The Old Testament and the Jewish Church* (1881), introduced the Wellhausen view to the public, whereas Samuel R. Driver, *Introduction to the Literature of the Old Testament* (1891), gave the documentary hypothesis its classical English formulation and George Adam Smith (1856-1942) applied the approach to the Old Testament prophets in his contribution to the *Expositor's Bible,* edited by W. R. Nicoll (1887ff). In the United States the most notable advocates of the new school were Charles Augustus Briggs (1841-1913), *The Higher Criticism of the Hexateuch* (1893) and his collaborator Henry Preserved Smith (1847-1927).[98]

During the twentieth century the general outlines of the Wellhausian theory continued to be taught in most nonconservative institutions, although some uncertainties were expressed concerning the comparative dating of the "documents" by W. O. E. Osterley and T. H. Robinson, *Introduction to the Books of the Old Testament* (1934), and other documents were identified. In general, however, such advocates as Julius A. Bewer, *Literature of the Old Testament* (1922), Robert H. Pfeiffer, *Introduction to the Old Testament*

97. Archer, *A Survey of Old Testament Introduction,* p. 87.
98. See Roger R. Nicole, "Introduction" to Archibald A. Hodge and Benjamin B. Warfield, *Inspiration;* pp. vi-xiv. Also see Gerhard Hasel, *Old Testament Theology: Basic Issues in the Current Debate,* pp. 29-30.

(1941, 1948), and others adhered to Wellhausen's theory. No other systematic account of the origin and development of the Old Testament has commanded the general acceptance of the scholarly world. Nevertheless, vigorous reaction to the documentary hypothesis, which undermines the unity of the Old Testament, and additional developments in Old Testament studies have culminated in the provocative challenge to the documentary hypothesis by Isaac M. Kikawada and Arthur Quinn.[99]

The first signs of a serious invasion of the rationalistic spirit into New Testament studies also came from Germany through the writings of Schleiermacher, Eichhorn, and the more radical criticism of F. C. Baur (1792-1860) at Tübingen. Baur reduced the authentic Pauline Epistles to four (Romans, 1 and 2 Corinthians, and Galatians) and denied the genuineness of most other New Testament books. Although his critical opinions fell into disrepute with the rejection of his historical reconstruction and presuppositions, other critics began from equally tenuous presuppositions. David Strauss, *The Life of Jesus* (1835), approached the gospel narratives in the belief that much of the material was mythical. His views were not acclaimed by contemporaries, but they have played an important role in subsequent developments. Most critical of all nineteenth century scholars were the Dutch radical critics W. C. van Manen and P. W. Schmiedel, who denied the authenticity of all the Pauline Epistles and ended in complete skepticism. Against such a background of critical scholarship, conservative scholars consistently upheld the authenticity of the text.[100]

During the past century many critical scholars have concentrated on seeking literary sources. Their most effective outlet has been in the liberal school that dominated the theological scene at the turn of the century under the leadership of Heinrich Julius Holtzmann (1832-1910), Adolf Harnack (1851-1930), Albert Schweitzer (1875-1965), and others. Two of the most dominating figures in New Testament studies in the first half of the twen-

99. Isaac M. Kikawada and Arthur Quinn, *Before Abraham Was: The Unity of Genesis 1-11*. Also see Gleason Archer, Jr., *A Survey of Old Testament Introduction*, pp. 87-88; Gerhard F. Hasel, *Old Testament Theology: Basic Issues in the Current Debate;* Meredith G. Kline, *The Structure of Biblical Authority;* Sid Z. Leiman, *The Canonization of Hebrew Scripture: The Talmudic and Midrashic Evidence;* Roger Beckwith, *The Old Testament Canon of the New Testament Church and Its Background in Early Judaism;* R. K. Harrison, *Introduction to the Old Testament*.

100. Donald Guthrie, "The Historical and Literary Criticism of the New Testament," pp. 439-41, in Frank E. Gaebelein, gen. ed., *The Expositor's Bible Commentary,* vol. 1, *Introductory Articles: General, Old Testament, New Testament*. Also see Gerhard F. Hasel, *New Testament Theology: Basic Issues in the Current Debate*, pp. 28-53.

tieth century have been Karl Barth (1886-1968) and Rudolf Bultmann (1884-1976).[101]

In the 1960s, two newer movements grew out of Bultmann's approach as they moved away from his historical skepticism. These "post-Bultmannians" went beyond his hermeneutic, particularly his adoption of the existentialism of the earlier Heidegger to criticize Bultmann's understanding of the way language functions in their pursuit of "new quest" and redaction criticism. Representatives of "new quest" seek to support some aspect of the historical as authentic without returning to the historical Jesus of the old liberal school. Among the leading "new quest" spokesmen are Ernst Käsemann, Gunther Bornkamm, and Ernst Fuchs.[102] The diversity of theories proposed by these critics have little in common, and they do not instill confidence in their quest. Redaction criticism has arisen directly out of form criticism and focuses attention on the evangelists as writers. Several German scholars, icluding Gunther Bornkamm, Willi Marxsen (who coined the term *Redaktionsgeschichte,* "form history"), Hans Conzelmann, and Ernst Haenchen, have devoted attention to Matthew, Mark, Luke, and Acts respectively. Their approach is much more positive than its earlier forebears, but that issue will be pursued in chapter 25.[103]

In recent times all of these trends have had their impact on the traditional doctrines of revelation, inspiration, and the authority of Scripture. Some evangelical scholars have attempted to incorporate various insights into the framework of the historical-grammatical method of interpreting. Others have not been able to avoid the adoption of an erroneous or untenable position in their

101. See Heinrich Johann Holtzmann, *Einleitung in das Neue Testament;* Adolf Harnack, *Das Wesen des Christentums* [*What Is Christianity?*]; Albert Schweitzer, *Von Reimarus zu Wrede* [*The Quest for the Historical Jesus*]; Karl Barth, *Romerbrief* [*The Epistle to the Romans*] and *Kirchliche Dogmatik* [*Church Dogmatics*]; and Rudolf Bultmann, *Die Geschichte der synoptischen Tradition* [*History of the Synoptic Tradition*], and *Theologie des Neuen Testaments* [*Theology of the New Testament*]. See Donald Guthrie, "The Historical and Literary Criticism of the New Testament," pp. 447-48; Gerhard F. Hasel, *New Testament Theology,* pp. 53-71. For a comprehensive survey of the liberal approach to this issue see Charles C. Anderson, *Critical Quests of Jesus.* See Carl. F. H. Henry, ed., *Jesus of Nazareth: Saviour and Lord,* for articles relating to the theological confusion following the breakdown of Bultmannianism.

102. See Carl F. H. Henry, "Cross-currents in Contemporary Theology," pp. 1-22, Ralph P. Martin, "The New Quest of the Historical Jesus," pp. 23-45, and Gordon H. Clark, "Bultmann's Historiography," pp. 213-23, in Carl F. H. Henry, ed., *Jesus of Nazareth: Saviour and Lord*; Guthrie, "The Historical and Literary Criticism of the New Testament," p. 448. Also see Ernst Käsemann, *Essays on New Testament Themes,* trans. W. J. Montague; Gunther Bornkamm, *Jesus of Nazareth,* trans. I. and T. Mchuskey with J. M. Robinson; Ernst Fuchs, *Studies on the Historical Jesus*; Martin Dibelius, *From Tradition to Gospel,* trans. B. L. Woolf.

103. Guthrie, "The Historical and Literary Criticism of the New Testament," pp. 448-49; Gerhard F. Hasel, *New Testament Theology,* pp. 53-71. Also see Gunther Bornkamm, G. Barth, and H. J. Held, *Tradition and Interpretation in Matthew,* trans. P. Scott; Willi Marxsen, *Mark the Evangelist,* trans. R. A. Harrisville; Hans Conzelmann, *The Theology of Luke,* trans. G. Buswell; Enst Haenchen, *Acts of the Apostles,* trans. B. Noble and G. Shinn, revised by R. McL. Wilson.

endeavor. For many of them an extensive use of the dialectical method is the vehicle employed to achieve their scholarly synthesis.[104]

Summary and Conclusion

Various creed-forms and confessional statements from across the broad and diverse ranks of Christianity indicate that Christians officially adhered to the traditional doctrine of the inspiration and authority of Scripture well into the twentieth century. Nevertheless, between the early seventeenth and the early twentieth centuries a series of changes in the climates of opinion gradually prepared the ground for a direct and open confrontation between religion and science over the issues of revelation, inspiration, and the authority of Scripture. As the impact of the rationalism of the Enlightenment tradition made itself felt on the question of authority (religious or otherwise), changes in the climates of opinion began to undermine the traditional doctrine of Scripture both within and without Christian churches. Sometimes those changes resulted from a reaction to the cold, formal orthodoxy that had a stultifying effect on personal experience. At other times they were the result of well-intended but incorrect attempts to defend the Christian faith in the face of challenges from science and philosophy.

On occasion doubt about the authority of Scripture would turn to skepticism and denial of Scripture when the methods of science were rigorously applied to specific problems of special revelation. When unsatisfactory results were achieved by those methods, the issue often yielded to the serious question of whether there were any revelation at all. Yet the haunting question remained: Had God indeed spoken to man through revelation? Some responded by taking refuge in human reason and declaring that they could not know with certainty that Scripture was revealed and inspired by God and authoritative. Others resorted to their subjective experience as the basis of their authority. Still others modified their faith into a virtual civil religion by compartmentalizing religion and culture. Finally, there were those whose emphasis on everyday life needs and concerns caused them to stress the need for a "leap of faith" in an attempt to avoid the paradoxical issue of authority in the realms of fact and value. In view of this conundrum, it is hardly unexpected that modern man entered into the twentieth century without a basic commitment to the traditional doctrine of the inspiration and authority of Scripture as the very Word of God.

104. As the previous discussion suggests, the dialectical method is widely used in the works of post-Wellhausian scholars. The "dialectical method" is employed extensively by Clark Pinnock, *The Scripture Principle* (San Francisco: Harper & Row, 1984), pp. 74, 106, 177, 184-86, 193-99. The impact of critical methodology is evident in the change of position by Bernard Ramm, *Protestant Biblical Interpretation: A Textbook of Hermeneutics*. 3d rev. ed. For examples of the widespread use of the dialectical method see Gerhard Hasel, *Old Testament Theology* and *New Testament Theology;* James Barr, *Holy Scripture* (Philadelphia: Westminster, 1983); Brevard S. Childs, *Introduction to the Old Testament as Scripture* (Philadelphia: Fortress, 1979) and *Introduction to the New Testament as Canon* (Philadelphia: Fortress, 1984); Robert K. Johnston, *The Use of the Bible in Theology* (Atlanta: John Knox, 1985).

10

Contemporary Theories of Revelation and Inspiration

Biblical scholars in the twentieth century continue to advocate the various views of Scripture held in the preceding centuries. But they have also produced some unique deviations of their own. In the following discussion, six different contemporary views will be investigated: liberal, fundamentalist, neo-orthodox, liberal-evangelical, neo-evangelical, and evangelical. The following discussion utilizes Protestant representatives. But similar examples may be found with Roman Catholicism.[1]

The Liberal View of Scripture

Following in the wake of Friedrich Schleiermacher (1768-1834) and other nineteenth-century liberal theologians, the twentieth-century liberal view of Scripture rests heavily on the consequences of negative higher criticism discussed in chapter 9. Two of their number reflect the liberal view of Scripture.

Harold DeWolfe (1905-)

Harold DeWolfe is typical of the old liberal view of Scripture. He says, "Strictly speaking, the Bible itself is not the pure Word of God."[2] For "it is evident that the Bible is a collection of intensely human documents." In fact, "most of the events described are activities of obviously fallible human beings. Many passages contradict one another or well-established knowledge. Many of the moral and religious ideas, especially in the more ancient documents, are distinctly sub-Christian."[3]

According to DeWolfe, "the writing of the Bible as a whole was accomplished by an extraordinary stimulation and elevation of the powers of men

1. See Bruce Vawter, *Biblical Inspiration*, and especially James T. Burtchaell, *Catholic Theories of Biblical Inspiration Since 1810*.
2. Harold DeWolfe, *The Case for Theology in Liberal Perspectives*, p. 17; see also Norman L. Geisler, *Decide for Yourself: How History Views the Bible*, pp. 57-61.
3. Harold DeWolfe, *A Theology of the Living Church*, p. 73.

who devoutly yielded themselves to God's will and sought, often with success unparalleled elsewhere, to convey truth useful to the salvation of men and nations." However, "the human fallibility of the Bible does not preclude the possibility of its divine inspiration nor of its unmatched moral and religious authority." But despite some inspired truths contained within Scripture, much is in error. For "while we are treating the fallibility of the Scriptures we must note that Jesus unhesitatingly and repeatedly sets Old Testament teaching at naught."[4]

DeWolfe believes that "some degree of accommodation to culture seems inevitable unless Christian teaching is to become a mere irrelevant echoing of ancient creeds—which were themselves products of some accommodation to Hellenic thought."[5] Thus "to the intelligent student who is more concerned with seeking out and declaring the truth than with maintaining a dogma it must be apparent that the Bible is by no means infallible." "In regard to many facts of minor importance there are obvious contradictions within the Bible."[6] In view of these errors, "the correcting of the text and the historical locating of the writing are but different aspects of one great task."[7]

It is clear that DeWolfe's rejection of much of Scripture is based on his anti-supernaturalistic bias. He declares,

> The insistence of some conservative Christians on a Biblical literalism that is rationally indefensible and an appeal based on the "proofs" of prophecy and miracles, in defiance of the natural sciences and the new historical understanding of Biblical times, needlessly drives from the Christian faith intelligent young people.[8]

The only sense in which DeWolfe is willing to speak of "miracles" is as a revealing event of nature. For "if a miracle were to be properly called a special revelation it could not be so-called because of its being any more an act of God than are the ordinary processes of nature, but only because it was more revealingly meaningful to men."[9]

In brief, the Bible merely contains the Word of God, along with many errors. One must use human reason and the "spirit of Christ" to determine which parts of Scripture are true and which are false. DeWolfe believes, of course, that the miracles recorded did not actually occur.

Harry Emerson Fosdick (1878-1969)

One of the most popular of the old liberals was the famous preacher of the

4. Ibid., pp. 76, 75, 73.
5. DeWolfe, *The Case for Theology,* p. 58.
6. Ibid., pp. 68-69.
7. Ibid., pp. 51-52.
8. Ibid., p. 43.
9. Ibid., p. 66.

Riverside Church in New York, Harry Emerson Fosdick. He is forthright in declaring that "the liberal emphasis rests upon experience; we regard that, rather than mental formulas, as the permanent continuum of the Gospel."[10] The Bible is not an absolute guide, for "any idea of inspiration which implies equal value in the teachings of Scripture, or inerrancy in its statements, or conclusive infallibility in its ideas, is irreconcilable with such facts as this book presents." What makes it necessary to reject the Bible? "The vast enlargement of the physical cosmos, the evolutionary origin of man, materialistic theories which endeavor to explain him, brutality of social life involving low conceptions of him, the innumerable masses of men such that old cynicisms gain new force ... tend in many minds to undo what the Hebrew-Christian development did."[11] However, "we are saved by it [biblical criticism] from the old and impossible attempt to harmonize the Bible with itself, to make it speak with unanimous voice, to resolve its conflicts and contradictions into a strained and artificial unity."[12]

Fosdick acknowledges the source of the modern liberal rejection of the Bible. "Get back to the nub of their difficulty and you find it in Biblical categories which they no longer believe—miracles, demons, fiat creation, apocalyptic hopes, eternal hell, or ethical conscience." This should be no surprise to us. For "it is impossible that a Book written two to three thousand years ago should be used in the twentieth century A.D. without having some of its forms of thought and speech translated into modern categories."[13]

Without Scripture as an unwavering authority, Fosdick falls back on human reason. For "the man who ministers ... must have an intelligible way of handling the Bible. He must have gone through the searching criticism to which the last few generations have subjected the Scriptures and be able to understand and enter into the negations that have resulted." There is one thing which reasons gleans from Scripture that is always useful: "So long as a man knows the whole road and judges every step of it by the spirit of Christ, who is its climax, he can use it all."[14]

But even Fosdick had second thoughts about his own radical view of Scripture. Near the end of his life he wrote,

> Today, however, looking back over forty years of ministry, I see an outstanding difference between then and now with regard to what is standard and who must do the adjusting. What man in his senses can now call our modern civilization standard? It is not Christ's message that needs to be accommodated to this mad scene; it is this mad scene into which our civilization has collapsed that needs to

10. Harry Emerson Fosdick, *Modern Use of the Bible,* p. 183; see also Geisler, *Decide for Yourself,* pp. 61-67.
11. Harry Emerson Fosdick, *A Guide to Understanding the Bible,* pp. xiv, 97.
12. Fosdick, *Modern Use of the Bible,* p. 24.
13. Ibid., pp. 5, 29.
14. Ibid., pp. 5-6, 30.

> be judged and saved by Christ's message. This is the most significant change distinguishing the beginning of my ministry from now. Then we were trying to accommodate Christ to our scientific civilization; now we face the desperate need of accommodating our scientific civilization to Christ.[15]

Shubert Ogden (1928-)

Working out of the background of Alfred North Whitehead (1861-1947) and Process Theology, Shubert Ogden is representative of the many new liberal thinkers who do not view the Scriptures as the verbally inspired Word of God. Instead they view the Bible as an errant human book. Ogden recognizes but rejects the view that "what the Bible says, God says." He writes:

> In Protestant orthodoxy, then, the developed doctrine of the verbal inspiration of the canonical writings entailed the assertion of their uniform authority, and thus made it possible to claim without qualification that "what Scripture says, God says." But, with the emergence of Protestant liberal theology and its commitment to the historical-critical method, as well as its insistence that Scripture neither is nor can be a sufficient authorization for the meaning and truth of theological assertions, this claim was abandoned, never again to be made by those who have led in the subsequent important developments in Protestant theology.[16]

Ogden's liberal theology is dependent on negative higher criticism. Thus he believes that " 'the historic, apostolic Christ,' just like 'the historic biblical Christ,' is every bit as historical as 'the so-called historical Jesus,' and to this extent there is no escaping the dependence of theology on the work of the historians." In fact, Ogden insists, "historical-critical inquiry is *theologically* necessary and legitimate."[17]

In his claim that the locus of the canon "cannot be the writings of the New Testament as such but can only be the earliest traditions of Christian witness accessible to us today by historical-critical analysis of those writings," Ogden rejects the New Testament as the canon. Rather, he believes "the canon of the church, and hence also the highest authority for theology, must now be located in what form critics generally speak of as the earliest layer of the Synoptic tradition, or what Marxsen in particular refers to as 'the Jesus-kerygma.' "[18]

Given his acceptance of negative higher criticism, it is not surprising to hear Ogden claim that "none of the New Testament writings, in its present form, was authored by an apostle or one of his disciples."[19] Ogden believes

15. Harry Emerson Fosdick, *A Great Time to Be Alive*, pp. 201-2.
16. Shubert Ogden, "The Authority of Scripture for Theology," *Interpretation* 30, no. 3 (July 1976):257.
17. Ibid., p. 256.
18. Ibid., p. 258.
19. Ibid., p. 251.

the norm for the church is not the New Testament but, rather, the *apostolic witness*. "This witness is, of course, found in the New Testament, but it is not identical with the New Testament. In the strict sense only the apostolic testimony to Jesus as the Divine revelation can be described as canonical." In rejecting the divine authority of Scripture, Ogden claims,

> We today must indeed recognize a higher theological authority than the canon of Scripture, and hence can no longer maintain that Scripture is in some sense the sole primary authority for Christian theology. The theological authority of Scripture, great as it may be, is nevertheless a limited authority, in that it could conceivably be greater than it is—namely, as great as that of the apostolic witness by which it itself is and is to be authorized."[20]

Besides rejecting the Bible as the supreme authority for faith, Ogden believes it has no intrinsic authority at all.[21] For him, the Bible has only a functional but not an essential authority. It is an authority insofar as it brings Christ to us. The Bible is "perfect" only "with respect to the end of man's salvation, and so to witnessing to all that is necessary to the attainment of that end."[22]

Process theologians do not believe God is infinite, all-powerful, or all-knowing. Nor do they believe the Bible contains infallible predictions about the future. As Lewis Ford observes,

> Divine providence cannot be understood as the unfolding of a predetermined course of events. Prophecy is not prediction, but the proclamation of divine intent, dependent for its realization upon the continued presence of those conditions which called forth that intent and upon the emergence of the means whereby that intent may be realized. ... God becomes the great improvisor and opportunist seeking at every turn to elicit his purpose from every situation: if not by the hand of Sennacherib, then by the hand of Nebuchadnezzar.[23]

Revelation, then, is not supernatural but only a divine "lure," or an attempt to persuade men. Indeed, as Ogden wrote, "*what* Christian revelation reveals to man is nothing new, since such truths as it makes explicit must already be known to him implicitly in every moment of existence."[24] Another Process theologian suggests that revelation is akin to physical resonance. He writes, "In keeping with Whitehead's premise to start from human experience in the world, I propose as a model for revelation an analogy with the physical phenomenon of resonance." He describes this resonance as "a physical phenomenon shown by a vibrating system, which responds with maximum am-

20. Ibid., pp. 251-52.
21. Ibid., p. 246.
22. Ibid., p. 245.
23. Lewis Ford, "Biblical Recital and Process Philosophy," p. 206.
24. Shubert Ogden, "On Revelation," in *Our Common History as Christians: Essays in Honor of Albert C. Outler.*

plitude under the action of a force applied with a frequency that is a natural frequency of the vibrating body."[25]

Not only does God not inform man in advance what will occur, God must be informed Himself. As one Process theologian frankly admits, "God, as it were, has to wait with bated breath until the decision is made, not simply to find out what the decision was, but perhaps even to have the situation clarified by virtue of the decision of that concrete occasion."[26] So for neo-liberals in the Process tradition, like Shubert Ogden, the Bible has no divine authority nor infallible predictions. It is a human document with only instrumental authority to bring about man's salvation.

A Fundamentalist View of Inspiration: John R. Rice (1895-1980)

The term *fundamentalist* covers a wide variety of beliefs regarding inspiration. Many contemporary theologians who call themselves fundamentalists accept the same view discussed later as the "evangelical" position. Both groups trace their roots back to Hodge and Warfield. There are others, however, whose positions are more conservative. John R. Rice was one of the best representatives of such a view.

The essence of Rice's position was that the Bible was *verbally dictated* by God. "All Scripture is 'God-breathed,' that is, the Scripture itself is breathed out from God."[27] And, he asserts, "if God gave all the words in the Bible, then is not that dictation?"[28] Rice hastened to say that it was not *mechanical dictation;* it was simply verbal dictation. His response to the identity of these two positions into one was to say, "This charge of 'mechanical dictation' against fundamental Bible believers is dishonest pretense."[29] After all, "a secretary is not ashamed to take dictation from man. Why should a prophet be ashamed to take dictation from God?"[30]

According to Rice, saying the Bible is verbally dictated does not mean it has no human dimension. "Certainly we admit gladly that there is a 'human side of the Bible—its style, language, composition, history and culture.' "[31] Just how did God get a word-for-word, verbal dictation recorded and yet use

25. Jerry Korsmeyer, "A Resonance Model for Revelation," p. 195.
26. Bernard Loomer, "A Response to David R. Griffin," p. 365.
27. John R. Rice, *Our God-Breathed Book—The Bible,* pp. 49.
28. Ibid., p. 286. A verbal dictation view is held by Muslims, who believe that the Koran was given by dictation from Gabriel to Muhammad out of the eternal book in heaven. See *The Glorious Koran,* an explanatory translation by M. M. Pickthall, Surah II, pp. 97-98. See Gleason L. Archer, Jr., *A Survey of Old Testament Introduction,* "Appendix 2: Anachronisms and Historical Inaccuracies in the Koran," pp. 498-500. A mechanical verbal dictation view may also be found in Occultism and Spiritism. In view of this see Archer, "Appendix 3: Anachronisms and Historical Inaccuracies in the Mormon Scriptures," pp. 501-4.
29. Ibid., p. 265.
30. Ibid., p. 287.
31. Ibid., p. 141.

the different styles of the Biblical writers? "God planned all that so that each one was chosen before he was born and fitted to be the instrument God wanted to use. The varying styles are all God's styles in the Bible. God made the men and made the styles, and used them according to plan."[32]

So "the Bible does not simply in some places 'contain the Word of God'; the Bible *is* the Word of God." That means the Bible is "absolutely correct when it speaks on matters of history or geography." Inerrancy does not extend to every copy of the Bible. "The original autographs of the Scriptures were infallibly correct."[33] Thus Rice rejected all higher criticism of the Bible, saying, "Higher criticism tends to sit in judgment on the Bible and let poor, sinning, frail, ignorant, mortal men pass judgment on the Word of God."[34] Instead of a fallible, mutilated word from God, Rice held to a verbally dictated, inerrant Book—the Bible.

The Neo-orthodox View of Inspiration

The orthodox believe the Bible *is* God's Word; liberals believe the Bible *contains* God's Word; neo-orthodox hold that the Bible *becomes* God's Word. Three names stand out in the rise and spread of the modern neo-orthodox view of inspiration: Karl Barth, Emil Brunner, and John Baillie.

Karl Barth (1886-1968)

Karl Barth did not believe "that the Word of God is tied to the Bible. On the contrary . . . the Bible is tied to the Word of God." Actually, for Barth the Bible "only 'holds,' encloses, limits and surrounds it: that is the indirectness of the identity of revelation and the Bible." Thus the human words "are the instruments by which [the Bible] aims at becoming a Word which is apprehended by men and therefore a Word which justifies and sanctifies men." The Bible "as such, of course, . . . is only a sign. Indeed, it is the sign of a sign, i.e., of the prophetic-apostolic witness of the revelation as the primary sign of Jesus Christ."[35] Thus " 'what stands there,' in the pages of the Bible, is the witness to the *Word of God,* the Word of God in this testimony of the Bible. Just how far it stands there, however, is a fact that demands unceasing discovery, interpretation, and recognition."[36]

God reveals Himself in acts, not in words. Hence, "To say 'the Word of God' is to say the work of God. It is not to contemplate a state or fact but to watch an event, and an event which is relevant to us, an event which is an act of God,

32. Ibid., p. 206.
33. Ibid., p. 88.
34. Ibid., p. 136.
35. Karl Barth, *Church Dogmatics,* 1:153; 1:492; 1:1223; 1:583; 1:527.
36. Karl Barth, *Evangelical Theology: An Introduction,* p. 36; see Geisler, *Decide for Yourself,* pp. 77-81.

an act of God which rests on a free decision."[37] According to Barth, the Bible is not a revelation but an *instrument* of divine disclosure. The human words of Scripture "are the instruments by which [the Bible] aims at becoming a Word which is apprehended by men and therefore a Word which justifies and sanctifies men, by which it aims at executing upon men the grace of God which is its content."[38] Indeed, the Bible is not the Word of God; it *becomes* the Word of God to the believer as Christ is revealed through it. For "by the Holy Spirit it *became* and *will become* to the Church a witness to divine revelation."[39]

The Word of God for Barth is personal, not propositional. It is Christ. The Bible is simply a witness to Christ. Christ is God's revelation; the Bible is only a fallible human record of that revelation. According to Barth, in the Bible "there are obvious overlappings and contradictions—e.g., between the Law and the prophets, between John and the Synoptists, between Paul and James." For "the prophets and apostles as such ... were real, historical men as we are, and therefore sinful in their action, and capable and actually guilty of error in their spoken and written word." And the "vulnerability of the Bible, i.e., its capacity for error, also extends to its religious or theological content."[40] In short, the Bible is an errant human instrument used by God as a witness to His divine Word who is Christ.

Emil Brunner (1889-1966)

Emil Brunner believed "the orthodox view of the Bible ... is an absolutely hopeless state of affairs."[41] For "literary criticism of the Bible brought to light the thousands of contradictions and human characteristics with which the Old and New Testaments abound. In this way the authority of the Bible was completely overthrown."[42] Hence, "Scripture is not a *formal* authority which demands belief in all it contains from the outset, but it is an *instrumental* authority." And "the Scriptures possess this authority because they are the *primary witness* to the revelation of God in Jesus Christ." In fact, "we believe in the Scriptures because, and in so far as they teach Christ. The authority of Scripture is not formal but material: Christ, the revelation."[43] For Brunner, to claim the Bible is infallible is to make it a "paper pope."

The authority of the Bible is identified by Brunner with the witness of the Holy Spirit. For "the word in Scripture, Christ, becomes the same as the word in the heart, the Holy Spirit." In fact, "there is no such thing as revelation-in-

37. Karl Barth, *Church Dogmatics,* 1:527.
38. Ibid., 1:223.
39. Ibid., 1.2:457.
40. Ibid., 1.2:509; 1.2:529; 1:509.
41. Emil Brunner, *Revelation and Reason,* p. 291; see Geisler, ibid., pp. 81-89.
42. Emil Brunner, *God and Man,* p. 36.
43. Emil Brunner, *The Christian Doctrine of God,* pp. 110, 45, 110.

itself, because revelation consists always of the fact that something is revealed to *me*." Thus, "revelation is . . . an act of God, an event involving two parties; it is a personal address."[44] Hence, "this 'revelation' is not a 'Word' but a Person—a human life fully visible within history."[45]

Brunner sees his view as essentially the same as Barth's, saying, "Fundamentally, Karl Barth's *Dogmatik* takes the same position: 'The Bible is not a book of sacred oracles; it is not an organ of direct communication. It is real witness.' " Brunner admits that "the doctrine of Verbal Inspiration was already known to pre-Christian Judaism . . . and was probably also taken over by Paul and the rest of the Apostles." He also says, "Calvin is already moving away from Luther toward the doctrine of Verbal Inspiration. His *doctrine* of the Bible is entirely the traditional, formally authoritative view."[46]

In addition, Brunner notes that "from the end of the sixteenth century onwards there was no other 'principle of Scripture' than this formal authoritarian one." Thus, "whatever development took place after this culminated in the most strict and most carefully formulated doctrine of Verbal Inspiration which is characteristic of orthodoxy proper—Lutheran as well as Reformed.[47]

Despite his accurate portrayal of the historic roots of the orthodox doctrine of inspiration, Brunner overconfidently asserts, "The orthodox doctrine of Verbal Inspiration has been finally destroyed. It is clear that there is no connection between it and scientific research and honesty: we are forced to make a decision for or against this view."[48] Thus, "we perceive that the labors of historical critics are . . . a help for the right understanding of the Word of God." Higher criticism "has pointed out various contradictions in the book of Acts, and has discovered various inconsistencies in the assignment of certain definite writings to well-known Apostles as their authors."[49]

John Baillie (1886-1960)

John Baillie and his brother Donald MacPherson Baillie[50] (1887-1954) were prominent Scottish theologians and ecumenists who reflect neo-orthodox developments in the English-speaking world. Baillie's influential book *The Idea of Revelation in Recent Thought* (1956) was delivered as a series of lectures at Columbia University. In it he states, "The weakness of Protestant orthodoxy has been that it could show no convincing reason for insisting on the plenary nature of the divine assistance to the Scriptural authors while as

44. Brunner, *God and Man*, pp. 28, 32.
45. Emil Brunner, *The Christian Doctrine of God*, p. 23.
46. Ibid., pp. 113, 101, 111.
47. Ibid., p. 111.
48. Emil Brunner, *The Mediator*, p. 105.
49. Brunner, *Revelation and Reason*, pp. 292, 285.
50. Donald MacPherson Baillie, *God Was in Christ*, is regarded as one of the most significant statements of neo-orthodox Christology.

firmly denying it to the mind of the Church in later days."[51] This is why he compares and summarizes the positions of modern theologians about the impact of the doctrine of revelation in men's lives. In his work he stresses the existential nature of man's role in the revelatory process, opposes the notion of propositional revelation, which he confuses with mechanical dictation,[52] and suggests that revelation is essentially personal encounter in the present moment.[53] He criticizes the Roman Catholic and Protestant tradition for its "simple identification of divine revelation with Holy Scripture."[54]

In stating his case, Baillie presents an incorrect dichotomy between non-verbal encounters and dictation when he asserts, "The propositions on the Scriptural page express the response of human witnesses to divine events, not a miraculous divine dictation."[55] In addition to his failure to distinguish between revelation, inspiration, and interpretation (terms discussed in chapter 2), Baillie overstates the role of the human in the revelatory process as he correlates these elements with the broader concept of communication. He writes, "For the deepest difficulty felt about the equation of revelation with communicated truths is that it offers us something less than personal encounter and personal communion; and that difficulty is in no way relieved by the proposal to replace communicated truths by implanted images."[56] The fact of the matter is, as a linear model of communication[57] suggests, a revelation may be disclosed whether or not it is received or understood by another. Moreover, there is no need to reject propositional revelation or verbal plenary inspiration in an attempt to avoid the mechanical dictation theory of inspiration.

By overemphasizing the human role in the communication process, and by confusing the elements of that communication process, Baillie places the entire task of determining what is inspired on a totally subjective, fallible, and human level. He holds that "all true knowledge is knowledge which is determined not by the subject [God] but by the object [man]."[58] This relegates God to a secondary role governed by the human recipient who may or may not have a receptive disposition or who is otherwise unable to distinguish be-

51. John Baillie, *The Idea of Revelation in Recent Thought*, p. 112. Also see his discussion on pp. 29-30.
52. Ibid., pp. 36, 40.
53. Ibid., pp. 24, 30, 32-33, 39, 105, 107-8. Also see the discussion in chap. 9, which shows Baillie's place in the existential tradition.
54. Ibid., pp. 29-32.
55. Ibid., p. 36.
56. Ibid., p. 39.
57. A linear model of communication would include disclosure, transmission, discovery, and understanding. Simply because one does not understand a disclosed message does not mean that the message was undisclosed in the first place. Numerous reasons could cause a message disclosed by a subject not to be received or understood by its intended object.
58. John Baillie, *The Idea of Revelation*, p. 20, brackets supplied since the subject of the divine revelation in Baillie's discussion as in the present context is God and the object of it is man.

tween essential truth and that which is peripheral. He criticizes thirteenth-century Christians for their over-reverence of the Scriptures as he states,

> On the other hand, the intelligent reading of the Bible—"in the Spirit but with the mind also," and the reading of it so as to understand how it *Christum treibt* [conveys Christ], depends entirely on our ability to distinguish what is central from what is peripheral; to distinguish its unchanging truth from its clothing in the particular cultural and cosmological preconceptions of the times and places in which it was written; to distinguish between its essential message and its numerous imperfections—historical inaccuracies, inaccurate or conflicting reports, misquotations or misapplied quotations from the Old Testament in the New, and such like; and withal to distinguish the successive levels of understanding both within the Old Testament and in the transition from that to the New.[59]

Baillie approves of the statement by C. H. Dodd, who quotes several passages from Isaiah and says, "Any theory of inspiration of the Bible which suggests that we should recognize such utterances as authoritative for us stands self-condemned. They are relative to their age. But I think we should say more. They are false and they are wrong."[60] Even more candidly, when speaking of the inadequacy of the events portrayed in Scripture to reveal God, Baillie himself asserts, "I could not know that God had revealed Himself to the prophets and apostles through these events, unless through His revelation of Himself to them He were now revealing Himself to me. I could know indeed that they claimed to have received such a revelation, but I can know that their claim is justified only if, as I read what they say, I too find myself in the presence of God."[61] As Leon Morris rightly observes, for Baillie and others in his tradition, "The propositions laid down in Scripture are unimportant, even irrelevant. What matters is the encounter the man of faith has with God."[62] This view is hardly compatible with what the Bible has to say for itself, and what has been taught by Christians throughout church history.

To sum it up, the neo-orthodox view is that the Bible is a fallible human book. Nevertheless, it is the instrument of God's revelation to us, for it is a record of God's personal revelation in Christ. Revelation, however, is personal; the Bible is not a verbally inspired revelation from God. It is merely an errant human means through which one can encounter the personal revelation who is Christ. In itself it is not the Word of God: at best, the Bible only becomes the Word of God to the individual when he encounters Christ through it.

59. Ibid., p. 120.
60. C. H. Dodd, *The Authority of the Bible*, p. 128.
61. John Baillie, *The Idea of Revelation*, p. 105.
62. Leon Morris, *I Believe in Revelation*, p. 113.

A Liberal-Evangelical View of Inspiration: C. S. Lewis (1898-1963)

Clive Staples Lewis held a view of inspiration that technically speaking is neither orthodox nor neo-orthodox. Since it is not a typical liberal view or an evangelical position, it is dubbed by the paradoxical term *liberal-evangelical*. According to Lewis, "the voice of God [is heard] in the cursing Psalms through all the horrible distortions of the human medium." Lewis believed "the human qualities of the raw materials show through. Naivety, error, contradiction, even (as in the cursing Psalms) wickedness are not removed. The total result is not 'the Word of God' in the sense that every passage, in itself, gives impeccable science or history." In fact, he believed some sections of the Bible to be even anti-religious. He wrote, "Nor would I (now) willingly spare from my Bible something in itself so anti-religious as the nihilism of Ecclesiastes. We get there a clear, cold picture of man's life without God."[63] Many Old Testament events—including Adam, Job, Esther, and Jonah—are mythological; their truth only becomes fully historical in the New Testament. For "the Hebrews, like other people, had mythology: but as they were the chosen people so their mythology was the chosen mythology—the mythology chosen by God to be the vehicle of the earliest sacred truths, the first step in that process which ends in the New Testament where truth has become completely historical."[64]

Lewis rejected the orthodox view of inspiration: "One can respect, and at moments envy, both the Fundamentalist's view of the Bible and the Roman Catholic's view of the Church. But there is one argument which we should beware of using for either position: God must have done what is best, this is best, therefore God has done this."[65] He therefore rejected the position "that inspiration is a single thing in the sense that, if present at all, it is always present in the same mode and the same degree." However, "the overall operation of Scripture is to convey God's Word to the reader (he also needs his inspiration) who reads it in the right spirit, I fully believe."[66] Nevertheless, Lewis believed that in one sense all inspiring writings are inspired. For "If every good and perfect gift comes from the Father of lights then all true and edifying writings, whether in Scripture or not, must be *in some sense* inspired." The process of "inspiration may operate in a wicked man without his knowing it, and he can then utter the untruth he intends . . . as well as truth he does not intend."[67]

Conceiving of inspiration as a process of literary elevation that has been

63. C. S. Lewis, *Reflections on the Psalms,* pp. 111-12, 114-15. In this volume there are extensive quotations of Herman Bavinck. Also see Geisler, *Decide for Yourself,* pp. 91-102.
64. C. S. Lewis, *Miracles,* p. 139 n. 1.
65. Lewis, *Reflections on the Psalms,* p. 112.
66. Cited in M. J. Christensen, *C. S. Lewis on Scripture,* p. 199.
67. Ibid., pp. 98-99.

providentially guided by God, Lewis asserted: "When a series of such retelling turns a creation story of almost no religious significance into a story which achieves the idea of a transcendent Creator (as *Genesis* does), then nothing will make me believe that some of the re-tellers, or some one of them, has not been guided by God." For in that way, he writes, "something originally merely natural . . . will have been raised by God above itself, qualified by Him and compelled by Him to serve purposes which of itself it would not have served."[68] Like much of the liberal position, the view of inspiration held by Lewis operated on a model similar to that of theistic evolution.

> For long centuries God perfected the animal form [by natural processes] which was to become the vehicle of humanity and the image of Himself. . . . Then, in the fullness of time, God caused to descend upon this organism, both on its psychology and physiology, a new kind of consciousness which could say 'I' and 'me,' which could look upon itself as an object, which knew God.[69]

In like manner, Lewis believed that when the natural development of a pagan and Hebrew myth has been perfected it is taken over into the service of God and elevated to its edifying and sacred heights in New Testament truth. In that way, wrote Lewis, "I have therefore no difficulty in accepting, say, the view of those scholars who tell us that the account of Creation in *Genesis* is derived from earlier Semitic stories which were Pagan and mythical." But eventually the mythology of the Old Testament becomes history in the New Testament. Thus the resurrection of Christ is a historical and very important event, "but the value of others (e.g. the fate of Lot's wife) hardly at all. And the ones, whose historicity matters, are, as God's will, those where it is plain."[70] Thus Lewis strongly attacked

> a theology which denies the historicity of nearly everything in the Gospels to which Christian life and affections and thought have been fastened for nearly two millennia—which, either denies the miraculous altogether or, more strangely, after swallowing the camel of the Resurrection strains at such gnats as the feeding of the multitudes.[71]

In summation, Lewis believed in a fallible Bible that manifests varying degrees of inspiration. He saw a process of development whereby myth becomes history. God providentially guided the natural and errant literary productions of the past. Then, at the appropriate moment, God adopted that natural myth and elevated it into the service of the Word of God. He now speaks through it to the edification of believers.

68. Lewis, *Reflections on the Psalms,* p. 110.
69. Ibid., pp. 65, 110.
70. Cited by Clyde S. Kilby, *The Christian World of C. S. Lewis,* p. 153.
71. C. S. Lewis, *Christian Reflections,* p. 153.

The Neo-evangelical View of Inspiration

Much of the debate about the Bible among contemporary Christians relates to the differences between the evangelical and what has been called the "neo-evangelical" view of Scripture. Evangelicals believe in unlimited inspiration; neo-evangelicals hold that inspiration is limited to redemptive truths and does not guarantee the correctness of all scientific and historical statements. The neo-evangelicals feel comfortable with the term *infallibility*, but most evangelicals insist on the word *inerrancy* as well. One of the foremost spokesmen for the neo-evangelical view is Jack B. Rogers, who follows basically the later position of G. C. Berkouwer. Their writings provide a sample of the neo-evangelical view on inspiration.

G. C. Berkouwer (1903-   )

G. C. Berkouwer followed in the train of J. Herman Bavinck (1895-1964), the Dutch Calvinist theologian who wrote, "Scripture is therefore not the revelation itself, but the description, the record, from which the revelation can be known."[72] After being influenced further by Karl Barth, Berkouwer rejected his earlier orthodox view of the Bible for a more neo-othodox position. Fundamental to this view of Scripture is what Berkouwer insists is "the contrast noted frequently in Scripture between the Word of God and the words of men, between relying on God and relying on man." That is, the Bible is not the Word of God essentially; the Bible is only the Word of God confessionally. For "it is truly a *confession* that continues to be filled with expectation in listening to the many voices within the one voice in this Scripture."[73]

Berkouwer rejects the orthodox tendency "to interpret the God-breathed character in an abstract supernaturalistic and 'miraculous' manner." Rather than inspiration involving a supernatural interruption of the natural world, "this divine taking-into-service has an aspect of triumph and sovereignty, yet it does not erase the weakness of the human word nor its limitations." Thus, the human authors of Scripture are spoken of as "becoming bearers of God's Word." Hence, "the speech of men in prophecy is the way of the reliable testimony of God."[74] According to Berkouwer's view, "the Word became Scripture and as Scripture subjected itself to the fate of all writing." (Cf. I. Howard Marshall on the subject of inspiration, chap. 2 of this book.) Berkouwer believes the orthodox view of Scripture is "docetic" in that it denies the humanity of Scripture. For "in its eagerness to maintain Holy Scripture's divinity, [it] does not fully realize the significance of Holy Scripture as a prophetic-apostolic, and consequently human, testimony."[75]

72. Herman Bavinck, *Our Reasonable Faith: A Survey of Christian Doctrine*, trans. Henry Zylstra.
73. G. C. Berkouwer, *Holy Scripture*, pp. 240, 168.
74. Ibid., pp. 170, 206, 146.
75. Ibid., 99, 22.

Because the Bible is a fully human book it suffers the fate of all other human books—it is errant. This view "means a greater degree of naturalness in speaking of Scripture, with a view to its nature and purpose." Thus "formal problems of correctness (inerrancy alongside infallibility) disintegrate with such a naturalness." Hence, "the concept of error in the sense of incorrectness is obviously being used on the same level as the concept of erring in the sense of sin and deception." The "truth" of Scripture should be understood as its unswerving *purpose* to save. For Berkouwer, error is not simply a falsehood but it is an intentional misleading or deception. Berkouwer himself believes the Scriptures to be free from error in that sense. In this way "the authority of Scripture is in no way diminished because an ancient world view occurs in it; for it was not the purpose of Scripture to offer revealing information on that level."[76]

Berkouwer sees his view as representing "the transition from a more 'mechanical' to a more 'organic' view of Scripture."[77] For him "organic inspiration [is] the unfolding and application of the central fact of revelation, the incarnation of the Word."[78] Such a view rejects the idea that

> every book of it, every chapter of it, every word of it, every syllable of it, every letter of it, is the direct utterance of the Most High. This statement . . . disregards all nuances of Scripture (consider the Psalms, Job, Ecclesiastes), as though it were a string of divine or supernaturally revealed statements, ignoring the fact that God's Word has passed through humanity and has incorporated its service.[79]

It is not all the *content* of the Bible that is inspired truth but the saving *intent* of the Bible. "Scripture is central because of its nature and intent. For this Scripture is only referred to because its sense and intent is the divine message of salvation."[80] In short, the Bible is only an instrument and confessional revelation of Christ. It is not a verbal and propositional revelation. For Berkouwer the Bible has an inspired purpose, but not inerrant propositions.

Jack B. Rogers (1934-)

Jack Rogers translated Berkouwer's work into English, and his view of inspiration is substantially the same as Berkouwer's. Rogers says the concept "called 'organic inspiration,' drew attention to the fact that there is a center and a periphery to Scripture."[81] By that he means it is "possible to define the meaning of biblical inerrancy according to the Bible's saving purpose and

76. Ibid., pp. 182, 181.
77. Ibid., p. 11.
78. Ibid., p. 199.
79. Ibid., pp. 23-24.
80. Ibid., p. 147.
81. Jack B. Rogers and Donald K. McKim, *The Authority and Interpretation of the Bible: An Historical Approach,* p. 391. Also see Clark Pinnock, *The Scripture Principle,* pp. xviii, 110, 115.

taking into account the human forms through which God condescended to reveal himself."[82]

In the view of the "organic" nature of inspiration, "the purpose of the Bible is to warn against human sin and offer us God's salvation in Christ. Scripture infallibly achieves that purpose. We are called, not to argue Scripture's scientific accuracy, but to accept its saving message."[83] Thus "the central saving message of Scripture could be received in faith without waiting for scholarly reasons. The supporting material of Scripture, the human forms of culture and language, were open to scholarly investigation." So "in order to communicate effectively with human beings, God condescended, humbled, and accommodated himself to human categories of thought and speech."[84]

So for Rogers the orthodox claim to a factually inerrant Bible is wrong. "It is historically irresponsible to claim that for two thousand years Christians have believed that the authority of the Bible entails a modern concept of inerrancy in scientific and historical details." Rogers believes it is "irresponsible to claim that the old Princeton theology of Alexander, Hodge, and Warfield is the only legitimate evangelical, or Reformed, theological tradition in America." In fact Rogers says, "Augustine, Calvin, Rutherford, and Bavinck, for example, all specifically deny that the Bible should be looked to as an authority in matters of science. To claim them in support of a modern inerrancy theory is to trivialize their central concern that the Bible is our sole authority on salvation and the living of a Christian life." He also says, "Scripture was not to be used as a source of information in the sciences to refute what the scholars were discovering."[85]

In summary, for a neo-evangelical the Bible is a religious book, a book of salvation. Its purpose is to save and it is infallible in accomplishing that purpose. But it is not inerrant in all its statements. Only the saving "core" is true, not the cultural "husk" in which it is presented. Inspiration is dynamic and "organic." It does not guarantee the inerrancy of all historical and scientific statements in Scripture but only the infallibility of the saving purpose of Scripture.

The Evangelical View of Scripture

The modern evangelical position on Scripture is heir of the traditional, orthodox position of historic Christianity from biblical times to the present.[86] Mainline evangelicals from all major denominations and most smaller

82. Jack B. Rogers, *Biblical Authority,* p. 45. Pinnock identifies these as "incidental or culturally conditioned aspects," *The Scripture Principle,* p. 110.
83. Ibid., p. 46. Also see Pinnock, *The Scripture Principle,* pp. xviii, 110, 115.
84. Rogers and McKim, *Authority and Interpretation of the Bible,* pp. 393, 10.
85. Rogers, *Biblical Authority,* pp. 44-45, 34. Also see Pinnock, *The Scripture Principle,* pp. 76, 77, 78, 96, 101.
86. See chaps. 3, 4, 5, and 6 for the biblical perspective and chaps. 7, 8, and 9 for the history of the doctrine into the twentieth century. Chap. 8 traces the formal train of this position in the confessions and creeds of Christendom since the Reformation.

groups accept the verbal inspiration of Scripture, as well as its divine authority and consequent inerrancy. Perhaps the most united manifestation of this confession is the Chicago Statement on Scripture (1978) published by the International Council on Biblical Inerrancy. It is a good representation of the views of evangelical leaders of the last part of the twentieth century, including such noted leaders as James Boice, John Gerstner, Carl F. H. Henry, Kenneth Kantzer, Harold Lindsell, John Warwick Montgomery, J. I. Packer, Robert Preus, Earl Radmacher, Francis Schaeffer, R. C. Sproul, John Wenham, and numerous others.[87]

The "Chicago Statement" will serve as a summary of the contemporary evangelical view on the inspiration and inerrancy of the Bible. An official commentary on these articles was written by R. C. Sproul, and a book covering the major addresses was published.[88]

Articles of Affirmation and Denial

Article I

We affirm that the Holy Scriptures are to be received as the authoritative Word of God.

We deny that the Scriptures receive their authority from the Church, tradition, or any other human source.

Article II

We affirm that the Scriptures are the supreme written norm by which God binds the conscience, and that the authority of the Church is subordinate to that of Scripture.

We deny that Church creeds, councils, or declarations have authority greater than or equal to the authority of the Bible.

Article III

We affirm that the written Word in its entirety is revelation given by God.

We deny that the Bible is merely a witness to revelation, or only becomes revelation in encounter, or depends on the responses of men for its validity.

87. The Chicago Statement was signed by nearly 300 scholars, representing almost every major evangelical organization in the United States and several foreign countries.
88. R. C. Sproul, *Explaining Inerrancy: A Commentary;* Norman L. Geisler, ed., *Inerrancy,* "Appendix," pp. 494-97.

Article IV

We affirm that God who made mankind in His image has used language as a means of revelation.

We deny that human language is so limited by our creatureliness that it is rendered inadequate as a vehicle for divine revelation. We further deny that the corruption of human culture and language through sin has thwarted God's work of inspiration.

Article V

We affirm that God's revelation in the Holy Scriptures was progressive.

We deny that later revelation, which may fullfil earlier revelation, ever corrects or contradicts it. We further deny that any normative revelation has been given since the completion of the New Testament writings.

Article VI

We affirm that the whole of Scripture and all its parts, down to the very words of the original, were given by divine inspiration.

We deny that the inspiration of Scripture can rightly be affirmed of the whole without the parts, or of some parts but not the whole.

Article VII

We affirm that inspiration was the work in which God by His Spirit, through human writers, gave us His Word. The origin of Scripture is divine. The mode of divine inspiration remains largely a mystery to us.

We deny that inspiration can be reduced to human insight, or to heightened states of consciousness of any kind.

Article VIII

We affirm that God in His Work of inspiration utilized the distinctive personalities and literary styles of the writers whom He had chosen and prepared.

We deny that God, in causing these writers to use the very words that He chose, overrode their personalities.

Article IX

We affirm that inspiration, though not conferring omniscience, guaranteed true and trustworthy utterance on all matters of which the Biblical authors were moved to speak and write.

We deny that the finitude or fallenness of these writers, by necessity or otherwise, introduced distortion or falsehood into God's Word.

Article X

We affirm that inspiration, strictly speaking, applies only to the autographic text of Scripture, which in the providence of God can be ascertained from available manuscripts with great accuracy. We further affirm that copies and translations of Scripture are the Word of God to the extent that they faithfully represent the original.

We deny that any essential element of the Christian faith is affected by the absence of the autographs. We further deny that this absence renders the assertions of Biblical inerrancy invalid or irrelevant.

Article XI

We affirm that Scripture, having been given by divine inspiration, is infallible, so that, far from misleading us, it is true and reliable in all the matters it addresses.

We deny that it is possible for the Bible to be at the same time infallible and errant in its assertions. Infallibility and inerrancy may be distinguished, but not separated.

Article XII

We affirm that Scripture in its entirety is inerrant, being free from all falsehood, fraud, or deceit.

We deny that Biblical infallibility and inerrancy are limited to spiritual, religious, or redemptive themes, exclusive of assertions in the fields of history and science. We further deny that scientific hypotheses about earth history may properly be used to overturn the teaching of Scripture on creation and the flood.

Article XIII

We affirm the propriety of using inerrancy as a theological term with reference to the complete truthfulness of Scripture.

We deny that it is proper to evaluate Scripture according to standards of truth and error that are alien to its usage or purpose. We further deny that inerrancy is negated by Biblical phenomena such as a lack of modern technical precision, irregularities of grammar or spelling, observational descriptions of nature, the reporting of falsehoods, the use of hyperbole and round numbers, the topical arrangement of material, variant selections of material in parallel accounts, or the use of free citations.

Article XIV

We affirm the unity and internal consistency of Scripture.

We deny that alleged errors and discrepancies that have not yet been resolved vitiate the truth claims of the Bible.

Article XV

We affirm that the doctrine of inerrancy is grounded in the teaching of the Bible about inspiration.

We deny that Jesus' teaching about Scripture may be dismissed by appeals to accommodation or to any natural limitation of His humanity.

Article XVI

We affirm that the doctrine of inerrancy has been integral to the Church's faith throughout its history.

We deny that inerrancy is a doctrine invented by Scholastic Protestantism, or is a reactionary position postulated in response to negative higher criticism.

Article XVII

We affirm that the Holy Spirit bears witness to the Scriptures, assuring believers of the truthfulness of God's written Word.

We deny that this witness of the Holy Spirit operates in isolation from or against Scripture.

Article XVIII

We affirm that the text of Scripture is to be interpreted by grammatico-historical exegesis, taking account of its literary forms and devices, and that Scripture is to interpret Scripture.

We deny the legitimacy of any treatment of the text or quest for sources lying behind it that leads to relativizing, dehistoricizing, or discounting its teaching, or rejecting its claims to authorship.

Article XIX

We affirm that a confession of the full authority, infallibility, and inerrancy of Scripture is vital to a sound understanding of the whole of the Christian faith.

We further affirm that such confession should lead to increasing conformity to the image of Christ.

We deny that such confession is necessary for salvation. However, we further deny that inerrancy can be rejected without grave consequences, both to the individual and to the Church.

Theories of Revelation and Inspiration: An Evaluation of the Non-orthodox Views

There are several elements common to non-orthodox and unorthodox views of Scripture. A few of them are noted here.

First, the non-orthodox views of inspiration do not fit the biblical data. The Bible claims to be verbally inspired. For it is the *writings (graphē)* that are inspired (2 Tim. 3:16). Paul speaks of "*words . . . taught* by the Spirit" (1 Cor. 2:13). God spoke to Isaiah of "My *words* which I have put in your mouth" (Isa. 59:21). David acknowledged, "The Spirit of the Lord spoke to me, and His *word* was on my tongue" (2 Sam. 23:2). But all the unorthodox views reject verbal inspiration. Hence, whatever else may be said in their favor, they are not biblical. (See chaps. 3-6 for a more complete treatment of this point.)

Second, the unorthodox views of Scripture are not supported by the Fathers of the church. The orthodox view of the inspiration of Scripture has dominated for nearly nineteen centuries of the Christian church (see chaps. 7-9 above). That is recognized by even non-orthodox scholars.

Third, behind most denials of the orthodox view is an antisupernatural bias (see chap. 9). They wrongly assume that because the Bible is written in a human *form* it must have a purely human *source*. It is understandable that someone who does not believe in God would deny the Bible is a God-breathed book, but it is unjustifiable for a theist to rule out the possibility. Furthermore, to assume that the Bible cannot have a supernatural *origin* because it has a natural *character* is like denying the deity of Christ because He appeared in "the form of a man" (Phil. 2:8).

Fourth, denial of inspired words is often based on the presupposition that revelation cannot be propositional (that is, that God cannot reveal Himself in words). This assumption can be satirized by the words of the psalmist who wrote, "He who planted the ear, does He not hear?" (Ps. 94:9), to which may be added, "He who made the tongue, does He not speak?" Surely the God who made speech can Himself speak. How can the creature have greater powers than the Creator? The effect cannot be greater than its cause any more than water can rise higher than its source.

Sometimes there is the implication that divine truth is somehow inexpressible in words: God is beyond words. If this means only that words cannot *exhaust* the meaning of God, there would be no problem. Unfortunately, the objection to verbal propositional revelation often means that no truth about God can be *expressed* in words. However, this view is wrong. Human understanding is incapable of *comprehending* God completely, but it is able to *apprehend* Him sufficiently. The language of Scripture is not a complete expression of God, but it is an adequate one. Indeed, it is ironic that those who insist that human language is an inadequate vehicle to express theological truth use human language to express that very theological position.

Fifth, the non-orthodox views ultimately deny any objective basis for divine authority. This issue revolves around the question of who will be the final arbiter—man or God. The Bible addresses this matter by saying, "Rather, let God be found true, though every man *be found* a liar, as it is written, 'That Thou mightest be justified in Thy words, and mightest prevail when Thou art judged' " (Rom. 3:4). Instead, man's reason or subjective experience becomes the authority. For all non-orthodox views agree that the objective language of the Bible is not in itself the Word of God. That is, they deny the formula "What the Bible says, God says." This being the case, even after one discovers what Paul (or Peter, or John, et al.) said in the text he must still ask the crucial question: "Indeed, has God said?" (Gen. 3:1). For once we drive a wedge between the words of Scripture and the Word of God, then after we discover the *meaning* of a passage it is left to our reason or experience to determine whether or not it is *true*. Thus the orthodox view is left with no objective basis in the text of Scripture for a divine authority. As Carl Henry states,

> Every critical effort that absolutely contrasts the Word of God and the words of Scripture contradicts our Lord's own representatives of the prophets as conveyors of the incarnate Word by turning Scripture into a nonauthoritative, fallible report, to be considered less trustworthy than the verdicts passed upon it by modern theologians and ethicists. However piously they frame representations of the transcendent Word toward which (supposedly errant) prophetic-apostolic words witness, or of the Word hidden and revealed in or under (supposedly fallible) scriptural words, concessive critics dissolve an authoritative prophetic-apostolic word, and simultaneously erode an authoritative divine Word somehow wholly distinguishable from, yet presumably based upon, an equivocating Scripture. On the premise that the Bible is not the unadulterated Word of God, many critical scholars have erected private theological distilleries for extracting a totally foolproof "Truth" from error-prone documents. But informed seminarians know the long list of learned analysts whose personal brand of criticism foundered because of a dilution of the biblical essence and the substitution of ersatz ingredients.[89]

Sixth, there is in some non-orthodox views a confusion between *revelation* (an objective disclosure of God) and *interpretation* (a subjective discovery of that objective truth). Truth is not personal; it is propositional. However, truth comes from a person to a person (or persons) and can be about a personal relationship (for example, a love letter). The Bible is a propositional revelation from a personal Being (God) to persons, about their personal relationship

89. Carl F. H. Henry, *God, Revelation and Authority,* vol. 4: *God Who Speaks and Shows: Fifteen Theses, Part Three,* p. 50.

to Him and to other persons. But the truth of the Bible about those personal relationships is not personal truth; rather it is propositional truth about persons. Thus, the revelation of God in Scripture is an objective, propositional revelation about personal relationships. When one properly interprets that objective revelation and by the help of the Holy Spirit (1 Cor. 2:14-16; Eph. 1:18) understands how it applies to his life, he has illumination.

Unfortunately non-orthodox views often confuse individual illumination (or even human intuition) with God's objective revelation in Scripture. To do so is to shift the locus of revelation from the *objective* written Word of God to the *subjective* experience of the believer. In the case of the neo-orthodox view, it is claimed that the Bible is only a revelation when man is receiving it. Their claim that God is not really speaking unless man is hearing is clearly contrary to the repeated exhortation in Scripture to receive what God has spoken. Jesus said "Have you not read" (Matt. 19:4), for "It is written" (4:4, 7, 10). He cried out, "O foolish men and slow of heart to believe in all that the prophets have spoken" (Luke 24:25).

Seventh, there is a tendency within the extreme fundamentalist view to deny in effect the human dimension of Scripture. This leads to a biblical "docetism," wherein the divine nature of Scripture is affirmed at the expense of its human aspect. Just as it is unorthodox to deny Christ's true humanity, it is also wrong to deny the truly human nature of Scriptures. Hence, it is necessary to affirm the ways in which the Bible is a truly human book.

(1) The Bible often uses *human sources* for its material: Luke may have used written sources for his gospel (Luke 1:1-4); the Old Testament often used non-canonical writings as sources (cf. Josh. 10:13); Paul quoted non-Christian poets three times (Acts 17:28; 1 Cor. 15:33; Titus 1:12); Jude cited material contained in non-canonical books (Jude 9, 14).

(2) Every book in the Bible was the composition of a *human writer,* about forty of them in all.

(3) The Bible manifests different *human literary styles,* from the mournful meter of Lamentations to the exalted poetry of Isaiah, from the simple grammar of John to the complex Greek of Hebrews.

(4) The Bible also manifests *human perspectives:* David spoke in Psalm 23 from a shepherd's perspective; Kings is written from a prophetic vantage point, and Chronicles from a priestly point of view; Acts manifests a historical interest and 2 Timothy a pastor's heart. Writers speak from an observer's perspective when they write of the sun rising or setting (Josh. 1:15).

(5) The Bible reveals *human thought patterns,* including memory lapses (1 Cor. 1:14-16).

(6) The Bible reveals *human emotions* (Gal. 4:14).

(7) The Bible reveals specific *human interests.* Indicated by their choice of images, Hosea had a rural interest, Luke a medical interest, and James an interest in nature.

The Bible is in every sense of the word a truly human book—*except* that it has no errors. Just as Christ the living Word of God was truly human, yet without sin (Heb. 4:15), even so the written Word of God is truly human, yet without error.

Summary and Conclusion

There are three main views within Christendom in the contemporary scene regarding the Bible. These views may be summarized as follows:

The Bible *is* the Word of God—orthodox.
The Bible *contains* the Word of God—liberal.
The Bible *becomes* the Word of God—neo-orthodox.

However, there is a sense in which many who do not hold the orthodox belief in the identity between the Bible and the Word of God do, nonetheless, admit to some truth in the expression "The Bible is the Word of God." Understood this way, the Bible is the Word of God in one of the following manners:

essentially (orthodox);
partially (liberals);
instrumentally (neo-orthodox, neo-evangelical).

Evangelical Christians, however, believe the *propositions* of the Bible are God's infallible words. Neo-evangelicals believe only the *purpose* is infallible. Whereas liberals believe one can find God's Word *here and there* in the Bible, evangelicals believe it is found *everywhere* in Scripture. Although neo-evangelicals hold that the Bible is God's Word *confessionally* (that is, it is a confession to God's Word), evangelicals hold that the Bible is God's Word *essentially.*

The difference between the orthodox and neo-orthodox (and neo-evangelical) views is this:

Orthodox: the Bible *is* a revelation;
Neo-orthodox: the Bible is only a *record* of revelation.

For the orthodox revelation is *propositional*. For the neo-orthodox revelation is *personal;* the Bible is only a record of personal, existential encounters with God.

There is no essential difference between the neo-evangelical and the neo-orthodox views of Scripture. Both deny an identity between the words of Scripture and the Word of God. Both deny the formula, "Whatever the Bible says, God says." Both claim the Bible is a human (and fallible) record. Both hold the Bible is only an instrument *through which* God speaks, not the words *in which* God speaks.[90] It should be no surprise that the neo-evangelical view is similar to the neo-orthodox view, because the main source of it is Jack Rogers, who follows G. C. Berkouwer, who was influenced by Karl Barth. Even non-evangelicals have noted the similarity.

The various positions can also be contrasted according to their beliefs about the *modus operandi* (means of operation) of inspiration. Accordingly, these views hold that God produced the Bible by:

Verbal dictation through secretaries (extreme fundamentalists)
Verbal inspiration through prophets (orthodox)
Human intuition through natural process (liberals)
Divine elevation of human literature (liberal-evangelical)
Human recording of revelational events (neo-orthodox)
Inspiration of only redemptive truths or purpose (neo-evangelical)

Neo-evangelicals vary on the issue of the precise *means* of inspiration. Some hold that God inspired the *idea,* and the writers put it into their own erring *words*. Others affirm that God inspired only the *core* redemptive truths, not the *cultural* mode in which it was expressed. Some stress that the *purposes* (intentions) of the Bible are inspired of God, but not all its *propositions* (affirmations). But all neo-evangelicals allow for actual errors (i.e., mistakes) in the biblical record. That is in strong contrast to the historic orthodox and contemporary evangelical view of the Bible as an infallible and inerrant record. The chart "Theories of Revelation and Inspiration" summarizes the major features of the various views discussed.

90. The neo-evangelical view of Scripture has been critiqued historically by John Woodbridge, *Biblical Authority: A Critique of the Rogers-McKim Proposal,* and *John Hannah, ed., Inerrancy and the Church;* philosophically by Norman L. Geisler, ed., *Biblical Errancy: Its Philosophical Roots;* and theologically by Gordon Lewis and Bruce Demarest, eds., *Challenges to Inerrancy.*

Theories of Revelation and Inspiration

View	Name	Proponents	Revelation	Errors in Originals?	Errors in Copies?	Means of Inspiration	Degree of Authority of Bible
Mechanical Dictation	Hyper-Fundamentalism	Muslims Spiritists Some Hyper-Fundamentalists	In Words (Individually)	None	None	By Dictation	Infallible and Inerrant
Verbal Dictation	Fundamentalism	John R. Rice	In Words (Individually)	None	Few	By Supernatural Molding of Writer's Style	Infallible and Inerrant
Verbal Inspiration	Fundamentalism Evangelicalism	B.B. Warfield F. Schaeffer ICBI	In Words (Holistically)*	None	Few	Supernatural Process	Infallible and Inerrant
Conceptual Inspiration	Neo-Evangelicalism	A.H. Strong D. Beegle J. Rogers	In Concepts (Not Words)	None theologically (or morally) Some factually	Few	Revealed Ideas Writer's Own Words	Infallible Not Inerrant
Instrumental Revelation	Liberal Evangelicalism	C.S. Lewis	Through Words (Not *in* Words)	Some (In both areas)	Some	Writer's Words "Elevated" by God	Authoritative Not Inerrant
Personal Revelation	Neo-Orthodoxy	Karl Barth Emil Brunner John Baillie	In Acts, Events (Not Words)	Some (In both areas)	Many	Revealed Acts Writer's Record	Usually Reliable Not Inerrant
Illuminationism	Liberalism	Harold DeWolf Harry E. Fosdick	By Illumination (No Revelation)	Many (In both areas)	Many	Divine Actualization of Natural Powers	Often Reliable Not Inerrant
Intuitionalism	Process Theology	Shubert Ogden	By Intuition (No Revelation)	Many (In both areas)	Largely	Purely Natural Powers	Sometimes Reliable Not Inerrant

*In words as parts of a whole sentence or proposition.

11

Evidences for the Inspiration of the Bible

The Word of God needs no proof. It has self-vindicating authority because it is God's Word. After all, God is the highest authority (Heb. 6:13). Hence, there is nothing greater than God to which one could appeal for authority. So the Word of God is its own authority. And if the Bible is God's Word, then the same is true of the Bible—it too would speak with ultimate authority.

However, the question as to whether or not the Bible is the Word of God is a matter of evidence. After all, there are other books, such as the Koran and the Book of Mormon, that claim to be the Word of God, and yet they contradict the Bible. But God cannot contradict Himself, and His Word cannot contradict itself. Because they contradict one another, only one of these competing books at best can be the Word of God. Hence, one must offer evidence in support of the claim that the Bible is the Word of God, as opposed to the other books that make contrary claims. One is obliged to obey the legitimate authority (Rom. 13:1-8) of a police officer provided he has evidence that he is really an officer, and not an imposter posing as an officer. Likewise, any book demanding obedience to it as the Word of God needs to support its claim to be the authentic voice of God. What, then, is the evidence that the Bible has divine authority?

It is one thing to claim divine inspiration for the Bible and quite another to provide evidence to confirm that claim. Before examining the supporting evidence for the inspiration of Scripture, a precise summary of what it is that inspiration claims is in order.

A Summary of the Claim for the Inspiration of the Bible

The inspiration of the Bible is not to be confused with a poetic inspiration. Inspiration as applied to the Bible refers to the God-given authority of its teachings for the thought and life of the believer.

Biblical Description of Inspiration

The Greek word for *inspiration* (*theopneustos*) means God-breathed, but in its broader theological usage it is often used to include the process by which the Scriptures or writings were invested with divine authority for doctrine and practice (2 Tim. 3:16-17). It is the writings that are said to be inspired. The writers, however, were Spirit-moved to record their messages. Hence, when viewed as a total process, inspiration is what occurs when Spirit-moved writers record God-breathed writings. Three elements are contained in the total process of inspiration: the divine causality, the prophetic agency, and the resultant scriptural authority.

The three elements in inspiration. The first element in inspiration is *God's causality.* God is the Prime Mover by whose promptings the prophets were led to write. The ultimate origin of inspired writings is the desire of the Divine to communicate with man. The second factor is the *prophetic agency.* The Word of God comes through men of God. God employs the instrumentality of human personality to convey His message. Finally, the written prophetic utterance is invested with *divine authority.* The prophet's words are God's Words (chap. 2).

The characteristics of an inspired writing. The first characteristic of inspiration is implied in the fact that it is an inspired writing; namely, it is *verbal.* The very words of the prophets were God-given, not by dictation but by the Spirit-directed employment of the prophet's own vocabulary and style.[1] Inspiration also claims to be *plenary* (full). No part of Scripture is without divine inspiration. Paul wrote, "All scripture is inspired by God" (2 Tim. 3:16). In addition, inspiration implies the *inerrancy* of the teaching of the original documents (called autographs). Whatever God utters is true and without error, and the Bible is said to be an utterance of God. Finally, inspiration results in the divine *authority* of the Scriptures. The teaching of Scripture is binding on the believer for faith and practice (chap. 3).

The Biblical Claim to Divine Inspiration

Inspiration is not something merely attributed to the Bible by Christians; it is something the Bible claims for itself. There are literally hundreds of references within the Bible about its divine origin.

The claim for the inspiration of the Old Testament. The Old Testament claims to be a prophetic writing. The familiar "thus says the Lord" fills its pages. False prophets and their works were excluded from the house of the Lord. Those prophecies that proved to be from God were preserved in a sacred place. The growing collection of sacred writings was recognized and even quoted by later prophets as the Word of God (chap. 4).

1. See discussions in chaps. 2 and 10.

Jesus and the New Testament writers held these writings in the same high esteem; they claimed them to be the unbreakable, authoritative, and inspired Word of God. By numerous references to the Old Testament as a whole, to its basic sections, and to almost every Old Testament book, the New Testament writers overwhelmingly attested to the claim of divine inspiration for the Old Testament (chap. 5).

The claim for the inspiration of the New Testament. The apostolic writings were boldly described in the same authoritative terms that denoted the Old Testament as the Word of God. They were called "Scripture," "prophecy," and so on. Every book in the New Testament contains some claim to divine authority. The New Testament church read, circulated, collected, and quoted the New Testament books right along with the inspired Scriptures of the Old Testament (chap. 6).

The contemporaries and immediate successors of the apostolic age recognized the divine origin of the New Testament writings along with the Old. With only heretical exceptions, all the great Fathers of the Christian church from the earliest times held to the divine inspiration of the New Testament. In brief, there is continuous claim for the inspiration of both Old and New Testaments from the time of their composition to the present (chaps. 7, 8, and 9). In modern times that claim has been seriously challenged by many from inside and outside Christendom (chaps. 9 and 10). The challenge calls for a substantiation of the claim for inspiration of the Bible.

Support for the Biblical Claim for Inspiration

Defenders of the Christian faith (apologists) have responded to the challenge in sundry ways. Some have transformed Christianity into a rational system, others have claimed belief in it because it is without reason, but the great mass of informed Christians through the centuries have avoided either rationalism or fideism. Claiming neither absolute finality nor complete skepticism, Christian apologists have given "an account for the hope that is in" them (1 Pet. 3:15).[2] The following is a summary of evidence for the biblical doctrine of inspiration.

Internal Evidence of the Bible's Inspiration

There are two lines of evidence to be considered on the inspiration of the Bible: the evidence flowing from within Scripture itself (internal evidence) and that coming from outside (external evidence). Several lines of internal evidence have been presented.

The prima facie evidence for inspiration. The Bible on its surface seems to be an inspired book. Like Jesus, the Bible speaks with authority

2. See Norman L. Geisler, *Christian Apologetics*, chaps. 16-18.

(John 7:46). It gives every appearance of having come from God. Not only does it claim to have a divine origin, but it seems to have a supernatural character. Although such is not full proof of the Bible's inspiration, it is at least an indication that merits examination. To rephrase the gospel writer, "never did a book speak the way this Book speaks" (cf. John 7:46). The Bible has the ring of truth. As such there is at least *prima facie* evidence for its inspiration. This *prima facie* credential calls for further examination of other evidence.

Evidence of the testimony of the Holy Spirit. Closely allied with the evidence of the *prima facie* authority of Scripture is the witness of the Holy Spirit. The Word of God is confirmed to the children of God by the Spirit of God. The inner witness of God in the heart of the believer who reads the Bible is evidence of its divine origin. The Holy Spirit not only bears witness to the believer that he is a child of God (Rom. 8:16) but that the Bible is the Word of God (2 Pet. 1:20-21). The same Spirit who communicated the truth of God also confirms to the believer that the Bible is the Word of God. That witness does not occur in a vacuum. The Spirit uses the objective Word to bring about subjective assurance.[3] But by the witness of the Spirit of God to the truth of the Word of God, there is certainty about its divine authority.

Evidence from the transforming ability of the Bible. Another so-called internal evidence is the ability of the Bible to convert the unbeliever and to build up the believer in the faith. The writer of Hebrews says, "The word of God is living and active and sharper than any two-edged sword" (4:12). Untold thousands have experienced this dynamic power. Drug addicts have been cured, derelicts have been transformed, hate has been turned to love by reading the Bible. Believers grow by studying it (1 Pet. 2:2). The sorrowing are comforted, sinners are rebuked, and the negligent are exhorted by the Scriptures. God's Word possesses the dynamic, transforming power of God. God vindicates the Bible's authority by its evangelistic and edifying powers.

Evidence from the unity of the Bible. A more formal evidence of the Bible's inspiration is its unity. Composed as it is of sixty-six books, written over a period of some fifteen hundred years by about forty authors using several languages and containing hundreds of topics, it is more than accidental or incidental that the Bible possesses an amazing unity of theme—Jesus Christ. One problem—sin—and one solution—the Savior—unify its pages from Genesis to Revelation. This is an especially valid point because no one person or group of men put the Bible together. Books were added as they were written by the prophets. They were then collected because they were considered inspired. It is only later reflection, both by the prophets themselves (cf. 1 Pet. 1:10-11) and later generations, that has discovered that the Bible is really one book whose "chapters" were written by men who had no explicit

3. See R. C. Sproul, "The Internal Testimony of the Holy Spirit," in Norman L. Geisler, ed., *Inerrancy*, chap. 11.

knowledge of the overall structure. Their individual roles could be compared to that of different men writing chapters of a novel for which none of them have even an overall outline. Whatever unity the book has must come from beyond them. Like a symphony, each individual part of the Bible contributes to an overall unity that is orchestrated by one Master.

External Evidences of the Bible's Inspiration

The internal evidence of inspiration is mostly subjective in nature. It relates to what the believer sees or senses in his experience with the Bible. With the possible exception of the evidence from the unity of the Bible, the internal evidences are available only inside Christianity. The nonbeliever does not sense the witness of His Spirit, nor experience the edifying power of Scripture in his life. Unless he steps by faith to the inside, these internal evidences may have little convincing effect on his life. This is where the external evidence plays a crucial role. It provides signposts indicating where the "inside" really is. It is public witness to something very unusual, which serves to draw attention to the voice of God in Scripture.

Evidence from the historicity of the Bible. Much of the Bible is historical and as such is subject to historical investigation. The most significant area of confirmation in this regard has come from the field of archaeology. The renowned archaeologist William F. Albright said, "There can be no doubt that archaeology has confirmed the substantial historicity of the Old Testament tradition."[4] Nelson Glueck adds, "It may be stated categorically that no archaeological discovery has ever controverted a Biblical reference. Scores of archaeological findings have been made which confirm in clear outline or exact detail historical statements in the Bible."[5] Millar Burrows notes that "more than one archaeologist has found his respect for the Bible increased by the experience of excavation in Palestine."[6] Clifford A. Wilson has added still more support to the historical reliability of the Bible.[7] No historical discovery is a direct evidence of any spiritual claim in the Bible, such as the claim to be divinely inspired; nevertheless the historicity of the Bible does provide indirect verification of the claim of inspiration. Confirmation of the Bible's accuracy in factual matters lends credibility to its claims when speaking on other subjects. Jesus said, "If I told you earthly things and you do not believe, how shall you believe if I tell you heavenly things?" (John 3:12).

Evidence from the testimony of Christ. In connection with the evidence from the historicity of the biblical documents is the evidence of the testimony of Christ. Since the New Testament has been documented as historical,

4. William F. Albright, *Archeology and the Religion of Israel,* p. 176.
5. Nelson Glueck, *Rivers in the Desert: A History of the Negev,* p. 31.
6. Millar Burrows, *What Mean These Stones?* p. 1
7. Clifford A. Wilson, *Rocks, Relics, and Biblical Reliability.*

and since those same historical documents provide the teaching of Christ about the inspiration of the Bible, one needs only to assume the truthfulness of Christ in order to argue for the inspiration of the Bible. If Christ possesses any kind of authority or integrity as a religious teacher, then the Scriptures are inspired, for He taught that they are God's Word. In order to falsify this contention, one must reject the authority of Jesus to make pronouncements on the subject of inspiration. The evidence from Scripture conclusively reveals that Jesus held to the full divine authority of the Scriptures (see chap. 6). Indications from the gospel records, with ample historical backing, show that Jesus was a man of integrity and truth. The argument, then, is this:

> If what Jesus taught is true,
> And Jesus taught that the Bible is inspired,
> Then it follows that it is true that the Bible is inspired of God.

In order to deny the authority of Scripture one must reject the integrity of Christ.[8]

Evidence from prophecy. Another forceful external testimony to the inspiration of Scripture is the fact of fulfilled prophecy. According to Deuteronomy 18, a prophet was false if he made predictions that were never fulfilled. No unconditional prophecy of the Bible about events to the present day has gone unfilled. Hundreds of predictions, some of them given hundreds of years in advance, have been literally fulfilled. The time (Dan. 9), city (Mic. 5:2), and nature (Isa. 7:14) of Christ's birth were foretold in the Old Testament, as were dozens of other things about His life, death, and resurrection (see Isa. 53). Numerous other prophecies have been fulfilled, including the destruction of Edom (Obad. 1), the curse on Babylon (Isa. 13), the destruction of Tyre (Ezek. 26) and Nineveh (Nah. 1-3), and the return of Israel to the Land (Isa. 11:11). Other books claim divine inspiration, such as the Koran, the Book of Mormon, and parts of the Veda. But none of those books contains predictive prophecy.[9] As a result, fulfilled prophecy is a strong indication of the unique, divine authority of the Bible.

Evidence from the influence of the Bible. No book has been more widely disseminated and has more broadly influenced the course of world events than the Bible. The Bible has been translated into more languages, been published in more copies, influenced more thought, inspired more art, and motivated more discoveries than any other book in history. The Bible has been translated into over one thousand languages representing more than ninety percent of the world's population. It has been published in billions of copies. There are no close seconds to it on the all-time bestseller list. The

8. See John W. Wenham, *Christ and the Bible*.
9. In this regard see Gleason L. Archer, Jr., *A Survey of Old Testament Introduction*, "Appendix 2: Anachronisms and Historical Inaccuracies in the Koran," pp. 498-500; "Appendix 3: Anachronisms and Historical Inaccuracies in the Mormon Scriptures," pp. 501-4.

2. *In fulfillment of prophecy (Obad. 1-4), Petra is today a deserted ruin. This is the so-called "Treasury" (Giovanni Trimboli)*

influence of the Bible and its teaching in the Western world is clear for all who study history. And the influential role of the West in the course of world events is equally clear. Civilization has been influenced more by the Judeo-Christian Scriptures than by any other book or series of books in the world. Indeed, no great moral or religious work in the world exceeds the depth of morality in the principle of Christian love, and none has a more lofty spiritual concept than the biblical view of God. The Bible presents the highest ideals known to men, ideals that have molded civilization.

Evidence from the apparent indestructibility of the Bible. Despite its importance (or maybe because of it), the Bible has suffered more vicious attacks than would be expected to be made on such a book. But the Bible has withstood all its attackers. Diocletian attempted to exterminate it (c. A.D.

302/3-305),[10] and yet it is the most widely published book in the world today. Biblical critics once regarded much of it as mythological, but archaeology has established it as historical. Antagonists have attacked its teaching as primitive, but moralists urge that its teaching on love be applied to modern society. Skeptics have cast doubt on its authenticity, and yet more men are convinced of its truth today than ever. Attacks on the Bible continue to arise from science, psychology, and political movements, but the Bible remains undaunted. Like the wall four-feet high and four-feet wide, attempts to blow it over accomplish nothing. The Bible remains just as strong after the attack. Jesus said, "Heaven and earth will pass away, but My words will not pass away" (Mark 13:31).

Evidence from the integrity of the human authors. There are no good reasons to suppose that the authors of Scripture were not honest and sincere men. From everything that is known of the disciples' lives—even their deaths for what they believed—they were utterly convinced that God had spoken to them. What shall be made of men—over five hundred of them (1 Cor. 15:6)—who claim as evidence for the divine authority of their message that they saw Jesus of Nazareth, crucified under Pontius Pilate, alive and well? What shall be made of the claim that they saw Him on about a dozen occasions over a period of a month and a half? That they talked with Him, ate with Him, saw His wounds, and handled Him, and even the most skeptical among them fell at His feet and cried, "My Lord and my God!" (John 20:28)? It stretches one's credulity to believe that the disciples were all drugged or deluded, especially in view of the number and nature of their encounters and the lasting effect on them. But granting their basic integrity, one is confronted with an unusual phenomenon of men facing death with the claim that God had given them the authority to speak and write. When men of sanity and noted integrity claim divine inspiration for their writings and offer as evidence that they have communicated with the resurrected Christ, then men of good will who seek the truth must take notice. In brief, the honesty of the biblical writers vouches for the divine authority of their writings.

Evidence from miracles. Another support for the inspiration of Scripture comes from miracles. A miracle is an act of God and confirms the Word of God by a prophet of God (see chap. 13). Nicodemus said to Jesus, "Rabbi, we know that You have come from God as a teacher; for no one can do these signs [miracles] that You do unless God is with him" (John 3:2). Peter said to the crowd at Pentecost, "Jesus the Nazarene, [was] a man attested to you by God with miracles and wonders and signs which God performed through Him" (Acts 2:22). The same is true of other spokesmen for God in the Bible. Moses, for example, was given the ability to perform miracles so that Egypt would believe his message was from God (Ex. 4:1-9). So were other prophets,

10. See discussions in chaps. 16 and 27.

such as Elijah (1 Kings 18) and Elisha (2 Kings 4). In the New Testament the apostles' message was confirmed by miracles. Hebrews says,

> How shall we escape if we neglect so great a salvation? After it was at the first spoken through the Lord, it was confirmed to us by those who heard, God also bearing witness with them, both by signs and wonders and by various miracles and by gifts of the Holy Spirit according to His own will. (Heb. 2:3-4)

The Bible is a prophetic book. Every book in it was written by a prophet or spokesman for God (see chaps. 3-6). And since there were miracles to confirm the prophetic messages given by authors of Scripture, then the Bible is confirmed to be the Word of God by acts of God (miracles).[11]

The argument from alternate possibility. One of the most interesting arguments for the inspiration of the Bible has been suggested by Charles Wesley.

> The Bible must be the invention either of good men or angels, bad men or devils, or of God.
>
> 1. It could not be the invention of good men or angels; for they neither would or could make a book, and tell lies all the time they were writing it, saying "Thus saith the Lord," when it was their own invention.
> 2. It could not be the invention of bad men or devils; for they would not make a book which commands all duty, forbids all sin, and condemns their souls to hell to all eternity.
> 3. Therefore, I draw this conclusion, that the Bible must be given by divine inspiration.[12]

Of course these arguments do not rationally demonstrate the divine origin of Scripture beyond all question. Even if they did objectively *prove* the inspiration of the Bible, it would not necessarily follow that they would *persuade* everyone. Rather, they are evidences, testimonies, and witnesses. As witnesses they must be cross-examined and evaluated as a whole. Then, in the jury room of one's own soul a decision must be made—a decision that is based not on rationally inescapable proofs but on evidence that is "beyond reasonable doubt."[13]

Perhaps all that need be added here is that the claim for the inspiration of the Bible is on trial, and each individual is part of a jury called upon for a verdict. That being the case, based on a comprehensive examination of the claim and alleged credentials of the Bible to be inspired, the jury would be

11. The argument here is not circular, since the Bible as a historically reliable document (supported by evidence) can be used as a basis for knowing these miracles occurred that confirm it to be the Word of God. See F. F. Bruce, *The New Testament Documents: Are They Reliable?* for evidence on the reliability of the New Testament.
12. Robert W. Burtner and Robert E. Chiles, *A Compend of Wesley's Theology,* p. 20.
13. For further evidence see Bernard Ramm, *Protestant Christian Evidences,* and Josh McDowell, *Evidence That Demands a Verdict.*

compelled to vote that the Bible is "guilty of being inspired as charged." The reader too must decide. For those who tend to be indecisive, one is reminded of the words of Peter: "Lord, to whom shall we go? You have the words of eternal life" (John 6:68). In other words, if the Bible—with its clear-cut claim to be inspired, as well as its incomparable characteristics and multiple credentials—is not inspired, then to what else can one turn? It has the words of eternal life.

Summary

The Bible claims to be and proves to be the Word of God. There are general claims for the Bible as a whole and more specific claims for sections and even individual books. This is true of both Old and New Testaments.

Support for the Bible's claim to be the written Word of God comes from many sources. First, there is *prima facie* evidence from the very nature of the Bible itself. Second, the *witness of the Spirit* to the heart of the believer adds further confirmation to the Bible's inspiration. Third, the *transforming ability* of Scripture is indication of its divine origin. Fourth, the very *unity* of the Bible amid all its diversity of authors, languages, and topics bespeaks of a divine Mind behind it. Fifth, the *historicity* of the Bible as confirmed by multitudinous archaeological discoveries, lends further support to its claim to divine authority. Sixth, the *testimony of Christ* is a clear indication it is the very Word of God. Seventh, uniquely the Bible offers numerous *fulfilled prophecies* as confirmation of its divine character. Eighth, the *influence of the Bible* has been more widespread than any other book in the world. Ninth, the *apparent indestructability* of the Bible is another indication it is from God. Tenth, the *integrity of the human authors* also lends support to their claims for inspiration. Eleventh, *miracles* confirm the Bible to be the Word of God. Twelfth, there is the argument from *alternate possibility,* suggesting the unlikeliness that it was invented by either good or evil creatures but rather that it truly came from God as claimed.

Some of these arguments alone are indecisive. But when all of them are taken together they form a very persuasive argument that the Bible is indeed the Word of God. In fact, no other book in the world has such widespread and unique support for its claim to be the inspired Word of God.

Part Two

CANONIZATION OF THE BIBLE

12

Determination of Canonicity

The first link in the chain of revelation "From God to Us" is inspiration, which concerns *what* God did, namely, that He breathed out (spirated) the Scriptures. The second link in the chain is canonization, which relates to the question of *which* books God inspired. Inspiration indicates how the Bible received its *authority,* whereas canonization tells how the Bible received its *acceptance*. It is one thing for God to give the Scriptures their authority, and quite another for men to recognize that authority.

Canonicity Defined

In the overall subject of canonicity, the first question to be considered is the determining principle: What is it that makes a book canonical? In his discussion of canonicity in the twentieth century, R. C. Leonard "distinguishes four main views: (*i*) the theory of canon as inspired word, rooted in prophecy, (*ii*) the theory of canon as history—the history of the acts of God in relation to Israel, and their interpretation, (*iii*) the theory of canon as law, rooted in the Pentateuch, with parallels in non-Israelite treaties and law-codes, and (*iv*) the theory of canon as a cultic phenomenon, rooted in worship."[1] Various answers have been presented concerning the determining principle of canonicity. Before they can be understood, it is necessary to trace briefly the development of the concept of the "canon."

Literally

The original meaning of the term *canon* can be traced to the ancient Greeks, who used it in a literal sense: a *kanon* was a rod, ruler, staff, or measuring rod. The Greek word *kanon* is probably a derivative of the Hebrew *kaneh* (reed), an Old Testament term meaning measuring rod (Ezek. 40:3;

1. R. C. Leonard, "The Origin of Canonicity in the Old Testament," (Ph.D. diss., Boston University, 1972), especially chaps. 6-9. This material provides the basis for the discussion in Roger Beckwith, *The Old Testament Canon of the New Testament Church and Its Background in Early Judaism,* pp. 63-104.

42:16).[2] This literal concept provided the basis for a later extended use of the word *kanon,* meaning "standard," "norm." Even in pre-Christian Greek, the word *kanon* bore a non-literal meaning,[3] as it does in the New Testament. In 2 Corinthians 10:13-16 it bears the sense of "sphere of action or influence."[4] Galatians 6:16 comes closest to the final theological significance of the word, as Paul says "Those who will walk by this rule [*kanon*], peace and mercy be upon them."

Theologically

From the literal "ruler," the word was extended to mean a rule or standard for anything. In early Christian usage, it came to mean rule of faith, normative writings, or authoritative Scripture. The Fathers, from the time of Irenaeus, referred to the *kanon* of Christian teaching, which they called "The *Kanon* of the Church," "The *Kanon* of the Truth," and "The *Kanon* of Faith."[5] However, the first clear application of the word to the Scriptures came at about A.D. 350, with Athanasius.[6] The word *kanon* was applied to the Bible in both an active and a passive sense: one in which it was the canon or standard, and the other in which it was canonized or recognized to be canonical by the church. In this chapter canonicity is viewed in the active sense in which the Scriptures are the ultimate norm.

Canonicity Described

The ancient Jews did not use the word *canon* (*kaneh*) in reference to their authoritative writings, although the theological concept of a canon or divine standard is certainly applicable to their sacred writings. Nevertheless, several other phrases or concepts used by the Jews are equivalent to the word *canon*.

Sacred Writings

An inspired or canonical writing was considered sacred and was kept by the Ark of the Covenant (Deut. 31:24-26). After the Temple was built, the sacred writings were kept in the Temple (2 Kings 22:8). This special attention and reverence paid to the Jewish Scriptures is tantamount to saying that they were considered canonical.

2. For the history of the word *canon* see Alexander Souter, *The Text and Canon of the New Testament,* pp. 154-56.
3. For example, it was used to describe a standard in ethics, art, literature, and even great epochs. See Brooke Foss Westcott, *A General Survey of the History of the Canon of the New Testament,* "Appendix A," p. 504.
4. Walter Bauer, *A Greek-English Lexicon of the New Testament and Other Early Christian Literature,* p. 403.
5. Westcott, *General Survey,* p. 506 and notes 1-2.
6. According to Westcott, pp. 508-9 and notes 1-2, p. 516, although certain derivatives of the Greek word were used by Origen.

Authoritative Writings

Another concept that is synonymous with canonicity is "authority." The rulers of Israel were to be subject to the authority of the Scriptures. The Lord commanded that when a king "sits on the throne of his kingdom, he shall write for himself a copy of this law on a scroll . . . and he shall read in it all the days of his life, that he may learn to fear the Lord his God" (Deut. 17:18-19). The Lord enjoined the same authoritative writings unto Joshua, saying, "This book of the law shall not depart from your mouth, but you shall meditate on it day and night" (Josh. 1:8).

Books That "Defile the Hands"

Some assert that in the later Talmudic tradition the canonical, or sacred, books were called those that "defile the hands" of the users, because the books were considered holy.[7] W. O. E. Osterley, and others since,[8] suggest that contact with the Scriptures really sanctified the hands, but it was called uncleanness because the hands had to be washed before touching other things, in accordance with Leviticus 6:27f; 16:23f, 26, 28. Still others, such as Roger Beckwith,

> fall back on the reason given by the Mishnah and Tosephta themselves, where Rabbi Johanan ben Zakkai answers the Sadducean objection to the teaching that the Scriptures make the hands unclean but the writings of Homer do not, by explaining that 'as their preciousness, so is their uncleanness' (M. Yadaim 4.6), and continuing, 'so that they may not be made into spreads for beasts' (Tos. Yadaim 2.19). By declaring that the Scriptures made the hands unclean, the rabbis protected them from careless and irreverent treatment, since it is obvious that no one would be so apt to handle them heedlessly if he were every time obliged to wash his hands afterwards.[9]

The books of the Old Testament, in contrast, do make the hands unclean, that is, they are canonical. Indeed, Paul refers to the inspired Old Testament as "sacred" writings (2 Tim. 3:15).

Books from the Prophetic Period

Josephus in his *Contra Apion* 1.8 says,

7. See for example Robert H. Pfieffer, *Introduction to the Old Testament,* p. 68 n. 10, who cites Tosefta Yadim 3.5 of the Talmud: "The Gospel and the books of the heretics are not canonical (lit., 'do not make the hands unclean'); the books of Ben Sira and whatever books have been written since his time are uncanonical."
8. W. O. E. Osterley, *The Books of the Apocrypha* (London: Scott, 1914), pp. 177-82. Also see the discussion in Sid Z. Leiman, *The Canonization of Hebrew Scripture: The Talmudic and Midrashic Evidence,* pp. 104-20, esp. pp. 117-20.
9. Beckwith, p. 280.

> From Artaxerxes until our time everything has been recorded, but has not been deemed worthy of like credit with what preceded, because the exact succession of the prophets ceased. But what faith we have placed in our own writings is evident by our conduct; for though so long a time has now passed, no one has dared to add anything to them, or to take anything from them, or to alter anything in them.

That is, only the books written from Moses to Malachi, in the succession of Hebrew prophets, were considered to be canonical. With that the statement of the Talmud (Seder Olam Rabba 30) agrees when it says, "Up to this point [the time of Alexander the Great] the prophets prophesied through the Holy Spirit; from this time onward incline thine ear and listen to the sayings of the wise."

Roger Beckwith notes the following rabbinical statements on the cessation of prophecy:

> 'With the death of Haggai, Zechariah and Malachi the latter prophets, the Holy Spirit ceased out of Israel' (Tos. Sotah 13.2: baraita in Bab. Yoma 9b, Bab. Sotah 48b and Bab. Sanhedrin 11a).
>
> 'Until then [the coming of Alexander the Great and the end of the empire of the Persians] the prophets prophesied through the Holy Spirit. From then on, "incline thine ear and hear the words of the wise" ' (Seder Olam Rabbah 30, quoting Prov. 22.17).
>
> 'Rab Samuel bar Inia said, in the name of Rab Aha, "The Second Temple lacked five things which the First Temple possessed, namely, the fire, the ark, the Urim and Thummim, the oil of anointing and the Holy Spirit [of prophecy]" ' (Jer. Taanith 2.1; Jer. Makkoth 2.4-8; Bab. Yoma 21b).
>
> 'Rabbi Abdimi of Haifa said, "Since the day when the Temple was destroyed, prophecy has been taken from the prophets and given to the wise" ' (Bab. Baba Bathra 12a).
>
> 'Rabbi Johanan said, "Since the Temple was destroyed, prophecy has been taken from prophets and given to fools and children" ' (Bab. Baba Bathra 12b).[10]

"In each of these five passages," Beckwith notes, "an era is in view, which is variously described as the death of Haggai, Zechariah and Malachi, the end of the empire of the Persians, the destruction of the First Temple or the transition from the First Temple to the Second."[11] So then, if a book were written after the prophetic period, it was not considered canonical. If it were written within the prophetic period, in the succession of Hebrew prophets, it was canonical.

In brief, what were later called canonical writings were by the Jews considered to be those sacred and authoritative writings of the Hebrew prophets from Moses to Malachi. So sacred were these holy writings that they were

10. Beckwith, p. 370.
11. Ibid.

preserved by the Ark of the Covenant in the Temple. To touch these holy writings was to defile one's hands; to break them was to defile one's life. The Hebrew canon, then, was that collection of writings which, because they possessed divine inspiration and authority, were the norm or rule for the believer's faith and conduct.

Numerous Other Titles

Many other titles were ascribed to the Old Testament canon by the first century A.D. Beckwith lists twenty-eight of these names as a minimum rather than a maximum when he writes,

> The collection is called (*i*) 'the Law and the Prophets and the Others that have followed in their steps', (*ii*) 'the Law and the Prophets and the Other Ancestral Books', (*iii*) 'the Law and the Prophecies and the Rest of the Books', (*iv*) 'the Law of Moses and the Prophets and the Psalms', (*v*) 'the Laws, and Oracles given by inspiration through the Prophets, and the Psalms', (*vi*) 'the Law and the Prophets', (*vii*) 'Moses and the Prophets', (*viii*) 'the Laws and the accompanying Records', (*ix*) 'the Law', (*x*) 'the (Most) Holy Scriptures', (*xi*) 'the Scriptures laid up in the Temple', (*xii*), 'the Scriptures', (*xiii*) 'Scripture', (*xiv*) 'the (Most) Holy Books', (*xv*) 'The Book of God', (*xvi*) 'the (Most) Holy Records', (*xvii*) 'the Records', (*xviii*) 'the Record', (*xix*) 'the Most Holy Oracles', (*xx*), 'the Divine Oracles', (*xxi*) 'the Inspired Oracles', (*xxii*) 'the Written Oracles', (*xxiii*) 'the Oracles of the teaching of God', (*xxiv*) 'the Oracles of God', (*xxv*) 'the Oracles', (*xxvi*) 'the Holy Word', (*xxvii*) 'the Divine Word', (*xxviii*) 'the Prophetic Word'.[12]

Canonicity Determined

In a real sense, Christ is the key to the inspiration and canonization of the Scriptures. It was He who confirmed the inspiration of the Hebrew canon of the Old Testament; and it was He who promised that the Holy Spirit would direct the apostles into all truth. The fulfillment of that promise resulted in the writing and collection of the New Testament. As Carl F. H. Henry writes,

> Jesus altered the prevailing Jewish view of Scripture in several ways: (1) he subjected the authority of tradition to the superior and normative authority of the Old Testament; (2) he emphasized that he himself fulfills the messianic promise of the inspired writings; (3) he claimed for himself an authority not below that of the Old Testament and definitively expounded the inner significance of the Law; (4) he inaugurated the new covenant escalating the Holy Spirit's moral power as an internal reality; (5) he committed his apostles to the enlargement and completion of the Old Testament canon through their proclamation of the Spirit-given interpretation of his life and work. At the same time he identified himself wholly with the revelational authority of Moses and the prophets—that is, with the Old

12. Beckwith, p. 105.

> Testament as an inspired literary canon—insisting that Scripture has sacred, authoritative and permanent validity, and that the revealed truth of God is conveyed in its teachings.[13]

This ongoing ministry of the Holy Spirit in the lives and work of the New Testament writers is manifest in several ways as has been indicated (chap. 7). Once it is understood what canonicity means, the question of how the biblical books received their canonicity must be considered. In order to do this, several inadequate views of canonicity will be examined in order to observe how they fall short of explaining what it is that really determines the canonicity of a book.

Some Inadequate Views on Old Testament Canonicity

Several insufficient suggestions have been offered as to the determining criteria of canonicity.

Age determines canonicity.[14] It has been suggested that canonicity is determined by antiquity. The general argument is that if the book were ancient it would have been venerated because of its age and placed among the prized collection of Hebrew literature. But, this view clearly does not measure up to the facts.

1. *Many ancient books are not in the canon.* That antiquity does not determine canonicity is apparent from the fact that numerous books, many of which are older than some canonical books, are not in the canon: "the Book of the Wars of the Lord" is mentioned in Numbers 21:14, and "the book of Jasher" in Joshua 10:13,[15] neither of which is part of the Hebrew canon.
2. *Many young books were placed in the canon.* Most, if not all, of the canonical books were received into the canon soon after they were written. Moses' writings were placed by the ark while he was yet alive (Deut. 31:24-26). Daniel, a younger contemporary of Jeremiah, had accepted Jeremiah's book as canonical (Dan. 9:2), and Ezekiel, another contemporary, made reference to the prophet Daniel (Ezek. 28:3). In the New Testament, Peter had a collection of Paul's books and considered them to be Scripture (2 Peter 3:15-16). Because many old books were not ac-

13. Carl F. H. Henry, *God, Revelation and Authority,* vol. 3: *God Who Speaks and Shows: Fifteen Theses, Part Two,* p. 47.
14. See W. H. Green, *General Introduction to the Old Testament: The Canon,* p. 34. He lists Wildeboer as holding this view and Hitzig as holding that Hebrew language is the test of canonicity (p. 29).
15. For a more complete list of extrabiblical books contained in the Old Testament, see chap. 15.
16. Some of the Apocryphal books found among the Dead Sea Scrolls were written in Hebrew, e.g., Tobit, Apocryphal Daniel, and Jubilees. Cf. Menahem Mansoor, *The Dead Sea Scrolls,* p. 203.

cepted in the canon, and many young books were received, age could not have been the determining factor of canonicity.

Hebrew language determines canonicity. It has also been suggested that the Hebrew language is the key to the Old Testament canon. If a book were written in the "sacred" language of the Jews, it would have been placed with their sacred Scriptures, and if not, it would have been rejected. This view breaks down on two counts.

1. *Many books in the Hebrew language are not in the canon.* Most of the books written by the Hebrews were obviously in the Hebrew language, but they were not all accepted in the canon. Even though some of these books were extant in the Hebrew language at the time of the recognition of the Old Testament Scriptures, for example, Ecclesiasticus and other Apocryphal books,[16] yet they were not received into the Hebrew canon (see chap. 15).
2. *Some books not totally written in the Hebrew language are in the canon.* Parts of some of the books that were received into the Jewish canon were not in Hebrew at all, but in Aramaic. This fact is not only true of Daniel 2:4*b*—7:28, but of Ezra 4:8—6:18 and 7:12-26 as well. The thesis that the Hebrew language determines canonicity, then, breaks down for two reasons: some books in Hebrew were not accepted, whereas books which had some parts written in other languages were accepted as canonical.

Agreement with the Torah determines canonicity. To the Jews, ultimate criterion for all doctrine was the Torah, the law of Moses. This being the case, it has been suggested that all Hebrew religious literature that agreed with the teachings of the Torah was accepted into the canon, and all those books that disagreed with it were not. Of course, no book that contradicted the Torah would be accepted, because the Torah was believed to be God's Word, and no subsequent word from God could contradict a previous one. What this view does not account for are the numerous books that did agree with the Torah yet were not accepted into the canon. There are no doubt many noncanonical Old Testament books (see chap. 15) that agree with the Torah in their teaching but were never considered to be canonical.[17] Shemaiah the prophet and others kept "records" that no doubt agreed with the Torah (2 Chron. 12:15), yet they are not in the canon. Mere agreement with the Torah, or previous revelation, is not enough. The Jews no doubt thought that the Talmud and Midrash (see chap. 27) agreed with the Torah, but did not thereby consider them to be canonical. Moreover, this view does not account for the manner by which the Torah itself came to be viewed as canonical. There were

17. The letter written by Elijah the prophet is not an example of an uncanonical writing because the contents are recorded in 2 Chron. 21:12-15.

no writings prior to the time of the Torah by which its canonicity could be judged.

Religious value determines canonicity. Still another view that merits consideration is that the religious value of a given book was the determining factor of its reception into the canon. It is almost redundant to say that a book would be rejected if it did not have any spiritual or religious value, for the canon was a religious canon, and only a book of religious value would be accepted as a part of it. The mistake in this view is similar to that of the preceding one, that is, it fails to take into account that there are many books of religious value that were not accepted into either the Old or New Testament collections. Any honest, objective reading of the Apocrypha will reveal much material of religious value (cf. Ecclesiasticus). Furthermore, even if it be conceded that a book was accepted because of its religious value, that in no way explains *how it received its religious value*. The real question to be asked is: How (or from whom) did the books of spiritual import that agreed with the Torah (and God's previous revelations) receive their valued truth to begin with? Or, for that matter, where did the previous revelation in the Torah receive its truth and authority?

The religious community determines canonicity. According to this view, the final determination of canonicity is its acceptance by the believing community. A book then is canonical because it was collected and preserved by the community of believers. As Paul J. Achtemeier says,

> A further implication of the nature of Scripture as we have outlined it consists in the realization that Scripture has been produced out of the experience of a community as it sought to come to terms with a God whose nature was totally beyond that community's human perceptions, and who therefore acted in ways unaccountable by contemporary social or political customs. Scripture reflects not only God's word to the community but also that community's response, both positive and negative, to that word. Scripture did not drop as a stone from heaven. It grew out of the life of a community chosen by a God it barely understood and often did not want to follow, yet who would not release his people to their own devices.[18]

There are several serious objections to this view. First, a book is not the Word of God because it is accepted by the people of God. Rather, it was accepted by the people of God because it is the Word of God. That is, God gives the book its divine authority, not the people of God. They merely recognize the divine authority which God gives to it. Further, this view shifts the "locus of authority" from God to man, from the divine to the human. Thus, the divine authority of Scripture is determined by man. Finally, the final

18. Paul J. Achtemeier, *The Inspiration of Scripture: Problems and Proposals*, pp. 90-91. This is contrary to the notion of revelation as "disclosure," not "discovery," as discussed in chap. 2. Also see discussion in chap. 13.

acceptance of a book by the church of God often did not come for many generations, even centuries. But according to this view a book would not possess canonical authority, even if it came from God, until the people of God gave it divine authority. But this is obviously false. For if God spoke the words of a book by means of a prophet, then it had immediate authority, even if the people of God did not acknowledge it immediately.

A Mistake Common to the Inadequate Views of Canonicity

Underlying all the insufficient views of what determined canonicity is the failure to distinguish between *determination* and *recognition* of canonicity.

Canonicity is determined by God. Actually, a canonical book is valuable and true because God inspired it. That is, canonicity is determined or fixed conclusively by authority, and authority was given to the individual books by God through inspiration. The real question is not where a book received its divine authority, for that can only come from God; but how did men recognize that authority?

Canonicity is recognized by men of God. Inspiration determines canonicity. If a book was authoritative, it was so because God breathed it and made it so. How a book *received* authority, then, is determined by God. How men *recognize* that authority is another matter altogether (see discussion in chap. 13). As J. I. Packer notes, "The Church no more gave us the New Testament canon than Sir Isaac Newton gave us the force of gravity. God gave us gravity, by His work of creation, and similarly He gave us the New Testament canon, by inspiring the individual books that make it up."[19]

A More Sufficient View of Canonicity

Precisely speaking, canonicity is determined by God. In other words, the reason there are only sixty-six books in the canon is that God inspired only that many. Only sixty-six books were found to have the stamp of divine authority, because God only stamped that many, or invested that number with authority for faith and practice.

A book is valuable because it is canonical. A given book is not canonical because it was found to be valuable. Rather, it was found to be valuable because it was determined to be canonical by God. In other words, a book is not inspired because it is inspiring; it is inspiring because it is inspired.

A book is canonical because it is inspired. Edward J. Young presents the correct view, that *inspiration determines canonicity,* as he writes,

> When the Word of God was written it became Scripture and, inasmuch as it had been spoken by God, possessed absolute authority. Since it was the Word of God, it was canonical. That which determines the canonicity of a book, therefore, is

19. J. I. Packer, *God Speaks to Man,* p. 81.

> the fact that the book is inspired by God. Hence a distinction is properly made between the authority which the Old Testament possesses as divinely inspired, and the recognition of that authority on the part of Israel.[20]

Although his discussion has primarily centered on the Old Testament, the principles are also applicable to the New Testament.

In brief, a book is canonical if it is prophetic, that is, if it was written by a prophet of God. In other words, *propheticity determines canonicity*. Of course one did not have to belong to the school of the prophets begun by Samuel (1 Sam. 19:20) or to be a disciple ("son") of a prophet (2 Kings 2:3). All one needed was a prophetic gift as Amos (7:14) or Daniel (7:1) possessed. A prophet was a mouthpiece of God. He was one to whom God spoke in visions, dreams, and sundry ways. Even kings such as David (2 Sam. 23:1-2) and Solomon (1 Kings 9:2) were prophets in this sense. It was necessary to have prophetic gifts in order to write canonical Scripture, because all inspired writing is "prophetic" (Heb. 1:1; 2 Pet. 1:19-20).

Canonicity Discussed

The Authors Were Apostles or Prophets

The same principle applies to the New Testament: *propheticity determines canonicity.* The church is "built upon the foundation of the apostles and prophets" (Eph. 2:20). Apostles, by their very office, were accredited spokesmen for God. It was they whom Jesus promised: "The Holy Spirit ... will teach you all things, and bring to your remembrance all that I said to you" (John 14:26) and "the Spirit of truth ... will guide you into all the truth" (John 16:13). It was the "apostles' teaching" in which the early church continued (Acts 2:42) and it was the apostles who were given special signs (miracles) to confirm their message (Heb. 2:3-4). Those confirmatory signs were given to other apostles than the twelve, such as the apostle Paul, who had "the signs of a true apostle" (2 Cor. 12:12). There was also the gift of prophecy (1 Cor. 12:10). Some "prophets," such as Agabus, even gave messages from God to apostles (Acts 11:27-28). John the apostle considered himself one of "the prophets" (Rev. 22:9). So, in the New Testament as well as the Old, the determining factor in whether a book was canonical was its propheticity.

Every New Testament book was written by an apostle or prophet. Thus each book has either apostolic *authorship* or apostolic *teaching*. And in either case it possesses apostolic authority. Matthew was an apostle. Mark is considered by many to be "Peter's gospel," because Mark was closely associated with the apostle Peter (1 Pet. 5:13). That relationship notwithstanding,

20. Edward J. Young, "The Canon of the Old Testament," in Carl F. H. Henry, ed., *Revelation and the Bible*, p. 156.

Mark had his own God-given ministry (Acts 12:25; 2 Tim. 4:11). The author of Luke was an associate of the apostle Paul (Col. 4:14; Philem. 24). Luke also wrote Acts (1:1). John was an apostle. He wrote John, three epistles bearing his name, and Revelation (Rev. 1:4, 9). Paul wrote at least the thirteen epistles that bear his name (Romans-Philemon). The author of Hebrews is not known for sure. But whoever its author was, he received revelation from God (Heb. 1:1), the truth of which was confirmed by the twelve apostles (Heb. 2:3-4). James was a half brother of Jesus (James 1:1; Gal. 1:19) and a leader in the apostolic church in Jerusalem (Acts 15:13; Gal. 2:9). The apostle Peter authored two epistles (see 1 Pet. 1:1; 2 Pet. 2:1), although he used Silvanus as a scribe to pen the first one (1 Pet. 5:12). This leaves only Jude, who was also a half brother of Jesus (Jude 1:1; cf. Matt. 13:55), and he too spoke with prophetic authority (vs. 3, 5, 20ff.).

There is good evidence that all twenty-seven books of the New Testament come from the apostles and their associates. Indeed, even some liberal scholars are now insisting on a very early apostolic date for the New Testament books. Bishop John A. T. Robinson, father of the so-called "Death of God" movement, has more recently concluded that "all the various types of the early church's literature ... were coming into being more or less concurrently in the period between 40 and 70."[21] The renowned archaeologist William F. Albright came to the same conclusion, declaring that "every book of the New Testament was written by a baptized Jew between the forties and the eighties of the first century A.D. (very probably some time between A.D. 50 and 75)."[22] Jesus died in A.D. 33,[23] so the New Testament was written during the lifetime of the apostles and eyewitnesses (see Luke 1:1-4; 1 Cor. 15:6).

Ample evidence confirms that all the books of the New Testament are apostolic or prophetic. The question that remains is whether all the apostolic books are in the New Testament. Two books in particular have been called into question: the so-called Epistle of the Laodiceans (Col. 4:16) and a Corinthian epistle some believe was written before 1 Corinthians (see 1 Cor. 5:9). These books pose a problem concerning canonicity because they were both prophetic and yet are allegedly not in the canon. If propheticity is the key to canonicity, how is it that some prophetic (or apostolic) books are not in the canon? There are two basic responses to this question.

First, it is possible that these books were not prophetic, for in addition to their divinely authoritative writings, the prophets and apostles had private or personal correspondence. They may even have had grocery lists, travel itineraries, or the like. Such items were not inspired. Shemaiah the prophet and Iddo the seer had some "records" (2 Chron. 12:15) that were probably not inspired. There seem to be two keys as to whether or not a writing by a person

21. John A. T. Robinson, *Redating the New Testament,* p. 352.
22. William F. Albright, "Toward a More Conservative View," p. 3 (359).
23. See Harold Hoehner, *Chronological Aspects of the Life of Christ,* p. 114.

(who was a prophet) was prophetic. First, it had to be a *public,* not strictly a private writing. That is, it had to be offered to the people of God and not merely a private record. For example, of Solomon's 3,000 proverbs and 1,005 songs only those publicly presented by Solomon were immediately recognized as authoritative (see chap. 13 discussion). Second, it had to be *teaching* something to the people of God. In short, it had to be a word from God for the people of God. Even Paul's so-called private epistles (1 and 2 Timothy, Titus, and Philemon) fit these criteria, as do 2 and 3 John, which many believe were written to individuals. All of these books contain instructions written to leaders of churches, and the books were obviously circulated and collected by the churches. Otherwise they would not have been part of the Bible through the centuries. The Bible does not guarantee that everything a prophet *says* or *writes* is from God but only that what he teaches as a truth from God is really from God. In short, a prophet is not infallible in his *private* utterance but only in his *prophetic* utterances. Hence it is possible that the prophets wrote other things which were not prophetic.

Second, it is possible that a book could be prophetic but still not canonic. For although all canonic writings are prophetic, it is possible that not all prophetic writings are canonic. That is, perhaps God did not intend that all prophetic books would be preserved for posterity but only those select few He deemed necessary for the believer's faith and practice. If that be so, then propheticity is only a *necessary* condition of canonicity but not a *sufficient* condition. In that case there would be another condition for canonicity. The most likely candidate for such a further condition would be *acceptance by the people of God* of the books they deemed of value to the broader Christian community. But this view would mean that there are (or could be) books that are inspired words of God but not part of the Inspired Word of God. This is not only unlikely but is also unnecessary.

There is another more plausible possibility: *all* prophetic books may be in the canon. That is, it is possible that no prophetic book has been left out of the canon. There are plausible explanations for the only known books that are apparent exceptions to this principle, as the following discussion indicates.

1. *The "Letter ... from Elijah"* (2 Chron. 21:12-15). This is a public prophetic exhortation. Hence, it had divine authority and thereby qualified for the canon. But as a matter of fact, the letter is in the canon. The letter is included as part of the text in 2 Chronicles 21:12-15. Because it is in the canon, it poses no difficulty.

2. *"The records of Shemaiah the prophet"* (2 Chron. 12:15). This book was definitely written by a prophet, and it seems certain that it is not identical to any of the existing books in the Old Testament. However, it is possible that the book, though written by a prophet, was not prophetic. It is called a "record." Perhaps it was a mere geneological enrollment without any implied or stated religious instruction or exhortation. In that respect it is unlike the

canonical books of Chronicles, in even which the geneological sections contain religious instructions and redemptive material, such as the messianic lineage (see 1 Chron. 5:25; 9:1, 22).

3. *"The Chronicles of Samuel . . . Nathan the prophet . . . and Gad the seer"* (1 Chron. 29:29). These books correspond to 1 and 2 Samuel in their content and coverage. Hence, it is possible that if their contents were prophetic they are contained within the confines of the canonical books of 1 and 2 Samuel. On the other hand, they may have been mere uninspired records kept by these public servants and used later as a factual basis for the inspired books of Samuel.

4. *"The vision of Isaiah the prophet"* (2 Chron. 32:32). This is an inspired writing, but it is probably the same as the canonical book of Isaiah, which was collected within a larger corpus called "the Book of the Kings of Judah and Israel" (v. 32; see also 33:18).[24]

5. *The "many" accounts referred to by Luke*. Luke said, "Many have undertaken to compile an account" of Jesus' life (Luke 1:1). There are two possible explanations for this comment. First, if Matthew and Mark (and even John) wrote before Luke, they could be the "many" others to whom Luke refers. The Greek word "many" (*polloi*) can mean as few as two or three. On the other hand, even if other gospel accounts are in view, those other records may not have been prophetic. That is, it is possible that they were not offered by an accredited prophet as a message from God for His people. Thus, being non-prophetic by nature, they would not be candidates to be included in the canon of Scripture.

6. *The so-called "real" 1 Corinthians* (1 Cor. 5:9). This book poses a much more serious threat to the theory that all truly prophetic writings are in the present canon of Scripture. For it was definitely written by an accredited apostle (Paul), and it did contain religious instruction and exhortation (1 Cor. 5:9-13). Hence, either this so-called "real" First Corinthians must be contained within one of the existing books of the Bible or else the theory fails. There are two possibilities for identifying the book to which Paul refers with an existing book of the Bible. First, he may be referring to part of the present 2 Corinthians (e.g., chapters 10-13), which was put together with another part of his Corinthian correspondence at a later time. Second Corinthians chapters 1-9 is definitely different in tone from the rest of the present book (chapters 10-13), which could indicate that it was originally written on a different occasion.

Second, there is also the possibility that Paul is referring to the present 1 Corinthians in 1 Corinthians 5:9, that is, to the very book he was then writing. It is true that he uses an aorist tense here, which could be translated "I wrote," thus identifying some previous letter. But the aorist tense could refer to the

24. See Keil and Delitzsch, *Biblical Commentary on the Old Testament, The Books of the Chronicles,* 7.28-38.

book at hand. Such a device is called an "epistolary aorist," because it refers to the very epistle in which it is being used. Although the aorist tense could be translated "I wrote," the aorist tense in Greek is not a past tense as such. The Greek aorist tense has primary reference to the *kind* of action, not the *time* of action it portrays. It identifies a completed action that may even require a long time to be accomplished (cf. John 2:20). Hence, Paul could be saying something like this: "I am now decisively writing to you." That would certainly fit the urgency of his message in the context. Further, the same epistolary use of the aorist is found elsewhere in this very letter (1 Cor. 9:15). Moreover, there is no indication from the early history of the church that any such letter (other than the existing 1 Corinthians) ever existed. The reference to Paul's enemies in 2 Corinthians 10:10 need not be taken to mean that he actually wrote many other letters to them. It may mean no more than "what Paul writes is weighty." The "now" (KJV) of 1 Corinthians 5:11 need not indicate a later letter. It can be translated "rather" (RSV) or "actually" (NASB). In short, it is not necessary to take 1 Corinthians 5:9 as a reference to any other epistle than the present 1 Corinthians, which is in the canon.

7. *The epistle of the Laodiceans* (Col. 4:16). This epistle is another authoritative book. It is clear from the facts within it that it was written by an apostle who enjoined both its reading and circulation among the churches (Col. 4:16). Hence, if this Laodicean book were not one of the present twenty-seven books of the New Testament, then a truly apostolic book would have been excluded in the canon. And if that be so, then one would have to reject the view that all prophetic books are in the canon. However, such a conclusion is not required. It is entirely possible that this letter is really the book of Ephesians. The following evidence may be offered in support of that thesis: (1) The text does not call it the epistle *of* the Laodiceans. Rather, it is called the "letter that is coming *from* Laodicea," whatever it may have been named. (2) It is known that Paul wrote Ephesians at the same time he wrote Colossians and sent it to another church in the same general area. (3) There is some evidence that Ephesians did not originally bear that title but was a kind of cyclical letter intended for the churches of Asia Minor in general. As a matter of fact, some early manuscripts do not have the expression "in Ephesus" (Eph. 1:1) in them. It is certainly strange that Paul, who spent three years ministering to the Ephesians (Acts 20:31), has no personal greetings in the book, if it were intended only for them. Paul had numerous personal greetings in Romans (chap. 16), and he never ministered there prior to writing that epistle. In view of all those factors, it makes sense to conclude that the so-called Laodicean letter is probably the canonical book of Ephesians. Add to this the fact that no "epistle of the Laodiceans" is referred to in early church writings, and one has a convincing case that no such apostolic book is missing from the New Testament canon. If so, then it is possible that not only all the canonic books are prophetic, but that all prophetic books are in the canon.

The Canon Is Closed

This statement raises an interesting question: What *if* a truly prophetic or apostolic book were found today: would it belong in the canon? Of course, the question is only hypothetical, and so the answer is only hypothetical, too. But it is an interesting question, and it does focus an important issue not yet stressed: *the providence of God*. It seems highly unlikely that God would have inspired a book He did not preserve. Why should He give a revelation for the church but not provide for the preservation of it? It is understandable that God might give special guidance to certain individuals, which He did not deem necessary to do for the broader body of believers. But to provide instruction in the Christian faith by way of a revelation He did not preserve for others is another matter altogether. Perhaps the question could be rephrased this way: Is the biblical canon closed? To this one should respond that the canon is closed theologically and historically, and is open only hypothetically.

Theologically the canon is closed. God has inspired only so many books and they were all completed by the end of the apostolic period (first century A.D.). God used to speak through the prophets of the Old Testament, but in the "last days" he spoke through Christ (Heb. 1:1) and the apostles whom He empowered with special "signs" (miracles). But because the apostolic age ended with the death of the apostles (Acts 1:22), and because no one since apostolic times has had the "signs of a true apostle" (2 Cor. 12:12) whereby they can raise the dead (Acts 20:10-12) and perform other unique supernatural events (Acts 3:1-10; 28:8-9), it may be concluded that God's "last day" revelation is complete (see Acts 2:16-18). This does not mean that God's *visitations* are over, because there are many other things yet to be fulfilled (see Acts 2:19-20). Nor does it mean that there will be no new *understanding* of God's truth after the first century. It simply means that there is *no new revelation* for the church. Indeed, this does not necessarily imply that there have been no miracles since the first century. Supernatural acts will be possible as long as there is a Supernatural Being (God). It is not the *fact* of miracles that ceased with the apostles but the special *gift* of miracles possessed by a prophet or apostle who could claim, like Moses, Elijah, Peter, or Paul, to have a new revelation from God. Such a prophet or apostle could back up his claim by dividing a sea, bringing down fire from heaven, or raising the dead. These were special gifts bestowed on prophets (apostles), and they are not possessed by those who are not the recipients of new revelation (Acts 2:22; Heb. 2:3-4).

Historically the canon is closed. For there is no evidence that any such special *gift* of miracles has existed since the death of the apostles. The immediate successors of the apostles did not claim new revelation, nor did they claim these special confirmatory gifts. In fact, they looked on the apostolic revelation as full and final (see chaps. 6, 16, and 17). When new cults have arisen since the time of the apostles, their leaders have claimed to be apostles in order that their books could gain recognition. Historically, the canon is closed with the twenty-seven books written in the apostolic period. They alone are and have been the books of the canon through all the intervening centuries. No other non-apostolic books have been accepted since the earliest centuries, and no new books written by the apostles have come to light. In His providence, God has guided the church in the preservation of all the canonical books.

The canonical books are those *necessary* for faith and practice of believers of all generations. It seems highly unlikely that God would inspire a book in the first century that is necessary for faith and practice and then allow it to be lost for nearly two thousand years. From a providential and historical standpoint the canon has been closed for nearly two thousand years.

Hypothetically the canon could be open. It is theoretically possible that some book written by an accredited apostle or prophet from the first century will yet be found. And what *if* such a prophetic book were found? The answer to this question will depend on whether or not *all* prophetic books are canonic. If they are, as has been argued, then this newly discovered prophetic book should be added to the canon. But that is unlikely for two reasons. First, it is *historically unlikely* that such a new book intended for the faith and practice of all believers, but unknown to them for two thousand years, will suddenly come to light. Second, it is *providentially improbable* that God would have inspired but left unpreserved for two millennia what is necessary for the instruction of believers of all generations.

Summary and Conclusion

The history of the word *canon* indicates a development from a literal rod or ruler to the concept of a standard for something. Subsequently the word was applied to the *rule of faith,* that is, the normative writings or authoritative Scriptures, which were the standard of faith and practice. Just how that standard or canon was determined is the subject of some misunderstanding. With that in view, the present chapter has discussed that which determined canonicity. Several insufficient views have been suggested, for example, (1) age decided the issue; (2) Hebrew language determined it; (3) agreement with the Torah did; (4) religious value determined whether or not a book was canonical; or (5) the religious community determines canonicity. However, all those views share one common weakness: they fail to distinguish between the *determination* of canonicity (a work of God) and the *recognition* of canonicity (a work of men). The biblical view is that inspiration determines canonicity; a book is valuable because it is inspired, and not inspired because men found it to be valuable.

So canonicity is determined by God, not by the people of God. The simple answer to the question "Why are there only these books in the Bible?" is that God inspired only these and no more. If God had given more books through more prophets, then there would be a larger canon. But, because *propheticity determines canonicity,* only the prophetic books can be canonical. Furthermore, it is probable that in God's providence He has preserved *all* the prophetic books. If so, then not only all canonical books are prophetic, but all prophetic books are canonical.

13
The Discovery and Recognition of Canonicity

How the Canon Was Determined

Definition

Canonicity is determined by God. A book is not inspired because men made it canonical; it is canonical because God inspired it. It is not the antiquity, authenticity, or religious community that makes a book canonical or authoritative. On the contrary, a book is valuable because it is canonical, and not canonical because it is or was considered valuable. Inspiration determines canonization, and confusion at this point not only dulls the edge of authority but it mistakes the effect (a canonical book) for the cause (inspiration of God). Canonicity is *determined* or established authoritatively by God; it is merely *discovered* by man.

Distinction

The distinction between God's determination and man's discovery is essential to the correct view of canonicity, and should be drawn carefully. This may be done by a careful comparison of the following two views. The

The Incorrect View	The Correct View
The Church Is Determiner of Canon	The Church Is Discoverer of Canon
The Church Is Mother of Canon	The Church Is Child of Canon
The Church Is Magistrate of Canon	The Church Is Minister of Canon
The Church Is Regulator of Canon	The Church Is Recognizer of Canon
The Church Is Judge of Canon	The Church Is Witness of Canon
The Church is Master of Canon	The Church Is Servant of Canon

comparison is shown in the accompanying chart. In the "Incorrect View"[1] the authority of the Scriptures is based upon the authority of the church; the correct view is that the authority of the church is to be found *in* the authority of the Scriptures. The incorrect view places the church *over* the canon, whereas the proper position views the church *under* the canon. In fact, if in the column title "Incorrect View," the word *church* be replaced by *God,* then the proper view of the canon emerges clearly. It is God who *regulated* the canon; man merely *recognized* the divine authority God gave to it. God *determined* the canon, and man *discovered* it. Louis Gaussen gives an excellent summary of this position:

> In this affair, then, the Church is a servant and not a mistress; a depository and not a judge. She exercises the office of a minister, not of a magistrate.... She delivers a testimony, not a judicial sentence. She discerns the canon of the Scriptures, she does not make it; she has recognized their authenticity, she has not given it.... The authority of the Scriptures is not founded, then, on the authority of the Church: It is the Church that is founded on the authority of the Scriptures.[2]

How the Canon Was Discovered

The Methodology Employed

In order for man to discover which books God determined to be canonical, an appropriate method of must be employed. Otherwise, the list of canonical books might be varied and incorrectly identified. Many procedures used in the study of the canon of the Old Testament have been marred by the use of fallacious methods. Several of these have been set forth succinctly by Roger Beckwith:

Five particular fallacies of method which have hitherto vitiated much writing on our theme deserve to be singled out:

- (i) failure to distinguish evidence that a book was known from evidence that a book was canonical;
- (ii) failure to distinguish disagreement about the canon between different parties from uncertainty about the canon within those parties;
- (iii) failure to distinguish between the adding of books to the canon and the removal of books from it;
- (iv) failure to distinguish between the canon which the community recognized and used, and the eccentric views of individuals about it;

1. It is not correct to identify this "Incorrect View" with that of the Roman Catholic Council of Trent or Vatican I or II. Vatican I pronounced that the books of the Bible are held by the church to be "sacred and canonical, not because, having been carefully composed by mere human industry, they were afterwards approved by her authority ... but because, having been written by the inspiration of the Holy Ghost, they have God for their author, and have been delivered as such to the Church herself."
2. Louis Gaussen, *Theopneustia,* p. 137.

(v) failure to make proper use of Jewish evidence about the canon transmitted through Christian hands, whether by denying its Jewish origins, or by ignoring the Christian medium through which it has come.[3]

The Principles Involved

It is all very well to assume that God gave authority and hence canonicity to the Bible, but another question arises, namely, *How* did man discover or become aware of what God had done? How did the church Fathers know when they had come upon a canonical book? The commonly accepted canonical books of the Bible themselves make reference to many other books that are no longer available, for example, the "Book of Jasher" (Josh. 10:13); "the Book of the Wars of the Lord" (Num. 21:14). Then there are the Apocryphal books and the so-called "lost books" of the Bible.[4] How did the Fathers know those were not inspired? Did not John (21:25) and Luke (1:1) indicate that there was a profusion of religious literature? Were there not false epistles (2 Thess. 2:2)? What were the earmarks of inspiration that guided the Fathers in their recognition and collection of the inspired books? How did they sort out the true from the false, and the canonical from the apocryphal? Perhaps the very fact that some canonical books were doubted at times, on the basis of one principle or another, argues both for the value of the principle and the caution of the Fathers in their recognition of canonicity. If so, it provides assurance that the people of God really included no books that God wanted excluded from the canon. In the following discussion, several foundational questions are raised that lie at the very heart of the discovery process.

Was the book written by a prophet of God? The most basic question asked about a book was: *Is it prophetic?* For as was discussed in chapter 12, propheticity determined canonicity. If it was written by a spokesman for God, then it was the Word of God. The characteristic words "And the word of the Lord came to the prophet," or "The Lord said unto," or "God spoke" so fill the prophetic pages of the Old Testament that they have become proverbial. These earmarks of inspiration are so clear and resounding in the prophets that it is hardly necessary to mark them as divine in their origin.

A prophet was the mouthpiece of God. His function is clarified by the various descriptions given him. He was called a man of God (1 Kings 12:22), revealing that he was chosen of God; a servant of the Lord (1 Kings 14:18), indicating his occupation; a messenger of the Lord (Isa. 42:19), designating his mission for God; a seer or beholder (Isa. 30:10), revealing apocalyptic source of his truth; a man of the Spirit (Hos. 9:7), showing by whose promptings he spoke; a watchman (Ezek. 3:17), manifesting his alertness to do the

3. Roger Beckwith, *The Old Testament Canon of the New Testament Church and Its Background in Early Judaism,* pp. 7-8.
4. See discussion in chap. 12.

work of God. By far and away, the most common expression was "prophet," or spokesman for God.

By his very calling, a prophet was one who felt as did Amos, "The Lord God has spoken; who can but prophesy?" (Amos 3:8); or, as another prophet who said, "I could not do anything, either small or great, contrary to the command of the Lord my God" (Num. 22:18). Aaron was a prophet or mouthpiece for Moses (Ex. 7:1), speaking "all the words which the Lord had spoken to Moses" (Ex. 4:30). Even so God's prophets were to speak only what He commanded them. God said of His prophets, "I will put My words in his mouth, and he shall speak to them all that I command him" (Deut. 18:18). Further, "You shall not add to the word which I am commanding you, nor take away from it" (Deut. 4:2). In short, a prophet was one who declared what God had disclosed to him. Thus, only the prophetic writings were canonic. Anything not written by a spokesman (prophet) of God was not part of the Word of God.

In view of the nature of religious exhortation by a prophet, it is reasonable to conclude that whatever is written by a prophet of God is the Word of God. In most cases it is simply a matter of establishing the authorship of the book. If it was written by an apostle or prophet (the prophetic principle), then its place in the canon is secured. Therefore, any historical or stylistic (external or internal) evidence that supports the genuineness of a prophetic book (see chap. 20) is also an argument for its canonicity. This was exactly the argument Paul used in the support of his epistle to the Galatians (Gal. 1:1-24). He argued that his message was authoritative because he was an authorized messenger of God, "an apostle not sent from men nor through the agency of man, but through Jesus Christ, and God the Father" (Gal. 1:1). He also turned the tables on his opponents who preached "a different gospel; which is really not another; only . . . to distort the gospel of Christ" (Gal. 1:6-7). His opponents' gospel could not be true because they were "false brethren" (Gal. 2:4). It should be noted in this connection that occasionally the Bible *contains* true prophecies from individuals whose status as men of God is questionable, such as Balaam (Num. 24:17) and Caiaphas (John 11:49). However, granted that their prophecies were consciously given,[5] these prophets were not writers of Bible books, but were merely quoted by the actual writer. Therefore, their utterances are in the same category as the Greek poets quoted by the apostle Paul (cf. Acts 17:28; 1 Cor. 15:33; Titus 1:12).

As previously mentioned, Paul used against the false teachers opposing him at Galatia the argument that a book from God must be written by a man of God. It was also used as a reason for rejecting a letter that was forged, or written under false pretenses, as the one mentioned in 2 Thessalonians 2:2. A book cannot be canonical if it is not genuine (see chap. 20). In this connec-

5. In the case of Caiaphas it would seem that the prophecy was given unwittingly.

tion, however, it should be noted that a book might use the device of literary impersonation with no intent to deceive, by which the writer assumes the role of another for effect. Some scholars feel such is the case in the book of Ecclesiastes, where *Koheleth* wrote autobiographically as though he were Solomon.[6] Such a view is not incompatible with the principle herein presented, provided it can be shown to be a literary device and not a moral deception. However, when an author pretends to be an apostle in order to gain acceptance of his unorthodox ideas, as the writers of many New Testament apocryphal books did, then it is moral deception (see chap. 17).

Because of this "prophetic" principle, 2 Peter was disputed in the early church.[7] On the basis of internal evidence (differences in the style of writing), it was felt by some that the author of 2 Peter could not be the same as the author of 1 Peter. But 2 Peter claimed to have been written by "Simon Peter, a servant and apostle of Jesus Christ" (2 Pet. 1:1). Thus, the epistle was either a forgery or there was great difficulty in explaining its different style. Those who were disturbed by such evidence doubted the genuineness of 2 Peter and it was placed among the Antilegomena books for a time (see chap. 17). It was finally admitted to be canonical, but only on the grounds that it was also Petrine. The differences in style between 1 and 2 Peter can be accounted for by the time lapse, different occasions, and the fact that Peter used an amanuensis for his first epistle (1 Pet. 5:13).

The benchmark of inspiration is so clear in the prophetic writings that it was hardly necessary to look for any other characteristic to show their divine origin and authority. Some books were rejected because of their absence of authority, as in the books of Pseudepigrapha (see chap. 14). These books did not have the "ring" of authority, or, if they claimed authority, the claim had a hollow sound. They provided no character to support their claim. In many cases the books were fanciful and magical, and hardly anyone mistook their divine claims to be dogmatic commands from God. Their shallow pretentions were clearly not sovereign intentions, and so they were emphatically rejected. This same principle of authority was the basis for some books' being doubted and spoken against, as in the Antilegomena books (see chap. 14). For a time the book of Esther, in which even the name of God is conspicuously absent, fell into this category. Finally, upon closer examination, Esther retained its place in the canon, but only because the Fathers were convinced that authority was present, although some did not consider it observably present.[8]

6. See Herbert Carl Leupold, *Exposition of Ecclesiastes* (Columbus,Ohio: Wartburg, 1952), pp. 8ff. for a defense of this view by a conservative scholar. Other orthodox scholars favor the Solomonic authorship. See Gleason L. Archer, Jr., *A Survey of Old Testament Introduction,* pp. 478-88.
7. Even Eusebius *Ecclesiastical History* 3.3, in the fourth century said, "But the so-called second Epistle we have not received as canonical, but nevertheless it has appeared useful to many, and has been studied with other Scriptures" (Loeb, ed., 1:193).
8. See chap. 15 for the discussion and support for Esther's canonicity.

Was the writer confirmed by acts of God? There were true prophets and false prophets (Matt. 7:15). Hence, it was necessary to have a divine confirmation of the true ones. Miracles were used for this purpose. Moses was given miraculous powers to prove his call of God (Ex. 4:1-9). Elijah triumphed over the false prophets of Baal by a supernatural act (1 Kings 18). Jesus was "attested to . . . by God with miracles and wonders and signs which God performed through Him" (Acts 2:22). Even Nicodemus, the ruler of the Jews, said to him, "Rabbi, we know that You have come from God as a teacher; for no one can do these signs that You do unless God is with him" (John 3:2). As to the apostle's message, "God [was] also bearing witness with them, both by signs and wonders and by various miracles and by gifts of the Holy Spirit according to His own will" (Heb. 2:4). Paul gave testimony to his apostleship to the Corinthians declaring, "the signs of a true apostle were performed among you with all perseverence, by signs and wonders and miracles" (2 Cor. 12:12). In short, a miracle is an act of God to confirm the Word of God given through a prophet of God to the people of God. It is the sign to substantiate his sermon; the miracle to confirm his message. Not every prophetic revelation was confirmed by a specific miracle. There were other ways to determine the authenticity of an alleged prophet.[9] So if there were any question about one's prophetic credentials it could be settled by divine confirmation, as indeed it was on numerous occasions throughout Scripture (Ex. 4; Num. 16-17; 1 Kings 18; Mark 2; Acts 5).

Did the message tell the truth about God? Only the immediate contemporaries had access to the supernatural confirmation of the prophet's message. Hence, other believers in distant places or subsequent times had to depend on other tests for the canonicity of a book. One such test was the *authenticity* of a book (see chap. 20). That is, does the book tell the truth about God and his world as known from previous revelations? God cannot contradict Himself (2 Cor. 1:17-18), nor can He utter what is false (Heb. 6:18). Hence, no book with false claims can be the Word of God. Moses stated this principle, saying,

> If a prophet or a dreamer of dreams arises among you and gives you a sign or a wonder, and the sign or the wonder comes true, concerning which he spoke to you, saying, "Let us go after other gods (whom you have not known) and let us serve them," you shall not listen to the words of that prophet or that dreamer of dreams. (Deut. 13:1-3)

So, any teaching about God contrary to what His people already knew to be true was to be rejected. Furthermore, any predictions made about the world which failed to come true indicated that a prophet's words should be rejected. As Moses said to Israel,

9. See discussion in chaps. 12 and 14.

> And you may say in your heart, "How shall we know the word which the Lord has not spoken?" When a prophet speaks in the name of the Lord, if the thing does not come about or come true, that is the thing which the Lord has not spoken. The prophet has spoken it presumptuously; you shall not be afraid of him. (Deut. 18:21-22)

In fact, any prophet who made such false claims was severely punished. For the Lord said, "The prophet who shall speak a word presumptuously in My name which I have not commanded him to speak, or which he shall speak in the name of other gods, that prophet shall die" (Deut. 18:20). That kind of punishment would not only assure no repeat performance by that prophet but would give other prophets pause before they said, "Thus says the Lord."[10]

Of course, simply because a book is not false does not make it canonical. Thus, this is more a test for the *inauthenticity* of a book than for its canonicity. That is, it is a negative test that could eliminate books from the canon. It is not a positive test to discover whether or not a book was canonical. This authenticity test was no doubt the reason that the Bereans searched the Scriptures to see whether Paul's teaching was true (Acts 17:11). If the preaching of the apostle did not accord with the teaching of the Old Testament canon, then it could not be of God. Agreement with the rest of the known Word of God does not necessarily make a book canonical, but disagreement would certainly relegate a book to a noncanonical status.

Much of the Apocrypha was rejected because it was not authentic (see chaps. 15 and 17). The Jewish Fathers and early Christian Fathers rejected, or considered second-rate, these books because they had historical inaccuracies and even moral incongruities. The Reformers rejected some because of what they considered heretical teaching.[11] The apostle John strongly urged that "truth" be tested by the known standard before it be received (1 John 4:1-6). Logically, a book from the God of truth *must* accord with the truth of God. If its claim is divine but its credentials are inauthentic, then the credentials must supersede the claim.

The test of authenticity was the reason a few of the canonical books, such as James and Jude, have been doubted by some. Some thought that Jude could not have been authentic, because it supposedly quoted from unauthentic Pseudepigraphal books (Jude 9, 14).[12] Martin Luther questioned the full canonicity of James because he thought the book taught salvation by works, and that teaching was contrary to the doctrine of salvation by faith as it was clearly taught in other Scriptures.[13] Historically and uniformly, Jude and James have been vindicated and their canonicity recognized, but only when their teaching had been harmonized with the rest of the body of Scripture.

10. See Neil Babcox, *A Search for Charismatic Reality,* for a vivid illustration of this point.
11. Such as praying for the dead, which 2 Maccabees 12:45 supports.
12. See Jerome *Lives of Illustrious Men* 4. See chapter 15 for discussion on the pseudepigrapha.

What has compounded the problem has been the failure of men to see that further truth can be complementary and supplementary without being contradictory to existing truth. But because the Fathers held a kind of "if in doubt throw it out" policy, the validity of their discernment of the canonical books is enhanced.

Does it come with the power of God? Another test for canonicity was the edifying effect of a book. Does it have the power of God? The Fathers believed the Word of God is "living and active" (Heb. 4:12),[14] and consequently ought to have a transforming force for edification (2 Tim. 3:17) and evangelization (1 Peter 1:23). If the message of a book did not effect its stated goal, if it did not have the power to change a life, then God was apparently not behind its message. A *message* of God would certainly be backed by the *might* of God. The Fathers believed that the Word of God can accomplish its purpose in the lives of the people of God (Isa. 55:11).

The apostle Paul applied this principle to the Old Testament when he wrote to Timothy, "And that from a child thou hast known the holy scriptures, which are able to make thee wise unto salvation" (2 Tim. 3:15, KJV). If it is of God, it will work—it will come to pass. This simple test was given by Moses to try the truth of a prophet's prediction (Deut. 18:20 ff.). If his prophecy did not materialize, then it was not from God.

On that basis, much heretical literature and even some good noncanonical apostolical literature was rejected from the canon of Scripture. Even those books whose teaching was spiritual, but whose message was at best only devotional, were deemed not to be canonical. Such is the case for the vast amount of literature written in the apostolic and subapostolic period (see chap. 17). As a result, those books were refused a place in the canon. When the transition is made from the canonical books of the New Testament to the other religious writings of the apostolic period, "one is conscious of a tremendous change. There is not the same freshness and originality, depth and clearness. And this is no wonder, for it means the transition from truth given by infallible inspiration to truth produced by fallible pioneers."[15] The noncanonical books lacked power; they were devoid of the dynamic aspects found in inspired Scripture. In short, they did not come with the power of God.

Because a book must come with edifying power in order to be considered canonical, some books (such as the Song of Solomon and Ecclesiastes) were

13. Luther placed James at the end of the New Testament, saying, "I do not regard it as the writing of an apostle; and my reasons follow. In the first place it is flatly against St. Paul and all the rest of Scripture in ascribing justification to works...therefore, I cannot include him among the chief books, though I would not thereby prevent anyone from including or extolling him as he pleases, for there are otherwise many good sayings in him." See E. Theodore Bachmann, ed., "Preface to Epistles of St. James and St. Jude," *Luther's Works,* 35:396-97.
14. Greek: "effectual, active, powerful," cf. Walter Bauer, *A Greek-English Lexicon of the New Testament and Other Early Christian Literature,* p. 265.
15. Louis Berkhof, *The History of Christian Doctrines,* p. 42.

the subject of occasional doubts. Could a book that is sensual or another that is skeptical be from God? Obviously not. And as long as these books were thought of in that manner, they could not be acclaimed as canonical. Eventually, the messages of those books were seen as spiritual and hence the books themselves were recognized as canonical.[16] The principle, nevertheless, was applied to all the books impartially. Some passed the test, whereas others failed. In the end, this much was certain: no book that lacked essential edificational or practical characteristics was considered canonical.

Was it accepted by the people of God? If a book was prophetic it was canonic. A prophet of God was confirmed by an act of God (miracle) and was a spokesman recognized by the people of God to whom he gave his message. Thus, the seal of canonicity was whether or not the book was accepted by the people of God. This does not mean that everybody in the community to which the prophetic message was addressed accepted it as divinely authoritative. On occasion even a prophet (see 1 Kings 17-19; 2 Chron. 36:11-16) or an apostle (Gal. 1) was initially rejected by some in the community. However, true believers in the community acknowledged the prophetic nature of the message, as did other contemporary believers familiar with the prophet. This acceptance by the people of God occurred in two stages: initial acceptance and subsequent recognition.

The *initial acceptance* of a book by the people to whom it was addressed is crucial. Paul said of the Thessalonians, "We also constantly thank God that when you received from us the word of God's message, you accepted it not as the word of men, but for what it really is, the word of God" (1 Thess. 2:13). For whatever subsequent debate there may have been about a book's place in the canon, the people in the best position to know its prophetic credentials were those who knew the prophet who wrote it. Hence, despite all later debate about the canonicity of some books, the definitive evidence is that which attests to its original acceptance by the contemporary believers. Of course some books were comprised of sections written over long periods of time (like Psalms) or by several authors (see Prov. 30:1; 31:1). But the individual parts of these books were recognized by their contemporaries to come from spokesmen of God.

There is ample evidence in Scripture that books were immediately accepted into the canon by contemporaries of the writers. For example, when Moses wrote, his books were immediately placed by the Ark (Deut. 31:26). Joshua's writing was accepted in like manner (Josh. 24:26). Following him there were books by Samuel and others (1 Sam. 10:25). Daniel even had a copy of Moses and the Prophets (Dan. 9:2, 10-11) which included the book of his contemporary Jeremiah (Dan. 9:2). Likewise, in the New Testament Paul quoted the gospel of Luke as "Scripture" (1 Tim. 5:18) and Peter had a

16. See discussion in chap. 15.

collection of Paul's "letters" (2 Peter 3:16). Indeed, the apostles exhorted that their letters be read and circulated among the churches (1 Thess. 5:27; Col. 4:16; Rev. 1:3).

Some have argued that Proverbs 25:1 is an exception to this thesis. On this assumption, some of Solomon's proverbs were not collected in the canon during his lifetime. They were collected when "the men of Hezekiah... transcribed" more of Solomon's proverbs (Prov. 25:1). Two comments are in order here.

First, it is possible that these additional proverbs (chaps. 25-29) were not officially presented to the believing community during Solomon's life (perhaps because of his later moral decline). However, since they are *authentic* Solomonic proverbs there is no reason they could not be later presented and then immediately accepted as authoritative by the believing community. In this case Proverbs 25-29 would not be an exception to the canonic rule that the authentic prophetic material was accepted immediately when it was presented. This is true even if it were not presented until after his death.

Second, it is also possible that these later chapters of Proverbs were presented and accepted as authoritative during Solomon's lifetime. Support for this view can be derived from the fact that the Solomonic part of the book may have been compiled in three sections (1:1; 10:1; 25:1), perhaps because it was preserved on separate scrolls. Thus the word "also" (Prov. 25:1; see John Peter Lange, *Commentary on the Holy Scriptures: Critical, Doctrinal and Homeletical,* 5.215) can refer to the fact that Hezekiah's men also copied this last section (scroll) along with the first two sections (scrolls). In this case all three sections (scrolls) were originally presented (in three parts) and accepted as divinely authoritative but were only copied later by the men of Hezekiah.

Because every preceding section of Scripture (and nearly all the books) are quoted in succeeding sections, and because each book of the Bible is quoted by some church Father or listed in some canon (see chap. 16), there is ample evidence to conclude that there was a continuity of conviction within the covenant community concerning the canon of Scripture. That is to say, the fact that certain books are in the canon today, and that they were written by prophets in biblical times, argues for their canonicity. Along with the evidence for a continuity of belief in the covenant community regarding the canon, this argues strongly for their canonicity from the very beginning. In brief, this means that the presence of a book in the canon down through the centuries is evidence that it was known by the contemporaries of the prophet who wrote it to be genuine and canonical, despite the fact that succeeding generations lack definitive knowledge of who the author was or what his prophetic credentials were. Surely God in His providence guided His people in the preservation of His Word.

Subsequent recognition of the canon of Scripture was the ratification of the initial acceptance of that canon. The later debate about certain books in the canon should not cloud the fact of their initial acceptance by the immediate contemporaries of the prophets. The true canonicity of the book was *determined* by God when He directed the prophet to write it, and it was immediately *discovered* (recognized) by the people of God to whom He wrote it.

Technically speaking, the discussion about certain books in later centuries was not a question of *canonicity* but of *authenticity* or *genuineness* (see chap. 20). Because they had neither access to the writer nor direct evidence of his supernatural confirmation, they had to rely on historical testimony about their prophetic credentials. Once they were convinced by the evidence that the books were written by an accredited spokesman for God, then the books were accepted by the church universal. But the decisions of church councils in the fourth and fifth centuries did not determine the canon, nor did they even first discover or recognize it. In no sense was the authority of the canonical books contingent upon the later church councils. All those councils did was to give *later, broader,* and *final* recognition to what was already a fact, namely, that God had inspired them and that the people of God had accepted them in the first century.

Several centuries went by before there was universal recognition of all the books in the canon. There are many reasons for that. First, communication and transportation were slow in those days. Hence, it took much longer for the believers in the West to become fully aware of the evidence for books first written and circulated in the East, and vice versa. Second, the first centuries of the church (prior to A.D. 313) were times of great persecution that did not provide the resources nor allow for research, reflection, and recognition concerning the first-century situation.[17] As soon as that was made possible (after A.D. 325), it was only a short time before there was general recognition of all the canonical books. That was accomplished by the councils of Hippo (A.D. 393) and Carthage (397). Third, there was no widespread need to list the precise books of the canon until there was serious challenge to the canonical books, which had already been accepted for centuries. That challenge did not become acute until Marcion published his heretical canon (with only Luke and ten of Paul's epistles) in the middle of the second century (see chart on p. 294). Along with his gnosticism there were the many apocryphal gospels and epistles written in the second and third centuries, which claimed to be apostolic. Since those books claimed divine authority, it was necessary for the universal church to define precisely the limits of the canon that had been determined by God and recognized earlier by the people of God.

17. See discussion in chap. 16.

How the Principles Were Employed

The principles involved. Lest the impression be gained that those five principles were explicitly and mechanically put into operation by some especially appointed committee of church Fathers commissioned to discover which books were inspired, a few words of explanation are needed. Just how did the principles operate in the history and consciousness of the early Christian church? Although the issue of the discovery of the canon centers about the Old and New Testaments alike, J. N. D. Kelly discusses these principles as they apply to the New Testament canon. He writes,

> The main point to be observed is that the fixation of the finally agreed list of books, and of the order in which they were to be arranged, was the result of a very gradual process. . . . Three features of this process should be noted. First, the criterion which ultimately came to prevail was apostolicity. Unless a book could be shown to come from the pen of an apostle, or at least to have the authority of an apostle behind it, it was peremptorily rejected, however edifying or popular with the faithful it might be. Secondly, there were certain books which hovered for long time on the fringe of the canon, but in the end failed to secure admission to it, usually because they lacked this indisputable stamp. . . . Thirdly, some of the books which were later included had to wait a considerable time before achieving universal recognition. . . . By gradual stages, however, the Church both in East and West arrived at a common mind as to its sacred books. The first official document which prescribes the twenty-seven books of our New Testament as alone canonical is Athanasius's Easter letter for the year 367, but the process was not everywhere complete until at least a century and a half later.[18]

Some are only implicitly present. It should be apparent that all of the criteria of inspiration are necessary to demonstrate the canonicity of each book. All of the five characteristics must be at least implicitly present, even though some of them are more dominant than others. For example, the dynamic ability is more obvious in the New Testament epistles than in the historical books of the Old Testament. Likewise, the authoritative nature is more apparent in the Prophets than the Poetry. That is not to say that there is not an implicit "thus says the Lord" in the Poetry, nor a dynamic in the redemptive history of the Old Testament. It does mean, however, that the Fathers did not always have in operation all of the principles in an explicit fashion.

Some are more important than others. Furthermore, it should be noted that some criteria of inspiration are more important than others, in that the presence of one implies another or is a key to others. For example, if a book is authoritative (i.e., if it is from God), then it will be dynamic. That is, if it is from God, it will be accompanied with the transforming power of God. In

18. J. N. D. Kelly, *Early Christian Doctrines,* pp. 59-60.

fact, when authority was unmistakably present, the other characteristics of inspiration were automatically assumed to be present also. So it was that with regard to the New Testament books, the proof of apostolicity (its prophetic nature) was often considered a virtual certainty of inspiration.[19] In addition, if the first test (is the book prophetic?) could be verified explicitly, it was conceded that this was sufficient to establish that the book was canonical. Generally speaking the church Fathers were only explicitly concerned with apostolicity and authenticity. The edificational characteristic and the universal acceptance of a book were then implicitly assumed unless some doubt was cast on the latter two that forced a reexamination of the former three tests for canonicity. This was the case with some of the Antilegomena (e.g., 2 Peter and 2 John). But even in those cases, as discussed in chapters 15 and 17, the positive evidence for the first three principles emerged victoriously over the supposed negative evidence on the latter two.

The witness of the Holy Spirit. The recognition of canonicity was not a mere mechanical matter settled by a synod or ecclesiastical council. It was a providential process directed by the Spirit of God as He witnessed to the church about the reality of the Word of God. Man of himself could not identify the Word of God, but the Holy Spirit opened the eyes of their understanding so that they could recognize God's Word. Jesus said, "My sheep hear My voice" (John 10:27). This is not to say that in some mystical way the testimony of the Holy Spirit in the hearts of believers settled the question of canonicity. The witness of the Spirit only convinced them of the reality of the canon, not its extent or limits.[20] The canon was recognized by a twofold method of faith and science. Objective principles were used, but the subjective testimony of the Holy Spirit used the objective evidence, thus confirming the reality of God's Word to His people.

The tests for canonicity were not mechanical means for measuring out the amount of inspired literature, nor did the Holy Spirit say, "This book or passage is inspired, that one is not." That would be a disclosure, not a discovery. The Holy Spirit neither witnessed to the exact extent of the canon nor settled the matters of textual criticism. He did providentially guide the process that gave assent to the limits of the canon as well as give witness to the people of God as to the reality of God's Word when they read or heard it.

Summary and Conclusion

The most important distinction to be made at this point is between the *determination* and the *discovery* of canonicity. God is solely responsible for

19. Benjamin B. Warfield, *The Inspiration and Authority of the Bible,* p. 415.
20. R. C. Sproul, "The Internal Testimony of the Holy Spirit," in Norman L. Geisler, ed., *Inerrancy,* pp. 337-54.

the first, and man is responsible merely for the last. *That* a book is canonical is due to *divine inspiration*. *How* that is known to be true is the process of *human recognition*. How men *discovered* what God had *determined* was by looking for the "earmarks of inspiration." It was asked whether the book (1) was written by a man of God, (2) who was confirmed by an act of God, (3) told the truth about God, man, and so on, (4) came with the power of God, and (5) was accepted by the people of God. If a book clearly had the first earmark, the remainder were often assumed. Of course the contemporaries of the prophet (apostle) knew his credentials and accepted his book *immediately*. But later church Fathers sorted out the profusion of religious literature, discovered, and gave official recognition to the books that, by virtue of their divine inspiration, had been determined by God as canonical and originally recognized by the contemporary believing community to which they were presented.

14
Development and History of the Old Testament Canon

The fact *that* the canon developed is indisputable, but *how* it developed and *when* it was completed is a matter that must also be considered. Although inspiration determines canonicity, men are actively involved in the recognition of the canon. The process of recognition is a historical study; hence a review of the development of the Old Testament canon is in order.

Preliminary Considerations

Much of the historical data necessary to provide a complete picture of the process of the canonization of the Old Testament is lost in the mists of antiquity. Enough information is available, however, to give a general overview of the development of the Hebrew canon.

The Three Steps

The principles operative in the historical process of canonization are three: (1) inspiration by God; (2) recognition by men of God; and (3) collection and preservation of the books by the people of God.

Inspiration by God. As the previous discussion reveals (see chap. 12), God took the first step in canonization when He inspired the books. Thus, the simple answer to the question as to why there are only thirty-nine books in the Old Testament canon (see chap. 1) is that those are all that God inspired. Obviously, if God did not inspire and thus give divine authority to a book, no council of men could ever do it.

Recognition by men of God. Once God gave a book its authority, men of God assented to that authority by their recognition of it as a prophetic utterance. There is every reason to believe that this recognition followed immediately upon the publication of the message. As Edward J. Young states, "There is no evidence that these particular books existed among the ancient Jews for many years before they were recognized as canonical. Indeed, if a book was actually revealed by God, is it conceivable that such a book would circulate for many years before anyone recognized its true nature?"[1] The evidence, in fact, is to the contrary. Moses' writings were received in his day (Ex. 24:3; Josh. 1:8). Joshua's book was added to the canon immediately (Josh. 24:26). Daniel, a contemporary of Jeremiah, had received the latter's book along with "*the* books" (Dan. 9:2).

Collection and preservation by the people of God. Moses' books were collected and preserved beside the Ark (Deut. 31:26). "Samuel told the people the ordinances of the kingdom, and wrote them in the book and placed it before the Lord" (1 Sam. 10:25). Daniel had a collection of "the books," and there is every indication throughout the Old Testament that prophetic writings were collected as soon as they were written. During Josiah's day, the "law of Moses" was "found in the house of the Lord" (2 Kings 23:24-25), where it had been stored. Proverbs 25:1 notes that "these . . . are the proverbs of Solomon which the men of Hezekiah, king of Judah, transcribed." Ezra the priest had preserved a copy of "the law of Moses" that he brought with him out of Babylon after the captivity (Ezra 7:6). Therefore, inspiration produced the canonical books, and subsequent recognition and collection preserved them for posterity.

Two Distinctions

Two other factors are to be kept in mind in the history of the Old Testament canon.

Distinction between the canon and other literature. A distinction must be made between the formal canon and other Hebrew literature, such as the book of Jasher (Josh. 10:13); the Book of the Wars of the Lord (Num. 21:14); the visions of Iddo the seer (2 Chron. 9:29); the book of the acts of Solomon (1 Kings 11:41) and many others.[2] Most of these books were part of Hebrew religious literature, but were never a part of their theological canon. There was evidently a profusion of religious lore in Hebrew, as is evident from the many noncanonical books (see chap. 15), but these were not a part of the "Law and Prophets," the "sacred Scriptures," considered to be divine and authoritative.

Immediate recognition did not guarantee against subsequent debate. Immediate recognition of a book as inspired did not thereby guarantee subsequent recognition by all. This will become apparent from the debate over certain books among later Jews. In fact, there was initial recognition and then, after a time lapse, subsequent doubts before all books received eventual

1. Edward J. Young, "The Canon of the Old Testament," in Carl F. H. Henry, ed., *Revelation and the Bible*, p. 163.
2. Willis J. Beecher lists twenty-five extracanonical books mentioned in Chronicles alone in his article s.v. "Chronicles," in James Orr, ed., *The International Standard Bible Encyclopaedia*, 1:630.

recognition. Apparently this did happen with some books, for example, Ecclesiastes and the Song of Solomon. In reality, the problems of *transportation, transmission* (making copies), and sometimes even *translation* tended to slow down the final and universal recognition of canonicity. The fact that a book had been accepted hundreds of years earlier did not guarantee that someone in succeeding generations would ever raise questions about it, since they did not have access to the original evidence to its prophetic credentials. That is especially understandable in a case such as the book of Esther, whose author is unknown to subsequent generations.

Progressive Collection of the Canon

The standard critical theory enunciated by Herbert E. Ryle and others asserts that the books of the Hebrew Scriptures were canonized in three stages, according to their dates of composition, into the Law (c. 400 B.C.), Prophets (c. 200 B.C.), and Writings (c. A.D. 100)[3] However, this view is untenable in light of the more recent developments and the arguments summarized by Sid Z. Leiman, Roger Beckwith, and others, which demonstrate that the canon was completed no later than the second century B.C. and possibly as early as the fourth century B.C.[4] In fact, a completed canon of the Hebrew Scriptures is evident from the testimony of the "Prologue of Ecclesiasticus" (c. 132 B.C.), Jesus, Philo, and Josephus well before A.D. 100. Furthermore, there is evidence that inspired books were added to the canon immediately as they were written. Hence, the Old Testament canon was actually completed when the last book was written and added to it by the fourth century B.C.

The older notion that the Old Testament canon was not finalized until the so-called "Council of Jamnia (Jabneh)" (c. A.D. 90) has been completely refuted in the works of Jack P. Lewis[5] and Sid Z. Leiman.[6] Roger Beckwith summarized the combined result of their investigations as follows:

> *(a)* The term 'synod' or 'council' is inappropriate. The academy at Jamnia, established by Rabbi Johanan ben Zakkai shortly before the fall of Jerusalem in AD 70, was both a college and a legislative body, and the occasion in question was a session of the elders there.

3. Herbert Edward Ryle, *The Canon of the Old Testament: An Essay on the Gradual Growth and Formation of the Hebrew Canon of Scripture*, 2d ed.; F. P. W. Buhl, *Canon and Text of the Old Testament*; Gerrit Wildeboer, *The Origin of the Canon of the Old Testament*.
4. See Roger Beckwith, *The Old Testament Canon of the New Testament Church and Its Background in Early Judaism*, pp. 138-66, especially pp. 164-66. Also see Sid Z. Leiman, *The Canonization of Hebrew Scripture: The Talmudic and Midrashic Evidence*, pp. 131-32.
5. Jack P. Lewis, "What Do We Mean by Jabneh?" *Journal of Bible and Religion* 32 (1964): 125-32.
6. Sid Z. Leiman, *The Canonization of Hebrew Scripture: The Talmudic and Midrashic Evidence*. Also see Sid Z. Leiman, ed., *The Canon and Masorah of the Hebrew Bible: An Introductory Reader*.

History of the Old Testament Canon

	National Events	Probable Date of Writing of Canonical Books	Suggested History of the Manuscripts and Copies
1500 B.C.			
	Exodus from Egypt	Original Pentateuch	Original scrolls of Moses stored beside ark
		Job (?)	
1400 B.C.	Conquest of Canaan		
	Ark kept at Shiloh	Joshua	Copy of Law available to Joshua
1300 B.C.			
1200 B.C.			
1100 B.C.			
	Shiloh destroyed by Philistines and Tabernacle moved		Original scrolls dispersed and new copies made (?)
	Israel's Kingdom established	Judges and Ruth	Samuel, David and Levites distribute copies throughout Israel. Apology for David's reign and his court annals
1000 B.C.	David captures Jerusalem	Davidic Psalms 1 & 2 Samuel Proverbs, Ecclesiastes, Song of Solomon	
	Division of Kingdom		

History of the Old Testament Canon (*continued*)

	National Events	Probable Date of Writing of Canonical Books	Suggested History of the Manuscripts and Copies
900 B.C.			
	Samaria made capital of Northern Kingdom	Obadiah Joel?	Copies brought to Northern Kingdom during Elijah's reform (?)
800 B.C.			
		Jonah Amos, Hosea	Kings written by a succession of prophets and collected, edited by Jeremiah (?)
	Assyrians capture Samaria		
		Micah	
700 B.C.	Revival under Hezekiah	Isaiah	Copies obtained for Samaritans by Israelite priest at order of Sargon II (2 Kings 17:27-28) ?
	Revival under Josiah Daniel taken hostage to Babylon	Nahum Zephaniah Habakkuk	Copy of Book of the Law recovered during Temple repair; and copies distributed to the people during Josiah's reform (2 Chron. 34:6-9, 21) ?
600 B.C. 587 B.C.	Ezekiel *et al.* taken captive Jerusalem destroyed	Jeremiah, Lam. 1 & 2 Kings Ezekiel	Copies taken to Babylon
	Cyrus captures Babylon Jewish returnees rebuild Temple	Daniel Haggai Zechariah	
500 B.C.			
			Copies brought back from Babylon
	Ezra returns to Jerusalem Nehemiah rebuilds walls	Ezra, Nehemiah, Esther Malachi, 1 & 2 Chronicles	Copies taken to Samaria at time of Nehemiah's exclusion (Neh. 13:28-30) ?
400 B.C.			

(b) The date of the session may have been as early as AD 75 or as late as AD 117.

(c) As regards the disputed books, the discussion was confined to the question whether Ecclesiastes and the Song of songs (or possibly Ecclesiastes alone) make the hands unclean, i.e. are divinely inspired.

(d) The decision reached was not regarded as authoritative, since contrary opinions continued to be expressed throughout the second century.

The assumption that the canon was closed at Jamnia about AD 90 has been elaborated by different writers in various ways. Some have seen it as part of the polemic against Christianity; and some, as a piece with the standardization of the Masoretic test. If however, the canon was not closed about AD 90 but a long time before, all these corollaries lose the premiss [sic] on which they depend. Similarly, any inference that the canon was decided by councils must be abandoned.[7]

The Law of Moses

Historically, Moses wrote first, so his books were the first to be recognized as canonical. The constant reference to "the law of Moses" by almost every canonical book after Moses' day demonstrates that the law of Moses was immediately received as authoritative and continuously recognized as such.

Joshua. The Lord enjoined the "book of the law" to Joshua (Josh. 1:8), "which Moses ... commanded" (Josh. 1:7) unto the people of his day (cf. also Josh. 8:31; 23:6).

David. David charged Solomon to keep the statutes, commandments, ordinances, and testimonies that were "written in the law of Moses" (1 Kings 2:3).

Solomon. Solomon, at the dedication of the Temple, urged the people, saying, "Let your heart therefore be wholly devoted to the Lord our God, to walk in His statutes and to keep His commandments" (1 Kings 8:61), which he had previously identified as the works of Moses (cf. vv. 53, 56).

Amaziah. It is written of King Amaziah that he acted not "according to what is written in the book of the law of Moses" (2 Kings 14:6).

Manasseh. The wicked Manasseh did not live "according to all the law that ... Moses commanded" (2 Kings 21:8).

Josiah. Josiah turned to the Lord "with all his soul and with all his might, according to all the law of Moses" (2 Kings 23:25).

Asa. In Asa's day Judah was commanded "to observe the law and the commandment" (2 Chron. 14:4).

Jehoshaphat. During Jehoshaphat's reign the priests "taught in Judah, having the book of the law of the Lord with them" (2 Chron. 17:9).

Jeremiah-Daniel. About the time of the Babylonian exile, Jeremiah referred to "the law of the Lord" (Jer. 8:8). Daniel made reference to "the curse" and "the oath which is written in the law of Moses" (Dan. 9:11; cf. 9:13).

7. According to Beckwith, pp. 276-77.

Ezra. In Ezra's time, the Levitical system was reinstituted "as it is written in the book of Moses" (Ezra 6:18).

Nehemiah. In Nehemiah's day, the priests "read aloud from the book of Moses in the hearing of the people" (Neh. 13:1).

Malachi. Malachi, the last Old Testament prophet, admonished the people to "remember the law of Moses My servant, even the statutes and ordinances which I commanded him in Horeb for all Israel" (Mal. 4:4).

From those passages, and others like them, it can readily be seen that the rest of the Old Testament after Moses considered his writings to be canonical.

The Prophets

The most common designation for the rest of the Old Testament is "the Prophets." This title, combined with "the Law," occurs about a dozen times in the New Testament (cf. Matt. 5:17; 7:12; Luke 24:27).

The character of a prophet. A true prophet was one who was a mouthpiece of God (see chaps. 2, 12, and 13). It is specifically said that Joshua (Josh. 24:26) and Samuel (1 Sam. 10:25) added writings to the canon.

In the general sense of the word, all of the books of the Old Testament were written by "prophets." Moses was a prophet according to Deuteronomy 18:15 and Hosea 12:13; Daniel and David are called prophets in the New Testament (Matt. 24:15; Acts 2:30). And, if the word *prophet* is broadly defined as one who receives and relates a revelation from God, King David is certainly to be regarded as a prophet, because he received a revelation "in writing by His hand upon me" (1 Chron. 28:19). Even Solomon was a prophet because God spoke to him in dreams, or visions (1 Kings 3:5; 11:9) and even revealed the future to him.

A priest could be a prophet (cf. Ezek. 2:2-5), as could a prince (cf. Dan. 1:3, 7). One did not have to belong to the "company of the prophets" (1 Sam. 19:20) or to be a "son of a prophet" (i.e., as student or apprentice of a prophet as Elisha was to Elijah, cf. 2 Kings 2:12) to be a prophet as the testimony of Amos confirms (Amos 7:14). In this broad sense of the word, then, all of the Old Testament writers, including men from Moses the lawgiver to Amos the vinedresser, were prophets.

The confirmation of a prophet. In addition to miracles as the divine confirmation of a true prophet,[8] numerous other tests were applied to indicate false prophets: (1) Do they ever give false prophecies (Deut. 18:21, 22)? (2) Do they contact departed spirits (Deut. 18:11)? (3) Do they use names of divination (Deut. 18:11)? (4) Do they use mediums or witches (Deut. 18:11)? (5) Do they follow false gods or use idols (Ex. 20:3-4; Deut. 13:1-3)? (6) Do they confess the humanity of Jesus Christ (1 John 4:1-2)? (7) Do they deny the deity of Jesus Christ (Col. 2:9)? (8) Do their prophecies center in Jesus

8. See chaps. 12 and 13.

Christ (Rev. 19:10)? (9) Do they advocate abstaining from foods (e.g., meats) (1 Tim. 4:3-4)? (10) Do they deprecate marriage (1 Tim. 4:3)? (11) Do they promote immorality (Jude 7)? (12) Do they encourage legalistic self-denial (Col. 2:16-23)?

The continuity of the prophets. A prophet was one who spoke for God, and it was that characteristic which bound together the ministry of the prophets from Moses to Malachi. The succession of prophets produced the continuous history contained in the canon of the Old Testament. The books of Chronicles, for instance, bear an unusual testimony to this fact, as the following survey indicates:

1. The history of David was written by Samuel, Nathan, and Gad (1 Chron. 29:29).
2. The history of Solomon was recorded by Nathan, Ahijah, and Iddo (2 Chron. 9:29).
3. The acts of Rehoboam were written by Shemaiah and Iddo (2 Chron. 12:15).
4. The history of Abijah was added by Iddo (2 Chron. 13:22).
5. Jehoshaphat's story was recorded by Jehu the prophet (2 Chron. 20:34).
6. Hezekiah's story was told by Isaiah (2 Chron. 32:32).
7. Manasseh's life story was recorded by unnamed seers (2 Chron. 33:19).
8. The other kings had their histories recorded in other books (2 Chron. 35:27).

To that list of writing prophets Jeremiah may be added, for his writings were added to theirs and the entire collection was designated "the books" by Daniel (Dan. 9:2).[9] R. Laird Harris says:

> This continuity of writing prophets may be the solution to the problem of how Moses and Joshua could have written the accounts of their own death in historical narratives (cf. Deut. 34, Josh. 24). Each book completes the preceding and links the prophetic history together. Ruth was originally appended to Judges, and the genealogy of Ruth may have been added after David's rise to power in order to link it to Samuel and the Kings, which are a unit. Likewise, the last chapter of Kings parallels the material of Jeremiah 52, 39, 40, and 41. Similarly, the book of Chronicles ends with the same two verses that the Ezra-Nehemiah unit begins.[10]

In other words, the Old Testament prophets undoubtedly recorded a continuous sacred history, tying their books together into a canonical unit as

9. See R. Laird Harris, *Inspiration and Canonicity of the Bible*, p. 166.
10. Ibid., p. 168.

they were individually written. That practice of connecting books or documents by a footnote or statement is known as the "colophon principle" and also was used in nonbiblical writings.[11]

The completion of the prophets. The continuity of the prophetic writings ended with Malachi. Several lines of evidence support this assertion.

1. There are intimations in some of the postexilic prophets that the next revelation from God would be just before the coming of Messiah (Mal. 4:5), and that there would be no true prophets in the intervening period (Zech. 13:2-5).

2. Furthermore, there is confirmation from the intertestamental period that there were indeed no prophets after Malachi. In the Maccabean period, the people were waiting "until a prophet should arise" (1 Mac. 4:45; 9:27; 14:41). *The Manual of Discipline* from the Qumran community (B.C.) also looked for the "coming of a prophet."[12]

3. Verification of this view also comes from Josephus;[13] the Talmud, which states, "After the latter prophets Haggai, Zechariah, and Malachi, the Holy Spirit departed from Israel";[14] and from the New Testament, which never quotes a post-Malachi book as canonical. In fact, Jesus uses the expression "from ... Abel to ... Zechariah" (Matt. 23:35) to identify the Old Testament. This reference encompasses all the books from Genesis to 2 Chronicles, which is the chronological arrangement of the entire Hebrew Old Testament (see chaps. 1 and 5). Harris summarizes this view well when he says, "The chain of prophets evidently wrote a chain of histories from Genesis through Nehemiah, and the writings of these prophets were accepted, one by one, through the centuries, until, when the Spirit of Prophecy departed from Israel, the canon was complete."[15]

The Writings

Twofold division at the time of canonization. The present Jewish arrangement of the Old Testament is threefold: Law, Prophets, and Writings. However, that was not the oldest Old Testament format. There is no intimation of it in the Old Testament itself, and only one possible allusion to it in the New Testament (Luke 24:44). Some books of the Prophets did not fit neatly into the continual sequence of the history of the prophets, such as the "four books of hymns and the precepts for human conduct" mentioned by Josephus.[16] That apparently led to a very early (possibly 200 B.C. or earlier)

11. See Alexander Heidel, *The Babylonian Genesis,* 2d ed., pp. 25 ff.
12. IQS, *The Manual of Discipline,* trans. P. Wernberg-Möller, 9. 11.
13. Josephus *Against Apion,* 1.8.
14. Michael L. Rodkinson, Tractate "Sanhedrin," *The Babylonian Talmud,* VII-VIII, 24.
15. Harris, pp. 168-69.
16. Josephus *Against Apion* 1.8.

arrangement of books into the later widely accepted threefold classification of Law, Prophets, and Writings (see chap. 1). The earliest mention of a third group of books is in the "Prologue to Ecclesiasticus" (c. 132 B.C.), but it does not enumerate the books. Josephus (A.D. 37-100) is more explicit, saying that there were only four books in the third section.[17] No doubt he considered Esther to be with the other prophetic histories, whereas Ruth and Lamentations were counted with Judges and Jeremiah respectively, which accounts for his numbering twenty-two books in the Hebrew canon. That would also mean that Daniel was listed with the prophets.[18] Whatever the origin or status of the threefold classification,[19] the Septuagint (LXX) (c. 250 B.C.) reflects no compunction whatever to follow it. Moreover, Origen (third century A.D.), who claimed to derive his list from the Jews, does not follow the threefold arrangement of books. Likewise, Melito (late second century A.D.), the earliest LXX manuscripts (Vaticanus, Sinaticus, and Alexandrinus), the lists of Epiphanius of Salamis (c. 315-403) and others do not follow the threefold arrangement.[20] Hence, it would seem best to agree with Robert Dick Wilson and R. Laird Harris that, so far as *canonization* is concerned, there were only two groups of books: the Law (five books) and the Prophets (seventeen books).[21]

Subsequent threefold classification. Having said that, it must also be admitted that there was an early (perhaps by the second cent. B.C.) *classification* of books into three groups: the Law, the Prophets, and the Writings. The reason for this is not altogether clear, but several observations are in order.

1. One possible explanation is the later distinction between men who held prophetic *office* and those who had only the prophetic *gift*. Thus the canon was divided into the Law, written by the lawgiver; the Prophets, written by those who held the office of prophet; and the Writings, written by those who were prophets by gift. Perhaps that would help explain why some of the books, for examples Ecclesiastes and Song of Solomon, were later disputed (see chap. 15). One problem with this view is that there is no evidence that every book in the Prophets was written by someone with the prophetic office. Amos, for example, seems to disavow being a prophet by training or office (Amos 7:14), yet his book is listed among the Prophets.
2. It may have been felt by some, at a later date, that the books in the third

17. These books were probably Psalms, Proverbs, Ecclesiastes, and Song of Solomon. See Beckwith, p. 253.
18. See Harris, p. 140.
19. See Beckwith, pp. 110-66.
20. Ibid., pp. 181-222. See also Sid. Z. Leiman, *The Canonization of Hebrew Scripture: The Talmudic and Midrashic Evidence*, pp. 37-50, 131-55, and 156 n. 195.
21. Harris modified his earlier view to permit an early threefold arrangement, perhaps as a variant practice: "Was the Law and the Prophets Two-Thirds of the Old Testament Canon?" p. 170.

category, that is, those not written by prophets by office, were for that reason not fully canonical; thus they were not to be placed in the same section with the writings of the Prophets. One problem with this position is that there is no evidence that the Writings were considered uncanonical. Some books always held to be canonical, such as Psalms and Daniel, were placed in the Writings section.

3. The view of most higher critical scholars (see chap. 25) that these books were placed in the canon at a late date because they were not written and/or accepted until a late date (second cent. B.C. or later) does not square with the established early dates for many of the Writings (e.g., Davidic Psalms and Proverbs, c. 1000 B.C.). Nor does it fit with the fact that Josephus had only four, rather than eleven, books in this section, as the later (A.D. 400) Talmud did. Indeed, Josephus placed Daniel among the Prophets, rather than with the Writings. That fact not only belies the late date (second cent. B.C.) higher critical scholars usually ascribe to Daniel, but it also conflicts with their late date for the acceptance of the Writings into the canon.

4. Another possible reason for the later threefold classification of the Old Testament arises from the topical and festal significance of the books. For example, the Five Rolls were read at the five annual feasts. Thus, to serve a more practical purpose, they were removed from the category of prophetic writings.
5. Roger Beckwith offers a plausible explanation for the origin of the threefold classification and the order of the books in each section. Ascribing the process of subdividing the non-Mosaic Scriptures (originally called "the Prophets") to form the "Prophets and Hagiographa," to Judas Maccabeus and his associates (c. 164 B.C.), he writes,

> The three sections of the canon are not historical accidents but works of art. The first consists of the Mosaic literature, partly historical and partly legal, arranged in chronological order. The other two sections of the canon also contain both historical and non-historical books. The historical books cover two further periods and are arranged in chronological order. The non-historical books (visionary or oracular in the case of the Prophets, lyrical and sapiental in the case of the Hagiographs) are arranged in descending order of size.[22]

Whatever the reason for the later threefold *classification,* it must be remembered that *canonization* was on a twofold basis: the Law and the Prophets. These divisions actually included all the same books that were later given a threefold classification in some circles, and that finally gained general

22. Beckwith, p. 165. Also see Leiman, *The Canonization of Hebrew Scripture: The Talmudic and Midrashic Evidence,* pp. 30-50.

acceptance among Jews by (or before) the fourth century A.D.

Confirmation of the Prophetic Model

Historical data by which a complete picture of the development of the Old Testament canon may be traced is currently lacking. Nevertheless, important historical facts that serve as checkpoints in the overall process are available as the following discussion illustrates.

Evidence of the Later Threefold Classification

Even though the Old Testament Scriptures were apparently not canonized in three groups and/or stages, there is early evidence of this alternate way to classify the canonical books.

Prologue to Ecclesiasticus. Possibly the earliest reference is in the "Prologue to Ecclesiasticus" (c. 132 B.C.), which may refer to the use of a threefold arrangement of the Old Testament by the writer's grandfather (c. 200 B.C.). However, no books are named. Hence, it is not known which books were in this section.

Jesus Christ. Jesus on one occasion alluded to a possible threefold arrangement of the Old Testament (Luke 24:44), although He spoke of a twofold classification as comprising "all the Scriptures" in the same chapter (Luke 24:27).

Philo. Just after the time of Christ (c. A.D. 40), Philo witnessed to a threefold classification, making reference to the Law, the Prophets (or Prophecies), as well as "hymns and the others which foster and perfect knowledge and piety."[23]

Josephus. Josephus attested to the same classification at about the same time (c. A.D. 37-100), and explicitly stated that the third section was made up of "hymns to God" and "precepts for the conduct of human life."[24] However, Josephus had only four books in this section compared to the Talmud, which listed eleven.

Babylonian Talmud. By (or before) the fourth century A.D., the Babylonian Talmud gave the modern threefold classification of Law (five books), Prophets (eight books), and Writings (eleven books). Thus the tendency to classify the canon into three sections, which possibly began as early as 200 B.C., became the accepted form by A.D. 400. That fact may be further confirmed at other checkpoints in the history of the Hebrew canon in this interval.

23. Philo *De Vita Contemplativa* 3.25. See F. H. Colson's translation of *The Contemplative Life*, in *Philo*, p. 127: "In each house there is a consecrated room which is called a sanctuary or closet and closeted in this they are initiated into the mysteries of the sanctified life. They take nothing into it, either drink or food or any other of the things necessary for the needs of the body, but [1] laws and [2] oracles delivered through the mouth of prophets, [3] and psalms and anything else which fosters and perfects knowledge and piety."

24. Josephus *Against Apion* 1.8. Several reasons for accepting the reliability of Josephus are enumerated by Beckwith, pp. 33-34.

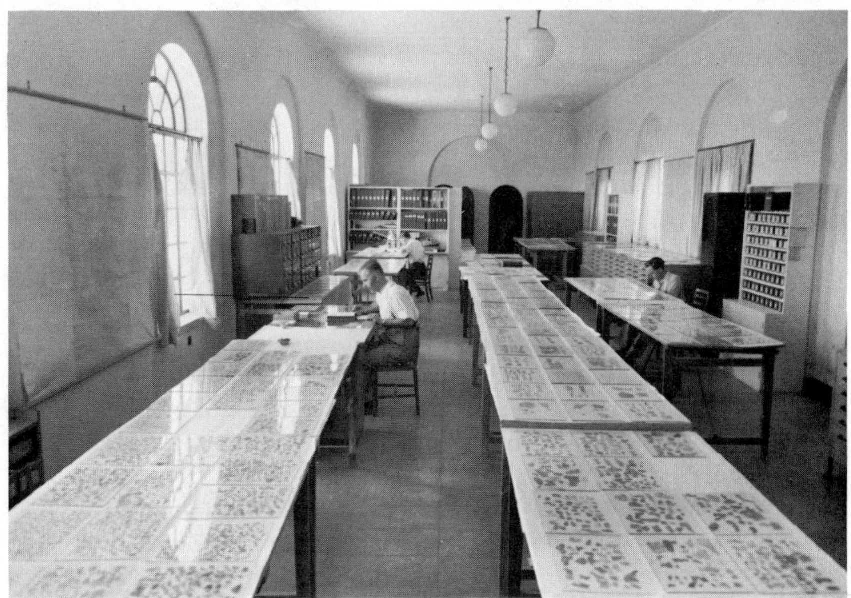

3. *Thus far all Old Testament books except Esther have been represented in the Dead Sea Scrolls. Here small Dead Sea Scroll fragments are under the scrutiny of scholars (Palestine Archaeological Museum)*

Confirmation of the Twofold Canonization

The Talmudic tractate Aboth (1.1-2) refers to "the men of the Great Synagogue" (400 B.C. ff.). The tradition of the Great Synagogue is that of those Jewish scholars (fifth to third centuries B.C.) who followed Ezra in the exposition of the Law (cf. Neh. 9-10). It is believed that they formed an assembly that was responsible for the recognition and preservation of the Old Testament canon.[25] There are several lines of evidence that support the contention that they classified and recognized the Old Testament canon as a twofold division of Law and Prophets.

Old Testament links them together. First of all, as indicated above, the historical books of the Old Testament give evidence that they have been linked together as a prophetic unity from the time of Moses to Nehemiah.

Repeated use of "Law and Prophets." There is also the repeated use of the description "Law and Prophets" in the New Testament, a common Talmudic phrase also used in the Maccabean period (cf. 2 Macc. 15:9) and by

25. See the Talmudic tractate Aboth (sometimes called Pirke Aboth, or "Chapters of the Fathers"), 1.1 ff., in Herbert Danby, trans., *The Mishnah,* pp. 446 ff.

the Dead Sea community at Qumran.[26]

Acknowledgment in Daniel. Then too, there is the acknowledgment in the Old Testament book of Daniel of the "law of Moses" (Dan. 9:11, 13) as well as a group called "the books" (9:2). The postexilic prophet, Zechariah, refers to the "former prophets" (Zech. 1:4; 7:7, 12), which also attests to a line of prophetic utterances.

Acknowledgment by succeeding prophets. The acid test, however, of the view that the canon developed gradually is the acknowledgment by succeeding prophets of the existence and/or authority of preceding prophetic utterances. For, if there were a gradually developing canon to which inspired books were added as they were written (presumably without a long delay), it is reasonable to expect not only continuity between the books but some recognition of the existence of the former books by the latter writers. It is unreasonable, however, to expect all the preceding books to be quoted in later Old Testament books any more than the New Testament quotes all Old Testament books.

A survey of important Old Testament passages is sufficient to confirm the general thesis of a twofold canon.

1. That the law of Moses was recognized and utilized by subsequent prophetic books is most evident from Joshua 1:7 to Malachi 4:4 (see above). There can be no doubt that all of the latter prophets stood in continuity with, and in dependence upon, the great prophet and lawgiver Moses. There is a constant reechoing of his truth and hearkening back to his precepts throughout the remaining pages of the Old Testament. It is evident that the rest of the Old Testament writers were aware that a great lawgiver lived, taught, and wrote a law that was reflected by other prophets of his nation for about a millennium after him.

2. The crucial question for consequent consideration is whether or not there is evidence of prophets since Moses' time who are in continuity with and/or have a recognition of the other biblical prophets that precede them. A careful look at a good cross-reference Bible or concordance will reveal that such evidence is widely manifest in the historical books.

   a. Both Joshua and events in the book by his name are referred to by the book of Judges (1:1, 20, 21; 2:8).

   b. Ruth, originally appended to Judges, refers to "the days when the judges ruled" (1:1).

   c. The book of 1 Samuel continues the history of Israel after Judges, and 2 Samuel formed a unit with 1 Samuel in the Hebrew canon.

   d. Both 1 and 2 Kings (one book in the Hebrew canon) refer to the "law of Moses" (2 Kings 14:6), and repeatedly speak of David as his life is told in 1 and 2 Samuel (1 Kings 3:14; 5:7; 8:16; 9:5).

26. IQS, *The Manual of Discipline* 1.3; 8.15; 9.11.

e. The books of 1 and 2 Chronicles, which give a parallel history to Samuel and Kings, likewise allude to former events. In fact, genealogies are traced all the way from the book of Genesis (1 Chron. 1), including the one that is recorded only in Ruth (1 Chron. 2:12-13).

f. Ezra-Nehemiah begin with the same two verses that close 2 Chronicles (36:22-23), refer to the "law of Moses" (Ezra 3:2; Neh 13:1), and review Israel's entire history as it is recorded from Genesis through the captivity and restoration (Neh. 9).

3. The remainder of the Old Testament provides the final aspect of the "acid test" of the twofold canonical thesis. What is the evidence that these prophetical and poetical books were recognized and accepted into the canon soon after they were written?

a. The date of the writing of the book of Job is uncertain.[27] Ezekiel mentions the notoriety of Job (Ezek. 14:14, 20), a fact that substantiates the existence of the book of Job by his day.

b. Portions of the Psalms also occur in the historical books (cf. 2 Sam. 22; 1 Chron. 16). There is also the acknowledged fact that David spoke by the Holy Spirit (2 Sam. 23:2).

c. The Solomonic writings (Song of Solomon, Proverbs, Ecclesiastes) are most likely included as part of the list in 1 Kings 4:32, namely, "He . . . spoke three thousand proverbs, and his songs were a thousand and five."

d. Many of the prophets also quote from or refer to the inspired writings of their predecessors. Daniel had a collection that he called "the books," which apparently included books from Moses (Dan. 9:13) to his contemporary Jeremiah (Dan. 9:2), and "the prophets" in between, who had spoken to the kings, princes, fathers, and all the people of the land (Dan. 9:6). Jeremiah 26:18 quotes Micah 3:12, and Micah 4:1-3 cites Isaiah 2:2-4 (or vice versa). There is also a dependence between Isaiah 2:4 and Joel 3:10; between Joel 3:16 and Amos 1:2; Obadiah 17*a* and Joel 2:32*b*, and many other instances. The prophets reflect a clear knowledge of Psalms; Jonah 2:2-9, for example, is filled with references from Psalms. Jonah 2:3, "All Thy breakers and billows passed over me," is from Psalm 42:7. Jonah 2:4 reflects a knowledge of Psalm 5:7, "I will look again toward Thy holy temple" (cf. also Jonah 2:5 with Ps. 18:4-6).

It could not be expected that every book of the Old Testament would be referred to by succeeding prophets; the New Testament as a whole does not refer to every book in the Old Testament. It is no more necessary for there to be an explicit reference to every book being added to the canon than to have an explicit claim for its own inspiration (e.g., Esther).

27. See "Introduction to the Book of Job," in *Ellicott's Commentary,* 4:4-5; Gleason L. Archer, Jr., *A Survey of Old Testament Introduction,* pp. 454-74, argues for a patriarchal date for the events of Job, though the book in its present form may have been composed at a later date.

However, there is substantial evidence to support the concept of *a growing canon:* books that were written by a man of God, accredited by acts of God to tell the truth about God, were *then and there* received by the people into the canon and preserved. Later the people of God universally came to recognize their canonicity.

Problems with the Redactional View of Canonicity

Canonicity is determined by God and only recognized by the people of God. The basic test for canonicity is propheticity. That is, a book was recognized by the people of God if it was known to come from a prophet of God.

The Redactional Canon Theory

Recent trends in critical views of the Old Testament have proposed a view that challenges the prophetic model of canonicity presented above.[28] They argue that "inspired redactors" made substantial changes in the writings of earlier biblical authors. Hence, the content of biblical writings underwent continual change until it reached its final form, often centuries after it had been uttered. In support of this position the following arguments are sometimes offered.

1. Someone after Moses, possibly Joshua, wrote the last chapter of Deuteronomy (Deut. 34), since it is not prophetic and it records Moses' death.
2. Certain sections of Deuteronomy (2:10-12; 2:20-23) show evidence of a later redactor because they are editorial (i.e., parenthetical) in nature, and they refer to a later time when Israel was in "the land of their possession" (Deut. 2:12).
3. The arrangement of Psalms into five books is undoubtedly the work of editors.
4. Proverbs passed through the hands of editors after Solomon (1:1; 10:1; 25:1; 30:1; 31:1), some of whom lived in Hezekiah's day, two hundred years after Solomon (25:1).
5. Some books, such as Jeremiah, survive in two substantially different versions. The longer Masoretic version is one-seventh larger than the shorter Septuagint (LXX) version (which survives in a Hebrew fragment from Qumran (4Q Jer[b]).
6. The books of Chronicles present themselves as being based on prior prophetic records (1 Chron. 9:1; 27:24; 29:29; 2 Chron. 9:29; 13:22;

28. See discussion in chap. 9 for parallel redaction theories in the New Testament. See also chap. 25.

16:11; 20:34; 25:26; 27:7; 28:26; 32:32; 33:19; 35:27; 36:8), which were redacted by the author(s) of Chronicles.

In support of this redactional canon view Emanual Tov is often quoted. On the alleged redactions of Jeremiah he wrote:

> Editor II [Masoretic text] took the liberty of adding and changing many minor details and a few major ones. These changes are visible in (1) text arrangement; (2) the addition of headings to prophecies; (3) repetition of sections; (4) addition of new verses and sections; (5) addition of new details; and (6) changes in content.[29]

Some redactional models have been proposed by evangelicals, including William Abraham, Paul Achtemier, and Bruce Waltke. Waltke claims "that the books of the Bible seem to have gone through an editorial revision after coming from the mouth of an inspired spokesman." In the same passage he speaks of "later editorial activity." Waltke claims "we have evidence of redaction over at least two millennia, from 1800 B.C. to A.D. 200.[30] However, respondents to Waltke's proposal have rejected his position on redaction criticsm, registering "strong disagreement with it."[31]

Objections to the Redaction Canon Theory

It should first be noted that none of the arguments advanced in support of the "inspired redaction" view of the canon is definitive.[32] All of them are capable of explanation in view of the prophetic view presented earlier in this chapter.

Response to redaction canon arguments. Responses to the inspired redaction view will be presented in order.

1. That Moses might not have written the account of his own death (Deut. 34) has long been accepted by conservative scholars (such as R. D. Wilson, L. Harris, G. Archer). This in fact supports the view of a continuity of writing prophets that the successor wrote the last chapter of his

29. Emanuel Tov, "The Literary History of the Book of Jeremiah in the Light of Its Textual History" in J. Togay, ed., *Empirical Models for Biblical Criticism,* p. 217.
30. Bruce K. Waltke, "Historical Grammatical Problems," in *Hermeneutics, Inerrancy and the Bible,* ed. Earl D. Radmacher and Robert D. Preus, pp. 78, 79, 92. See also Waltke, "The Textual Criticism of the Old Testament," in *Expositor's Bible Commentary,* pp. 211-16.
31. See Waltke, "Historical Grammatical Problems," p. 133. The very book in which Waltke's article appears reminds the readers in the introduction that "ICBI [International Council of Biblical Inerrancy] does not endorse every point made by the authors of this book."
32. Some have quoted Merrill Unger in favor of the redaction theory of canonicity. In fact Unger said "the difficulties involved [in such a view] are inseparable" (*Introductory Guide to the Old Testament*, p. 231). He said that some may "fondly dream" such a view is plausible, but only in vain. The most Unger would grant was slight "editorial additions to the Pentateuch, regarded as authentically Mosaic" (ibid.). But he flatly rejected the notion that later non-Mosaic additions were made on the Pentateuch by redactors, inspired or not (ibid., 231-32).

predecessor's book.

2. The parenthetical sections in Deuteronomy 2 need not be non-Mosaic simply because they are editorial. Authors often use editorial (i.e., parenthetical) material in their own writings. The "land of their possession" referred to in Deuteronomy 2:13 is, as Keil and Delitzsch noted,

   > The land to the east of the Jordan (Gilead and Bashan), which was conquered by the Israelites under Moses, and divided among the two tribes and a half, and which is also described in chap. iii. 20 as the "possession" which Jehovah had given to these tribes.[33]

   Even if they are later additions, they may possibly be uninspired changes that are subject to the same textual debate as Mark 16:9-20 and John 7:53—8:11.

3. Simply adding and rearranging inspired writings (individual psalms) is not proof of the redaction model. Adding psalms to the psalter as they were written fits perfectly with the prophetic model of the canon. What the redactional model would have to prove is that later allegedly inspired editors made deliberate content changes in psalms (or other books) already in the canon and did not simply rearrange what was already there. There is no proof of such content changes in the Psalms.[34] Furthermore, small editorial additions to a text are one thing, but the inspired redactor view believes in substantial changes in the content of the text; this is quite another matter for which no proof is offered.

4. None of the passages cited from Proverbs prove that the original author's writing, whether Solomon's (1-29), Agur's (30), or Lemuel's (31), was not accepted by the believing community immediately and continued subsequently without deliberate content changes. "Copied out" (25:1, KJV) does not mean "changed in content" but merely transcribed onto another manuscript.

5. Conservative scholars have long acknowledged that there may have been two versions (editions) of Jeremiah, one that came from Jeremiah himself (on which the LXX is based), and a later larger one (on which the Masoretic Text is based) with more of his prophecies collected by his scribe, Baruch.[35] Thus there is no need to posit a later inspired redactor of Jeremiah after his time.

6. The passages cited in Chronicles do not mean that the writer of Chronicles (possibly Ezra) was redacting some other books but merely that he

33. C. F. Keil and F. Delitzsch, *Commentary on the Old Testament,* 1:293.
34. The evidence for this was provided by Kenneth Barker in response to Waltke's proposal (Radmacher, ibid., 134, 135).
35. See Gleason Archer, Jr., *A Survey of Old Testament Introduction,* pp. 361-62.

was using them as sources to write his own book. For example, Daniel (Dan. 9) uses Jeremiah (Jer. 25), and 2 Sam. 22 uses Psalm 18. Further, it is not necessary to take all the books Chronicles cites as inspired writings. Some were simply court records (e.g. 1 Chron. 9:1; 27:24; 2 Chron. 20:34). The books by "Samuel the Seer and Nathan the Prophet" (1 Chron. 29:29) may be the prophetic writing now known as 1 Samuel. Still others may have been uninspired commentaries (e.g., 2 Chron. 13:22).

Problems with the redaction canon theory. Inasmuch as the redaction canon theory involves inspired redactors who allegedly made deliberate and substantial changes in the content of previous prophet material decades, even centuries after the original author died, it is unacceptable for many reasons.

1. It is contrary to the repeated warning God gave not to "add to the word which I [God] am commanding you" (Deut. 4:2; cf. Prov. 30:6; Rev. 22:18-19). This of course does not mean that another prophet could not get his own revelation, which was later placed along with a previous prophet's writing in the canon of Scripture. But it does mean that no one was later permitted to change (redact) the revelation God had already given.

2. The redaction theory confuses canonicity and textual criticism. The question of scribal changes in transmitting a manuscript of an inspired book is one of textual criticism, not canonicity. Likewise, if there is some sizeable material added later that is not found in earlier manuscripts, then, as in the case of Mark 16:9-20 and John 7:53—8:11, it is a matter of textual criticism to determine whether or not it was in the original writing. This is not properly a question of canonicity.

3. The "inspired redactor" theory is contrary to the bibical use of the word "inspired" (2 Tim. 3:16). The Bible does not speak of inspired writers, but only inspired *writings* (see chap. 2). If the authors were inspired, then they would be *infallible (and inerrant) men,* not simply authors of an infallible (and inerrant) book. Furthermore, inspired *(theopneustos)* does not mean to "breathe into" the writers, but to "breath out" the writings.

4. The redaction theory is contrary to the evangelical view that only the *autographa* (original writings) are inspired. The words "original writings," and "original manuscripts" are used interchangeably with the word "autographs." But if it is only the final redacted version that is inspired, then the original writings were not the ones breathed out by God. To accept inspired redactors would necessitate a rejection of the evangelical view of a definite written original autograph, which God breathed out by the prophets. Instead, fixed "autographs" would be transformed into a fluid process of manuscript changes by many hands over many centu-

ries. It would in effect transform mere scribes into prophets. This is why 2 Peter 1:20-21 affirms that all "prophecy" (not the prophets) comes from God. God would have to breathe out the copies (with their errors) as well as the original prophetic writing. It would in fact result in God-breathed (inspired) errors!

5. Inspired redaction would also eliminate the means by which a prophetic utterance could be tested by those to whom it was given. Typically the redaction theory asserts that the written prophetic work as such was not presented to the contemporary believing community of the prophet through whom God gave it but by someone decades (or even centuries) later. Hence, there was no way to confirm whether that writing (in its eventual edited form) actually came from a prophet of God. Only if the original and unchanged message was confirmed by the original audience can we have assurance of its rightful place in the canon. As I. Howard Marshall aptly notes, "the weakness of the view is that it locates inspiration as an activity in the process of composition of the Bible and does not really tackle the issue of the inspiredness of the resulting book."[36]
6. The redaction model shifts the locus of divine authority from the original prophetic message (given by God through the prophet) to the community of believers generations later. It is contrary to the true principle of canonicity that God *determines* canonicity and the people of God merely *discover* what God determined or inspired (see chap. 13). In effect the redaction model locates the authority in the church rather than in the God-given prophetic message.
7. A redaction model of canonicity entails acceptance of deception as a means of divine communication. It asserts that a message or book that claims to come from a prophet (such as Isaiah or Daniel) did not really come from him in its entirety, but rather from later redactors. As applied to the gospels, redaction criticism claims that Jesus did not necessarily say or do what the gospel writers claim He did.[37] They literally put their words in Jesus' mouth. But that involves an intentional misrepresentation on their part, which is deceptive and contrary to their own assertions (Luke 1:1-4; John 20:30-31). The same applies to whatever later redactors allegedly changed what a stated prophet wrote. To do such would be a deception, misleading the reader to believe that the God-directed original writers had said that. But God cannot lie (Titus 1:2; Heb. 6:18).

36. I. Howard Marshall, *Biblical Inspiration,* p. 38.
37. Robert Gundry was asked to resign from the Evangelical Theological Society over this very issue. He claimed that the expressions " 'Jesus said' or 'Jesus did' need not always mean that in history Jesus said or did what follows, but sometimes may mean that in the account at least partly constructed by Matthew himself Jesus said or did what follows" (Robert Gundry, *Matthew: A Commentary on His Literary and Theological Art,* p. 630).

8. The redaction model of the canon confuses legitimate scribal activity, involving grammatical form, updating of names, and arrangement of prophetic material with the illegitimate redactional changes in actual content of a previous prophet's message. It confuses acceptable scribal transmission with unacceptable redactional tampering with the inspired text.

9. The redaction theory assumes there were inspired redactions of the Old Testament well beyond the period in which there were no prophets (namely the fourth century B.C.). There can be no inspired works unless there are living prophets. And the Jews recognized no prophets after the time of Malachi (c. 400 B.C.; see material earlier in this chap.). Thus any changes in the Old Testament text after that time could not be inspired. As a result such changes would be a matter of textual criticism, not canonicity.

Summary and Conclusion

There are three steps to canonization: (1) inspiration by God; (2) recognition by the people of God; and (3) collection and preservation by the people of God. The history of the canon indicates a gradual development of the collection of prophetic books which were added continually to the Law as they were written.

The Old Testament canon was probably completed about 400 B.C., and perhaps by about 200 B.C. the twenty-four books that had undergone this process of canonization began to assume an alternate threefold classification: the Law, the Prophets, and the Writings. One suggestion is that a third category may have been created for liturgical reasons (to fit their festal year). A more plausible approach is that the threefold classification is a result of topical arrangement into legal, historical, and nonhistorical books.

Whatever the reason for a threefold classification, there are several lines of evidence to support the view that the Old Testament was originally canonized into the twofold division of the Law (five books) and the Prophets (seventeen books): (1) the way in which the historical books are linked together into a unit; (2) the most common New Testament designation of the Old Testament, "Law and Prophets"; (3) the reference in Daniel to the Law and "the books" (Dan. 9:2); and (4) the recognition of the "Former" prophetic books by the "Latter." Nevertheless, because of the early tendency to separate the Prophets into two groups, the final form of the Hebrew canon eventually became threefold: the Law, the Prophets, and the Writings.

15
The Old Testament Apocrypha and Pseudepigrapha

Once the "What?" (nature) and the "How?" (history) of the canon have been considered, the question "Which?" (extent of the canon) demands attention. Historically, the *number* of books in the canon has been nearly as difficult a problem as the *nature* of the canon. To borrow the terminology of the New Testament Fathers (see chap. 17), the Old Testament books may be arranged into four groups: (1) those accepted as canonical by virtually everyone, called Homologoumena (one word, agreement); (2) those that at one time or another have been disputed by some of the Fathers, called Antilegomena (spoken against); (3) those that were rejected by virtually everyone, called Pseudepigrapha (false writings, spurious); and (4) those that were accepted by some, called Apocrypha (hidden, secret). Each of these various classifications requires individual treatment.

The Books Accepted by All—Homologoumena

The Nature of the Homologoumena

The Homologoumena are books which once they were accepted into the canon were not subsequently questioned or disputed. They were recognized not only by early generations but by succeeding generations as well.

In view of the divine origin of the Scriptures, it is not at all surprising to find them described as "holy" in the literature of the intertestamental period. Moreover, the Temple was the repository for these sacred writings. With the destruction of the Temple in the second century B.C., these Temple Scriptures were disbursed. Roger Beckwith observes, "Even if it became possible, after the destruction of the Temple, to add certain *disputed* books to the canon (which is conceivable), the *undisputed* books, in all three sections of the canon, must have been canonical before the Temple was destroyed, and not just a little while before, but for a very long while."[1]

The Number of the Homologoumena

In all, the Homologoumena comprise thirty-four of the thirty-nine books in the English versions of the Protestant Old Testament. All of the Old Testament except the Antilegomena are in this body of books. That is, the Homologoumena include every book of the Protestant English Old Testament except Song of Solomon, Ecclesiastes, Esther, Ezekiel, and Proverbs. Because the Homologoumena are not involved in the debate about the Old Testament, no space need be devoted to discussing them in this context. The question of the Antilegomena is important, however, and requires additional treatment.

The Books Disputed by Some—Antilegomena

The Nature of the Antilegomena

Several books that were initially, and ultimately, considered canonical, were for one reason or another, at one time or another, disputed by some of the rabbis. Moses Stuart has drawn attention to the conservative tendency that must have resulted from the rivalry among the Pharisees, Sadducees, and Essenes to the effect that

> any attempt to add to the canon, or to take away from it, by one of these groups, would almost certainly have been resisted by one or both of the others, and even if the resistance had been unsuccessful, the controversy involved might never have been appeased, and could be expected to have left its mark on history.[2]

These books classified as Antilegomena were originally accepted into the canon and were only subsequently disputed. That is, these canonical books had their character and/or claims brought into question by later rabbis.

The Number of the Antilegomena

As has been stated, there are five books that fall into this category, and each one deserves individual treatment.

Song of Solomon. This book "is included in the canon of Aquila, and ranked as Scripture by Melito and Tertullian. It is also quoted, with standard formulas for citing Scripture, in the Mishnah (Taanith 4.8; Abodah Zarah 2.5)."[3] The basic reason that this book was challenged is that it seemed *sensual* to some. The school of Shammai (first cent. A.D.) expressed doubt

1. Roger Beckwith, *The Old Testament Canon in the New Testament Church and Its Background in Early Judaism,* p. 86.
2. Moses Stuart, *Critical History and Defence of the Old Testament Canon,* section 10, as cited in Beckwith, pp. 86-87.
3. Beckwith, pp. 321-22.

about its canonicity, but eventually the view of Rabbi Akiba ben Joseph (c. 50-132) prevailed, when he said,

> God forbid!—No man in Israel ever disputed about the Song of Songs [that he should say] that it does not render the hands unclean [i.e., is not canonical], for all the ages are not worth the day on which the Song of Songs was given to Israel; for all the Writings are holy, but the Song of Songs is the Holy of Holies. And if aught was in dispute the dispute was about Ecclesiastes alone.[4]

However, as H. H. Rowley observes, the very fact that such a statement was necessary implies that there was some doubt concerning it.[5] If those doubts centered in the alleged sensual character, they were based upon a misunderstanding. Nevertheless, it is entirely possible "that God has placed this Song in the canon in order to teach us the purity and the sanctity of that estate of marriage which He Himself has established."[6] Whatever questions may arise about the interpretation of the Song, there ought to be none about its inspiration and consequent canonization. Moreover,

> since the Song of Songs was not (like Ecclesiastes and Esther) one of the more hotly disputed books, the absence of direct evidence is less serious, and the indirect evidence for its canonicity is sufficient. For it is evidently one of Josephus's 22 canonical books, which he says had been accepted by all Jews for a long time, and it is presumably also one of the 24 canonical books mentioned by 2 Esdras (4 Ezra) and perhaps alluded to by the Revelation of John. And if, as we have argued, the standard numbers 24 and 22 for the canonical books go back to the second century BC, the canonicity of the books in question must go back equally far, for standard numbers would only have been adopted after the identity of the books was settled, thus allowing them to be counted in an agreed way.[7]

Ecclesiastes. One of the main objections to this book was that it seemed *skeptical*. Some have called it the "Song of Skepticism."[8] Rabbi Akiba admitted that "if aught was in dispute [about Song of Solomon and Ecclesiastes] the dispute was about Ecclesiastes alone."[9] However, there is no necessity to come to that conclusion about the book. Ecclesiastes itself comes to a spiritual conclusion: "Fear God and keep His commandments; because this applies to every person" (12:13). There may be some doubt about man "under the sun," but there need be none about the ultimate teaching of the book, which goes "above and beyond the sun" and comes as the "words of truth ... given by one Shepherd" (Eccles. 12:10-11). For after such an affirmation, it adds a

4. *The Mishnah,* trans. Herbert Danby, Yadaim 3.5, pp. 178-82.
5. H. H. Rowley, "The Interpretation of the Song of Songs," pp. 337-63.
6. Edward J. Young, *An Introduction to the Old Testament,* p. 355.
7. Beckwith, p. 322.
8. As cited in Herbert Carl Leupold, *Exposition of Ecclesiastes,* p. 19.
9. Yadim 3.5, in *The Mishnah,* pp. 781-82; also see discussion in R. K. Harrison, *Introduction to the Old Testament,* pp. 1079-84, and Eduroth 5.3 in Danby, p. 431.

warning of the unprofitableness of books that are earthly in their origin: "But beyond this, my son, be warned: the writing of many books is endless, and excessive devotion *to books* is wearying to the body" (Eccles. 12:12). "Add to this the fact that Ecclesiastes was evidently in the canon of Josephus, which he declares had been fixed for a long time; also that it was in the canon of Aquila, and that it is quoted, with standard formulas for citing Scripture, in the Mishnah (Sukkah 2.6; Hagigah 1.6; Kiddushin 1.0) and the other tannaitic literature."[10]

Esther. Because of the conspicuous absence of the name of God, this book encountered some difficulty in retaining its position in the Hebrew canon. The basis of challenge lay in the fact that the book seemed to be *unspiritual*. The primary question asked was: How can the book be God's Word when it does not even mention God's name? There are two possible explanations that merit mention at this point. Some have suggested that because the Jews of the Persian exile "were no longer in the Theocratic line, so to speak, the *Name* of the covenant God is not associated with them."[11] Others have thought the omission of God's name to be an intentional one, to protect the book from pagan plagiarization and the substitution of the name of a heathen god. In support of that contention is the observation of W. G. Scroggie, who indicates that the name of Jehovah (YHWH) may be seen four times in acrostic form in the book, in such a way and in such places that would place it beyond the realm of mere probability.[12] In any event, the absence of God's name is more than conpensated for by the presence of His power and grace in the deliverance of His people, a fact which gives canonical worth to the book (cf. Esther 4:14; 9:20-22).

Roger Beckwith summarizes the historical evidence in support of the canonicity of Esther as he writes,

> Josephus's attestation of Esther is direct. He tells us that the 22 canonical books trace the course of history from the Creation to the time of Artaxerxes the successor of Xerxes, whom he identifies with the Ahasuerus who married Esther.... Esther was in the canon of Aquila, and it was probably accepted in the Western Christian church from the beginning.... It is quoted in the Mishnah and the other tannaitic literature, in the latter case with the standard formulas for citing Scripture.[13]

10. Beckwith, p. 321.
11. Young, p. 378.
12. W. Graham Scroggie, *Know Your Bible*, vol. 1: *The Old Testament*, p. 96. The Jewish scholars did not doubt the canonicity of the Song of Solomon on the same grounds, for although no name or term for God appears in an English translation of the Song of Solomon except in the *New American Standard Bible*, the Hebrew name for God, *Yah*, occurs at the end of 8:6. No other recent major translation of the Old Testament into English follows the lead of the NASB translators.
13. Beckwith, p. 322.

Ezekiel. This book was questioned by some because of its apparent *anti-Mosaical* teachings. The school of Shammai thought that the teaching of the book was not in harmony with the Mosaic law, and that the first ten chapters exhibited a tendency toward gnosticism.[14] However, no specific examples have been supplied that do in fact contradict the Torah. If there were actual contradictions, then of course the book could not be considered canonical. Hence, as in the case of the other disputed books, the arguments were centered about interpretation rather than inspiration (see chap. 2).

From the historical perspective, as Beckwith observes,

> evidence in favour of the canonicity of Ezekiel is so ample and so early that the book is something of an embarrassment to those who hold the common view about the date of the closing of the canon. Ezekiel certainly claims to be by a divinely-commissioned prophet, and...the book is probably or certainly acknowledged as prophetic, biblical or divine by Tobit, Ecclesiasticus, 4 Maccabees, the Dead Sea Scrolls, the Revelation of John, 1 Clement and Josephus. Its revelations and predictions are endorsed, its prophetic authorship is acknowledged, it is quoted with standard formulas for citing Scripture, and it is included in 'the Law and the Prophets' and the 22 books. There is also possible attestation from Philo and from Jesus in the Gospel of John....Pharisaic, Essene and Christian opinion all support it, and the support goes back at least to the second century BC, as is shown by the evidence of Tobit and Ecclesiasticus, and by the Essene evidence, which (though it may not itself go back quite so far) suggests that the book was already canonical before the Essenes broke way in that century. Then, too, the fact that it belongs not to the Hagiographa, like the other four disputed books, but to the Prophets, is significant, since no one really believes the canon of the Prophets was still open in the first century AD. The case could scarcely be more complete.[15]

Proverbs. The disputation over this book was based on the grounds that it is *illogical* (contradictory within itself). This charge is clear in the Talmud, which states, "The book of Proverbs also they sought to hide, because its words contradicted one to another."[16] The supposed contradiction is found in Proverbs 26:4-5, where the exhortation is both to "answer a fool according to his folly" and not to do so. However, as the rabbis have observed, the obvious meaning intended is that there are occasions when a fool should be answered and others when he should not. Because the statements are in successive verses and in couplet form, it would appear that they carry an implicit impact similar to the current expression, "On the one hand—and on the other hand." In any event, the remainder of the verses give different reasons for the two kinds of advice, respectively; and, as a result, there is no contradiction to stand in the way of canonicity.

14. Young, p. 257.
15. Beckwith, p. 318. Also see the discussion in chap. 14.
16. Tractate Shabbath, 30b, Talmud, as cited in Young, p. 332.

Additional witness to the canonicity of Proverbs is again substantial. As Beckwith observes,

> The book of Proverbs is certainly or probably treated as Scripture by Ecclesiasticus, 4 Maccabees, the Dead Sea Scrolls, Philo, the Epistle to the Romans, the Epistle of James, 1 Clement and Josephus. It was in the canon of Aquila, and is frequently quoted with standard formulas for citing Scripture, in the Mishnah, (Peah 5.6; 7.3; 8.9; Shabbath 9.2; Shekalim 3.2; Yoma 3.11; Taanith 4.8, etc.)....Finally, in pseudo-Philo's *De Sampsone* 44, perhaps written in the first century AD, either Prov. 26.27 or Eccles. 10.8 is quoted with the formulas 'Scripture says'.
>
> Once again, it will be observed that the book has Pharisaic, Essene and Christian support, and that the support goes back to the second century BC, as is shown by the evidence of Ecclesiasticus and its prologue, and by the Essene evidence, which suggests that the book was already canonical before the Essene schism.[17]

The Books Rejected by All—Pseudepigrapha

There are a vast number of false and spurious writings that deserve mention at this point; not because anyone would seriously contend for their authority, but because they do represent the religious lore of the Hebrews in the intertestamental period. The New Testament writers make use of a number of these books, for example, Jude 14-15 have a possible quotation from the Book of Enoch (1:9) and the Assumption of Moses (1:9); and an allusion from the Penitence of Jannes and Jambres is found in 2 Timothy 3:8. Of course, it should be remembered that the New Testament also quotes from the heathen poets Aratus (Acts 17:28); Menander (1 Cor. 15:33); and Epimenides (Titus 1:12).[18] Truth is truth no matter where it is found, whether uttered by a heathen poet, a pagan prophet (Num. 24:17), or even a dumb animal (22:28). Nevertheless, it should be noted that no such formula as "it is written" or "the Scriptures say" is connected with these citations. It should also be noted that neither the New Testament writers nor the Fathers have considered these writings canonical.

The Nature of the Pseudepigrapha

The Pseudepigrapha books are those that are distinctly spurious and unauthentic in their overall content (see chap. 20). Although they claim to have been written by biblical authors, they actually express religious fancy and magic from the period between about 200 B.C. and A.D. 200. In Roman Catholic circles these books are known as the Apocrypha, a term not to be confused with an entirely different set of books known in Protestant circles

17. Beckwith, p. 319.
18. William H. Green, *General Introduction to the Old Testament: The Canon*, pp. 146 ff.

by the same name (see below); although at times Protestants have referred to these same books as the "wider Apocrypha," or "Apocalyptic Literature." Most of these books are comprised of dreams, visions, and revelations in the apocalyptic style of Ezekiel, Daniel, and Zechariah. A notable characteristic of these books is that they depict the bright future of the Messianic kingdom, as well as the questions of creation, angels, sin, suffering, and rewards for faithful living.

The Number of the Pseudepigrapha

The actual number of these books is not known certainly, and various writers have given different numbers of important ones. There are eighteen worthy of mention,[19] and they may be classified as follows:

Legendary	1. The Book of Jubilee 2. The Letter of Aristeas 3. The Book of Adam and Eve 4. The Martyrdom of Isaiah
Apocalyptic	1. 1 Enoch 2. The Testament of the Twelve Patriarchs 3. The Sibylline Oracle 4. The Assumption of Moses 5. 2 Enoch, or the Book of the Secrets of Enoch 6. 2 Baruch, or The Syriac Apocalypse of Baruch 7. 3 Baruch, or The Greek Apocalypse of Baruch
Didactical	1. 3 Maccabees 2. 4 Maccabees 3. Pirke Aboth 4. The Story of Ahikar
Poetical	1. The Psalms of Solomon 2. Psalm 151
Historical	1. The Fragment of a Zadokite Work

19. Seventeen are in Robert Henry Charles, *The Apocrypha and Pseudepigrapha of the Old Testament in English*. Psalm 151 may be found in *The Septuagint Version of the Old Testament*. A Hebrew copy of Psalm 151 was found at Qumran. Also see Willis Barstone, ed., *The Other Bible*. This work is based on ancient esoteric texts from the Pseudepigrapha, the Dead Sea Scrolls, the early Kabbalah, the Nag Hammadi Library, and other sources.

The Books Accepted by Some—Apocrypha

Some books, referred to collectively as the Apocrypha, were mistakenly viewed as part of the Old Testament canon. Several factors concerning these books must be considered.

The Meaning of "Apocrypha"

Part of the mystery that surrounds these "extra" books concerns the meaning of their very name, "Apocrypha."

Classical and *Hellenistic Greek*. The word *apocrypha* was used to describe something "hard to understand," or "hidden."

Patristic Greek. Later the word was used with the connotation of "esoteric," that is, something understood only by the initiated, or those within the inner circle of believers.

Early Fathers. Some of the early Fathers, for example Irenaeus and Jerome, were among the first to apply the word *Apocrypha* to the list of noncanonical books, including the Pseudepigrapha.

Post-Reformation. Since the time of the Reformation, the word *Apocrypha* has come to mean "Old Testament Apocrypha." The basic etymology of the word is clear, meaning "hidden." The disputation about the Apocrypha centers in the reason for its being so labeled. Is "hidden" to be used in a good sense, indicating that these books were hidden in order to be preserved, or in the sense that their message was deep and spiritual? Or, is the word *hidden* used in the bad sense, indicating that the books were of doubtful authenticity, spurious? In order to answer those questions, the individual books must be examined carefully.

The Mix-up About the Apocrypha

The confusion over the present issue about the Apocrypha revolves about the two traditions of the Old Testament canon. The Palestinian Canon contains twenty-two books in Hebrew (thirty-nine in English), and the so-called "Alexandrian Canon" contains an additional fourteen (or fifteen) books in its collection. The Palestinian Canon is the Hebrew canon that arose in Palestine and was recognized by the Jews. The Alexandrian collection is the Greek listing of Old Testament books, and it allegedly arose in Alexandria, Egypt, where the Hebrew Scriptures were translated into the Greek Septuagint (LXX) about 250 B.C. and following (see chap. 1).

It has been thought by some that there were actually two canons: a broader canon containing the Apocrypha, and a narrower one without it. That two-canon hypothesis is based on the fact that the earliest extant copies of the Greek Septuagint (LXX, c. 4th cent. A.D.) contain some of the apocryphal

4. *Skyline of Alexandria, where the Septuagint was produced (Egyptian State Tourist Administration)*

books whereas the Hebrew Bible has only the familiar thirty-nine books.

Arguments in favor of accepting the Alexandrian list. The Alexandrian list contains the following fourteen (or fifteen) additional books, commonly called Apocrypha, interwoven among the other thirty-nine books of the Old Testament (see chart on p. 266). Only eleven of the fourteen (or twelve of fifteen) books are accepted as canonical by the Roman Catholic Church, which includes all but 1 and 2 Esdras (called 3 and 4 Esdras by Roman Catholics) and the Prayer of Manasseh. However, according to the numbering of books in the Douay and The New American Bible Old Testaments, only seven additional books are listed in the table of contents, making the total forty-six. The reason for that is that Baruch and the Letter of Jeremiah were combined into one book, having six chapters; the additions to Esther were added at the end of the book of Esther; the Prayer of Azariah was inserted between the Hebrew Daniel 3:23 and 24, making it Daniel 3:24-90 in the Douay and New American Bible texts; Susanna was placed at the end of the book of Daniel (as chap. 13); and Bel and the Dragon was attached as chapter 14 of Daniel. Because three of the fifteen books were rejected, the remaining twelve books were incorporated into eleven, and because four of those books were added to the existing Old Testament books (by combining Baruch and the Letter of Jeremiah), only seven extra books appear in the Douay and the New American Bible Old Testament table of contents. Nonetheless, the Roman Catholic Church has actually added eleven (twelve if Baruch is separated from the Letter of Jeremiah) pieces of apocryphal literature to the Hebrew canon, in contrast to the Protestants who followed the Hebrew canon (see chap. 1).

Type of Book	Revised Standard Version	The New American Bible
Didactic	1. The Wisdom of Solomon (c. 30 B.C.)	Book of Wisdom
	2. Ecclesiasticus (Sirach) (132 B.C.)	Sirach
Religious Romance	3. Tobit (c. 200 B.C.)	Tobit
	4. Judith (c. 150 B.C.)	Judith
Historic	5. 1 Esdras (c. 150-100 B.C.)	3 Esdras*
	6. 1 Maccabees (c. 110 B.C.)	1 Maccabees
	7. 2 Maccabees (c. 110-70 B.C.)	2 Maccabees
Prophetic	8 Baruch (c. 150-50 B.C.)	Baruch chaps. 1-5
	9. Letter of Jeremiah (c. 300-100 B.C.)	Baruch chap. 6
	10. 2 Esdras (c. A.D. 100)	4 Esdras*
Legendary	11. Additions to Esther (140-130 B.C.)	Esther 10:4–16:24
	12. Prayer of Azariah (second or first century B.C.) (Song of Three Young Men)	Daniel 3:24-90
	13. Susanna (second or first century B.C.)	Daniel 13
	14. Bel and the Dragon (c. 100 B.C.)	Daniel 14
	15. Prayer of Manasseh (second or first century B.C.)	Prayer of Manasseh*

*Books not accepted as canonical at the Council of Trent, 1546.

The reasons generally advanced in favor of this broader Alexandrian list, which includes the apocryphal books, are as follows:

1. The New Testament reflects the thought of the Apocrypha, and even refers to it (cf. Heb. 11:35 with 2 Macc. 7, 12).

2. The New Testament quotes mostly from the Greek Old Testament, the Septuagint (LXX), which contained the Apocrypha.
3. Some of the early church Fathers quoted and used the Apocrypha as Scripture in public worship.
4. Some of the early church Fathers accepted all of the books of the Apocrypha as canonical, for example, Irenaeus, Tertullian, and Clement of Alexandria.
5. Catacomb scenes depict episodes from the Apocrypha, showing it was part of the early Christian's religious life.
6. The great Greek manuscripts (א, A, and B) interpose the Apocrypha among the Old Testament books.
7. The Syriac church accepted them in the fourth century.
8. Augustine and the councils he influenced at Hippo (393) and presided over at Carthage (397) accepted them.
9. The Eastern Orthodox church accepts them.
10. The Roman Catholic church proclaimed them canonical at the Council of Trent (1546).
11. The apocryphal books continued in the Protestant Bibles as late as the nineteenth century.
12. Some apocryphal books written in Hebrew have been found among other Old Testament canonical books in the Dead Sea community at Qumran.

Arguments against accepting these apocryphal books.[20] In response to the alleged support for considering the apocryphal books as canonical, the following reasons may be proffered, answering point by point the arguments presented in the previous discussion.

1. There may be New Testament *allusions* to the Apocrypha, but there are no clear New Testament *quotations* from it. In any event, the New Testament never refers to any of the fourteen or fifteen apocryphal books as authoritative or canonical.
2. It is not certain that the Greek Old Testament, Septuagint (LXX), of the first century contained the Apocrypha. The earliest Greek manuscripts that include them date from the fourth century A.D. (see chaps. 21 and 22). Even if they were in the LXX of apostolic time, Jesus and the

20. See Norman L. Geisler, "The Extent of The Old Testament Canon," for a current critique of the so-called Alexandrian Canon.

apostles implied their view of them by never once quoting them, although they are supposed to have been included in the very version of the Old Testament that they cited.

3. Citations of the church Fathers in support of the canonicity of the Apocrypha must be done with care. As Beckwith observes,

> When one examines the passages in the early Fathers which are supposed to establish the canonicity of the Apocrypha, one finds that some of them are taken from the alternative Greek text of Ezra (1 Esdras) or from additions or appendicies to Daniel, Jeremiah or some other canonical book, which...are not really relevant; that others of them are not quotations from the Apocrypha at all;[21] and that, of those which are, many do not give any indication that the book is regarded as Scripture.[22]

4. Although some individuals in the early church had a high esteem for the Apocrypha, no council of the entire church during the first four centuries favored them, and there were many individuals who vehemently opposed them, for example, Athanasius, Cyril of Jerusalem, Origen, Jerome.

5. Scenes from the catacombs do not prove the canonicity of the books whose events they depict. Such scenes need not indicate any more than the religious significance that the portrayed events had for early Christians.

6. None of the great Greek manuscripts (א, A, and B) contain all of the Apocryphal books. In fact, only four (Tobit, Judith, Wisdom, and Ecclesiasticus) are found in all of them, and the oldest manuscript (Vaticanus) totally excludes the books of Maccabees. Furthermore, no Greek manuscript has the exact list of Aprocryphal books accepted by the Council of Trent (1545-63).[23]

7. The Syrian church did not accept these books until the fourth century A.D. In the second century A.D. the Syrian Bible (Peshitta) did *not* contain the Apocrypha (see chaps. 27 and 28).

8. Augustine is the single significant voice of antiquity that recognized the Apocrypha. But his opinion was unfounded for several reasons: (a)

21. "Thus, Epistle of Barnabas 6.7 and Tertullian, *Against Marcion* 3.22.5, are not quoting Wisd. 2.12 but Isa. 3.10 LXX, and Tertullian, *On the Soul* 15, is not quoting Wisd. 1.6 but Ps. 139.23, as a comparison of the passages shows. Similarly, Justin Martyr, *Dialogue with Trypho* 129, is quite clearly not quoting Wisdom but Prov. 8.21-5 LXX. The fact that he calls Proverbs 'Wisdom' is in accordance with the common nomenclature of the earlier Fathers" (Beckwith, p. 427 n.208).
22. Beckwith, p. 387.
23. See Beckwith, pp. 194, 382-83.

His contemporary Jerome, a greater biblical authority than Augustine, rejected the Apocrypha. (b) Augustine recognized that the Jews rejected these books.[24] (c) Augustine reasoned that the apocryphal books should be in the Bible because of their mention "of extreme and wonderful suffering of certain martyrs." But on that ground *Foxe's Book of Martyrs*[25] should also be in the canon. (d) Augustine rejected a book because it was not written by a prophet, yet he accepted apocryphal books that actually deny being prophetic (1 Macc. 9:27). (e) Augustine's acceptance of the Apocrypha seems to be connected with his mistaken belief in the inspiration of the Septuagint (LXX), which contained them.[26]

9. The Greek church has not always accepted the Apocrypha, nor is its present position unequivocal. At the synods of Constantinople (1638), Jaffa (1642), and Jerusalem (1672) these books were declared canonical. But, even as late as 1839 their Larger Catechism expressly omitted the Apocrypha on the grounds that they did not exist in the Hebrew Bible.

10. The Council of Trent (1545-63) was the first official proclamation of the Roman Catholic church on the Apocrypha, and it came a millennium and a half after the books were written, in an obvious polemical action against Protestantism. Furthermore, the addition of books that support salvation by works and prayers for the dead at that time—only twenty-nine years after Luther posted his Ninety-five Theses—is highly suspect.

11. Apocryphal books appeared in Protestant Bibles prior to the Council of Trent, and were generally placed in a separate section because they were not considered to be of equal authority. Even Roman Catholic scholars through the Reformation period made the distinction between the Apocrypha and the canon. Cardinal Ximenes made that distinction in his *Complutensian Polyglot* (1514-17) on the very eve of the Reformation. Cardinal Cajetan, who opposed Luther at Augsburg in 1518, published a *Commentary on all the Authentic Historical Books of the Old Testament* that did not include the Apocrypha in A.D. 1532. Luther spoke against the Apocrypha in his Bible published in 1543 by placing its books in the back.[27]

24. Augustine *The City of God* 19.36-38.
25. John Foxe (1516-87), *Acts and Monuments of Matters Happening in the Church* (1563).
26. Because he accepted the inspiration of the Septuagint Augustine also accepted the Apocrypha. His later acknowledgment of the superiority of Jerome's Hebrew text should have led him to accept the authority of Jerome's Hebrew canon as well (cf. chap. 29).
27. Bruce M. Metzger, *An Introduction to the Apocrypha*, pp. 181 ff.

12. The discoveries at Qumran included not only the community's Bibles but their library with fragments of hundreds of books. Among those were some of the Old Testament apocryphal books. The fact that no commentaries were found on apocryphal books and that only canonical books, not the apocryphal, were found in the special parchment and script indicates that the apocryphal books were not viewed as canonical by the Qumran community.[28]

Therefore, all of the arguments urged in favor of the canonicity of the apocryphal books merely prove that these books have been given varied degrees of esteem and recognition, usually falling short of full canonicity, until the Roman Catholic church officially pronounced them canonical at the Council of Trent. That belated recognition falls far short of the initial and continued support accorded the thirty-nine books of the Old Testament. Hence, the overwhelming arguments in favor of rejecting the Apocrypha as part of the canon provide convincing evidence that the books are not God-breathed.

Arguments in favor of accepting the Palestinian Canon. The true canon is the Palestinian Canon. It was the canon of Jesus, Josephus, and Jerome and, for that matter, the canon of most qualified witnesses from before the time of Christ to the present. The arguments for accepting the Palestinian Canon (only the thirty-nine books of the Old Testament) as canonical are:

1. Some of the additional books have teaching that is *unbiblical* or heretical. Two of the main doctrines in dispute during the Reformation are supported by the Apocrypha: prayers for the dead (2 Macc. 12:45-46) and salvation by works (Tobit 12:9). The canonical books of the Bible are against praying for the dead (Heb. 9:27; Luke 16:25-26; 2 Sam. 12:19). They are also strongly against salvation by works (Gen. 15:6; Rom. 4:5; Gal 3:11).[29]

2. Some of the apocryphal stories are *extrabiblical* and fanciful. The story of Bel and the Dragon is a case in point. In it, the pagan priests of Bel try to deceive Daniel by using a trap door to go in and consume the food offered to Bel to prove that Bel is a "living God" who "eats and drinks every day" (v. 6). So, in order to assist the "living God," Bel, "in the night the priests came with their wives and children, as they were accustomed to do, and ate and drank everything" (v. 15). The same unauthentic ring

28. Menahem Mansoor, *The Dead Sea Scrolls,* p. 203, lists the following fragments from the Apocrypha and Pseudepigrapha: Tobit, in Hebrew and Aramaic; Enoch in Aramaic; Jubilees, in Hebrew; Testaments of Levi and Naphtali, in Aramaic; Apocryphal Daniel literature, in Hebrew and Aramaic; Psalms of Joshua. See *New Catholic Encyclopedia,* 2:390. See also M. Burrows, *More Light on the Dead Sea Scrolls,* p. 178: "There is no reason to think that any of these works were venerated as Sacred Scripture." Also see chap. 21.

may be heard in the other legendary books of Additions to Esther, Prayer of Azariah, and Susanna, as well as Tobit and Judith.

3. Much of the teaching of the Apocrypha is *subbiblical* and, at times, even immoral. Judith was allegedly assisted by God in a deed of falsehood (Judith 9:10, 13), and both Ecclesiasticus and Wisdom teach a morality based on expedience.

   Besides this low morality, the subbiblical nature of the Apocrypha can be seen in its historical and chronological errors. It is claimed that Tobit was alive when the Assyrians conquered Israel (722 B.C.) as well as when Jeroboam revolted against Judah (931 B.C.), yet his total life-span was only 158 years (Tobit 14:11; cf. 1:3-5). Judith speaks of Nebuchadnezzar as reigning in Nineveh instead of Babylon (Judith 1:1). William H. Green concisely summarizes the evidence: "The books of Tobit and Judith abound in geographical, chronological, and historical mistakes, so as not only to vitiate the truth of the narratives which they contain, but to make it doubtful whether they even rest upon a basis of fact."[30]

4. Most of the Old Testament Apocrypha was written in Judaism's *postbiblical,* intertestamental period. According to Josephus, the prophets wrote from Moses to Artaxerxes, and he adds, "It is true our history hath been written since Artaxerxes very particularly but hath not been esteemed of the like authority with the former by our forefathers, because there hath not been an exact succession of the prophets since that time."[31] The Talmud adds a similar thought as it records, "After the latter prophets Haggai, Zechariah ... and Malachi, the Holy Spirit departed from Israel."[32] Because the apocryphal books were written long after Artaxerxes' time (Malachi's day, 400 B.C.), namely, after about 200 B.C., then they could not be considered inspired. Not only does the Talmud testify to that end, but the canonical books of the Old Testament also imply it (see Zech. 1:5; Mal. 4:5), as do some of the statements in the apocryphal books themselves (see chap. 14). In fact, there is no claim within the Apocrypha that it is the Word of God. It is sometimes asserted that Ecclesiasticus 50:27-29 lays claim to divine inspiration, but a closer examination of the passage indicates that it is illumination not inspiration that the author claims to have.

   Briefly then, with the possible exception of 2 Esdras, all of the apocryphal books are postbiblical for Judaism because they were written after the time that the prophetic spirit had departed from Israel but before

29. Also see Wisdom 11:17, which teaches creation *ex hula* (out of preexisting matter) rather than *ex nihilo* (out of nothing), as in John 1:1-3 and Heb. 11:3.
30. Green, p. 195.
31. Josephus *Against Apion* 1.8.
32. Tractate Sanhedrin, trans. Michael L. Rodkinson, *Babylonian Talmud,* VII-VIII, 24.

the prophet cried, "Make ready the way of the Lord" (Matt. 3:3), and "the fulness of the time came" (Gal. 4:4) when God spoke through His Son.

5. Finally, all of the books of the Apocrypha are *nonbiblical* or uncanonical because none of them was ever accepted by the people of God as the canonical books were. In order for a book to be canonical, it must satisfy the tests of canonicity:

   a. Was it written by a "prophet" of God? There is neither claim nor proof that they were.

   b. Was its writer confirmed by an act of God? Because the apocryphal books were not written by prophets (see 1 Macc. 9:27), they were obviously not supernaturally accredited by God.

   c. Did it have the power of God? There is nothing transforming about the apocryphal books. Their truth is not exhilarating, except as they are a repetition of canonical truth in other books.

   d. Did it tell the truth about God, man, etc.? As was mentioned above, there are contradictions, errors, and even heresies in the Apocrypha. These books do not stand the test of canonical truth.

   e. Was it accepted by the people of God? There was no continuous or universal acceptance of these books by the church of God.

Testimony of antiquity against accepting Apocrypha. There is an almost unbroken testimony of antiquity *against* accepting the Apocrypha into the canon:

1. Philo, Alexandrian Jewish philosopher (20 B.C.-A.D. 40), quoted the Old Testament prolifically and even recognized the threefold classification of books, but he never quoted from the Apocrypha as inspired.
2. Josephus (A.D. 30-100), Jewish historian, explicitly excludes the Apocrypha, numbering the books of the Old Testament as twenty-two. Neither does he quote the apocryphal books as Scripture.
3. Jesus and the New Testament writers never once quote the Apocrypha although there are hundreds of quotes and references to almost all of the canonical books of the Old Testament.
4. The Jewish scholars of Jamnia (A.D. 90) did not recognize the Apocrypha.
5. No canon or council of the Christian church recognized the Apocrypha as inspired for nearly four centuries.
6. Many of the great Fathers of the early church spoke out against the Apocrypha, for example, Origen, Cyril of Jerusalem, Athanasius.
7. Jerome (340-420), the great scholar and translator of the Latin Vulgate, rejected the Apocrypha as part of the canon. Jerome said that the church

reads them "for example of life and instruction of manners," but does not "apply them to establish any doctrine."[33] He disputed across the Mediterranean with Augustine on this point. At first Jerome refused even to translate the apocryphal books into Latin, but later he made a hurried translation of a few of them. After his death and "over his dead body" the apocryphal books were brought into his Latin Vulgate directly from the Old Latin Version (see chap. 29).

8. Many Roman Catholic scholars through the Reformation period rejected the Apocrypha.
9. Luther and the Reformers rejected the canonicity of the Apocrypha.
10. Not until A.D. 1546, in a polemical action at the counter-Reformation Council of Trent (1545-63), did the apocryphal books receive full canonical status by the Roman Catholic church.
11. The acceptance of the Apocrypha at the Council of Trent is suspect because:

    a. It was used against Luther in support of the Roman Catholic position (e.g., 2 Macc. 12:45-46, which favors prayers for the dead). Later, the Council added the Apocrypha in a counter-Reformation attempt to refute Luther.

    b. Not all of the Apocrypha was accepted. Only eleven of the fourteen books were, and one of those omitted books (2 Esdras)[34] is against prayers for the dead (cf. 7:105).

    c. In fact, the very history of this section of 2 Esdras is suspect. It was written in Aramaic by an unknown Jewish author (c. A.D. 100) and circulated in the Old Latin versions (c. A.D. 200). The Latin Vulgate printed it as an appendix to the New Testament (c. A.D. 400). Then it disappeared from Western Bibles until Protestants, beginning with Johann Haug (1726-42), began to print it in the Apocrypha based on Aramaic texts. In 1874 a long section (seventy verses from chap. 7) was found by Robert L. Bently in a library at Amiens. That material was the first known Latin manuscript containing 7:36-105 (as renumbered), and, as Metzger observes, "It is probable that the lost section was deliberately cut out of an ancestor of most extant Latin Manuscripts, because of dogmatic reasons, for the passage contains an emphatic denial of the value of prayers for the dead."[35] From 1895 to the present that section has been printed in the Protestant Apocrypha.

33. As cited in Beckwith, p. 343.
34. Named 4 Esdras in the Vulgate to distinguish it from Nehemiah, which the Vulgate labeled 2 Esdras.
35. Metzger, p. 23.

Therefore, for some fifteen hundred years the Apocrypha was not accepted as canonical by the people of God. Then, in 1546, just twenty-nine years after Luther posted his Ninety-Five Theses, the Council of Trent elevated the Apocrypha, or rather the part of it that supported the council's position, to the level of inspired Scripture, saying,

> The Synod . . . receives and venerates . . . all the books (including the *Apocrypha*) both of the Old and of the New Testament—seeing that one God is the Author of both . . . as having been dictated, either by Christ's own word of mouth or by the Holy Ghost . . . if anyone receive not as sacred and canonical the said books entire with all their parts, as they have been used to be read in the Catholic Church . . . let him be anathema.[36]

This stand was reaffirmed by Vatican I and Vatican II (see chap. 13, n. 1).

The Value of the Apocrypha

Even though the Apocrypha cannot be afforded a place in the canon of inspired books, it should not be dismissed as having no value. Some, such as Jerome and Rufinus (A.D. 410), have held the Apocrypha to be a kind of "ecclesiastical" canon containing books to be preserved, read, and used by the church. For many it has served as a sort of "homiletical" or "devotional" canon from which many of the Fathers have drawn illumination for life, for art, and for preaching. Almost all agree that the Apocrypha has some historical value. It provides a most important source of information about the history and religion of the Jewish church in the intertestamental period. Nevertheless, it is probably going too far to give the Apocrypha a semicanonical status, as did the Church of England, or a quasi-canonical status, as did the Eastern Orthodox Church. Whatever place it may be accorded below this level, it clearly is not part of the theological canon, which alone should be used for faith and practice.

Summary and Conclusion

Thirty-four of the thirty-nine books of the Old Testament are accepted by all Christians as part of the canon, called Homologoumena. The other five books, called Antilegomena, have been disputed by some but have retained their place in the canon. The Pseudepigraphical books have been rejected as spurious by virtually everyone. A real battle has raged, however, over the fourteen (or fifteen) books of the Apocrypha written between 200 B.C. and A.D. 100. The Roman Catholic church canonized them at Trent (1546); Protestants have rejected them; and the Church of England and the Eastern Orthodox church have given them a status in between these positions. Whereas

36. Philip Schaff, ed., *The Creeds of Christendom,* 2:81.

there is no doubt a devotional and even homiletical and historical value in them, yet they are not part of the theological canon to which the other thirty-nine books of the Old Testament belong because:

1. Some of their teaching is *unbiblical* or heretical.
2. Some of their stories are *extrabiblical* or fanciful.
3. Much of their teaching is *subbiblical,* at times even immoral.
4. Most of the Apocrypha was written in the *postbiblical* or intertestamental period.
5. Finally, all of the Apocrypha is *nonbiblical* or uncanonical, because it was not received by the people of God.

16
Development and History of the New Testament Canon

Preliminary Considerations

The history of the New Testament canon is similar to that of the Old Testament, although there is happily much more data available on the subject. Before that evidence is examined, a preliminary distinction must be made between the source and the stimuli for canonization.

The Source of Canonization

It has already been indicated that God is the source of canonicity (chap. 12). A book is canonical because it is inspired, and it is inspired because God moved in and through the men who wrote it. In this sense, canonicity is passive; it is something received from God. There is also an active sense of the word *canonization,* the sense in which the people of God were active in the recognition and collection of the books God had inspired. The historical process of canonization is concerned with this latter sense.

The Stimuli for Collection

From the human point of view there were several stimuli for the collection and final canonization of inspired books.

Books were prophetic. The initial reason for collecting and preserving the inspired books was that they were prophetic. That is, since they were written by an apostle or prophet of God, they must be valuable, and if valuable, they should be preserved. This reasoning is apparent in apostolic times, by the collection and circulation of Paul's epistles (cf. 2 Peter 3:15-16; Col. 4:16). The postapostolic period continued to reflect this high regard for the apostolic writings of the New Testament by their voluminous and authoritative quotations from those inspired books.

Demands of early church. Closely connected with the foregoing reason for preserving the inspired books were the theological and ethical demands of the early church. That is, in order to know which books should be read in the churches (cf. 1 Thess. 5:27 and 1 Tim. 4:13) and which books could be definitely applied to the theological and practical problems of the Christian church (cf. 2 Tim. 3:16-17), it became necessary to have a complete collection of the books that could provide the authoritative norm for faith and practice.

Heretical stimulus. On the negative side there was the heretical stimulus. At least as early as A.D. 140 the heretical Marcion accepted only limited sections of the full New Testament canon. Marcion's heretical canon, consisting of only Luke's gospel and ten of Paul's epistles, pointed up clearly the need to collect a complete canon of New Testament Scriptures.

Missionary stimulus. On the positive side, there was the missionary stimulus. Christianity had spread rapidly to other countries, and there was the need to translate the Bible into those other languages (see chaps. 27-29). As early as the first half of the second century the Bible was translated into Syriac and Old Latin. But because the missionaries could not translate a Bible that did not exist, attention was necessarily drawn to the question of which books really belonged to the authoritative Christian canon.

Persecutions and politics. The final phase of full and general recognition of the whole canon of New Testament writings also involved a negative and political stimulus. The Diocletian persecutions of about A.D. 302/303-5 provided forceful motivation for the church to sort, sift, and settle on the New Testament Scriptures. For certainly the books they would risk their lives to preserve must have been considered sacred to them.

The great persecution of Diocletian and Maximian (302/3-313) befell Christians all across the Roman Empire. An eyewitness account to the outbreak of persecution in Nicomedia, the capitol of the Roman province of Bythinia (in Asia Minor) has been preserved. Lactantius (c. 240-c. 320), a native of North Africa, was officially summoned to Nicomedia to teach rhetoric during the reign of Diocletian (284-305). He was converted to Christianity and he lost his position there when persecution broke out in February 302:

> A fit and auspicious day was sought for the accomplishment of this undertaking, and the festival of the god Terminus, celebrated on the twenty-third of February was chosen, in preference to all others, to "terminate," as it were, the Christian religion.
>
> That day, the harbinger of death arose,
> First cause of ill, and long-remembered woes,
>
> which befell not only the Christians, but the whole earth. When the day dawned, in the eighth consulship of Diocletian and the seventh of Maximian, suddenly, while it was hardly light, the prefect, together with chief commanders, tribunes

and officers of the treasury, came to the church in Nicomedia; they forced the doors and searched everywhere for an image of the god. The Holy Scriptures were found and burnt; the church was abandoned to general pillage: all was rapine, confusion, tumult. That church, situated on rising ground, was within view of the palace, and Diocletian and Galerius stood on a watch-tower disputing long whether it ought to be set on fire. The sentiment of Diocletian prevailed, who was afraid that once so great a blaze had started, some part of the city might be burnt; for there were many large buildings round the church. Then Praetorian Guards came in battle array, with axes and other tools; they were let loose everywhere, and in a few hours, leveled that very lofty edifice to the ground.

Next day an edict was published, depriving the Christians of all honours and dignities; ordaining also that, without any distinction of rank or degree, they should be subject to torture, and that every suit of law should be received against them; while, on the other hand, they were debarred from being plaintiffs in questions of wrong, adultery, or theft; and finally, that they should neither be capable of freedom, nor have the right of suffrage.[1]

Eusebius of Caesarea relates another incident from March 303 when he writes,

It was in the nineteenth year of the reign of Diocletian, and the month of Dystrus, or March, as the Romans would call it, in which, as the festival of the Saviour's Passion was coming on, an imperial letter was everywhere promulgated, ordering the razing of the churches to the ground and the destruction by fire of the Scripture, and proclaiming that those who held high positions would lose all civil rights, while those in households, if they persisted in their profession of Christianity, would be deprived of their liberty. Such was the first document against us. But not long afterwards we were further visited with other letters, and in them the order was given that the presidents of the churches should all, in every place, be first committed to prison, and then afterwards compelled by every kind of device to sacrifice.[2]

In still another part of the Roman Empire, the Christian clergy were compelled under pain of death to surrender their church possessions and their sacred books to the Roman magistrates. An inquisition that occurred a few months later in northern Africa is recorded by A.H.M. Jones. The following excerpt from that narrative reveals the intensity of the effort to rid the world of Christians, their possessions, and their Scriptures.

In the eighth and seventh consulships of Diocletian, 19th May, from the records

1. Lactantius *On the Deaths of the Persecutors* 12-13, as printed in J. Stevenson, ed., *A New Eusebius: Documents illustrative of the history of the Church to* A.D. *337,* p. 286. Also see Phillip Schaff and Henry Wace, eds., *Ante-Nicene Fathers,* 7:303-6.
2. Eusebius *Ecclesiastical History* 8.2, Loeb, ed., 2:257-59. Also see Joseph Cullen Ayer, ed., *A Source Book for Ancient Church History,* pass.; and Ray C. Petry, ed., *A History of Christianity: Readings in the History of the Early and Medieval Church,* pp. 35-58. In ancient Rome, the new year began in March instead of January as it does in the modern Western world.

of Munatius Felix, high priests of the province for life, mayor of the colony of Cirta. Arrived at the house where the Christians used to meet, the Mayor said to Paul the bishop: "Bring out the writings of the law and anything else you have here, according to the order, so that you may obey the command."

The Bishop: "The readers have the scriptures, but we will give you what we have."
The Mayor: "Point out the readers or send for them."
The Bishop: "You all know them."
The Mayor: "We do not know them."
The Bishop: "The municipal office knows them, that is, the clerks Edusius and Junius."
The Mayor: "Leaving over the matter of the readers, whom the office will point out, produce what you have."

Then follows an inventory of the church plate and other property, including large stores of male and female clothes and shoes, produced in the presence of the clergy who include three priests, two deacons, and four subdeacons, all named, and a number of "diggers."

The Mayor: "Bring out what you have."
Silvanus and Carosus (two of the subdeacons): "We have thrown out everything that was here."
The Mayor: "Your answer is entered in the record."

After some empty cupbords had been found in the library, Silvanus then produced a silver box and a silver lamp, which he said he had found behind a barrel.

Victor (the mayor's clerk): "You would have been a dead man if you hadn't found them."
The Mayor: "Look more carefully, in case there is anything left here."
Sylvanus: "There is nothing left. We have thrown everything out."

And when the dining room was opened, there were found there four bins and six barrels.

The Mayor: "Bring out the scriptures that you have so that we can obey the orders and command of the emperors."

Catullinus (another subdeacon) produced one very large volume.

The Mayor: "Why have you given one volume only? Produce the scriptures that you have."
Marcuclius and Catullinius (two subdeacons): "We haven't any more, because we are subdeacons; the readers have the books."
The Mayor: "Show me the readers."

> *Marcuclius and Catullinius:* "We don't know where they live."
> *The Mayor:* "If you don't know where they live, tell me their names."
> *Marcuclius and Catullinius:* "We are not traitors: here we are, order us to be killed."
> *The Mayor:* "Put them under arrest."
>
> They apparently weakened so far as to reveal one reader, for the Mayor now moved on to the house of Eugenius, who produced four books.
> The Mayor now turned on the other two subdeacons, Silvanus and Carosus:
>
> *The Mayor:* "Show me the other readers."
> *Silvanus and Carosus:* "The bishop has already said the Edusius and Junius the clerks know them all: they will show you the way to their houses."
> *Edusius and Junius:* "We will show them, sir."
>
> The Mayor went on to visit the six remaining readers. Four produced books without demur. One declared he had none, and the Mayor was content with entering his statement in the record. The last was out, but his wife produced his books; the Mayor had the house searched by the public slave to make sure that none had been overlooked. This task over, he addressed the subdeacons: "If there has been any omission, the responsibility is yours."[3]

As these examples illustrate, the destruction of biblical manuscripts during the pre-Constantine persecutions, especially under Decius (249-51) and Diocletian (302/3-305), was widespread throughout the Roman Empire. Even after Diocletian abdicated (305), the persecution begun in his reign continued until the Edict of Toleration (311) and the Edict of Milan (313). Diocletian's Edict in 302 was followed by the systematic destruction of the Scriptures and other church books, which resulted in the loss of untold numbers of biblical manuscripts. Only the library at Caesarea (in the East) was spared. This library housed a collection of thirty thousand books that were used by Origen, Pamphilius, Eusebius of Caesarea, and Jerome. Later, even this great library was destroyed by the Moslems (A.D. 638) as they took control of much of the territory of the ancient Roman Empire. That loss is of inestimable value.[4]

3. A.H.M. Jones, *Constantine and the Conversion of Europe,* pp. 51-54. According to *The Oxford Classical Dictionary,* 2d ed., p. 242, the full name of the colony of Cirta (located in modern Algeria) during the Roman Empire was *Colonia Iulia Iuvenalis Honoris et Virtutis Cirta.* It was the center of a unique confederation that included three other colonies, Rusicade, Chullu, and Milev. There was a large community of Christians at Cirta, and it was very prosperous during the second and third centuries A.D. Cirta was damaged during civil wars in the fourth century before Constantine restored and renamed it *Constantina* and it became the capital of Numidia.
4. See Michael W. Holmes, "The 'Majority text debate': New Form of an Old Issue," *Themelios* 8.2 (January 1983), p. 16. Also see W. H. C. Frend, *Martyrdom and Persecution in the Early Church,* pp. 372-77.

Ironically enough, within twenty-five years of the edict to destroy the Scriptures, Constantine took positive action to preserve them. He commissioned Eusebius, the historian, to prepare fifty copies of the Scriptures at imperial expense in the following letter, from "Victor Constantinus, Maximus Augustus, to Eusebius":

> I have thought it expedient to instruct your Prudence to order fifty copies of the sacred Scriptures, the provision and use of which you know to be most needful for the instruction of the Church, to be written on prepared parchment in a legible manner, and in a convenient, portable form, by professional transcribers thoroughly practiced in their art. The catholicus of the diocese has also received instructions from our Clemency to be careful to furnish all things necessary for the preparation of such copies; and it will be for you to take special care that they are completed with as little delay as possible.[5]

Both of those political actions prompted a careful examination and scrutiny of all religious writings in order to discover which were truly authoritative. And, in the same century as Diocletian's persecutions and Constantine's letter, the church began to give official recognition to the twenty-seven books of the New Testament, that is, in A.D. 363 (at Laodicea), and in A.D. 397 (at Carthage).

Progressive Collection

Although the church did not give official recognition to the canon prior to the late fourth century, it is misleading to say there was no recognition before then. As with the Old Testament books, there is ample evidence available to confirm that the inspired books were received immediately as such, circulated, and even collected. The problem of the New Testament is somewhat different, however, in that the New Testament books were written during a half-century period by some eight or nine different writers, having destinations ranging from individuals (e.g., Philemon) to groups of churches (e.g., 1 Peter) located in centers extending from Jerusalem to Rome. The problems of transportation and translation would tend to obscure the authority and authenticity of books even though they had already gained recognition by the original recipients.

Of course there is no record that each book was recognized as canonical immediately by its original audience. But it is no more necessary for an explicit reference to the acceptance of each book than it is for an explicit claim for its inspiration (cf. 2 and 3 John). It is sufficient that the book was written by an apostle (or prophet) and that it was copied, collected, and cited from earliest times. To also have direct confirmation of the immediate recog-

5. Philip Schaff, ed., *The Nicene and Post-Nicene Fathers*, 1:549. For the impact of these events on the transmission of the New Testament text, see the discussions in chaps. 22, 24, and 26.

nition of specific books is sufficient evidence that the other books were immediately accepted as well.

New Testament Indications

Within the New Testament itself, there is evidence of the concept of a developing canon of inspired books. This may be observed in the principle and progress of canonization in the New Testament.

The principle of canonization. The determining factor in New Testament canonization was inspiration, and the primary test was apostolicity (see chap. 12). If it could be determined that a book had apostolic authority, there would be no reason to question its authenticity or veracity (see chap. 20). In New Testament terminology, the church was "built upon the foundation of the apostles and prophets" (Eph. 2:20) whom Christ had promised to guide unto "all the truth" (John 16:13) by the Holy Spirit. The church at Jerusalem was said to have continued in the "apostles' teaching" (Acts 2:42). The term *apostolic* as used for the test of canonicity does not necessarily mean "apostolic authorship," or "that which was prepared under the direction of the apostles,"[6] unless the word "apostle" be taken in its nontechnical sense, meaning someone *beyond* the twelve apostles or Paul. In this nontechnical sense, Barnabas is called an apostle (Acts 14:14, cf. v. 4), as is James (Gal. 1:19), and evidently others too (Rom. 16:7; 2 Cor. 8:23; Phil. 2:25).

It appears rather unnecessary to think of Mark and Luke as being secretaries of apostles, or to argue that the writer of James was an apostle, to say nothing of Jude or the writer of Hebrews. In fact, the writer of Hebrews disclaims being an apostle, saying that the message of Christ "was attested to us [readers and writer] by those [the apostles] who heard him" (Heb. 2:3). It seems much better to agree with Louis Gaussen, B. B. Warfield, Charles Hodge, J. N. D. Kelly, and most Protestants that it is apostolic authority, or apostolic approval, that was the primary test for canonicity, and not merely apostolic authorship.[7] In the terminology of the New Testament, a book had to be written by an apostle or prophet (cf. Eph. 2:20). The real question, then, was, "Is a book prophetic?" that is, "Was it written by a prophet of God?" The apostles were, of course, granted a prophetic ministry (John 14-16): John called himself "a fellow servant [with] ... the prophets" (Rev. 22:9), and Paul considered his books prophetic writings (cf. Rom. 16:25-26; Eph. 3:3-5). Individuals in the New Testament besides those called apostles were granted a prophetic ministry, in accordance with the promise on the day of Pentecost

6. R. Laird Harris attempts to defend this view, however, making Mark and Luke to be secretaries to Peter and Paul, respectively, etc.; see *Inspiration and Canonicity of the Bible*, p. 270.
7. Louis Gaussen, *Theopneustia*, p. 319; Benjamin B. Warfield, *The Inspiration and Authority of the Bible*, p. 455; Charles Hodge, *Systematic Theology*, 1:153; J. N. D. Kelly, *Early Christian Doctrines*, pp. 59-60.

Major English Bible Translations

Original Bible Manuscripts
Old Testament in Hebrew and Aramaic
15th-5th cent. B.C.

Greek translation
of Old Testament
Septuagint (c. 250 B.C.)

Original Bible mss
New Testament in Greek
c. A.D. 30-100
Council of Jamnia (A.D. 90)
Old Testament Canon fixed

Syriac, Old Latin, and
Coptic translations
(2d-4th centuries)

New Testament Canon
fixed (4th cent.)

Latin Vulgate
Jerome (c. A.D. 400)

Anglo-Saxon
Paraphrases (c. 700-1000)
Gospel of John
Bede (735)

9th-century Bible mss
Oldest known until 1947

English Bible
Wycliffe (c. 1380-1384)

Printed Latin Bible
Gutenberg (c. 1456-1457)

Printed Hebrew OT
(1482)

Printed Greek NT
Erasmus (1516)

Printed English NT
Tyndale (1525, 1535)
English Pentateuch

Printed Latin Bible
Pagninus (1528)

German NT
Luther (1522)

German OT
Luther (1534)

Printed English Bible
Coverdale (1535)

Matthew's Bible (1537)

Great Bible
(1539)

Taverner Bible
(1539)

Greek New Testament
Stephanus (1550)

MAJOR ENGLISH BIBLE TRANSLATIONS *(continued)*

Greek New Testament
Beza (1557)

Geneva Bible (1560)
Bishops Bible (1568)

Rheims NT (1582)

King James Bible [KJV] (1611)

Douay OT (1610)

Textus Receptus (1624)

Important Manuscripts Discovered (1840)

English Revised NT [RV] (1881)
English Revised OT [RV] (1885)

Papyri Discovered (1897)

American Standard Version [ASV] (1901)
Weymouth New Testament (1902)
Centenary New Testament (1904)

English Old Testament
Jewish Publication Society [JPS] (1917)

Papyri Discovered (1930)

Moffatt Bible (1924-1926, 1935)
Smith-Goodspeed Bible (1927, 1935)

Revised Standard Version
New Testament (1946, 1952)

Confraternity New Testament
Roman Catholic (1946)

Dead Sea Scrolls Discovered (1947)

Revised Standard Version
Old Testament, Apocrypha (1952)
NT in Plain English
Williams (1952)
NT in Modern English, Phillips (1958)

The Modern Language Bible
Berkeley (1959)
The Amplified Bible (1958-1965)

Anchor Bible (1964)
New American Standard Bible [NASB] (1966)
New English Bible [NEB] (1970)
The Living Bible (1971)
Good News Bible [TEV] (1976)

New International Version [NIV] (1979)
New King James Version [NKJV] (1982)

The Holy Bible
Knox (1944-1955)
Confraternity Bible
(1952, 1955)
The Authentic New Testament
Schonfield (1955)
The New World Translation
Jehovah's Witnesses
(1953-1960, 1961)
The New Jewish Version
JPS (1962-1982)

Jerusalem Bible (1966)
New American Bible [NAB] (1970)

Readers Digest Bible (1982)

JPS Tanakh [OT] (1985)
New Jerusalem Bible (1985)

(Acts 2:17-18), as was manifest in Agabus and the other prophets from Jerusalem (Acts 11:27-28), not to mention the "gift of prophecy" evident in the New Testament church (cf. 1 Cor. 12:29).

The process of canonization. A close look at the New Testament reveals that these prophetic writings were being sorted from among the nonprophetic writings, even from oral traditions, and a canon was being formed during apostolic times. Several procedures were involved in this process.

1. *Selecting procedure.* John implies that there was a selecting process going on among the apostles themselves, dealing with the problem of which particular truths should be preserved in written form. He writes that "many other signs therefore Jesus also performed . . . which are not written in this book" (John 20:30); and "if they were written in detail," he adds, "I suppose that even the world itself would not contain the books which were written" (John 21:25). Luke speaks of other accounts of the life of Christ, from which he compiled "an accurate account" based on "eyewitnesses" in order that "the exact truth" might be known (Luke 1:1-4). This evidence seems to imply that there were other written records of Christ's life that were not entirely true. There are several references to the authority of apostolic oral tradition or teaching (cf. 1 Thess. 2:13; 1 Cor. 11:2). These "traditions" meant that there was authoritative teaching by original eyewitnesses to Christ's life. Some have suggested that that was in fact the *kerygma* (authoritative apostolic pronouncement about Christ), or a sort of "canon within the canon."[8] Whether or not that *kerygma* was used as the test for canonicity is uncertain, but it is clear that there were apostolic criteria for sorting out oral traditions of an apocryphal nature. John speaks of a false belief regarding his own death, which "went out among the brethren" as a distortion by Jesus' own disciples of something spoken from the lips of Jesus (John 21:23-24). No doubt there were other incidents of this nature. However, though they may have been believed among the early disciples, they were nowhere taught as apostolic truth, at least not in the canonical writings. They were not part of the authoritative oral message of the eyewitnesses and therefore never became part of the teaching of the written record.

2. *Reading procedure.* Another indication within the New Testament itself that a canon was being formed is the repeated injunction that certain books should be read to the churches. Paul commanded that 1 Thessalonians be "read to all the brethren" (5:27). Revelation 1:3 promised a blessing to all who read "the words of the prophecy" and kept it; in fact, it gave a warning to those who "hear the words of the prophecy" of this

8. See Herman Ridderbos, "The Canon of the New Testament," in Carl F. H. Henry, ed., *Revelation and the Bible,* pp. 191ff. Also see Kelly, *Early Christian Doctrines,* pp. 29-31.

book and do not keep them. The key to canonicity implicit in those injunctions appears to be authority, or prophecy. If a writing was prophetic, it was to be read with authority to the churches.

3. *Circulating procedure.* Those writings that were read as authoritative to the churches were circulated and collected by the churches. The book of Revelation was circulated among the churches of Asia Minor, as John was told to "write in a book what you see, and send it to the seven churches" (Rev. 1:11). Paul commanded the Colossians, saying, "When this letter is read among you, have it read also in the church of the Laodiceans; and you, for your part read my letter that is coming from Laodicea" (Col. 4:16).[9] This is a crucial passage, because it indicates that the authority of one epistle included a larger audience than just the one to which it was written. Thus, as the book of Revelation was circulated throughout the churches, so other epistles were to be exchanged, and prophetic messages were to be read with all authority.

4. *Collecting procedure.* The circulating procedure no doubt led to the habit of collecting prophetic and apostolic writings, such as those alluded to in 2 Peter 3:15-16, where the author speaks of "all his [Paul's] letters" as being on a level with "the rest of the Scriptures." As has already been noted (see chap. 5), the apostles considered the collection of Old Testament writings to be divine Scripture; therefore, as the New Testament prophets wrote inspired books, those were added to the collection of "the other Scriptures." Thus, by the time of 2 Peter (c. A.D. 66)[10] Paul's epistles were in the canon.[11] Since most of the general epistles were written after Paul's, it cannot be expected that they would be mentioned. Nevertheless, Jude probably is referring to Peter's book, and he seems to regard it as Scripture (cf. Jude 17-18 and 2 Peter 3:2-3). As Edward Lohse observes, "The early Christian writings, originally written for particular situations, were gathered into collections very early."[12]

5. *Quotation procedure.* If Jude quoted from Peter's writing when he said, "You must remember, beloved, the predictions of the apostles of our Lord Jesus Christ" (v. 17), then he not only verified that Peter's writing was accepted into the canon by that time, but that the books received were

9. Some scholars believe that this letter from Laodicea is the epistle called Ephesians in modern English Bibles. Cf. discussion of this matter in F.F. Bruce and E.K. Simpson, *Commentary on the Epistles to the Ephesians and Colossians*, pp. 310-11. Others, however, have suggested that it is Philemon instead of Ephesians. See discussion in Everett F. Harrison, *Introduction to the New Testament*, pp. 308-9. Also see previous discussion in chap. 12.
10. Harrison, p. 140.
11. Lewis Foster argues that Luke made the earliest collection of Paul's epistles as a kind of third volume following his gospel and Acts sequence. See his article "The Earliest Collection of Paul's Epistles," pp. 44-53.
12. Eduard Lohse, *The Formation of the New Testament*, p. 19.

immediately and authoritatively quoted as Scripture. Paul (1 Tim. 5:18) quoted from the gospel of Luke (10:7) with the same formula he used to quote the Old Testament. It would be too much to expect that every book of the New Testament would be verified in this way, but enough of them are referred to (at least some of Paul's, one of Luke's and perhaps one of Peter's—a substantial part of the New Testament) in order to demonstrate that there was a canon of New Testament books even during New Testament times. The absence of any quotation from some of the smaller and more personal epistles may be explained by their size and nature.

In summary, the primary test of canonicity in New Testament times was apostolic or prophetic authority. Those writings that came to local churches (or individuals) were read, circulated, collected, and even quoted as a part of the canon of the Scriptures. Those writings supplemented and formed an integral part of the inspired Word of God along with the previously recognized Old Testament Scriptures.

Apostolic Fathers

What has been said of the development of the New Testament canon, as seen in the inspired writings of the New Testament itself, is even more apparent in the writings of the younger contemporaries, the apostolic Fathers. A sample survey will suffice to show that by the middle of the second century every book of the New Testament was referred to, as authoritative (canonical), by at least one of these Fathers.

The Gospels.

1. Matthew was quoted by the *Epistle of Pseudo-Barnabas* (c. 70-79) on several occasions, for example, 4:14 (Matt. 20:16, 22:14); 5:12 (Matt. 26:31); 6:13 (Matt. 19:30; 20:16); 7:3 (Matt. 27:34) and 12:11 (Matt. 22:45); in addition to several allusions. The *Didache* (c. 70-130) quotes Matthew rather extensively (cf. Matt. 6:9-13).

2. Mark was cited by the *Epistle of Pseudo-Barnabas* in only one clear example, 5:9 (Mark 2:17), but 12:11 quotes the parallel passage in Matthew 22:45 and/or Luke 20:44. Papias (c. 70-163) wrote five treatises entitled *Interpretation of the Oracles of the Lord* (c. 120), which included the four gospels.[13]

3. Luke was revised by the Gnostic Marcion (c. A.D. 140) and appeared in his sharply abridged canon of Scriptures. *The Muratorian Fragment* (c. 170-80) began with Mark, and refers to Luke as the third gospel and follows with John, Acts, etc.[14]

13. See Eusebius *Ecclesiastical History* 3:39. Loeb ed., 1:291.
14. See Caspar René Gregory, *Canon and Text of the New Testament*, pp. 129-33.

4. John was cited by Papias and listed in the Muratorian Canon. It was also cited and alluded to in the epistles of Ignatius (c. 110-17), for example, his *Ephesians* 5:2 (John 6:33) and 17:1 (John 12:3). Clement of Rome (c. 95-97) cited John 17:3 in his *Epistle to the Corinthians* 43:5.

Acts. Acts appeared in the *Muratorian Fragment,* and was quoted by Polycarp (69-155), the disciple of John, in his *Philippians* 1:2 (Acts 2:24). The *Shepherd* of Hermas quotes Acts in several instances for example, Vision 2: 2.7 (Acts 10:35); Vision 3: 7.3 (Acts 2:38; 10:48; 19:5); Similitude 9: 28.2 (Acts 15:26); 10: 2.3; 4.1 (Acts 2:11, 2:1).

The Epistles.

1. Romans is frequently cited by Clement of Rome in his *Epistle to the Corinthians* (also identified as *1 Corinthians* of Clement of Rome), for example, 33:1 (Rom. 6:1); 35:6 (Rom. 1:29-32); 50:6 (Rom. 4:7-9). Polycarp quotes Romans on several occasions in his *Epistle to the Philippians,* for example, 5:2 (Rom. 8:17); 6:1 (Rom. 12:17); 6:3 (Rom. 14:10, 12); 10:1 (Rom. 13:8). The *Didache* (5:1-2) cites Romans 1:29-30 and 12:9, respectively.

2. First Corinthians was cited in the *Didache* 10:6 (1 Cor. 16:22); 13:1-2 (1 Cor. 9:13-14); and 16:6 (1 Cor. 15:22; cf. Matt. 24:30-31). The *Shepherd,* Mandate 3:6 (1 Cor. 7:11; cf. Matt. 5:32; 19:9; and Mark 10:11); and Mandate 4:4.1 (1 Cor. 7:38-40) also cites 1 Corinthians.

3. Second Corinthians was cited by Polycarp in his *Philippians* 2:2 (2 Cor. 4:14); 4:1 (2 Cor. 6:7), as it was by the *Shepherd,* Similitude 9:13, 7-8 (2 Cor. 13:11); and the *Epistle to Diognetus* (c. 150), 5:7 (2 Cor. 10:3); 5:12 (2 Cor. 6:9-10); 5:15-16 (2 Cor. 4:12; 6:10).

4. Galatians was frequently quoted by many writers such as Polycarp, his *Philippians* 3:3 (Gal. 4:26); 5:1 (Gal. 6:7); 5:3 (Gal. 5:17); *Epistle to Diognetus* 6:5 (Gal. 5:17); and 10:5 (Gal. 6:2).

5. Ephesians, one of Paul's prison epistles, was cited by Clement of Rome in his *1 Corinthians* 46:6 (Eph. 4:4-6); 59:3 (Eph. 1:18); by Ignatius in his *Smyrnaeans* 1:2 (Eph. 2:16); *Polycarp* 1:3 (Eph. 4:2); 5:1 (Eph. 5:25, 29); and alluded to in *Pseudo-Barnabas* 6:10 (Eph. 2:10; 4:22-24).

6. Philippians was often quoted by Polycarp in his *Philippians* 9:2 (Phil. 2:16); 11:3 (Phil. 4:15); 12:3 (Phil. 3:18); and *Shepherd,* Similitude 5:3.8 (Phil. 4:18); 9:13. 7-8 (Phil. 2:2; 3:16; 4:2); and by Ignatius, *Smyrnaeans* 4:2 (Phil. 4:13); 11:3 (Phil. 3:15).

7. Colossians was cited by Polycarp, *Philippians* 10:1 (Col. 1:23); 11:2 (Col. 3:5); Ignatius, *Ephesians* 10:2 (Col. 1:23); *Trallians* 5:2 (Col. 1:16); and *Epistle to Diognetus* 10:7 (Col. 4:1).

8. First Thessalonians 5:13 was cited several times in the *Shepherd,* Vision 3:6.3; 3:9.2, 10; Similitude 8:7.2; the *Didache* 16:7 also quotes this epistle (1 Thess. 4:16); it is used by Ignatius, *Ephesians* 10:1 (1 Thess. 5:17); and *Romans* 2:1 (1 Thess. 2:4).

9. Second Thessalonians is less frequently cited, but Igantius uses it as the basis of his statement in his *Philadelphians* 4:3 (2 Thess. 3:5). Polycarp also uses this epistle in his *Philippians* 11:3 (2 Thess. 1:4) and 11:4 (2 Thess. 3:15). *Dionysius of Corinth* (c. A.D. 170) also quotes this epistle.

10. First Timothy was repeatedly used by Clement of Rome in his *1 Corinthians,* as it was in Polycarp's *Philippians*. The *Shepherd,* Similitude 8:2.9, cites 1 Timothy 2:4, and the *Didache,* 13:1-2, quotes 1 Timothy 5:17-18.

11. Second Timothy is used in *Pseudo-Barnabas* 5:6 (2 Tim. 1:10), as it is in the *Shepherd,* Mandate 3:2 (2 Tim. 1:14).

12. Titus is frequently quoted by Clement of Rome in his *1 Corinthians; Pseudo-Barnabas* 1:4-6 and 14:5 cite Titus 1:1-3, 7 and 2:14, respectively, as does the *Epistle to Diognetus* 9:1-2 (Titus 3:3-5).

13. Philemon was a personal letter, and its nature is reflected in its use: Ignatius makes allusions to it, and the *Muratorian Fragment* lists thirteen of Paul's epistles, which would include Philemon.

14. Hebrews was frequently cited by Clement of Rome in his *1 Corinthians;* it was also quoted in the *Ancient Homily* (often called *2 Corinthians* of Clement of Rome) 11:6 (Heb. 10:23); the *Shepherd* frequently used this epistle, for example, Vision 2:2.7 (Heb. 11:33); Vision 2:3.2 (Heb. 3:12).

15. James is repeatedly used in the *1 Corinthians* of Clement of Rome, as it is in the *Shepherd,* Vision 3:9.6 (James 5:4); Mandate 2:2.7 (James 4:11; 1:27); 11:5 (James 3:15).

16. First Peter is used in *Pseudo-Barnabas* 4:12 (1 Peter 1:17); 6:2 (1 Peter 2:6) 7:2 (1 Peter 4:5); the *Shepherd* quotes 1 Peter 5:7, 4:13, 15-16; 4:14 in Vision 3:11.3, Similitude 9:28.5, and 9:28.6, respectively.

17. Second Peter (2:6-9) is quoted in *1 Corinthians* 11:1 by Clement of Rome. It is also used in *Pseudo-Barnabas* 15:4 (2 Peter 3:8).

18. First John is cited in the *Shepherd,* Mandate 3:1 (1 John 2:27); Similitude 6:5-6 (1 John 3:22).

19. Second John is listed in the *Muratorian Fragment,* and is cited in Polycarp, *Philippians* 7:1 (2 John 7).

20. Third John is listed in the *Muratorian Fragment*.

21. Jude is listed in the *Muratorian Fragment* and is cited in *The Martyrdom of St. Polycarp, Bishop of Smyrna*. Preface (Jude 2).

Revelation. The book of Revelation was cited in the *Didache* 10:3 (Rev. 4:11); 16:4 (Rev. 13:2, 13), as well as in the *Shepherd,* Vision 4:2.1 (Rev. 21:2). Papias accepted the authority of Revelation, and it was cited in the *Ancient Homily* 17:7 (Rev. 11:13) and by Justin Martyr and Dionysius of Corinth.

Although many of these citations may be disputed if modern critical approaches are used, it should be noted that by the standards of classical civilization they would be considered legitimate quotations. Therefore, works are regarded as quoted when they would possibly be misquoted or alluded to in modern parlance. As a result, the first hundred years of the existence of the twenty-seven books of the New Testament reveal that virtually every one of them was quoted as authoritative and recognized as canonical by men who were themselves the younger contemporaries of the Apostolic Age.

Practical Completion and Verification

Of course there was not universal agreement by all the early Fathers, in either the second or even the third century, on all of the canonical books. Nevertheless, some Fathers and canons recognized almost all of the books before the end of the second century, and the church universal was in agreement before the end of the fourth century.

Recognition by Individuals

Some outstanding Fathers of the second century show their acceptance of most of New Testament canon, and there is no reason to believe they did not also accept the rest of it. Four examples may serve as representative of the period, which had widespread witness to the inspiration and text of the New Testament (see discussions in chaps. 7 and 22).

Polycarp (c. A.D. 150). The younger contemporary and disciple of the apostle John, Polycarp quotes from Matthew, John, the first ten of Paul's epistles, 1 Peter, and 1 and 2 John. Because most of the rest of the books were small, it could not be expected that he would refer to them. As a result, the argument from silence that Polycarp did not know or accept them is a weak one at best.

Justin Martyr (c. A.D. 140). Justin Martyr considered all the gospels as Scripture, plus most of Paul's epistles, as well as 1 Peter and Revelation. It is noteworthy that Justin had occasion to refer to Mark, Luke, John, and Revelation, not cited by Polycarp, and not to refer to Philippians or 1 Timothy, which would tend to confirm the thesis that both men accepted more books than those from which they quoted.

Irenaeus (c. A.D. 170). The first early Father who himself quoted almost every book of the New Testament was Irenaeus. As a young boy he had heard Polycarp, and the experience made a lasting impact on this first great missionary to France (see chap. 7) He quoted or considered as authentic twenty-three of the twenty-seven books, omitting only Philemon, James, 2 Peter, and 3 John.

Clement of Alexandria (c. A.D. 200) has almost an identical list, with the exception of his omission of 2 Timothy and 2 John. Philemon and 3 John may not have been quoted because of their brevity, leaving only 2 Peter and James in question. In that connection it is interesting to note that the *Shepherd* (c. A.D. 140) referred to James, and the book of 2 Peter had already been quoted as Scripture in Jude. Thus, before the end of the second century some individuals had recognized almost all of the twenty-seven books, and the remainder were recognized by others even before that time.

Recognized in Canonical Lists (and Translations)

Another confirmation that the New Testament canon was formed as early as the second century comes from canonical lists and translations (see chaps. 27, 28, and 29); and it goes without saying, a translation assumes a canon by those individuals doing the translation.

The Old Syriac. This translation of the New Testament was in circulation in Syria about A.D. 400, but represented a text dating from the end of the second century.[15] It included all of the twenty-seven New Testament books except 2 Peter, 2 and 3 John, Jude, and Revelation. Brooke Foss Westcott notes: "Its general agreement with our own [canon] is striking and important; and its omissions admit of easy explanation."[16]

The Old Latin. This was translated prior to A.D. 200 and served as the Bible of the Western church as the Syriac did in the East. This Latin version contained all the New Testament books except Hebrews, James, and 1 and 2 Peter.[17]

The Muratorian Canon (A.D. 170). Aside from Marcion's heretical canon (A.D. 140), the earliest canonical list is in the *Muratorian Fragment*. This list coincides exactly with the Old Latin, omitting only Hebrews, James, and 1 and 2 Peter. Westcott argues for the probability of a break in this manuscript that may once have included those books.[18] It does seem strange that Hebrews and 1 Peter should be omitted while Philemon and 3 John were included. This feature is the opposite of the lists of Irenaeus and Clement of Alexandria.

15. See chap. 28; Bruce M. Metzger, *The Text of the New Testament*, p. 69.
16. Brooke Foss Westcott, *A General Survey of the History of the Canon of the New Testament*, p. 245.
17. Ibid., p. 258. Also see chap. 29.
18. Ibid., p. 219; also see "Appendix C: The Muratorian Fragment on the Canon," pp. 521-38.

Recognition by Councils

As can be seen from the examination of quotations by individuals and canonical lists, a few books were rather persistently unrecognized. Eusebius summed up the situation in the early-fourth century by acknowledging all twenty-seven books, but stating that James, 2 Peter, 2 and 3 John, and Jude were "spoken against" (Greek: *Antilegomena*).[19] Nevertheless, whatever doubts existed in his day gradually faded during the next fifty years, when Athanasius (c. 367), the "Father of Orthodoxy," clearly and emphatically listed all twenty-seven books as canonical, saying,

> Again it is not tedious to speak of the books of the New Testament. These are, the four gospels, according to Matthew, Mark, Luke and John. Afterwards, the Acts of the Apostles and Epistles (called Catholic), seven, viz. of James, one; of Peter, two; of John, three; after these, one of Jude. In addition, there are fourteen Epistles of Paul, written in this order. The first, to the Romans; then two to the Corinthians; after these, to the Galatians; next, to the Ephesians; then to the Philippians; then to the Colossians; after these, two to the Thessalonians, and that to the Hebrews; and again, two to Timothy; one to Titus; and lastly, that to Philemon. And besides, the Revelation of John.[20]

The synods at Hippo (A.D. 393) and Carthage (A.D. 397) were under the influence of Augustine. At those regional councils the New Testament canon that was ratified agreed with the present-day canon of twenty-seven books;[21] however, they accepted a variation of the Alexandrian Canon of the Old Testament.[22] The canon adopted by Hippo and Carthage is verification of the contention of Athanasius with regard to the New Testament.[23] Therefore, the councils followed the example of leading individuals and canons in recognizing those New Testament books which God had inspired.

19. Eusebius 3.25. Loeb ed., 1:257-59.
20. Athanasius, *Letters,* no. 39 (Easter 367), paragraph 5, in Philip Schaff, ed., *The Nicene and Post-Nicene Fathers,* 4:552.
21. This also agreed with Augustine's list in his treatise *On Christian Doctrine* 2.8, 13 as translated in Schaff, ed., *The Nicene and Post-Nicene Fathers* (1st series), 2:538-39.
22. See chap. 15. Also see Philip Schaff, *History of the Christian Church,* 3:608-9; also see Augustine *The City of God* 18.36.
23. The complete list of Old and New Testament books for Hippo (393) and Carthage (397) is also given in Canon 24 of the Council of Carthage (419), and is commonly known as the "African Code"; cf. Schaff, *The Nicene and Post-Nicene Fathers,* 14:453-54; also see F. L. Cross and E. A. Livingston, eds., *The Oxford Dictionary of the Christian Church,* s.v. "Carthage, Councils of," p. 244.

The New Testament Canon During The First Four Centuries

BOOK	INDIVIDUALS																
	PSEUDO-BARNABAS (c. 70-130)	CLEMENT OF ROME (c. 95-97)	IGNATIUS (c. 110)	POLYCARP (c. 110-50)	HERMAS (c. 115-40)	DIDACHE (c. 120-50)	PAPIAS (c. 130-40)	IRENAEUS (c. 130-202)	DIOGNETUS (c. 150)	JUSTIN MARTYR (c. 150-55)	CLEMENT OF ALEXANDRIA (c. 150-215)	TERTULLIAN (c. 150-220)	ORIGEN (c. 185-254)	CYRIL OF JERUSALEM (c. 315-86)	EUSEBIUS (c. 325-40)	JEROME (c. 340-420)	AUGUSTINE (c. 400)
Matt.	X	X		X	X	X		O		X	X	X	X	O	O	O	O
Mark	X			X	X			O		X	X	X	X	O	O	O	O
Luke	X			X		X		O		X	X	X	X	O	O	O	O
John		X		X			X	O		O	X	X	X	O	O	O	O
Acts				X	X			O		X	X	X	X	O	O	O	O
Rom.		X		X		X		O		X	O	X	X	O	O	O	O
I Cor.		O		X	X	X		O		X	O	X	X	O	O	O	O
II Cor.				X	X			O	X	X	O	X	X	O	O	O	O
Gal.				X				O	X	X	O	X	X	O	O	O	O
Eph.	X	X	X	X				O		X	X	X	X	O	O	O	O
Phil.			X	X	X			O			O	X	X	O	O	O	O
Col.			X	X				O	X	X	O	X	X	O	O	O	O
I Thess.			X	X	X	X		O		X	X	X	X	O	O	O	O
II Thess.			X	X				O		X	X	X	X	O	O	O	O
I Tim.		X		X	X	X		X			O	X	X	O	O	O	O
II Tim.	X				X			X				X	X	O	O	O	O
Titus	X	X						X	X		O	X	X	O	O	O	O
Philemon			X											O	O	O	O
Heb.	X	X			X			X			O	X	?	O	O	O	O
James		X			X									O	?	O	O
I Peter	X			X	X			O		X	O	X	O	O	O	O	O
II Peter	X	X											?	O	?	O	O
I John				X	X			O			O	X		O	O	O	O
II John				X				X					?	O	?	O	O
III John													?	O	?	O	O
Jude								X			O	X		O	?	O	O
Rev.					X	X	O	O		X	O	X	O		O	O	O

BOOK	CANONS					TRANSLATIONS			COUNCILS			
	MARCION (c. 140)	MURATORIAN (c. 170)	APOSTOLIC (c. 300)	CHELTENHAM (c. 360)	ATHANASIUS (367)	TATIAN DIATESSARON (c. 170)	OLD LATIN (c. 200)	OLD SYRIAC (c. 400)	NICEA (c. 325-40)	HIPPO (393)	CARTHAGE (397)	CARTHAGE (419)
Matt.		O	O	O	O	O	O	O	O	O	O	O
Mark		O	O	O	O	O	O	O	O	O	O	O
Luke	O	O	O	O	O	O	O	O	O	O	O	O
John		O	O	O	O	O	O	O	O	O	O	O
Acts		O	O	O	O		O	O	O	O	O	O
Rom.	O	O	O	O	O		O	O	O	O	O	O
I Cor.	O	O	O	O	O		O	O	O	O	O	O
II Cor.	O	O	O	O	O		O	O	O	O	O	O
Gal.	O	O	O	O	O		O	O	O	O	O	O
Eph.	O	O	O	O	O		O	O	O	O	O	O
Phil.	O	O	O	O	O		O	O	O	O	O	O
Col.	O	O	O	O	O		O	O	O	O	O	O
I Thess.	O	O	O	O	O		O	O	O	O	O	O
II Thess.	O	O	O	O	O		O	O	O	O	O	O
I Tim.		O	O	O	O		O	O	O	O	O	O
II Tim.		O	O	O	O		O	O	O	O	O	O
Titus		O	O	O	O		O	O	O	O	O	O
Philemon	O	O	O	O	O		O	O	O	O	O	O
Heb.			O		O			O	O	O	O	O
James			O		O			O	?	O	O	O
I Peter			O	O	O			O	O	O	O	O
II Peter			O	?	O				?	O	O	O
I John		O	O	O	O		O	O	O	O	O	O
II John		O	O	?	O		O		?	O	O	O
III John		O	O	?	O		O		?	O	O	O
Jude		O	O		O		O		?	O	O	O
Rev.		O		O	O		O		O	O	O	O

X = Citation or allusion
O = Named as authentic
? = Named as disputed

Summary and Conclusion

God is the source of canonicity, and in His providence He utilized several stimuli that finalized the recognition and ratification of all twenty-seven books of the New Testament. Those stimuli—practical, theological, and political in nature—were instrumental in the collection and transmission of the New Testament Scriptures. It should be remembered, however, that the canon was actually completed when the last New Testament book was written. Within the New Testament itself may be seen the process of selecting and reading the prophetic and apostolic writings that were then being circulated, collected, and even quoted in other inspired writings. In support of this view of canonization, the apostolic Fathers may be cited as referring to all of the New Testament books within about a century of the time they were written. Individuals, translations, and canons show that all but a very few books were generally recognized as canonical before the end of the second century. During the next two centuries the controversy over those Antilegomena books gradually erased all doubts, and there was a final and official recognition of all twenty-seven books of the New Testament by the church universal.

17
The New Testament Apocrypha and Pseudepigrapha

During the third century Origen, like Clement of Alexandria, was faced with the problem that no conclusively fixed boundary between the canonical and noncanonical books of the Bible had been recognized by the church. He set about classifying Christian writings so that they fell into three basic groupings: (a) *anantireta* ("unobjectionable") or *homologoumena* ("acknowledged"), which were in general use in the church, (b) *amphiballomena* ("included/contested"), which were contested, and (c) *psethde* ("false"), which included books that were rejected as falsifications and therefore the products of heretics.[1] This classification was later reformulated by Eusebius of Caesarea during the fourth century as (a) *homologoumena* ("acknowledged"), (b) *antilegomena* ("disputed"), which were divided into two subcategories—*gnorima* ("acquainted with"), for those most Christians acknowledged, and *notha* ("illegitimate"), for those regarded as inauthentic, and (c) *apocrypha* ("hidden"), which were viewed as spurious. These arrangements of books have become settled in four categories: (a) *Homologoumena,* books accepted by virtually everyone as canonical; (b) *Antilegomena,* books disputed by some; (c) *Pseudepigrapha,* books rejected by virtually everyone as unauthentic; and (d) *Apocrypha,* books accepted by some as canonical or semicanonical.

Books Accepted by All—Homologoumena

The Nature of the Homologoumena

The Homologoumena are those books that have been universally acclaimed as canonical from their beginning. They have appeared in virtually every ancient version and orthodox canonical list, as well as having been widely quoted as Scripture. None of these books was deliberately deleted from the circulating canon in orthodox circles or brought into question by

1. Eduard Loshe, *The Formation of the New Testament,* p. 23.

any prominent Father. Of course, the exact number of these books will vary depending on one's definition of "orthodox" and "prominent"; but for the most part, there is little disagreement on this point.

The Number of the Homologoumena

Generally speaking, twenty of the twenty-seven books of the New Testament canon are considered to be undisputed. This includes all of the books from Matthew through Philemon, plus 1 Peter and 1 John. It is true that some have also included the latter three books (Philemon, 1 Peter, 1 John) among the disputed books; however, it is probably better to refer to those as omitted rather than disputed books (see chap. 16). A disputed book is characterized as one that is retained and yet questioned, not merely one that is not quoted nor included in a given list. Unless there is clear evidence that a book was absent from a canonical list or from a Father's quotation (or enumeration) because it was considered of doubtful authenticity or authority, it would be better not to classify it as Antilegomena. In either event, if the seven disputed books were extended to ten, they, interestingly enough, would still be among the last books in the order of the New Testament canon.

The Disputed Books—Antilegomena

The Nature of the Antilegomena

It has already been implied that the reason for certain books having been classed as Antilegomena consists in the fact that these books possessed neither uniform nor universal recognition in the early church. They were books that became the subject of canonical controversity and had, as it were, their canonical "ups" and "downs." It should be said, however, that these books were seldom considered anticanonical, or even uncanonical. Instead, they were given a sort of semicanonical status, as has sometimes been accorded to the Old Testament Apocrypha (see chap. 15).

The Number of the Antilegomena

There are seven books in the Antilegomena, that is, seven books that may be properly called "disputed books." Concerning the possibility of including three more books in this list, it should be noted that there is good early evidence for the canonicity of 1 Peter, 1 John, and even the brief epistle to Philemon (see chap. 16). Certainly there is almost no evidence that those who possessed the three books did not consider them authentic and apostolic. The seven books that came in question for various reasons are Hebrews, James, 2 Peter, 2 and 3 John, Jude, and Revelation. In order to clearly understand the issue at stake, the books "spoken against" (Antilegomena) must be considered carefully and individually.

Hebrews. This book was questioned because of its *anonymity.* In the East, where it was considered Pauline, it was readily received. The West was slower, however, because of uncertainty as to its apostolic authorship, and possibly because individuals in the heretical Montanist sect appealed to Hebrews for one of their erroneous doctrines.[2] In the fourth century, through the influence of Jerome and Augustine, the West finally recognized the epistle as canonical. One other reason that the West was slow in its deliberation was its stress upon *apostolic authorship* rather than *apostolic authority* as the correct test of canonicity (see chap. 15).

James. James was questioned as to its *veracity,* although some questioned its authorship as well. The supposed conflict with Paul on justification by faith held back full acceptance as late as the time of Eusebius.[3] Even during the Reformation period, Luther had doubts about James, calling it "flatly in contradiction to St. Paul and all the rest of Scripture."[4] Luther placed it at the end of his New Testament, along with Hebrews, Jude and Revelation, in a lesser position. As a result of the work of Origen, Eusebius (who personally favored James), Jerome, and Augustine, the West finally recognized its complementary nature to Paul's epistles and hence, its canonicity.

2 Peter. The *genuineness* of 2 Peter was questioned. In fact, no other book in the New Testament has been questioned as persistently. Even Calvin seemed to be unsure of it. Jerome stated that the hesitancy to accept 2 Peter was due to dissimilarity of style with 1 Peter.[5] Whether, as Jerome thought, this characteristic is due to a different amanuensis may never be fully settled. It is clear, however, that ample evidence is now available to attest that this epistle is rightly attributed to the apostle Peter.[6]

1. Another reason for rejecting 2 Peter has been the claim that it is a second century work. However, W.F. Albright has pointed out the reminiscences of Qumran literature in 2 Peter and dates it before A.D. 80.[7]
2. The discovery of the Bodmer manuscript (P^{72}), which contains the earliest known copy of 2 Peter (late third century), reveals that it was in use and highly respected by Coptic Christians in Egypt during the third century.[8]

2. Everett F. Harrison, *Introduction to the New Testament,* p. 345; Donald Guthrie, *New Testament Introduction: Hebrews to Revelation,* pp. 11-18.
3. Eusebius *Ecclesiastical History* 2.23. Loeb ed., 1:179.
4. M. Reu, *Luther and the Scriptures,* p. 24.
5. Jerome *Catalogus Scriptorum Ecclesiasticorum,* as cited by Harrison, p. 389.
6. Harrison, pp. 386 ff. and Guthrie, pp. 137 ff.
7. William F. Albright, *From the Stone Age to Christianity,* pp. 22-23.
8. See chap. 22. Also see Marchant A. King, "Notes on the Bodmer Manuscript of Jude and 1 and 2 Peter," pp. 54-57; or see "The Text of I Peter in Papyrus 72," p. 253.

3. Besides the possible allusions to 2 Peter in *Pseudo-Barnabas* 15:4 (cf. 2 Peter 3:8), there is the testimony of Origen, Eusebius, Jerome, and Augustine, which finally triumphed. Benjamin B. Warfield perceptively observes that there is more evidence for 2 Peter than there is for Herodotus and Thucydides.[9]
4. Furthermore, there is positive internal evidence for the authenticity of 2 Peter. For although there are some marked differences, there are some close similarities to 1 Peter both linguistically and doctrinally.[10]

2 and 3 John. These books were also questioned as to their *genuineness* (see chap. 20). Because of their private nature and limited circulation, they did not enjoy a widespread acceptance. The author identified himself not as an apostle but as an "elder," another fact that hindered its acceptance. All these difficulties notwithstanding, these two epistles were more widely recognized than 2 Peter, being acknowledged in the Muratorian Canon as well as by some of the Fathers in the second century. Furthermore, the similarity of style and thought to 1 John, and the use of "elder" by apostles on other occasions (1 Peter 5:1), argues strongly for the Johannine authorship.

Jude. This was disputed on the question of *authenticity* (see chap. 20). The majority of those who questioned Jude did so on the basis of its alleged references to the Pseudepigraphical *Book of Enoch* (vv. 14-15; cf. Enoch 1:9), and possibly also to the *Assumption of Moses* (v. 9). Origen hints at this, and Jerome specifically says this is the reason it was challenged.[11] It is interesting to note that Tertullian defended Jude as authoritative because it *did* refer to Enoch.[12] However, "the explanation which has most commended it is that Jude's citation of Enoch does not demand approval of the work as a whole, but extends only to those portions that he utilizes for his purpose. This situation is not materially different from Paul's references to pagan poets (Acts 17:28; 1 Cor. 15:33; Titus 1:12)."[13] The external evidence for Jude is widespread from the time of Irenaeus (c. A.D. 170). Like 2 Peter, the Bodmer papyrus manuscript P^{72} from Egypt confirms the use of Jude during the third century. In fact, traces of Jude's influence may be found in the *Didache* (2:7).

Revelation. The Apocalypse (Revelation) was included in the Antilegomena because its *authenticity* was challenged. The doctrine of *chiliasm* (millennialism) was the focal point of the controversy, which lasted longer than that over any other New Testament book. It is a curous thing that Revelation was one of the first books to be recognized in existing writings of the apostolic Fathers, and one of the last to be questioned.

9. Benjamin B. Warfield, *Syllabus on the Special Introduction to the Catholic Epistles*, pp. 116-17.
10. J.D. Douglas, ed., *The New Bible Dictionary*, p. 978.
11. Origen *Commentary on Matthew* 18-30; Jerome *Lives of Illustrious Men* 4.
12. Tertullian *On the Apparel of Women* 1.3, in *Ante-Nicene Fathers*, 4:16-17.
13. See chap. 13; Harrison, p. 404.

Evidence for the immediate reception of Revelation in the first century is understandable, because the "seven churches" (Rev. 2-3) to which it was addressed would naturally want to preserve a work that related to them so directly. There is external evidence for its recognition from the time of the *Shepherd* of Hermas, continuing on into the second century until the Montanists began to attach their unique form of millennialism to it. Around the middle of the third century, Dionysius, the bishop of Alexandria, raised his influential voice against the Apocalypse. His views prevailed through the time of Eusebius of Caesarea to the time of Athanasius and the Council of Carthage (A.D. 397) when this trend was reserved. It seems clear that the question was not one of inspiration, but interpretation and association with particular doctrinal emphases that occasioned the dispute. Once this was understood, the authentic apostolic authority of Revelation was vindicated.

As with Revelation, so with all of the disputed books: once the question of authenticity or genuineness was settled, there was no problem about their canonicity. If it was clear that a book was written by a prophet of God, and it told the truth about God, man, and so on, then it was recognized to be the Word of God.

The Books Rejected by All—Pseudepigrapha[14]

The Nature of the Pseudepigrapha

During the first few centuries, numerous books of a fanciful and heretical nature arose that are neither genuine nor valuable as a whole. Eusebius of Caesarea called these "totally absurd and impious." Virtually no orthodox Father, canon, or council considered these books to be canonical and, so far as the church is concerned, they are primarily of historical value. These books indicate the heretical teaching of gnostic, docetic, and ascetic groups, as well as the exaggerated fancy of religious lore in the early church. At best, these books were revered by some of the cults and referred to by some of the orthodox Fathers, but they were never considered canonical by the mainstream of Christianity.

The Number of the Pseudepigrapha

There was apparently a large number of non-canonical books even in the first century (cf. John 21:25; 2 Thess. 2:2). By the ninth century Photius listed some 280 of them, and more have subsequently been discovered. The

14. Although most writers call these books *Apocrypha* in the wider sense of that term, they are labeled Pseudepigrapha here because they were rejected by all orthodox Fathers who sought to distinguish them from those books which were accepted by some and identified as Apocrypha. Also see Willis Barnstone, ed., *The Other Bible.*

following list includes some of the more important Pseudepigraphal books of the New Testament.

Gospels

There are more than fifty Pseudepigraphal gospels. However, many are known only by name and others by a few scattered citations in the church Fathers.[15] A discussion of the more significant of these follows.

The Gospel of Thomas (early second century). *The Gospel of Thomas* was known to Hippolytus, Origen, Cyril of Jerusalem, and Irenaeus. There were at least two versions of this collection of sayings, one of which shows Gnostic influence. Like other accounts of the infancy of Christ, the *Gospel of Thomas* contains fanciful stories of alleged childhood miracles of Jesus:

> This little child Jesus when he was five years old was playing at the ford of a brook: and he gathered together the waters that flowed there into pools, and made them straightway clean, and commanded them by his word alone. And having made soft clay, he fashioned thereof twelve sparrows. . . . Jesus clapped his hands together and cried out to the sparrows and said to them: Go! and the sparrows took their flight and went away chirping. (2:1-4)

Another tells how He cursed a lad to wither like a tree:

> And when Jesus saw what was done, he was wroth and said unto him: O evil, ungodly, and foolish one, what hurt did the pools and the waters do thee? Behold, now also thou shalt be withered like a tree, and shalt not bear leaves, neither root, nor fruit. And straightway that lad withered up wholly, but Jesus departed and went unto Joseph's house.(3:2-3)

Again, when a "child ran and dashed against his shoulder, Jesus is said to have been provoked and said unto him: 'Thou shalt not finish thy course (lit., go all thy way). And immediately he fell down and died.' "[16] These accounts reflect a dimension of personality in Jesus that is utterly at variance with that as set forth in the New Testament gospel accounts.

The Gospel of the Ebionites (second century). This work was noted by Epiphanius in his *Refutation of All Heresies* (fourth cent.). The Ebionites were a Jewish sect of Christians who stressed the law of Moses, denied the deity of Christ, and are said to have accepted only one gospel.[17] They were vegetarians and rejected the idea that John the Baptist ate locusts, claiming:

15. M.R. James published a collection of these apocryphal writings in 1924 in *The Apocryphal New Testament*. The more recent collection of Edgar Hennecke and Wilhelm Schneemelcher (*New Testament Apocrypha*) provides additional information about the Pseudepigraphal gospels.
16. James, pp. 14-15.
17. *The Oxford Dictionary of the Christian Church*, pp. 438-39.

> John was baptizing, and there went out unto him Pharisees and were baptized, and all Jerusalem. And John had raiment of camel's hair and a leathern girdle about his loins: and his meat (it saith) was wild honey, whereof the taste is the taste of manna, as a cake dipped in oil.[18]

The Ebionites also believed that Jesus was a mere man whom God adopted at the time of His baptism:

> After the people were baptized, Jesus also came and was baptized by John; and as he came up from the water, the heavens were opened, and he saw the Holy Ghost in the likeness of a dove that descended and entered into him: and a voice from heaven saying: Thou art my beloved Son, in thee I am well pleased: and again: This day have I begotten thee. And straightway there shone about the place a great light.[19]

According to the *Gospel of the Ebionites,* it was

> on this account they say that Jesus was begotten of the seed of a man, and was chosen; and so by the choice of God he was called the Son of God from the Christ that came into him from above in the likeness of a dove. And they deny that he was begotten of God the Father, but say that he was created, as one of the archangels, yet greater, and that he is Lord of angels and of all things made by the Almighty.[20]

The Gospel of Peter (second century). Origen, Eusebius, and Theodoret all refer to this Pseudepigraphal gospel. Only fragments of it have been preserved. Eusebius identified it as docetic, which means it denied the true humanity of Christ.[21]

The *Gospel of Peter* teaches several things that fail to concur with the New Testament. That includes the following examples:[22] (1) That Pilate was guiltless for the death of Jesus and only the Jews were answerable for it. (2) That Jesus felt no pain when crucified. "And they brought two malefactors and crucified the Lord in the midst between them. But he held his peace, as if he felt no pain." (3) That Jesus referred to the Father as "My power." And the Lord called out and cried, "My power, O power, thou hast forsaken me!" (4) That Jesus' "brothers and sisters" were from a first marriage of Joseph, a view long held by Roman Catholic scholars.

In addition, the *Gospel of Peter* contains an embellished account of the resurrection of Jesus, which asserts that

> in the night in which the Lord's day dawned, when the soldiers, two by two in

18. James, p. 9.
19. Ibid.
20. Ibid., p. 10.
21. Eusebius *Ecclesiastical History* 6.12.6.
22. 4.10; 5.19; in Hennecke and Schneemelcher, *The Apocryphal New Testament,* 2:179-80, 184.

> every watch, were keeping guard, there rang out a loud voice in heaven, and they saw the heavens opened and two men come down from there in a great brightness and draw nigh to the sepulchre. That stone which had been laid against the entrance to the sepulchre started of itself to roll and give way to the side, and the sepulchre was opened, and both the young men entered in. When now those soldiers saw this, they awakened the centurion and the elders—for they also were there to assist at the watch. And whilst they were relating what they had seen, they saw again three men come out from the sepulchre, and two of them sustaining the other, and a cross following them, and the heads of the two reaching to heaven, but that of him who was led of them by the hand overpassing the heavens. And they heard a voice out of the heavens crying, "Thou hast preached to them that sleep", and from the cross there was heard the answer, "Yea."[23]

Protevangelium of James (late second century). This book is mentioned by Clement of Alexandria, Origen, and many other early Fathers. Only one manuscript copy is preserved, in the Bodmer papyrus collection at Oxford University. It is characterized by a particular devotion to Mary. Among its many features are the following:[24] (1) A very early form of devotion to Mary, which included belief in her miraculous birth (not the immaculate conception) and her perpetual virginity. (2) That Mary was born after only six months in the womb and walked (seven steps) only six months after birth. (3) That "Mary was sixteen years old when all these mysterious things [virgin birth, accouncement, conceptions] happened." (4) The text contains one of the most outlandish miracle stories found anywhere. Speaking of Jesus' birth it says,

> And I looked up at the vault of heaven, and saw it standing still and the birds of the heaven motionless. And I looked at the earth, and saw a dish placed there and workmen lying round it, with their hands in the dish. But those who chewed did not chew, and those who lifted up anything lifted up nothing, and those who put something to their mouth put nothing (to their mouth), but all had their faces turned upwards. And behold, sheep were being driven and (yet) they did not come forward, but stood still; and the shepherd raised his hand to strike them with his staff, but his hand remained up. And I looked at the flow of the river, and saw the mouths of the kids over it and they did not drink. And then all at once everything went on its course (again).[25]

The Gospel of the Hebrews (second century). *The Gospel of the Hebrews* is a false gnostic gospel that was known to Irenaeus, Clement of Alexandria, Origen, Eusebius, and Jerome. It was mistakenly believed by some that this was the original Hebrew version of the gospel of Matthew, which many believe to have been written prior to the Greek version. Accord-

23. 9.35—10.42; in Hennecke and Schneemelcher, 2:185-86.
24. 5.2; 6.1; 12.3; in Hennecke and Schneemelcher, 2:373, 381.
25. 18.2; in Hennecke and Schneemelcher, 2:383-84.

ing to Irenaeus, it was used by the Ebionites to exalt the Old Testmament law and to repudiate the apostle Paul. Some claimed this gospel was the same as the *Gospel of the Ebionites* (based on Epiphanius's statement) but the two have significant differences, including dissimilar accounts of the baptism of Christ.[26]

Some of the features of the *Gospel of the Hebrews* include the following:[27] (1) A special appearance of Christ to James, who, contrary to the canonical gospels, is said to have been at the Last Supper. (2) Reference to the Holy Spirit as our "mother." Jesus said, "Even now did my mother the Holy Spirit take me by one of mine hairs, and carried me away unto the great mountain Thabor." (3) That Mary was only seven months pregnant with Jesus. (4) It embellishes the voice at the baptism of Christ, saying, "My Son, in all the prophets was I waiting for thee that thou shouldest come and I might rest in thee. For thou art my rest; thou art my first-begotten Son that reignest for ever." (5) An account of the Shroud of Christ, which says,

> And when the Lord had given the linen cloth to the servant of the priest, he went to James and appeared to him.... And shortly thereafter the Lord said: Bring a table and bread! And immediately it is added: he took the bread, blessed it and brake it and gave it to James the Just and said to him: My brother, eat thy bread, for the Son of man is risen from among them that sleep.

The Gospel of the Egyptians (second century). This spurious gospel is mentioned by Clement of Alexandria and Origen. It survives in only a few fragments. Like most of the Pseudepigraphical gospels, the *Gospel of the Egyptians* is heretical. It purports that Jesus "showed his disciples that the same person was Father, Son, and Holy Spirit." There seems to be an early ascetic tendency in the cult that produced the work, as reflected in a dialogue between Salome (the mother of James and John) and Jesus: "when she had said, 'I have done well, then, in not bearing children?' (as if childbearing were not the right to accept) the Lord answers and says: Every plant eat thou, but that which hath bitterness eat not."[28] In addition, this gospel has a gnostic disdain for Jesus' body that is evident on several occasions. For example it states, "When Salome inquired when the things concerning which she asked should be known, the Lord said: When ye have trampled on the garment of shame, and when the two become one and the male with the female is neither male nor female." In another instance it asserts, "The Lord said to Salome when she inquired: How long shall death prevail? 'As long as ye women bear children', not because life is an ill, and the creation evil: but as showing the sequence of nature: for in all cases birth is followed by decay."[29]

26. James, p. 10.
27. Hennecke and Schneemelcher, 1:159, 163-65.
28. James, pp. 11-12.
29. Ibid., p. 11.

The Gospel of the Nazaraeans (early second century). *The Gospel of the Nazaraeans* is closely related in content and compass to the synoptic gospels. It was referred to by Jerome as "the Gospel which the Nazarenes use,"[30] or more often as "the Jewish Gospel." Some of its features include the following:[31] (1) That the man with a withered hand was a mason who said, "I was a mason and earned [my] livelihood with [my] hands; I beseech thee, Jesus, to restore to me my health that I may not with ignominy have to beg for my bread." (2) It says (contrary to Matthew 12:40) that Jesus did not spend "three days and three nights" in the grave. (3) It declares, as Jerome notes, that "in the Gospel which is written in Hebrew characters we read not that the veil of the temple was rent, but that the lintel of the temple of wondrous size collapsed."[32] (4) It claims that thousands were converted at the cross when Jesus said, "Father, forgive them" (Luke 23:34): "At this word of the Lord many thousands of the Jews who were standing round the cross became believers."[33] (5) It gives the reason that John was known by the high priest was that "he had often brought fish to the palace of the high priests Annas and Caiaphas."[34] (6) There is an embellishment in the story of the rich young ruler:

> But the rich man then began to scratch his head and it [the saying] pleased him not. And the Lord said to him: How canst thou say, I have fulfilled the law and the prophets? For it stands written in the law: Love thy neighbor as thyself; and behold, many of thy brethren, sons of Abraham, are begrimed with dirt and die of hunger—and thy house is full of many good things and nothing at all comes forth from it to them!

The Gospel of Philip (second century). This is a gnostic gospel known only by one citation until a fourth-or fifth-century manuscript was found in the Gnostic library at Nag Hammadi, Egypt (1945). It narrates the manner of the ascent of a soul through seven successive spheres of hostile "powers" (planetary archons). Its expressions resemble the neoplatonic philosopher Porphyry (c. 232-c. 303), a disciple of Plotinus (c. 205-70) who was a fellow classmate of Origen (c. 185-c. 254). It contains some noncanonical sayings of Christ, such as, "A disciple one day asked the Lord about something worldly. He replied: Ask thy mother, and she will give thee strange things."[35]

The Book of Thomas the Athlete. A gnostic-like gospel containing an alleged dialogue of Jesus and Thomas that occurred between the resurrection

30. Jerome *Commentary on Matthew* 23.35.
31. Hennecke and Schneemelcher, 2:148-49.
32. Jerome, *Epist. 120 to Hedibia* and *Commentary on Matthew* (on Matt. 27:51); in Hennecke and Schneemelcher, 2:150.
33. Haimo of Auxerre, *Commentary on Isaiah 53:2,* in Hennecke and Schneemelcher, 2:150.
34. Hennecke and Schneemelcher, 2:152.
35. Ibid., 2:276; 1:277.

and ascension, this book contains condemnations of the flesh, womanhood, sexuality, and promises of a future rest in the kindgom of heaven. It begins, "The secret words spoken by the Saviour to Judas Thomas, and which I have written down, I, Matthew, who heard them while they spoke together."[36]

The Gospel According to Mathias: The Traditions of Mathias. Here is another work known to Origen, Eusebius, Ambrose, and Jerome. Quotations from it are preserved by Clement of Alexandria:[37] (1) "Wonder at what is present." (2) "Strive with the flesh and misuse it, without yielding to it in any way to unbridled lust, but to increase the soul through faith and knowledge." Again there is a Gnostic influence manifest.

The Gospel of Judas (late second century). This gospel was known to Irenaeus and Epiphanius (c. 315-403), bishop of Salamia. The product of an antinomian Gnostic sect, it may have contained "a Passion story setting forth the 'mystery of the betrayal' (*proditionis mysterium*) and explaining how Judas by his treachery made possible the salvation of all mankind."[38]

Epistle of an Apostle [*Epistula Apostolorum*] (second century). Unknown before a Coptic text was found in Cairo in 1895, this presents a dialogue between Christ and the eleven disciples after the resurrection. Hennecke summarizes its contents as follows:

> He entered into the womb of Mary in the disguise of the angel Gabriel. After his resurrection also He sent His power in the form of Gabriel to free Peter from the prison for one night. The reality of Christ's body is strongly maintained (against Cerinthus and Simon, whom the apostles warn against), but at the same time the unity of the Son and the Father is so strongly emphasized that one could justifiably speak of identity. During Christ's descent He took on, in each of the heavenly spheres, the form of the angel residing there, in order to reach the earth without being recognized (as also described in the *Ascension of Isaiah*.) As the Logos took on real flesh and also after the resurrection appears to His disciples with flesh that can be felt (so that Peter as well as Thomas can put his fingers into the nailprints of His hands), so too will His redeemed rise again in the flesh, "a garment that will not pass away." Christ has also proclaimed the message of salvation in the underworld.[39]

Another passage about the Incarnation reads,

> At that time I appeared in the form of the archangel Gabriel to (the virgin) Mary and spoke with her, and her heart received (me); she believed and laughed; and I, the Word, went into her and became flesh; and I myself was servant for myself, and in the form of the image of an angel; so I will do after I have gone to my Father.[40]

36. Ibid., 1:307-8.
37. Ibid., 1:308-9.
38. Ibid., 1:313.
39. Ibid., 1:190.
40. Ibid., 1:199.

The Apocryphon of John (second century). This is a Pseudepigraphal post-resurrection dialogue between a disciple and the Revealor, who says,

> I am [the Father]; I am the Mother, I [am the Son]. I am the eternally Existing, the unmixable, [since there is none who] mingles himself with him. [Now am I come] to reveal to thee [what] is, what [was], and what [shall] be, that [thou mayest know] the invisible things like [the] visible, and [to instruct thee] concerning the perfect [man].[41]

The Gospel of Truth (second century). This early gnostic gospel may have been written by the gnostic theologian Valentinus (c. A.D. 140-145). It was the first work from the Nag Hammadi discovery to be translated.[42] This gospel narrative begins, "The Gospel of Truth is joy for those who have received from the Father of Truth the grace of knowing Him through the power of the Word, which has come forth from the Pleroma, (the Word)."

The basic theme is found in the words, "this ignorance concerning the Father produced anguish and terror. And the anguish became dense like a mist, so that no one could see. For this reason Error waxed strong." Speaking of salvation by knowledge (*gnosis*), it reads:

> Thus the Word of the Father proceeds forth into the All, being the fruit of His heart and a form of His will. It upholds the All, it chooses it, and also takes (upon itself) the form of the All, purifying it and causing it to return to the Father and to the Mother, Jesus of the infinite gentleness. The Father reveals His breast; but His breast is the Holy Spirit. He reveals that of Himself which was hidden (that of Himself which was hidden was His Son) in order that through the compassion of the Father the aeons might know Him, and cease to torment themselves in search of the Father, resting in Him since they know that this is rest.

The *Gospel of Truth* concludes as follows:

> This is the place of the blessed; this is their place.... But therein shall I be, and devote myself at all times to the Father of the All, and to the true brethren, upon whom the love of the Father is poured out, and in whose midst nothing of Him is lacking. These are they who are manifest in truth ... and which is in His Heart and in the pleroma, while His Spirit rejoices in Him and glorifies Him in whom it was for, He is good. And His children are perfect, and worthy of His name, for it is children of this kind that He, the Father, loves.

Additional Pseudepigraphal gospels. More than fifty Pseudepigraphal gospels have been cataloged and edited by Edgar Hennecke and Wilhelm Schneemelcher into several categories. A modification of their list follows.

I. ISOLATED SAYINGS OF THE LORD

41. Ibid., 1:322.
42. From ibid., 1:523, 525-26, 531.

II. PAPYRUS FRAGMENTS OF PSEUDEPIGRAPHAL GOSPELS

1. An unknown gospel of synoptic type (Oxyrhynchus Papyrus 840)
2. An unknown gospel with Johannine elements (Egerton Papyrus 2)
3. Sayings—collections on papyrus
   Introduction
   (a) Oxyrhynchus Papyrus 654
   (b) Oxyrhynchus Papyrus 1
   (c) Oxyrhynchus Papyrus 655
4. Other Greek papyrus fragments
   (a) Oxyrhynchus Papyrus 1224
   (b) Cairo Papyrus 10 735
   (c) The so-called Fayyum Fragment

III. JEWISH-CHRISTIAN GOSPELS

1. The gospel of the Nazaraeans
2. The gospel of the Ebionites
3. The gospel of the Hebrews

IV. THE GOSPEL OF THE EGYPTIANS

V. THE GOSPEL OF PETER

VI. CONVERSATIONS BETWEEN JESUS AND HIS DISCIPLES AFTER THE RESURRECTION

1. The Freer logion
2. Epistula apostolorum
3. A gospel fragment from the Strasbourg Coptic papyrus

VII. GNOSTIC GOSPELS AND RELATED DOCUMENTS

A. Gospels Under General Titles
   1. The Gospel of the Four Heavenly Regions or of the Four Corners of the World
   2. The Gospel of Perfection
   3. The Gospel of Truth

B. Gospels Under the Name of an Old Testament Figure

C. Gospels Current, Directly or Indirectly, Under the Name of Jesus, and Similar Works
   1. The Sophia Jesu Christi
   2. The Dialogue of the Redeemer
   3. The Pistis Sophia
   4. The Two Books of Jeu

D. Gospels Attributed to the Twelve as a Group

1. The Gospel of the Twelve (or Twelve Apostles)
2. The (Kukean) Gospel of the Twelve
3. The Memoria Apostolorum
4. The (Manichean) Gospel of the Twelve Apostles
5. The Gospel of the Seventy
6. Other "Gospels of the Twelve Apostles"

E. Gospels Under the Name of an Apostle
1. The Gospel of Philip
2. The Gospel of Thomas
3. The Book of Thomas the Athlete
4. The Gospel According to Matthias
   The Traditions of Matthias
5. The Gospel of Judas
6. The Apocryphon of John
7. Fragments of a Dialogue Between John and Jesus
8. The Apocryphon of James (Apocryphon Jacobi)
9. The Gospel of Bartholomew

F. Gospels Under the Names of Holy Women
1. The Questions of Mary
2. The Gospel According to Mary
3. The "Genna Marias"

G. Gospels Attributed to an Arch-heretic
1. The Gospel of Cerinthus
2. The Gospel of Basilides
3. The Gospel of Marcion
4. The Gospel of Apelles
5. The Gospel of Bardesanes
6. The Gospel of Mani

H. Gospels Under the Names of Their Users

VIII. INFANCY GOSPELS
1. The Protevangelium of James
2. The Infancy Story of Thomas
3. Gnostic Legends
4. Later Infancy Gospels
   A. Extracts from the Arabic Infancy Gospel
   B. Extracts from the Gospel of Pseudo-Matthew
   C. Extract from the Latin Infancy Gospel in the Arundel Manuscript
   D. Extract from the Life of John According to Serapion

IX. THE RELATIVES OF JESUS

X. THE WORK AND SUFFERINGS OF JESUS
1. Jesus' Earthly Appearance and Character
2. The Alleged Testiomony of Josephus
3. The Abgar Legend
4. The Gospel of Nicodemus, Acts of Pilate, and Christ's Descent into Hell.
5. The Gospel of Bartholomew
   A. The Questions of Bartholomew
   B. Coptic Texts of Bartholomew
6. The Gospel of Gamaliel

By comparison with the canonical gospels, these Pseudepigraphal writings fall far short of the quality of the inspired Word of God. Edwin Yamauchi's summary is direct and to the point:

> The apocryphal [pseudepigraphal] gospels, even the earliest and soberest among them, can hardly be compared with the canonical gospels. The former are all patently secondary and legendary or obviously slanted. Commenting on the infancy gospels, Morton Enslin concludes: "Their total effect is to send us back to the canonical gospels with fresh approval of their chaste restraint in failing to fill in the intriguing hidden years."

Yamauchi cites the editors of the *Ante-Nicene Fathers,* O. Roberts and J. Donaldson: "The predominant impression which they leave on our minds is a profound sense of the immeasurable superiority, the unapproachable simplicity and majesty, of the Canonical Writings." Quoting Joachim Jeremias with approval, Yamauchi concludes, "The extra-canonical literature, taken as a whole, manifests a surprising poverty. The bulk of it is legendary, and bears the clear mark of forgery. Only here and there, amid a mass of worthless rubbish, do we come across a priceless jewel."[43]

Acts

In addition to Pseudepigraphal gospels there are also numerous Apocryphal accounts of the Acts of the Apostles.[44]

A. Second- and third-century acts of apostles
   Introduction
   1. The Acts of John
   2. The Acts of Peter (contains the legend of Peter being crucified upside down.)
   3. The Acts of Paul (Paul is here described as a short, bald man with a large nose and bowlegged.)

43. Edwin Yamauchi, "The Word from Nag Hammadi," p. 22.
44. For the following lists see Hennecke and Schneemelcher 2:19-21.

4. The Acts of Andrew
5. The Acts of Thomas

B. The pseudo-clementines

C. Later acts of apostles
1. The Continuation of the Early Acts of Apostles
2. Later Acts of Other Apostles

EPISTLES ("Apostolic Pseudepigrapha")

1. The Kerygma Petrou
2. The Kerygmata Petrou
3. The Epistle to the Laodiceans
4. The Apocryphal Correspondence Between Seneca and Paul
5. The Pseudo-Titus Epistle

APOCALYPSES

A. Apocalyptic in Early Christianity
1. Introduction
2. The Ascension of Isaiah
3. Apocalypse of Peter

B. Apocalyptic Prophecy of the Early Church
Introduction
1. The Fifth and Sixth Books of Esra
2. Christian Sibyllines
3. The Book of Elchasai

C. Later Apocalypses
Introduction
1. Apocalypse of Paul
2. Apocalypse of Thomas

BOOKS ACCEPTED BY SOME—APOCRYPHA

THE NATURE OF THE APOCRYPHA

The distinction between the Pseudepigrapha and the Apocrypha in most cases is a valid one, but it becomes rather tenuous in some instances. For the most part, these books were not received as canonical and, like the Pseudepigrapha, they were used heretically by the sects and were even quoted by some orthodox writers. Nonetheless, on the whole they have one further characteristic, namely, they were not only part of the religious literature quoted by the Fathers, but sometimes appeared in local ecclesiastical canons and Bible translations. The first seven in the following discussion are what Alexander Souter called "Books of Temporal and Local Canonicity," or books that "had canonicity, or something very like it, in a particular church for a particular period, but were afterward dropped."[45] Some of the Fathers and churches considered several of these books to be canonical. Nevertheless the testimony of the church in general, as well as the final canonical decisions, reveals that partial and local judgment was faulty. Still, local acceptance and wide circulation of some of these books manifest their value as well as their esteem.

The Number of the Apocrypha

Here again, the number is somewhat arbitrary, because it is based on two distinctions that are difficult to determine precisely, that is, the difference between the "orthodox" and "heretical" Fathers. In a general way, the latter may be determined by the canons and creeds of the church councils of the first five centures, while the former by whether or not the book was used only homiletically, or theologically and authoritatively. The following list, and perhaps more, fits into the category of books used at least ecclesiastically, and possible canonically.

Epistle of Pseudo-Barnabas (c. A.D. 70-79). This widely circulated epistle is found in the Codex Siniaticus (א) (c. 340), and mentioned in the table of contents of Codex Bezae (D) (c. 450 or c. 550; see chap. 22). It was quoted as Scripture by Clement of Alexandria and Origen. It parallels the canonical epistle to the Hebrews in style although it is more allegorical and mystical than Hebrews, and there is some debate as to whether it is a first or second century document. Nonetheless, it may be concluded with Brooke Foss Westcott that "while the antiquity of the Epistle is firmly established, its Apostolicity is more than questionable."[46]

Epistle to the Corinthians (c. A.D. 96). Dionysius of Corinth (160-80) says that this epistle *1 Corinthians* by Clement of Rome, was read publicly at Corinth and elsewhere,[47] and it is found in Codex Alexandrinus (A) [the Alexandrian manuscript] of the New Testament (c. 450; see chap. 22). Herbert T. Andrews sums up the situation on this epistle, saying,

> Today no one would put in a plea for its recognition as Scripture, yet from a historical point of view the Epistle has no little interest for us.... It gives us a very good conception of the Christian belief at the time.... It contains explicit references to Paul's first Epistle to the Corinthians, and gives several quotations from

45. Alexander Souter, *The Text and Canon of the New Testament,* pp. 178-81.
46. Brooke Foss Westcott, *A General Survey of the History of the Canon of the New Testament,* p. 41.
47. Cf. Eusebius, 4.23. Loeb, ed., 1:383.

the Epistle to the Hebrews, and so proves that these books were widely circulated and recognized before the close of the first century.[48]

Ancient Homily, or the so-called Second Epistle of Clement (c. A.D. 120-40). This was known and used in the second century and is also called *2 Corinthians* of Clement of Rome. In the Alexandrian manuscript (A) it is placed after the book of Revelation, with *1 Clement* and the *Psalms of Solomon* as a sort of appendix. There is no clear evidence, however, that it was considered fully canonical, at least on any broad scale.

Shepherd, of Hermas (c. A.D. 115-40). This is the most popular of all the noncanonical books of the New Testament. It is found in Sinaiticus (א), in the table of contents of Bezae (D), in some Latin Bibles, quoted as inspired Scripture by Irenaeus and Origen, and Eusebius recognized that "it was publicly read in the churches" and "deemed most necessary for those who have need of elementary instruction." The *Shepherd* has been aptly called the "Pilgrim's Progress" of the early church. Like Bunyan's great allegory, it ranks second only to the canonical books in its circulation in the early church and in its dramatization of spiritual truths. In other words, it is like Ecclesiasticus (Sirach) of the Old Testament Apocrypha—ethical and devotional, but not canonical (see chap. 15).

Didache, or *Teaching of the Twelve* (c. A.D. 100-120). The *Didache* was held in high regard by the early church. Clement of Alexandria quoted it as Scripture, and Athanasius listed it among the sacred writings along with Judith and Tobit. This book is of great importance from the historical point of view, giving the opinion of the church of the early second century on the essential truths of Christanity, and it forms a bridge between the New Testament and the patristic literature;[49] nevertheless, the verdict of history is at one with Eusebius, who placed it among the "rejected books."

Apocalypse of Peter (c. 150). This is perhaps the oldest of the noncanonical New Testament apocalypses, and it enjoyed great popularity in the early church. It is mentioned in the *Muratorian Fragment,* in the table of contents of Bezae (D), and is quoted by Clement of Alexandria. Its description of heaven is picturesque, and its pictures of hell are grotesque, depicting it as a lake of "flaming mire" or a "lake of pitch and blood and boiling mire." Its imagery had a wide influence on medieval theology, and was a source from which Dante's *Inferno* was derived. As to its authenticity, even the *Muratorian Fragment* raised questions, saying that some would not permit it to be read in the churches. The church in general has agreed with that conclusion.

48. Herbert T. Andrews, *An Introduction to the Apocryphal Books of the Old and New Testaments,* p. 102.
49. An illustration may be seen in the case of baptism, where the use of affusion instead of immersion may have been alluded to, in *Didache* 7.1-4.

The Acts of Paul and Thecla (170). *The Acts of Paul and Thecla* was quoted often by Origen and is in the table of contents of Bezae (D). Stripped of its mythical elements, it is the story of the conversion and testimony of an Iconian lady, Thecla, based on Acts 14:1-7. It no doubt embodies a genuine tradition, as such noted scholars as William M. Ramsay and G. A. Deissmann have argued, but most scholars are inclined to agree with Adolf Harnack, who said it contains "a great deal of fiction and very little truth."

Epistle to the Laodiceans (fourth century?). Although the *Epistle to the Laodiceans* was known to Jerome, and was included in many Latin Bibles from the sixth to the fifteenth centuries, it is a forgery based on the reference of Paul in Colossians 4:16. A book by this name is mentioned in the *Muratorian Fragment,* although it may be another name for Ephesians,[50] which does not have "to the Ephesians" (in 1:1) in some early manuscripts (א , B, P^{46}). To quote J.B. Lightfoot, "The Epistle is a centro of Pauline phrases strung together without any definite connection or any clear object."[51] As late as A.D. 787, the Council of Nicea (II) warned against it, terming it "a forged epistle." It reappeared as late as the Reformation era in German and even in English Bibles.[52] "Unlike most forgeries it had no ulterior aim.... It has no doctrinal peculiarities. Thus it is quite harmless, so far as falsity and stupidity combined can ever be regarded as harmless."[53]

The Gospel According to the Hebrews (A.D. 65-100). Probably the earliest noncanonical gospel, *The Gospel According to the Hebrews* has survived only in a few fragmentary quotes culled from various Fathers of the church.[54] According to Jerome, some called it "the true Matthew," although this seems unlikely from its quotations, which bear little relation to the canonical Matthew. In fact, it is questionable whether it deserves to be called Apocryphal rather than Pseudepigraphal, because there is no evidence that it had any more than a homiletical usage. And, even if evidence be educed that it had a limited ecclesiastical use, it certainly was not canonical; as a matter of fact, it is not even extant.

Epistle of Polycarp to the Philippians (c. A.D. 108). In one sense, Polycarp is the most important of the apostolic Fathers. He was a disciple of the apostle John. He lays no claim to inspiration for himself, but says that he "always taught the things he had learned from the apostles, and which the Church has handed down, and which alone are true."[55] There is very little originality in this epistle, as it borrows both matter and style from the New Testament, and particularly from Paul's epistle to the Philippians. Even though

50. Harrison, pp. 310-11.
51. J.B. Lightfoot, *Saint Paul's Epistles to the Colossians and to Philemon,* p. 285.
52. See discussions in chaps. 28-31.
53. Lightfoot, p. 285.
54. Andrews, p. 109.
55. Irenaeus *Against Heresies* 3.3.4.

it was not considered canonical, it is a valuable testimony to the existence of most of the New Testament canon, which he interweaves into his writing.[56]

The Seven Epistles of Ignatius (c. A.D. 110). These letters indicate a definite familiarity with the teachings of the New Testament, but have a marked peculiarity of style. Their teaching shows a strong belief in the unity of the visible church, with a bishop-centered government. Bishop J.B. Lightfoot has ably defended the genuineness of these epistles, but vitually no one contends for their canonicity.

Evaluation of the New Testament Apocrypha and Pseudepigrapha

A brief evaluation of each classification of this vast body of early Christian literature will serve to focus on each one's significance in the early church as well as for the church today.

The Value of the New Testament Pseudepigrapha. In general, these books have no positive theological value, and almost no historical value, except as they reflect the religious consciousness of the church during early centuries. Their value may be summarized as follows:

1. They contain, no doubt, the kernel of some correct traditions that, by careful "demythologizing," may furnish some supplementary historical facts about the early church.
2. They reflect the ascetic, docetic and gnostic tendencies, and heresies of early Christianity.
3. They show a popular desire for information not given in the canonical gospels, such as information about the childhood of Jesus, and the lives of the apostles.
4. They manifest an illegitimate tendency to glorify Christianity by means of pious frauds.
5. They display an unhealthy desire to find support for doctrinal interests and heretical teachings under the guise of apostolic authority.
6. They reveal an unwholesome attempt to fill up supposed lacks in the canonical writings.
7. They demonstrate the incurable tendency of depraved curiosity to arrive at heretical and fanciful embellishments of Christian truth (e.g., Mary worship).

The Value of the New Testament Apocrypha. There is no doubt that the theological and historical value of most of these books is much higher than that of the Pseudepigrapha. In brief, they are valuable, but not canonical.

56. Westcott, pp. 36-37.

1. They provide the earliest documentation of some of the canonical books of the New Testament.
2. They reveal beliefs within the subapostolic church.
3. They form a bridge between the apostolic writings of the New Testament and the patristic literature of the third and fourth centuries, thus providing some clues to that transition.
4. They possess hints as to the rise of later unorthodox teachings (e.g., allegorical interpretation in *Pseudo-Barnabas,* or baptismal regeneration in the *Shepherd*).
5. They contain much of historical value about the practices and policies of the early church.

With the above values in mind, it should be emphasized that none of these books is to be considered canonical or inspired. Several reasons may be proffered in support of that contention. (1) None of them enjoyed any more than a temporary or local recognition. (2) Most of them never did have anything more than a semicanonical status, being appended to various manuscripts or mentioned in tables of contents. (3) No major canon or church council included them as inspired books of the New Testament. (4) The limited acceptance enjoyed by most of these books is attributable to the fact that they attached themselves to references in canonical books (e.g., Laodiceans to Col. 4:16), because of their alleged apostolic authorship (e.g., Acts of Paul). Once these issues were clarified, there remained little doubt that these books were not canonical.

Summary and Conclusion

On the question of New Testament canonicity, twenty of the twenty-seven books were never seriously questioned in orthodox circles, namely, the Homologoumena. The other seven books, called Antilegomena, were questioned by some Fathers for a time, but were finally and fully recognized by the church generally. There are numerous books that were never accepted by anyone as authentic or canonical, which are called Pseudepigrapha. The final class of books is called Apocrypha. These books were of good quality and integrity that had a local and temporary acceptance, although they were never widely nor finally considered to be canonical.

Part Three

TRANSMISSION OF THE BIBLE

18
Languages of the Bible

There are four links in the chain "from God to us": inspiration, canonization, transmission, and translation. In the first, God gave the message to the prophets who received and recorded it. Canonization, the second link, dealt with the recognition and collection of the prophetic writings. In effect, the objective disclosure was complete when the sixty-six books of the Bible were written, and then recognized by their original readers. However, in order for succeeding generations to share in this revelation the Scriptures had to be copied, translated, recopied, and retranslated. This process not only provided the Scriptures for other nations, but for other generations as well. The third link is known as transmission of the Bible.

Because the Scriptures have undergone some two thousand years of transmission, it is only natural to ask: How much has the Bible suffered in the process? Or, to put it more precisely: Is the twentieth-century English Bible an accurate reproduction of the first-century Greek Testament and the Hebrew Old Testament? The answer to that question comes from the science of textual criticism, which will now be traced in terms of the transmission of the biblical text.

Why God Chose Written Languages

Several alternatives were open to God in His choice of a means for communication of His truth to men. As a matter of fact, a wide variety of the media of communication were actually utilized by God "in time past," as He "spake unto the fathers by the prophets" (Heb. 1:1, KJV).

What God Could Have Used

God could have chosen to continue to communicate with men as He did initially in biblical times.

Sometimes God spoke through angels. (Cf. Gen. 18-19, 22: Ex. 3.) In fact, their very name means "messenger." Their ministry began in Genesis (chaps. 18-19), and continued through the very last chapter of the Bible (Rev.

22:8-9). However, the very nature of their celestial intrusion into the terrestrial made it a special revelation that did not lend itself to permanence. There were certain distinct limitations in having to call upon angels to convey everything that God wished to say to every man under every circumstance in every age. One could imagine quite an endless invasion from outer space in order to care for all the details of truth transmitted to billions of people, many of which have short memories.

Visions and dreams. This was another means of communication that God occasionally chose to utilize (cf. Dan. 7:1; Gen. 41). Visions and dreams had more potential for universality and individuality than did angels. This is because it did not involve the mass of heavenly traffic and it could even be worked into one's personal experience more readily. However, this method also has serious handicaps. For one thing, visions and dreams tend to be subjective and personal rather than objective and universal. For another, even their ecstatic impact could wear off and be forgotten.

The Urim and Thummim and the lot. These methods were sometimes used to determine God's will (see Ex. 28:30; Prov. 16:33). However, they were limited in the scope of the content of truth they could convey. Apparently, all they could indicate was a yes or no answer to questions that men happened to direct toward God. Thus, their scope was quite limited when compared with a detailed description of God's declarations to men found in other media of transmission.

The moral law and creation.[1] God has revealed Himself by the moral law "written in the heart" (Rom. 2:15) as well as through creation (Ps. 19:1 ff.) to all men. But the amount of truth available here is limited and subject to corruption. Romans 1:18-19 says that although the truth from creation is "evident within them," men "suppress the truth in unrighteousness." Their consciences also distort the moral law (Rom. 2:15; cf. 1 Tim. 4:2). Further, even though this general revelation is sufficient for man's condemnation (Rom. 1:20; 2:12), only through special revelation has salvation come to light (Heb. 1:1; Rom. 10:9 f.).

The audible voice and the direct miracle. These were also media of divine communication (see 1 Sam. 3 and Judges 6:40), but they suffered from the same intrinsic difficulties that other means had, namely, they were good ways for God to speak to one man on one occasion and for one specific purpose. Nevertheless, it would be a strain on the divine economy to expect a repeat performance of these feats in speaking to all men everywhere. This is not to say that all of these methods were not good; they were in fact the ways by which God did speak to the prophets. There was, however, a better way to

1. For an extended treatment of general revelation see Bruce A. Demarest, *General Revelation: Historical Views and Contemporary Issues.*

communicate; it was a more precise, more permanent, and more easily disseminated revelation, which was just as personal.

WHAT GOD CHOSE TO USE

It was no doubt desirable to speak *to* the prophets "in divers manners," but the best way to speak to the men of all ages through the prophets was to *record* the communication. Although no one can doubt that language, whether written or spoken, is not a "perfect" means of communication, it seems evident that it was the "best" means available, not that the best means was "adequate." It is incongruous that the scholars who raise a voice against the adequacy of language have found language adequate enough to convey their view that language is not adequate! The time-tested superiority of a written record of truth was the one God chose to use in order to make permanent and immortalize His message to men. There were several decided advantages to this medium of revelation.

Precision. One of the advantages of language over the other media of communication mentioned is the matter of precision. It is a common experience that thoughts become more precise as they are expressed. In this connection it may be said that a student can understand better with a pencil than with any other instrument; because, if a thought can be apprehended and expressed in writing, it must have been clearly understood. Another illustration of the precision of language is the difference between one's active and his passive vocabularies. It is possible to read and understand, in a general way, more words than one can use or write in a specific way. This is true because the accurate usage of words requires a more precise understanding of them, and precision is attained by expression. The proof of that point is the fact that mankind's most treasured knowledge to date is in the form of written records and books. It is understandable, then, that God should choose to have His truth conveyed by books as precisely as is possible.

Propagation. There is another advantage to written revelation, namely, the matter of propagation. It is possible to make more precise copies of a written medium than a spoken one. No one will disagree that a written copy can be, and usually is, a much more accurate reproduction than an oral tradition. No matter how careful the communication is made orally, there is always a greater chance for change and corruption of the original than with a written record. A simple experiment will suffice to convince the skeptic. The word-of-mouth story passed around a circle of friends returns with amazing emendations in a few short minutes. In fact, it is astounding to note that Jesus' disciples misinterpreted and mistransmitted a simple oral tradition that they thought they had heard Jesus say (John 21:23). Thus, in order to transmit revealed truth accurately, written records were made and copied by hand, until the invention of movable type in the printing process. Once the movable type had been invented (in the fifteenth century), the advantage of the printed page, and ability to reproduce it on a mass scale, became most apparent.

Preservation. Another advantage of writing is the matter of preservation. Failing memories are sometimes a blessing, but they are a decided disadvantage in the retention of the repertoire of revelation. It is always better to "make a note of it," or to "put it on record." As a matter of fact, it is difficult to imagine the adjudication of justice in a court without a record of testimony, to say nothing of the vacillation of memory in other realms. A written record has one additional advantage as well, namely, it can stimulate memory and conjure up within the individual's imagination a host of personal implications that are latent within the given symbols or words of that record. Words, then, are not so wooden as to prevent a "personal blessing" for the individual reader, particularly in light of the fact that biblical words are the objective vehicle through which the Holy Spirit applies truth personally and subjectively to each reader individually (cf. John 16:13; 1 Pet. 1:11).

Which Languages God Chose

Having discussed why God chose to commit His truth to men by way of writing, it is only natural to examine which languages He chose. Ostensibly, it could be expected that He who "works all things after the counsel of His will" (Eph. 1:11) and who brought forth Christ "when the fulness of time came" (Gal. 4:4), would have chosen languages that were particularly suited to the purpose of His revelation. Happily, such is the case with the biblical languages as the following examination will reveal.

Old Testament Languages: The Semitic Family

Two important language groups trace their origins to the descendants of Noah: Shem and Ham. On the basis of phonological and morphological features that they share, Semitic and Hamitic languages are thought by many scholars to be related through a hypothetical common ancestor, Hamito-Semitic. To the Hamitic group, which is essentially North African, belong Egyptian (called Coptic after the third century of the Christian era), the Berber dialects of North Africa, and various Cushitic dialects spoken along the upper Nile. Coptic is the language used in the liturgy of the early Christian church in Egypt. South of the Sahara languages are usually classified into three main divisions: Sudanese, Bantu, and Hottentot and Bushman. The Semitic group of languages includes four divisions.[2]

The Eastern Division. Akkadian, called Assyrian in the periods of the oldest texts, and later Babylonian are spokesmen of this division. Akkadian was the common language of all Southwest Asia during the height of the Old

2. Thomas Pyles, *The Origins and Development of the English Language*, p. 83.

Babylonian and Assyrian empires, a fact evidenced by the Amarna Letters, which were sent by petty kings in Syria and Palestine to the Pharaohs in Egypt around 1400-1360 B.C. These languages are not used in the Old Testament.

The Southern Division. This division has two major languages: Arabic and Ethiopic. Neither of those languages is used in the Old Testament. Ethiopic was the language of Ethiopia (Cush), a country referred to in each section of the Old Testament (cf. Gen. 10:7-8; Isa. 45:14; Ps. 68:31). Arabic is the most widely spoken Semitic language in the modern world, being spoken by large numbers of people over a vast area. In the sixteenth century Arabic became the official language of Egypt.

The Northern Division. Amorite and Aramaic,[3] which was the language of Jesus and the disciples, are representatives of the northern division. The Amorites inhabited Palestine before and during Israel's occupation (cf. Gen. 10:16; 15:16; Deut. 7:1; Josh. 10:6; 2 Chron. 8:7), but their language was not used in the writing of the Old Testament. Aramaic, the language of the Syrians, appears in all three sections of the Old Testament either in writing or in place names (cf. Gen. 10:22; 31:47; 2 Kings 18:26; Ezra 4:7—6:1; 7:12-26; Isa. 36:11; Jer. 10:11; Dan. 2:4—7:28).

The Northwest Division. This division of the Semitic family includes the Canaanite subdivision as well as Aramaic elements, and is represented by four dialects: Ugaritic, Phoenician, Moabite, and Hebrew.

Ugaritic is not used in the Old Testament, but it has been instrumental in further study of the cognate Hebrew language of the Old Testament. It was the language of the Ras Shamra Tablets, discovered in Northern Syria since 1929, which provide another key to the Canaanite dialects.

Phoenician is another important language that was not used in the Old Testament, although Phoenicians are mentioned in all three sections (cf. Gen. 10:8-12; 1 Kings 5:6; Neh. 13:16; Ezek. 27:9; Zeph. 1:11). The contribution of the Phoenicians is a major one, because it was they who introduced the alphabet to other languages,[4] thus making writing much less cumbersome than it was for the Akkadians.

Lot's descendants developed two dialects of Hebrew: Moabite by way of his oldest daughter, and Ammonite by way of the younger. Neither of these languages were used in the Old Testament; however, their nations are referred to repeatedly in all three sections of the Old Testament. The Moabite Stone (c. 850 B.C.) is the first really long inscription in any Canaanite language that

3. Many scholars oversimplify the divisions of the Semitic branch to the point of error, which is both ill-advised and unnecessary, e.g., Mario A. Pei, *The World's Chief Languages*, pp. 29-30; *Encyclopedia Britannica* 20:314-18; Philip Babcock Gore, ed., *Webster's Third International Dictionary*, p. 38; and even Pyles, pp. 82-83.
4. See F. F. Bruce, *The Books and the Parchments*, pp. 15-32, for an excellent discussion on "The Bible and the Alphabet."

has been discovered (found in 1868 at Dibon) and is the account of the Moabite king, Mesha, concerning the revolt mentioned in 2 Kings 1:1; 3:4-27.

Hebrew is by far the most important language of the Old Testament.[5] Most of the Old Testament is written in it, and it is called "Judean" (2 Kings 18:26, 28), as well as "the language of Canaan" (Isa. 19:18). Except for the portions mentioned above (cf. Aramaic in particular), the Old Testament was written in Hebrew. During its long history, Hebrew has developed into the Biblical, Mishnaic, Rabbinic, Medieval, and Modern dialects.

New Testament Languages: Semitic Family and Indo-European Family

There is no need to retrace the various divisions of the Semitic family, and the Indo-European family is traced in more detail at a later point (see chap. 30); hence, the present discussion deals with the individual languages involved in the New Testament.

The Semitic Family. This is represented by both Hebrew and Aramaic (Syriac). Most of the Hebrew influence is seen in the Greek translation of the former's idiom. This may be seen in the use of the expression "and it came to pass," the use of two nouns rather than an adjective and a noun (cf. 1 Thess. 1:3, Eph. 1:13), and calling someone a child or son of a given quality if he has that quality (cf. Luke 10:6; Eph. 2:3).[6] Aramaic was no doubt the spoken language of the Lord and His disciples. It was the source of such words as Cephas, Matthew, Abba (Mark 14:36), and Maranatha (1 Cor. 16:22). It is also noteworthy that in the very hour of His agony on the cross, Jesus cried out in His native Aramaic tongue, " 'Eli, Eli, lama sabachthani?' that is, 'My God, my God, why has Thou forsaken Me?' " (Matt. 27:46).

The Indo-European Family. Even more prominent are Latin and Greek. Although Latin was used in the Eastern Roman Empire mostly by the legions, it made its influence felt in the Rabbinical Hebrew, spoken Aramaic, and Greek writings.[7] Its influence in the New Testament is found mainly in loanwords, for example, centurion (Mark 15:39, 44-45); tribute (Matt. 17:25; Mark 12:14, KJV); legion (Matt. 26:53). In addition to that, the inscription on the cross was written in Latin, Hebrew, and Greek.[8] The Greek of the New Testament has been quite problematic through the centuries. The basic language of the New Testament, it has gone through a series of changes similar to Latin, Hebrew, and English. There are five basic periods of Greek: Homeric, Attic, Koine, Byzantine, and Modern. Until the late nineteenth century, the language of the New Testament (Koine) was considered a sort of special

5. Ibid., pp. 33-47 discusses "The Hebrew Language."
6. See Joseph Angus, *The Bible Handbook,* pp. 181-84.
7. Bruce, pp. 48-57.
8. For a comprehensive list of New Testament Latinisms, see ibid., pp. 72-73, as well as the discussion in chap. 23.

"Holy Ghost" language because it was not specifically identifiable with any of the other four periods, and the vocabulary was somewhat different. However, with the discovery in the late nineteenth century of first-century letters and other documents in Egypt, that view began to give way to the current view, that the New Testament was written in the language of the common people. It should be pointed out that Koine, or Hellenistic Greek, "is not confined to the vernacular speech. There was a flourishing *koinē* literature in the centuries before and after the time of Christ."[9] It was this language that was most widely known throughout the world: its alphabet was derived from the Phoenicians, its language and culture were not limited to a given geographical area, it became the official language of the empires into which Alexander's conquests were divided, and even the Romans used Greek in their literature as fluently as they did Latin. Koine Greek was not a special "Holy Ghost" language, but its appearance was certainly providentially directed, as Paul implied in his statement "When the fulness of the time came, God sent forth His Son" (Gal. 4:4).

Why God Chose These Languages

Now that the background and development of the biblical languages have been traced, it remains to examine how they fit God's purpose of revelation. What was it that made these languages, above others, particularly appropriate channels for God's truth? In theorizing about this point, it would be imprudent to overlook a very practical purpose for God's choice of both major and minor languages, namely, they were the primary languages of the times and the people to whom God was speaking.

Minor Languages

Aramaic. This language, which shows influence in both vocabulary and form in the New Testament, was the local language of the land of Palestine and much of Syria when Jesus and the apostles lived and ministered. It was no doubt the language that Jesus used in day-to-day conversation.[10] Furthermore,

9. Ibid., p. 65, but also see his entire chapter, entitled "The Greek Language," pp. 58-73, as well as the discussion in chap. 23.
10. Some have argued that the gospels were originally written in Aramaic (cf. C. C. Torrey, *The Four Gospels* [New York: Harper, 1933]). Although certain others have shared that view, there are serious objections against it. W. F. Albright has pointed out that "there is absolutely no trace so far of a continuous Aramaic literary tradition spanning the interval between the Achaemenian and earliest Hellenistic period on the one hand, and the second century A.D. on the other" ("Recent Discoveries in Palestine and the Gospel of St. John," p. 155). Besides the fact that there has been no objective evidence for the existence of Aramaic originals of the gospels, the view is rendered improbable by the broad Greek constituency of the early church, as well as by the commission of Christ that His followers take the gospel into all the world. Greek, and not Aramaic, was the only language spoken throughout the Mediterranean world.

Aramaic had been the lingua franca of the Near East in the sixth through fourth centuries B.C., until the conquests of Alexander the Great. This was the language of the documents, mostly papyri, left by the Jewish colony at Elephantine (near modern Aswan, Egypt) during the fifth century B.C.

Latin. On the other hand, Latin, which made its influence felt in the New Testament,was the military and political language of the Roman Empire. The Empire included Herod's Palestine; and it was only natural that the New Testament would include the use of Latin and Latinisms to some degree.

Major Languages

It would be too much to suppose, however, that Hebrew and Greek, the major biblical languages, were chosen by God because they just happened to be the ones available when He decided to speak to man. The Christian theist who believes in special as well as general providence will expect that God planned the very languages to fit the message and the age to which the message was addressed. On this assumption, an inquiry into these purposes may be briefly pursued.

Hebrew: its biographical suitability. The Old Testament is primarily the biography of a people and God's dealings with them. Hebrew was the primary language in which the Old Testament was written, and it was particularly suited for this kind of biographical expression for at least two reasons.

1. It is a *pictorial* language, speaking with vivid, bold metaphors that challenge and dramatize the story. The Hebrew language possesses a facility to present "pictures" of the events narrated. "The Hebrew thought in pictures, and consequently his nouns are concrete and vivid." In addition, "Compound words are lacking.... There is no wealth of adjectives...."[11] The language shows "vast powers of association and, therefore, of imagination."[12] Some of this is lost in the English translation, but even so, "much of the vivid, concrete, and forthright character of our English Old Testament is really a carrying over into English of something of the genius of the Hebrew tongue."[13] As a pictorial language, Hebrew presents a vivid picture of the acts of God among a people who became examples or illustrations for future generations (cf. 1 Cor. 10:11). Because the Old Testament was intended as a biographical book for believers, it was fitting for those truths to be presented graphically in a "picture-language."

2. Further, Hebrew is a *personal* language. It addresses itself to the heart and emotions rather than merely to the mind or reason. Sometimes even

11. Elmer W. K. Mould, *Essentials of Bible History,* p. 307.
12. Mary Ellen Chase, *Life and Language in the Old Testament,* p. 87.
13. Bruce, p. 45.

nations are given personalities (cf. Mal. 1:2-3). Always the appeal is to the person in the concrete realities of life and not to the abstract or theoretical. Hebrew is a language through which the message is felt rather than thought. As such, the language was highly qualified to convey to the individual believer as well as to the worshiping community the personal revelation of the living God in the events of the Jewish nation. It was much more qualified to record the realization of revelation in the life of a nation than to propositionalize that revelation for the propagation among all nations. F.F. Bruce sums up these characteristics well:

> Biblical Hebrew does not deal with abstractions but with the facts of experience. It is the right sort of language for the record of the self-revelation of a God who does not make Himself known by philosophical propositions but by controlling and intervening in the course of human history. Hebrew is not afraid to use daring anthropomorphisms when speaking of God. If God imparts to men the knowledge of Himself, He chooses to do so most effectively in terms of human life and human language.[14]

Greek: its evangelistic suitability. The foundation of God's revelation of Christ was laid in the biography of the Old Testament. The interpretation of the revelation of Christ was made in the theological language of the New Testament. New Testament Greek was appropriately adapted to the end of propositionalizing and propagating the truth about Christ for two basic reasons.

1. Greek was an *intellectual* language. It was more a language of the mind than of the heart, a fact to which the great Greek philosophers gave abundant evidence. Greek was more suited to codifying a communication or reflecting on a revelation of God in order to put it into simple communicable form. It was a language that could more easily render the credible into the intelligible than could Hebrew. It was for this reason that New Testament Greek was a most useful medium for expressing the propositional truth of the New Testament, as Hebrew was for expressing the biographical truth of the Old Testament. Because Greek possessed a technical precision not found in Hebrew, the theological truths that were more generally expressed in the Hebrew of the Old Testament were more precisely formulated in the Greek of the New Testament.

2. Furthermore, Greek was a nearly *universal* language. The truth of God in the Old Testament, which was initially revealed to one nation (Israel), was appropriately recorded in the language of that nation (Hebrew). But the fuller revelation given by God in the New Testament was not restricted in that way. In the words of Luke's gospel, the message of Christ was to "be proclaimed in His name to all nations" (Luke 24:47). The language

14. Ibid.

most appropriate for the propagation of that message was naturally the one that was most widely spoken throughout the world. Such was the common (Koine) Greek, a thoroughly international language of the first-century Mediterranean world.

It may be concluded, then, that God chose the very languages to communicate His truth which had, in His providence, been prepared to express most effectively the kind of truth He desired at that particular time, in the unfolding of His overall plan. Hebrew, with its pictorial and personal vividness, expressed well the biographical truth of the Old Testament. Greek, with its intellectual and universal potentialities, served well for the doctrinal and evangelistic demands of the New Testament.

Summary and Conclusion

The written word, with all of its limitations, was by far the most adequate means of conveying the truth of God because it could be more precisely presented, more easily preserved from corruption, and more effectively propagated. Therefore, when God—who spoke to the prophets by visions, dreams or angels—desired to speak through the prophets to succeeding generations, He chose to have them *write* their revelation. In the providence of God the Hebrew and Greek languages were prepared to express most appropriately the kind of revelation God desired for their particular days. Hebrew is a language well fitted to depict God's deeds in the biography of the Old Testament, and Greek is particularly suited to the expression and propagation of the doctrines of the New Testament.

19
Writing Materials

Before proceeding to the mechanics of transmission, it is needful to consider the materials used by the men of God in their communication of the message of God. This study involves the development of writing, the description of materials, and the divisions of the text in order to make it more usable.

The Development of Writing

The Old Testament has nothing to say about the origin of writing, which seems to have been invented early in the fourth millennium B.C.,[1] but it does assume writing on the part of Moses,[2] who wrote the Law not earlier than about 1450 B.C.[3] Many earlier records of writing have been discovered in various places. But, what was the character of those records? Were they drawings? Symbols? If so, what did they symbolize?

Advances in the Development of Writing

Three stages in the development of writing may be discerned: pictograms, ideograms, and phonograms.

Pictograms. These were representations that long antedated the origin of writing and played a role in the development of it. They were actually crude pictures that represented objects such as the sun, an old man, an eagle, an ox, a lion. As long as pictograms represented nothing other than the objects themselves, there was no difficulty in using them. However, as time passed the use of pictures to depict ideas appeared, and pictograms lost their dominant position in recorded communication.

Ideograms. Ideograms superseded pictograms. They were pictures that actually represented ideas rather than objects. Here the picture of the sun might represent heat; an old man might represent old age; an eagle, power; an

1. See Samuel Noah Kramer, *History Begins at Sumer,* or any basic up-to-date work on the subject of writing in Sumer and/or Egypt.
2. F. F. Bruce, *The Books and the Parchments,* p. 15.
3. See for example, Alan R. Millard, "The Practice of Writing in Ancient Israel," *Biblical Archaeologist* 35:4 (December 1972): 98-111.

ox, strength; a lion, regality. Thus, a long stride toward writing was taken, although writing in the modern sense was still a long way off. But ideograms, actually a particular use of pictograms, were not the only extension of pictograms.

Phonograms. Still another extension of pictograms, phonograms were really representations of sounds rather than objects or ideas. Thus, a representation of the sun might speak of a son rather than the sun; a picture of a bear might be used to express "the verb 'to bear'; the picture of a bee to express the verb 'to be.' "[4] As a result, another step was taken in the direction of written languages, but there was still a long succession of events necessary before writing in the modern sense was achieved.

Ideographic and phonographic writings were later intermingled with simple syllabic writing, and that with a more sophisticated system of cuneiform, wedge-shaped signs was used by the Sumerians. Merrill F. Unger adequately summarizes the situation:

> Those who first attempted to reduce human speech to writing did not at once perceive the chasm that separates the spoken words from the characters in which they are symbolized. They wrote as they spoke in unbroken succession, inscribing the letters in closest proximity to each other, without separating them into words, much less into sentences, paragraphs and chapters.[5]

Although letters were used in writing by the time of Moses, they were consonants only, as vowels were added much later. Hence, an unbroken succession of consonants covering an entire tablet, later a scroll, and still later a codex (sheets of papyrus bound into a book form) would appear before the reader of a given text. Needless to say, even that was still far from the modern concept of writing.

Age of Writing

Although the witnesses to writing in antiquity are far from abundant, there is sufficient evidence available to indicate that it was the hallmark of cultural achievement. During the second millennium B.C. there were several experiments that led to the development of the alphabet and written documents. In Palestine itself there have been very few documents that have survived from the preexilic period, but the evidence from surrounding territories makes it reasonable to assume that the Israelites shared in the act of writing even earlier than the beginning of the Davidic kingdom. Several lines of evidence may be called upon to witness to the fact that writing was most certainly practiced by the Israelites prior to the time of the Moabite Stone of Mesha, king of Moab, which dates from about 850 B.C. It was this item that was used

4. Bruce, p. 23.
5. Merrill F. Unger, *Introductory Guide to the Old Testament,* p. 115.

5. *Cuneiform (Assyrian) inscription in stone from the palace of King Sargon II, eighth century* B.C. *(The Louvre)*

by the late-nineteenth-century higher critical writers, for example, Graf and Wellhausen, as the earliest example of writing in Palestine. As a matter of fact, the negative higher critical view was formulated prior to the discovery of the material discussed below. The testimony of these discoveries overwhelmingly disproves that position.

Evidence from Mesopotamia. This dates from about 3500 B.C. and includes cuneiform tablets of the Sumerians. The successors to the Sumerians used the latter's cuneiform script in developing their own individual languages.[6] Leonard Woolley discovered many temple tablets in the ruins of ancient Ur of the Chaldees that date from about 2100 B.C.; however, they are antedated by many other tablets, including some dating to about 3500 B.C. found in Uruk (the Erech of Gen. 10:10) and Kish. The Sumerian flood narrative found at Nippur dates from about 2100 B.C.

Egyptian discoveries. These confirm those found in Mesopotamia, and they are dated about 3100 B.C. The hieroglyphic script first appeared in Egypt just prior to the founding of Dynasty I (c. 3100 B.C.), whereas its successors, the hieratic and demotic scripts, both appeared prior to the exilic period in

6. Bruce, pp. 9-21, for a discussion on the whole problem of alphabets, languages, etc. Also see Sir Frederic G. Kenyon, *Our Bible and the Ancient Manuscripts,* pp. 3-15; P. Kyle McCarter, "The Early Diffusion of the Alphabet," *Biblical Archaeologist* 37:3 (December 1974): 54-68.

Israel's history. Among the early Egyptian writings are *The Teachings for Kagemni* and *The Teaching of Ptah-Hetep,* which date from about 2700 B.C. There are, in addition to those witnesses, other testimonies that illustrate the use of writing in Egypt prior to the time of Moses, Joseph, and even Abraham, regardless of the dates ascribed to each of those individuals. Furthermore, the Israelites must have been aware of writing techniques prior to their exodus from Egypt, for Moses was raised as a child with great position in the household of the pharaoh during the New Kingdom period. The New Testament record indicates the Hebrew traditional position, as Stephen bears witness in his famous sermon when he relates that "Moses was educated in all the learning of the Egyptians, and he was a man of power in words and deeds" (Acts 7:22). That learning most likely included writing on papyrus, as papyrus was used in writing earlier than Dynasty V (c. 2500 B.C.).

East Mediterranean testimony. Evidence from about 2500 B.C., shows that pictographic signs were used in Byblos (Gebal) and Syria. As early as about 3100 B.C. there was writing used on cylinder seal impressions in Byblos. Leonard Woolley's discoveries at Atchana (in northern Syria) appear to have been contemporaneous to the records found by Sir Arthur Evans at Knossos, Crete. These records date into the mid-second millennium B.C., and they indicate that connection between the mainland of Asia and the island bridge of Europe, namely, Crete.

Early Palestinian and Syrian contributions. From 1947 to 1976, excavations at Tell-Mardikh (ancient Elba) south of Aleppo in northern Syrian uncovered over 15,000 clay tablets inscribed in the cuneiform script with an early northwest Semitic dialect of c. 2300 B.C. The tablets are from the time of the Babylonian king Naram-Sin (equated by some with Nimrod of Gen. 10:9) who campaigned in the area. Included among the tablets are portions of the Epic of Gilgamesh and other kinds of literature from later Syria (Ugarit). Thus they attest to an early literary tradition, as already well known from Babylonia. In addition, they have caused Old Testament scholars to reevaluate the accuracy of the Bible patriarchs as well as names and events recorded in Genesis. Mitchell Dahood provides specific examples of clarification of the Hebrew text from Eblaic evidence in his article "Ebla, Ugarit, and the Bible."[7]

7. Mitchell Dahood, "Afterword: Ebla, Ugarit, and the Bible," pp. 271-321. See also D. J. Wiseman, "Archeology and the Old Testament," p. 314. Additional information may be obtained from Ignace J. Gelb, "Thoughts About Elba: A Preliminary Evaluation, March 1977," pp. 1-30. Also see Robert Biggs, "The Ebla Tablets: An Interim Perspective," pp. 76-86; as well as the "Elba Update" articles in *Biblical Archaeology Review,* 1977 ff.; and Eugene Merrill, "Ebla and Biblical Historical Inerrancy," and Chaim Bermant and Mitchell Weitzman, *Ebla: An Archaeological Enigma*. Edwin M. Yamauchi, "Unearthing Ebla's Ancient Secrets," pp. 18-21, brings the account up to date and includes some observations about the controversy that has arisen between Paolo Matthiae, *Ebla: An Empire Rediscovered;* and Giovanni Pettinato, *The Archives at Ebla: An Empire Inscribed in Clay.*

6. *The Moabite Stone. Oriental Institute Museum cast C2, taken from the original Museeé du Louvre AO 5066 (Courtesy of The Oriental Institute of The University of Chicago)*

In addition, alphabetic inscriptions from the turquoise mines in southern Sinai date from about 1500 B.C. A pottery fragment from Gezer is dated from about 1800 to 1500 B.C.; the Lachish dagger inscription is contemporary, as are inscriptions from Shechem, Beth-Shemesh, Hazor, and Tel el-Hesi. The Ras Shamra tablets, from the coastal site in northwest Syria identified as Ugarit, date from about 1500 to 1300 B.C. There they employed the same diplomatic language as the Tel el-Amarna tablets (c. 1380 B.C.) from the ancient Egyptian capital of Amenhotep IV (Akhenaton). At Ras Shamra were also found specimens of the Canaanite language written in alphabetic form. Those writings were made by inscribing unique cuneiform signs on clay tablets, known as the Ugaritic tablets (see chap. 18).

All of the above evidence is extant from the period prior to the Moabite Stone of Mesha, king of Moab. The event recorded on the Moabite Stone is that revolt against Israel recorded in 2 Kings 1:1 and 3:4-27. Although the preceding evidence is not direct, it is overwhelming in its denunciation of the negative higher critical position. It is also overwhelming in its demarcation of the history of writing before the time of Moses. As a result, the more than 450 biblical references to writing may be seen as reflective of the cultural diffusion between Israel and her neighbors.

Activity of Biblical Writers Within Literate History

The foregoing discussion makes the assertion that "Moses and the other biblical writers wrote during the literate age of man" almost redundant. Nevertheless, the biblical record itself asserts that its writers wrote. Several of the more 450 biblical references may be called upon to indicate this fact.

The Law. The *Torah* (Law) makes reference to several kinds of writing done by Moses and his predecessors (cf. Gen. 5:1[8]; Ex. 17:14; 24:4; 34:27-28; Num. 17:2-3; Deut. 31:9, 19, 22, 24).

The Prophets. The Prophets (*Nevi'im*) indicate that writing was employed by several individuals even prior to the time of the Moabite Stone (cf. Josh. 8:30-34; 18:4-9; 24:26; Judg. 8:14; 1 Sam. 10:25), which further militates against the negative higher critical view.

The Writings. These *Kethuvím* (Writings) also relate that individuals were writing before the time of the Moabite insurrection recorded in 2 Kings 1:1 and 3:4-27 (cf. Prov. 1:1 with 22:20; 2 Chron. 35:4).

The Description of Materials and Instruments

Writing Materials

The materials upon which the ancients wrote were also used by the writers of Scripture. Several of these items may be indicated.

Clay. Clay was not only used in ancient Sumer as early as about 3500 B.C., but it was used by Jeremiah (17:13) and Ezekiel (4:1). This material would be inscribed while it was still damp or soft. It would then be either dried in the sun or baked in a kiln to make a permanent record.

8. The clause "this is the account of" or "the book of the generations of" occurs twelve times in Genesis and probably indicates the divisions of early family records of the patriarchs; cf. Gen. 2:4; 5:1; 6:9; 10:1, 31; 11:10, 27; 25:12-13, 19; 36:1, 9; 37:2.

Stone. This was used in Mesopotamia, Egypt, and Palestine, as is evidenced by the Code of Hammurabi, the Rosetta Stone, and the Moabite Stone. The biblical writers also made use of stone as a writing material (cf. Ex. 24:12; 31:18; 32:15-16; 34:1, 28; Deut. 5:22; 27:2-3; Josh. 8:31-32). Also, at the Dog River in Lebanon and at Behistun in Iran royal inscriptions were carved on cliff faces.

Papyrus. Papyrus was used in ancient Gebal (Byblos) and Egypt from about 3100 B.C. It was made by pressing and gluing two layers of split papyrus reeds together in order to form a sheet. A series of papyrus sheets were joined together to form a scroll. It is that type of papyrus "scroll" that is mentioned in Revelation 5:1 (though it is translated "book" in NASB). The apostle John used papyrus for his epistles (cf. 2 John 12).

Vellum, parchment, leather. These are various quality grades of writing material made from animal skins of calf or antelope, sheep or goat, and cow or bull, respectively. Although these substances are not mentioned directly as writing materials in the Bible, some kind of animal skin may have been in mind in Jeremiah 36:23. It could hardly have been vellum, for Frederic Kenyon has indicated that vellum was not known prior to about 200 B.C.[9] Most likely it was leather, for the king used a knife on it. Parchments are, on the other hand, clearly mentioned in Paul's request to Timothy (2 Tim. 4:13). The chief difference in the use of these materials seems to be that leather was prepared for writing on *one* side only (as a scroll), whereas parchment or vellum was prepared on *both* sides (as in a codex).

Miscellaneous items. Writing also was done in the biblical narrative upon such things as metal (Ex. 28:36; Job 19:24; Matt. 22:19-20); a wooden writing board recessed to hold a wax writing surface (cf. Isa. 8:1; 30:8; Hab. 2:2; Luke 1:63); precious stones (Ex. 28:9, 11, 21; 39:6-14); and potsherds (Job 2:8), better known as ostraca, as found in such locations as Samaria and Lachish in Palestine. Still another item used in ancient writing in Egypt, Greece, Etruscan and Roman Italy, but not mentioned in the Bible, was linen.

Writing Instruments

Several different instruments were necessary in the production of written records on the various materials mentioned above:

Stylus. A three-sided instrument with a beveled head, the stylus was used to make incursions into clay and wax tablets. It was sometimes called a "pen," as in Jeremiah 17:1.

Chisel. A chisel was used in making inscriptions in stone, as in Joshua 8:31-32. Job wished that his words might be engraved with "an iron stylus" in the rock forever (Job 19:24).

9. Kenyon, pp. 43 f.

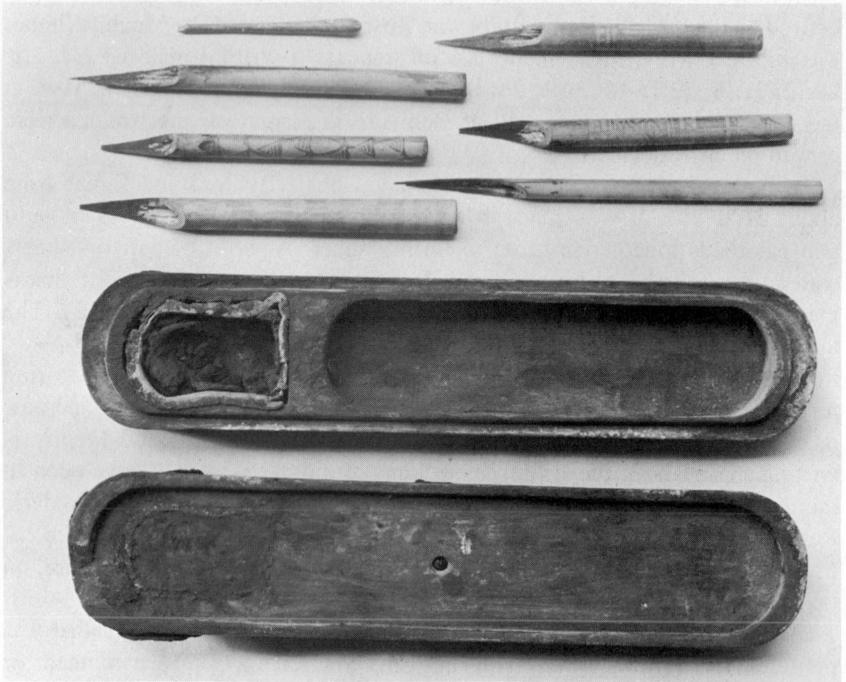

7. *Ancient writing equipment from Egypt. Biblical writers may have used something similar (Reproduced by courtesy of the Trustees of the British Museum)*

Pen. A pen was employed in writing on papyrus, vellum, leather, and parchment, as indicated in 3 John 13.

Penknife. This was used in Jeremiah 36:23 to destroy a scroll, the material of which was probably tougher than papyrus. It was also used to sharpen the writer's pen after it had begun to wear down.

Inkhorn and ink. These were necessary concomitants of the pen, and they served as the container and fluid used for writing on papyrus, vellum, leather, and parchment. Thus, just as writing and its materials were available for the biblical writers, so were the instruments necessary for their vital task.

The Divisions of the Text

Writing material and instruments were the means by which revelation could be expressed in the media of language. However, the ancients for the most part felt no need for dividing the text into such smaller and meaningful units as chapters, paragraphs, or verses. These divisions came into being much later than the time when the Scriptures began to be preserved in written form. Because the procedure of textual division did not take place in both Testaments simultaneously, each will be treated separately before they are observed jointly.

The Old Testament

Chapters (sections). There were apparently some divisions in the autographs of the Old Testament: for example, the book of Lamentations and Psalm 119,[10] which are indicated by the use of the letters of the Hebrew alphabet. These cases are not numerous but they do reflect at least some natural divisions in the Hebrew text.

1. *Palestinian sections* were begun prior to the Babylonian captivity (586 B.C.), and consisted of 154 sections for the Pentateuch. These sections were called *sedarim (seder,* singular), and were designed to provide lessons sufficient to cover a three-year cycle of reading.[11]

2. *Babylonian sections* appeared during the captivity (prior to 536 B.C.), when the Torah was divided into fifty-four sections called *parashiyyoth (parashah,* singular). These were later subdivided into 669 sections for reference purposes. These sections were utilized for a single-year cycle.

3. *Maccabean sections* appeared during the period at about 165 B.C. These fifty-four sections, corresponding with the *sedarim* of the Law, covered the Prophets and were called *haphtarahs.*

4. *Reformation sections.* After the Protestant Reformation, the Hebrew Bible for the most part followed the same chapter divisions as the Protestant Old Testament. These divisions were first placed in the margins in 1330. They were printed into the text of the *Complutensian Polyglot* (1517), and the text was divided in the edition of Arias Montanus (1571).

Verses.

1. *Ancient verse* indications were merely spaces between words, as the words were run together continuously through a given book. Each book was separate, and there were no vowel points until the Masoretes added them (fifth to tenth century A.D.). After the Babylonian captivity, for the purpose of public reading and interpretation, space stops were employed, and still later additional markings were added. These "verse" markings were not regulated, and differed from place to place. It was not until about A.D. 900 that the markings were standardized.

10. W. Graham Scroggie, *Know Your Bible,* 1:122-23.
11. H. S. Miller, *A General Biblical Introduction,* p. 165, seems to imply that this sectioning was not the earliest; he favors making the *parashiyyoth (parashah)* antedate it instead. However, Bruce, p. 121, indicates the view followed in the text.

2. *Reformation verse indications* appeared in the sixteenth century. In the Bomberg edition (1547), every fifth verse was indicated; in 1571 Montanus indicated each verse in the margin for the first time.

The New Testament

Ancient sections. The autographs of the New Testament were undoubtedly written in an unbroken manner, similar to the Old, especially since they consisted mostly of shorter books than the gospels and Acts. However, there was an early sectioning that took place, and it is commonly referred to as the old Greek division into paragraphs (*kephalaia*). These divisions appeared prior to the Council at Nicea (325), and differed from modern chapter divisions; for example, Matthew 2:1-15 (1); 2:16-23 (2); 3:1—4:16 (3); 4:17-22 (4).[12] During the fourth century, the Codex Vaticanus (B) utilized another system of marking sections, for example, Matthew 1:1-5 (1); 1:6-11 (2); 1:12-16 (3); 1:17 (4); 1:18-23 (5); 1:24-25 (6). In total there were 170 sections in Matthew, 62 in Mark, 152 in Luke, and 50 in John. That system is not completely known today, as the Vaticanus manuscript is broken off at Hebrews 9:14. As a result, only the *kephalaia* markings down to that point are known. "Another system of chapter divisions is found in Codex Alexandrinus (A) of the fifth century as well as in most other Greek manuscripts. According to this capitulation in Matthew there are 68 *kephalaia,* in Mark 48, in Luke 83, and in John 18.[13] The historian Eusebius of Caesarea attempted still another means of sectioning the New Testament. He devised a system of short paragraphs, which he cross-referenced on a series of tables, for the gospels. Those paragraphs were longer than modern verses but shorter than current chapters. In his work, Mathew had 335 sections, Mark had 233 (later changed to 241), Luke had 342, and John 232.[14]

Modern sections.

1. *The English New Testament.* It was not until the thirteenth century that those sections were changed, and then only gradually. Stephen Langton, a professor at the University of Paris and afterward Archbishop of Canterbury, divided the Bible into the modern chapter divisions (c. 1227).[15] That was prior to the introduction of movable type in printing. Since the Wycliffe Bible (1382) followed that pattern, those basic divisions have been the virtual base upon which the Bible has been printed to this very

12. Eberhard Nestle, *Novum Testamentum Graece (Editio vicesima quinta),* pp. 82-83, of his introduction, explains its markings of these old Greek paragraphs (*kephalaia*) and the old Greek descriptive headings (*titloi*) in its apparatus.
13. Bruce M. Metzger, *The Text of the New Testament, Its Transmission, Corruption, and Restoration,* p. 22.
14. Miller, p. 165, is apparently incorrect in his tabulations at this point. For the correct totals see Nestle, pp. 82-83 in his introduction.

day, as the Wycliffe Bible has been basic to subsequent versions and translations.

2. *The Latin New Testament (Vulgate)*. The Vulgate New Testament was printed by Gutenberg in 1456 and is known as the Mazarin Bible. This edition followed the thirteenth-century chapter divisions and paved the way for such sectioning in the Rheims-Douay Version (1581-1609), which became the authoritative English edition by decree of Pope Sixtus V in 1585. The only major revision it experienced was by Bishop Challoner (1691-1781).

3. *The Greek New Testament*. This was first printed in 1516, by Desiderius Erasmus. It was done in an effort to beat Cardinal Ximenes to the market, as the latter's work was already printed but bogged down in ecclesiastical machinery in the matter of publication. Erasmus followed the chapter divisions of the Mazarin Bible (1456) and therefore gave the same chapter divisions to the Protestant world that Mazarin gave to the Catholics. That provided a valuable common ground for cross-references of biblical texts between Catholics and Protestants.

Modern verses. These were actually developed later than the chapters, apparently in an effort to further facilitate cross-references and make public reading easier. The markings first occur in the fourth edition of the Greek New Testament published by Robert Stephanus, a Parisian printer, in 1551. These verses were introduced into the English New Testament by William Whittingham of Oxford in 1557.[16] In 1555, Stephanus introduced his verse divisions into a Latin Vulgate edition, from which they have continued to the present day.

The Whole Bible

Latin Vulgate. The first Bible to use both the modern chapter and verse divisions was the Latin Vulgate edition of Robert Stephanus (1555). He had previously used those divisions in his Greek New Testament (1551).

Geneva Bible. The first English Bible to incorporate both the modern chapter and verse divisions was the Geneva Bible (1560). It was actually done

15. The traditional view has been stated in the text, but others have held that Cardinal Hugo of St. Cher (d. 1263) was the pioneer in this effort, in the preparation of a concordance (c. 1244). Cf. Kenyon, p. 190, for the former view; Bruce, p. 121, for the latter. Miller, pp. 10-11, presents both views. M. H. Black, "The Printed Bible," in S. L. Greenslade, ed., *The Cambridge History of the Bible,* 2:419, avoids the problem altogether by saying, "The chapters had always been divided in printed Bibles; the division itself, Berger says, dates from the thirteenth century."
16. F. F. Bruce, *The English Bible: A History of Translations,* pp. 85-86, indicates that Whittingham was married to John Calvin's sister (or sister-in-law), and succeeded John Knox as the pastor of the English church in Geneva; hence, his influential position in the preparation of the Geneva Bible (1560).

in two parts: in 1557, the New Testament was done by Whittingham, as a stopgap measure, and, in 1560, the entire Bible was completed in the same tradition. It employed modern chapter and verse divisions, and even introduced italicized words into the text where English idiom required fuller treatment than a simple Greek translation. More of that is considered later. It is sufficient to note here that the Bible had attained its "modern" character before the translation work of either the Rheims-Douay or the so-called "authorized" versions of the Bible.

Summary and Conclusion

A brief history of the development of writing indicates a progressive development from pictograms, through ideograms, to phonograms, before the time of the biblical writers. Hence, the Bible is correct in assuming the development of writing; and the late nineteenth-century view that Moses and others lived in preliterate history is totally unfounded in the light of modern archaeological discoveries, namely, from Mesopotamia, Egypt, Western Asia, Crete, and even Palestine. With the development of writing, there must have been a development of writing materials and instruments. Those too appeared in ample time to be utilized in the recording of divine revelation.

The divisions of the autographs were quite different from those of modern Bibles; a survey of the divisions of the record reveals that the process began over a half millennium before the earthly ministry of Christ and took almost two millennia to come to its current form. The divisions, it has been shown, are *not of divine origin,* but are rather the efforts of man to "find his way" more adequately through that revelation which *is* of divine origin.[17] It was also indicated that the period that evidenced a rise in opposition to papal authority had, as a concomitant, the rise in making the Bible a more practically workable source of authority. Most of the innovations were well established before the translation of either the Rheims-Douay or the so-called "authorized" versions of the Bible.

17. Archibald T. Robertson, *An Introduction to the Textual Criticism of the New Testament,* p. 100, states accordingly, "The first step in interpretation is to ignore the modern chapters and verses."

20
Manuscript Transmission, Preparation, and Preservation

In order to appreciate fully the total process by which the Bible was transmitted from the first to the twentieth century, certain mechanical items must be discussed (e.g., preparation, age, and preservation of manuscripts). Along with these technical matters of transmission, certain definitions are basic to the understanding of this crucial "link" in the chain "from God to us." The following discussion is an overview of the next several chapters (21-26) and is intended as an introduction to the whole subject of transmission and translation (chaps. 27-32).

The Process of Transmission

Genuineness and Authenticity Distinguished

As the terms *authority* and *canonicity* were basic to Sections 1 and 2, the words *genuineness* and *authenticity* are fundamental to this third section. Unfortunately, there is some confusion about the meaning of these terms, as their usage is somewhat interchangeable in theological circles.

Genuineness. As used here, genuineness refers to the truth of the *origin* of a document, that is, its authorship. It answers the question, Is this document really from its alleged source or author? Is it genuinely the work of the stated writer? As such, genuineness is primarily the subject of Special Introduction, which on the whole deals with such things as the authorship, date, and destiny of the biblical books. General Introduction, on the other hand, is concerned with the topics of authority, canonicity, and authenticity.

Authenticity. This refers to the truth of the facts and *content* of the documents of the Bible. Authenticity deals with the integrity (trustworthiness) and credibility (truthfulness) of the record. A book may be genuine without being authentic, if the professed writer is the real one, even if the content is untrue. Then, again, a book may be authentic without being genuine, if the content is true but the professed writer is not the actual one. In such a case, the book would be called forged or spurious, regardless of the truthfulness or falsity of its content. Biblical books of course must be both genuine and authentic or they cannot be inspired, because in either case there would be a falsehood. However, General Introduction does not deal explicitly with genuineness (authorship); it deals with the integrity of the text based on its credibility and authority. It is assumed that a biblical book, which has divine authority, and hence credibility, and has been transmitted with integrity, will automatically have genuineness. If there be a lie in the book regarding its origin and/or authorship, how can its content be believed?

Guarantee of Authenticity (and Genuineness)

The whole chain of revelation must be examined in order to demonstrate with certainty that the fact and route of revelation are found in the history of the Bible known to Christians today. A complete chain "from God to us" will consist of the following necessary "links."

Deity. This is the first link in the chain of revelation. The existence of a God who desires to communicate Himself to man is the one irreducible axiom of this entire study. Evidence that there is such a God is the subject of theology and philosophy,[1] but this fact is assumed at this juncture.

Apostolicity. The next link is apostolicity. That God accredited and directed a group of men known as prophets and apostles to speak authoritatively for Him is the repeated claim of the biblical writers (see chaps. 3-4, 6; the evidence that what they wrote was God's Word is examined in chap. 11).

Canonicity. A somewhat parenthetic but necessary link is canonicity. It answers the historical question, Which are the inspired prophetic and apostolic books and how are they known? They are those books that were written by men of God, confirmed by acts of God, that came with the authority and power of God, that told the truth about God, man, and so on, and that were accepted and collected by the people of God (see chaps. 12-17).

Authority. The direct result of apostolicity is authority, as circumscribed by the limits of canonicity. The teaching of men who were divinely accredited for that purpose is divinely authoritative teaching. In that sense, authority is just a logical link, consequent upon apostolicity as apostolicity is, in turn, dependent upon deity, or, rather, upon God's desire to communicate to men.

Authenticity. Likewise, authenticity is the necessary result of authority, which is derived from apostolicity, deity, and so on. Whatever is spoken of God must be true, because God is the very standard of truth itself (cf. Heb. 6:18). The Scriptures are authentic (true in content) if they are the prophetic voice of God.

1. For a thorough defense of the standard arguments for the existence of God, see Stuart Cornelius Hackett, *The Resurrection of Theism*, William L. Craig, *The Existence of God*, and N. L. Geisler, *Christian Apologetics*.

Integrity. This is the historic evidence that links authenticity and credibility. Anything authentic or true is of course credible. The question is, Does the twentieth-century Bible possess integrity? To put it another way, Does it adequately and accurately reproduce the original apostolic writings known as the autographs?

1. *Autographs.* Sometimes these were inaccurately called "originals" and sometimes incorrectly defined as the original writing from the hand of an apostle or prophet. In reality the authentic apostolic writings produced under the direction and/or authorization of a prophet or apostle are the autographs.

   a. An autograph would not necessarily have to be written by an apostle's own hand. Paul often used a secretary (cf. Rom. 16:22), as did Jeremiah (cf. Jer. 36:27).

   b. Nor does an autograph necessarily have to be the "first edition" of a book. Jeremiah, for example, produced two editions of his scroll to Jehoiakim (cf. Jer. 36:28). Similarly, some students of the gospels have suggested that Mark may have had two editions.[2] In such cases both editions are inspired, but the latter supersedes the former in a supplementary and complementary sense, in somewhat the same way that the New Testament does the Old Testament.

2. *Ancient versions.* The autographs are not extant. (For a suggested reason as to why God permitted the autographs to perish, see pp. 43-44). So they must be reconstructed from early manuscripts and versions. The earliest Old Testament translation into Greek is the Septuagint (LXX) begun in Alexandria, Egypt, during the third century B.C. The earliest versions, or translations of the New Testament into other languages, for example, the Syriac and Latin, extend back to the threshold of the second century. They began to appear just over a generation from the time the New Testament was completed (see chaps. 27-28).

3. *Citations of the Fathers.* The corroborative quotations of the church Fathers from the first few centuries, totaling over 36,000, include almost every verse of the New Testament. Some of these citations begin in the first century, and they continue in an unbroken succession from that time (cf. chap. 24).

4. *Manuscript copies.* These were in Greek and extended practically to the first century in fragmentary form and to the third and fourth centuries in completed copies. The earliest manuscripts, known as uncials, were written in capital letters throughout. Later manuscripts, known as minuscules, were written in lower case letters or in flowing letters, cursives. Some manuscripts were written on scrolls and others as books,

2. Merrill C. Tenney, *New Testament Survey*, p. 157.

codex form, from which they are known as codices (chaps. 21-22).

5. *Modern versions.* The ancient manuscripts are the most important witnesses to the autographs and, by the method of textual criticism (chaps. 25-26), they form the basis for the modern versions of the Bible (chaps. 31-32). Some early modern versions were based on medieval versions (cf. chaps. 29-30); however, since the discoveries of the great manuscripts of the New Testament and other miscellaneous items, most recent versions and translations are based on the latter. These discoveries form the basis of the critical Greek text rather than the so-called Received Text used as the authority of the earlier modern versions. In the minds of most modern textual scholars, that so-called "critical" text represents an objective attempt to reconstruct the autographs. It is a scientific approach to the question of integrity, and it concludes that the present Greek text (after the Nestle/United Bible Societies Text) is probably over 99 percent accurate in reproducing the exact words of the autographs. Others maintain that the Received Text, or "Majority Text," is preferred. An extended discussion of the relative merits of the various textual traditions appears in chapters 25-26.

Credibility. The right to be believed—credibility—is based on the authenticity of the text. This, in turn, is founded upon divine authority, which is guaranteed by the ministry of the Holy Spirit and the integrity of the text.

1. *Objective credibility.* This is based on (1) the integrity of the text via the science of textual criticism, which yields a Bible that is probably over 99 percent trustworthy, or credible. (2) There is the objective evidence supplied by apologetics, which likewise confirms the Bible to be the Word of God (cf. chap. 11). (3) The providence of God and the witness of the Holy Spirit provide assurance to the believer that the chain is unbroken. They are the "welds" for what may seem to be "cracks" in the chain for critics who stress the weakness of the link of integrity that is only "probably" some "99 percent" sure, and not "actually" a full "100 percent" certain.

2. *Subjective assurance.* Before discussing the subjective assurance that welds together any potential cracks in the chain of the Bible's transmission, it should be emphasized that a 99 percent probability is as good as can be obtained by the historical method. Similar textual methods applied to other ancient documents yield a much lower percent of certitude (see chap. 25). (1) In fact, human beings do not require any more assurance for credibility. The game of life is played, and must be, quite often on much lower odds. (2) The providence of God, a characteristic that is

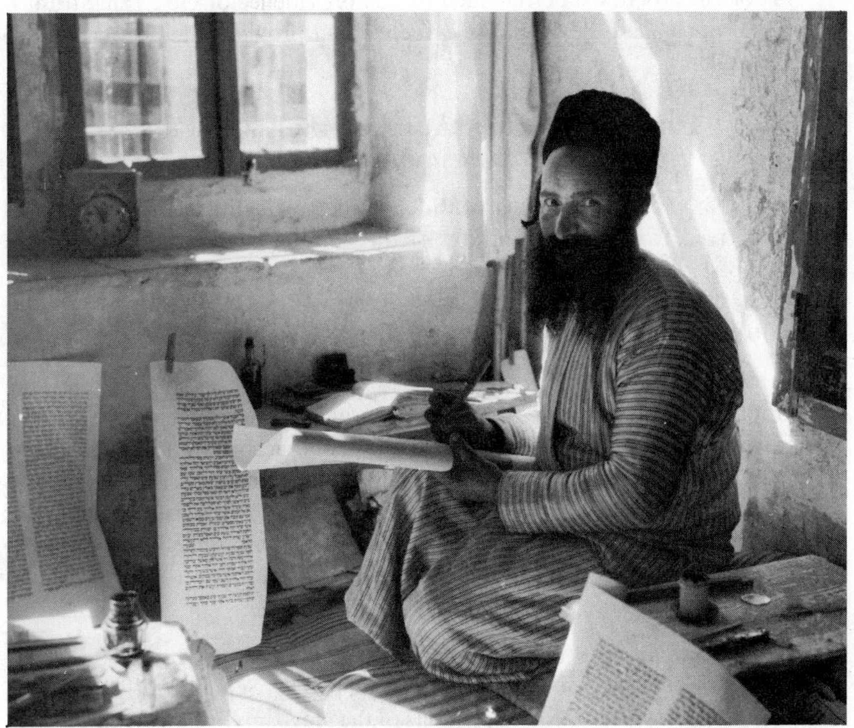

8. *An orthodox Jewish scribe in Jerusalem transcribing the Torah on parchment (The Matson Collection, The Episcopal Home)*

consonant with a self-revealing God, is the force that welds together the entire chain of communication. Any alleged "cracks" are welded by God, who providentially planned the process of communication and, therefore, is the One who perfects its product. The chain, then, has no real "cracks" because it is God who bonds it together. (3) Finally, there is, transcending the entire chain, the witness to the hearts of the children of God by the Spirit of God that the Bible is the Word of God. However, this subjective witness should not be used to "short circuit" the objective evidence; rather it is used to complete the circuit that brings the power and truth of God to man. History is replete with illustrations of the danger of mysticism as well as rationalism. Any attempt to bypass God's truth in its objective form, whether in its original oral form or its final written form, is doomed to the dismal dungeon of defeat. The Spirit of God speaks through the Word of God, and the Word of God has been transmitted by a historical process superintended by the providence of God. That truth is based upon the best objective evidence and provides the best subjective certitude.

The Preparation, Age, and Preservation of Manuscript Copies

Another factor that enhances confidence in the fidelity of the transmitted text is derived from a consideration of the copying and subsequent care of manuscripts.

The Preparation of Manuscript Copies

The Old Testament. Although it is impossible to fix with certainty the beginning of Hebrew writing, it was pre-Mosaic. Thus, from an early date the Scriptures were copied. These copies were made according to different criteria, depending on the purpose of the manuscript being copied. There are no manuscripts in existence dating from before the Babylonian captivity (586 B.C.), but there was a great flood of copies of the Scriptures dating from the Talmudic period (c. 300 B.C.-A.D. 500). During that period there were two general classes of manuscript copies.

1. *The synagogue rolls* were regarded as "sacred copies" of the Old Testament text and were used in public meeting places. Separate rolls contained the Torah (Law) on one roll, portions of the Nevi'im (Prophets) on another, the Kethuvim (Writings) on two others,[3] and the Megilloth ("five rolls") on five separate rolls. The Megilloth were no doubt produced on separate rolls to facilitate their being read at the annual feasts.[4] Strict rules were employed so that these rolls would be copied scrupulously. Samuel Davidson related these rules rather meticulously when he wrote,

> [1] A synagogue roll must be written on the skins of clean animals, [2] prepared for the particular use of the synagogue by a Jew. [3] These must be fastened together with strings taken from clean animals. [4] Every skin must contain a certain number of columns, equal throughout the entire codex. [5] The length of each column must not extend over less than 48 nor more than 60 lines; and the breadth must consist of thirty letters. [6] The whole copy must be first-lined; and if three words should be written without a line, it is worthless. [7] The ink should be black, neither red, green, nor any other colour, and be prepared according to a definite recipe. [8] An authentic copy

3. Three of these books were on one roll of poetry: Job, Psalms, and Proverbs; and three other books were on the other: Daniel, Ezra-Nehemiah, and Chronicles.
4. At the Passover, the Song of Songs was read; at Pentecost, it was Ruth; Tabernacles featured Ecclesiastes; Purim used Esther; and on the Anniversary of the Destruction of Jerusalem, Lamentations was read.

> must be the exemplar, from which the transcriber ought not in the least deviate. [9] No word or letter, not even a *yod,* must be written from memory, the scribe not having looked at the codex before him. . . . [10] Between every consonant the space of a hair or thread must intervene; [11] between every new *parashah,* or section, the breadth of nine consonants; [12] between every book, three lines. [13] The fifth book of Moses must terminate exactly with a line; but the rest need not do so. [14] Besides this, the copyist must sit in full Jewish dress, [15] wash his whole body, [16] not begin to write the name of God with a pen newly dipped in ink, [17] and should a king address him while writing that name he must take no notice of him.[5]

2. *The private copies* were regarded as "common copies" of the Old Testament text and were not used in public meetings. These rolls, although not governed by such strict rules as the synagogue rolls, were prepared with great care. They were frequently ornamented, often took a codex form, sometimes included marginal notes and commentaries. Because they were private copies, the desires of the purchaser were paramount in choosing such things as the size, material, form, and ink color. Seldom did an individual have a collection of scrolls that contained the entire Old Testament.

The New Testament. Although the autographs of the New Testament have long since disappeared, there is enough evidence to warrant the statement that those documents were written in rolls and books made of papyrus. The Old Testament had been copied into the "books and the parchments," but the New Testament was probably written on papyrus[6] between about A.D. 50 and 100.[7] During this period, papyrus rolls were used, and papyrus survived long periods of time only when placed in rather unusual circumstances. By the early second century, codices were introduced but they too were still generally made of papyrus.[8] As a by-product of the persecutions, culminating with the Edict of Diocletian in 302/3, the Scriptures were jeopardized and not systematically copied. It was with the Letter of Constantine to Eusebius (see chap. 16) that systematic copying of the New Testament began in the West. From that time, vellum and parchment were used along with the papyrus. It was not until the Reformation era that printed copies of the Bible became available.

The Age of Manuscripts

Because there was no printing process available at the time of manuscript copying of the Scriptures, the age of manuscripts must be determined by

5. Samuel Davidson, *The Hebrew Text of the Old Testament,* p. 89, as cited in James Hastings, ed., *A Dictionary of the Bible,* 4:949.
6. F. F. Bruce, *The Books and the Parchments,* rev. ed., pp. 176-77.
7. Sir Frederic G. Kenyon, *Our Bible and the Ancient Manuscripts,* pp. 98-102.
8. Papyrus was much less expensive to obtain than was vellum or parchment.

other means than a publisher's date. The process of dating is not nearly so accurate as finding the publication date printed on the title page of a modern book, but it is relatively accurate.

Materials. The materials of a given manuscript copy may provide the basis for discovering its date. Chapter 19 mentioned such materials as stone (not used for manuscripts), papyrus, vellum, parchment, and leather. For present purposes, only those materials that could be utilized in making rolls and/or books will be considered.

1. *Skins* were possibly the earliest materials used, and they were at first of coarse texture and made rather heavy, bulky rolls. These materials were used early in Hebrew history and led to refinements in the postcaptivity period.
2. *Papyrus rolls* were used in the New Testament period, largely because of their inexpensive character when compared with vellum and parchment.
3. *Papyrus codices* were introduced when attempts at collecting the individual rolls revealed that there was a need to make them less cumbersome to handle. Formerly each book or group of books was written on a single roll, but this multiplicity of rolls was replaced by codices in the early second century.
4. *Vellum* was prepared from animal skins, chiefly from lambs and young goats, and was rather costly. It was used for more expensive copies of manuscripts.
5. *Parchment* was used as early as the days of the New Testament composition (cf. 2 Tim. 4:13). Because there are various qualities of parchment and vellum writing material made from animal skins, they were often used during the same period of time. Codices of the two materials did not appear generally until after the Edict of Diocletian and were the primary materials used in manuscript copying in the Middle Ages.
6. *Redressed parchment* was used for copying manuscripts after the original writing had become faded. Sometimes parchments were "erased" and "rewritten," as in the case of the Codex Ephraemi Rescriptus (C), also known as a *palimpsest* (Greek, "rubbed again") *rescriptus* (Latin, "rewritten"). Needless to say, these manuscripts would be of a later date than the earlier text on the parchment.
7. *Paper* was invented in China in the second century A.D.; it was introduced into Eastern Turkestan as early as the fourth century, manufactured in Arabia in the eighth century,[9] introduced into Europe in the tenth century, manufactured in Europe in the twelfth century, and became common by

9. After the Arabs captured Samarkand (704); see *The Catholic Encyclopedia,* 9:615.

the thirteenth century. There were, of course, developments in the manufacture of paper, for example, with hemp, flax, linen, and rag content. Thus, the materials used in the manufacture of writing material on which manuscripts were copied assist in determining their age.

Letter size and form. Evidence is also provided by letter size and form for the date of a given manuscript. The earliest form of Hebrew writing was in the prong-like letters of the old Phoenician alphabet. This style prevailed until the return from the Babylonian captivity in Nehemiah's time (c. 444 B.C.).[10] After Nehemiah the Jews apparently adopted the Aramaic script, as it became the vernacular language during the fifth century B.C. At that time, the Hebrew Old Testament was translated into Aramaic; then, after about 200 B.C., it was copied in the square letters of Aramaic script. The square characters of extant manuscripts are not identical to those of that early period, but they are direct descendants.[11] The discovery of the Dead Sea Scrolls of Qumran in 1947 brought even more precision to the study of Hebrew paleography, as it has brought a large quantity of early biblical and nonbiblical manuscripts to light. These manuscripts have provided the first examples of Hebrew texts from pre-Christian times, a thousand years earlier than the oldest Hebrew Old Testament manuscripts previously available. The Qumran manuscripts reveal three main types of text and indicate differences in matters of spelling, grammatical forms and, to some extent, wording from the Masoretic text.[12] By the time of the Masoretes (c. A.D. 500-1000), the principles of the late Talmudic period (c. A.D.300-500) became rather stereotyped.[13]

Greek manuscripts were written in two general styles during the New Testament period: literary and nonliterary. The New Testament was probably written in nonliterary style. In fact, for the first three centuries, the New Testament was undoubtedly circulated outside the channels of ordinary book trade. Whereas the literary hand was well-rounded, graceful, and handsome, the nonliterary was smaller, square lettered, sprinkled with variants, and exhibited a general lack of literary exactness. The written repositories of Christian tradition were not plentiful during the first three centuries, and the records that were preserved included various oral and written traditions according to the individual interpreters involved in the given historical situation. Coupled with the tenuous position of the church prior to the time of Constantine's letter to Eusebius in the fourth century, the period of the establishment of the canon witnessed attempts at textual emendation and alteration according to the prevailing fashions or whims among scribes. Not until the late third or

10. Bruce, p. 22; also see Merrill F. Unger, *Introductory Guide to the Old Testament,* pp. 123-25.
11. Hastings, 4:949.
12. For further study of this matter see Millar Burrows, *More Light on the Dead Sea Scrolls,* and Frank Moore Cross, Jr., *The Ancient Library of Qumran and Modern Biblical Studies.*
13. Hastings, 4:949.

early fourth century were serious attempts at recension of the manuscripts actually tried with success, and those have left little direct historical evidence. These matters belong to the discipline of textual criticism and restoration, however, and require no further elaboration at this juncture. The style of writing was slow and laborious during the early centuries of the church, as the letters were capital (uncial),[14] written separately, and without breaks between words or sentences. Uncial manuscripts were copied through the tenth century; but before they became less prominent, a new form of writing was introduced into the field, which is called minuscule or cursive writing. By the tenth century, the demand for manuscript copies caused the more fluid cursive style to outstrip the cumbersome uncial style. Thus, by the golden age of manuscript copying, the eleventh through fifteenth centuries, this new running hand employing small and connected letters was the dominant form of manuscript copying. It was superseded in the fifteenth century by printed manuscripts, after the introduction of movable typeset by Johann Gutenberg.

During the centuries when handwriting underwent its gradual process of development, one form gave way to another almost imperceptibly. Considerable time is generally required to produce significant changes in the shapes of letters and the general appearance of the script. Bruce M. Metzger observes the quite marked differences in the average hand from about A.D. 900 to 1300. As time went on, there was a very great increase in the number of ligatures; there was a general decline in the minuscule hand as scribes apparently devoted less care to their handiwork and copied rapidly; considerable diversity developed in handwriting; and in some cases the writing became irregular, with letters that varied considerably in size. At the same time, the beginning of certain features or practices can be identified. For example, infralinear writing appeared as early as A.D. 917 and became common by the middle of the tenth century; however, the letters were sometimes still written on the line as late as 975. The shape of breathing marks changed from square to round shape between 1000 and 1300. In addition to the evolution of minuscule script there was an intrusion, in ever greater numbers, of uncial forms of certain letters which replaced the corresponding minuscule forms. Never-the-less, many scholars confess that it is extremely difficult to be confident in determining within narrow limits the date of a minuscule manuscript between 1050 and 1350. As a result, two considerations must be kept in mind when considering whether a manuscript is uncial or minuscule. (1) A scribe sometimes took an earlier hand as his model and produced an archaic script that was not characteristic of his time. (2) Because the style of a person's handwriting may remain more or less constant throughout his life, it is unrealistic to fix upon a date narrower than a fifty-year spread. As Metzger

14. "Uncial letters were an adaptation of the lapidary capitals used for inscriptions in stone, tablets, and the like; miniscule letters, as the name implies, were smaller and more akin to ordinary cursive hands." See chap. 22 discussion; Bruce, p. 182; and Kenyon, p. 15 n. 1.

observes, however, "in spite of the preceding caveats it still remains useful to attempt to date the handwriting of an undated manuscript by comparing it with dated manuscripts."[15]

Punctuation. Further light is added to the age of a given manuscript by its punctuation. At first, words were run together, and very little punctuation was used. "During the sixth and seventh centuries, scribes began to use punctuation marks more liberally."[16] The actual process of change proceeded from spaceless writing, to spaced writing, addition of end punctuation (periods), commas, colons, breath and accent marks (seventh-eighth centuries), interrogation marks, and so on. It was a long slow process that was rather complete by the tenth century, in time for the miniscules and the golden age of manuscript copying.

Text divisions. The text divisions into sections, chapters, and verses have been treated in chapter 19 and need only be mentioned at this point. It was not until the thirteenth century that modern chapter divisions appeared, and not until the sixteenth century that modern verses were introduced. But this development occurred prior to the mass distribution of the printed Bible, and it augmented the influence of the Rheims-Douay and King James Version of the English Bible.

Miscellaneous factors. Also involved in the dating of a given manuscript were such miscellaneous factors as the size and shape of letters within the uncial miniscule groupings of manuscripts.[17] Ornamentation is another factor in dating of manuscripts; from the fourth to the late ninth centuries the ornamentation of manuscripts became more elaborate in the uncial manuscripts. After that time, they became less ornate and less carefully copied. These factors helped to increase the popularity of the miniscules, which went through a similar development. Spelling was modified during the centuries, just as it is in living languages, and that helps date manuscripts. The color of the ink used is another important factor. At first only black ink was used, but green, red, and other colors were added later. Finally, the texture and color of parchment help date a manuscript. The means of parchment production changed, quality and texture were modified, and the aging process added another cause for color change in the material.

15. Bruce M. Metzger, *Manuscripts of the Greek Bible: An Introduction to Greek Paleography,* 49-51. Metzger indicates that Robert Devreesse, *Introduction a l'etude des manuscrits grecs,* pp. 286-320, has "a chronological list of several hundred dated Greek manuscripts, extending from about A.D. 512 to 1593." Also see Edward Maunde Thompson, *A Handbook of Greek and Latin Paleography.*
16. Bruce M. Metzger, *The Text of the New Testament,* p. 26; also see his book *en passim* for a fuller treatment of the subject of punctuation in manuscripts.
17. For a brief, thorough description of the changing character of writing in manuscripts, see Hastings, 4:953.

The Preservation of Manuscripts

Although manuscripts give information as to their date, and their quality is governed by their preparation, the preservation of given manuscripts adds vital support to their relative value for the textual critic and student of the Bible. That may be illustrated by a cursory treatment of manuscript preservation in general.

The Old Testament manuscripts. These manuscripts generally fall into two general periods of evidence.

1. *The Talmudic period* (c. 300 B.C.-A.D. 500) produced a great flood of manuscripts that were used in the synagogues and for private study. In comparison to the later Masoretic period, for the Temple and synagogues there were very few, but they were careful "official" copies. By the time of the Maccabean revolt (168 B.C.), the Syrians had destroyed most of the existing manuscripts of the Old Testament. The Dead Sea Scrolls (c. 167 B.C.-A.D. 133) have made an immense contribution to Old Testament critical study. There were many manuscript copies, confirming for the most part the textual tradition of the Masoretes (see chap. 21).
2. *The Masoretic period* (flourished c. A.D. 500-1000) of Old Testament manuscript copying indicates a complete review of established rules, a deep reverence for the Scriptures, and a systematic renovation of transmission techniques.

The New Testament manuscripts. New Testament manuscripts fall into four general periods of development.

1. *The first three centuries* witnessed a composite testimony as to the integrity of the New Testament Scriptures. Because of the illegal position of Christianity, it cannot be expected that many, if any, complete manuscripts from that period are to be found. Therefore, textual critics must be content to examine whatever evidence has survived, that is, nonbiblical papyri, biblical papyri, ostraca, inscriptions, and lectionaries that bear witness to the manuscripts of the New Testament (see chap. 21).
2. *The fourth and fifth centuries* brought a legalization of Christianity and a multiplication of manuscripts of the New Testament. These manuscripts, on vellum and parchment generally, were copies of earlier papyri and bear witness to this dependence (see chap. 22).
3. *From the sixth century onward,* monks collected, copied, and cared for New Testament manuscripts in the monasteries. This was a period of rather uncritical production, and it brought about an increase in manuscript quantity, but with a corresponding decrease in quality (see chap. 26).

4. *After the tenth century,* uncials gave way to miniscules, and copies of manuscripts multiplied rapidly (see chap. 26).

The classical writings of Greece and Rome. These writings illustrate the character of biblical manuscript preservation in a candid fashion (see chap. 25). In contrast to the total of 5,366 (see chap. 22) partial and complete New Testament manuscripts known today, the *Iliad* of Homer has only 643, *The Peloponnesian War* of Thucydides only eight, while Tacitus's works rely on but two manuscripts. The abundance of biblical evidence would lead one to conclude with Sir Frederic Kenyon that "the Christian can take the whole Bible in his hand and say without fear or hesitation that he holds in it the true word of God, handed down without essential loss from generation to generation throughout the centuries."[18] Or, as he goes on to say,

> The number of manuscripts of the New Testament, of early translations from it, and of quotations from it in the oldest writers of the Church, is so large that it is practically certain that the true reading of every doubtful passage is preserved in some one or other of these ancient authorities. This can be said of no other ancient book in the world.[19]

Summary and Conclusion

Between the autograph and the modern Bible extends an important link in the overall chain "from God to us" known as *transmission.* It provides a positive answer to the question: Do Bible scholars today possess an accurate copy of the autographs? Obviously, the authenticity and authority of the Bible cannot be established unless it be known that the present copies have *integrity.* In support of the integrity of the text, an overwhelming number of ancient documents may be presented. For the New Testament, beginning with the second century ancient versions and manuscript fragments and continuing with abundant quotations of the Fathers and thousands of manuscript copies from that time to the modern versions of the Bible, there is virtually an unbroken line of testimony. Furthermore, there are not only countless manuscripts to support the integrity of the Bible (including the Old Testament since the discovery of the Dead Sea Scrolls), but a study of the procedures of preparation and preservation of the biblical manuscript copies reveals the fidelity of the transmission process itself. In fact, it may be concluded that no major document from antiquity comes into the modern world with such evidence of its integrity as does the Bible.

18. Kenyon, p. 55.
19. Ibid.

21
Old Testament Manuscripts

The original manuscripts (autographa) of the Old Testament are not available, but the Hebrew text is amply represented by both pre- and post-Christian manuscripts.[1] As a result, the reliability of the Hebrew text can be evaluated from available manuscript evidence.

But what are the nature and amount of the documentary evidence for the original text of the Old Testament? Sir Frederic Kenyon posed this "great, indeed all important question" when he wrote, "Does this Hebrew text which we call Masoretic[2] faithfully represent the Hebrew text as originally written by the authors of the Old Testament books?"[3] The answer to that question arises from a careful examination of the number and nature of Hebrew manuscripts of the Old Testament.

The Number of Hebrew Old Testament Manuscripts

The first collection of Hebrew manuscripts, made by Benjamin Kennicott (A.D. 1776-1780) and published by Oxford, listed 615 manuscripts of the Old Testament. Later Giovanni de Rossi (1784-1788) published a list of 731 manuscripts. The main manuscript discoveries in modern times are those of the Cairo Geniza (c. 1890ff.) and the Dead Sea Scrolls (1947ff.) In the Cairo synagogue attic storeroom alone were discovered some 200,000 manuscripts and fragments,[4] some 10,000 of which are biblical.[5] According to J. T. Milik, fragments of about 600 manuscripts are known from the Dead Sea Scrolls, not all biblical. Moshe Goshen-Gottstein estimates that the total number of

1. Much of the following discussion is updated from Norman L. Geisler, "Bible Manuscripts," in *Wycliffe Bible Encyclopedia,* 1:248-52.
2. The standard edition of the Masoretic Text was first published under the editorship of a Hebrew Christian, Jacob Ben Chayyim (c. 1525). It was essentially a recension of the text of the Masorete Ben Asher (flourished c. A.D. 920). See chap. 25 discussion.
3. Frederic G. Kenyon, *Our Bible and the Ancient Manuscripts,* p. 88.
4. Paul E. Kahle, *The Cairo Geniza,* p. 13; Ernst Würthwein, *The Text of the Old Testament: An Introduction the Biblia Hebraica,* p. 25.
5. Moshe Goshen-Gottstein, "Biblical Manuscripts in the United States," p. 35.

Old Testament Hebrew manuscript fragments throughout the world runs into the tens of thousands.[6]

Major Collections of Old Testament Manuscripts

Of the 200,000 Cairo Geniza manuscript fragments, some 100,000 are housed at Cambridge. The largest organized collection of Hebrew Old Testament manuscripts in the world is the Second Firkowitch Collection in Leningrad. It contains 1,582 items of the Bible and Masora on parchment (725 on paper), plus 1,200 additional Hebrew manuscript fragments.[7] The British Museum catalog lists 161 Hebrew Old Testament manuscripts. At Oxford, the Bodleian Library catalog lists 146 Old Testament manuscripts, each one containing a large number of fragments.[8] Goshen-Gottstein estimates that in the United States alone there are tens of thousands of Semitic manuscript fragments, about 5 percent of which are biblical—more than 500 manuscripts.[9]

Description of Major Old Testament Hebrew Manuscripts

The most significant Hebrew Old Testament manuscripts date from between the third century B.C. and the fourteenth century A.D.

Nash Papyrus. Besides those unusual finds, which are about a thousand years older than most of the earliest Old Testament Hebrew manuscripts, there is extant one damaged copy of the Shema (from Deut. 6:4-9) and two fragments of the Decalogue (Ex. 20:2ff.; Deut. 5:6ff.). It is dated between the second century B.C.[10] and the first century A.D.

Orientales 4445. This British Museum manuscript is dated by C[hristian] D. Ginsburg between A.D. 820 and 850, the Masora notes being added a century later. But Paul E. Kahle[11] argues that both consonantal Hebrew texts and pointing (the added vowel points or marks) are from the time of Moses ben Asher (tenth century). Because the Hebrew alphabet consists only of consonants, Hebrew writing normally shows only those letters, with a few of the letters being used in varying degrees to represent some of the vocalic sounds. This manuscript contains Genesis 39:20—Deuteronomy 1:33 (less Numbers 7:47-73 and Numbers 9:12—10:18).

Codex Cairensis. A codex is a manuscript in book form with pages. According to a colophon, or inscription at the end of the book, this Cairo Codex

6. Ibid., p. 31.
7. The Antonin Collection, Würthwein, p. 23.
8. Kahle, p. 5.
9. Goshen-Gottstein, p. 30.
10. William F. Albright, "A Biblical Fragment from the Maccabean Age: The Nash Papyrus," pp. 145-76.
11. Kahle, in Würthwein, p. 118.

was written and vowel-pointed in A.D. 895 by Moses ben Asher in Tiberias in Palestine.[12] It contains the Former Prophets (Joshua, Judges, 1 and 2 Samuel, 1 and 2 Kings) and the Latter Prophets (Isaiah, Jeremiah, Ezekiel, and the Twelve). It is symbolized C in *Biblia Hebraica Stuttgartensia* (BHS).[13]

Aleppo Codex of the Whole Old Testament. This was written by Shelomo ben Baya'a,[14] but according to a colophon it was pointed (i.e., the vowel marks were added) by Moses ben Asher (c. A.D. 930). It is a model codex, and although it was not permitted to be copied for a long time and was even reported to have been destroyed,[15] it was smuggled from Syria to Israel. It has now been photographed and will be the basis of the *New Hebrew Bible* to be published by the Hebrew University.[16] It is a sound authority for the Ben Asher text.

Codex Leningradensis ($B19^{A}$). According to a colophon, or note at the end, this was copied in Old Cairo by Samuel ben Jacob in A.D. 1008 from a manuscript (now lost) written by Aaron ben Moses ben Asher c. A.D. 1000,[17] whereas Ginsburg held it was copied from the Aleppo Codex.[18] It represents one of the oldest manuscripts of the complete Hebrew Bible that is known.[19] Kittel adopted it as the basis for the third edition of his *Biblia Hebraica* (BHK), and it continues to be used as such in *Biblia Hebraica Stuttgartensia* (BHS), where it is represented under the symbol L.

Babylonian Codex of the Latter Prophets (MS Heb. B3). This is sometimes called the Leningrad Codex of the Prophets[20] or the [St.] Petersburg Codex.[21] It contains Isaiah, Jeremiah, Ezekiel, and the Twelve. It is dated A.D. 916, but its chief significance is that through it punctuation added by the Babylonian school of Masoretes was rediscovered. It is symbolized as $V(ar)^{P}$ in *Biblia Hebraica Stuttgartensia.*

Reuchlin Codex of the Prophets. Dated A.D. 1105, this is now at Karlsruhe. Like the British Museum manuscript Ad. 21161 (c. A.D. 1150), it contains a recension of Ben Naphtali, a Tiberian Masorete. These have been of great value in establishing the fidelity of the Ben Asher text.[22]

Cairo Geniza Manuscripts. Of the approximately 10,000 biblical manuscripts and fragments from the Geniza (storehouse for old manuscripts) of the

12. Würthwein, p. 25.
13. K. Elliger and W. Rudolph, eds., *Biblia Hebraica Stuttgartensia* is the successor of R. Kittel and P. Kahle, eds., *Biblia Hebraica,* 7th ed., and is regarded as the most authoritative Hebrew text based on the Masoretic text tradition.
14. Kenyon, p. 84.
15. Würthwein, p. 25.
16. Goshen-Gottstein, p. 13.
17. Kahle, p. 110.
18. Ginsburg, pp. 243f.
19. Kahle, p. 132.
20. Kenyon, p. 85.
21. Würthwein, p. 26.
22. Kenyon, p. 36.

Cairo synagogue now scattered throughout the world, Kahle identified more than 120 examples copied by the Babylonian group of Masoretes. In the Firkowitch Collection are found 14 Hebrew Old Testament manuscripts dating between A.D. 929 and 1121. Kahle contends also that the 1,200 manuscripts and fragments of the Antonin Collection come from the Cairo Geniza.[23] He provided a list of 70 of these manuscripts in the prolegomena to *Biblia Hebraica*, seventh edition. There are other Geniza manuscripts scattered over the world. Some of the better ones in the United States are in the Enelow Memorial Collection housed at the Jewish Theological Seminary, New York.[24]

Erfurt Codices (E 1, 2, 3). These are listed in the University Library in Tübingen as Manuscript Orientale 1210/11, 1212, 1213. Their peculiarity is that they represent more or less (more in E 3) the text and Masora of the Ben Naphtali tradition. E 1 is a fourteenth-century manuscript containing the Hebrew Old Testament and the Targum. E 2 is also of the Hebrew Old Testament and Targum Ontelos, probably from the thirteenth century. E 3 is the oldest, being dated by Kahle and others before A.D. 1100.[25]

Some Lost Codices. There are a number of significant but now lost codices whose peculiar readings are preserved and referred to in *Biblia Hebraica Stuttgartensia*. Codex Severi (Sev.) is a medieval list of thirty-two variants of the Pentateuch (cf. critical apparatus to Gen. 18:21; 24:7; Num. 4:3), supposedly based on a manuscript brought to Rome in A.D. 70 that Emperor Severus (A.D. 222-35) later gave to a synagogue he had built. Codex Hillel (Hill.) was supposedly written c. A.D. 600 by Rabbi Hillel ben Moses ben Hillel. It is said to have been accurate and was used to revise other manuscripts. Readings from that manuscript are cited by medieval Masoretes and are used in the critical apparatus of *Biblia Hebraica Stuttgartensia* in Genesis 6:3; 19:6; Exodus 25:19; Leviticus 26:9.[26] A critical apparatus lists the variant readings to the text that the editor considers are significant for translators or necessary for establishing the text.

Dead Sea Scrolls (DSS)

The most remarkable manuscripts are those of the Dead Sea Scrolls, which date from the third century B.C. to the first century A.D. They include one complete Old Testament book (Isaiah) and thousands of fragments, which together represent every Old Testament book except Esther. Before showing how the amazing new evidence from Qumran bears on the state of the Hebrew text, a word should be said about the discovery of the scrolls, which are

23. Kahle, p. 7.
24. Cf. Goshen-Gottstein, p. 44f.
25. Cf. Würthwein, p. 26.
26. Ibid., p. 27.

viewed by W. F. Albright as "the greatest manuscript discovery of modern times."[27]

Discovery of the Dead Sea Scrolls

Ironically, and perhaps providentially, this great manuscript discovery was hit upon by chance when an Arab shepherd boy (Muhammad adh-Dhib) was pursuing a lost goat seven and one-half miles south of Jericho and a mile west of the Dead Sea. Here in a cave he found some jars containing several leather scrolls. Later explorations in this and nearby caves produced thousands of manuscript fragments which had once constituted about four hundred books thought to belong to the library of the Essenes. The Essenes were a Jewish religious sect dating from about the time of Christ. They had broken away from the Temple-centered worship at Jerusalem and had established their own monastic and messianic community in the Judean desert near Qumran.

The first discovery was made in March 1947, and subsequent explorations produced amazing finds through 1956. In all there were eleven caves containing scrolls and/or fragments excavated near Qumran between February 15, 1949 and February 1956. Much material of interest to the archaeologist was discovered, but the discussion here is limited to the manuscripts that bear on the text of the Old Testament.

Description of the Dead Sea Scroll Discoveries

Cave I. Cave I was discovered first by the Arab shepherd boy. From it he took seven more or less complete scrolls and some fragments including the following:

1. St. Mark's Monastery Isaiah Scroll (Isaiah A, or IQIs[a]). It is a popular copy with numerous corrections above the line or in the margin and is the earliest known copy of any complete book of the Bible.
2. Manual of Discipline, a scroll containing rules and regulations of the Qumran sect.
3. Commentary on the book of Habakkuk, containing the text of the first two chapters of the Prophet Habakkuk with a running interpretation.
4. Genesis Apocryphon, first known as the Lamech Scroll, containing Apocryphal accounts in Aramaic of some of the patriarchs of Genesis.
5. Hebrew University Isaiah (Isaiah B, or IQIs[b]) is incomplete but its text agrees more closely with the Masoretic text than does Isaiah A.
6. War Scroll, whose full title is War of the Sons of Light Against the Sons

27. J. C. Trever, "The Discovery of the Scrolls," *Biblical Archaeologist* 11 (Sept. 1948), 55.

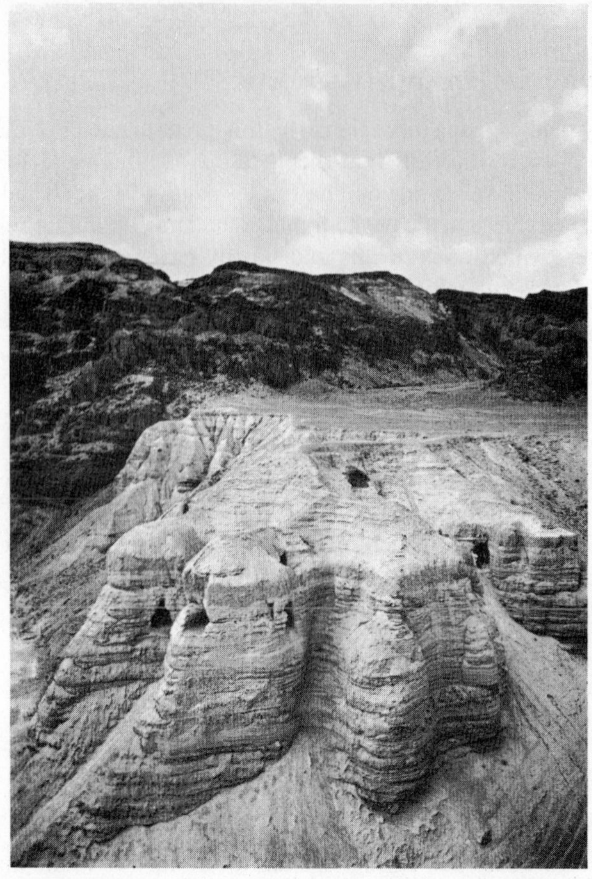

9. *Qumran caves where the Dead Sea Scrolls were found (Giovanni Trimboli)*

of Darkness, gives an account of preparation for the end-time war between the Qumran sect and their enemies.

7. Thanksgiving Hymns contain about thirty hymns, which resemble Old Testament psalms.[28]

Cave I was officially excavated between February 15 and March 9, 1949. It yielded fragments of Genesis, Leviticus, Deuteronomy, Judges, Samuel, Isaiah, Ezekiel, Psalms, and some nonbiblical works including Enoch, Sayings of Moses (previously unknown), Book of Jubilee, Book of Noah, Testament

28. Taken from Menahem Mansoor, *The Dead Sea Scrolls,* pp. 2-3.

of Levi, Tobit, and the Wisdom of Solomon. An interesting fragment of Daniel, containing 2:4 (where the language changes from Hebrew to Aramaic), also comes from this cave. Fragmentary commentaries on Psalms, Micah, and Zephaniah were also found in Cave I.[29]

Cave II. This cave, first discovered and pilferred by the Bedouin, was excavated between March 10 and 29, 1952. Fragments of about a hundred manuscripts, including two of Exodus, one of Leviticus, four of Numbers, two or three of Deuteronomy, one of Jeremiah, Job, Psalms, and two of Ruth, were found. However, nothing so spectacular as the manuscripts found in some of the other caves was uncovered.

Cave III. Cave III was found by the archaeologists and searched on March 14, 1952. It disclosed two halves of a copper scroll with directions to sixty or sixty-four sites containing hidden treasures. These sites were mostly in and around the Jerusalem area, ranging from north of Jericho to the Vale of Achor. Thus far, search for the treasures has been unfruitful. Various views have emerged to explain this scroll. It has been suggested that it is the work of a crank, or part of the people's folklore, or possibly a record of the deposits of the tithe money and sacred vessels dedicated to the Temple service.[30]

Cave IV. This cave (Partridge Cave), after being ransacked by the Bedouin, was searched in September, 1952, and it proved to be the most productive cave of all. Literally thousands of fragments were recovered either by purchase from the Bedouin or by the archaeologists' sifting the dust on the floor of the cave. These scraps represent hundreds of manuscripts (nearly four hundred of which have already been identified), including about one hundred copies of Bible books (all except Esther). The fragment of Samuel ($4QSam^b$) is thought to be the oldest known piece of biblical Hebrew, dating from the third century B.C. Also found were a few fragments of commentaries of the Psalms, Isaiah, and Nahum. The entire collection of Cave IV is believed to represent the scope of the Qumran library, and judging from the relative number of books found, their favorite books seemed to be Deuteronomy, Isaiah, Psalms, the Minor Prophets, in that order, and Jeremiah ($4QJer^b$). An interesting fragment containing some of Daniel 7:28, 8:1 (where the language changes back from Aramaic to Hebrew) was found.

Cave V. This cave was excavated in September 1952. Fragments of Tobit and some biblical books, all in an advanced stage of deterioration, were found.

Cave VI. This cave was investigated on September 27, 1952, and produced,

29. For a more detailed list of the manuscript fragments from the various caves see *Biblical Archaeologist* (Sept. 1965), pp. 87-100. Also see Gleason L. Archer, Jr., *A Survey of Old Testament Introduction,* "Appendix 4: Inventory of the Biblical Manuscripts from the Dead Sea Caves," pp. 505-9.
30. See John M. Allegro, *The Treasure of the Copper Scroll,* 2d rev. ed.

10. The Qumran Community, where the Dead Sea Scrolls were produced (Giovanni Trimboli)

strangely enough, mostly papyrus instead of leather fragments. Papyrus pieces of Daniel, 1 Kings, and 2 Kings were among the finds.

Caves VII–X. These caves were examined between February 2 and April 6, 1955. The contents are interesting to the expert archaeologist but not relevant to the present study of textual criticism.

Cave XI. This cave was excavated in January or February 1956. It produced a well-preserved copy of some of the Psalms, including the apocryphal Psalm 151, which was hitherto known only in Greek texts. Altogether, this manuscript contains the whole or part of thirty-six canonical psalms, ranging from Psalm 93 through 150. In addition to these, a very fine scroll of part of Leviticus, some large pieces of an Apocalypse of the New Jerusalem, and an Aramaic Targum (paraphrase) of Job were discovered.

Murabba'at Discoveries. Prompted by the original finds, the Bedouin have pursued their search and found caves to the southeast of Bethlehem, which have produced self-dated manuscripts and documents from the Second Jewish Revolt (A.D. 132-135). Systematic exploration and excavation of these caves

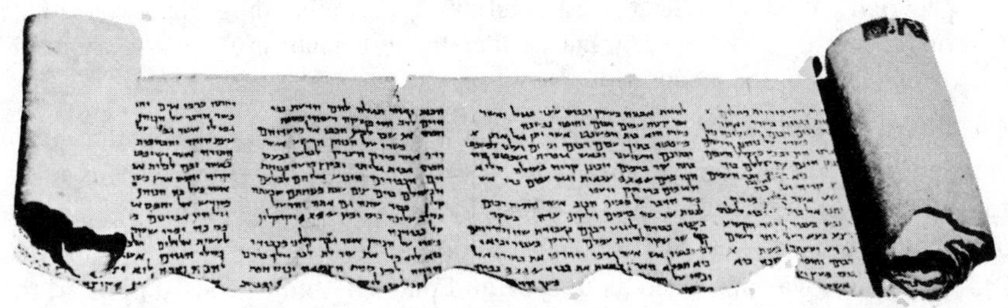

11. The Habakkuk Commentary (Y. Yadin and The Shrine of the Book)

began on January 21, 1952. The dated manuscripts proved to be later and helped to establish the antiquity of the Dead Sea Scrolls. From these caves came another scroll of the Minor Prophets (the last half of Joel through Haggai), which closely supports the Masoretic Text. The oldest known Semitic papyrus (a palimpsest), inscribed the second time in the ancient Hebrew script (dating from the seventh-eighth centuries B.C.), was found here.[31] As can readily be seen, there is now a mass of material of the Old Testament text, more than scholars will be able to absorb in some decades. Much of this material has already been published,[32] but much more from Caves IV and XI still remains to be published.

Dating the Dead Sea Scroll Discoveries

The question of dating these manuscripts from the Dead Sea has been settled by several lines of evidence.

Carbon 14. This was applied to half of a two-ounce piece of linen wrapping from one of the scrolls in Cave I by Dr. W. F. Libby of the University of Chicago in 1950. Results indicated an age of 1,917 years with a two-hundred-year (10 percent) variant, which left the date somewhere between 168 B.C. and A.D. 233.

Paleography and Orthography. Another means of dating was found in paleography (ancient writing forms) and orthography (spelling), which indicated a date for some of the manuscripts before 100 B.C. Photographs of the complete Isaiah scroll mailed to him by John Trever were examined by W. F.

31. See D. Barthelemy and J. T. Milik, *Ten Years of Discovery in the Judean Wilderness*. Another site known as Khirbet Mird has produced manuscript materials. On April 3, 1960, a parchment fragment (first century A.D.) of Psalm 15 and part of Psalm 16 was discovered at Wadi Murabba'at. See T. L. Cass, *Secrets from the Caves*, p. 164.
32. See Geza Vermes, trans., *The Dead Sea Scrolls in English*.

Albright, who wrote,

> There is no doubt in my mind that the script is more archaic than the Nash papyrus. . . I should prefer a date around 100 B.C. . . . What an absolutely incredible find! And there can happily not be the slightest doubt in the world about the genuineness of the manuscript.[33]

Archaeology. Collaborative evidence for an early date came from archaeology. The accompanying pottery was analyzed as Late Hellenistic (c. 150-63 B.C.) and Early Roman (c. 63 B.C. to A.D. 100). The coins found in the monastery ruins proved by their inscriptions to extend from 135 B.C. to A.D. 135. The cloth was analyzed as to type and pattern, and it, too, supported the early date. Final evidence came from the Murabba'at Discoveries south of Bethlehem, where self-dated manuscripts were discovered in 1952. Bearing dates from A.D. 132-135, these proved to be paleographically younger than the Dead Sea Scrolls. Practically the only source of evidence urged against the great antiquity of the scrolls was internal evidence, but that proved to be a double-edged argument.[34] There can be no reasonable doubt that the Qumran manuscripts came from the century before Christ and the first century A.D. Thus, they are one thousand years older than the Masoretic manuscripts of the tenth century. Before 1947, the Hebrew text was based on three partial and one complete manuscript dating from about A.D. 1000. Now, thousands of fragments are available, as well as complete books, containing large sections of the Old Testament from one millennium before the time of the Masoretic manuscripts. The recent discovery of fourth-century B.C. papyri in Aramaic cursive in caves southeast of Samaria shows by paleography that datings proposed for 40 Ex^{f} (c. 250 B.C.) and 4Q Sam^{b} (c. 225 B.C.) now appear to be minimal.[35]

Details of the Dead Sea Scroll Texts

The nature and number of these finds are of critical value for establishing the true text. With innumerable fragments of the entire Old Testament, there are abundant samples from which to draw comparisons with the Masoretic Text. What does such a comparison reveal? All of the evidence has not been critically analyzed to date, but a decade and a half of scholarship has produced the following general conclusions.

Similarity to the Masoretic Text. The scrolls give an overwhelming confirmation of the fidelity of the Masoretic Text. Millar Burrows, in his valuable work entitled *The Dead Sea Scrolls,* writes, "It is a matter of wonder that through something like a thousand years the text underwent so little altera-

33. Trever, p. 55.
34. See Solomon Zeitlin, *The Dead Sea Scrolls and Modern Scholarship.*
35. *Biblical Archaeologist* (Dec., 1963), pp. 119 ff.

tion. As I said in my first article on the scroll, 'Herein lies its chief importance, supporting the fidelity of the Masoretic tradition.' "[36] R. Laird Harris points out that "evidently the difference between the standard text of A.D. 900 and the text of 100 B.C. is not nearly so great as that between the Neutral and Western text in the New Testament study."[37] Gleason Archer observes that the two copies of Isaiah discovered in Qumran Cave I "proved to be word for word identical with our standard Hebrew Bible in more than 95% of the text. The 5% of variation consisted chiefly of obvious slips of the pen and variations in spelling."[38] To return to the original and "all important question" that Kenyon stated a generation ago, as to whether "this Hebrew text which we call Masoretic faithfully represents the Hebrew text as originally written by the authors of the Old Testament," it may now be more confidently asserted than ever before that the Dead Sea discoveries have enabled us to answer this question in the affirmative with much greater assurance than was possible before 1948.[39]

Difference from Masoretic Text. Next to the substantial agreement between the scrolls and the Masoretic Text, the most important contribution these Dead Sea manuscripts make to textual criticism of the Old Testament is in the area of variant readings which they provide. Millar Burrows states, "I still feel that the amount of agreement with the Masoretic text is the manuscript's most significant feature, but having said that, I agree that the variants constitute its second point of importance."[40] This raises the question of what some of the variants are and what constitutes their significance.

Some of the important variants show a close parallel to the Greek text (Septuagint [LXX]).

1. A fragment from Cave IV containing Deuteronomy 32:8 reads, "according to the number of the sons of God," which is translated "angels of God" by the LXX, as in Genesis 6:4 (margin); Job 1:6; 2:1; and 38:7. The Masoretic Text reads, "according to the number of the children of Israel."

2. The Masoretic Text of Exodus 1:5 reads "seventy souls," whereas the LXX and the New Testament quote taken from it (cf. Acts 7:14) read "seventy-five souls." A fragment of Exodus 1:5 from the Qumran Scrolls reads "seventy-five souls," in agreement with the LXX.

3. Hebrews 1:6 (KJV), "Let all the angels of God worship him," is a quote from the LXX of Deuteronomy 32:43. This quotation is not in agree-

36. Millar Burrows, *The Dead Sea Scrolls,* p. 304.
37. R. Laird Harris, *Inspiration and Canonicity of the Bible,* p. 99.
38. Gleason L. Archer, Jr., *A Survey of Old Testament Introduction,* p. 19.
39. See F. F. Bruce, *Second Thoughts on the Dead Sea Scrolls,* pp. 61-69.
40. Burrows, p. 304.

ment with the Masoretic Text, but one of the scroll fragments containing this section tends to confirm the Greek text (LXX).

4. The famous Isaiah 7:14 passage reads, "she shall call his name" in the Masoretic Text, but the LXX and now the great Isaiah scroll read, "His name shall be called," a matter of one less consonant of the Hebrew alphabet.
5. The Greek version of Jeremiah is sixty verses (one-eighth) shorter than the Hebrew text of Jeremiah. The fragment of Jeremiah (4Q Jerb) supports some of these omissions.
6. In Cave XI a copy of Psalm 151 was found, which was previously unknown in the Hebrew text although it appeared in the Septuagint. There were also some apocryphal books found in the Hebrew manuscripts of the Qumran caves, which had previously been known only in the LXX.[41]

This should by no means be construed as a uniform picture, since there are not many deviants in the Dead Sea Scrolls from the Masoretic Text to begin with, and in some cases the variants do not consistently agree with the LXX, whereas in a few cases they do not agree at all. However, even Orlinsky, who is one of the foremost defenders of the Masoretic Text against proposed emendations based on the Dead Sea Scrolls, admits, "But this much may be said: The LXX translation, no less than the Masoretic Text itself, will have gained considerable respect as a result of the Qumran discoveries in those circles where it has long—overlong—been necessary."[42]

Samaritan Pentateuch (SP)

The separation of the Samaritans from the Jews was an important event in the history of the post-exilic period of the Old Testament. It occurred probably during the fifth or fourth century B.C., and was the culmination of a long process. At the time of the schism one would suspect that the Samaritans took with them the Scriptures as they then existed, with the result that there came into being a second Hebrew recension or revised text of the Pentateuch. This Samaritan Pentateuch is not a version in the strict sense of the word, but rather a manuscript portion of the Hebrew text itself. It contains the five books of Moses and is written in a Paleo-Hebrew script quite similar to that found on the Moabite Stone, the Siloam inscription, the Lachisch letters, and in particular some of the older biblical manuscripts from Qumran. Because the Samaritan script is a derivative of the Paleo-Hebrew script that was revived in the Maccabean era of nationalist archaizing, and because of the

41. Vermes, *The Essene Writings of Qumran,* p. 296.
42. Harry M. Orlinsky, "The Textual Criticism of the Old Testament," in G. E. Wright, ed., *The Bible and the Ancient Near East,* p. 121.

full orthography of the Samaritan Pentateuch, Frank M. Cross, Jr., believes that the Samaritan Pentateuch branched off from the pre- or proto-Masoretic text in the second century B.C.[43]

A form of the Samaritan Pentateuch text seems to have been known to such early church Fathers as Eusebius of Caesarea and Jerome. It did not become available to scholars in the West, however, until 1616, when Pietro della Valle discovered a manuscript of the Samaritan Pentateuch in Damascus. A great wave of excitement arose among biblical scholars. The text was published in an early portion of the Paris Polyglot (1632) and later in the text of the London Polyglot (1657). It was quickly regarded as being superior to the Masoretic Text (MT); but it became relegated to relative obscurity after Wilhelm Gesenius in 1815 adjudged it to be practically worthless for textual criticism. In more recent times the value of the Samaritan Pentateuch has been reasserted by such scholars as A. Geiger, Paul E. Kahle, and Frederic G. Kenyon.

So far as is known, no manuscript of the Samaritan Pentateuch is older than the eleventh century A.D. Although the Samaritan community claims that one roll was written by Abisha, the great-grandson of Moses, in the thirteenth year after the conquest of Canaan, their authority is so spurious that the claim may safely be dismissed. The oldest codex of the Samaritan Pentateuch bears a note about its sale in A.D. 1149-50, but the manuscript itself is much older. One manuscript was copied in 1204, another dated 1211-1212 is now in the John Rylands Library at Manchester, and still another, dated c. 1232, is in the New York Public Library.

The standard printed edition of the Samaritan Pentateuch is in five volumes by A. von Gall, *Der Hebräische Pentateuch der Samaritaner* (1914-1918). It provides an eclectic text based on eighty late medieval manuscripts and fragments. Although von Gall's text is in Hebrew characters, the Samaritans wrote in an alphabet quite different from the square Hebrew. Nevertheless, their script, like the Hebrew, descended from old Paleo-Hebrew characters.

In all there are about six thousand deviations of the Samaritan Pentateuch from the Masoretic Text, many of them being merely orthographic and trivial. In about nineteen hundred instances the Samaritan text agrees with the LXX[44] against the Masoretic Text. It must be argued, however, that some of the deviations from the Masoretic Text are alterations introduced by the Samaritans in the interests of preserving their own cultus as well as the northern Israelitic dialectal peculiarities, whereas the Masoretic Text perpetuates any Judean dialectal features and traditions.

In the early Christian era a translation of the Samaritan Pentateuch into the Aramaic dialect of the Samaritans was made and is known as the Samaritan

43. Frank Moore Cross, Jr., *The Ancient Library of Qumran and Modern Biblical Studies*, pp. 127f.

44. See chap. 27.

Targum. It was also translated into Greek, called the *Samaritikon,* from which about fifty citations are preserved in the notes on Origen's *Hexapla.* After the eleventh century several translations of the Samaritan Pentateuch were made into Arabic.[45]

Nature of Old Testament Manuscripts

Types of Manuscript Errors

Although the official text of the Old Testament was transmitted with great care, it was inevitable that certain copyist errors would creep into the texts over the hundreds of years of transmission into thousands of manuscripts. There are several kinds of copyist errors that produce textual variants.[46] *Haplography* is the writing of a word, letter, or syllable only once when it should have been written more than once. *Dittography* is writing twice what should have been written only once. *Metathesis* is reversing the proper position of letters or words. *Fusion* is the combining of two separate words into one. *Fission* is the dividing of a single word into two words. *Homophony* is the substitution of a word for another that is pronounced like it (e.g., "two" for "to"), or the misreading of similarly shaped letters. *Homoeoteleuton* is the omission of an intervening passage because the scribe's eye skipped from one line to a similar ending on another line. *Accidental omissions* occur where no repetition is involved (as "Saul was ... year(s) old," 1 Sam. 13:1, RSV), or vowel letters are misread for consonants.

Rules for Textual Criticism

Scholars have developed certain criteria for determining which reading is the correct or original one. Seven rules may be suggested.[47] (1) The older reading is to be preferred, because it is closer to the original. (2) The more difficult reading is to be preferred, because scribes were more apt to smooth out difficult readings. (3) The shorter reading is to be preferred, because copyists were more apt to insert new material than omit part of the sacred text. (4) The reading that best explains the other variants is to be preferred. (5) The reading with the widest geographical support is to be preferred, because such manuscripts or versions are less likely to have influenced each other. (6) The reading that is most like the author's usual style is to be preferred. (7) The reading that does not reflect a doctrinal bias is to be preferred.[48]

45. Cf. Kahle, pp. 51-57.
46. Gleason L. Archer, Jr., *A Survey of Old Testament Introduction,* pp. 55-57.
47. Ibid. pp. 51-53.
48. Cf. Würthwein, pp. 80-81, for further textual principles.

HISTORY OF THE OLD TESTAMENT TEXT

The Sopherim (from Hebrew meaning "scribes") were the Jewish scholars and custodians of the Old Testament text between the fifth and the third centuries B.C. whose responsibility it was to standardize and preserve it. They were followed by the Zugoth ("pairs" of textual scholars) in the second and first centuries B.C. The third group were Tannaim ("repeaters" or "teachers"), whose work extended to A.D. 200. The work of Tannaim can be found in the *Midrash* ("textual interpretation"), *Tosefta* ("addition"), and *Talmud* ("instruction"), which latter is divided into *Mishnah* ("repetitions") and *Gemara* ("the matter to be learned"). The Talmud gradually was written between A.D. 100 and 500.

Between A.D. 500 and 950 the Masoretes added the vowel pointings and pronunciation marks to the consonantal Hebrew text received from the Sopherim, on the basis of the *Masora* ("tradition") that had been handed down to them. The Masoretes were scribes who codified and wrote down the oral criticisms and remarks on the Hebrew text. There were two major schools or centers of Masoretic activity, each largely independent of the other, the Babylonian and the Palestinian. The most famous Masoretes were the Jewish scholars living in Tiberias in Galilee, Moses ben Asher (with his son Aaron) and Moses ben Naphtali, in the late ninth and tenth centuries A.D. The ben Asher text is the standard text for the Hebrew Bible today as best represented by Codex Leningradensis $B19^{A}$ (L) and the Aleppo Codex.

PRINTED HEBREW BIBLES[49]

1. The Bologna edition of the Psalms (A.D. 1477).
2. The Soncino edition of the complete Old Testament with vowel pointing (A.D. 1488). There were also editions in Naples (1491-1493) and Brescia (1494).
3. The Complutensian Polyglot Bible by Cardinal Ximenes at Alcala, Spain (1514-1517), in Hebrew, Greek, Aramaic, Targum, and Latin. A polyglot is a multiple-columned edition containing the original language and various other translations for means of comparison.
4. The Antwerp Polyglot (1569-1572).
5. The Paris Polyglot (1629-1645), ten volumes.
6. The London Polyglot (1654-1657), six folio volumes.

49. See Kenyon, pp. 86-88; Goshen-Gottstein, pp. 8-10; Würthwein, pp. 27-30; and *Biblia Hebraica Stuttgartensia*, pp. I-LV.

7. The First Rabbinic Bible (1516-1517), was produced by Felix Pratensis and published by Daniel Bomberg. It was a considerable critical achievement (in four volumes) and served as the basis of the Second Rabbinic Bible.

8. The Second Rabbinic Bible (1524-1525), by Jacob ben Chayyim and published by Daniel Bomberg in four volumes. It was based on late manuscripts that provide the basis of the *Textus Receptus,* a text presumed to be identical to that of the original manuscripts. Until 1929 it was found in Kittel's first and second editions of *Biblia Hebraica* (where it is called Bombergiana or B).

9. The J. H. Michaelis edition (M^1) (A.D. 1720). Michaelis was a Protestant Pietist of Halle who followed in the main the text of Jablonski's 1699 edition. The critical apparatus contains the most important readings of the Erfurt manuscripts.

10. The B. Kennicott edition (1776-1780) used 615 manuscripts (mostly late) and 52 printed editions. The text follows the edition of van der Hooght (1705).

11. Meit Halevi Letteris (1852). This is a two-volume Hebrew Bible based to a marked extent on manuscript Erfurt 3, readings of which are found in Michaelis (1720). He may have used manuscript or folio 121 of Marburg.[50]

12. G. B. De Rossi (1784-1788) produced not an edition but a collection of variants from 1,475 manuscripts and editions. The collection is greater than Kennicott's, but most variants are not substantial.

13. S. Baer (B) (1869-1895), with the collaboration of Franz Delitzsch, endeavored to produce a correct form of the Masoretic Text using old manuscripts and editions. Their methods of "correcting" the text are questionable, according to Kahle and Würthwein. They followed the text of Wolf Heidenheim (1757-1832).

14. The C. D. Ginsburg edition (1894) used earlier and better manuscripts.

15. C. D. Ginsburg (G) produced for the British and Foreign Bible Society (1926) a new edition of Ginsburg's earlier work (1894). It contained variants of seventy manuscripts and nineteen printed editions (mostly thirteenth-century), including Orientales 4445, which Ginsburg dated A.D. 820-50.

16. R. Kittel and P. Kahle, *Biblia Hebraica* (1929), first and second editions were based on Bomberg (1524-1525) and contained variants from the

50. Goshen-Gottstein, p. 8.

tenth and eleventh centuries. *Codicis Jemensis* (V[ar][1]) was edited by R. Hoerning (1889).

17. R. Kittel and P. Kahle, *Biblia Hebraica* (1937), third edition and following, were based on Codex Leningradensis B19^{A} (L) (from A.D. 1008) with the small Masora of Ben Asher in the margin. Their seventh edition includes Dead Sea Scrolls Isaiah and Habakkuk variants for the first time.

18. Karl Elliger and Wilhelm Rudolph, *Biblia Hebraica Stuttgartensia* (1967/77) is the successor to the Kittel-Kahle *Biblia Hebraica*. It continues to be based on Codex Leningradensis B19^{A} (L) and includes Dead Sea Scroll variants. The differences between the *Biblia Hebraica* and the *Biblia Hebraica Stuttgartensia* include the moving of 1 and 2 Chronicles to the end, a remaking of type face (due to the destruction of the original plates in the bombing of Leipzig), use of the latest band of L as the basis of the text, use of the Masora of Codex L in its entirety, and a complete revision of the critical apparatus.

Family Tree of Old Testament Text-Types

The discovery of the Dead Sea Scrolls, with their variant readings, reopened the whole question of the Old Testament textual traditions. As a result, some attempts to reconstruct a family tree of those manuscripts have been made.[51] Because the Masoretic Text (between 500 and 950 A.D.) stemmed from a single source that was standardized by Hebrew scholars at about A.D. 100, the discovery of manuscripts antedating that period casts new light on the history of the Old Testament text before that recension. From among the Dead Sea Scrolls several textual traditions can be observed.

The Proto-Masoretic Text-Type

This textual type, which was the predecessor of the later Masoretic Text, is clearly represented at Qumran, chiefly in Isaiah, Ezekiel, and the Twelve (the Minor Prophets), although fragments from among the Law and historical books also preserve this text-type. Most of the manuscripts of the Law from Cave IV are aligned with the Proto-Masoretic type. With the exception of the Writings (whose textual type has not been clearly determined as yet), the remaining books of the Old Testament are represented among the scrolls and fragments in a Proto-Masoretic text-type.

The Proto-Septuagint Text-Type

The Proto-Septuagint text-type is represented at Qumran by manuscripts

51. The discussion here is taken from Cross, pp. 121-45. See also D. Barthelemy and J. T. Milik, eds., *Discoveries in the Judean Desert of the Jordan,* chap. 2, and Archer, chap. 3.

of Joshua, Samuel (e.g. 4QSam^{a,b}), and Jeremiah (e.g., 4QJer^{a}). The text of 4QSam^{b} agrees systematically with the LXX against the Masoretic Text by a ratio of thirteen to four. In 4QSam^{a} the ratio of agreement with the LXX text-type is even higher. The other historical books (Joshua and Kings), insofar as they are preserved by the fragments, also support the Proto-Septuagint text-type. A few manuscripts of the Pentateuch from Cave IV also support this tradition, for example, the Exodus manuscript (4QEx^{a}) and the manuscript containing Deuteronomy 32:43. From the Prophets there is a Jeremiah fragment (4QJer^{b}) that follows the LXX very closely. In the LXX, Jeremiah is one-eighth shorter than in the Masoretic Text, and in Jeremiah 10 of this Qumran manuscript four verses are omitted and one shifted, exactly as it is in the Qumran literature. Hitherto there were no Hebrew manuscripts supporting the shorter LXX version of Jeremiah.

The Proto-Samaritan Text-Type

This is also known among the Dead Sea Scrolls. From Cave IV came a Paleo-Hebrew manuscript of Exodus[52] and one of the Numbers (4QNum^{b}) in "square" script, which give collateral witness to a Samaritan type of text. The Numbers manuscript is not a consistent witness to the Samaritan text or even to a Proto-Samaritan type, because it shows striking contact with the LXX tradition. Some scholars indicate the possibility of a fourth main manuscript family called "a neutral family," which stands more or less midway among the conflicting traditions of the other three families.[53] The accompanying chart is an attempt to show these family histories.

The Quality of the Old Testament Manuscripts

Several reasons have been suggested for the scarcity of early Hebrew manuscripts. The first and most obvious reason is a combination of antiquity and destructibility. Two or three thousand years is a long time to expect the elements and the destructiveness of man to leave these ancient documents unmolested. With this in mind, the next logical question to be asked is, How good are the Hebrew manuscripts that remain? Several lines of evidence suggest that their quality is very good.

Relatively Few Variants

There are very few variants in the texts available because the Masoretes

52. Published by Patrick W. Skehan, "Exodus in the Samaritan Recension from Qumran," pp. 182-87.
53. Archer, *A Survey of Old Testament Introduction*, p. 41.

History of the Old Testament Text*

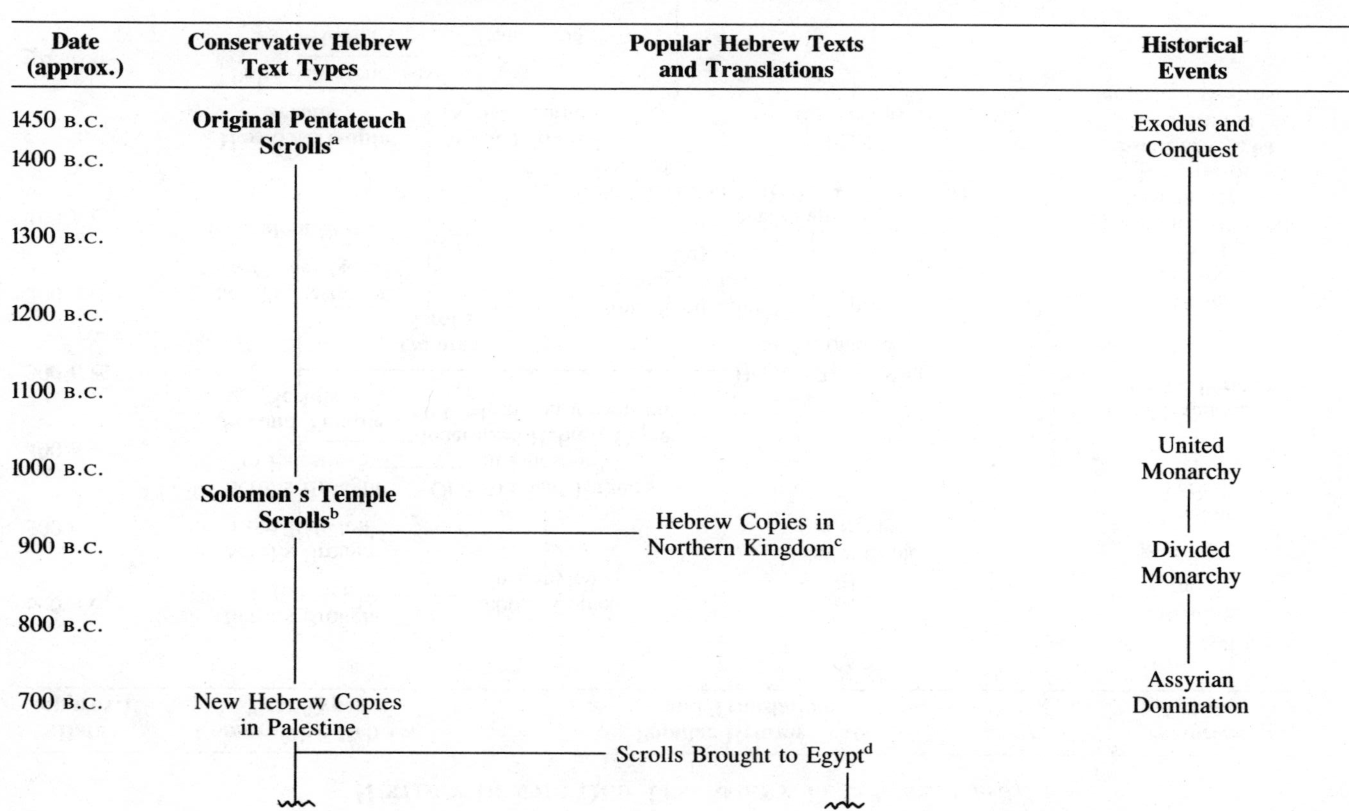

Date (approx.)	Conservative Hebrew Text Types	Popular Hebrew Texts and Translations	Historical Events
1450 B.C.	**Original Pentateuch Scrolls**[a]		Exodus and Conquest
1400 B.C.			
1300 B.C.			
1200 B.C.			
1100 B.C.			
1000 B.C.	**Solomon's Temple Scrolls**[b]		United Monarchy
900 B.C.		Hebrew Copies in Northern Kingdom[c]	Divided Monarchy
800 B.C.			
700 B.C.	New Hebrew Copies in Palestine	Scrolls Brought to Egypt[d]	Assyrian Domination

History of the Old Testament Text* *(continued)*

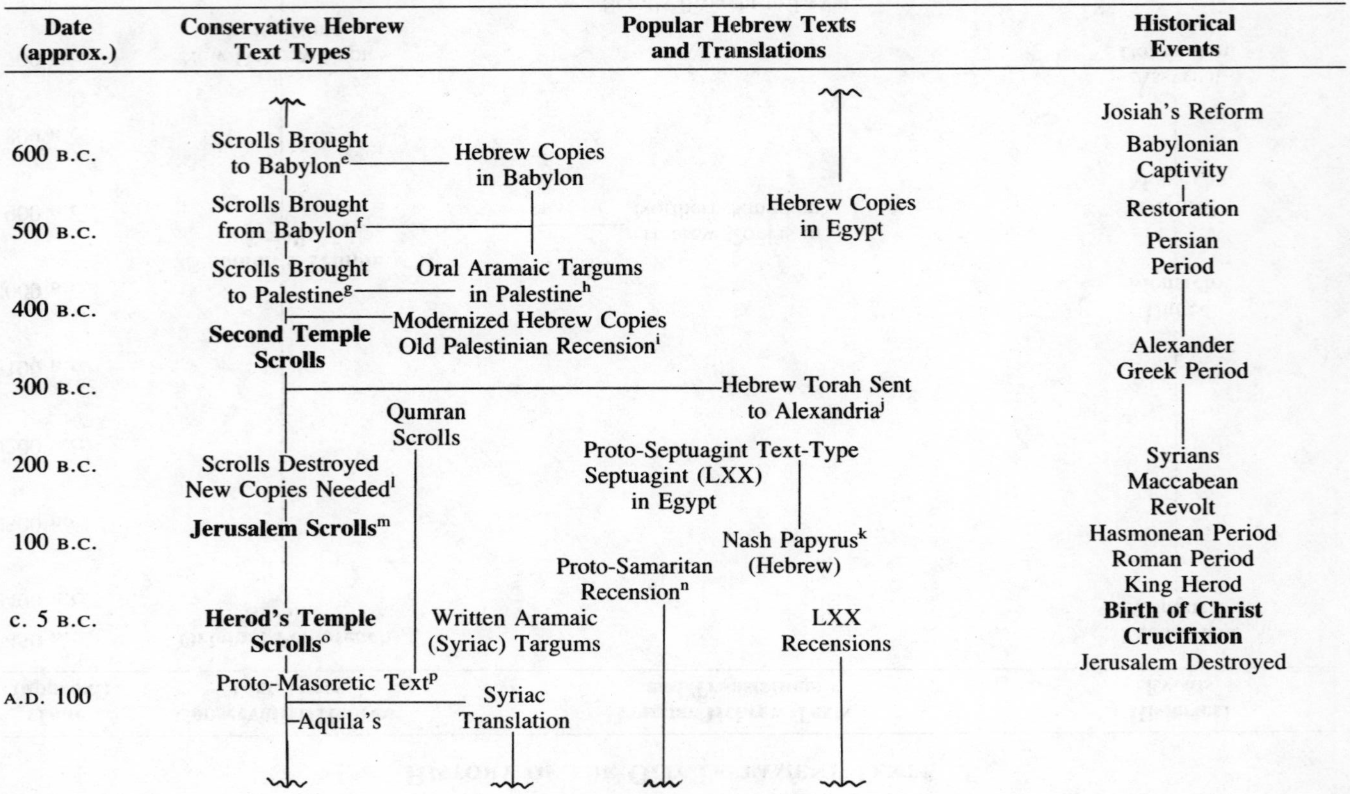

Date (approx.)	Conservative Hebrew Text Types	Popular Hebrew Texts and Translations	Historical Events
			Josiah's Reform
600 B.C.	Scrolls Brought to Babylon[e]	Hebrew Copies in Babylon	Babylonian Captivity
500 B.C.	Scrolls Brought from Babylon[f]	Hebrew Copies in Egypt	Restoration; Persian Period
400 B.C.	Scrolls Brought to Palestine[g]; **Second Temple Scrolls**	Oral Aramaic Targums in Palestine[h]; Modernized Hebrew Copies Old Palestinian Recension[i]	
300 B.C.		Hebrew Torah Sent to Alexandria[j]; Qumran Scrolls	Alexander Greek Period
200 B.C.	Scrolls Destroyed New Copies Needed[l]	Proto-Septuagint Text-Type Septuagint (LXX) in Egypt	Syrians Maccabean Revolt
100 B.C.	**Jerusalem Scrolls[m]**	Nash Papyrus[k] (Hebrew); Proto-Samaritan Recension[n]	Hasmonean Period; Roman Period; King Herod
c. 5 B.C.	**Herod's Temple Scrolls[o]**	Written Aramaic (Syriac) Targums; LXX Recensions	**Birth of Christ**; **Crucifixion**; Jerusalem Destroyed
A.D. 100	Proto-Masoretic Text[p]; Aquila's	Syriac Translation	

HISTORY OF THE OLD TESTAMENT TEXT* *(continued)*

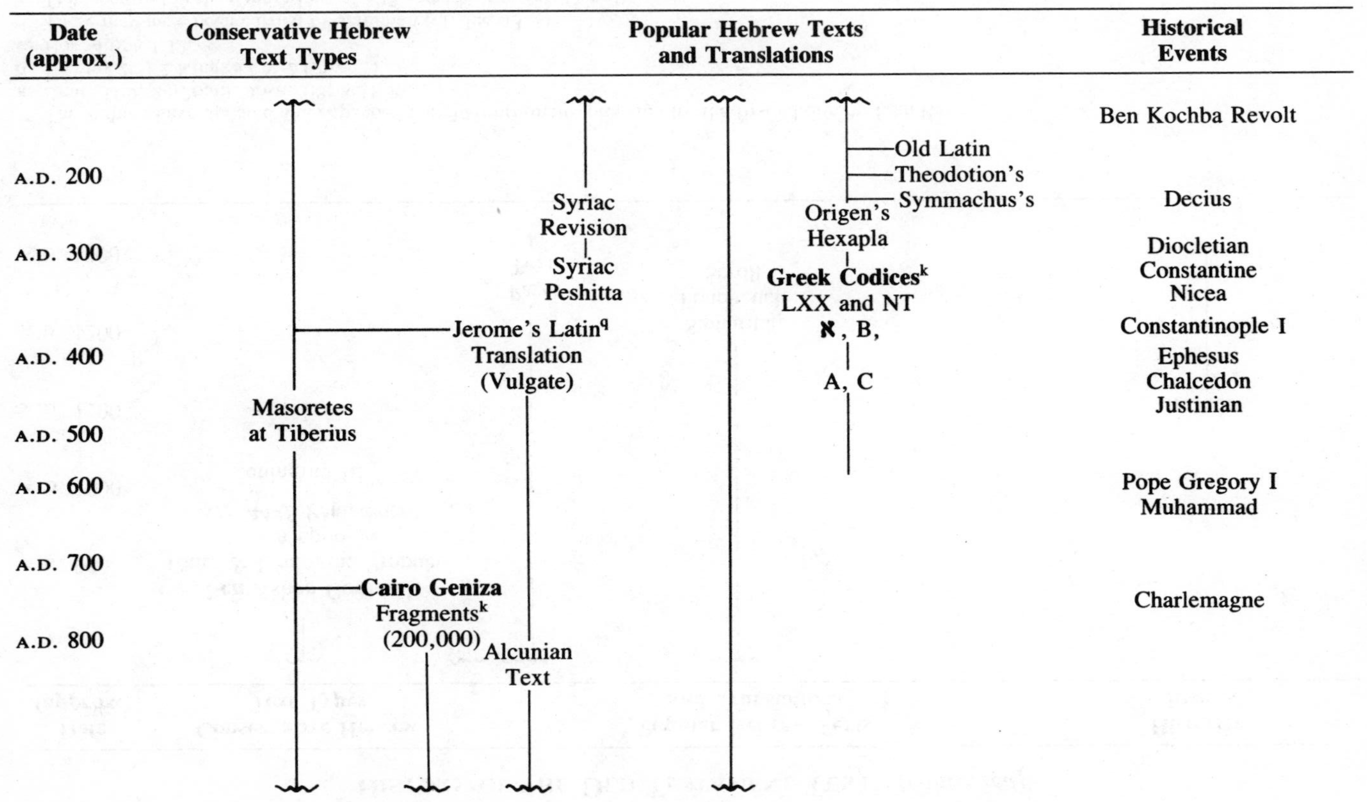

History of the Old Testament Text* *(continued)*

Date (approx.)	Conservative Hebrew Text Types	Popular Hebrew Texts and Translations		Historical Events
	Ben Asher Codices[k]			
A.D. 900	Cairo & Leningrad Prophets Aleppo Or. 4445 Pentateuch			
A.D. 1000	Leningrad B^{19A}			
A.D. 1100				Crusades
A.D. 1200			Samaritan Pentateuch Scroll	
A.D. 1300		Paris Text		

* The authors have updated and expanded the chart originally prepared for the first edition by John Rea.

a. Deut. 31:9, 24-26; cf. Josh. 1:8; 8:31-35.

b. 1 Kings 2:3; 2 Kings 14:6; 2 Chron. 17:9.

c. Hos. 4:6; 8:1,12.

d. These may have been carried by Jeremiah (cf. Jer. 43-44).

e. This occurred in the deporations of 597 and 586 B.C. (cf. Dan. 9:2).

f. Perhaps Zerubbabel brought Hebrew manuscripts with him in 535 B.C. when he and others returned to Palestine from Babylon (cf. Ezra 2:1-70).

g. Ezra 7:6, 10; Neh. 8:1-8.

h. Oral Aramaic Targums were used in Palestine (cf. Ezra 8:7-8) and in Babylon by Daniel (cf. Dan. 9:2) and possibly by Ezekiel as they explained their prophecies (and Scripture?).

i. Some argue that this recension was used by the chronicler when citing the Pentateuch and the books of Samuel. See Frank Moore Cross, "New Directions in Dead Sea Scroll Research, I: The Text Behind the Text of the Hebrew Bible," *Bible Review,* 1:2 (Summer 1985): 12-25, and "New Directions in Dead Sea Scroll Research, II: Original Biblical Research Reconstructed from Newly Found Fragments," *Bible Review,* 1:3 (Fall 1985): 26-35.

j. According to *The Letter of Aristeas,* which purports to tell how the Septuagint (LXX) originated.

k. Existing manuscript copy.

l. See 1 Macc. 1:56f; 2 Macc. 2:13.

m. Hillel's work (c. A.D. 100) produced a Proto-Rabbinic text type of standardized Hebrew text by comparing all existing manuscript copies.

n. This recension (c. 100 B.C.) utilized a particular form of Old Hebrew script that was current during the Hasmonean revival.

o. This authoritative Pharisaic text was completed before A.D. 70 and reflects Hebrew manuscritps from Masada as well as the great manuscripts from the caves of the Wadi Murabba'at (Hebrew Minor Prophets) and the Nahal Hever (Minor Prophets Scroll in Greek). See Cross, *Bible Review,* 1:2, p. 19.

p. The Proto-Masoretic standardization of the consonantal Hebrew text as a result of the studies at the synod at Jabneh (Jamnia) and the exegesis of Rabbi Akiba.

q. See the Latin Vulgate version edited by H.F.D. Sparks and W. Thiele, with a brief critical apparatus by Robert Weber, *Biblia Sacra: Iuxta Vulgatam Versionem,* editio minor (Stuttgart: Deutsch Bibelgesellschaft, 1984), follows *Biblia Sacra: Iuxta Vulgatam Version,* 3d ed. (Stuttgart: Deutsch Bibelgesellschaft, 1983). The small edition also contains manuscript evidence from major codices and editions of the Vulgate text.

systematically destroyed old manuscripts once they were carefully copied. Kenyon illustrates the paucity of variations in the Masoretic Text by contrasting the Leningrad Codex of the Prophets, which is Babylonian (Eastern), with the standard Palestinian text (Western) of Ezekiel, where the Masoretic Text is sometimes corrupt. A critical comparison reveals that there are only sixteen real conflicts between the two texts.[54] The fidelity of the New Testament text depends upon the multiplicity of manuscripts, whereas in the Old Testament the accuracy of the text results from the ability and reliability of the scribes who transmitted it.

Reverence for the Bible

With respect to the Jewish Scriptures, however, it was not scribal accuracy alone that guaranteed their product. Rather, it was their almost superstitious reverence for the Bible. According to the Talmud, there were specifications not only for the kind of skins to be used and the size of the columns, but there was even a religious ritual necessary for the scribe to perform before writing the name of God. Rules governed the kind of ink used, dictated the spacing of words, and prohibited writing anything from memory. The lines, and even the letters, were counted methodically. If a manuscript was found to contain even one mistake, it was discarded and destroyed (cf. chap. 20). This scribal formalism was responsible, at least in part, for the extreme care exercised in copying the Scriptures. It was also the reason there were only a few manuscripts (as the rules demanded the destruction of defective items), as well as why those which are extant are of good quality.

Comparison of Duplicate Passages

Another line of evidence for the quality of the Old Testament manuscripts is found in the comparison of the duplicate passages of the Masoretic Text itself. Several psalms occur twice (e.g., Pss. 14 and 53); much of Isaiah 36-39 is also found in 2 Kings 18-20; Isaiah 2:2-4 is almost exactly parallel to Micah 4:1-3; Jeremiah 52 is a repeat of 2 Kings 25; and large portions of Chronicles are found in Samuel and Kings. An examination of those passages shows not only a substantial textual agreement but, in some cases, almost a word-for-word identity. Therefore it may be concluded that the Old Testament texts have not undergone radical revisions, even if it were assumed that these parallel passages had identical sources.

Support from Archaeology

A substantial proof for the accuracy of the Old Testament text has come

54. Kenyon, pp. 45, 70-72.

from archaeology. Numerous discoveries have confirmed the historical accuracy of the biblical documents, even down to the occasional use of obsolete names of foreign kings.[55] These archaeological confirmations of the accuracy of Scripture have been recorded in numerous books.[56] Archaeologist Nelson Glueck asserts, "As a matter of fact, however, it may be stated categorically that no archaeological discovery has ever controverted a Biblical reference. Scores of archaeological findings have been made which confirm in clear outline or exact detail historical statements in the Bible."[57]

Furthermore, the Septuagint was the Bible of Jesus and the apostles. Most New Testament quotations are taken from it directly, even when it differs from the Masoretic Text. These differences will be discussed subsequently, but on the whole the Septuagint closely parallels the Masoretic Text and is a confirmation of the fidelity of the tenth-century A.D. Hebrew text.

Close Parallel Between the LXX and Masoretic Text

If no other evidence were available, the case for the fidelity of the Masoretic Text could be brought to rest with confidence upon the foregoing lines of evidence alone. It appeared to be a careful and correct reproduction of the autographs. But with the discovery of the Dead Sea Scrolls in 1947 and thereafter, there is now another and almost overwhelming substantiation of the received Hebrew text of the Masoretes. Critics of the Masoretic Text charged that the manuscripts were few and late; now, however, there is available, through the Dead Sea Scrolls, many and early manuscript fragments that provide a check on nearly the whole Old Testament. Those checks date about a thousand years before the great Masoretic manuscripts of the tenth century A.D. Before the discoveries in the Cairo Geniza and the Dead Sea caves, the Nash Papyrus (a fragment of the Ten Commandments and Shema, Deut. 6:4-9), dated between 150 B.C. and A.D. 100, was the only known scrap of the Hebrew text dating from before the Christian era.

Agreement with the Samaritan Pentateuch

Despite the many minor variants between the Samaritan Pentateuch and

55. The reference to "So king of Egypt" (2 Kings 17:4) has been used to illustrate the total ignorance of the writer of the book. No such king of Egypt was known to history. Now it is known, from the Egyptian spelling of the city of Sais—the capital of an Egyptian province in the western delta of that time (c. 725 B.C.)—that the text should read "To So [Sais], to the king of Egypt." Hans Goedicke, "The End of 'So,' King of Egypt," pp. 64-66, and William F. Albright, "The Elimination of King 'So,' " p. 66.
56. William F. Albright, *Archaeology of Palestine;* E. M. Blaiklock and R. K. Harrison, eds., *The New International Dictionary of Biblical Archaeology;* Gleason L. Archer, Jr., *Encyclopedia of Biblical Difficulties;* and a good popular summary by Clifford Wilson, *Rocks, Relics, and Biblical Reliability.*
57. Nelson Glueck, *Rivers in the Desert: A History of the Negev,* p. 31.

the Hebrew text of the Old Testament, there is substantial agreement between them. The Samaritan Pentateuch contains about six thousand variants from the Masoretic Text, but most of those are a matter of orthography (spelling, etc.). Some nineteen hundred of the variants agree with the LXX (e.g., in the ages given for the patriarchs in Gen. 5 and 11). Some of the Samaritan Pentateuch variants are sectarian, such as the command to build the Temple on Mt. Gerizim, not at Jerusalem (e.g., after Ex. 20:17). It should be noted, however, that most manuscripts of the Samaritan Pentateuch are late (13th-14th cent.), and none is before the tenth century.[58] But in chapter after chapter and verse after verse, the Samaritan Pentateuch is a confirmation of the general text of the Hebrew Old Testament.

Crosscheck by the Dead Sea Scrolls

With the discovery of the Dead Sea Scrolls, scholars have Hebrew manuscripts one thousand years earlier than the great Masoretic Text manuscripts, enabling them to check on the fidelity of the Hebrew text. The result of comparative studies reveals that there is a word-for-word identity in more than 95 percent of the cases, and the 5 percent variation consists mostly of slips of the pen and spelling.[59] To be specific, the Isaiah scroll (1Q Is[a]) from Qumran led the Revised Standard Version translators to make only thirteen changes from the Masoretic Text; eight of those were known from ancient versions, and few of them were significant.[60] More specifically, of the 166 Hebrew words in Isaiah 53 only seventeen Hebrew letters in 1Q Is[b] differ from the Masoretic Text. Ten letters are a matter of spelling, four are stylistic changes, and the other three compose the word for "light" (add in v. 11), which does not affect the meaning greatly.[61] Furthermore that word is also found in that verse in the LXX and 1Q Is[a].

Conclusion

The thousands of Hebrew manuscripts, with their confirmation by the LXX and the Samaritan Pentateuch, and the numerous other crosschecks from outside and inside the text provide overwhelming support for the reliability of the Old Testament text. Hence, it is appropriate to conclude with Sir Frederic Kenyon's statement, "The Christian can take the whole Bible in his hand and say without fear or hesitation that he holds in it the true word of God, handed down without essential loss from generation to generation throughout the centuries."[62]

58. Archer, *Survey of Old Testament Introduction,* p. 44.
59. Ibid., p. 24.
60. Burrows, *Dead Sea Scrolls,* pp. 305ff.
61. Harris, *Inspiration and Canonicity,* p. 124.
62. Kenyon, p. 55.

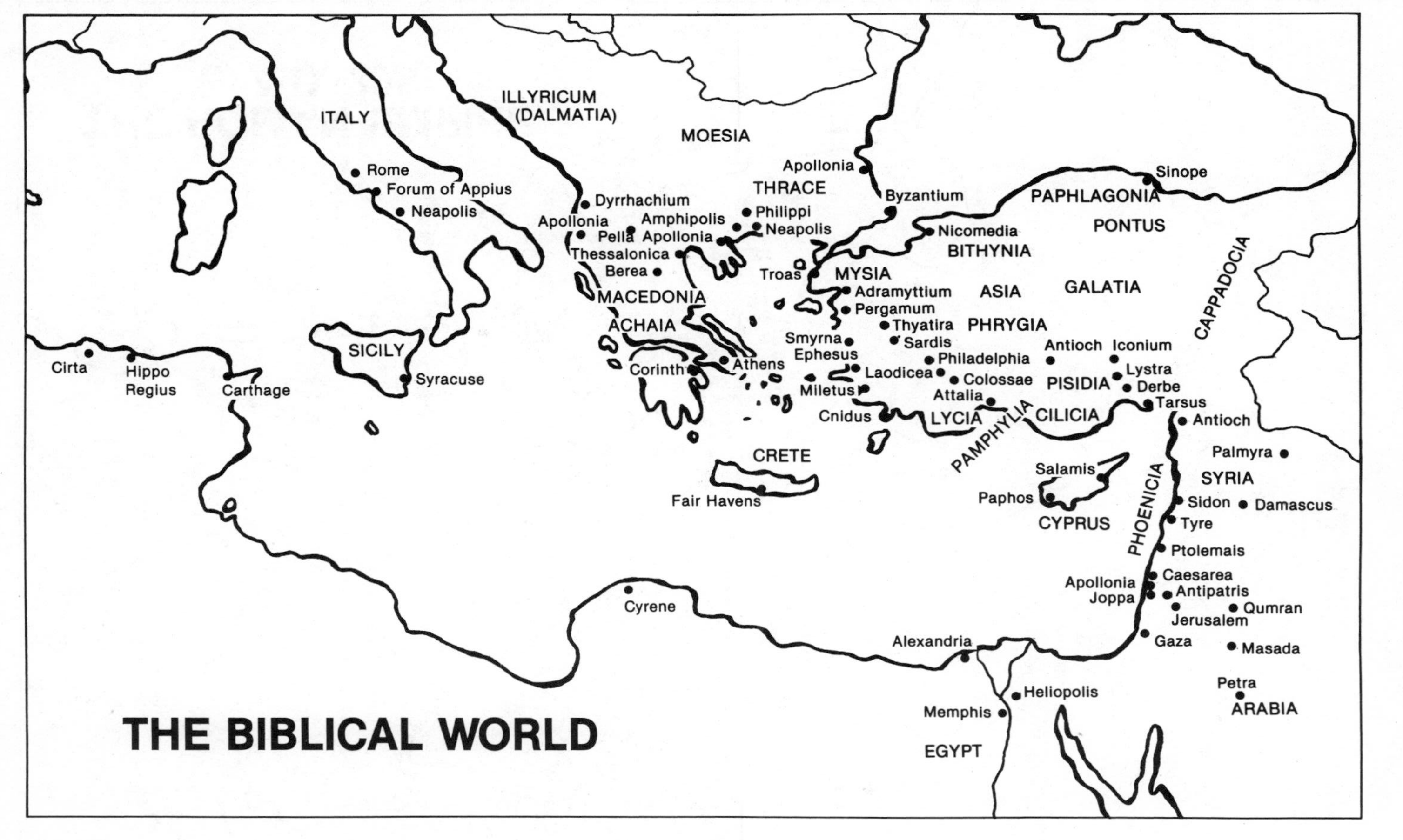
THE BIBLICAL WORLD
ITALY
ILLYRICUM (DALMATIA)
MOESIA
Rome
Forum of Appius
Neapolis
Dyrrhachium
Apollonia
Amphipolis
Pella
Apollonia
Thessalonica
Berea
MACEDONIA
ACHAIA
Corinth
Athens
THRACE
Apollonia
Philippi
Neapolis
Byzantium
Nicomedia
BITHYNIA
PAPHLAGONIA
Sinope
PONTUS
CAPPADOCIA
GALATIA
Troas
MYSIA
Adramyttium
Pergamum
ASIA
Thyatira
Sardis
Smyrna
Ephesus
PHRYGIA
Philadelphia
Laodicea
Colossae
Miletus
Cnidus
Attalia
LYCIA
PAMPHYLIA
Antioch
Iconium
Lystra
Derbe
PISIDIA
CILICIA
Tarsus
Antioch
Palmyra
SYRIA
Sidon
Damascus
Tyre
Ptolemais
Caesarea
Antipatris
Apollonia
Joppa
Qumran
Jerusalem
Gaza
Masada
Petra
ARABIA
PHOENICIA
Salamis
Paphos
CYPRUS
CRETE
Fair Havens
SICILY
Syracuse
Cirta
Hippo Regius
Carthage
Cyrene
Alexandria
Heliopolis
Memphis
EGYPT

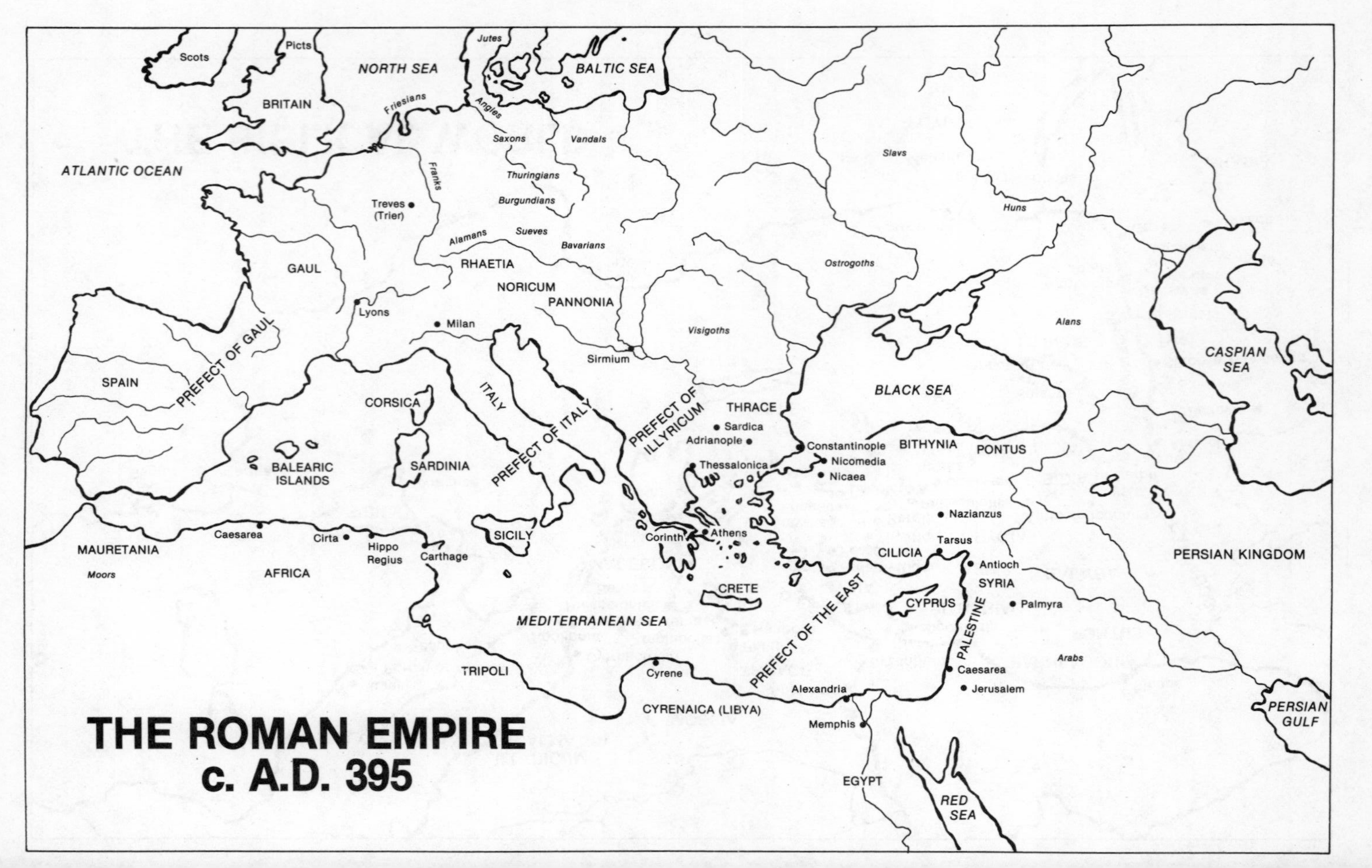
Scots
Picts
BRITAIN
NORTH SEA
Jutes
BALTIC SEA
Friesians
Angles
Saxons
Vandals
ATLANTIC OCEAN
Franks
Thuringians
Burgundians
Treves
(Trier)
Alamans
Sueves
Bavarians
GAUL
RHAETIA
NORICUM
PANNONIA
Lyons
Milan
Sirmium
PREFECT OF GAUL
SPAIN
CORSICA
ITALY
PREFECT OF ITALY
PREFECT OF ILLYRICUM
THRACE
Sardica
Adrianople
Thessalonica
Constantinople
Nicomedia
Nicaea
BITHYNIA
PONTUS
BLACK SEA
Slavs
Huns
Ostrogoths
Visigoths
Alans
CASPIAN SEA
BALEARIC ISLANDS
SARDINIA
SICILY
Corinth
Athens
CRETE
Nazianzus
Tarsus
CILICIA
Antioch
SYRIA
CYPRUS
PALESTINE
Palmyra
PERSIAN KINGDOM
MAURETANIA
Moors
Caesarea
Cirta
Hippo
Regius
Carthage
AFRICA
MEDITERRANEAN SEA
PREFECT OF THE EAST
Arabs
TRIPOLI
Cyrene
CYRENAICA (LIBYA)
Alexandria
Caesarea
Jerusalem
Memphis
EGYPT
RED SEA
PERSIAN GULF
THE ROMAN EMPIRE
c. A.D. 395

22
New Testament Manuscripts

Introductory Considerations

The integrity of the Old Testament text had been established in the transmission of the Masoretic tradition and was confirmed with the discovery of the Dead Sea Scrolls. The accuracy of the Old Testament text is largely the result of the meticulous care taken by rabbinical scholars in the transmission process.

The fidelity of the New Testament text, however, rests on a different basis altogether. The New Testament rests on a multitude of manuscript evidence. Counting Greek copies alone, the New Testament text is preserved in some 5,366 partial and complete manuscript portions that were copied by hand from the second through the fifteenth centuries.[1] By way of contrast, most other books from the ancient world survive in only a few and late manuscript copies (see comparison later in this chapter).

A few of the New Testament manuscript fragments are very early, dating from the second century. By contrast, the manuscripts for most other ancient books date from about a thousand years after their original composition. Some 362 New Testament uncial manuscripts and 245 uncial lectionaries[2] date from the second through the tenth centuries, constituting nearly 11 percent of all New Testament and lectionary manuscripts. Those early uncial manuscript witnesses are extremely valuable in establishing the original text of the New Testament (as will be shown in chap. 26). The other 89 percent of manuscripts are minuscule, dating between the ninth and fifteenth centuries; those provide the basis for the text family similar to the so-called Received Text.[3]

1. Chaps. 20, 21, 24, 25, and 26 provide extended discussions of the issues summarized here.
2. Lectionaries are collections of Scripture texts grouped together for reading in public worship services.
3. Chap. 26 considers these textual traditions, which provide the basis for modern translations of the Bible discussed in chaps. 31 and 32.

Definition of Manuscript

A manuscript is a handwritten literary composition, in contrast to a printed copy. An original manuscript is the first one produced, usually called an autograph. There are no known extant original manuscripts of the Bible. However, the abundance of manuscript copies makes it possible to reconstruct the original with complete accuracy. Nor is there a known manuscript containing the entire Bible, referred to as a *pandect* (Gr. *pandektās*).

At one time the uncial codex manuscripts א, A, B, and C were complete in both Testaments, but none of these have survived intact. Nevertheless, it is possible to reconstruct the original text of the Bible with complete accuracy. The differences between existing translations reflect differences of opinion regarding what was in the original text and what was added later. Those decisions are made through the process of textual criticism, using the manuscripts that have survived and are catalogued for use by textual scholars.

Different Kinds of Manuscripts

New Testament manuscripts written in a formal printed style somewhat similar to capital letters are known as uncials (or majuscules).[4] Uncial manuscripts of Greek and biblical literature flourished from the third to the seventh centuries A.D. Gradually, during the next two centuries, the style degenerated until a reform in handwriting was initiated, consisting of smaller letters in a running hand called "minuscules."[5] Minuscule manuscripts in Greek are dated from the ninth to the fifteenth centuries; nevertheless, this running hand, known also as "cursive," was employed by the Greeks for nonliterary, everyday documents from antiquity. The cursive hand proved to be more practical than the more formal "book hand" (uncial), and became popular almost immediately throughout Western Europe, with the exception of some liturgical writers who employed uncials as late as the tenth and eleventh centuries.

Testimony to the fidelity of the New Testament text comes primarily from three sources: Greek manuscripts, ancient translations, and patristic citations. The first source is the most important and can be subdivided into four classes, commonly termed papyri, uncials, minuscules, and lectionaries. The most distinguishing characteristic of each of those classes has been chosen as its designation. The papyrus manuscripts and over two hundred lectionaries were written in uncial letters. The second and third classes are differentiated by the style of writing, because both were written on vellum or

4. The word *uncial* is derived from the Latin *uncia,* meaning "a twelfth part," implying that the letter was one-twelfth the size of a normal line. Cf. chap. 20, n. 14; *Classical Philology,* 30 (1935): 247-54.
5. *Minuscule* is derived from the Latin *minuscules,* meaning "rather small."

parchment. At present there are 88 catalogued papyri manuscripts, an additional 274 uncial manuscripts in codex format, and 245 lectionaries in uncial script. In addition, 2,795 manuscripts and 1,964 lectionaries in minuscule script have been catalogued.[6]

New Testament Manuscript Distribution by Century and Manuscript Type*

Cent.	2	3	4	5	6	7	8	9	10	11	12	13	14	15	16	17	18	19	Totals
Papyri	1	31	20	8	9	13	3												85
Uncial		3	16	44	60	29	27	47	18	1									245
Min.			1	1	3	4	22	13	125	436	586	569	535	248	138	44	16	4	2,745
Lect.								116	143	241	490	398	313	168	194	73	11		2,147

*This arrangement is an adaptation by Darrell L. Bock of material from Kurt Aland and Barbara Aland, *Der Text des Neuen Testaments: Einführung in die wissenschaftlichen Ausgaben sowie in Theorie und Praxis der modernen Textkritik* (Deutsche Bibelgesellenschaft, 1982), p. 90. There is an apparent conradiction in the totals summarized in the Aland list (5,222 items) and the evidence presented by Metzger (5,366 items). Aland and Aland seem to have excluded from their list manuscripts whose century is uncertain, whereas Metzger, UBS, and Nestle (26th ed.) include all catalogued papyri and uncials but incorporate selected minuscule and lectionary evidence into their lists.

6. See discussion in chap. 20. Bruce M. Metzger, "Appendix III: Statistics Relating to the Manuscripts of the Greek New Testament," in *Manuscripts of the Greek Bible,* pp. 54-56, identifies the four categories of New Testament manuscripts officially catalogued as of 1976 as follows:

Manuscripts Catalogued	Uncial Script	Minuscule Script
Papyri P[1]-P[88]	88	
Uncial MSS 01-0274	274	
Minuscule MSS 1-2795		2795
Lectionaries *l*1-*l*2209	245	1964
Totals	607	4759

Total number of N.T. lectionaries: 2,209
Total number of N.T. manuscripts: 5,366

This alters the 1964 figures in Metzger, *The Text of the New Testament,* pp. 31-33, where he listed 76 papyri, 250 uncials, 2,646 minuscules, and 1,997 lectionaries for a total of 4,969 manuscripts. He based the earlier figures on Kurt Aland's *Kurzgefasste Liste* (1963), which is the official list of New Testament Greek manuscripts. His 1981 figures are based on Aland's *Kurzgefasste Liste* and Aland's supplements to that list in *Materialien zur neutestamentlichen Handschriften* (Berlin, 1969), pp. 1-37, *Bericht der Stiftung zur Forderung der neutestamentlichen Textforschung für die Jahre 1972 bis 1974* (Munster, Westfalen, 1974), pp. 9-16, and *Bericht der Stiftung zur Forderung der neutestamentlichen Textforschung fur die Jahre 1975 und 1976* (Munster/Westfalen, 1977), pp. 10-12. J. Harold Greenlee, *An Introduction to New Testament Textual Criticism,* p. 62, adds that about 95 percent of these date from the eighth century onward. That would leave a chain of some 250 manuscripts stretching back to the early second century.

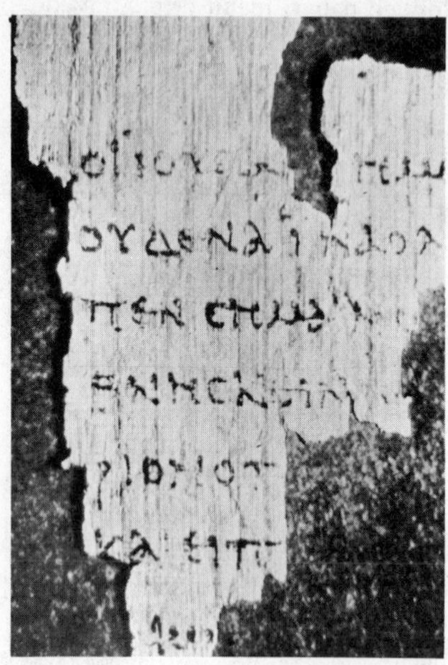

12. The John Rylands Fragment of John 18:31-33 (John Rylands Library)

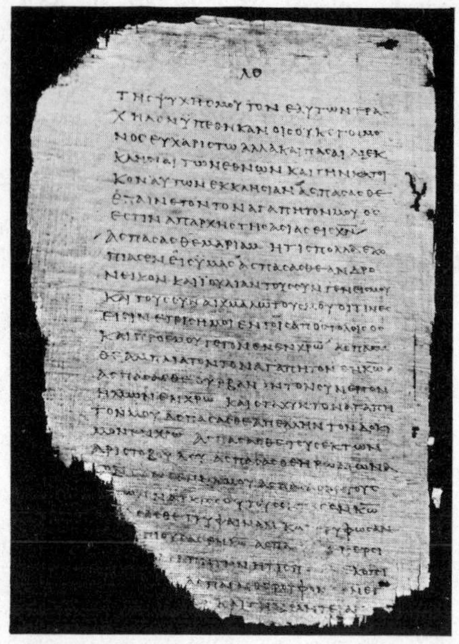

13. A page of Romans from a Beatty-Michigan papyrus dating about A.D. 200 (The Department of Rare Books and Special Collections, The University of Michigan Library)

MANUSCRIPTS ON PAPYRUS (SECOND-THIRD CENTURIES)[7]

P^{52}, JOHN RYLANDS FRAGMENT (c. A.D. 117-138)

This papyrus fragment (2½ by 3½ inches) from a codex is the earliest known copy of any portion of the New Testament. It dates from the first half of the second century, probably A.D. 117-138. Adolf Deissmann argues that it may be even earlier.[8] The papyrus piece, written on both sides, contains

7. Unless otherwise noted, the following discussion and dating system are after Bruce M. Metzger, *The Text of the New Testament*. Supplemental information appears in Kurt Aland, Matthew Black, Carlo M. Martini, Bruce M. Metzger, and Alan Wikgren, eds., *The Greek New Testament*, pp. xi-liii. In addition, see Bruce M. Metzger, *Manuscripts of the Greek Bible: An Introduction to Greek Paleography,* especially pp. 3-5, where Metzger identifies the modern tools for paleographic research as well as locations of microfilm copies of the manuscript collections that are available.
8. Metzger, *The Text of the New Testament,* p. 39 n. 2.

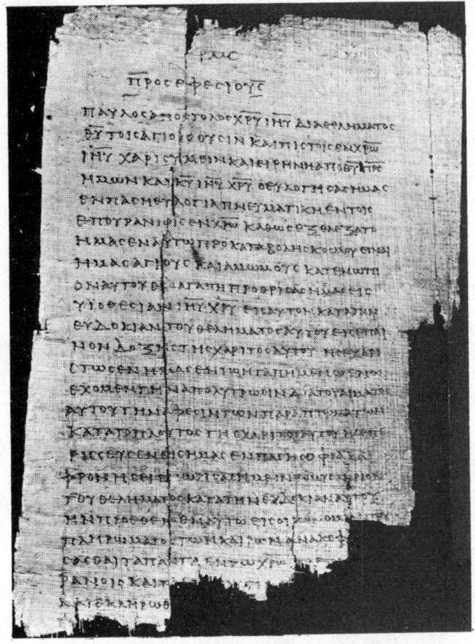

14. The first page of Ephesians from a Beatty-Michigan papyrus dating about A.D. 200 (The Department of Rare Books and Special Collections, The University of Michigan Library)

15. The Bodmer Papyrus (P^{66}) dates from about A.D. 250. John 1:1-14 is pictured (Bodmer Library)

portions of five verses from the gospel of John (18:31-33, 37-38). Although this is a short fragment, it has proved to be the closest and most valuable link in the chain of transmission. Because of its early date and its location (Egypt) some distance from the traditional place of composition (Asia Minor), this portion of the gospel of John tends to confirm the traditional date of the composition of the gospel before the end of the first century. The fragment belongs to the John Rylands Library at Manchester, England.

P^{45}, P^{46}, P^{47} Chester Beatty Papyri (c. a.d. 250)

This important collection of New Testament papyri now resides in the Beatty Museum near Dublin. It consists of three codices and contains most of the New Testament. P^{45} is made up of pieces of thirty leaves of a papyrus codex: two from Matthew, two from John, six from Mark, seven from Luke, and thirteen from Acts. The original codex consisted of some 220 leaves, measuring ten by eight inches each. Several other small fragments of Matthew from those papyri have appeared in a collection at Vienna.[9] The type of text represented in Mark is nearer to the Caesarean family.[10] The other gospels stand between the Alexandrian and Western text-types. Acts is clearly nearer to the Alexandrian family of manuscripts. P^{46} consists of eighty-six slightly mutilated leaves (11 by 6½ inches), stemming from an original that contained 104 pages of Paul's epistles, including Romans, Hebrews, 1 Corinthians, 2 Corinthians, Ephesians, Galatians, Philippians, Colossians, 1 Thessalonians, and 2 Thessalonians. Portions of Romans and 1 Thessalonians, and all of 2 Thessalonians, are missing from the present manuscripts, which were arranged in descending order according to size. Like P^{45}, P^{46} dates from about A.D. 250. In general, the text is closer to the Alexandrian type. P^{47} is made up of ten slightly mutilated leaves of the book of Revelation, measuring 9½ by 5½ inches. Of the original thirty-two leaves, only the middle portion, 9:10—17:2, remains. In general, it agrees with the Alexandrian text of Codex Sinaiticus (א), but shows frequent independence. This papyrus dates from about A.D. 250 or later. Thirty of the leaves are owned by the University of Michigan, Ann Arbor.

P^{66}, P^{72}, P^{75} Bodmer Papyri (A.D. second-third century)

The most important discovery of New Testament papyri since the Chester Beatty manuscripts was the acquisition of the Bodmer Collection by the Library of World Literature at Culagny, near Geneva. P^{66}, dating from about A.D. 200 or earlier, contains 104 leaves of John 1:1—6:11; 6:35*b*—14:26; and fragments of forty other pages, John 14—21. The text is a mixture of the Alexandrian and Western types, and there are some twenty alterations between the lines that invariably belong to the Western family.[11] P^{72} is the earliest known copy of Jude, 1 Peter, and 2 Peter. It dates from the third century and contains several apocryphal and canonical books, in the following order: Nativity of Mary, apocryphal Correspondence of Paul to the Corinthians, the Eleventh Ode of Solomon, the epistle of Jude, Melito's Homily on the Passover, a Fragment of a Hymn, the Apology of Phileas, Psalm 33, Psalm 34, 1 Peter, and 2 Peter. This papyrus was apparently a private codex measuring 6 by 5¾ inches, prepared by some four scribes and having definite affinities to the Alexandrian textual tradition and particularly the Sahidic version.[12] P^{75} is a codex of 102 pages (originally 144) measuring 10¼ by 5⅓ inches, containing most of Luke and John in clear and carefully printed uncials, and dated between A.D. 175 and 225. It consequently is the earliest known copy of Luke. Its text is very similar to Codex Vaticanus (B), although

9. Ibid., p. 37 n. 2.
10. For a discussion of the meaning of "textual families," see chap. 25.
11. Metzger, *The Text of the New Testament*, p. 40.
12. Ibid., pp. 40-41.

it occasionally agrees with the Sahidic version.[13]

Actually, there are some eighty-eight[14] papyri manuscripts of portions of the New Testament, of which the foregoing are merely the most important representatives. The papyri witness to the text is invaluable, ranging chronologically from the very threshold of the second century—within a generation of the autographs—and including the content of most of the New Testament. All are extant from within the first two hundred years after the New Testament itself was written.[15]

Uncial Manuscripts on Vellum and Parchment (Fourth-Ninth Centuries)

The most important manuscripts of the New Testament are generally considered to be the great uncial codices that date from the fourth and following centuries. These appeared almost immediately following the conversion of Constantine and the authorization to make multiple copies of the Bible at the Council of Nicea (325), as discussed in chapter 16.

Codex Vaticanus (B) (c. 325-350)

The Codex Vaticanus is perhaps the oldest uncial on parchment or vellum (c. 325-350), and one of the most important witnesses to the text of the New Testament. This manuscript copy of the whole Bible was probably written by the middle of the fourth century; however, it was not known to textual scholars until after 1475, when it was catalogued in the Vatican Library. For the next four hundred years scholars were prohibited from studying it.[16] After that time, a complete photographic facsimile was made of it (1889-90), and another of the New Testament in 1904. It includes most of the LXX version of the Old Testament and most of the New Testament in Greek. Missing are 1 Timothy through Philemon, Hebrews 9:14 to the end of the New Testament, and the General Epistles. The Apocrypha is included with the exceptions of 1 Maccabees, 2 Maccabees, and the Prayer of Manasses. Also missing is Genesis 1:1—46:28, 2 Kings 2:5-7 and 10-13, and Psalms 106:27—138:6. Mark

13. A more detailed analysis appears in Metzger, *The Text of the New Testament, p. 42*.
14. See "Check-list of the Greek Papyri of the New Testament," ibid., pp. 247-56. Also see Metzger, *Manuscripts of the Greek Bible,* p. 54. A listing of "The Greek Manuscript Evidence" is also available in Aland, Black, Martini, Metzger, and Wikgren, eds., *The Greek New Testament,* pp. xi-liii.
15. See chaps. 16 and 27 for discussions related to the systematic destruction of biblical manuscripts by the enemies of Christianity during this period, and especially under the Roman Emperor Diocletian.
16. Constantin Tischendorf (in 1843-1866) and S. P. Tregelles (in 1845) were permitted to look at it for a few hours. They were not permitted to copy the manuscript, but Tregelles secretly memorized much of it. For a more complete story of Codex Vaticanus (B), see G. L. Robinson, *Where Did We Get Our Bible?* p. 111.

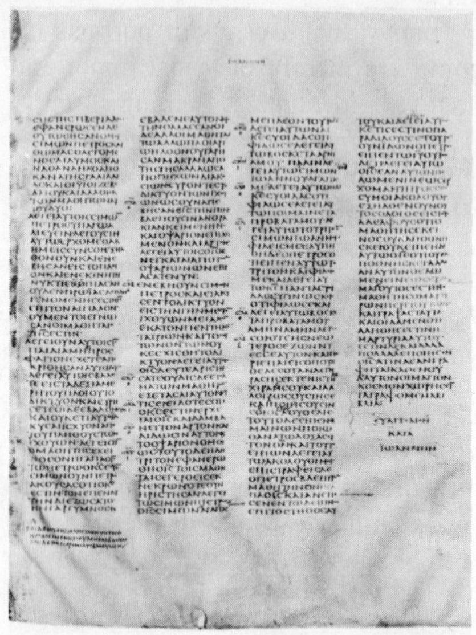

16. *Codex Sinaiticus opened to John 21:1-25 (By permission of the British Library)*

17. *The Monastery of St. Catherine of Mount Sinai is a repository of ancient manuscripts (Courtesy of* Biblical Archaeologist, *a publication of the American Schools of Oriental Research)*

16:9-20 and John 7:53—8:11 were purposely omitted from the text. This codex was written in small and delicate uncials on fine vellum. It has three columns of forty-two lines per page, except for the Old Testament poetical books, which have only two columns. It contains 759 leaves measuring 10 by 10½ inches: 617 in the Old Testament, and 142 in the New. The manuscripts are divided into sections: Matthew has 170 sections, Mark has 61, Luke 152, John 80, and so on. Codex Vaticanus is a possession of the Roman Catholic Church, and is housed in the Vatican Library, Vatican City. This manuscript is generally regarded as an excellent example of the Alexandrian text-type.

Codex Sinaiticus (א [Aleph]) (c. 340)

This fourth-century Greek manuscript is generally considered to be the most important witness to the text because of its antiquity, accuracy, and lack of omissions. The story of the discovery of א is one of the most fascinating and romantic in textual history.[17] It was found in the monastery of St. Cather-

17. For the details of this story see Metzger, *The Text of the New Testament*, pp. 42-45.

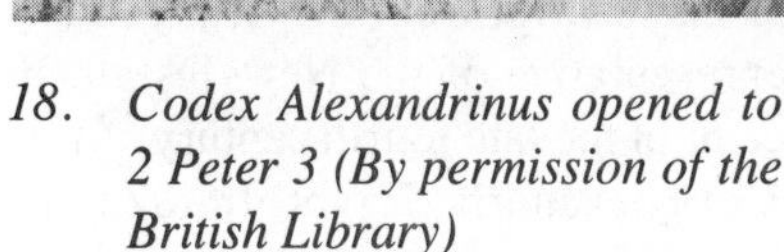

18. Codex Alexandrinus opened to 2 Peter 3 (By permission of the British Library)

19. Papyrus 1532. This third-century fragment shows Hebrews 12:1-11 (By permission of the British Library)

ine at Mount Sinai by the German Count Lobegott Friedrich Constantine von Tischendorf (1815-1874), who was living in Prussia by permission of the czar. On his first visit (1844), he discovered forty-three leaves of vellum, containing portions of the LXX (1 Chronicles, Jeremiah, Nehemiah, and Esther), in a basket of scraps that the monks were using to light their fires. He secured it and took it to the University Library at Leipzig, Germany. It remains there, known as the Codex Frederico-Augustanus. Tischendorf's second visit, in 1853, proved unfruitful; but in 1859, under the authority of Czar Alexander II, he returned again. Just as he was about to return home empty-handed, the monastery steward showed him an almost complete copy of the Scriptures and some other books. These were subsequently acquired as a "conditional gift"[18] to the czar. This manuscript is now known as the famous Codex

18. Actually, Tischendorf pulled a bit of ecclesiastical diplomacy in convincing the monastery that it would be to their advantage for them to give the manuscript to the czar, whose influence as protectorate of the Greek church could be to their advantage. In return for the manuscript, the czar gave them a silver shrine, 7,000 rubles for the library at Sinai, 2,000 rubles for the monks in Cairo, and conferred several Russian decorations on the authorities of the monastery.

Sinaiticus (א). It contains over half the Old Testament (LXX), and all of the New, with the exception of Mark 16:9-20 and John 7:53—8:11. All of the Old Testament Apocrypha, with the addition of the *Epistle of Barnabas* and a large portion of the *Shepherd* of Hermas, are also included. This codex was written in large clear Greek uncials on 364½ pages (plus the forty-three at Leipzig), measuring 13½ by 14 inches. Each page has four columns about 2½ inches wide, except the Old Testament poetical books where there are only two wider columns per page. The material is good vellum, made from antelope skins. Originally the manuscript underwent several scribal "corrections," known by the seglum $א^{c}$, and then, at Caesarea in the sixth or seventh century a group of scribes introduced a large number of alterations known as $א^{ca}$ or $א^{cb}$. In 1933 the British government purchased א for the British Museum for £100,000, about $500,000 at that time. It was published in a volume entitled *Scribes and Correctors of Codex Sinaiticus* (London, 1938). The text-type is Alexandrian in general but has definite strains of Western readings.

Codex Alexandrinus (A) (c. 450)

Codex Alexandrinus is a well-preserved manuscript from the fifth century that ranks second only to B and א as representative of the New Testament text. Though some have dated this manuscript in the late fourth century,[19] it is probably the result of fifth-century scribes of Alexandria, Egypt. In 1078 this codex was presented to the Patriarch of Alexandria, after whom it was named. In 1621 it was taken to Constantinople by Cyril Lucar, who was transferred to patriarchal duties there. Lucar gave it to Sir Thomas Roe, English ambassador to Turkey in 1624, to present to King James I. James died before it reached England, and the manuscript was given to Charles I in 1627, too late for use in the King James Version of 1611. In 1757, George II presented it to the National Library of the British Museum. It contains the whole Old Testament, except for several mutilations (Gen. 14:14-17; 15:1-5, 16-19; 16:6-9; 1 Kingdoms [1 Sam.] 12:18—14:9; Pss. 49:19—79:10), and most of the New Testament (only Matt. 1:1—25:6; John 6:50—8:52 and 2 Cor. 4:13—12:6 are missing). However, the manuscript also contains 1 and 2 Clement and the Psalms of Solomon, with some parts missing. The manuscript contains 773 leaves, 639 of the Old Testament and 134 of the New. The page size is 10¼ by 12 inches, and is written in two columns of fifty or fifty-one lines per page. The large square uncials are written on very thin vellum, and are divided into sections marked by large letters. Codex Alexandrinus is in the possession of the National Library of the British Museum. The text is of varied quality. The Gospels are the oldest example of the Byzantine text, which is generally

19. Sir Frederic G. Kenyon, *Our Bible and the Ancient Manuscripts*, p. 129. Cf. Metzger, *The Text of the New Testament*, p. 49.

regarded as inferior. The remainder of the New Testament, which was probably copied from a different source, ranks with א and B as a representative of the Alexandrian type of text.[20]

Codex Ephraemi Rescriptus (C) (c. 345)

The Ephraemi Rescriptus Codex probably originated in Alexandria, Egypt. It was brought to Italy by John Lascaris at about 1500 and was later purchased by Pietro Strozzi. Catherine de Medici, an Italian who was the wife and mother of French kings, acquired it about 1533. At her death, the manuscript was placed in the Bibliothèque Nationale at Paris, where it remains today. Most of the Old Testament is missing from this codex, except parts of Job, Proverbs, Ecclesiastes, Song of Solomon, and two apocryphal books: The Wisdom of Solomon, and Ecclesiasticus. The New Testament lacks 2 Thessalonians, 2 John, and parts of other books.[21] The manuscript is a *palimpsest* (rubbed out, erased) *rescriptus* (rewritten). It originally contained the Old and New Testaments, but they were erased by Ephraem, who wrote his sermons on the leaves. By chemical reactivation, Tischendorf was able to decipher the almost invisible writing.[22] Only 209 leaves survive: 64 from the Old and 145 (of an original 238) from the New Testament. The pages are 9½ by 12¼ inches, with one wide column of forty to forty-six lines (usually forty-one). Located in the Bibliothèque Nationale, Paris, C is a compound of all the major textual types, agreeing frequently with the inferior Byzantine family. The manuscript has been corrected by two scribes, in texts referred to as C^2 or C^b (sixth-century Palestine) and C^3 or C^c (ninth-century Constantinople).

Codex Bezae (D [Codex Cantabrigiensis]) (c. 450 or c. 550)

This is the oldest known bilingual manuscript of the New Testament. It was written in Greek and Latin and may have originated in southern Gaul (France) or northern Italy. It was found in 1562 by Théodore de Bèze (Beza), the French theologian, at St. Irenaeus Monastery, Lyons, France. In 1581 Beza gave it to Cambridge University. This manuscript contains the four gospels, Acts, and 3 John 11-15, with variations from other manuscripts indicated. Present omissions in Greek include Matthew 1:1-20; 6:20—9:2; 27:2-12; John 1:16—3:26; Acts 8:29—10:14; 21:2-10, 15-18; 22:10-20; and 22:29—28:31. In Latin, Matthew 1:1-11; 6:8—8:27; 26:65—27:1; 1 John 1:1—3:16; Acts 8:20—10:4; 20:31—21:2; 21:7-10; 22:2-10; and 22:20—28:31 are omit-

20. Cf. Metzger, *The Text of the New Testament,* pp. 47, 49.
21. F. H. A. Scrivener, *A Plain Introduction to the Criticism of the New Testament,* 1:121, lists these in detail.
22. For correction of Tischendorf's edition (Leipzig, 1843), see Robert W. Lyon, "Re-examination of Codex Ephraemi Rescriptus," pp. 266-72.

ted. There are 406 leaves (8 by 10 inches), with one column of thirty-three lines to the page. The Greek text is on the left page, and the Latin on the right. The order of the books is Matthew, John, Luke, Mark, and so on. Third John 11-15 is found in Latin only. In each book the first three lines are in red ink. The manuscript is located in the Cambridge University Library. The gospels are Western in type but, as Metzger points out, "no manuscript has so many and such remarkable variations from what is usually taken to be the normal New Testament Text."[23]

Codex Claromontanus (D^2 or D^{p2})[24] (c. 550)

Codex Claromontanus is a sixth-century complement of D, containing much of the New Testament missing in Codex Bezae. D^2 seems to have originated in Italy or Sardinia.[25] It was named after a monastery at Clermont, France, where it was found by Beza. After Beza's death, the codex was owned by several private individuals. Finally, King Louis XIV purchased it for the Bibliothèque Nationale at Paris in 1656. Tischendorf fully edited it in 1852. It contains all of Paul's epistles and Hebrews, although Romans 1:1-7, 27-30 and 1 Corinthians 14:13-22 are missing in Greek, 1 Corinthians 14:8-18 and Hebrews 13:21-23 are missing in the Latin. Like D, D^2 is a bilingual manuscript, containing 533 pages, seven by nine inches. It was written in a single column of twenty-one lines. It was artistically written on thin, high quality vellum. The Greek is good, but the Latin is grammatically inferior in some places. The manuscript is now located in the Bibliothèque Nationale, Paris. D^2 is distinctly Western, although the readings in the Epistles are not so striking as those in the Gospels and Acts.

Codex Basilensis (E)

This is an eighth-century manuscript of the four gospels on 318 leaves. It is presently in the library of the University of Basel, Switzerland, and has a Byzantine text-type.

Codex Laudianus 35 (E^2 or E^a)

Codex Laudianus dates from the late sixth or early seventh century. It contains Acts in both Greek and Latin, arranged in very short lines of one to three words. The text-type is mixed, sometimes agreeing with D, but more

23. Metzger, *The Text of the New Testament,* p. 50. See discussion in chap.26.
24. D^{p2} stands for D^{Paul} because it supplements D with the Pauline epistles.
25. Kenyon, *Our Bible and the Ancient Manuscripts,* pp. 207-8. Also see Alexander Souter, *The Text and Canon of the New Testament,* p. 28.

often with the Byzantine family.[26] It is the earliest known manuscript containing Acts 8:37.

Codex Sangermanensis (E^3 or E^p)

This is a ninth-century copy of D^2 in Greek and Latin and therefore has no independent value for the textual critic.

Codex Boreelianus (F)

Codex Boreelianus contains the four gospels, dates from the ninth century, and is a typically Byzantine text-type. It is located at Utrecht.

Codex Augiensis (F^2 or F^p)

This is a ninth-century manuscript of Paul's epistles in Greek and Latin (with large omissions) but Hebrews is in Latin only. It is now at Trinity College, Cambridge. The text is Western and was published by F.H.A. Scrivener in 1859.

Codex Wolfii A (G)

Also called Codex Harleianus, this codex dates to the tenth century. It contains the four gospels with many lacunae (omissions).

Codex Boernerianus (G^3 or G^p)

Dating from the ninth century, this codex contains Paul's epistles in Greek with a literal Latin translation between the lines (interlinear). It has the name but not the narration of the apocryphal Epistle to the Laodiceans. The text is closely akin to F^2. It is possibly of Irish origin and apparently was part of the same codex as Δ (see Codex Sangallensis).

Codex Wolfii B (H)

This codex contains the four gospels with many lacunae. It dates from the ninth or tenth century and now resides in the Public Library, Hamburg. The text is Byzantine.

Codex Mutinensis (H^2 or H^a)

This is a ninth-century copy of Acts (seven chapters missing), now in the Grand Ducal Library at Mondena, Italy. The text is Byzantine.

26. Constantin Tischendorf edited it in 1870.

Codex Coislinianus (H^3 or H^p)

This is an important codex of Paul's epistles, dating from the sixth century. The forty-three leaves known to exist today are divided among the libraries at Paris, Leningrad, Moscow, Kiev, Turin, and Mount Athos. The text is Alexandrian.

Codex Washingtonianus II (I)

Codex Washingtonianus II is a manuscript of the Pauline epistles in the Freer Collection at the Smithsonian Institution. There are 84 surviving leaves of the original 210. It dates from the fifth or sixth century and has portions of all of Paul's letters and Hebrews, except Romans. The text is a good representative of the Alexandrian family, agreeing more closely with א and A than B.

Codex Cyprius (K)

This is a ninth- or tenth-century complete copy of the four gospels with a typically Byzantine text.

Codex Mosquensis (K^2 or K^{ap})

This is a ninth- or tenth-century codex of Acts, the general epistles, and Pauline epistles with Hebrews. The text is a form of Von Soden's I-text (see chap. 26).

Codex Regius (L)

Codex Regius is an eighth-century codex of the gospels. It is badly written but represents a good text-type, often agreeing with B. Its unique feature is the presence of two endings to the gospel of Mark. The first is the shorter ending, reading as follows:

> But they [the women] reported briefly to Peter and those with him all that they had been told. And after this, Jesus himself sent out by means of them, from east to west, the sacred and imperishable proclamation of eternal salvation.[27]

The second ending is the traditional verses 9-20 found in the King James Version and the *New King James Version* (see discussion in chaps. 26 and 32).

27. As translated by *Revised Standard Version* in note on Mark 16:8. See discussion in chapter 26. Also see chaps. 31 and 32 for other modern speech translations as they treat these passages.

Codex Angelicus (L^2 or L^{ap})

This codex is a ninth-century copy of Acts, the general epistles, and the Pauline epistles. It is a Byzantine text-type.

Codex Pampianus (M)

Codex Pampianus contains the four gospels. It is a Byzantine text, with admixtures of Caesarean. It dates from the ninth century.

Codex Purpureus Petropolitanus (N)

This codex, written in the sixth century in silver letters on purple vellum, is a deluxe parchment of the gospels. Of the 462 original leaves, some 230 known leaves are scattered around the world. The text is dominantly Byzantine, although B. H. Streeter regarded it as a weak member of the Caesarean family.[28]

Codex Sinopensis (O)

Codex Sinopensis is another sixth-century deluxe edition of the gospels, written with gold ink on purple vellum. It is now in Bibliothèque Nationale, Paris. It contains forty-three leaves of Matthew 13-24, and five smaller leaves in Caesarean text-type.

Codex Porphyrianus (P^2 or P^{apr})

This is one of the few uncial manuscripts containing the book of Revelation. It also contains Acts and the general and Pauline epistles; however there are omissions. The text is Koine (Byzantine), with sporadic I (Western) readings in Acts, and Alexandrian in the other books. It is now in Leningrad.

Codex Nitriensis (R)

Now in the British Museum, this codex is a palimpsest of Luke from the sixth century, over which an eighth- or ninth-century treatise of Severus of Antioch was written. It also contains four thousand lines of Homer's *Iliad*. The text is Western.

Codex Vaticanus 354 (S)

This is one of the earliest self-dated manuscripts of the gospels, A.D. 949. It resides in the Vatican library (No. 354), and the text is Byzantine.

28. B. H. Streeter, "Codices 157, 1071 and the Caesarean Text," in *Quantulacumque, Studies Presented to Kirsopp Lake* (1937), pp. 149-50.

Codex Borgianus (T)

This is a valuable fifth-century fragment of Luke 22-23 and John 6-8. The text closely resembles B.

Codex Mosquensis (V)

Now in Moscow, this codex is a nearly complete copy of the four gospels from the eighth or ninth century. The manuscript is in uncials to John 8:39, where it shifts to thirteenth-century minuscules. The type of text is Byzantine.

Codex Washingtonianus I (W)

This dates from the fourth or early fifth century. It was purchased by Charles F. Freer of Detroit in 1906 from a dealer in Cairo, Egypt. Professor H. A. Sanders, of the University of Michigan, edited it between 1910 and 1918. The manuscript contains the four gospels, portions of all the Pauline epistles except Romans, Hebrews, Deuteronomy, Joshua, and Psalms. The portions missing from the codex are Mark 15:13-38; John 14:25—16:7; some of Paul's epistles; Deuteronomy 5:16—6:18; Joshua 3:3—4:10; and some of the psalms. The gospels manuscript has 187 leaves, 374 pages of good vellum. Each page (5⅝ by 8¼ inches) has one column of thirty lines, consisting of small, slanting uncials clearly written. The gospels include Matthew, John, Luke, and Mark, in that order. Mark has the long ending (16:9-20) attached; however, a most noteworthy insertion follows Mark 16:14:

> And they excused themselves, saying, "This age of lawlessness and unbelief is under Satan, who does not allow the truth and power of God to prevail over the unclean things of the spirits. Therefore reveal thy righteousness now"—thus they spoke of Christ. And Christ replied to them, "The term of years for Satan's power has been fulfilled, but other terrible things draw near. And for those who have sinned I was delivered over to death, that they may return to the incorruptible glory of righteousness which is in heaven."[29]

The manuscript of Deuteronomy and Joshua has 102 leaves (10½ by 12½ inches), with two columns per page, and is written on thick vellum. The mutilated manuscript of Psalms has portions of 107 leaves that originally measured eleven by fourteen inches, written in single columns. This codex is located in the Smithsonian Institution, Washington, D.C. As to text-type, it is mysteriously mixed, as though it were compiled from various manuscripts of different families. Matthew and Luke 8:13—24:25 are Byzantine, but Mark 1:1—5:30 is Western, resembling the Old Latin. Mark 5:31—16:20 is Caesarean, like P^{45}, whereas Luke 1:1—8:12 and John 5:12—21:25 are Alexandrian.

29. As cited by Metzger, *The Text of the New Testament*, p. 54. Also see Bruce M. Metzger, *A Textual Commentary on the Greek New Testament*, pp. 122-28.

John 1:1—5:11, which was added in the seventh century, is a mixture of Alexandrian and Western readings.

Codex Dubliensis (Z [*Zeta*])

This is a palimpsest of 299 verses from Matthew. It dates from the fifth or sixth century, and agrees chiefly with א.

Codex Sangallensis (Δ [*Delta*])

This is a ninth-century Greek-Latin interlinear manuscript of the four gospels (John 19:17-35 missing). It agrees with the Alexandrian text in Mark, and the Byzantine elsewhere.

Codex Koridethi (Θ [*Theta*])

This is a ninth-century copy of the Gospels. It is very much like the Byzantine text in Matthew, Luke, and John. Mark, however, is akin to the third- or fourth-century text used by Origen and Eusebius of Caesarea.

Codex Tischendorfianus III (Λ [*Lambda*])

This codex contains the text of Luke and John, and is of the Byzantine type. A ninth-century manuscript, Λ is located at Oxford.

Codex Zacynthius (Ξ [*Xi*])

This is a twelfth- or thirteenth-century palimpsest preserving most of Luke 1:1—11:33. It is an Alexandrian text-type akin to B, and is the earliest known New Testament manuscript with a marginal commentary.

Codex Petropolitanus (Π [*Pi*])

This is an almost complete ninth-century copy of the four gospels. With a Byzantine text-type, it heads a subfamily akin to A.

Codex Rossanensis (Σ [*Sigma*])

This is a sixth-century copy of Matthew and Mark. It is the earliest known Bible adorned with watercolored pictures. The text often agrees with the Byzantine, but has certain Caesarean readings.

Codex Beratinus (Φ [*Phi*])

This is another sixth-century deluxe edition, containing Matthew and Mark (with large lacunae). It is a mixed textual type (Koine, Western, and Caesarean).

Codex Athous Laurae (Ψ [*Psi*])

This is an eighth- or ninth-century manuscript containing the gospels from Mark 9 onward, Acts, the general epistles, Pauline epistles, and Hebrews. The ending of Mark is the same as L. The text is primarily Byzantine, with some portions of Alexandrian.

Codex Athous Dionysiou (Ω [*Omega*])

This dates from the eighth or ninth century and is a virtually complete copy of the four gospels. It is one of the oldest examples of the Byzantine text.

There are 362 uncial manuscripts of sections of the New Testament, of which only the more important ones have been listed, and 245 uncial lectionaries. The most important of the uncial manuscripts are א, B, A, and C, none of which were available to the King James translators. The only great Greek uncial manuscript available in 1611 was D, and it was used only slightly in the preparation of the King James Version (KJV). That fact alone indicated the need for a Revised Version based on earlier and better manuscripts long before it was actually accomplished.

Minuscule Manuscripts (Ninth—Fifteenth Centuries)

As their dates would indicate, most minuscule manuscripts do not possess the high quality of the earlier uncials. However, that is not always the case, because some minuscules are late copies of good and early texts. Their main importance rests in the accent they place on the textual families (see discussions of textual families in chaps. 25 and 26) and not in their multitude, there being some 2,795 of them and 1,964 minuscule lectionaries. Metzger asserts, "Of the total number of minuscule manuscripts only 34 are complete without lacunae for the entire New Testament; a list of these by century indicates that 14 belong to the fourteenth century."[30] In sum, there are 362 manuscripts and 245 lectionaries in uncial script, 2,795 manuscripts and 1,964 lectionaries in minuscule script, totaling 5,366 officially catalogued portions of the Greek New Testament (see comparison and chart at the end of this chapter, "History of the New Testament Text").

The Alexandrian Family

This is represented by manuscript 33, the "Queen of the Cursives," dating from the ninth or possibly the tenth century. It contains the entire New Testament except Revelation and is now in the possession of the Bibliothèque

30. Metzger, *Manuscripts of the Greek Bible*, p. 54. See above, n. 6.

Nationale, Paris. Although it is predominantly Alexandrian text-type, it shows traces of Byzantine in Acts and the Pauline epistles.

The Caesarean Text-Type

Some scholars find a "Caesarean" text-type in some manuscripts of the Gospels. It is found in P^{45}, W, Θ, family 1, family 13, and citations of Mark in Origen.[31] Although family 1 includes manuscripts 1, 118, 131, and 209, all of which date from the twelfth to the fourteenth centuries, an analysis of Mark reveals a textual type similar to Θ, family 13, and citations from Origen. Hence, it harks back to the Caesarean text of the third and fourth centuries.

An Italian Subfamily of Caesarean

This is represented by about a dozen manuscripts known as family 13 (including 13, 69, 124, 230, 346, 543, 788, 826, 828, 983, 1689, and 1709).[32] These manuscripts were copied between the eleventh and fifteenth centuries. One of their interesting characteristics is that they contain the section about the adulterous woman (John 7:53—8:11) following Luke 21:38 instead of after John 7:52.

Manuscript 28. This is an eleventh-century copy of the gospels having many noteworthy readings, especially in Mark where the text follows the Caesarean type.

Manuscript 61. This consists of the entire New Testament, dating from the late fifteenth or early sixteenth century. It was the first manuscript found containing 1 John 5:7, the single basis by which Erasmus was compelled to insert that doubtful passage into his Greek New Testament in 1516.

Manuscript 69. This contains the entire New Testament and dates from the fifteenth century. It is an important member of family 13.

Manuscript 81. This was written in A.D. 1044 and is one of the most important of all minuscules. Its text in Acts agrees frequently with the Alexandrian text-type.

Manuscript 157.[33] This is a twelfth-century codex of the Gospels following the Caesarean type.

Manuscript 383. This is thirteenth-century codex of Acts and the Epistles having the Western text-type in Acts.

Manuscript 565. This is one of the most beautiful of all known manuscripts. It has all the Gospels on purple vellum in gold letters. Mark is closely

31. See Gordon Fee, "The Textual Criticism of the New Testament," p. 424.
32. The first four manuscripts in this list were formerly thought to be of the "Syrian" text-type. Cf. Kenyon, *Our Bible and the Ancient Manuscripts*, p. 153.
33. A colophon, found in Λ, 20, 164, 215, 262, 300, 376, 428, 565, 686, 718, and 1071, states that they were copied and corrected "from ancient manuscripts at Jerusalem." This item is known as the "Jerusalem colophon"; see *Journal of Theological Studies* 14 (1913): 78ff., 242ff., 359 ff.

akin to Θ, in support of the Caesarean text.

Manuscript 579. This is a thirteenth-century copy of the Gospels. Matthew belongs to the late Byzantine group, whereas the other gospels belong to a good Alexandrian text, often agreeing with B, א, and L.

Manuscript 614. This is a thirteenth-century copy of Acts and the Epistles, with a great number of pre-Byzantine readings. Many of those readings agree with the Western text-type.

Manuscript 700. This is an eleventh- or twelfth-century codex that is remarkable for its divergent readings. It has some 2,724 deviations from the Received Text, and some 270 not found in any other manuscript.[34]

Manuscript 892. This is a ninth- or tenth-century codex of the Gospels, with remarkable readings of an early (Alexandrian) type.

Manuscript 1241. This contains the whole New Testament except Revelation. It dates from the thirteenth century, and the text often agrees with C, L, Δ, Ψ, and 33.

Manuscript 1224. This includes the whole New Testament, dates from the ninth or tenth century, and heads a host of members into family 1224, which witnesses to the Caesarean text.

Manuscript 1739. This is a very important codex from the tenth century based directly on a fourth-century Alexandrian type of manuscript. It has marginal notes taken from the writings of Irenaeus, Clement, Origen, Eusebius, and Basil.

Manuscript 2053. This is a thirteenth-century copy of Revelation. Together with codices A, C, and 2344, it is one of the best sources for the text of the Apocalypse.

Manuscript 2344. This is an eleventh-century codex of the New Testament, minus the Gospels and parts of the Old Testament. It agrees frequently with Manuscript 2053.

Summary and Conclusion

Whereas there are many variant readings in New Testament manuscripts (see chap. 25), there are a multitude of manuscripts available for comparison and correlation of those readings in order to arrive at the correct one. Just how that is done is discussed in detail in chapter 26. It is sufficient to remember at this point that whereas there are only 643 manuscripts by which the *Iliad* is reconstructed, 9 or 10 good ones for Caesar's *Gallic Wars,* 20 manuscripts of note for Titus Livy's *History of Rome,* and only 2 by which Tacitus is known to the modern world, yet there are 5,366 Greek manuscript witnesses that attest to part or all of the New Testament text.[35]

34. Metzger, *The Text of the New Testament,* p. 64.
35. See previous discussion and n. 6.

Furthermore, the time lapse between the original composition and the earliest manuscript copy is very significant. The oldest manuscript for the *Gallic Wars* is some nine hundred years later than Caesar's day. The two manuscripts of Tacitus are eight and ten centuries later, respectively, than the original. In the case of Thucydides and Herodotus, the earliest manuscript is some thirteen hundred years after their autographs. But with the New Testament it is very different.[36] In addition to the complete manuscripts only three hundred years later (B, א), most of the New Testament is preserved in manuscripts less than two hundred years from the original (P^{45}, P^{46}, P^{47}), some books of the New Testament dating from little over one hundred years after their composition (P^{66}), and one fragment (P^{52}) comes within a generation of the first century.

The chart "Reliability of the New Testament Documents" shows by comparison the integrity of the New Testament. Not only are there thousands more manuscripts and portions of the New Testament than other ancient books, but the oldest New Testament manuscript portions are centuries earlier. Consequently, the original New Testament can be reconstructed with a greater degree of accuracy than those other ancient books. So definite is the evidence for the New Testament that no less a scholar than Sir Frederic Kenyon could write:

> The interval then between the dates of original composition and the earliest extant evidence becomes so small as to be in fact negligible, and the last foundation for any doubt that the Scriptures have come down to us substantially as they were written has now been removed. Both the *authenticity* and the *general integrity* of the books of the New Testament may be regarded as finally established.[37]

Add to their proximity to the autographs not only the multiplicity of the New Testament manuscripts, but the prolific quotation by the early church Fathers (chap. 24) and the plurality of early versions (chaps. 27-29), and without entering into the mechanics by which the character of the New Testament text is established (chaps. 25 and 26), it can be readily understood why no book from the ancient world comes to us with more abundant evidence for its integrity than does the New Testament.

36. On this point compare the excellent little book by F. F. Bruce, *The New Testament Documents, Are They Reliable?* pp. 16-20.
37. Sir Frederic G. Kenyon, *The Bible and Archaeology,* pp. 288f.

History of the New Testament Text

Date	Greek Manuscripts	Versions and Translations[a]
A.D. 50		
	Original Manuscripts Written	
A.D. 100		
(c. 117-138)	P^{52} 1st extant ms [John 18:31-33, 37-38]	
A.D. 200	P^{32} P^{45} P^{46} P^{47} P^{64} P^{66}	Beginnings of Coptic,
	P^{67} P^{75} [papyrus mss]	Syriac, & Itala Versions
Decius (c. 250)	[Persecution—mss destroyed]	[mss appear later]
		I[b] C[c]
A.D. 300 Diocletian (c. 302)	[Persecution—mss destroyed]	S[d]
Nicean Council (325)	[Eusebius commissioned to make 50 copies]	
	Papyri mss [mostly Alexandrian, some Western]	G[e]
	ℵ , B [uncial codices; Alexandrian]	V[f]
A.D. 400	C [uncial eclectic codex; some Byzantine]	Arm[g]
	A [uncial codex; Alexandrian]	Geo[h]
	D [uncial codex; Western]	
	l 1053[i] [earliest lectionary]	
A.D. 500		
	N [uncial codex; Byzantine]	E[j]
	Most uncials	
A.D. 600		
A.D. 700		Ara[k] A-S[l]

History of the New Testament Text *(continued)*

Date	Greek Manuscripts	Versions and Translations[a]
A.D. 800	Ψ [uncial; Byzantine, some Alexandrian] 33 [minuscule; Alexandrian-Byzantine mixture] K, M [uncials; Byzantine]	
A.D. 900	Most minuscules [80 percent Byzantine]; Most lectionaries [mostly Byzantine]	
	S [uncial; Byzantine]	
A.D. 1000		
A.D. 1100	Family 1, 13 [evidence 3d-4th century Caesarean text]	
A.D. 1200		

a. See the discussion of the versions, translations, etc. in chaps. 27, 28, 29 and 30. Also see Bruce M. Metzger, *The Early Versions of the New Testament,* and Darrell L. Bock, "Textual Criticism Notes."
b. The Coptic versions appeared in the third and fourth centuries in Sahidic, Bohairic, Fayyumic, Achmimic, and Sub-Achmimin dialects.
c. The Itala or Old Latin versions appeared during the second to fourth centuries before they were superseded by Jerome's Vulgate version. The earliest of these manuscripts are Itala[a] (4th century) and Itala[k] (4th-5th century).
d. The Syriac versions began to appear in the fourth—seventh centuries, first in Old Syriac and then in Peshitta and Later Syriac.
e. The Vulgate version of Jerome became the dominant text of the Bible in the Western church during the fourth and fifth centures. Presently there are more than 8,000 manuscripts of the Vulgate.
f. The Gothic version (earliest manuscript is fourth century; others continue into fifth-sixth centuries).
g. The Armenian version translated from the Old Syriac version.
h. The Georgian version translated from the Armenian version.
i. The earliest lectionary (fifth century).
j. The Ethiopic version was translated as a result of the Monophysite controversy (fifth-sixth century).
k. The Arabic version arose from earlier translations following the rise of Islam in the seventh century.
l. The Anglo-Saxon versions were based on Old Latin and Vulgate versions. For translations of the Bible into English see chaps. 30-32 and Appendix.

RELIABILITY OF THE NEW TESTAMENT DOCUMENTS

Author/ Book	Date Written	Earliest Copies	Time Gap	No. of Copies	Percent Accuracy
Hindu *Mahābhārata*	13th cent. B.C.				90
Homer, *Iliad*	800 B.C.			643	95
Herodotus, *History*	480-425 B.C.	c. A.D. 900	c. 1,350 yrs.	8	?
Thucydides, *History*	460-400 B.C.	c. A.D. 900	c. 1,300 yrs.	8	?
Plato	400 B.C.	c. A.D. 900	c. 1,300 yrs.	7	?
Demosthenes	300 B.C.	c. A.D. 1100	c. 1,400 yrs.	200	?
Caesar, *Gallic Wars*	100-44 B.C.	c. A.D. 900	c. 1,000 yrs.	10	?
Livy, *History of Rome*	59 B.C.- A.D. 17	4th cent. (partial) mostly 10th cent.	c. 400 yrs. c. 1,000 yrs.	1 partial 19 copies	?
Tacitus, *Annals*	A.D. 100	c. A.D. 1100	c. 1,000 yrs.	20	?
Pliny Secundus, *Natural History*	A.D. 61-113	c. 850	c. 750 yrs.	7	?
New Testament	A.D. 50-100	c. 114 (fragment) c. 200 (books) c. 250 (most of N.T.) c. 325 (complete N.T.)	±50 yrs. 100 yrs. 150 yrs. 225 yrs.	5366	99+

23
Papyri, Ostraca, Inscriptions, and Lectionaries

The transmission of the New Testament text can be traced rather clearly and completely from the late second and early third centuries to modern times by means of the great biblical manuscripts (see chap. 22). Although the textual evidence linking those manuscripts with the first century is scant, consisting of a few fragments like P^{52} and some quotations from the apostolic Fathers, there is evidence that the type of Greek (i.e., vocabulary, grammar, style, etc.) represented by the New Testament is that of the first century. Support for that thesis has come from the nonbiblical papyri and ostraca discovered at Oxyrhynchus and elsewhere in Egypt since 1896.

The Nonbiblical Papyri

The epoch-making discovery of the papyri, ostraca, and inscriptions was destined to transform the world's understanding of the New Testament background. It also led to the classification of the New Testament as a book of the common man of the first century, instead of some especially mysterious writing that was given to man in a "Holy Ghost" language. Several scholars stand out in the epochal task of reclassification: James Hope Moulton in England (see J. H. Moulton and G. Milligan's *Vocabulary of the Greek New Testament, Illustrated from the Papyri and Other Non-Literary Sources,* 1914-29), Archibald T. Robertson in the United States (see A. T. Robertson, *A Grammar of the Greek New Testament in the Light of Historical Research),* and Adolf Deissmann in Germany, who wrote the results of his work in *Light from the Ancient East.*[1] The works of those men and others point indisputably to the conclusion that the New Testament was not written as classical literature, nor was it written in a special "Holy Ghost" language, but it is a lucid example of first century colloquial speech—Koine Greek.

1. Unless otherwise noted, the factual content of this chapter is dependent upon the monumental work of Adolf Deissmann, *Light from the Ancient East*.

Discoveries Bearing on the Language of the New Testament

There is a wealth of evidence that the New Testament was not written in a "perfect language," as some of the Latin Fathers contended. Examples may be cited from the nonliterary papyri in several areas to demonstrate that the New Testament is really a record in late colloquial Greek.

Phonology. Without engaging in the phonological trifles of the papyri, it will be sufficient to mention here that the same accent and inflections found in the New Testament (which differ from classical Greek), which were once thought to be a special "New Testament" or "biblical Greek" phenomenon, are known in abundance from the papyri.[2] So extensive is the evidence, says Deissmann, "as to make it impossible any longer to ignore the morphological identity of the 'New Testament idiom' with the Hellenistic colloquial language."[3]

Vocabulary. The field of linguistics abounds with evidence that confirms the contention that the New Testament, known from second and third century manuscripts, was the work of first-century writers. Formerly there were some 550 words thought to be "biblical," that is, unique to the LXX and the New Testament. The list has been narrowed to about 50 (1 percent of the New Testament) since the discovery of the papyri. As a result of this evidence, Deissmann concludes that "unless a word is recognized as Christian or Jewish at sight, we must consider it ordinary Greek until the contrary is proved." He goes on to cite two examples to illustrate this point: *agapē* (love) and *apokalupsis* (unveiling). The former is a typical "biblical word," and the latter was mistakenly limited to the Bible by Jerome, although Plutarch (A.D. 46-125) used it.[4] Now, because of the papyri, they are known to be common words in secular literature as well. As a matter of fact, *agapē* is found in the prayer of a devotee to the god Isis. It is no doubt true that the New Testament adopted and modified the meaning of those words, but the words were not created by the New Testament writers. They were common, current words in the culture of the first century.[5]

Syntax. Several phrases formerly thought to be "Hebraisms" have been found in the papyri; for example, *blepein apo* (beware of) and *duo duo* (two by two). *Pleres* (full), which was once held to be a nominative of the Holy

2. According to Deissmann, two of the classical works on this aspect of the Koine Greek are Winer's *A Grammar of the Idiom of the New Testament Greek* and Karl Dieterich's *Researches on the History of the Greek Language from the Hellenistic Period to the Tenth Century A.D.*
3. Deissmann, p. 73.
4. Ibid., p. 78.
5. Ibid., p. 707.

Spirit from John 1:14,[6] has its parallel in the papyri along with many others.[7]

Style. The paratactic style of John may be singled out as a test case on style because it is so often considered Semitic. The "I am's" and even the "and ... and" construction have their parallel in the Fayum papyrus number 108,[8] the inscription of Asclepius in Rome, and many others. Hence, even the style of John may not be as Semitic as it once seemed.

The verdict, then, of historical philology based on the contemporary nonliterary texts is that the "sacred books are so many records of popular Greek, in its various grades" and "taken as a whole the New Testament is a book of the people."[9]

Discoveries Bearing on the New Testament as Literature

Was the New Testament "something written for the public cast in artistic form," or was it the "product of life and not art," being literature only in a secondary sense? To answer that question the papyri and letters written on other materials provide numerous samples of the "everyday" correspondence and other nonliterary writings of the first century or before.

Leaden tablet from Chaidari, near Athens. This is the oldest known Greek letter, coming from the third or fourth century B.C. The notable feature of this letter is its epistolary form. It illustrates that the praescript is not part of the address; the address was printed on the outside after the thin lead tablet was folded. According to Deissmann that was doubtless the case with Paul's letters as well.

Letter to Appolonius from Zoilus. From the third century B.C. comes a piece of religious correspondence that provides a remarkable parallel to the form of religious experiences reflected in Paul's letters. The writer, a religious devotee of the god Serapis, expressed a very similar attitude toward his god as Paul did toward Christ.[10]

Ostracon letter to Portis. This is a private receipt from an Egyptian landowner to his tenant; it employed the apparently common custom of using an amanuensis. Deissmann suggests that this letter may parallel Galatians 6:11, in that a secretary could write a better letter than could the slow, large, working hand of Paul or another author.[11]

From Apion to Epimachus. This is an interesting letter having a typical

6. The adjective *pleres* in John 1:14, "full of grace and truth," seems to be in the nominative case, whereas it should be genetive to agree with *tēn doxan autou,* "his glory." It was once claimed that the Holy Spirit led the apostle to write the nominative because Jesus is always our Nominative. But inscriptions show that the word had become indeclinable by the first century.
7. Deissmann, pp. 122-24.
8. Ibid., p. 134.
9. Ibid., p. 143.
10. Ibid., pp. 154-61.
11. Ibid., p. 166. It is also possible that Paul said, "See how large letters I have written with my own hand," for effect, and not because he could not write well.

"Pauline" beginning. Like Paul's letters, it begins, "I thank God. . . ."

Numerous other letters. There is a letter, written by a farmer, having an uncial body and a cursive signature, just the reverse of Galatians. Very similar to Luke 15 is a letter containing a prodigal's confession to his mother.[12]

From these and many other examples it has been concluded that the New Testament epistles were really letters written in the form, style, and vocabulary current at the time of the first century.[13] The New Testament is a book "of the people, by the people, and for the people." It was written in the lingo of the *laos* (laity).

Discoveries Bearing on the Cultural and Religious Background of the New Testament

Another area illuminated by the papyri is the cultural and religious backdrop of the first century. Indications of this context are found in Jesus' handling of the Roman denarius (Matt. 22:19), Paul's preaching on the Athenian inscription (Acts 17:23), and the burning of the magical books at Ephesus (Acts 19:19).

Cultural similarity. Basically the same Hellenistic culture prevailed throughout the Mediterranean world, as is illustrated by the common census tax (Luke 2:3), the procedure of delivering a criminal to the people (cf. Barabbas, Matt. 27:15), and even the price of a sparrow (Luke 12:6). These very same customs and practices are known from the papyri to have existed in Egypt as well as Palestine and throughout the Mediterranean world.

Competing cults. Judaism, imperial religion, and the mystery religions were all missionary religions. The dispersed Jews left ample evidence of their religious activities; the *Letter to Zoilus* illustrates the religious zeal of the heathen religions, and the monuments have yielded enough information to reconstruct the beliefs of Mithraism.[14] It was into this caldron of religious missionary zeal that Christianity inserted its claim to be a world religion.

Private devotions. One of the most significant areas of illumination from the papyri is the private devotions of unnumbered individual personalities, which have become an open book for the world. In these nonliterary texts there arise, as it were, the living voices of a soldier, a wife, a religious propagandist, and others. This evidence is so clear that Deissmann concludes,

12. Ibid., pp. 172ff, 187ff.
13. Deissmann overdraws his conclusion when he says that these letters were only raised to the level of epistles when the church later canonized them and promulgated their contents as the sacred text (p. 240). Although these letters were not artistic literature, they were intended for the church public and for circulation (see chap. 16), and there is no reason a "letter" cannot communicate God's truth as well as an "epistle."
14. See Franz Cumont's monumental work, *Textes et Monuments figurés relatifs aux Mystères de Mithra*.

"Anyone coming from the soul life of the New Testament to the papyri finds himself in no strange world."[15]

Language of moral expressions. To the biblical student familiar with the phraseology of the New Testament, it will be no surprise to find among the inscriptions the well-known "I have fought a good fight," "Love your husbands," and "Rebuke not an elder."[16] The list of sins (excepting idolatry and covetousness) are also similar. It seems that both Christian and pagan writers shared a common core of culture and terminology, which was imbued with the content of their own unique experience and meaning.

Language of popular religion. One of the marks of the popular style of Paul is his employment of technical phraseology common to the technical language of magic. A Leyden papyrus has a parallel to the Galatians 6:17 expression "the marks of Jesus." First Corinthians 5:5 is exemplar to the formula of the ancient custom of execration, or the devoting of a person to the gods of the lower world. Likewise, technical expressions were adapted from the ritual of cursing, for example, "delivered to Satan" (1 Tim. 1:20), which has been found in the London Magical papyrus.[17]

Language of popular law. The inscriptions and papyri provide outstanding illustrations of Paul's famous analogies from slavery. Manumission (release from slavery) is described by Paul in such terms as "you have been bought with a price" (1 Cor. 6:20; 7:23) and "it was for freedom that Christ set us free" (Gal. 5:1). This legal language, which provided Paul with some of his most illustrative metaphors, is abundantly evident in temple inscriptions and the nonliterary papyri.

Language of emperor worship. One of the closest parallels, and the one that caused the greatest difficulty to Christianity, was the similarity of phraseology applied to Christ by Christians with that applied to Caesar by the Romans. The Christian antipathy toward emperor worship was strongly rooted in its monotheistic heritage (cf. Deut. 6:4). The following phrases, applied by the New Testament to Christ, were also appellations used in reference to Caesar:[18]

1. "Lord" was used of Nero.
2. "Lord's Day" was a direct contrast to "Imperial Day," or "Augustus' Day."
3. "Parousia" and "epiphany" were used to refer to the presence or appearance of Caesar.
4. Many of the Caesars (e.g., Domitian, Nero) claimed deity for themselves and received worship.

15. Deissmann, p. 299.
16. Ibid., pp. 309 ff.
17. Ibid., pp. 301-2.
18. Ibid., pp. 347, 354, 359, 370.

It was this identity of terms that occasioned the tremendous persecution and martyrdom of so many of the early Christians.

Conclusions

Avoidable conclusion. Lest the conclusion be drawn that common language necessitates common meaning and experience, it should be indicated at this point that the New Testament used modes of expression of its day but did not necessarily use the same meanings. The meaning of a word must be determined by the usage of that word in its context, as representative of the experience of the author. Christian content is obviously different from pagan content and usage. The same words used by the different religions could, at best, only be expected to have a parallel, not an identical meaning, in Christianity. In other words, the Christian's experience was different from the heathen's, even though the form of expression may have been similar. Certainly Paul used the language of the *heathen,* but he invested it with the meaning of *heaven* (cf. Acts 17:22-32).

Unavoidable conclusions. Although it need not be concluded that the New Testament reflects the same meaning as the contemporary profane usage of first-century words, there are some conclusions that do seem unavoidable in light of the papyri.

1. The New Testament was not written in any so-called "Holy Ghost" Greek. Instead, it was written in the common (Koine) trade language of the Roman world. The language of the masses, the merchants, and the marketplace was the instrument used in transmitting the Greek New Testament.

2. The "Pauline" and other styles of Greek syntax, and even the New Testament vocabulary, were all commonly used in the first century. In fact, so decisive were the papyri discoveries for New Testament studies that new standard Greek lexicons (dictionaries) have come into existence.[19] That in turn has led to the publishing of new commentaries.

3. The conclusion sometimes overlooked, yet implicit in the foregoing conclusions, is the fact that if the Greek of the New Testament was the common language of the first century, then *the New Testament must have been written in the first century.*[20] Obviously the New Testament was written in the language of its day, and that day was the first century. A book that reflects first-century vocabulary and literary forms, and that

19. The work of Joseph Henry Thayer, *A Greek-English Lexicon of the New Testament,* has been superseded by the translation of Walter Bauer's *Griechisch-Deutsches Wörterbuch zu den Schriften des Neuen Testaments und der übrigen urchristlichen Literatur* by William F. Arndt and F. Wilbur Gingrich, *A Greek-English Lexicon of the New Testament and Other Early Christian Literature.*

20. Millar Burrows has seen this point. See his book *What Mean These Stones?* pp. 53-54.

resembles first-century religious modes of expression, can scarcely be a second or third-century fraud.[21] In fact, the papyri have provided the biblical scholar with the "missing link" in his chain of transmission from the autographs to the modern Bible. Manuscript evidence is very good, dating back into the second century. From that point, thousands of papyri[22] take the stylistic evidence to the very hands of the apostles in the first century.

Biblical and Related Papyri, Ostraca and Inscriptions

To complete the picture, brief mention should be made of some of the other papyri and ostraca that relate to the understanding of the Bible text. Because the most important papyri manuscripts were previously treated (see chap. 22), only a few supplementary and related finds need be mentioned here.

New Testament Ostraca Fragments

Ostraca are broken pieces of pottery that were frequently used as a writing material by the poorer classes in antiquity, as they could not afford papyrus. There is an interesting find of twenty pieces of a seventh-century copy of the gospels on ostraca, which probably represents a poor man's Bible. Ostraca were long overlooked by scholars, who apparently desired not to condescend in their academic pursuits to the rubbish lest they be called a "potsherd among the potsherds" (Isa. 45:9, RV). But from the rubbish heaps has come additional light on the biblical text. In Wilkens's *Greek Ostraca,* some 1,624 specimens of these humble records of history are listed.[23]

New Testament Inscriptions

The wide distribution and variety of ancient inscriptions testifies to the existence and importance of the biblical texts. There is an abundance of engravings on walls, pillars, coins, monuments, and other things that have preserved a witness to the New Testament. For the most part, however, these are not of importance in establishing the text of the New Testament; their role is merely that of a supplementary witness to the already abundant evidence of other New Testament manuscriptions.

21. John Wenham, "The Origin of the Gospels," *Trinity Journal.* (7) 1978.
22. According to Allen P. Wikgren, there are some 25,000 papyri (biblical and nonbiblical) that shed light on the biblical text and early Christianity; about half of these have been published. See his article "Papyri, Biblical and Early Christian," in *The Twentieth Century Encyclopedia of Religious Knowledge,* ed. Lefferts A. Loetscher, vol. K-Z, p. 839.
23. Deissmann, p. 50 n. 5, also lists several other sources of Egyptian, Coptic, and Greek ostraca.

The Sayings of Jesus

A group of noncanonical sayings of Jesus has been discovered among the papyri. These writings are known as the "Logia of Jesus" (Grenfell and Hunt), a few samples of which follow:

> Jesus saith: Unless you fast to the world, you will not find the Kingdom of God; and unless you "sabbatize" the Sabbath, you will not see the Father.
>
> Jesus saith: Lift the stone and there you will find me, split the wood and I am there.
>
> Jesus saith: I stood in the midst of the world, and I appeared in the flesh, and I found all drunken, and I found none thirsty among them, and my soul grieves over the sons of men for they are blind in their hearts and do not see.[24]

A comparison of these "sayings" with familiar canonical quotes manifests their apocryphal tone. Even in New Testament times there was an abundance of oral "sayings" of Christ (cf. John 21:23, 25); many of them are recorded in the four gospels, and at least one more is found in Acts 20:35. There can be little doubt that many more "sayings" took on a local and even heretical flavor as time passed, and they in turn gave rise to collections of "sayings."

Lectionaries

A final testimony to the text of the New Testament, which has hitherto been generally undervalued, are the numerous lectionaries, or church service books, containing selected readings from the New Testament. These lectionaries served as manuals, and they were used throughout the church year for liturgical purposes.[25]

Nature

The great majority of the lectionary readings consisted of passages taken from the Gospels.[26] The rest of them contained portions of Acts, either with or without the Epistles. They were often elaborately adorned and sometimes even included musical notations. It may be admitted with Wikgren that:

> The origin of the lectionary still remains obscure. We are ignorant of the exact circumstances and date of the transition from early usage of nonlectionary manuscripts ... to lectionary proper. ... However, various converging lines of evidence

24. See Robert M. Grant, *The Secret Sayings of Jesus,* pp. 47ff.
25. For a brief discussion of the development of the Greek lectionary system, see Bruce M. Metzger, *Lessons from Luke in the Greek Gospel Lectionary* (Chicago, 1944), pp. 11ff.
26. Morton Enslin, *Christian Beginnings,* pp. 496ff., suggests that lectionaries originate from the first century, and that this idea was borrowed from the practice of the Jewish synagogue.

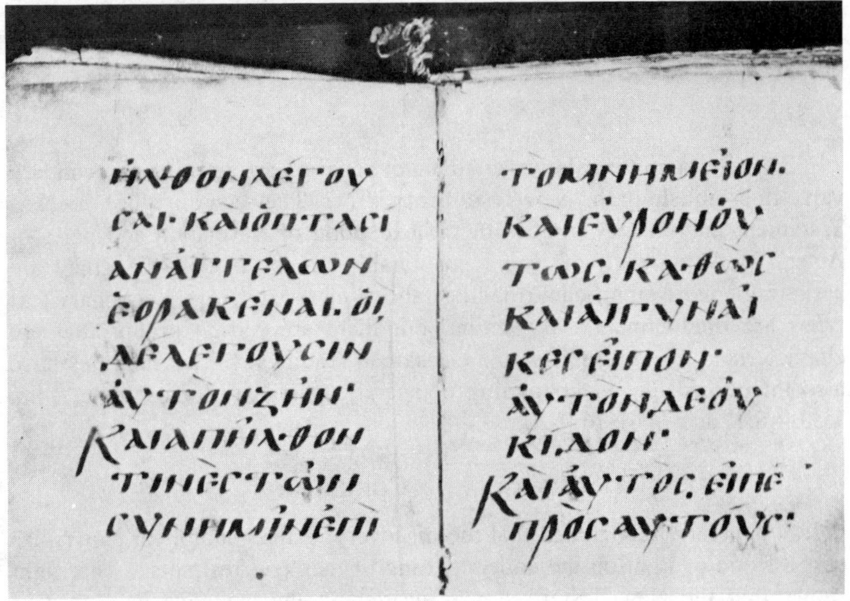

20. *A seventh-century lectionary, now in the library of St. Catherine's Monastery, showing Luke 24:23-25 (Courtesy of* Biblical Archaeologist, *a publication of the American Schools of Oriental Research)*

historical, liturgical and textual, point to Syria, possibly Antioch, in the mid-fourth century as a likely place and date for this event.[27]

Date

Since there was a continued ecclesiastical use of uncial manuscripts long after the minuscule type had superseded them, the lectionaries are difficult to date on the basis of paleography alone. Most lectionaries probably originated at a date ranging from the seventh to the twelfth centuries, with a dozen leaves and fragments dating from the fourth to the sixth centuries, five or six of which are papyri.[28]

Number

Although Caspar Gregory listed about 1,545 known in his day,[29] there are

27. Wikgren, p. 650.
28. Ibid.
29. Caspar René Gregory, *Canon and Text of the New Testament*, pp. 384-93.

over 2,209 Greek lectionaries presently identified and catalogued.[30] Consequently, Greek lectionaries have come to play a more prominent role in New Testament textual criticism.[31]

Value

It must be admitted, however, that lectionaries are only of a secondary value in establishing the New Testament text. (1) They contain all of the New Testament many times over, with the exception of Revelation and parts of Acts. (2) As a result of recent scholarship on the lectionaries, they are assuming a more significant role in establishing the true text. Lectionary text types are predominantly Byzantine, but there are certain groups that are characterized by Alexandrian and Caesarean readings. (3) Lectionaries have also influenced the understanding of specific passages, for example, John 7:53—8:11 and Mark 16:9-20.[32]

Summary and Conclusion

It is generally recognized that the discovery of the nonbiblical papyri has cast a flood of light on the understanding of the New Testament. That light shows that the New Testament was written in the language and style of first-century colloquial Greek. In the past it has been overlooked sometimes that this fact, at the same time, indicates that the Greek New Testament, as it is known to scholars from third and fourth century manuscripts, was *written in the first century*. The nonliterary papyri provide another link between the apostles and the early manuscript copies. That link has hitherto been made up of small fragments and quotations, but it is now supported by thousands of papyri manuscripts. Further support for the text of the New Testament may be found in the ostraca, inscriptions, and hundreds of lectionaries.

30. Bruce M. Metzger, *The Text of the New Testament*, p. 33, lists 1,997 Greek lectionaries, but this has been updated as of 1976 to 2,209 (245 uncial and 1,964 minuscule) in his *Manuscripts of the Greek Bible*, p. 54.
31. Greek lectionaries have been systematically cited in the textual apparatus of the United Bible Society's *Greek New Testament*, 3d ed. (1975), based on the fresh collations made for it at the University of Chicago and the Greek lectionary project there.
32. See John W. Burgon, *The Last Twelve Verses of the Gospel According to St. Mark*, chap.10.

24

Patristic Witnesses to the Text of Scripture

The Purpose for Using the Church Fathers

In addition to possessing the manuscripts, including the miscellaneous items, and versions of the Old and New Testaments, the student of textual criticism has available the patristic citations of those Testaments, which aid him in his search for the true text of the Bible. The Fathers lived during the early centuries of the church, and their witness to the original text assists in locating the precise area, date, and type of text used throughout the early church. This evidence assists the textual critic in ascertaining the authentic text of the originals.

When the Fathers Lived

Because the Old Testament canon was closed and recognized prior to the time of Christ, it is only necessary to mention with B. F. Westcott:

> In the direct citation of Scripture the usage of the Apostolic fathers agrees generally with that of the Apostles. They continued to look upon the Old Testament as a full and lasting record of the revelation of God. In one remarkable particular they carried this belief yet further than it had been carried before. With them the individuality of the several writers falls into the background. They practically regarded the whole Book as one Divine utterance; and, with the exception of Barnabas, no one of them ever makes a distinct reference by name to any book of the Old Testament.[1]

When considering their use of the New Testament, the picture is much more diverse and the role of the Fathers is much more important, for the recognition of the canon by the church was not finally completed until the fourth

1. Brooke Foss Westcott, *The Bible in the Church*, pp. 83-84.

century.[2] With that in view, it is necessary to trace the historical process of the recognition of the canon in a cursory manner in order to bring the position of the Fathers into sharper focus.[3]

First century. Even in the last half of the first century, there was already in progress the selecting, sorting (1 Thess. 2:13), reading (1 Thess. 5:27), circulating (Col. 4:16), collecting (2 Peter 3:15-16), and quoting (1 Tim. 5:8) of apostolic literature (see chap. 16). In brief, all twenty-seven books were written, copied, and began to be disseminated among the churches before the end of the first century.

First half of the second century. During this period the apostolic writings became more generally known and more widely circulated, because the apostles had all passed off the scene, and their teachings were carried on through written copies instead of their voices. At this time almost every New Testament book was cited as Scripture explicitly; however, "up to A.D. 150 the quotations in extant ecclesiastical writers, though important in their bearing on questions of the date and acceptance of the New Testament Scriptures, are of little value for purely textual purposes."[4] The writings of the Fathers were read in the churches, and they tell much of the history, doctrine, and practices of the church. It was in this period that the writings of the Fathers quoted Scripture with authority in struggles with heretical groups, dialogues with the heathen, and exhortations against vice.

Second half of the second century. As the church spread throughout this period, the New Testament books were widely recognized as Scripture as was the Old Testament. This was a time of missionary activity, as the church spread beyond the confines of the empire, and the Scriptures, Old and New Testaments, were translated into other languages. It was during these years that commentaries began to appear. Among them were Papias's *Exposition of the Lord's Oracles,* Heracleon's commentary on the Gospels, and Melito's commentary on the Apocalypse of John. This was also the period in which Tatian compiled his *Diatessaron* (see chap. 28). The writings of the Fathers make profuse citations of the New Testament as the authoritative Scriptures, and the Muratorian Fragment (c. 170) lists all but five of the books of the modern New Testament.[5]

Third century. During this century the New Testament books were collected into a single catalog of "recognized books," and separated from other species of Christian literature. It was this century that evidenced the great rise in intellectual activity within the church, as Origen's *Hexapla* and other works indicate. The recognition of the New Testament's authority, its collec-

2. See chap. 14 on the Old Testament canon and chap. 16 on the New Testament canon.
3. The following discussion follows G.T. Manley, ed., *The New Bible Handbook,* pp. 33-38.
4. Sir Frederic G. Kenyon, *Handbook to the Textual Criticism of the New Testament,* p. 199.
5. No conclusive evidence against the inclusion of the five missing books can be made from this fragment, as it is what its name implies, "incomplete."

tion as a valuable unit, its translation as a missionary tool, and its commentaries as teaching aids all combine to illustrate the need for distinguishing between the Christian Scriptures and other religious literature. No longer were there only two classes of Christian literature (Scripture and the writings of the Fathers); there was also a body of apocryphal and pseudepigraphical literature emerging. The abundance of religious literature gave rise to the application of sorting and sifting tests to all religious literature in the church. Those tests, and others (see chap. 16), led to the ultimate recognition of the canonical New Testament and the erasure of doubts concerning the Antilegomena books of the New Testament.

Fourth century. By this time the New Testament canon was fully recognized and settled. The writings of the Fathers present the general agreement of all Christians on the canon of the New Testament. It was this period which gave rise to the various classifications of books mentioned in chapters 16-17.

What the Fathers Did

It should be pointed out that several considerations must be kept in view when the textual critic attempts to use patristic citations to recover the original texts. Although the witness of the Fathers is quite early, actually older than the best codices, it is not always reliable. As a case in point, a patristic writer may have quoted a variant reading from one of the manuscripts that existed at the time. Another factor is that the writing of the particular Father may have been altered or modified during the history of its transmission in a manner similar to the Greek text of the New Testament.[6]

A third factor to be considered is whether the patristic author was quoting the New Testament verbatim, loosely, as a paraphrase, or possibly in a mere allusion to the original. Again, if it was an attempt to quote verbatim, the question must be asked whether or not the quote was made from memory rather than by consulting a manuscript. Often the writer was a member of a group that held heretical doctrines, and that factor needs to be kept in view as well. Still another consideration appears if a Father cites the same passage more than once, namely, are the quotes identical or divergent?

Finally, as in the case of Origen, an amanuensis would listen to dictation and hunt the passage of Scripture at a later time. His available manuscripts could result in a variety of readings for any given passage. But, the above difficulties notwithstanding, the evidence of the patristic writers "is of such great importance in tracing the history of the transmission of the text that the labour of refining the ore from the dross is well worth the effort."[7] Their

6. Bruce M. Metzger, *The Text of the New Testament,* p. 87, indicates that scribes were tempted to assimilate the reading of the citation into agreement with their New Testament manuscripts, and thus were prone to copy the later ecclesiastical text (Koine, Textus Receptus, or Vulgate).
7. Ibid., p. 88.

importance may be summarized as showing the history of the text of the New Testament, rendering the best evidence as to the canon of the New Testament, providing a means of dating the manuscripts of the New Testament, and assisting in determining just when translations, versions, and revisions of the text occur. With this information in hand, the following discussion may be more adequately considered.

The Principal Fathers of the Church and Their Witness[8]

The Apostolic Fathers (c. 70-c. 150)

The writers of this period all wrote in the Greek language. Their writings, for the most part, have been compiled in two excellent volumes of the Loeb Classical Library.[9] The citations of these Fathers must be weighed in light of the factors cited above, and their precision in quotation is far from modern standards, as some of their quotes would be regarded as mere allusions, and their allusions are often quite remote by modern standards.

The Epistle of Pseudo-Barnabas (c. 70-79). This makes many quotations and allusions to New Testament books. It cites Matthew 22:14, 44-45; and 26:31 (in 4.14: 12.11; and 5.16, respectively), while alluding to Matthew 20:16 in 6.13. In 11.10; 13.7; and 15.4, this same epistle, falsely ascribed to Paul's associate, quotes John 6:51; Romans 4:11; and 2 Peter 3:8, respectively. Again, these quotations are rather loose, perhaps from memory rather than from a manuscript copy.

Corinthians (by Clement of Rome, c. 95-97). This contains several quotations from the New Testament, including the synoptic gospels. His citations are more precise than those attributed to Barnabas, but they still lack modern precision. Among his many citations from the gospels are Matthew 5:7; 7:1-2 (in his chap. 13); 13:3 (chap. 24); 18:6; 26:24 (chap. 46). Mark 4:3 or Luke 8:5 may have been in view when Clement cited the gospels in chapter 24, and Mark 9:42 and 14:21 or Luke 17:1-2 and 22:22 may have been in view in his chapter 46. Acts 20:35 and Titus 3:1 were both cited in Clement's epistle (chap. 2), as were 1 Corinthians 2:9 (chap. 34); Hebrews 1:3-5, 7, 13 (chap. 36); 3:5 (chaps. 17, 43); 1 Peter 4:8 (chap. 49); and 5:5 (chap. 30). It is possible that Clement was alluding to Revelation 22:12 when he wrote 34.3-4.

Seven Epistles (by Ignatius, c. 110-117). Ignatius wrote these while en route to martyrdom in Rome. Although his references to the New Testament

8. Ibid., pp. 88-89; Metzger has an alphabetical listing of thirty additional important church Fathers, covering basically the same period, which may also be consulted.
9. *The Apostolic Fathers*, Kirsopp Lake, ed. Other useful English translations of the apostolic Fathers are C. C. Richardson, ed., *Christian Fathers*, vol. 1: *Library of Christian Classics* and a reprint edition of J. B. Lightfoot, *Apostolic Fathers*, 2 vols.

are either loose quotations from memory or allusions, they do indicate his wide selection of Bible materials for his own letters, in which he sought to strengthen respect for bishops and presbyters, and protested against the docetic heresy. In his *Ephesians* letter, Ignatius quoted Matthew 12:33 (chap. 14); Romans 6:4 (chap. 19); 1 Corinthians 1:20 (chap. 18); Galatians 5:21 (chap. 16); Colossians 1:23 (chap. 10); James 4:6 (chap 5); and 1 Peter 5:5 (chap. 5). In his letter *Magnesians,* he cited Matthew 27:52 (chap. 9); John 5:19, 30 (chap. 7); and Acts 1:25 (chap. 5). The *Trallians* letter quoted Matthew 15:13 (chap. 11); 1 Corinthians 4:1 (chap. 2); 9:27 (chap. 12); 15:12ff. (chap. 9); and Colossians 1:16 (chap. 5). In writing *Romans,* Ignatius used John 4:10; 7:38, 42 (chap. 7); 1 Corinthians 15:8-9 (chap.. 9); 1 Thessalonians 2:4 (chap. 2); 2 Thessalonians 3:5 (chap. 10); and 2 Timothy 2:8 (chap. 7). His *Philippians* epistle cited Matthew 15:13 (chap. 3); John 3:8 (chap. 7); and 1 Corinthians 2:10 (chap. 7); 6:9-10 (chap. 5); and 10:16-17 (chap. 4). He then wrote *Smyrnaeans* and cited Matthew 3:16 (chap. 1); 19:12 (chap. 6); Luke 24:39 (chap. 3); Acts 10:41 (chap. 3); Romans 1:3 (chap. 1); Ephesians 2:16 (chap. 1); Philippians 3:15 (chap. 11); 4:13 (chap. 4); and 2 Timothy 1:16 (chap. 10). In his personal letter to Polycarp, Ignatius cited several of the same books, for example, Matthew 8:17 (chap. 1); 10:16 (chap. 2); Ephesians 4:2 (chap. 1); 5:25, 29 (chap. 5); 1 Timothy 6:2 (chap. 4); and 2 Timothy 2:4 (chap. 6). It is advisable to mention again that quotation technique has changed throughout the course of history, as has the work of translation. That, along with the fact that modern scholars employ different criteria in distinguishing a citation from an allusion, may provide a basis for disagreement on just *what* is a quotation.

Philippians (by Polycarp, c. 110-135). The disciple of the apostle John, Polycarp wrote an epistle to the *Philippians* which contains a large number of citations, as did Clement's *Corinthians*. Among his quotations are the following: Matthew 5:3, 10 (chap. 2); 5:44 (chap. 12); 6:13 (chap. 7); Mark 9:35 (chap. 5); 14:38 (chap. 7); Acts 2:24 (chap. 1); 10:42 (chap. 2); Romans 12:10 (chap. 10); 14:10ff. (chap. 6); 1 Corinthians 6:2 (chap. 11); 14:25 (chap. 4); 15:58 (chap. 10); 2 Corinthians 3:2 (chap.11); 4:14 (chap. 2); 8:21 (chap. 6); Galatians 1:1 (chap. 12); 4:26 (chap. 3); 5:17; 6:7 (chap. 5); Ephesians 2:8ff. (chap. 1); 4:26 (chap. 12); 5:21 (chap. 10); 6:18 (chap. 12); Philippians 2:16 (chap. 9); 3:18 (chap. 12); 2 Thessalonians 1:4; 3:15 (chap. 11); 1 Timothy 2:1; 4:15 (chap. 12); 6:7, 10 (chap. 4); 2 Timothy 2:12 (chap. 5); 4:10 (chap. 9); 1 Peter 1:8 (chap. 1); 1:13, 21 (chap. 2); 2:11 (chap. 5); 2:12, 17 (chap. 10); 2:22, 24 (chap. 8); 3:9 (chap. 2); 4:7 (chap. 7); 1 John 4:2-3 or 2 John 7 (chap. 7). His work shows strong apostolic influence, and his prominence is noted in that Ignatius wrote a letter to him, and the church of Smyrna wrote a letter to the church of Philomelium entitled *The Martyrdom of Polycarp*.

The Shepherd (of Hermas c. 115-140). "Free" quotations from memory and allusion to the New Testament make themselves more evident in this writing than in the previous works. Nevertheless, all three portions of the *Shepherd* cite the New Testament. Matthew 26:24 appears in Vision 4.2.6, although it may be the parallel passage in Mark 14:21. In Mandate 4.6, Matthew 19:9 was quoted, while Mark 5:23-24 was used in Similitude 9.20.2-3. Whereas many other passages were quoted in the *Shepherd,* only a sampling is listed at this point: 1 Corinthians 7:40 (Mandate 4.4.2); Hebrews 11:33 (Vision 4.2.4); James 1:21 (Similitude 6.1.1); 2:7 (Similitude 7.6.4); 4:7 (Mandate 12.5.2); 4:12 (Mandate 12.6.3); 1 Peter 1:7 (Vision 4.3.4); 5:7 (Vision 3.11.3); 1 John 2:27 (Mandate 3.1); Revelation 21:14 (Vision 3.5.1).

The Didache, or *Teaching of the Twelve* (c. 120-150). This was widely used in the early church as a religious handbook. It followed the loose quote and allusion pattern of the *Shepherd* but gave wide variety to its quotations, as the following survey testifies. Matthew 5:5 (chap. 3); 5:26, 39-42, 46 (chap. 1); 6:9-13, 16 (chap. 8); 7:6 (chap. 9); 10:10 (chap. 13); 21:9 (chap. 12); 22:37, 39 (chap. 1); 24:10-13, 24, 30 (chap. 16); 25:13 (chap. 16); 28:19; Mark 11:9 (chap. 12); and Luke 6:27-35 (chap. 1); 9:2-4 (chap. 8); 12:35, 40 (chap. 16); 19:38 (chap. 13); 21:12 (chap. 16) witness to the widespread use of the gospels. Other portions of the New Testament cited in the *Didache* include Acts 4:32 (chap. 4); Romans 12:9 (chap. 5); 1 Corinthians 16:22 (chap. 10); Hebrews 8:7 (chap. 4); 1 John 4:18 (chap. 10); Jude 22 (chap. 2).

Epistle to Diognetus (c. 150). This epistle makes a few direct quotations from the New Testament, but it makes loose quotes or allusions mostly. Among the former are 1 Corinthian 8:1 (chap. 12); 1 Peter 3:18 (chap. 9); and 1 John 4:9, 19 (chap. 10). Among the latter are passages in John 1:1 (chap. 11); 3:17 (chap. 7); 17:11, 14 (chap. 6); Acts 17:24-25 (chap. 3); 1 Corinthians 4:12 (chap. 5); 2 Corinthians 6:9-10 (chap. 5); Ephesians 4:22-24 (chap. 2); Philippians 3:20 (chap. 5); 1 Timothy 3:16 (chap. 11); Titus 3:4 (chap. 9); and 1 John 1:1 (chap. 11).

Exposition of the Lord's Oracles (c. 130-140). In this period, Papias, who fits into this period chronologically but not topically, wrote his *Exposition of the Lord's Oracles*. It survives in fragments only. Among the fragments is his reference to Revelation 12:9 (Fragment 9), thus lending support to the quotations of the Apocalypse by other apostolic Fathers. From the above citations, it may be observed that every book of the New Testament was quoted clearly before A.D. 150, with the possible exception of Philemon and 3 John.[10]

THE ANTE-NICENE FATHERS (c. 150-c. 300)

In contrast to the apostolic Fathers, the Ante-Nicene Fathers wrote in

10. In his *Philippians,* 7.1, Polycarp may have used 2 John 7 as his authority instead of 1 John 4:2-3. If he did, only two "personal" letters were unquoted; if not, three "personal" letters were omitted as far as this study has revealed.

Greek, Syriac, and Latin. The writers in this period include such individuals as Marcion (d. c. 160), the heretic who mixed Gnosticism and orthodox Christianity into a dualistic and sharply anti-Judaistic sect, and Montanus, a second-century convert from Cybele worship in Phrygia who fancied himself "the inspired organ of the promised Paraclete or Advocate, the Helper and Comforter in these last times of distress."[11] Although heretical individuals and groups such as these, including the Donatists and the Novatians, may be appealed to in support of the present thesis, the treatment limits itself to the more notable Fathers of the Ante-Nicene period.

Justin Martyr (d. 165). Justin lived and worked at Rome, where he confronted Marcion at about 150. He later took a trip to Ephesus, where he wrote *Dialogues with Trypho, a Jew.* Upon his return to Rome (c. 165) he was arrested and martyred. But he had written two apologies in which he presented Christianity as the oldest, truest and most divine of all philosophies. He quoted the Scriptures very loosely, especially the Old Testament, and a Western text of the New Testament. In his writings, Justin quoted the gospels of Matthew (3:17; 7:23; etc.); Luke (3:33; 22:19; etc.); and John (3:3-5; etc.). He alluded to several of Paul's epistles (Romans, 1 Corinthians, Ephesians, Colossians, etc.), but did not mention Paul by name. Justin also cited the Apocalypse in his free style. More than 330 citations of the New Testament are in Justin's work, with an additional 266 allusions.[12]

Tatian (c. 110-172). Tatian wrote his *Oratio* as a defense of the Christian faith and a condemnation of the pagan philosophies. He is better known, however, for his *Diatessaron,* a harmony of the gospels. His work will be considered in chapter 28, and need not be discussed at this point, especially because he came under the influence of Gnosticism after the death of Justin. His writings were written in Syriac, or translated into it from Greek.

Irenaeus (c. 130-c. 202). Irenaeus wrote in Greek and was the first Father to make full use of the New Testament in his writings. His greatest work, *Against Heresies,* was written in Gaul (c. 185), and was a defense against Gnosticism and other heresies. He freely quoted the New Testament and demonstrated its unity with the Old. Although there are some differences, "we shall not err greatly in concluding that Irenaeus's copy of the Gospel was practically equivalent to an early ancestor of the Greek side of Codex Bezae, excelling the latter by a greater freedom from corruption." This situation prevails in the Acts as well.[13] In addition to the clarity of Irenaeus's text, there is manifold witness to his use of Scripture, as he makes more than eighteen hundred quotations from the New Testament alone. Also interesting

11. Philip Schaff, *History of the Christian Church,* 2:418.
12. See chart on p. 431 for totals on some of the following writers.
13. Alexander Souter, *The Text and Canon of the New Testament,* pp. 73-74. See chap. 22 discussion of this codex.

is the fact that Irenaeus's writings indicate that the canon of the New Testament was recognized in his day to be practically the same as it is today.[14]

Clement of Alexandria (c. 150-c. 215). Clement became head of the Catechetical School in Alexandria shortly before A.D. 200. Although he was not careful in his citation of Scripture, he left evidence that his text was also basically related to Codex Bezae.[15] He wrote several works in Greek, which were repetitious and lacking in clarity and sometimes even permitted error to creep into his theology. His works included an *Exhortation to the Heathen; Pedagogus,* which contains the earliest extant hymn of the church; and the *Stromata,* miscellaneous writings. His quotations were taken from both Testaments, and he cited all of the New Testament books except Philemon, James, and 2 Peter. There are some twenty-four hundred citations of the New Testament, including over one thousand from the gospels and over one thousand from the Pauline epistles. It is interesting to note that Clement quoted all of the Old Testament books except Song of Solomon and Ruth.

Tertullian (c. 160-c. 220). A contemporary to Clement of Alexandria, Tertullian is known as the "Father of Latin Christianity," as he was the first Father to write a body of Christian literature in Latin. His writings were in both Greek and Latin, as he served in the vital area of North Africa. His work was apologetical, polemical, practical, and pro-Montanist. He was a schismatic adherent to Montanism and used his powerful pen and pulpit to reprove what he considered to be compromise and worldliness within the Old Catholic church. His writings were prolific, and his use of Scripture was profuse but not always accurate. Many of his quotations were made from an Old Latin manuscript, basically following b,[16] although he often cited and/or translated a Greek manuscript closely akin to that used by Clement of Alexandria and Origen. That text, the furthest removed from Codex B among the Greek manuscripts, was closely related to D. In his writings, he makes more than seventy-two hundred New Testament citations, with more than thirty-eight hundred arising from the gospels, whereas more than twenty-six hundred were from the Pauline epistles.

Hippolytus (c. 170-c.236). Hippolytus lived in or near Rome and wrote in Greek, although little of his work has survived in the original language. His text type appears to be based upon a good Western copy of the gospels, but he may have also used Tatian's *Diatessaron* in his writing. In the Pauline Epistles he follows the Western text. "In the Apocalypse his text is particularly important: there he is found to agree with the best authorities."[17] In his writings, more than thirteen hundred New Testament citations appear. Of

14. See discussion in chap. 16.
15. Souter, pp. 74-75. Also see chap. 22 discussion.
16. See chap. 29 discussion.
17. Souter, p. 75.

those, more than seven hundred are from the gospels, nearly four hundred are Pauline, and almost two hundred are from the Apocalypse.

Origen (c. 185-c. 254). Origen succeeded Clement of Alexandria at the Catechetical School. He was by far the most prolific writer in the early church, as he wrote more than six thousand items and books. In his writings he made nearly eighteen thousand New Testament quotations. Among his outstanding works are the *Hexapla* and *De Principiis*. The former will be treated in chapter 27, and the latter is of importance as well, for it was his great work on the basic doctrines of Christianity. Still another work, *Against Celsus,* is a polemic in eight volumes, which has been preserved in Greek. It is interesting to observe that of Origen's citations of the New Testament, more than 95 percent were taken from the Gospels and Pauline Epistles, whereas only 205 were taken from the Apocalypse, and a mere 120 were taken from the General Epistles. When his views met with the theological bias of the West during the late fourth century, his writings were almost entirely neglected. That sad situation has resulted in the survival of only a few late and poor manuscripts to the present. The loss is tragic, as Origen had practically every existing text-type at his disposal when he wrote. Hence, it is significant that his manuscript basis was closely allied with that of Clement of Alexandria and Tertullian.

Cyprian (c. 195 or 200-258). Cyprian of Carthage wrote some eighty-one letters and twelve long treatises in Latin. He was one of the most careful and accurate quoters of the Bible in the early church. In his writings, Cyprian made about 740 Old and 1,030 New Testament quotations. He cited all the New Testament books except Philemon and 2 John. The quotations of Cyprian from the gospels adhere to the Old Latin k text-type.[18]

A brief inventory at this point will reveal that there were some thirty-two thousand citations of the New Testament prior to the time of the Council of Nicea (325). Those thirty-two thousand quotations are by no means exhaustive, and they do not even include the fourth-century writers. Just adding the number of references used by one other writer, Eusebius, who flourished prior to and contemporary with the Council at Nicea, will bring the total citations of the New Testament to over thirty-six thousand. Hence, prior to the period of the Nicene and Post-Nicene Fathers, there is overwhelming evidence in the manifold witness of the outstanding church Fathers to the text of the New Testament.

The Nicene and Post-Nicene Fathers (c. 300-c. 430)

The Nicene-Post-Nicene period of church history must be discussed at this point, because the New Testament canon had not yet been formally recog-

18. See chap. 29.

nized by the entire church in A.D. 325 (see chap. 16). During the period prior to the Council at Nicea, the church had gone through a series of local and imperial persecutions. As late as 302/3 the Emperor Diocletian had decreed that all copies of the Scriptures be destroyed and those people having them in their possession be punished (often unto death).[19] Thus, the Fathers of the period under discussion appeared *after* the Edict of Galerius (311) and the Edict of Milan (313), with the exception of Eusebius of Caesarea, who bridged the transition from "the persecuted to the patronized Church."

Eusebius of Caesarea (c. 263 or 265-c. 340). Eusebius was the bishop of Caesarea (315-340) and historian of the early church. He wrote, in Greek, such items as *Ecclesiastical History, Chronicles, Life of Constantine,* and a tract on *Martyrs of Palestine,* which earned for him the title "Father of Church History." Much of his work has survived to the present, and his role in the copying of the Scriptures is of great importance (see discussion in chap. 16). The literary value of his writing is not nearly so great as its historical value, and his use of the Scriptures in his writing follows the pattern of his forebears. He cited the New Testament more than five thousand times, and follows the basic text-type of Origen's sources. Eusebius was not a satisfactory quoter of Scripture, however, as he rarely cited long passages and, when he did quote, usually quoted loosely or from memory. His citations from the Gospels number more than thirty-two hundred with more than fifteen hundred from the Pauline Epistles. But it is with Eusebius that a new era opens in the transmission and citation of the biblical text.

Athanasius of Alexandria (c. 295-c. 373). Athanasius is known as the "Father of Orthodoxy" as a result of his role at the Council at Nicea (325) and his opposition to Arius and his followers. The writings of Athanasius were quite varied, as he spent some forty-six years as bishop of Alexandria and "defender of the faith" against Arianism. He was exiled five times, a total of twenty years, and did much of his writing in Greek during that period. Alexander Souter indicates that the text of Athanasius's New Testament, from which he made a vast number of citations, corresponded almost identically with Westcott and Hort's "Neutral text," as pointed out by Hermann von Soden.[20]

Cyril of Jerusalem (c. 315-386). Cyril wrote a series of lectures in Greek, *Twenty-three Catechises,* which he gave to candidates for baptism. He was later elected bishop of Jerusalem (350), but was deposed several times because of his personal prejudices. Each time he was reinstated, and he rose to a position of high esteem in the church because of his knowledge of Scripture and his general education. Cyril died in 386 after having spent sixteen

19. See chaps. 16 and 20 discussions.
20. Souter, p. 77.

years in exile and being recalled and highly esteemed. He was known for his willingness to suffer for his beliefs, and he freely quoted the New Testament in his catechises, which were actually a compendium of the Christian religion. The text of Cyril was basically that of Eusebius of Caesarea.[21]

The Three Cappadocian Fathers: Basil of Caesarea, "the Great" (c. 329-79), *Gregory of Nazianzus* (330-c. 390), and Basil's younger brother, *Gregory of Nyssa* (d. c. 395). These men are called the "Three Cappadocian Fathers." Their works were written in Greek and were widespread, influential, and beneficial. They were archdefenders of orthodoxy and wrote numerous items attacking Arianism. The text-type underlying their numerous citations of the New Testament was basically that of "the official ecclesiastical text associated with Constantinople and the regions under her influence."[22] There were, however, more ancient elements still preserved in their text, which they quoted rather carefully.

John Chrysostom (c. 347-407). Chrysostom was the first great writer to use the fully ecclesiastical text of the New Testament. He exerted much influence in his role as Metropolitan of Constantinople, and his support of the ecclesiastical text carried much weight. The numerous Greek commentaries written by Chrysostom included Matthew, John, Acts, all of Paul's Epistles, and Hebrews. He also wrote more than six hundred exegetical homilies. All of those works are saturated with citations of the New Testament text. Other outstanding leaders in the East, for example, Theodoret of Cyrrhus (c. 399-c. 466), and John of Damascus (c. 675-c. 749), used the same basic text as Chrysostom.

Ambrose of Milan (340-397). Ambrose represents the voice of the church in the West during this period. He was born into an aristocratic family and became bishop of Milan. Although his works were written in Latin, he based them on Greek sources. Thus, the vast number of quotations in his *Letters* are relatively poor samples of the Latin Bible. His text-type followed the Old Latin d and g, as seen in the Latin side of Codex Boernerianus.[23] It may have been this very text-type that was used by Jerome in his revision of the Old Latin New Testament. Ambrose left a tremendous impact on the church in the West, as he was the "spiritual father" of the "Medieval Monolith," Augustine.

Jerome (c. 340-420). Jerome will be considered and needs only to be mentioned in passing. Even prior to the death of Ambrose, Jerome was translating the Hebrew Old Testament into Latin (see chap. 29). His text-type for the gospels was the Old Latin a, while he turned to other Old Latin manuscripts for the remainder of the New Testament. It was this revision that

21. Cf. Kenyon, p. 366; also Souter, pp. 121-24.
22. Souter, p. 77.
23. See chap. 29.

became the "standard" for the Western church in the Middle Ages, and especially after the Council at Trent (1546-1563).

Augustine of Hippo Regius (c. 365-430). Augustine is one of the greatest scholars of this entire period. He wrote many extant Latin works, including *The City of God* and *The Confessions*. In his writings Augustine quoted profusely from both the Old and New Testaments. Prior to about 400, he followed the text of the Old Latin e in the gospels. After that time he turned to Jerome's Vulgate for his long citations, using memorized portions in shorter quotes. The remainder of his New Testament quotations appear to follow the Old Latin text of h or r.[24] His role in history has been amply seen before, but it should be pointed out that he was not a great philologist. His early opposition to Jerome's Vulgate was later reversed (see discussions in chaps. 16 and 29).

Summary and Conclusion

The patristic citations of Scripture are not primary witnesses to the text of the New Testament, but they do serve two very important secondary roles. First, they give overwhelming support to the existence of the twenty-seven authoritative books of the New Testament canon. It is true that their quotations were often loose, although in the case of some Fathers they were very accurate, but they do at least reproduce the substantial content of the original text. Second, the quotations are so numerous and widespread that if no manuscripts of the New Testament were extant, the New Testament could be reproduced from the writings of the early Fathers alone. Sir David Dalrymple's curiosity was aroused on this subject when once he was asked, "Suppose that the New Testament had been destroyed, and every copy of it lost by the end of the third century, could it have been collected together again from the writings of the Fathers of the second and third centuries?" Having given himself to research on this question, he was later able to report,

> Look at those books. You remember the question about the New Testament and the Fathers? That question roused my curiosity, and as I possessed all the existing works of the Fathers of the second and third centuries, I commenced to search, and up to this time I have found the entire New Testament, except *eleven verses*.[25]

In brief, J. Harold Greenlee was right when he wrote, "These quotations are so extensive that the New Testament could virtually be reconstructed from them without the use of New Testament Manuscripts."[26] Compare, for ex-

24. See chap. 29.
25. Charles Leach, *Our Bible: How We Got It*, pp. 35-36.
26. J. Harold Greenlee, *An Introduction to New Testament Textual Criticism*, p. 54.

ample, the numerous quotations given in Burgon's index, in the case of a few of the earlier and more important writers.[27]

EARLY CITATIONS OF THE NEW TESTAMENT

Writer	Gospels	Acts	Pauline Epistles	General Epistles	Revela- tion	Totals
Justin Martyr	268	10	43	6	3	330 (266 allusions)
Irenaeus	1,038	194	499	23	65	1,819
Clement Alex.	1,017	44	1,127	207	11	2,406
Origen	9,231	349	7,778	399	165	17,922
Tertullian	3,822	502	2,609	120	205	7,258
Hippolytus	734	42	387	27	188	1,378
Eusebius	3,258	211	1,592	88	27	5,176
Grand Totals	19,368	1,352	14,035	870	664	36,289

27. Cf. also Leach, pp. 35-36; Joseph Angus, *The Bible Handbook,* p. 57; Kenyon, p. 264.

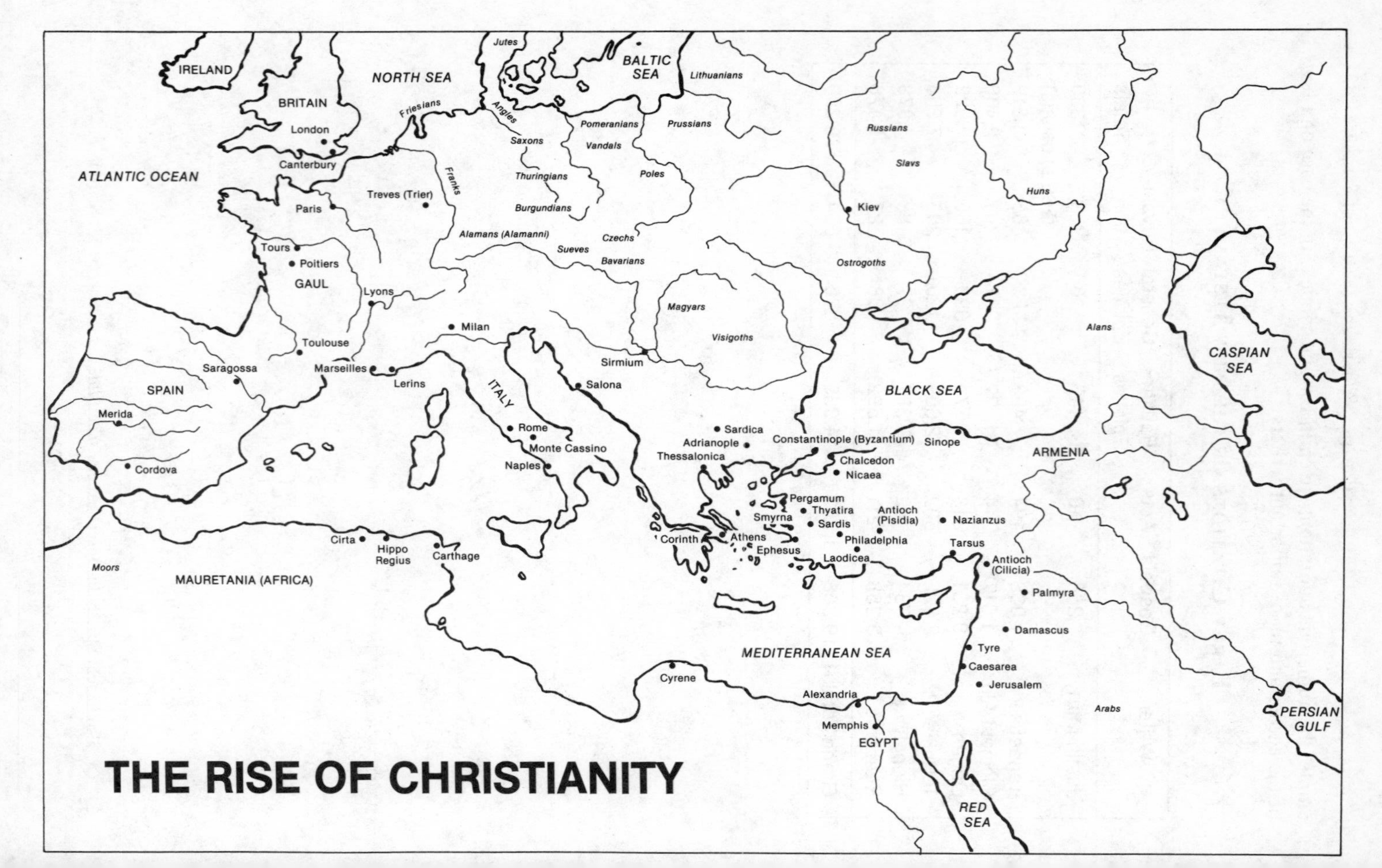
THE RISE OF CHRISTIANITY
IRELAND
BRITAIN
London
Canterbury
NORTH SEA
Jutes
BALTIC SEA
Lithuanians
Friesians
Angles
Saxons
Pomeranians
Vandals
Prussians
Russians
Slavs
ATLANTIC OCEAN
Franks
Treves (Trier)
Paris
Thuringians
Poles
Burgundians
Huns
Kiev
Alamans (Alamanni)
Czechs
Sueves
Bavarians
Tours
Poitiers
GAUL
Ostrogoths
Lyons
Magyars
Milan
Visigoths
Alans
Toulouse
CASPIAN SEA
Saragossa
Marseilles
Sirmium
SPAIN
Lerins
ITALY
Salona
BLACK SEA
Merida
Rome
Sardica
Monte Cassino
Adrianople
Constantinople (Byzantium)
Sinope
Naples
Thessalonica
Chalcedon
ARMENIA
Cordova
Nicaea
Pergamum
Thyatira
Smyrna
Sardis
Antioch (Pisidia)
Nazianzus
Cirta
Hippo Regius
Carthage
Corinth
Athens
Ephesus
Philadelphia
Tarsus
Laodicea
Antioch (Cilicia)
Moors
MAURETANIA (AFRICA)
Palmyra
Damascus
MEDITERRANEAN SEA
Tyre
Caesarea
Cyrene
Jerusalem
Alexandria
Arabs
PERSIAN GULF
Memphis
EGYPT
RED SEA

25
Development of Textual Criticism

Textual and Higher Criticism Distinguished

There has been much confusion and controversy over the matter of "higher" and "lower" criticism of the Bible. Much of this misunderstanding is a result of the semantic difficulty involved. "Criticism" in its grammatical sense means merely the exercise of judgment. When criticism is applied to the Bible, it is used in the sense of exercising judgment about the Bible itself. There are two basic kinds of criticism and two basic attitudes about each kind. In addition, there are six main branches within the two kinds of criticism of biblical criticism. The titles ascribed to the kinds of criticism have nothing whatsoever to do with their importance, although there are significant distinctions among the various branches.

When scholarly judgment is applied to the *genuineness* of the biblical text, it is classified as "higher" or "historical" criticism. This judgment is applied to the date of the text, its literary style and structure, its literary form, its historicity, its sources, and its authorship. As a result of the issues involved, higher criticism is not really an integral part of "General Introduction" but actually the very essence of "Special Introduction" to the Bible. For many, the outcome of higher critical approaches to the Old Testament by the heirs of the "destructive theology" of the late-eighteenth century has been a kind of "destructive criticism" of the Bible.[1] The development and expression of these approaches and criticism is discussed in chapters 8, 9, 10, and 20.

When scholarly judgment is applied to the *authenticity* of the biblical text, it is classified as "lower" or "textual" criticism. Lower criticism is concerned with the form or text of the Bible and attempts to restore the readings of the original text, the autograph. Not to be confused with higher criticism, which

1. These views arose as early as the time of Richard Simon (1638-1712), who is the so-called "father" of biblical criticism, as the discussion and notes of chap. 9 indicate. Also see Edgar Krentz, *The Historical-Critical Method*.

studies the value of a document, lower critics study the form of the words and structure of a document. Many examples of lower criticism may be observed in the history of the transmission of the Bible text. Some of the practitioners were sharp opponents, whereas others were staunch supporters of orthodox Christianity.[2] Since textual criticism is based on the assumption that the Bible is the inspired and inerrant Word of God, textual critics are interested in obtaining the original textual reading by applying certain criteria or standards of quality. Whether textual critics are constructive or destructive in their objective, they all approach the biblical text in an attempt to discover the original rendition of the autographs.

Because many adherents of higher criticism have also spent considerable time and energy in the study of textual criticism, there has been in the past a tendency to classify all textual critics as "modernists," destructive critics, or higher critics. Such an attitude tends to "throw out the baby with the bathwater." To avoid textual criticism simply because it has been practiced by certain destructive higher critics is hardly a justifiable reason for refraining from using the methods to discover the original reading of the Bible text. As Sir Frederic Kenyon has aptly observed, "the question of importance is not whether the criticism is 'higher,' but whether it is sound; and that is a question of evidence and argument, not of *a priori* assumptions or of impeaching the motives of those whose views we find unpalatable or consider to be unsound."[3] The following overview of the main branches within biblical criticism is presented in this frame of reference.

Within the tradition of biblical criticism six main branches may be distinguished: textual criticism, historical criticism, literary or source criticism, form criticism, tradition criticism, and redaction criticism.[4] These six main branches constitute the disciplines of "higher" and "lower" criticism. Although they arose from criticism studies of the Old Testament, the methods came to be applied to the New Testament as well. Throughout the branches of biblical criticism a basic theme common to the modern world remains constant. It is the question of authority in general and biblical authority in particular. Although some critics accept a higher degree of authority than others, more subjective methodologies (e.g., those of more extreme form criticism) tend to dispense with the notion of authority altogether. An over-

2. Also see J. N. Birdsall, "The New Testament Text," in P. R. Ackroyd, ed., *The Cambridge History of the Bible,* vol. 1, *From the Beginnings to Jerome,* pp. 308-77.
3. Sir Frederic Kenyon, *Our Bible and the Ancient Manuscripts,* p. 30.
4. Gordon Wenham, "1. History and the Old Testament," in Colin Brown, ed., *History, Criticism and Faith: Four Exploratory Studies,* pp. 13-75.

view of the main branches of biblical criticism will demonstrate their relationships to one another.

Textual criticism, also called "lower criticism," is concerned with recovering the original text of a literary document. By it, scholars attempt to seek and eliminate errors by using plausible explanations for emendations that have crept into the text. Through the study of numerous manuscripts, principles of textual criticism have been formulated that are applied to many different sorts of literary works. Textual criticism is discussed at length later below and in chapter 26).[5]

Historical criticism is a broad term that may be limited to three areas: techniques of dating documents and traditions; verification of events contained in those documents; and the writing of history, the reconstruction of events and their explanation. The "French Oratorian priest Richard Simon published a series of books in which he applied the critical method to the Bible (1678ff.) to become the direct founder of the historical-critical study of the Bible," although it was not until Eichhorn and Johann David Michaelis (1717-91) that the modern historical-critical pattern was set.[6] They were influenced by the secular historical research of Barthold Georg Niebuhr (1776-1831), Leopold von Ranke (1795-1886), and others who developed and refined its techniques.[7] Among those influenced by these methods was Johann Christian Konrad von Hofmann (1810-77), who combined elements of Schelling, Schleimeracher, and orthodox Lutheranism with history and the critical study of Scripture to make a fresh biblical-theological synthesis stressing "superhistorical history," "holy history," or "salvation history" (*Heilsgeschichte*) that would impact Karl Barth, Rudolf Bultmann, and others in the twentieth century.[8] Toward the close of the nineteenth century, capable orthodox scholars challenged "destructive criticism" and its rationalistic the-

5. For general issues related to textual criticism, see chaps. 18-20; Old Testament, chaps. 21 and 26; and New Testament, chaps. 22, 25, and 26. Also see Bruce K. Waltke, "The Textual Criticism of the Old Testament," pp. 211-28, R. K. Harrison, "Historical and Literary Criticism of the Old Testament," pp. 231-50, and Gordon D. Fee, "The Textual Criticism of the New Testament," pp. 417-33, all in Frank E. Gabelein, gen. ed., *The Expositor's Bible Commentary,* vol. 1; see as well F. M. Cross, "The Contribution of the Qumran Discoveries to the Study of the Biblical Text," *Israel Exploration Journal* 16 (1966): 81-95; and R. W. Klein, *Textual Criticism of the Old Testament.*
6. Krentz, p. 15. Also see Gerhard Maier, *The End of the Historical-Critical Method,* as well as the discussion and notes earlier in the present chapter. The specific titles were J. G. Eichhorn, *Einleitung in das Alte Testament* (3 vols., 1780-83), and the fourth edition (1788) of Johann David Michaelis (1717-91), *Einleitung in das Neue Testament* (1750). Krentz indicates that Semler is usually regarded as the father of historical-critical theology rather than Johann August Ernesti (1707-81), who wrote a decade earlier, "since Ernesti denied the possibility of divine Scripture ever erring" (p. 19).
7. Among works of significant influence were Barthold Georg Niebuhr, *Romische Geschichte* (1811-12), Leopold von Ranke, *Geschichte der romanischen und germanischen Volker von 1494-1535.* For a history of these developments see especially George Peabody Gooch, *History and Historians of the Nineteenth Century.*

ology. Among these more conservative scholars were George Salmon, Theodor von Zahn, R. H. Lightfoot, and others who used the methods of "higher criticism" to form the basis of "constructive criticism." This constructive criticism manifests itself most openly when it consders such matters as miracles, the virgin birth of Jesus, and the bodily resurrection of Christ. Historical criticism is today taken for granted in biblical studies. Much recent work in historical criticism manifests rationalistic theology that at the same time claims to uphold traditional Christian doctrine. As a result, it has given rise to several later developments.

Source criticism, also known as literary criticism, is the attempt to discover and define the literary sources used by the biblical writers. It is concerned predominantly with such matters as underlying literary sources, types of literature, and questions relating to authorship, unity, and date of the various Old and New Testament materials.[9] Some literary critics tend to decimate the biblical text and pronounce certain books inauthentic, and they even reject the notion of verbal inspiration altogether. In addition, some scholars have carried their rejection of authority to the point that they have modified the idea of the canon (e.g., with regard to pseudonymity) in order to accommodate the conclusions of their own theories.[10] Nevertheless, this difficult but important undertaking can be a valuable aid to biblical interpretation since it has bearing on the historical value of the biblical writings. In addition, careful literary criticism can also prevent historical misinterpretations of the biblical text.

Source criticism in the New Testament over the past century has focused on the so-called "Synoptic Problem," since it relates to difficulties surrounding attempts to devise a scheme of literary dependence to account for the combinations of similarities and dissimilarities among the synoptic gospels (Matthew, Mark, and Luke). Theories that one source, *Q* or *Quelle* (Ger. "Source"), was used by the three evangelists, who wrote in various sequences with the second depending on the first and the third on the other two. These theories were typical forerunners of the *Two-Source theory* advanced by B. H. Streeter, which asserted the priority of Mark and eventually gained wide acceptance among New Testament scholars. Streeter's argments have been questioned, and his thesis has been challenged by others.[11]

8. See the discussion in Werner Georg Kümmel, *The New Testament: The History of the Investigation of Its Problems,* trans. S. McLean Gilmour and Howard C. Kee; Krentz, pp. 17-32; Bernard Ramm, *Protestant Biblical Interpretation,* pp. 79-92.
9. Harrison, "Historical and Literary Criticism of the Old Testament," p. 239. Also see Wenham, "History and the Old Testament," pp. 36-37. See Harrison, pp. 243-46, for a discussion on developments in the role of literary criticism on the authorship, date, and unity of Isaiah as well as the book of Daniel.
10. See Donald Guthrie, "The Historical and Literary Criticism of the New Testament," pp. 454-56, in Frank E. Gaebelein, gen. ed., *The Expositor's Bible Commentary,* vol. 1.
11. See B. H. Streeter, *The Four Gospels: A Study of Origins,* pp. 150-360. Also see Robert L. Thomas, "An Investigation of the Agreements Between Matthew and Luke Against Mark,"

Form criticism is concerned with the study of literary forms, such as essays, poems, myths, and so on, since different writings have different forms. Often the form of a piece of literature can tell a great deal about the nature of a literary piece and its background. Technically this is termed "in its life setting" (*Sitz im Leben*). The classical liberal position with regard to Pentateuchal source-analysis was established by Wellhausen and his followers. They actually attempted to mediate between traditionalism and skepticism, dating the Old Testament books in a less supernaturalistic manner by applying the "documentary theory." These documents are identified as the Jehovistic (*J*), dated in the ninth century B.C., Elohistic (*E*), dated about a century later, Deuteronomic (*D*), from about the time of Josiah (640-609 B.C.), and Priestly (*P*), from perhaps the fifth century B.C. So attractive was the evolutionary concept in literary criticism that the source theory of Pentateuchal origins began to prevail over all opposition. A mediating position of some aspects of the theory was expressed by C. F. A. Dillman (1823-94), Rudolph Kittle (1853-1929), and others. Opposition to the documentary theory was expressed by Franz Delitzsch (1813-90), who rejected the hypothesis outright in his commentary on Genesis, William Henry Green (1825-1900), James Orr (1844-1913), A. H. Sayce, Wilhelm Möller, Eduard Naville, Robert Dick Wilson, and others.[12] Sometimes form-critical studies are marred by doctrinaire assumptions, including that early forms must be short and later forms longer, but, in general, form criticism has been of benefit to biblical interpretation. Form criticism has been most profitably used in the study of the Psalms.[13]

Twentieth-century form criticism was introduced into New Testament study of the gospels as *Formgeschichte* ("form history") or "form criticism" in English. Following in the tradition of Heinrich Paulus, Wilhelm De Wette, and others, scholars at Tübingen applied similar principles to the New Testament. Building on the foundation of source criticism theory, advocating the priority of Mark, and discontent with the limitations of multiple written sources (and hypothetical written sources), William Wrede (1859-1906) and

Journal of the Evangelical Theological Society 19 (1976): 103-12; Robert L. Thomas and Stanley N. Gundry argue that the Two-Source theory is inadequate and that the synoptic gospels arose in relatively independent circumstances ("Source Criticism," in *A Harmony of the Gospels with Explanations and Essays: Using the Text of the New American Standard Bible*, pp. 274-79); Krentz, *The Historical-Critical Method;* William R. Farmer, *The Synoptic Problem*, pp. 1-198 argues the primacy of Matthew; E. P. Sanders, *The Tendencies of the Synoptic Tradition*, indicates that the times, places, and circumstances of each gospel were sufficiently scattered to constitute them as independent witnesses to the life of Jesus. On the relationship of the gospel of John to the Synoptic Problem see Robert L. Thomas and Stanley N. Gundry, "Criticism of the Gospel of John," in *A Harmony of the Gospels*, pp. 295-301.

12. See Harrison, "Historical and Literary Criticism of the Old Testament," pp. 239-41; Gleason L. Archer, Jr., *A Survey of Old Testament Introduction*, passim; Robert H. Pfeiffer, *Introduction to the Old Testament*, passim.
13. Wenham, "History and The Old Testament," p. 40.

other form critics sought to eliminate the chronological-geographical framework of the Synoptic Gospels and to investigate the twenty-year period of oral traditions between the close of New Testament events and the earliest written accounts of those events. They attempted to classify this material into "forms" of oral tradition and to discover the historical situation (*Sitz im Leben*) withn the early church that gave rise to these forms. These units of tradition usually reflect more of the life and teaching of the early church than the life and teachng of Jesus. The "forms" in which the units are cast are clues to their relative historical value. The fundamental assumption of form criticism is typified by Dibelius and Bultmann. By creating new words and deeds of Jesus as the situation demanded, the evangelists arranged the units or oral tradition and created artificial contexts to serve the purposes of their own compositions. In challenging the authorship, date, structure, and style of other New Testament books, "destructive criticism" denied Pauline authorship of most of his epistles except Romans, 1 Corinthians, 2 Corinthians, and Galatians, and arrived at similar conclusions.[14] Thoroughgoing form critics hold two basic assumptions: (1) the early Christian community had little or no genuine biographical interest or integrity so it created and transformed oral tradition to meet its own needs; (2) the evangelists were merely editors of the individual, isolated units of tradition that they arranged and rearranged for their own purposes without regard for historical reality.[15]

Tradition criticism is primarily concerned with the history of traditions before they were recorded into writing and incorporated into literary sources. The stories of the patriarchs, for example, were probably passed down through generations by word of mouth either in the tribe or in the sanctuary until they were written down into a continuous narrative. Sometimes these oral traditions may have been changed in the long process of transmission. It is of great interest to the biblical scholar to know what changes were made and how the later tradition, now enshrined in a literary source, differs from the earliest oral one. Tradition criticism, although important, is less certain or secure than literary criticism for two reasons: (1) it begins where literary criticism leaves off, with conclusions that are in themselves uncertain, and (2) it is very difficult to check the hypotheses about the development of

14. See discussions in chapters 4, 9, and 11. Also see Zane C. Hodges, "Form-Criticism and the Resurrection Accounts," *Bibliotheca Sacra* 124 (1967): 339-48. On developments utilizing computer technology in biblical criticism see A. Q. Morton and James McLeman, *Christianity in the Computer Age*. For a critique of the fallacious presuppositions of the Morton-McLeman work see Reinier Schipper, "Paul and the Computer," *Christianity Today* (4 December 1964), p. 48. Surveys of these developments appear in the series of articles that conclude Robert L. Thomas and Stanley N. Gundry, eds., *A Harmony of the Gospels;* and Kenneth S. Kantzer and Stanley N. Gundry, eds., *Perspectives in Evangelical Theology;* Frank C. Gaebelein, ed., *Expositor's Bible Commentary,* vol. 1.
15. See Robert L. Thomas and Stanley N. Gundry, who identify Martin Dibelius, Rudolf Bultmann, Burton S. Easton, R. H. Lightfoot, Vincent Taylor, and D. E. Nineham as New Testament form critics, "Form Criticism," in *A Harmony of the Gospels,* pp. 281-82.

ancient oral tradition.[16] Even more tenuous is the "liturgical tradition" enunciated by S. Mowinckel and his Scandinavian associates who argue that literary origins were related to preexilic sanctuary rituals and sociological phenomena. An offshoot of the liturgical approach is the "myth and ritual" school of S. H. Hooke, which argues that a distinctive set of rituals and myths were common to all Near Eastern peoples, including the Hebrews. Both of these approaches use Babylonian festival analogies to support their variations on the classical literary-critical and tradition-critical themes.[17] As indicated in the previous discussion, form criticism is closely aligned with tradition criticism in New Testament studies. A review of many of the basic assumptions in view of the New Testament text have been made by Oscar Cullman and I. Howard Marshall.[18]

Redaction criticism is more closely associated with the text than is tradition criticism and, as a result, is less open to the charge of subjective speculation. Redaction (editorial) critics can achieve absolute certainty only when all the sources are used that were at the disposal of the redactor (editor), since the task is to determine how a redactor utilized sources, what was omitted, what was added, and what particular bias was involved in the redaction process. At best, the critic has only part of the sources available, such as the books of Kings used by the writers of Chronicles. Elsewhere, in both the Old and New Testaments, the sources must be reconstructed out of the edited work itself. Then redaction criticism becomes much less certain as a literary device.[19]

Redaction critics generally do not follow traditional viewpoints about authorship. Instead, they tend to favor a view that originators of biblical books are later theological editors to whom the various book names were attached for the sake of prestige. In Old and New Testament studies this view arose from historical criticism, source criticism, and form criticism. As a result, it adopts many of the same presuppositions, including the documentary hypothesis in the Old Testament, and the priority of Mark in the New Testament.

16. Wenham, "History and the Old Testament," pp. 40-41.
17. Harrison, "Historical and Literary Criticism of the Old Testament," p. 241.
18. Oscar Cullmann, *The Christology of the New Testament;* I. Howard Marshall, *The Origins of New Testament Christology.* Also see I. Howard Marshall, *I Believe in the Historical Jesus.* Also see the discussions in Brevard S. Childs, *Introduction to the Old Testament as Scripture* and *Introduction to the New Testament as Canon*; Gerhard Hasel, *Old Testament Theology: Basic Issues in the Current Debate,* and *New Testament Theology: Basic Issues in the Current Debate.*
19. See chap. 14 discussion. Also see Wenham, "History and the Old Testament," pp. 40-41. Also see Norman Perrin, *What is Redaction Criticism?;* I. Howard Marshall, *Luke: Historian and Theologian;* Everett F. Harrison, "*Gemeindetheologie:* The Bane of Gospel Criticism," in Carl F. H. Henry, ed., *Jesus of Nazareth,* pp. 157-73; Robert L. Thomas and Stanley N. Gundry, "Redaction Criticism," in *A Harmony of the Gospels,* pp. 287-94. A Christianity Today Institute Forum was moderated by Kenneth S. Kantzer and published as "Redaction Criticism: Is It Worth the Risk?" *Christianity Today,* 18 October 1985, pp. 55-66. Also see D.A. Carson, *Redaction Criticism: The Nature of an Interpretive Tool* (Carol Stream, Ill.: Christianity Today Institute, 1985).

A Critique of Destructive New Testament Criticism

As was noted earlier, not all higher criticism is negative and destructive. Criticism merely means to exercise scholarly judgment. This can be very helpful for a Christian, as long as it does not go contrary to the teaching of Scripture. However, much of modern biblical criticism springs from unbiblical philosophical presuppositions,[20] such as deism, materialism, skepticism, agnosticism, idealism (Hegelianism), and existentialism (see chap. 9). Beneath all these is a prevailing naturalism or antisupernaturalism that is intuitively suspicious of any document containing miracle stories (see chap. 10). As a result of the influence of this naturalistic bias, a negative (destructive) form of higher criticism arose that can be contrasted to positive (constructive) criticism in the following mutually exclusive categories:

	POSITIVE (CONSTRUCTIVE) CRITICISM	NEGATIVE (DESTRUCTIVE) CRITICISM
BASIS	Supernaturalistic	Naturalistic
RULE	"Innocent till proven guilty"	"Guilty till proven innocent"
RESULT	Bible is wholly true	Bible is only partly true
FINAL AUTHORITY	Word of God	Mind of Man
ROLE OF REASON	Man discovers truth (rationality)	Man determines truth (rationalism)

Some of the presuppositions of this negative criticism call for scrutiny, especially as they relate to the gospel record. This analysis is especially relevant to source citicism, form criticism, and redaction criticism as they challenge the genuineness, authenticity, and consequently the divine authority of the Bible. This kind of biblical criticism is unfounded for several reasons.

1. It is based on an unjustified antisupernatural bias which it superimposes on the biblical documents. Indeed, the originator of modern negative criticism was an incorrigible antisupernaturalist, Benedict Spinoza (see chap. 9). He declared that Moses did not write the Pentateuch, nor Daniel the whole book of Daniel, nor did any miracles recorded in the Bible actually occur, because miracles, he claimed, were scientifically and rationally impossible.

In the wake of Spinoza, negative critics concluded that Isaiah did not write the whole book of Isaiah, since that would involve supernatural predictions (including some about king Cyrus by name) over a hundred years in advance. Likewise, negative critics concluded Daniel could not have been written until c. 165 B.C., which would place it *after* the detailed description of world governments and rulers down to Antiochus IV Ephiphanes (d. 163 B.C.). Here too they assumed Daniel could not be giving supernatural predictions of

20. For a critical evaluation see Gerhard Maier, *The End of the Historical Critical Method*.

coming events. The same naturalistic bias was applied to the New Testament by David Strauss, Albert Schweitzer, and Rudolf Bultmann with the same devastating results.

The foundations of this antisupernaturalism have crumbled with the discovery of quantum physics and "Big Bang" theory. For according to modern physics, extraordinary events (such as miracles) cannot be ruled out. Even agnostics, such as Robert Jastrow,[21] speak of "supernatural" forces at work in the creation of the universe, and atheists admit the universe came into being from nothing.[22] Since antisupernaturalism has been thoroughly discussed elsewhere,[23] it is sufficient to note here that with the demise of modern antisupernaturalism there is no philosophical basis for such negative (destructive) criticism. Apart from the antisupernatural issue, other problems confront biblical critics of both Testaments (see chap. 9). New Testament examples will illustrate these problems.

2. *It either neglects or minimizes the role of the apostles and eyewitnesses who recorded the events*. Of the four Gospel writers, Matthew, Mark, and John were definitely eyewitnesses of the events they report. Luke was a contemporary and careful historian (Luke 1:1-4).[24] Indeed, every book of the New Testament was written by a contemporary or eyewitness of Christ. Even such critics as the "Death-of-God" theologian, Bishop John A. T. Robinson, admit that the Gospels were written between A.D. 40 and 65,[25] during the life of eyewitnesses.

But if the basic New Testament documents were composed by eyewitnesses, then much of destructive criticism fails. For it assumes a much later date in order for the alleged "myths" and distortions to occur. For studies have revealed that it takes at least two generations for a myth to develop.[26]

3. *It assumes wrongly that the New Testament writers did not distinguish between their own words and those of Jesus*. That a clear distinction was made between Jesus' words and those of the Gospel writers is evident from the ease by which a "red letter" edition of the New Testament can be made. Indeed, the apostle Paul is clear to distinguish his own words from those of Jesus (see Acts 20:35; 1 Cor. 7:10, 12, 25). So is John the apostle in the Apocalypse (see Rev. 1:8, 11, 17*b*-20; 2:1f.; 3:1f.; 22:7, 12-16, 20*b*). In view of this the New Testament critic is unjustified in assuming that the Gospel record is not actually reporting what Jesus said and did.

21. See Robert Jastrow, "A Scientist Caught Between Two Faiths," *Christianity Today*, 6 August, 1982, p. 18.
22. See Anthony Kenny, *The Five Ways: St. Thomas Aquinas' Proof of God's Existence*, p. 66.
23. See Norman L. Geisler, *Miracles and Modern Thought*.
24. See Sir William Ramsay, *St. Paul the Traveller and the Roman Citizen*.
25. John A. T. Robinson, *Redating the New Testament*, p. 352. The whole New Testament was written between A.D. 40 and 70. See chap. 12, n. 21.
26. See A. N. Sherwin-White, *Roman Society and Roman Law in the New Testament*, p. 190. Also see I. Howard Marshall, *The Origins of New Testament Christology*.

4. It incorrectly assumes that the New Testament stories are like folklore and myth. In actuality there is a vast difference between the simple New Testament account of miracles and the embellished myths of the second and third centuries A.D., as can be seen by comparing the accounts (see chap. 17 discussion). In point of fact, the New Testament writers explicitly disavow myths. Peter declared: "For we did not follow cleverly devised tales (*mythos*) when we made known to you the power and coming of our Lord Jesus Christ, but we were eyewitnesses of His majesty" (2 Pet. 1:16). Paul also warned against belief in myths on several occasions (1 Tim. 1:4; 4:7; 2 Tim. 4:4; Titus 1:14).

One of the most telling arguments against the myth view was given by a famous modern myth writer himself:

> First then, whatever these men may be as Biblical critics, I distrust them as critics. They seem to me to lack literary judgement, to be imperceptive about the very quality of the of the texts they are reading.... If he tells me that something in a Gospel is legend or romance, I want to know how many legends and romances he has read, how well his palate is trained in detecting them by the flavour; not how many years he has spent on that Gospel.... I have been reading poems, romances, vision-literature, legends, myths all my life. I know what they are like. I know that not one of them is like this.[27]

5. It undermines the integrity of the New Testament writers by claiming that Jesus never really said (or did) what they claim he said (or did). Even some confessed evangelical critics have gone so far as to claim that " 'Jesus said' or 'Jesus did' need not always mean that in history Jesus said or did what follows, but sometimes may mean that in the account at least partly constructed by Matthew himself Jesus said or did what follows."[28] But this clearly undermines confidence in the Gospel records, and in the truthfulness of the events recorded in them.

On this critical view the Gospel writers become *creators* of the events, not *recorders*. Indeed, one writer claimed that Matthew created the Magi story (Matt. 2) out of the turtledove story (of Luke 2). For according to Robert Gundry, Matthew "changes the sacrificial slaying of 'a pair of turtledoves or two young pigeons,' which took place at the presentation of the baby Jesus in the Temple (Luke 2:24; cf. Lev. 12:6-8), into Herod's slaughtering the babies in Bethlehem (cf. As. Mos. [Assumption of Moses] 6:2-6)."[29] But such a view not only overlooks the integrity of the Gospel writers but also undermines the authenticity and authority of the Gospel record.

One biblical scholar, Paul K. Jewett, went so far as to assert that what the

27. C. S. Lewis, *Christian Reflections,* pp. 154-55.
28. Robert Gundry, *Matthew: A Commentary on His Literary and Theological Art,* p. 630.
29. Ibid., pp. 34-35.

apostle Paul affirmed (in 1 Cor. 11:3)[30] was wrong. If this is so, then the time-honored truth that "what the Bible says, God says" is not so. Indeed, if Jewett is right, then even when one discovers what the author of Scripture is affirming, he must then ask one more question: "Hath God said?" (cf. Gen. 3:1). In short, if "what the Bible says, God says" is not so, then the divine authority of all Scripture is cast in doubt.

6. It is based on the implausible premise that the early church had no real biographical interest. It is highly improbable on the face of it that the New Testament writers, impressed as they were with the belief that Jesus was the long-promised Messiah, the Son of the living God (Matt. 16:16-18), would have no real interest in recording accurately what he actually said and did.

Indeed, it is contrary to their own clear statements. For John claimed that "Jesus did" the things recorded in his Gospel (John 21:25). Elsewhere John said "What... we have heard, we have seen with our eyes, we beheld and our hands handled... we proclaim to you also" (1 John 1:1-2). In fact, Luke clearly manifest the widespread biographical interest of the earliest Christian communities when he wrote:

> Inasmuch as many have undertaken to compile an account of the things accomplished among us, just as those who from the beginning were eyewitnesses and servants of the Word have handed them down to us, it seemed fitting for me as well, having investigated everything carefully from the beginning, to write it out for you in consecutive order, most excellent Theophilus; so that you might know the exact truth about the things you have been taught. (Luke 1:1-4)

Hence, to claim, as the critics do, that the New Testament writers lacked interest in recording real history is both implausible and contrary to their own statements.

7. It neglects the role of the Holy Spirit in activating the memories of the eyewitnesses. Much of the rejection of the gospel record is based on the assumption that the writers could not be expected to remember sayings, details, and events 20-40 years after the events. For Jesus died in A.D. 33, and the first gospel records probably come from between c. A.D. 50-60.[31]

But here again the critic is rejecting or neglecting the clear statement of Scripture. For Jesus promised his disciples that "The Helper, the Holy Spirit, whom the Father will send in My name, He will teach you all things, and bring to your remembrance all that I said to you" (John 14:26).

So even on the unlikely assumption that no one recorded anything Jesus said during His lifetime or immediately after, the critics would have us believe that eyewitnesses whose memories were later supernaturally activated by the Holy Spirit did not accurately record what Jesus did and said. It seems far

30. Paul K. Jewett, *Man as Male and Female,* pp. 134-35.
31. John W. Wenham, "Gospel Origins," *Trinity Journal* 7 (1978): 112-34.

more likely that the first-century eyewitnesses were right and the twentieth-century critics are wrong, than the reverse.

Of course biblical scholarship need not be destructive. But the biblical message must be understood in its theistic (supernatural) context and its actual historical and grammatical setting. Positive guidelines for evangelical scholarship are set forth in "The Chicago Statement on Biblical Hermeneutics." It reads in part as follows:[32]

Article XIII. WE AFFIRM that awareness of the literary categories, formal and stylistic, of the various parts of Scripture is essential for proper exegesis, and hence we value genre criticism as one of the many disciplines of biblical study.

WE DENY that generic categories which negate historicity may rightly be imposed on biblical narratives which present themselves as factual.

Article XIV. WE AFFIRM that the biblical record of events, discourses and sayings, though presented in a variety of appropriate literary forms, corresponds to historical fact.

WE DENY that any such event, discourse or saying reported in Scripture was invented by the biblical writers or by the traditions they incorporated.

Article XV. WE AFFIRM the necessity of interpreting the Bible according to its literal, or normal sense. The literal sense is the grammatical-historical sense, that is, the meaning which the writer expressed. Interpretation according to the literal sense will take account of all figures of speech and literary forms found in the text.

WE DENY the legitimacy of any approach to Scripture that attributes to it meaning which the literal sense does not support.

Article XVI. WE AFFIRM that legitimate critical techniques should be used in determining the canonical text and its meaning.

WE DENY the legitimacy of allowing any method of biblical criticism to question the truth or integrity of the writer's expressed meaning, or of any other scriptural teaching.

32. See Norman L. Geisler, *Summit II: Hermeneutics,* pp. 10-13. See also chap. 10 above and Earl D. Radmacher and Robert D. Preus, *Hermeneutics, Inerrancy, and the Bible,* especially Appendixes A, B, and C, pp. 881-914.

TEXTUAL CRITICISM IN THE ANCIENT PERIOD OF CHURCH HISTORY (TO C. 325)

From as early as the third century B.C., scholars in Alexandria attempted to restore the texts of the Greek poets and writers of prose. It will be recalled that this center also produced the Septuagint (LXX) version of the Old Testament at about 250-150 B.C. In addition, Alexandria was a center of Christianity during the early centuries of the church. The city retained its position of scholarly leadership until the rise of Islam in the late-sixth and early-seventh centuries. As a result, it is understandable that it would be a center of activity during attempts at restoring the biblical text prior to about A.D. 325. Basically, however, there was no real textual criticism of the New Testament books in this period; it was a "period of reduplication" of the manuscripts rather than one of evaluation of them. On the other hand, there was diligent textual work done in Palestine by the rabbis on the Old Testament between A.D. 70-100.

COPIES OF THE AUTOGRAPHS (to c. 150)

Most of the New Testament books were written during the second half of the first century. Those manuscripts were written under the direction of the Holy Spirit and were inerrant. They were undoubtedly written on papyrus and have all subsequently been lost. Nevertheless, the autographs of the New Testament were providentially copied and circulated before they became illegible or lost. These copies were made as early as A.D. 95. If copying had not begun very soon after the autographs were written, there would be no Bible today because papyrus survives for long periods of time only under exceptional conditions. Just as the autographs were written on papyrus rolls, so the earliest copies were probably written on papyrus rolls. Soon, however, papyrus codices were produced, and parchment and vellum were employed still later. Very few, if any, of the early copies are extant today, for basically the same reasons as indicated with regard to the autographs (see chap. 20).

Although there were many early copies of the autographs, they are not all of the same quality, for as soon as a manuscript was copied misprints began to creep into the text. Some of the early copies were highly accurate and quite expensive, as they were copied by professional scribes. Manuscript copies made by less capable scribes were less expensive, but they were of a generally poorer quality and wider distribution. Still other copies made in this early period were quite poor in quality, as they were often copied by nonprofessionals and were often all that an individual or group could afford to have made. Gordon Fee correctly calls this a *"Period of Confusion (to A.D. 400)"* and adds that

> during the second century in particular, when each NT book was being transmit-

ted independently of the others and when there was wide geographical distribution of these documents with little or no "controls," such scribal errors proliferated. Once an error was introduced into the text, it was then copied by the next scribe as his "received" text. Quite often a scribe "corrected" what he thought to be errors and in doing so created errors of his own.[33]

Copies of the Copies (c. 150-c. 325)

After the period of the Apostolic and Subapostolic Fathers, copies were made of the copies of the New Testament autographs. During these years there were widespread local persecutions of Christians, as well as two imperial persecutions (under Decius and Diocletian). During those persecutions Christians were confronted with intense suffering and even death. In addition, their sacred writings were often confiscated and destroyed on an Empire-wide basis.[34] As a result of their widespread destruction, the Scriptures were in danger of being lost to the church. Therefore, Christians often made copies of the manuscripts to take the place of those that had been destroyed. Many of these copies were made hastily, as the scribes were in danger of persecution if apprehended, and quite often they were copied "unprofessionally," or in an amateur fashion, by members of a given church.[35] Thus, the possibility of errors within the copies was multiplied at the same time numbers of manuscripts and older copies were being systematically destroyed. All of this was going on during a period when the church was progressively collecting, sifting, sorting, and recognizing the canonical books of the New Testament (see discussion in chap. 16). It was this situation that, according to Kenyon, "may be summarily characterized as the period when the textual problems came into being, which we have to try to solve with the help of the evidence afforded by the later periods."[36]

During this period of persecution of the church on the local level, the church in Alexandria began to do pioneer work in the comparison and publication of the texts (c. 200-c. 250). This leadership was extended to other areas of the Empire as well, and some basic work in textual criticism was done by the time of persecution under the Emperor Decius (249-51). Work on the Old Testament was done by Origen in Alexandria. His *Hexapla* was never published in its entirety, but it was a masterful attempt at textual criticism of

33. Gordon D. Fee, "The Textual Criticism of the New Testament," in Frank E. Gaebelein, ed., *The Expositor's Bible Commentary,* p. 425.
34. See discussion in chap. 16 as well as Brooke Foss Westcott, *A General Survey of the History of the Canon of the New Testament,* pp. 411-25. Textual scholars who follow Burgon overlook this crucial fact in their argumentation.
35. Bruce M. Metzger, *The Text of the New Testament,* pp. 14-16, describes the scribal practices in this period and the impact they had on textual quality. He mentions, among other things, the wage-fixing edict of Diocletian (A.D. 301) for scribes who reached at least two levels of quality in manuscript production.
36. Sir Frederic G. Kenyon, *Handbook to the Criticism of the New Testament,* p. 40.

the Old Testament (see chap. 27). In addition to his Old Testament work, Origen also wrote many New Testament commentaries in which he functioned as one of the first New Testament critics.[37] Other examples of early textual criticism would also include such works as the *Lucian Recension,* Julius Africanus's work on *Susanna,* and the *Song of Songs* by Theodore of Mopsuestia, who represents the school of theology having its center in Caesarea. The work of these early textual critics notwithstanding, the early church witnessed a period of casual, unsystematic, and largely unintentional creation of variants in the text of the New Testament. It also witnessed a conscious, though often elementary, selection and editorial revision of the text materials.

Textual Criticism in the Medieval Period (c. 325-c. 1500)

When the church was released from the threat of persecution, after the Edict of Milan (313), the influence was soon felt on the copying of the manuscripts of the Bible. This period was marked by the introduction of parchment and vellum codices, and paper books toward the close of the Middle Ages. During the medieval period, the Greek uncials gave way to minuscules, and printing gave way to cursive writing. Throughout the entire period, critical revisions of the texts of the Bible were relatively rare, except for the efforts of such scholars as Jerome (c. 340-420) and Alcuin of York (735-804). Nevertheless, the period from about 500 to 1000 produced scholars who were revising the Old Testament and adding finer points to the Hebrew text. Those scholars, the Masoretes, produced the Masoretic Text, which is still the authoritative text of the Hebrew Scriptures (see chap. 21).

The letter of Constantine to Eusebius, instructing him to make fifty copies of the Christian Scriptures,[38] marked a new direction in the history of textual criticism, the period of standardization of the text. The New Testament began to be carefully and faithfully copied from existing manuscripts. The text of a given area was copied by the copyists in that area. Hence, in A.D. 330, when Constantine moved the seat of the Roman Empire to the city named after him (Constantinople), and it became the dominant city in the Greek-speaking world, it was only reasonable that the ecclesiastical text of that imperial city would become the dominant text of the church. This is especially true in light of the emperor's patronage in producing careful copies of the New Testament text. It is undoubtedly true that other great cities of the Empire must have followed a similar pattern.

37. The choice of manuscripts at his disposal made his selection of a text guide significant; cf. chap. 24.
38. See chap. 16 for the text of the letter to Eusebius, written during the first third of the fourth century.

As a result of the precedent established by Constantine, great numbers of carefully copied manuscripts were produced in the Middle Ages. But official critical comparison and careful, planned revision were relatively rare in that manifold transmission of the text. J. Harold Greenlee correctly observes this point as he writes,

> The evidence of the mss. indicates that the processes of standardization of the text and consequent displacement of the older text-types continued from the fourth century until the eighth, by the end of which time the standardized or "Byzantine" text had become the accepted form of the text.
>
> Approximately 95 percent of the existing mss. of the N.T. are from the eighth and later centuries, and very few of these differ appreciably from the Byzantine text. This means that the witnesses from the pre-Byzantine text of the N.T. consist of a relatively small percentage of the mss., mostly from the period earlier than the eighth century.[39]

Once a standardized text was developed, there was little need for classification and critical evaluation of the earlier manuscripts of the text. As a result, the text remained relatively unchanged throughout the entire period, for the standardization had been the result of a comparison and mixing of these earlier manuscripts. Again, Greenlee states the situation with insight, as he writes,

> There was apparently some comparison of this text with other texts, resulting in something of a mixed type of text. The text seems to have been subjected to some editing, with parallel accounts tending to become harmonized, grammatical irregularities corrected, and abrupt transitions modified, producing a generally smooth text.[40]

Toward the end of the period a completely standardized text with an unlimited number of more-or-less identical copies became possible with the introduction of cheap paper and the printing press. Paper copies of the text had begun to appear in abundance after the twelfth century, and then in about 1454 Johann Gutenberg introduced movable type into the printing process. Thus, the door was open for the efforts of more careful textual criticism during the Reformation era.

Textual Criticism in the Reformation Period (c. 1500-c. 1648)

From their origins until the sixteenth century, books of the Bible were circulated in manuscript (handwritten) form, thus making each copy to some

39. J. Harold Greenlee, *An Introduction to New Testament Textual Criticism*, p. 62.
40. Ibid.

extent a different unit. In the Reformation era, however, the Bible text entered into a "period of crystallization" in printed rather than manuscript form.[41] Often attempts were made at revising and editing existing manuscripts in order to publish printed texts of the Bible as accurately as possible. Frequently Bibles were published in polyglot (multilingual) form, including such titles as the Complutensian Polyglot (1514-1517), the Antwerp Polyglot (1569-1572), the Paris Polyglot (1629-1645), and the London Polyglot (1657-1669). During this time, a standard edition of the Masoretic Text was published. It was printed under the editorship of Jacob Ben Chayyim, a Hebrew Christian, at about 1525, and was based on manuscripts dating from the fourteenth century. This text was essentially a recension of the Masorete Ben Asher text (c. A.D. 920), and it became the basis for all subsequent copies of the Hebrew Bible, whether in manuscript or printed editions. Work on the New Testament text in particular was more varied in this era, as well as being more sweeping in its outreach, as the results of Gutenberg's invention were felt.

Cardinal Francisco Ximenes de Cisneros (1437-1517)

Cardinal Francisco Ximenes de Cisneros of Spain planned the first printed Greek New Testament to come off the press. It was planned in 1502 as a part of the Complutensian Polyglot, consisting of the Hebrew, Aramaic, Greek, and Latin texts. It was printed in the university town of Alcalá (*Complutum* in Latin), after which the polyglot was named, and printed in 1514 (Old Testament in 1517). Although this was the first printed New Testament, it was not the first to be placed on the market. Pope Leo X did not give his sanction for publication until March 1520. The Greek manuscripts underlying the Complutensian Polyglot have never been adequately determined, and there is some question about Ximenes's statements in his dedication about the manuscripts used in the polyglot.[42]

Desiderius Erasmus (1466-1536)

Desiderius Erasmus of Rotterdam, the Dutch scholar and humanist, had the honor of editing the first Greek New Testament actually to be published. As early as 1514, Erasmus had discussed such a work with the printer Johann Froben of Basle. In July 1515, Erasmus journeyed to Basle looking for Greek manuscripts that would be usable to typeset as copy along with his own Latin translation. Although he could find only manuscripts that required editing before use, he proceeded with his task. On October 2, 1515, printing was

41. See Metzger, *The Text of the New Testament,* pp. 95-118; also see Sir Frederic G. Kenyon, *The Text of the Greek Bible,* pp. 122-84; Gordon D. Fee, "The Textual Criticism of the New Testament," pp. 419-26.
42. See the discussion of this point in Metzger, *The Text of the New Testament,* p. 98, and the references listed therein. Also see Kenyon, *The Text of the Greek Bible,* p. 174.

begun, and on March 1, 1516, the first edition was completed. This edition contained numerous errors, including hundreds of typographical and mechanical errors. Some of the problems Erasmus bypassed in his hasty work have been summarized by Metzger:

> Since Erasmus could not find a manuscript which contained the entire Greek Testament, he utilized several for various parts of the New Testament. For most of the text he relied on two rather inferior manuscripts in the university library at Basle, one of the Gospels and one of the Acts and Epistles, both dating from about the twelfth century. Erasmus compared them with two or three others of the same books and entered occasional corrections for the printer in the margins or between the lines of the Greek script. For the Book of Revelation he had but one manuscript, dating from the twelfth century, which he borrowed from his friend Reuchlin. Unfortunately, this manuscript lacked the final leaf, which had contained the last six verses of the book. For these verses, as well as at numerous passages throughout the book where the Greek text of the Apocalypse and the adjoining Greek commentary with which the manuscript was supplied are so mixed up as to be almost indistinguishable, Erasmus depended upon the Latin Vulgate, translating this into Greek. As would be expected from such a procedure, here and there in Erasmus' self-made Greek text are readings which have never been found in any known Greek manuscript but which are still perpetuated today in printings of the so-called Textus Receptus of the Greek New Testament.[43]

This evidence demonstrates that Erasmus's text, which was part of the basis for the so-called "Received Text," or Textus Receptus (after 1633), was not based on earlier manuscripts, not reliably edited, and consequently not as trustworthy as later editions. In fact, the Textus Receptus (TR) itself is derived from a few works of the Renaissance period.[44]

The reception of Erasmus's edition of the Greek New Testament was quite mixed. Because of the hundreds of printing errors in it, a new edition was issued in 1519. The second edition, like the first, was a diglot, and it was probably the basis of Martin Luther's German translation. One additional manuscript was used in the preparation of that second edition. In 1522 Erasmus produced his third edition, in which he reluctantly inserted 1 John 5:7.[45] It is about that edition that Frederick G. Kenyon writes, "For English readers ... the first English-printed New Testament, produced by Tyndale in 1526, was translated from the text of Erasmus; and this, with Latin and German Bibles, was the basis of Coverdale's successive Bibles from 1535 to 1541."[46] In 1527 Erasmus employed many of the readings of the Compluten-

43. Metzger, *The Text of the New Testament*, pp. 99-100.
44. See discussion in Metzger, *The Text of the New Testament*, pp. 103-6; D. A. Carson, *The King James Version Debate: A Plea for Reason*, pp. 33-37.
45. See the discussion of this passage in chap. 26.
46. Kenyon, *The Text of the Greek Bible*, p. 174.

sian Polyglot, which he saw just after publishing his third edition. Théodore de Bèze (Theodore Beza) published nine editions of the Greek New Testament that differed little from Erasmus's fourth edition. In 1535 a fifth and final edition of Erasmus's Greek text was published. It was still based on the Byzantine text-type, contained readings from very late manuscripts, and included the spurious reading of 1 John 5:7-8 as well as his translations back into Greek from Latin of the verses in Revelation.

Robert Estienne (Stephanus)

The royal printer of Paris, Robert Estienne (French, Étienne, Latinized as Stephanus), published the Greek New Testament in 1546, 1549, 1550, and 1551. The third edition of this Greek New Testament (1550) was the earliest edition to contain a critical apparatus, using fifteen manuscripts. It was based on Erasmus's fourth (1527) and fifth (1535) editions and along with Beza's editions became the basis for the Textus Receptus. In the fourth Stephanus edition (1557), the printer announced his conversion to Protestantism, and he demonstrated for the first time the modern verse divisions of the New Testament that he had produced. After its publication, this fourth edition of the Stephanus Greek text became dominant in England. It was used for the Geneva Bible (1557 and 1560) and the King James Version of 1611. In both of those translations, Stephanus's verse-division was adopted.[47] The situation is summarized by Kenyon when he writes,

> By 1550, therefore, scholars in Western Europe possessed the Greek New Testament substantially in the form which had become standardized in the Eastern Church during the later Middle Ages. From this point in the history of the text consists of the record of the labours of scholars in collecting materials for its revision, and of attempts from time to time made to revise it—labours and attempts that continue to the present day.
>
> For a century and more after the pioneer work of Ximenes and Erasmus very little was done to test the authenticity of the printed text by comparison with other manuscripts, and no stress was laid on the comparative age of these manuscripts. How many MSS were consulted for the Complutensian is not known. Erasmus, as we have seen, used very few. Neither of them gave any apparatus of various readings. Stephanus in 1550 did give in his margin variants from his fifteen MSS; but this remained a solitary exception for over a hundred years.[48]

Théodore de Bèze (Beza) (1519-1605)

Théodore de Bèze (Theodore Beza) was the successor to John Calvin at Geneva. He published nine editions of the New Testament after the death of his famous predecessor (1564), plus a posthumous tenth edition in 1611. The

47. See the discussion in chaps. 30-31.
48. Kenyon, *The Text of the Greek Bible*, pp. 174-75.

most outstanding edition to come from Beza was published in 1582, in which he included only a few of the readings of the Codex Beza (D) and the Codex Claromontanus (D^2). The sparse use of those manuscripts may be because they departed too radically from the Erasmusan and Complutensian texts. Thus, Beza's Greek New Testament editions were in general agreement with the 1550 edition of Robert Estienne, and their continued influence resulted from their tendency to popularize and stereotype the Textus Receptus. In 1611 the translators of the King James Version (KJV) relied largely on Beza's editions of 1588-1589 and 1598, along with Erasmus's Greek text. Still later the Elzevirs, Bonaventure and his nephew Abraham, published a compact Greek New Testament (1624), which was largely that of Beza. In 1633 a second edition of the Elzevir text was published, which is known as the Textus Receptus.

The Textus Receptus

While the Greek text of Stephanus held sway over England, Bonaventure Elzevir and his nephew Abraham produced the most popular editions of it to appear on the Continent. They were quite enterprising as publishers, and their company in Leiden published seven Greek editions between 1624 and 1787. The 1624 edition was drawn basically from Beza's 1565 edition. The second edition (1633) is the source of the title given to their text, as their preface reads, *"Textum ergo habes, nunc ab omnibus receptum: in quo nihil immutatum aut corruptum damus."*[49] Thus, the publisher's "blurb" became the catchword (Textus Receptus, "Received Text") to designate the Greek text that they had incorporated from the editions of Stephanus, Beza, and Ximenes. Their Greek text was almost identical to that of Stephanus, which lay as the basis of the New Testament in the King James Version (1611) and the *New King James Version* (1979)[50] because it was regarded as "the only true text" of the New Testament. However, the textual basis was actually very late, from only a handful of manuscripts, and several passages were inserted that had no actual authority supporting them. Only new manuscript discoveries, classification, and comparison could remedy this state of affairs.

Textual Criticism in the Post Reformation Period (c. 1648-present)

With the close of the Reformation period, the Bible entered into a "period of criticism and revision." This period actually revolves around four shorter periods, each of which is characterized by an important phase of criticism

49. "The reader has the text which is now received by all, in which we give nothing changed or corrupted." Cf. Metzger, *The Text of the New Testament,* p. 106.
50. See the discussion in chap. 32.

and revision, namely, preparation, progression, purification, and the present situation. It is important to remember that "constructive" rather than "destructive" criticism is in view in this discussion.

The Period of Preparation (c. 1648-c. 1831)

This period was characterized by the gathering of textual materials and their systematic collection.[51] Thus, when Brian Walton (1600-1661) edited the London Polyglot in 1655-1657, he included the variant readings of Estienne's 1550 edition. That polyglot contained the New Testament in Greek, Latin, Syriac, Ethiopic, Arabic, and Persian (in the gospels). In its footnotes appeared the variant readings of the recently discovered (1627) Codex Alexandrinus, as well as a critical apparatus prepared by Archbishop Ussher. In 1675 an anonymous edition of the Greek New Testament appeared at Oxford. This work was done by John Fell (1625-1686), who first presented evidence from the Gothic and Bohairic versions. In 1707 John Mill (1645-1707) reprinted Estienne's text of 1550, with the addition of some 30,000 variants from nearly 100 manuscripts. Mill's epochal work, published just two weeks before his death, provided all subsequent scholars with a broad basis of established textual evidence.

Richard Bentley (1662-1742) had established himself as an outstanding scholar in the classics before he began to work on the New Testament. In 1720 he issued a prospectus for his work, which he never completed. He did, however, produce a specimen of his proposed text from the last chapter of Revelation. In his manuscript, he forsook the Textus Receptus over forty times. Although he did not complete his work, he did challenge other scholars to take up the task.

One of the scholars so challenged was Johann Albrecht Bengel (1687-1752). He was disturbed by the thirty thousand variants of Mill's text and began to study the transmission of the text. He gathered all the editions, manuscripts, and early translations available to him for study. Then he developed a canon of textual criticism that has been approved by almost all textual critics since his day in one form or another. That canon is that "the difficult reading is to be preferred to the easy," as scribes were more likely to make a reading easier than more difficult.

One of Bentley's collators had been Johann Jakob Wettstein (1693-1754). He showed an early disposition for textual criticism and was the first to publish an apparatus with the uncials indicated by capital Roman letters and minuscules by Arabic numerals. He also advocated the sound principle that

51. The discussion follows Metzger, *The Text of the New Testament,* pp. 107-24. Also see Kenyon, *The Text of the Greek Bible,* pp. 175-84; Fee, "Textual Criticism of the New Testament," pp. 426-27.

"manuscripts must be evaluated by their weight, not by their number.[52] He published the fruits of forty years' work in 1751-52 at Amsterdam. A reprint of Wettstein's *Prolegomena* was made in 1764 by Johann Salomo Semler (1725-1791), known as the "Father of German Rationalism." He followed Bengel's pattern of classifying manuscripts by groups, but carried the process further. He was also the first to apply the term "recension" to groups of New Testament witnesses, as he indicated three: Alexandrian, Eastern, and Western. All later materials were regarded as mixtures of those three recensions.[53]

The individual who actually carried Bengel's and Semler's principles into their fruition was Johann Jakob Griesbach (1745-1812). He classified the New Testament manuscripts into three groups (Alexandrian, Western, Byzantine) and laid the foundations for all subsequent work on the Greek text of the New Testament. He showed great skill in evaluating the evidence of variant readings and developed fifteen canons of criticism. Shortly after Griesbach published the first edition of his New Testament (1775-1777), several other scholars published collations that greatly increased the availability of New Testament textual evidence from the church Fathers, early versions, and the Greek text.

Christian Friedrich Matthaei (1744-1811) published a valuable critical apparatus in his Greek and Latin New Testament, which otherwise was of little value. He added evidence, which appeared for the first time, from the Slavic version of the New Testament. Frary Karl Alter (1749-1804), a Jesuit scholar in Vienna, added evidence from Slavic manuscripts, from twenty additional Greek manuscripts, and from other manuscripts as well. Andrew Birch (1758-1829) published the results of the textual work done by a group of Danish scholars in four volumes (1788-1801). This work presented readings from the Codex Vaticanus (B), which appeared for the first time in print.

Meanwhile, two Roman Catholic scholars were intense in their work of textual criticism. Johann Leonhard Hug (1765-1846) and his pupil Johannes Martin Augustinus Scholz (1794-1852) developed the theory that a "common edition" *(Koinē ekdosis)* appeared after the degeneration of the New Testament text in the third century. Scholz added 616 new manuscripts to the body of materials available and stressed for the first time the importance of ascertaining the geographical provenance represented by several manuscripts. This last point was elaborated in 1924 by B. H. Streeter in his theory of "local texts." After some time Scholz adopted Bengel's classification of manuscripts, and published a New Testament in 1830-1836 that marked a retrogression toward the Textus Receptus, as he followed the Byzantine text rather than the

52. Metzger, *The Text of the New Testament,* p. 114, "*codices autem pondere, non numero estimandi sunt.*"
53. Ibid., p. 115.

Alexandrian. Only in 1845 did he retract this view in favor of the Alexandrian readings.

The Period of Progression (c. 1831-c. 1881)

Although some progress had been made earlier, it was this period that brought the constructive critics to the fore in their grouping of textual materials. In this period the first complete break with the Textus Receptus occurred,[54] made by such men as Karl Lachmann (1793-1851), who published the first Greek New Testament edition to rest wholly on the application of textual criticism and variant reading evaluation; Lobegott Friedrich Constantin von Tischendorf, the man to whom modern textual critics owe most;[55] Samuel Prideaux Tregelles (1813-1875), who was chiefly instrumental in leading England away from the Textus Receptus during the mid-nineteenth century; and Henry Alford (1810-1871), who is well known for his commentaries as well as his efforts to bring about the "demolition of the unworthy and pedantic reverence for the received text, which stood in the way of all chance of discovering the genuine word of God."[56]

Several other scholars must be mentioned at this point, as they have played key roles in the development of textual criticism. Caspar René Gregory finished the last edition of Tischendorf's Greek Testament with a prolegomenon (1894). This work "provided the chief magazine of textual materials on which scholars still depend; and his catalogue of manuscripts ... is, with the continuations of von Dobschütz and Lietzmann, the universally accepted official list."[57] Two Cambridge scholars, Brooke Foss Westcott (1825-1901) and Fenton John Anthony Hort (1828-1892), rank with Tischendorf as making outstanding contributions to the study of the New Testament text. In 1881-82 they published *The New Testament in the Original Greek* in two volumes. The text of that work had been made available to the revision committee that produced the English Revised New Testament in 1881.[58] Their views were not original but were based on the work of Lachmann, Tregelles, Griesbach, Tischendorf, and others. The use of their text in the English Revised Version and the thoroughness of the explanation of their views in their introduction added to the acceptance of their critical text.

However, the Textus Receptus had some scholarly advocates who spared no efforts in arguing against the Westcott and Hort text. Three of those scholars

54. See Kenyon, *The Text of the Greek Bible,* pp. 177-84; Fee, "Textual Criticism of the New Testament," p. 427.
55. In addition to purchasing manuscripts and producing more critical editions of the New Testament than anyone else, Tischendorf was instrumental in seeking out many valuable manuscripts; cf. chap. 22.
56. Henry Alford, "Prolegomena," *The Greek Testament,* 1:76.
57. Kenyon, *Our Bible and the Ancient Manuscripts,* p. 122.
58. See discussion in chap. 31. For their impact on other translations of the New Testament into English, see chap. 32 discussion.

were John W. Burgon (1813-1888), who was vehement in his denunciation of the critical text; F. H. A. Scrivener (1813-1891), who was milder than Burgon in his criticism; and George Salmon (1819-1904), who decried the lack of weight Westcott and Hort ascribed to purely "Western" readings. More recent advocates have devised a different text for the New Testament called the "Majority Text"; it will be discussed shortly.

The "genealogical theory" of Westcott and Hort divided the textual materials into four text-types: the Syrian, Western, Neutral, and Alexandrian. The Syrian text-type included the Syrian, Antiochian, and Byzantine texts. Some of the manuscripts in the Syrian text were A, E, F, G, H, S, V, Z, and most of the miniscules. The Western text of Westcott and Hort had its roots in the Syrian church but was carried farther west. Some of the Western manuscripts included Δ, Old Latin, Syriac^{c}, and the Θ family so far as it was known. The Neutral text was supposedly of Egyptian origin, and included the codices B and א. The fourth text-type, the Alexandrian, was made up of a small number of witnesses in Egypt that were not of the Neutral type. This family included C, L, family 33, the Sahidic, and the Bohairic texts. According to Westcott and Hort there was a common ancestor (X) to both the Neutral and Alexandrian families, and it was quite early and pure. The accompanying chart illustrates these family (text-type) relationships to each other and to the autographs of the New Testament.

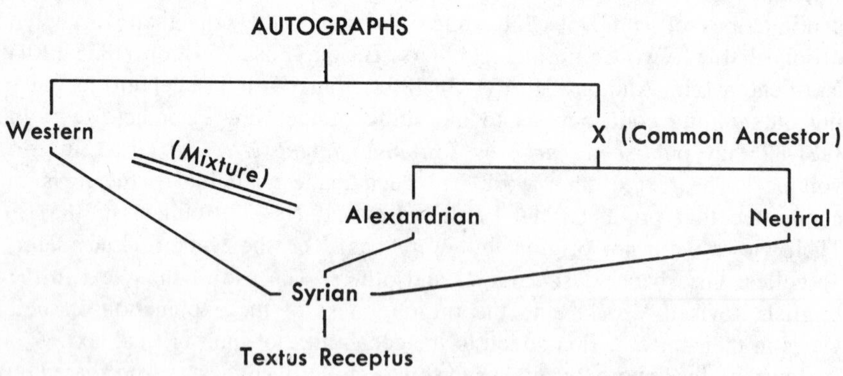

The Period of Purification (c. 1881-present)

The period since 1881 has witnessed some reaction against the Westcott and Hort theory, which had all but dethroned the Textus Receptus, as well as the growth in the amount of materials available for textual criticism.[59] The chief opponents to the Westcott-Hort theory were J.W. Burgon and F.H.A.

59. Kenyon, *The Text of the Greek Bible*, pp. 185-207; Fee, "Textual Criticism," pp. 428-29.

Scrivener and others, while its proponents included Bernhard Weiss (1827-1918), Alexander Souter, and others. In the meantime, Hermann Freiherr von Soden (1852-1914) also opposed the Westcott-Hort theory. He began his own work, which, although bolstered by tremendous financial assistance, was quite disappointing in its results. Von Soden started from a different basis but confirmed many of the findings of Westcott and Hort. Following the deaths of Burgon and Scrivener, opposition to the critical text fell from serious consideration for an extended period. At one time, for example, Harold Greenlee cited a scholarly work by Edward F. Hills that favored the Textus Receptus as "hardly more than a scholarly curiosity."[60] The situation for the traditional text proponents has changed dramatically since then, however, as is evidenced by numerous articles and books[61] culminating in the publication of *The Greek New Testament, According to the Majority Text* (1982, 2d ed., 1985).[62]

Arguments raised by Majority Text (M-Text) proponents against the critical text address three areas: theoretical, historical, and methodological. Those arguments may be summarized as follows: (1) the traditional text of the church for fifteen hundred years must be correct because of its duration; (2) the traditional text had hundreds of manuscripts in its favor, whereas the critical text has only a few early ones; and (3) the traditional text is actually superior to the critical text because it is older. Opponents of the Westcott-Hort theory argue the last point based on their perception that Westcott and Hort presented a view of the Syrian recension of the text that is not acceptable, and that the Syrian text may have represented an earlier and better text that has become lost.

Although the basic position of the Textus Receptus/Majority Text advocates is similar, their differences are sufficient to warrant that they be distinguished into two groups. Michael W. Holmes observes:

60. Greenlee, p. 82. He refers to Edward F. Hills, *The King James Version Defended!*

61. These items include, among others, Wilbur N. Pickering, *The Identity of the New Testament Text,* much of which is based on the author's Th.M thesis, "An Evaluation of the Contribution of John William Burgon to New Testament Textual Criticism." Pickering's thesis was published in an edited form along with other articles defending the Authorized Version (KJV) in David Otis Fuller, ed., *Which Bible?* Also see David Otis Fuller, *True or False?: The Westcott-Hort Theory Examined;* Harry A. Sturz, *The Byzantine Text-Type and New Testament Textual Criticism.* Zane C. Hodges, "A Defense of the Majority Text, contains some mathematical formulations in support of his thesis. In the meantime, Russell Paul Hills, "A Brief Introduction to New Testament Textual Criticism Containing a Defense of the Majority Text," argues uncritically in support of the TR.

62. Zane C. Hodges and Arthur L. Farstad, eds., *The Greek New Testament, According to the Majority Text.* Although argumentation for this Greek text follows along the same lines as the Textus Receptus, it should be noted that they are not to be confused. The Textus Receptus is viewed as a late and corrupted text within the Majority Text tradition. Several of the contributors to the volumes identified in the previous note were editors and consulting editors to the Hodges-Farstad Greek New Testament.

> Prominent among the first group, which defends the Textus Receptus, are Terence Brown, David Otis Fuller, J. J. Ray, and E. F. Hills. In contrast to Burgon, their champion, who was a scholar and indefatigable textual critic whose writings were based on tiresome work on original manuscripts, most of these men betray little if any first-hand acquaintance with either the materials of textual criticism or any of the scholarly literature of the last fifty years. Their writings largely consist of reprints or extracts from earlier writings, especially Burgon, who are quoted as if every line they wrote were true. Their attacks on the theories of Westcott and Hort consist primarily of *ad hominem* accusations (they are variously called papists, Arians, Origenists, rationalists, and naturalists) and leading questions left unanswered. The points adduced in favour of the Textus Receptus are theological rather than historical and are related to an extreme form of the doctrine of divine preservation.[63]

The second of these groups does not support the Textus Receptus but the Majority Text (of which the Textus Receptus is only a corrupt late representative), and its leading proponents include Zane C. Hodges, Wilbur Pickering, and Jakob van Bruggen.[64] These spokesmen offer "a much more sophisticated and creditable-appearing line of approach. The *ad hominem* arguments have largely (though not entirely) disappeared and *a priori* theological statements no longer form the basis of their arguments."[65] They address the problems of the Westcott-Hort theory and attempt to establish the preference for the Majority Text on some historically-grounded basis. Their efforts have resulted in a debate with D.A. Carson, E.C. Colwell, Gordon Fee, Richard A. Taylor, and others[66] who may be designated as Nestle-Aland (critical text) or "eclectic" text advocates. The direct interaction between the proponents of these opposing views constitutes the current "Majority Text debate"—primarily a debate over text *and method*.[67]

In his representation of the debate arguments, Holmes evaluates the Majority Text position as being inadequate on four grounds: (1) it is based on

63. Michael W. Holmes, "The 'Majority text debate': new form of an old issue" [*sic*], p. 13. The Greek Orthodox church is identified as the channel through which the Scripture text is preserved. Russell Paul Hills, "Brief Introduction," also argues for the Majority Text from a divine providence perspective.
64. Jakob van Bruggen, *The Ancient Text of the New Testament*.
65. Holmes, "Majority text debate," p. 14.
66. D. A. Carson, *The King James Debate: A Plea for Realism;* E. C. Colwell and Gordon Fee, "A Critique of W. N. Pickering's *The Identity of the New Testament Text:* A Review Article," pp. 165-67, and "Modern Textual Criticism and the Revival of the *Textus Receptus,*" pp. 19-33, and "Modern Textual Criticism and the Majority Text: A Rejoinder," pp. 157-60; Richard A. Taylor, "Queen Anne Resurrected? A Review Article," pp. 377-81, and " 'Queen Anne' Revisited: A Rejoinder," pp. 169-71. In response to these articles see Zane C. Hodges, "Modern Textual Criticism and the Majority Text: A Response," pp. 143-55, and "Modern Textual Criticism and the Majority Text: A Surrejoinder," pp. 161-64; Wilbur N. Pickering, " 'Queen Anne . . .' and All That: A Surrejoinder," pp. 165-67.
67. The present discussion relates to the text issue; see chart in chap. 26 for the various schools of New Testament textual critics as it relates to method.

erroneous evaluation of data (agreeing with Fee versus Pickering); (2) it confuses between *readings* and *text-type* (Pickering); (3) the single crucial assumption of Hodges, that the transmission process has been "reasonably normal," is invalid; and (4) some dominant readings in the early church are minority readings today and vice versa.[68]

In response to criticisms against their theory and the discovery of new manuscript evidence, textual scholars have continued to reevaluate the textual materials used by Westcott and Hort. The result of that scholarly investigation and constructive criticism has been a reclassification of the text-types. The Syrian family of manuscripts has been renamed "Byzantine" or "Antiochian" because of its possible confusion with the Old Syriac Version of the New Testament.[69] In addition, there is now general agreement that there was more intermixture between the Alexandrian text-type and the Neutral text-type, which resulted because they are actually slightly different variations of the same textual family. The Alexandrian text-type now includes manuscripts from both groups.

In their reevaluation, scholars have come to view three subgroups within the Western text-type (Codex D, Old Latin, and Old Syriac). They have also come to the opinion that readings within the Western text-type are not generally reliable when they stand alone. Another textual family has been discovered since the time of Westcott, Hort, and von Soden: the Caesarean text-type.[70] Although it lies between the Western and Alexandrian text-types, it is actually closer to the Western family. Study of theological tendencies in certain groups of variants by individual scholars has shown that not all textual variation is accidental or theologically unbiased.[71] In addition, there has been research in the writings of the church Fathers as well as early versions of the Bible.[72] The accompanying chart, by Harold Greenlee, indicates the distribution of textual materials among the various text-types.[73] Recent collations of catalogued manuscripts in English are found in Metzger's *Manuscripts of the Greek Bible*.[74] His findings are based on Kurt Aland's official list of New

68. Holmes, "Majority text debate," pp. 15-17. D. A. Carson identifies eight substantial criticisms directed at Pickering's study in an appendix entitled, "A Critique of the Identity of the New Testament Text," *King James Debate*, pp. 105-23.
69. For discussion concerning the Old Syriac Version, see chap. 28.
70. This text-type boasts a unique mixture of Alexandrian and Western readings, which has prompted some scholars to question the value of identifying it as a separate text-type. The issue is further clouded by the fact that the Caesarean text-type covers only the gospels and Acts (see Greenlee's chart on textual materials).
71. C. S. C. Williams, *Alterations to the Text of the Synoptic Gospels and Acts;* E. J. Epp, *The Theological Tendency of Codex Bezae Cantabrigiensis*.
72. See Bruce M. Metzger, *Early Versions of the New Testament: Their Origin, Transmission and Limitations*.
73. Greenlee, pp. 117-18.
74. Bruce M. Metzger, *Manuscripts of the Greek Bible: An Introduction to Greek Paleography.*

Distribution of New Testament Manuscript by Family

	Gospels	Acts	Catholic Epistles	Paul, Hebrews	Revelation
Alexandrian	P^{1} P^{3} P^{4} P^{5} P^{7} P^{22} P^{34} P^{39} (P^{66}) P^{75}	P^{8} (P^{50})	P^{20} P^{23} P^{72}	P^{10} P^{13} P^{15} P^{16} P^{27} P^{32} P^{40} P^{65}	P^{18} P^{2} P^{47}
	ℵ B C L Q T (W-Luke 1–John 8:12) Z Δ Ξ Ψ 054 059 060 0162	ℵ A B C Ψ 048 076 096	ℵ A B C P Ψ 048 056 0142 0156	ℵ A B C H I M P Psi 048 081 088 0220	ℵ A C P 0207 0169
	220 33 164 215 376 579 718 850 892 1241 (1342 Mark)	6 33 81 104 326 1175	33 81 104 323 326 424c 1175 1739 2298	6 33 81 104 326 424c 1175 1739 1908	61 59 94 241 254 1006 1175 1611 1841 1852 2040 2053 2344 2351
	Boh (Sah)	Boh (Sah)	Boh (Sah)	Boh (Sah)	
	Ath Cyr-Alex (Or)	Ath Cyr-Alex Clem-Alex? (Or)	Ath Cyr-Alex Clem-Alex? (Or)		
Caesarean	P^{37} P^{45} Θ (W-Mark 5 ff.) N O Σ Φ Fam 1 Fam 13 28 565 700 7071 1604	P^{45}? I? I?	(Text type not determined in the remainder of the New Testament)		
	Geo Arm Pal-Syr Eus Cyr-Jer (Or)	Cyr-Jer?			
Western	P^{25}	P^{38} P^{41} P^{48}	P^{38}		
	D (W-Mark 1–5?) 0171	D E 066	D E	D E F G	F?
		257 440 614 913 1108 1245 1518 1611 1739 2138 2298		88 181 915 917 1836 1898 1912	
	It, especially k e Sin-Syr Cur-Syr	It Hark-Syr mg	It Hark-Syr mg	It	It?
	Tert Ir Clem-Alex Cyp (Aug)		Ir Tert Cyp Aug Eph		
Byzantine	A E F G H K M S U V (W-Matt., Luke 8:12 ff.) Y Γ Λ Π Ω	H L S P	H K L S 42 398	K L	046 82 93 429 469 808 920 2048
	Most minuscules	Most minuscules	Most other minuscules	Most other minuscules	Most other minuscules
	Goth Later versions	Goth Later versions	Goth Later versions	Goth Later versions	Goth Later versions
	Later Fathers	Later Fathers	Later Fathers	Later Fathers	Later Fathers

From J. Harold Greenlee, *Introduction to New Testament Textual Criticism*, pp. 117-18. Used by permission.

Testament Greek manuscripts.[75] Those lists are also published in the most recent editions of Eberhard Nestle (edited by Erwin Nestle and Kurt Aland), *Novum Testamentum Graece*, and K. Aland and others (eds.), *The Greek New Testament*, of the United Bible Societies.[76] Metzger has used these collations in *A Textual Commentary on the Greek New Testament*. According to their

75. Kurt Aland, *Kurzgefasste Liste der griechischen Handschriften des Neuen Testaments*, as supplemented in Kurt Aland, *Materialien zur neutestamentlichen Handschriften*, pp. 1-37, and Kurt Aland, *Bericht der Stiftung zur Forderung der neutestamentlichen Textforschung für die Jahre 1972 bis 1974*, pp. 9-16, and *Bericht.... 1975 und 1976* (1977), pp. 10-12.
76. Both of these books are available from the American Bible Society. The two textual traditions have been brought together into a single text with the 26th edition of the Nestle-Aland text and the 3d edition of the United Bible Societies text.

reckoning, the manuscript families are ranked in the following order of importance: Alexandrian, Western, Caesarean, and Byzantine. Since the Textus Receptus follows the Byzantine text-type basically, it is almost redundant to say that its authority is not highly regarded by many textual critics.

The Present Situation

At present there are two basic textual traditions that command serious scholarly followings: the Textus Receptus/Majority Text and the Nestle-Aland text. New Testament textual critics may be placed in one of these two positions or on a spectrum between them. Those who advocate the Majority Text position may be represented by Zane C. Hodges, who co-edited, with Arthur L. Farstad, *The Greek New Testament, According to the Majority Text* (1982, 2d ed., 1985). Their position asserts that textual scholarship has gone awry during the past century, and that textual critics should return to the text of the large majority of manuscripts, which contain a Greek text very much like that used by the translators of the King James Version of 1611. Although viewing the Textus Receptus as only one late example of the Majority Text position, Hodges argues that the Majority Text view can answer, in ascending order of importance, three specific charges placed against it: (1) the oldest manuscripts do not support the Majority Text; (2) the Majority Text is a revised, and hence secondary, form of the Greek text; (3) the readings of the Majority Text are repeatedly inferior to those of the earlier manuscripts.[77]

Elsewhere, Hodges acknowledges the lateness of the manuscript evidence for the Majority Text position. Yet he defends the Majority Text by arguing the likelihood that an original would produce a majority of manuscript copies sharing the original reading. He uses mathematical formulae "to show an 'idealized' situation which does not represent what actually took place."[78] He adds that the Majority Text can be explained as the outcome of a "process" that resulted in the gradual formation of a numerically preponderant text-type. Hodges rejects the ability of such a process to explain an Alexandrian textual priority in the face of the Byzantine manuscript majority. He writes, "No one has shown a detailed explanation of exactly what the process was, how it began, or how—once begun—it achieved the result claimed for it."[79] The climatic conditions in Egypt are important to the position of the Majority Text, because they provide the basis for the absence of surviving Byzantine manuscripts from the third or fourth century. He states that Egypt alone

77. Zane C. Hodges, "The Greek Text of the King James Version," in Fuller, *Which Bible?* pp. 25-38. Sturz, *Byzantine Text-Type*, differs somewhat from Hodges in that he argues that the Byzantine Text should be held in equal value to the other textual families (see chap. 26).
78. Zane C. Hodges, "A Defense of the Majority-Text," p. 10. The issues in this paper follow a nine-page presentation of the Majority Text argument with mathematical formulations by David M. Hodges.
79. Ibid., p. 12.

has a climate favorable to the preservation of most ancient texts. But the existence of Byzantine texts at a date earlier than the dates of its extant representatives can be demonstrated in other ways.[80] Hodges goes on to argue that changes in current textual criticism away from the Westcott-Hort model have made several old arguments for Alexandrian textual priority either moot or subjectively based.[81] He then makes the following summation.

> The recent significant accessions of papyrus manuscripts have virtually destroyed confidence in all previous reconstructions of textual history. Virtually every major dictum of the last generation of textual critics is now open to question and debate. In this context, those who use modern critical editions must admit the possibility that a future *consensus of scholars* could radically alter the text which they now read.
>
> By contrast, those who read the Textus Receptus are reading the text resting upon a *consensus of manuscripts*....
>
> It remains to add only one point. When the history of the New Testament text is interpreted in this way, the widespread uniformity of the manuscripts at once becomes a potent tribute to the providence of God in preserving His Word. There is no other interpretation of textual history that can make this claim without serious reservations. For if the mass of witnesses is corrupt, 80% of tradition is corrupt. And no one is quite sure how to use the remaining 20%.
>
> True, this argument will no doubt appeal only to men of faith. But to what better kind of man could appeal be made?[82]

In the meantime many textual scholars, dissatisfied with the results achieved by weighing external evidence for variant readings, have turned to another method for determining the reading that best accounts for the rise of the others. That method is properly called "eclectic," or "reasoned eclecticism." It simply means that the "original" text of the New Testament is to be chosen variant by variant, using all the principles of critical judgment without regarding one manuscript or text-type as necessarily preserving the original. Most recent eclectics tend to lean toward the Alexandrian text family. Despite a few notable exceptions, most of the differences that remain in renderings made by eclectic textual critics result from a varying degree of weight

80. Ibid., pp. 14-16. This point is also made in Hodges and Farstad, eds., *The Greek New Testament,* "Introduction."
81. Ibid., pp. 16-17. These arguments concern the lack of support for the Majority Text in the ancient versions of the Fathers, the moot questions about the existence of the so-called Western-text, and the transcriptional inferiority of the Majority Text. Hodges cites E. C. Colwell, "Scribal Habits in Early Papyri: A Study in the Corruption of the Text," *The Bible in Modern Scholarship,* pp. 370-89, to show that it is impossible to generalize about scribal propensities. He then finds G. D. Kilpatrick, a recent supporter of Majority Text renderings, using arguments to support the position that were once used against it. Finally, Hodges asserts that the arguments on both sides are subjective, but positive conclusions one way or the other must be reached based on other factors, unless the position is taken "that no conclusion is valid which cannot be empirically tested!" (p. 17).
82. Hodges, "Defense of the Majority-Text," pp. 17-18.

given the external evidence. The eclectic method has been utilized in the most recent translations of the Bible into English done by committees.[83] There are other proponents to this method who advocate what may be called a "rigorous eclectic" method, for they use *only* internal evidence without regard to external evidence whatever.[84] "Rigorous eclecticism" tends to make subjective judgments about internal criteria and downplays objective textual data.

"Reasoned eclecticism" may be represented by D. A. Carson, *The King James Version Debate: A Plea for Realism*. He presents fourteen theses in his argument against the Textus Receptus position, although a few of them also apply to the Majority Text advocates. In presenting his theses, Carson makes several relevant points. He correctly observes that there is no unambiguous evidence that the Byzantine text-type was known before the middle of the fourth century. He argues that the appeal to the fact that most extant manuscripts of the Greek New Testament attest to the Byzantine text-type is logically fallacious and historically naive, that the Byzantine text-type is demonstrably a secondary text, and that the Alexandrian text-type has better credentials than any other text-type now available. According to Carson, an argument saying in effect that what the majority of believers in the history of the church have believed is true, is an ambiguous argument at best and a theologically dangerous argument at worst. When such an argument is applied to textual criticism, it proves nothing very helpful anyway. So too is the appeal to the providence of God to defend the Byzantine text. Carson argues that to deny the possibility that the Byzantine text is a conflation by appealing to fourth-century writing practices, is fallacious. Also erroneous is the charge that the non-Byzantine text-types are theologically aberrant. He warns the unwary reader that the Byzantine text-type must not be regarded as the precise equivalent of the Textus Receptus. He notes that textual arguments dependent upon adopting the Textus Receptus and comparing other text-types with it are guilty, methodologically speaking, of begging the issue and presenting less than the whole truth. Carson points out that tying the adoption of the Textus Receptus to verbal inspiration is logically and theologically fallacious. He also asserts that arguments attempting to draw textual conclusions from a prejudicial selection of not immediately relevant data, or from a slanted use of terms, or by a slurring appeal to guilt by association, or by

83. See discussion in chap. 32. Also see Metzger, *The Text of the New Testament*, pp. 175-79, and Fee, "Textual Criticism of the New Testament," pp. 429-33.
84. G. D. Kilpatrick, "An Eclectic Study of the Text of Acts," in J. N. Birdsall and R. W. Thomson, eds., *Biblical and Patristic Studies in Memory of C.R. Casey,* pp. 64-77. Also see G. D. Kilpatrick, "The Greek New Testament Text of Today and the Textus Receptus," in H. Anderson and W. Barclay, eds., *The New Testament in Historical and Contemporary Perspective: Essays in Memory of G. H. C. MacGregor,* pp. 189-208; J. K. Elliott, *The Greek Text of the Epistles to Timothy and Titus*.

repeated appeal to false evidence, are not only misleading but ought to be categorically rejected.[85]

This state of affairs leaves one on the horns of a dilemma with regard to the selection of one textual tradition over the other. Perhaps it is best to conclude the discussion of the present situation by looking to what A.W. Adams has to say about a matter that is strongly reinforced by what has been learned from the papyri with regard to the texts of classical authors. In view of the uncontrolled and widespread distribution of biblical manuscripts in the early church, and the deliberate and widespread attempts by Diocletian and others to systematically destroy the Christian Scriptures, and then the proliferation of the Scripture texts following the conversion of Constantine and the Council at Nicea, his words are most appropriate. He writes:

> The natural conclusion, then, is that while one family may in the overwhelming majority of cases be found to preserve the original text, it is probable that readings found in other families will sometimes be right. This is the conclusion to which all the evidence derivable from the early papyri points, and notably the Chester Beatty and Bodmer papyri. For the present purpose it matters not whether the text of these papyri be regarded as good or bad. What is significant is that they prove that in Egypt in the early part of the third century readings were in circulation which were derived from, or which eventually became attached to, all the principal families, together with a not inconsiderable number of which no other witness has survived. We must therefore be prepared to find that the best manuscript or family is not always right.[86]

Summary and Conclusion

The history of the New Testament text may be divided into several basic periods: (1) the period of reduplication (to c. 325), (2) the period of standardization of the text (c. 325-c. 1500), (3) the period of crystallization (c. 1500-c. 1648), and (4) the period of criticism and revision (c. 1648-present). During the period of criticism and revision, the struggle between proponents of the "Received Text" and the "Critical Text" has been waged. In the final analysis, there is no substantial difference between their texts. Their differences are mainly technical and methodological, not doctrinal, for the textual variants are doctrinally inconsequential. Nevertheless, the "critical" readings are often exegetically helpful to Bible students. Thus, for all practical purposes, both texts convey the *content* of the autographs, even though they are separately garnished with their own minor scribal and technical differences. Consequently, many textual scholars have turned to a "reasoned eclecticism" as they seek to ascertain the actual reading of the biblical text.

85. D. A. Carson, *The King James Version Debate,* see especially pp. 43-78.
86. Kenyon, *The Text of the Greek Bible,* p. 255.

26
Restoration of the Scripture Text

The Problem of Textual Criticism

It has already been stated that there are no known extant autographs of the New Testament.[1] There are available, however, numerous biblical manuscript copies (chaps. 21, 22, 23), versions (chaps. 27, 28), and quotations (chap. 24) by which the text can be restored. This process is known as textual criticism, or lower criticism. Before dealing with this process, however, a survey of manuscript evidence is in order.

Manuscript Evidence

Biblical manuscripts. The Old Testament has survived in few complete manuscripts, most of which date from the ninth century A.D. or later. There are, however, abundant reasons for believing that those are substantially *good* copies. Support for this position has existed for years from several lines of evidence: (1) the few variants in the existing Masoretic manuscripts; (2) the widespread literal agreement of most of the LXX with the Masoretic Hebrew text; (3) the scrupulous rules of the scribes; (4) similarity of parallel Old Testament passages; (5) archaeological confirmation of the fidelity of historical details in the text; and (6) the agreement, by and large, of the Samaritan Pentateuch. (7) The most phenomenal confirmation of the fidelity of the Hebrew text, however, is much more direct than any of these witnesses. The Dead Sea Scrolls included hundreds of Hebrew manuscripts that are a thousand years earlier than those previously possessed. From the Qumran caves have come fragments, sometimes complete copies, of almost every book of the Old Testament, some of which date as far back as the fourth century B.C. (cf. chap. 21). Those fragments often agree almost exactly with the corresponding copies of the Old Testament text that are 1,000 years later in the

1. See chap. 2 for suggested reasons God has permitted the autographs to perish.

history of the transmission of that text.[2]

The manuscripts of the New Testament are numerous, but so are the variant readings. Consequently, the science of textual criticism is much more crucial in the restoration of the New Testament text. There are a total of 3,157 Greek manuscripts containing part or all of the New Testament, excluding 2,209 catalogued lectionaries dating from the second century onward.[3] Hence, whereas the fidelity of the Old Testament is based on relatively *few* but *good* manuscripts, the integrity of the New Testament is derived by a critical comparison of *many* manuscripts that are of *poorer* quality (i.e., they possess more variant readings).

Versions. Other lines of evidence for the biblical text are the ancient and medieval versions. The Old Testament is represented by the LXX, the Samaritan Pentateuch, and the Babylonian Targums, as well as all of the major ancient versions that contain both the Old and New Testaments. Into this category may be placed the Old Syriac, the Old Latin, the Coptic, Sahidic, Latin Vulgate, and others (see chaps. 28-29). Of those versions, there are more than ten thousand manuscript copies of Jerome's Latin Vulgate available to scholars today.[4]

Quotations. A third line of evidence for the reconstruction of the Bible is derived from the quotations of the Fathers. Rabbinic quotations of the Old Testament are numerous in the Hebrew Talmudic writings. Other Jewish quotations, such as those by Philo the philosopher and Josephus the historian, are also found in proliferation. The patristic citations of the New Testament have survived in even greater abundance, as the extant writings of the Fathers of the second and third centuries alone contain more than thirty-six thousand citations of verses of the New Testament. In fact, if there were no biblical manuscripts available today, the entire New Testament could be reconstructed from the writings of the church Fathers of the first three centuries with the exception of eleven verses.[5]

Lectionaries. One further source of evidence that applies to the reconstruction of the New Testament text is the church service books, known as lectionaries.[6] Recent counts indicate that there are more than 2,209 Greek lectionaries. Revived interest in the lectionaries has demonstrated their value in textual reconstruction and their use in the diacritical apparatus that pertains thereto (see chap. 23). There are, then, a grand total of over 15,000

2. R. Laird Harris, "The Dead Sea Scrolls and the Old Testament Text," pp. 201-11, in J. Barton Payne, ed., *New Perspectives on the Old Testament* (Waco, Tex.: Word, 1970), details these findings; see especially pp. 204-11.
3. See chap. 22, n.6, for a tabulation of catalogued manuscripts of the New Testament text.
4. Bruce M. Metzger, *The Early Versions of the New Testament: Their Origins, Transmission and Limitations*, p. 293; pp. 295-308, 461-64 present a checklist of Old Latin manuscripts.
5. See chap. 24 discussion and chart for the extent of these citations.
6. See chap. 22, n. 6.

Greek and Latin manuscripts containing New Testament texts.[7] In addition to these manuscripts there are more than 36,000 patristic citations containing almost every verse of the New Testament. These are the materials that provide the data by which the textual critic attempts to reconstruct the original New Testament text.

Multitude of Variants

The multiplicity of manuscripts produces a corresponding number of variant readings, for the more manuscripts that are copied the greater will be the number of copyist's errors. However, as will be seen, what at first seems to be a grave hindrance to the reconstruction of the biblical text actually becomes extremely beneficial.

Old Testament variants. The variant readings of the Old Testament are relatively few for several reasons.

1. Copies were made by an official class of sacred scribes who labored under strict rules.
2. The Masoretes systematically destroyed all copies with "mistaken" and/or variant readings.[8] The Samaritan Pentateuch, however, contains about 6,000 variants from the Hebrew Masoretic text, but most of these are matters of spelling. Some 1,900 of those variants agree with the LXX against the Masoretic text (e.g., in the ages given for the patriarchs). The most significant variants are Samaritan sectarian insertions used to indicate that the Lord actually chose Mount Gerizim rather than Mount Zion, and Shechem rather than Jerusalem as His sacred sites.[9]

7. See chaps. 22, 24, and 29 for further discussion of these 5,366 plus Greek and 10,000 plus Latin manuscript items.
8. Critical study in the Old Testament has not been as necessary or as extensive as in the New. The first collection of evidence was made by Bishop Kennicott (1776-1780), who published a critical text at Oxford based on 634 Hebrew manuscripts. Later, in 1784-1788, the Italian scholar De Rossi published a collation of 825 more manuscripts. The critical edition of the Hebrew Bible edited by C. D. Ginsberg for the British and Foreign Bible Society (1926) was superseded by Rudolf Kittel and Paul E. Kahle, eds., *Biblia Hebraica* (1929-37). The Kittel-Kahle text went through three major revisions before it became outdated by the discovery of the Dead Sea Scrolls. A new edition of the Masoretic text, incorporating this new line of evidence, was published by Karl Ellinger and Wilhelm Rudolf, eds., *Biblia Hebraica Stuttgartensia* (1967-77). It is regarded as the most authoritative edition of the Hebrew text of the Old Testament. A complete "Editio Minor" [Small Edition] was published in 1983.
9. Gleason L. Archer, Jr., *A Survey of Old Testament Introduction*, p. 44.

New Testament variants.[10] Because the New Testament manuscripts are so numerous, and because there were many private and "unofficial" copies made, there are more variants in the New Testament than in the Old Testament.

1. *How many variants are there?* The gross number of variants increases with every new manuscript discovery.

   a. In 1707 John Mill estimated about 30,000 variants in the known New Testament manuscripts.[11] Many of the great manuscripts were discovered after that time.[12]

   b. By 1874, F. H. A. Scrivener counted nearly 50,000 variants.[13]

   c. To date there are over 200,000 known variants,[14] and this figure will no doubt increase in the future as more manuscripts are discovered.

2. *How are the variants counted?* There is an ambiguity in saying that there are some 200,000 variants in the existing manuscripts of the New Testament because those represent only 10,000 places in the New Testament. If one single word is misspelled in 3,000 different manuscripts, it is counted as 3,000 variants or readings. Once this counting procedure is understood, and the mechanical (orthographic) variants have been eliminated, the remaining significant variants are surprisingly few in number. It should be remembered that the production of multiple copies of manuscripts by printing and photocopying are relatively recent developments in the production of books.[15]

3. *How did variants occur?* In order to understand fully the significance of variant readings, and to determine which are the correct or original readings, it is necessary to examine first just how those variants came into the text. Careful students of textual criticism have suggested two classes of errors: intentional and unintentional.[16]

   a. Unintentional changes of various kinds all arise from the imperfection of some human faculty. These constitute by far the vast majority of all transcriptional errors (see chap. 21).

10. R. L. Clarke, Alfred Goodwin, and W. Sanday, eds., *The Variorum Edition of the New Testament of Our Lord and Saviour Jesus Christ,* may be consulted for a comprehensive listing of variants. More recent lists of variants are found in Kurt Aland, Matthew Black, Carlo M. Martini, Bruce M. Metzger, and Allen Wikgren, eds., *The Greek New Testament,* 3d ed., and Eberhard Nestle, Edwin Nestle, and Kurt Aland, eds., *Novum Testamentum Graece,* 26th ed., (New York: American Bible Society, 1979).
11. James Hastings, ed., *A Dictionary of the Bible,* 4 vols. plus one extra volume, 4:735.
12. The great period of manuscript discovery began at 1650 and continues to the present. See discussion in chap. 25.
13. Hastings, *Dictionary,* 4:735.
14. Neil R. Lightfoot, *How We Got the Bible,* p. 53.
15. See the discussion in chaps. 20, 25, and 30.
16. See Bruce M. Metzger, *The Text of the New Testament,* pp. 150ff.

(1) *Errors of the eye.*

(a) *Wrong division* of words actually resulted in the formation of new words. Early manuscripts were not punctuated and letters were not separated into words by spaces (see chap. 20). As a result, HEISNOWHERE could either mean HE IS NOW HERE or HE IS NOWHERE. A more amusing example is DIDYOUEVERSEEABUNDANCEONTHETABLE.[17]

(b) *Omissions* of letters, words, and even whole lines occurred when the astigmatic eye mistook one group of letters or words for another, sometimes located on a different line. That error is known as a *homeoteleuton* (similar ending). When only one letter is missing, it is called a *haplography* (single writing).

(c) *Repetitions* result in the opposite error to omissions. Hence, when the eye picked up the same letter or word twice and repeated it, it is called *dittography.* Such an error may be why some miniscules read, "Whom do you want me to release for you, (Jesus) Barabbas or Jesus?" (Matt. 27:17).

(d) *Transposition* is the reversal of position of two letters or words. This is technically known as *metathesis.* In 2 Chronicles 3:4, the transposition of letters would make the measurements of the porch of Solomon's Temple out of proportion, for example, 120 cubits instead of 20 cubits as in the LXX.

(e) *Other confusions* of spelling, abbreviation or scribal insertion account for the remainder of scribal errors. This is especially true about Hebrew letters, which were used for numbers and could be easily confused. These errors of eye may account for many of the numerical discrepancies in the Old Testament; for example, the reading of 40,000 stalls in 1 Kings 4:26 rather than 4,000 in 2 Chronicles 9:25 is undoubtedly an error of this kind, as is the 42 years in 2 Chronicles 22:2 in contrast to the correct reading of 22 in 2 Kings 8:26.[18]

(2) *Errors of the ear* occurred only when manuscripts were copied by listening to someone read them. This may explain why some manuscripts (fifth century onward) read *kamelos* (a rope) instead of *kamēlos* (a camel) in Matthew 19:24. In 1 Corinthians 13:3, *kauthē-*

17. Suggested by Alexander Souter, *The Text and Canon of the New Testament,* p. 103.

18. For a brief but good discussion of the types of manuscript errors in the Old Testament, see Archer, pp. 54-57, where he lists ten categories: haplography, dittography, metathesis, fusion, fission, homophony, misreading of similar appearing letters, homeoteleuton, accidental omission of words in situations where no repetition is involved, and misreading of vowel letters as consonants. Also see J. Barton Payne, "The Validity of Numbers in Chronicles," *Bulletin of the Near East Archaeological Society,* new series, 11 (1978): 5-58; and William E. Nix, "Joshua," "Judges," "1 Chronicles," and "2 Chronicles," in W. A. Criswell, ed., *The Criswell Study Bible* (Nashville: Nelson, 1979), pp. 267-96, 297-326, 482-519, and 520-61.

somai (he burns) was confused with *kauchēsomai* (he boasts). This kind of confusion occurred sometimes among the manuscripts, and some of them drastically affect the meaning of given passages. The confusion between the long vowel *omega* (ω) and the short vowel *omicron* (ο) arose as pronunciation changes occurred throughout church history, and this gave rise to such variants as *echōmen* and *echomen* in Romans 5:1, and *hōde* and *hode* in Luke 16:25. Another example of a long vowel *eta* (η) becoming a short vowel *epsilon* (ϵ) is seen in Codex D, which erroneously records *mē* instead of *me,* changing the reading in Mark 14:31 from "If I must die . . ." to "If it is *not* necessary to die. . . ." The interchange of personal pronouns in manuscript copying from oral readings was frequent. *Hēmon* (our) and *humon* (your) are quite similar in sound; hence, it would be difficult to determine whether 1 John 1:4 says, "that *your* joy may be complete," or "that *our* joy may be complete." First Peter records at least seven such confusions (1:3,12; 2:21 [2]; 3:18,21; 5:1).[19] Anyone who has written "their" for "there," or mistaken "here" for "hear," can readily understand this kind of error.

(3) *Errors of memory.* These are not so numerous, but occasionally a scribe might forget the precise word in a passage and substitute a synonym. Perhaps he might be unconsciously influenced by a parallel passage or truth. For example, Ephesians 5:9 has "the fruit of the Spirit" in the Byzantine manuscripts and P^{46} rather than "fruit of light," as in other early and diversified witnesses representing both the Alexandrian and the Western text-types.[20] The confusion is probably with Galatians 5:22. Sometimes letters within words are transposed and result in a different word altogether. Mark 14:65 is such an example, in which *elabon* became *ebalon* and then *eballon.*[21] Quite often today popular quotations of Hebrews 9:22 (KJV) will add ". . . there is no remission [of sins]." Thus, the memory may almost automatically transcribe a passage

19. See Metzger, *The Text of the New Testament,* pp. 190-93, for a more detailed treatment.
20. See Bruce M. Metzger, *A Textual Commentary on the Greek New Testament,* pp. 608-9.
21. See Kurt Aland, et al., eds., *The Greek New Testament,* 3d. ed., and Eberhard Nestle, et al., eds., *Novum Testamentum Graece,* 26th ed., which have been brought into textual conformity to provide the basis for translations based on this so-called critical text (also identified as the "Nestle-Aland" or "UBS" Text). In their marginal notes, the editors of the New King James Version identify this text as "NU-Text" after the common text of Nestle-Aland and the United Bible Societies. The NKJV editors use the acronym "M-Text" to refer to that produced by Zane C. Hodges and Arthur L. Farstad, eds., *The Greek New Testament, According to the Majority Text.* An earlier *Greek New Testament,* regarded by some to be a corrupted form of the Majority Text, was called the *Textus Receptus* (TR) and was the basis of the King James Version and other English Bible translations prior to 1881 as well as *Holy Bible: The New King James Version.* See Harry A. Sturz, *The Byzantine Text-type and New Testament Textual Criticism.*

in one gospel to conform to another. However, variants of this kind have more frequently been found to be intentional emendations.

(4) Errors of judgment. The most common error of this kind is caused by dim lighting or poor eyesight. Sometimes marginal notes were incorporated into the text under the misapprehension that they were part of the text. A. T. Robertson suggests that this is the explanation of the angel's disturbing the water (John 5:4).[22] The textual note at Romans 8:1 in the NKJV (which follows the KJV) indicates another illustration where the last portion of a verse was added to the text. It may have been added as an explanatory note at first, and then it became part of the manuscript texts that were the basis of the Textus Receptus reading. A comparison of the RV, ASV, RSV, NAB, NASB, and NIV renditions will show that they all adopt the shorter reading (see the discussion of these translations in chap. 32). An obvious example of a judgmental error by a sleepy scribe who added to a miniscule copy is found in 2 Corinthians 8:4-5, as the scribe interpolated into the text, "it is found thus in many copies,"[23] as though it were part of Paul's admonition to the Corinthians instead of a marginal annotation. It is difficult to determine whether some variants are caused by faulty judgment or intentional doctrinal changes. No doubt 1 John 5:7 and Acts 8:37 fall into one of these categories. John 7:53—8:11 will be considered elsewhere in this chapter.

(5) Errors of writing. If a scribe, due to imperfect style or accident, wrote indistinctly or imprecisely, he would set the stage for future error of sight or judgment. Rapid copying was no doubt responsible for many errors in writing. This is viewed especially in the parallel accounts of the Kings-Chronicles corpus.[24]

b. Intentional changes. Although most of the variant readings resulted from unintentional errors arising from human limitations, there were also a good number that occurred as a result of scribal intentions. Good intentions, no doubt, but nonetheless deliberate.

(1) Grammatical and linguistical. The orthographical variations in spelling, euphony, and grammatical form are abundantly illustrated in the papyri. Each scribal tradition had its own stylistic and linguistic idiosyncracies, and a scribe tended to modify his manuscript to conform to them. This included the spelling of proper

22. Archibald T. Robertson, *An Introduction to the Textual Criticism of the New Testament,* p. 154. Zane C. Hodges, "The Angel at Bethesda—John 5:4," 25-39, disagrees with Robertson's analysis.
23. Benjamin B. Warfield, *An Introduction to the Textual Criticism of the New Testament,* p. 100.
24. See Payne, "Validity of Numbers," pp. 5-58. Also see Nix, "1 Chronicles," 428-519, and "2 Chronicles," 520-61.

names, verb forms, the smoothing out of rough grammar, the changing of genders to agree with their referents, and other syntactical alterations. These changes were akin to recent efforts to change the older English "which" to "whom," and "shall" to "will."

(2) *Liturgical changes*. The lectionaries provide abundant examples of these changes. At the beginning of a given section of a lectionary, minor changes were made in order to summarize the preceding context. Some of those changes crept into biblical manuscripts. For example, "Joseph and Mary" came to be inserted in the place of "his parents" (Luke 2:41). Outside of the lectionaries, minor textual alterations were made in order to conform to ecclesiastical usage. The "doxology" of the "Lord's Prayer" (Matt. 6:13) probably arose in this manner.[25]

(3) *Harmonizational changes*. This kind of change is sometimes encountered in the gospels. The account of the "Lord's Prayer" in Luke 11:2-4 was made to agree with the more popular version in Matthew 6:9-13. Some manuscripts have made Acts 9:5-6 agree more literally with Acts 26:14-15. In like manner, quotations from the Old Testament were enlarged in some manuscripts to conform with the LXX (cf. Matt. 15:8 with Isa. 29:13; the phrase "this people" is added). To Paul's list of four commandments in Romans 13:9, another, "You shall not bear false witness," is added in some manuscripts.

(4) *Historical and factual changes*. Well-meaning scribes sometimes "corrected" manuscripts by changing what they thought was an error. This is no doubt what happened in Revelation 1:5, where a scribe changed *lusanti,* "loosed [us from our sins]," to *lousanti,* "washed [us from our sins]."[26] The change of "sixth hour" to "third hour" in John 19:14 in some manuscripts was probably an attempt to correct what the scribe considered to be an inaccuracy. Geographical corrections can be found among the manuscripts. Origen changed "Bethany" to "Bethabara" in order to explain a geographical difficulty.

25. Metzger, *Textual Commentary,* pp. 16-17, provides a plausible discussion of how this longer reading came to be added to the late manuscripts of the Textus Receptus tradition. The NKJV (following the KJV) does not mention the textual variation in the marginal notes, but the last half of the verse is omitted in the RV, ASV, NEB, NAB, and NIV, and it is placed in brackets in the RSV and NASB. See the discussion of these translations in chap. 32.

26. Metzger, *Textual Commentary,* p. 729, shows why the Nestle-Aland text reading is preferred over the Textus Receptus tradition on the basis of its superior manuscript support, its accord with Old Testament imagery, and because it better supports the idea in verse 6*a*, although the Textus Receptus and Majority Text follow most of the minuscule manuscripts and several early versions in their reading. The note in the NKJV errs in identifying the Majority Text and Nestle-Aland Text readings as the same. Since the vowels *u* and *ou* also sound similar when they are read aloud, the change may have been unintentional.

(5) *Conflational changes.* Conflation is the combining of two or more variants into one reading. The clause, "And every sacrifice will be salted with salt" (Mark 9:49), is probably a conflation.[27] The "unto all and upon all" of Romans 3:22 (KJV, "to ... to" in NKJV) is probably another example of combining two alternative readings (the ASV, RSV, NEB, NASB, NAB and NIV have only "for all" or its equivalent).[28]

(6) *Doctrinal changes.* Most deliberate doctrinal changes have been in the direction of orthodoxy, as is the reference to the Trinity in 1 John 5:7.[29] The addition of "fasting" to "prayer" in Mark 9:29 and the long ending to Mark (16:9-20),[30] if they were deliberate, may not have been so orthodox. In 1 Corinthians 6:20, the addition of "and in your spirit, which are God's" (KJV, NKJV) and "who walk not after the flesh ..." (Rom. 8:1) are possibly later interpolations introduced into later manuscripts.[31] Other passages of this variety may include John 1:18, "only begotten son" instead of "only begotten God," and Acts 20:28, "church of the Lord which he obtained with his blood" instead of "church of God, which he [God] hath purchased with his own [God's] blood" (KJV, NKJV).[32] It is well to add Greenlee's observation that "no Christian doctrine, however, hangs upon a debatable text; and the student of the New Testament must be aware of wanting his text to be more orthodox or doctrinally stronger than is the inspired original."[33]

4. *How significant are the variants?* It is easy to leave the wrong impression by speaking of 200,000 "errors" that have crept into the text by scribal mistakes and intended corrections. It has been mentioned previously that there were only 10,000 places where these 200,000 variants occur. The next question is: "How significant are those 10,000 places?" Textual critics have attempted to answer that question by offering percentages and comparisons.

27. Metzger, *Textual Commentary,* pp. 102-3, discusses the fact that the variants in Mark 9:49 appear in three principle forms. The difference in textual preference is again seen in the KJV and NKJV and the ASV, RSV, NEB, NASB, NAB, and NIV as discussed in chap. 32.
28. Metzger, *Textual Commentary,* p. 508, shows how the Textus Receptus reading is based on late and secondary manuscripts to produce this essentially redundant and tautological expression followed also by the M-Text and the NKJV.
29. See subsequent discussion of this passage.
30. "Fasting" is also added in Acts 10:30 and 1 Cor. 7:5. The Mark 16:9-20 passage will be discussed elsewhere in this chapter.
31. See Metzger, *Textual Commentary,* p. 515. The KJV and NKJV follow the TR (and the M-Text generally); the ASV, RSV, NEB, NASB, NAB, and NIV again follow the NU-Text.
32. See Metzger, *Textual Commentary,* for reasons the Nestle-Aland/United Bible Societies' Text (NU-Text) text follows the older manuscripts that are more broadly-based geographically than the Textus Receptus (TR) and Majority Text (M-Text) tradition. The modern English translations discussed in chap. 32 follow the same lines as elsewhere.
33. J. Harold Greenlee, *An Introduction to New Testament Textual Criticism,* p. 68.

a. Westcott and Hort estimated that only about one-eighth of all the variants had any weight, as most of them are merely mechanical matters such as spelling or style. Of the whole, then, only about one-sixtieth rise above "trivialities," or can in any sense be called "substantial variations."[34] Mathematically that would compute to a text that is 98.33 percent pure whether the critic adopts the Textus Receptus, Majority Text, Nestle-Aland Text, or some eclectic text of the New Testament.

b. Ezra Abbott gave similar figures, saying about 19/20 (95 percent) of the readings are "various" rather than "rival" readings, and about 19/20 (95 percent) of the remainder are of so little importance that their adoption or rejection makes no appreciable difference in the sense of the passage.[35] Thus the degree of substantial purity would be 99.75 percent.

c. Philip Schaff surmised that of the 150,000 variations known in his day, only 400 affected the sense; and of those only 50 were of real significance; and of this total not one affected "an article of faith or a precept of duty which is not abundantly sustained by other and undoubted passages, or by the whole tenor of Scripture teaching."[36]

d. A. T. Robertson suggested that the real concern of textual criticism is of a "thousandth part of the entire text."[37] That would make the reconstructed text of the New Testament 99.9 percent free from real concern for the textual critic. Hence, as Warfield observed, "the great mass of the New Testament, in other words, has been transmitted to us with no, or next to no variations."[38] At first, the great multitude of variants would seem to be a liability to the integrity of the Bible text. But just the contrary is true, for the larger number of variants supplies at the same time the means of checking on those variants. As strange as it may appear, the corruption of the text provides the means for its own correction.

e. The forthgoing discussion cannot be fully appreciated unless it is contrasted with the textual integrity of other books from the ancient world. The first comparison to consider is that of the number or quantity of manuscripts. The Greek manuscripts of the New Testament alone total more than three thousand, and there are more than two thousand lectionaries and more than ten thousand copies of Jerome's Latin Vulgate, in addition to all of the various versions;[39] whereas some of the greatest

34. Brooke Foss Westcott and Fenton John Anthony Hort, *The New Testament in the Original Greek,* 2.2.
35. Warfield, *Introduction,* pp. 13-14.
36. Philip Schaff, *Companion to the Greek Testament and the English Version,* p. 177. In fact, the idea goes back to J.A. Bengel; see chap. 25 discussion and Metzger, *The Text of the New Testament,* p. 112.
37. Archibald T. Robertson, *An Introduction to the Textual Criticism of the New Testament,* p. 22.
38. Warfield, *Introduction,* p. 14.
39. See chap. 22 for the precise numbers of Greek manuscripts. Also see Bruce M. Metzger, *The Early Versions of the New Testament: Their Origins, Transmission and Limitations.*

writings of antiquity have survived in only a handful of manuscripts (see chap. 20). Furthermore, a comparison of the nature or quality of the writings sets the fidelity of the biblical text in bold relief. Bruce M. Metzger's excellent study of Homer's *Iliad* and the Hindu *Mahābhārata* demonstrates that their textual corruption is much greater than that of the New Testament.

(1) The *Iliad* is particularly appropriate because it has the most in common with the New Testament. Next to the New Testament, there are more extant copies of the *Iliad* (643)[40] than any other book. Both the *Iliad* and the Bible were considered "sacred," and both underwent textual changes and criticism of their Greek manuscripts. The New Testament has about 20,000 lines; the *Iliad* about 15,600. Only 40 lines (or about 400 words) of the New Testament are in doubt, whereas 764 lines of the *Iliad* are questioned. Thus, the 5 percent textual corruption of the Iliad compares with one-half of 1 percent (or less) of similar emendations in the New Testament.

(2) The national epic of India, the *Mahābhārata,* has suffered even more corruption. It is about eight times the size of the *Iliad* and the *Odyssey* together, roughly 250,000 lines. Of these, some 26,000 lines have textual corruptions (10 percent).[41] The New Testament, then, has not only survived in more manuscripts than any other book from antiquity, but it has survived in purer form than any other great book.

The Principles of Textual Criticism

The full appreciation of the arduous task of reconstructing the New Testament text from thousands of manuscripts containing tens of thousands of variants can be derived, in part, from a study of just how textual scholars proceed. The evidence available for textual criticism is of two kinds: external and internal.

40. Bruce M. Metzger, *Chapters in the History of New Testament Textual Criticism,* p. 144, lists 453 papyri, 2 uncials, and 183 minuscules, after the computation of Kurt Aland of Münster, July 11, 1962.

41. Even the Koran, which did not originate until the seventh century A.D., has suffered from a large collection of variants that necessitated the Orthmanic revision. In fact, there are still seven ways to read the text (vocalization and punctuation), all based on Orthman's recension, which was made about twenty years after the death of Muhammad. Cf. Arthur Jeffrey, *Materials for the History of the Quran Text,* and the more recent work of Richard Bell, *Introduction to the Qu'ran.*

External Evidence

There are three kinds of external evidence. With few exceptions, textual scholars agree that "knowing the age or geographical distribution of early witnesses in no way guarantees finding the original text."[42] This is the reason most scholars employ an "eclectic" approach to textual criticism, as the discussion in chapter 25 indicates. Nevertheless, as Gordon Fee attests, "it is noteworthy that for most scholars over 90 percent of all the variants of the NT text are resolved, because in most cases the variant that best explains the origin of the others is also supported by the earliest and best witnesses."[43]

Chronological. The date of the text type (not necessarily the manuscript) is important. In general, earlier text-types are preferred to later ones.

Geographical. A wide distribution of independent witnesses that agree in support of a variant are generally preferred to those having closer proximity or relationship.

Genealogical. Witnesses to variants are to be weighed rather than merely counted to indicate their merits. The "weight" of the evidence for a textual reading is based on the same basic considerations that apply to manuscript families and individual manuscripts.

1. *The relative order of the families*. Of the four major textual families (see chart at the end of chap. 25)—Alexandrian, Caesarean, Western and Byzantine—(1) the Alexandrian is generally considered to be the most reliable text, although it sometime shows "learned" corrections.[44] However, (2) readings supported by good representatives of two or more text-types are generally preferred to those found in single text-types. In other words, a Byzantine-Western agreement could outweigh a well-attested Alexandrian reading. (3) The Byzantine text-type is generally considered to be the least preferred because in the judgment of most textual critics it is a derived text-type.[45]

2. *Consideration of individual manuscripts within the families*. When the manuscripts within an individual text-type are divided in their support of a variant, the correct reading of the family is probably (1) the reading of the manuscripts that are generally the most faithful to their own text-type (i.e., the best witnesses within a family of texts), (2) the reading that is most difficult but has good manuscript support within the family, and/or

42. Gordon D. Fee, "The Textual Criticism of the New Testament," in Frank E. Gaebelein, ed., *The Expositor's Bible Commentary,* 1:430.
43. Ibid.
44. The discussion here follows Greenlee, pp. 115f.
45. For an alternative view see Sturz, *Byzantine Text-type,* and various contributions by Zane C. Hodges and others as presented in the discussion on the development of textual criticism in chap. 25. Sturz and Hodges differ on their view of the Byzantine text. Sturz treats the Byzantine text as an equal to the other families whereas Hodges sees the Byzantine text as the best text.

(3) the reading that is most characteristic of the family to which it belongs (i.e., what the family as a whole appears to adopt as the preferred reading). The final step in determining a reading is comparing the family readings to one another by considering date and character, geographical or family distribution, and the strength of the unity of any reading within a family.

Internal Evidence

There are also two kinds of internal evidence—transcriptional (depending on the habits of the *scribes),* and intrinsic (depending on the characteristics of the *author).*

Transcriptional evidence is also called "transcriptional probablity," since it is concerned "with scribal errors and is based on certain inductively derived criteria."[46]

1. *The more difficult reading* (for the scribe) is to be preferred, particularly if it is sensible. The tendency of scribal emendations is to produce a superficially improved reading by combining "the appearance of improvement with the absence of its reality."[47]
2. *The shorter reading* is to be preferred unless it arose from an accidental omission of lines due to similar ends *(parablepsis),* or an intentional deletion of material on grammatical, liturgical, or doctrinal grounds. The premise is that a scribe is more likely to add for clarification than to delete material from the text.
3. *The more verbally dissonant readings* of parallel passages, whether they invoke Old Testament quotations or different accounts of the same events (as in the gospels), are to be preferred. There was a scribal tendency to harmonize divergent accounts of a given event recorded in Scripture.
4. *The less-refined grammatical construction,* expression, word, and so on, is preferred, because scribes tended to smooth out the rough grammar and improve the expression of Scripture.

Intrinsic evidence is also called "intrinsic probability," which "is the most subjective element in the methodology of textual criticism."[48] This depends upon the probablity of what the author is more likely to have written, and is determined by considering the following: (1) the style of the author throughout the book (and elsewhere), (2) the immediate context of the passage, (3) the harmony of a reading with the author's teaching elsewhere (as well as

46. Fee, "Textual," p. 430.
47. Westcott and Hort, *New Testament,* p. 27.
48. Fee, "Textual," p. 430.

with the other canonical writings),[49] and (4) the influence of the author's background, for example, Aramaic background of Jesus' teaching.[50]

As may be imagined, the consideration of all the external and internal factors involved in the process of textual criticism is not only a technical science but it is also a delicate art. This is especially true when there is conflict in the evidence. A few observations, however, may assist the beginner in getting acquainted with the process of textual criticism. (1) In general, external evidence is more important than internal evidence, because it is more objective than the latter. (2) Nevertheless, decisions must take both lines of evidence into account and carefully evaluate them. In other words,

> if the two are apparently contradictory, a satisfactory solution must be sought. To disregard external evidence and depend too completely on internal evidence may lead to unduly subjective decisions. At the same time, one must not depend upon external evidence without proper regard to internal considerations, since no manuscript or text-type is perfectly trustworthy.[51]

(3) "Since textual criticism is an art as well as a science, it is understandable that in some cases different scholars will come to different evaluations of the significance of the evidence,"[52] just as they do over other matters where both objective and subjective factors are involved. (4) Gleason Archer arranges the factors of external and internal evidence into the following rules or canons and cautiously suggests that, should a conflict occur, *priority* should be given in the following order:

1. The older reading is to be preferred.
2. The more difficult reading is to be preferred.
3. The shorter reading is to be preferred.
4. The reading that best explains the variants is to be preferred.
5. The reading with the widest geographical support is to be preferred.
6. The reading that most conforms to the style and diction of the author is to be preferred.
7. The reading that reflects no doctrinal bias is to be preferred.[53]

In addition to these general rules, Archer suggests that the excellent methodology proposed by Ernst Würthwein, involving the Masoretic Text (MT) in Old Testament textual criticism, be utilized:

> 1. Where the MT and the other witnesses offer the same text and it is an

49. Harmony with other biblical teachings is only a secondary consideration, unless the passage has an ideological contradiction with other biblical teaching instead of a mere verbal difference.
50. Metzger, *The Text of the New Testament,* p. 210, also adds two other considerations: (1) the priority of the gospel of Mark, and (2) the influence of the Christian community on the formulation and transmission of a given passage.
51. Greenlee, *Introduction,* p. 119.
52. Metzger, *The Text of the New Testament,* p. 211.
53. Archer, pp. 57-60.

intelligible and sensible reading, it is inadmissible to reject this reading and resort to conjecture (as too many critics have done).

2. Where there is a genuine deviation from the MT on the part of the other witnesses (and the deviation is not simply a matter of translator's interpretation) and both readings seem equally sensible, then the preference should normally be given to the MT (unless one of the canons intervenes to give clear preference to the other reading).

3. Where the text of the MT is doubtful or impossible because of factors of language, or sense-in-context, and where at the same time other witnesses offer a satisfactory reading, then the latter should be given favorable consideration. Especially is this so if it can be seen how the MT reading might have been corrupted through some familiar scribal error. . . .

4. Where neither the MT nor the other witnesses offer a possible or probable text, conjecture may legitimately be resorted to. . . .

5. In all textual-critical work, due regard must be given to the psychology of the scribe himself. We must always ask ourselves the question, How might this error—if error there be—have originated from his hand? Does this accord with his type or habit of mind as observed elsewhere in his work?

By means of this careful formula, Würthwein attempts to set up a method of objectivity and scientific procedure that will eliminate much of the reckless and ill-considered emendation which has so often passed for bona fide textual criticism.[54]

The Practice (Praxis) of Textual Criticism

There is not as much divergence of opinion over the criticism of the Old Testament text as there is over the New Testament text. For the Old Testament the most recent basic critical edition of the text is the *Biblia Hebraica Stuttgartensia* (BHS) [1967/77]. For the New Testament there are three basic textual traditions now available to the critic: the so-called Textus Receptus (TR) tradition, the so-called Critical Text tradition—the Nestle-Aland Text (NU-Text), or text of the Nestle-United Bible Societies (or UBS)—and the so-called Majority Text (M-Text) tradition.[55] The most practical way to observe the results of the principles of textual criticism is to compare the differences between the Old Testament translations based on the Masoretic Text (MT), LXX, Samaritan Pentateuch (SP), and Dead Sea Scroll (DSS) witnesses, and New Testament translations based on the Textus Receptus or Majority Text tradition, those based on the Nestle-Aland tradition, and "eclectic" approaches to it. To the Textus Receptus/Majority Text (TR/M-Text) tradition belong the King James Version (KJV) of 1611 and the New King

54. Archer, pp. 60-61, which follows Ernst Würthwein, *The Text of the Old Testament*, pp. 80-81.
55. Those familiar with the Hebrew and Greek languages will of course make reference to *Biblia Hebraica Stuttgartensia* (BHS), and *The Greek New Testament, According to the Majority Text*, and either Nestle's *Novum Testamentum Graece*, or the United Bible Societies *The Greek New Testament*.

James Version (NKJV) of 1979, 1982. Those based on the Nestle-Aland Text tradition or some "eclectic" approach to it include the English Revised Version (RV) of 1881, 1885, the *American Standard Version* (ASV) of 1901, the *Revised Standard Version* (RSV) of 1946, 1952, the *New English Bible* (NEB) of 1963, 1970, the *New American Standard Bible* (NASB) of 1963, 1972, the *New American Bible* (NAB) of 1970, and the *New International Version* (NIV) of 1973, 1978.[56] The difference between the approach of the Textus Receptus/ Majority Text tradition and the approach of the Nestle-Aland tradition is that the TR/M-Text tends to favor readings of the Byzantine family of texts, whereas the NU-Text text generally favors the readings of the Alexandrian family. Most New Testament textual critics favor the Alexandrian family (e.g., Metzger, Aland, Fee) over the Byzantine; but a few have called for the Byzantine family either to be treated with greater respect (Sturz) or to be given the place of priority (Hodges). The arguments involved are historical and complex, but it would appear that the Alexandrian text is the better family because of age and absence of harmonization of readings.[57] A survey of several passages will serve to illustrate the procedures of reconstructing the original text when significant textual variants are involved.

Old Testament Examples

Zechariah 12:10. This illustrates that translators sometimes use *weaker subjective* (internal) evidences weightier than external evidence. The Masoretic text in concurrence with the LXX reads, "They shall look upon me [Jehovah speaking] whom they have pierced." This rendition is followed by the KJV, RV, ASV, NEB, NASB, TANAKH (NJV),[58] NIV, and NKJV. The RSV, *Jerusalem Bible*,[59] and NAB follow Theodotion's revision (c. 180-190),[60] and the reading in John 19:37 in rendering it, "When they look on him whom they have pierced." Preference for the Masoretic and LXX reading is based on the following reasons:

1. It is based on earlier and better manuscripts.
2. It is the more difficult reading.

56. See the discussion in chap. 32 concerning the principles and procedures involved in these translations and others.
57. See the discussions in chaps. 16 and 25 concerning historical factors and other issues that must be considered. Also see Sturz, *Byzantine Text-Type;* Wilbur Pickering, *The Identity of the New Testament Text*, and D. A. Carson, *The King James Version Debate: A Plea for Realism*.
58. The Jewish Publication Society sponsored *The New Jewish Version* (NJV), 1962-1982. It was published in a one-volume edition, *TANAKH: A New Translation of the HOLY SCRIPTURES According to the Traditional Hebrew Text* (Philadelphia: The Jewish Publication Society, 5746/1985). See chap. 32 discussion on this new translation of the Old Testament into English.
59. See the discussion in chap. 32.
60. See discussion of this revision in chap. 27.

3. It can explain the other reading, namely (1) theological prejudice against the deity of Christ and/or (2) the influence of the New Testament which, when quoting this passage, changes the personal pronoun from the first person (me) to the third person (him) in order to apply it to Christ (cf. John 19:37).
4. In addition, it conforms to the methodology suggested by Ernst Würthwein.

Exodus 1:5. In the Masoretic Text this reads that "seventy" descended into Egypt. This has been a longstanding and perplexing problem because the LXX and the New Testament (Acts 7:14) read "seventy-five souls." Here the Dead Sea Scrolls cast light on the difficulty. A fragment of Exodus from Qumran reads, "seventy-five souls." It is possible that the LXX and DSS fragment preserve the true text. The problem has occasioned many ingenious attempts at harmonization, including the counting of five grandsons, or of alleging that Stephen was wrong in his sermon (but not Luke's record of it). This first explanation cannot be considered purely harmonistic because it still faces the statement in Genesis 46:27 that the number was "seventy." At least there is now a Hebrew manuscript to support the rendering of Exodus 1:5 as "seventy-five souls." Most modern translations follow the Masoretic Text, but those that have annotations generally indicate the variant reading.

Deuteronomy 32:8. This provides another interesting exercise in Old Testament textual criticism. The Masoretic Text, followed by KJV, ASV, and TANAKH, reads, "The Most High gave to the nations their inheritance. . . . He set the bounds of the peoples according to the number of the children of Israel." The RSV followed the LXX and a fragment from Qumran, which reads, "According to the number of the sons [or angels] of God." The LXX reading is an attempt to bring the text into harmony with the patriarchal description of angels as "sons of God" (cf. Job 1:6; 2:1; 38:7 and possibly even Gen. 6:4). The modern rendition that follows it is an example of "eclectic" interpretation of the Old Testament text that is quite at variance with the principles stated by the translators of the NIV. Their introduction indicates how capricious translators may become when they introduce their subjective interpretation or doctrinal position into the process of textual criticism without following the commonly accepted canons and methodology as presented in previous discussion.[61]

New Testament Examples

Before looking into specific examples of New Testament textual criticism, it is helpful to recall that the differences in the manuscript evidence between the Old and New Testaments has resulted in more divergence of opinion

61. See *New International Version,* Introduction, pp. viii-ix.

among textual critics who employ an "eclectic" approach to deriving the original reading. Gordon Fee is sensitive to those difficulties when he describes the debate among various approaches to the "eclectic" method utilized by most New Testament textual critics. He writes,

> With the rejection of Hort's genealogical method, by which the reading of the Alexandrian witness was adopted except where internal evidence proved it secondary, there has emerged a method that may properly be called "eclectic." Essentially, this means that the "original" text of the NT is to be chosen variant by variant, using all the principles of critical judgment without regarding one MS or text-type as necessarily preserving that "original."
>
> Despite a few notable exceptions, most of the differences that remain among critical texts result from a varying degree of weight given the external evidence.
>
> On the one hand, there is a kind of eclecticism that, when all other criteria are equal, tends to follow Hort and to adopt the readings of the Alexandrian witnesses. This may be observed to a greater degree in the UBS edition and to a somewhat lesser degree in the Greek texts behind the RSV and NEB, where early Western witnesses are given a little more consideration.
>
> Another kind of textual theory was advocated by M-E. Boismard and was used in D. Mollat's translation of John in the Jerusalem Bible. This is a kind of "eclectic Western" method. . . .
>
> On the opposite side is the method of "rigorous eclecticism" practiced by G.D. Kilpatrick and his student J.K. Elliott. They advocate placing no weight on the MSS at all, but making every choice solely on the basis of internal principles. . . .
>
> While, as has already been said, we may grant that not all of the principles of textual criticism are applicable to each variant, contemporary critics generally agree that questionable internal evidence should usually be asked first and that the weight of the MS evidence should be applied secondarily. What becomes obvious, however, is that on the grounds of internal evidence certain MSS tend to support the "original" text more often than others and that those MSS are the early Alexandrian. Therefore, when internal evidence cannot decide, the safest guide is to go with the "best" MSS.[62]

Various Schools of New Testament Textual Criticism

Westcott-Hort Text	Critical Text	Eclectic Text	Majority Text	Received Text
⇨	⇨		⇦	⇦
Tends toward Alexandrian Family		Takes each variant individually	Tends toward Byzantine Family	

(The purpose of textual criticism is to ascertain the original reading.)

62. Fee, "Textual," pp. 430-31.

Keeping these distinctions in view, it appears that the positions of modern textual critics fit somewhere on a continuum as illustrated in the chart, "Various Schools of New Testament Textual Criticism." Although they move from different starting points on that continuum (Textus Receptus/Majority Text on the one hand and Westcott-Hort/Critical Text on the other), they tend to converge on the original textual reading of the New Testament as they apply the principles of textual criticism to the individual textual variants.[63] This suggests that the original reading of the New Testament may be recovered by the proper application of the canons of textual criticism as previously outlined. Their application to several New Testament examples will make the process evident.

1 John 5:7-8 (KJV, NKJV). The Textus Receptus reads, "For there are three that bear record in heaven, the Father, the Word, and the Holy Ghost: and these three are one. And there are three that bear witness in the earth." The Nestle-Aland Text and the Majority Text render this passage as "For there are three that bear witness," and make appropriate notation of the textual variations. The RV, ASV, RSV, NEB and NAB omit the entire sentence without explanation, although the NASB and NIV add an explanatory for the omission of the longer reading, whereas the NKJV notes the textual variant but includes the longer reading. The longer reading has virtually no support among Greek manuscripts, although there is ample support for it in copies of the Latin Vulgate,[64] and its appearance in a few late Greek manuscripts is based on an interesting scene in the history of textual criticism. Desiderius Erasmus omitted the longer reading from the first two editions of his Greek New Testament (1516, 1519) and was challenged for making that omission. He hastily replied that he would include the reading in his next edition if anyone could produce even one Greek manuscript that included the reading. One sixteenth-century Greek minuscule (the 1520 manuscript of the Franciscan friar Froy, or Roy) was found, and Erasmus complied with his promise and inserted the longer reading in his 1522 edition. The King James translators followed the text of Erasmus that contained this rendering, and on the basis of the testimony that appears in insignificant and late minuscule manuscripts,[65] all the weight and authority of hundreds of uncial and minuscule manuscripts that omit it, as do the Greek Fathers, and the manuscripts of all the ancient versions (including the Old Latin and Vulgate) is disregarded. The earliest instance of this longer reading being quoted as a part of the actual text of 1 John comes in a fourth-century Latin treatise attributed to either the Spanish

63. See the discussion throughout this chapter as well as chaps. 10 and 25 for representative approaches among these various schools.
64. See the discussion on chap. 29.
65. The four manuscripts that support the longer reading are ms. 61 (sixteenth century), ms. 88 (twelfth century), ms. 629 (fourteenth or fifteenth century), and ms. 635 (eleventh-century manuscript with the passage written in its margin during the seventeenth century).

heretic Priscillian or to his follower Bishop Instantius.[66] In fact, the acceptance of the longer rendering as a genuine part of the text of 1 John violates almost every major canon of textual criticism.

Luke 11:2 (KJV, NKJV). Translations based on the Greek text of the Textus Receptus/Majority Text tradition read, "Our Father which art in heaven." Those which follow the Nestle-Aland Text and "eclectic" scholars read, "Father, hallowed be thy name," and relegate the longer reading to a note (RV, ASV, NEB, NASB, and NIV) or omit it altogether (RSV, NAB). A consideration of the canons of textual criticism previously discussed is relevant to arriving at the correct reading of the original text. In favor of the Nestle-Aland Text is canon #1 (the oldest reading is best), because Codices א and B omit the longer phrase. By the same token, canon #3 also supports the Nestle-Aland Text because it is the shorter reading. Likewise, the longer reading shows a clear harmonistic attempt to bring the passage in line with the parallel passage in Matthew 6:9, possibly as a result of liturgical usage of the Matthean form of the prayer, and canon #4 shows this to be the reading that best explains the variants. Furthermore, the shorter reading in the Nestle-Aland text is supported by the chief representatives of the purest textual family (Alexandrian), as well as the leading manuscripts in the Caesarean (f^1 and 700), and the Western family (SY^8 and Tertullian).[67]

John 7:53-8:11 (KJV, NKJV). This passage, concerning the woman taken in adultery, presents one of the most interesting and perplexing problems in New Testament textual criticism. The proponents of the Nestle-Aland Text and "eclectic" scholars place the passage in brackets with a note that most ancient authorities omit it.[68] The RV, ASV, RSV,[69] NASB, NAB, and NIV follow that approach, but the NEB transposes the passage in question to the end of John's gospel under a caption "An incident in the temple."[70] A review of the procedures of textual criticism should provide assistance in discovering

66. See Metzger, *Textual Commentary,* pp. 715-16, for an extended review of the external and internal evidence on this passage.
67. Ibid., pp. 154-56.
68. So the Nestle-Aland *Greek New Testament* and Metzger's *Textual Commentary,* pp. 355-537, which is based on it.
69. Since its 1971 revision, the RSV has included the pericope but has it set off distinctively apart from the text with a note appended.
70. In a footnote the NEB translators write, "This passage, which in the most widely received editions of the New Testament is printed in the text of John 7.53—8.11, has no fixed place in our witnesses. Some of them do not contain it at all. Some place it after Luke 21.38, others after John 7.36, or 7.52, or 21.24." The RV, ASV, RSV, and NAB also indicate that the passage in question is placed at various locations among the manuscript witnesses that contain it. The NASB and NIV merely indicate that it does not occur in the earliest and most reliable manuscripts. This suggests a difference in approach among the proponents of the Nestle-Aland Text and the "eclectic" tradition as indicated earlier.

whether or not this pericope is actually part of John's gospel.[71]

1. The passage in question does not appear in the oldest and most reliable Greek manuscripts, including P^{66}, P^{75}, ℵ, A^{vid}, B, C^{vid}, L, N. T, W, X, Δ, Θ, Ψ, 0141, 0211, 22, 33, 157, 209, 565, 892, 1230, 1241, 1253, 1333*, 2193, 2768, family 1424, and others.[72]
2. Neither Tatian nor the Old Syriac betrays any knowledge of it, nor do the best manuscripts of the Peshitta. Likewise, it is omitted by the Coptic (Sahidic and Bohairic), and several Gothic and Old Latin manuscripts.
3. No Greek writer comments on this passage until the twelfth century.
4. It is not included in Diatessaron, Clement, Tertullian, Origen, Cyprian, Chrysostom, Nonnus, Cyril, Cosmas, or Theophylact.
5. Its style and interruption do not fit the fourth gospel.
6. The earliest known Greek manuscript to contain it is Codex D (5th-6th cent.).[73]
7. Scribes have placed it in several other locations: some after John 7:36 (ms. 225); after John 21:24 (family 1, 1076, 1570, 1582); after John 7:44 (eleventh-century revision of the Old Georgian Version); or after Luke 21:38 (family 13).
8. Many of the manuscripts that have included it have marked it with an obelus, thus indicating it to be spurious. These manuscripts include E, S, Λ, Π, *l*077, *l*443, *l*445, $l69^{m}$, $l70^{m}$, $l185^{m}$, $l211^{m}$, $l1579^{m}$, and $l1761^{m}$.

Although it is possible that the pericope of the woman taken in adultery preserves a true story, it seems best to conclude with Metzger, RSV, NEB, NASB, NAB, and the NIV translation committees that from the standpoint of textual criticism, it should be regarded as an addition to John's gospel with no fixed place in the ancient witnesses that include it.[74] *The Reader's Digest Bible* (RDB), which is based on the RSV and Bruce M. Metzger as its general editor (see chap. 32), includes the pericope without comment. This suggests that there is no attempt on the part of Nestle-Aland Text or "eclectic" propo-

71. Metzger, *Textual Commentary,* pp. 219-23. In an extended discussion of John 7:53—8:11, Metzger says, "The evidence for the non-Johannine origin of the pericope of the adultress is overwhelming." Zane C. Hodges, "The Woman Taken in Adultery," pp. 41-53, and in the *Greek New Testament,* Introduction, pp. xxiii-xxxii, represents the Textus Receptus/Majority Text tradition as he argues that more than 900 manuscripts contain John 7:53—8:11.
72. See discussion of the manuscripts in chap. 22. These manuscripts are listed in Metzger, *The Text of the New Testament,* p. 223.
73. Metzger, *The Text of the New Testament,* p. 50, comments on Codex D (also known as Codex Bezae or Cantabrigiensis) saying, "No known manuscript has as many and such remarkable variations from what is usually taken to be the normal New Testament text." Also see discussion in chap. 22.
74. Ibid., p. 224. Also see the various translation notes to this effect.

nents to eliminate the pericope from Scripture. Their concern is for the correct rendering of the text.

Mark 16:9-20 (KJV, NAB, NKJV). This is another perplexing problem in New Testament textual criticism. Unlike John 7:53—8:11, however, this passage represents one of four endings current in the manuscripts, and some of that manuscript evidence is quite old. As might be expected, advocates against the inclusion of the long ending and those favoring inclusion are sharply divided over the issue.[75] The translators of the RV, ASV, NEB, NASB, and NIV all include the so-called longer ending (verses 9-20), whereas the RSV places it in a footnote. All of these translations provide an explanatory note and indicate that there is a textual problem. I. Howard Marshall summarizes the consensus of Nestle-Aland Text and "eclectic" proponents as he writes,

> Mark briefly recounts how some women found the empty tomb of Jesus and fled from it in confusion after the angelic vision (16:1-8). Then the story in Mark terminates abruptly without describing any appearances of the risen Lord. So it seems likely that the original ending of the Gospel has been lost. On the other hand, many scholars think the sudden ending is deliberate."[76]

Advocates of the Textus Receptus/Majority Text tradition, on the other hand, generally follow the position reflected in William F. Farmer, *The Last Twelve Verses of Mark*. The NAB includes the passage and makes the following annotation:

> 16:9-20: This passage, termed "the longer ending" to the Marcan gospel by comparison with a much briefer conclusion found in some manuscripts, has traditionally been accepted as an inspired part of the gospels. Early citations of it by the Fathers indicate that it was composed in the first century, although the vocabulary and style argue strongly that it was written by someone other than Mark. It is a general resumé of the material concerning the appearances of the risen Jesus, reflecting, in particular, traditions found in Luke (24) and John (20).[77]

Again, a survey of the evidence following the canons of textual criticism should be of assistance in resolving the question.

75. See Metzger, *The Text of the New Testament*, p. 122-28, for an extended discussion of the various endings to Mark and the variant readings within the text of Mark 16:9-20, and a verdict that this long ending "has no claim to be original" (p. 124). Also see William F. Farmer, *The Last Twelve Verses of Mark* (Cambridge: Cambridge U., 1974), who leans moderately toward inclusion.
76. I. Howard Marshall, "Jesus in the Gospels," in Gaebelein, ed., *Expositor's Bible Commentary*, 1:540.
77. *The New American Bible*, p. 1104. At the conclusion of verse 20, the NAB editors also include, "The Shorter Ending," with the note that it is "found after Mark 16,8 before the Longer Ending, in some late Greek manuscripts as well as some ancient versions" (p. 1105). In addition, they add "The Freer Logion," with a note that it is "found after Mark 16, 14 in a fourth century manuscript preserved in the Freer Gallery of Art, Washington, D.C. This ending was known to Jerome." This Freer manuscript is Codex W (see chap. 22).

1. These verses (9-20) are lacking in many of the oldest and most reliable Greek manuscripts,[78] including ℵ, B, Old Latin manuscript k, the Sinaitic Syriac, many Old Armenian manuscripts and a number of Ethiopic manuscripts.
2. Many of the ancient Fathers show no knowledge of these verses (e.g., Clement, Origen, Eusebius, et al.). Jerome admitted that "almost all Greek copies do not have this concluding portion."[79] Among some of the witnesses that have these verses, there is also an asterisk or obelus to indicate it is a spurious addition to the text.
3. There is another ending in addition to verses 9-20 that occurs in several uncials (L, Ψ, 099, 0112), a few miniscules (279^{mg}, 579), and several manuscript copies of ancient versions (k, $Syr^{h\ mg}$, $Coptic^{pt}$, Eth^{codd}).[80] This shorter passage reads, "But they reported briefly to Peter and those with him all that they had been told, from east to west, the sacred and imperishable proclamation of eternal salvation."
4. The familiar long ending of the KJV, NAB and NKJV reflected in the Textus Receptus/Majority Text tradition is found in a number of uncial manuscripts (C, D, L, W), most miniscules, most Old Latin manuscripts, the Vulgate, and in some Syriac and Coptic manuscripts.[81]
5. The long ending of verses 9-20 is expanded after verse 14 in Codex W (chap. 22). According to the NAB this "Freer Logion" reads,

> They offered this excuse: "This lawless and faithless age is under Satan, who does not allow what is unclean and dominated by spirits to grasp the true power of God. Therefore," they said to Christ, "reveal your just authority now." Christ replied: "The measure of years of Satan's power has been fulfilled, but other terrible things are imminent. Yet it was for the sake of sinners that I was handed over to death, that they might return to the truth and sin no more, and inherit the spiritual and immortal glory of justification in heaven."[82]

Which reading is the original ending? Metzger concludes that "none of these four endings commends itself as original,"[83] because of limited textual evidence, the aprocryphal flavor, and the non-Marcan style (e.g., it contains seventeen non-Marcan words). On the other hand, if none of those is genuine, it is difficult to believe with Metzger that Mark 16:8 is not the original ending. Defense of the Textus Receptus reading, including verses 9-20, has

78. See discussion of manuscripts in chap. 22.
79. Metzger, *The Text of the New Testament,* p. 226.
80. Ibid., p. 226.
81. Farmer, *Last Twelve Verses,* pp. 31-35, has an extensive list of witnesses for the inclusion of Mark 16:9-20.
82. *The New American Bible,* p. 1105. The "Freer Logion" appears in Codex W, which is dated in the late-fourth to early-fifth century (see chap. 22 discussion).
83. Metzger, *The Text of the New Testament,* p. 227.

been made by John W. Burgon,[84] and more recently by M. van der Valk,[85] in addition to William F. Farmer's moderate support for inclusion.

It is admittedly difficult to arrive at the conclusion that any of these readings is original. But, on the basis of known manuscript evidence, it seems likely that the position of I. Howard Marshall is most plausible: either Mark 16:8 is the real ending or that the original ending is not extant. Of these two options, the former is more compatible with the concept of a complete canon. In the final analysis, the textual critic is left to internal evidence as the basis for making a final judgment.[86] With the exception of the NAB and NKJV, most major twentieth-century English translations have tended to follow the approach of Marshall, Metzger, and others by using an "eclectic" approach to exclude verses 9-20 from the text.[87]

Acts 20:28 (KJV, NASB, NAB, NIV, NKJV and RDB). At issue in this passage is the rendering "feed the church of God, which he [God] hath purchased with his own [God's] blood." The RV, ASV, RSV and NEB, record the wording, "... church of the Lord." On the basis of the rules of textual criticism, however, this last reading is not preferred. Several observations will indicate that those translators did not follow the canons appropriately.

1. The external evidence is singularly balanced between the variants "church of God" and "church of the Lord."
2. Paleographically, there is only one letter at issue between the readings. The reading "church of the Lord and God" is an obvious conflation, thus reflecting a secondary reading.
3. The reading "church of the Lord" reflects influence from the LXX (where it is used seven times), not the New Testament (where it does not occur).
4. The reading "God" is more difficult because it raises the theological question, Does God have blood?
5. Furthermore, "God" is Alexandrian (א, B, etc.), the more reliable tradition, as opposed to the Western (P^{74}, A, D, etc.) reading "Lord."
6. In light of the Arian controversy over the deity of Christ, it is easy to see how "God" could have been toned down to "Lord."[88]

84. John W. Burgon, *The Last Twelve Verses of the Gospel According to St. Mark*.
85. M. van der Valk, "Observations on Mark 16:9-20 in Relation to St. Mark's Gospel," as cited in Metzger, *The Text of the New Testament*, p. 229.
86. Ned B. Stonehouse argues convincingly from internal evidence that Mark intended to end his gospel at verse 8, *The Witness of Matthew and Mark to Christ*, pp. 87-114.
87. The RV, ASV, NEB, NASB, and NIV set the long ending (16:9-20) apart from the text of Mark with a notation, whereas the NAB and NKJV (following the KJV) incorporate the long ending with a notation. Only the NAB includes the reading of the "Freer Logion" in its apparatus.
88. This is the position argued by Henry Alford, *The Greek New Testament*, Prolegomena, 1:83 n.1.

It is apparently for the same reason that the editorial committee of the RV, ASV, RSV and NEB chose to consider the *weaker subjective* evidence to be weightier than the *external objective* evidence plus *internal* transcriptional factors. It seems appropriate to follow other recent translations (NASB, NAB, NIV, NKJV, and the RDB) in choosing "church of God" as their reading.

Summary and Conclusion

Textual criticism is the art and science of reconstructing the original text from the multiple of variants contained in the manuscripts. It is significant that the Bible has not only been preserved in the largest number of manuscripts of any book from the ancient world, but that it also contains fewer errors in transmission. Actually, the variant readings which significantly affect the sense of a passage are less than ten percent of the New Testament, and none of these affect any basic doctrine of the Christian faith. Textual critics have made studied judgments on many of these significant variants, so that for all practical purposes the modern critical editions of the Hebrew and Greek texts of the Bible represent, with their footnotes, exactly what the autographs contained—line for line, word for word, and even letter for letter. Their objective has been to find God's Word as it was written in the autographs. This ideal is a worthy goal, for it assumes that the Word of God as originally written is a perfect treasure of God's revelation to men.

Part Four

TRANSLATION OF THE BIBLE

27

Translations Containing the Old Testament Text

In addition to the multitude of manuscript copies of the biblical text and the miscellaneous materials, the great ancient versions provide a very important witness to the text of the Scriptures. These combine to form the fourth link in the chain "from God to us"—the translation of the Bible text into various languages. The present chapter is primarily concerned with the great ancient translations of the Old Testament: the Samaritan Pentateuch, the Aramaic Targums, and the LXX. Before those works are viewed, however, several basic definitions and distinctions must be considered.

Definitions

There are two basic components of language that are emphasized by modern scholars: form and meaning. Those are the essential elements to be considered in the transmission of God's Word through history.[1] As a result, more precise definitions of some of the basic words are required than are generally followed in popular usage. The careful scholar will avoid confusing these terms.

Translation, Literal Translation, and Transliteration

Translation. A translation is simply the rendering of a given composition from one language into another. As an example, if the New Testament were translated into Spanish, it would be a translation. If, in turn, this Spanish translation were translated into French, or even back into Greek, it would result in another translation. To be specific about translations, Erasmus published the first printed Greek New Testament in 1516; however, the whole Apocalypse was not found in the original Greek, so he translated the Latin text into Greek. Hence, he published a translation of the Apocalypse.[2]

1. See John Beekman and John Callow, *Translating the Word of God;* Mildred Larson, *A Manual for Problem Solving in Bible Translation*.
2. See discussion in chaps. 25 and 26.

Literal translation. This is a specific kind of translation. It is one that expresses, as far as is possible, the exact meaning of the original words. It is a word-for-word translation and therefore is more rigid in its renderings than a mere translation. Consequently, a literal translation reveals the influence of Hebraisms and Greek idioms because it translates the precise word order rather than the idea contained in the original text. Examples of literal translation are Robert Young, *Young's Literal Translation of the Holy Bible*; *American Standard Version* (ASV); *New American Standard Bible* (NASB).

Transliteration. This is the rendering of the letters of one language into the corresponding letters of another. This results in many foreign words being introduced into a given language. To illustrate, the Greek words *angelos* and *euangelion* may be cited. *Angelos* is translated into English as "messenger," but it is transliterated as "angel." Likewise, *euangelion* is translated "gospel" and transliterated "evangel." It was the process of transliteration that rendered the Greek word *biblos*, through Latin and French, into English as "Bible" (see chap. 1).

Version

A version is a translation from the original language of a literary text into another language. In this sense, the King James Version and the Rheims-Douay Version are actually not even versions, the former being the fifth revision of Tyndale's Version and the latter being a translation of the Latin Vulgate. Both Tyndale's Version and Jerome's Vulgate, on the other hand, are versions of the original languages and qualify according to this definiton of a version because they were translated from the original languages. Modern versions, following this definition, are represented by the *New English Bible* (1961, 1970), *The Holy Bible: New International Version* (1973, 1978), the *New American Bible* (1970, 1983), and *TANAKH: A New Translation of THE HOLY SCRIPTURES According to the Traditional Hebrew Text* (1985).[3]

Revision, or Revised Version

Those works that are actually translated from one language, usually the original, and have been carefully and systematically reviewed and examined for the purpose of correcting errors or making other necessary emendations are called revisions or revised versions. Tyndale's "diligently corrected" edition of 1534, following an earlier printing of his New Testament made earlier that year by George Joye, the King James Version (1611), and the *New American Standard Bible* (1963, 1967, 1971) are examples of such a revision. Using

3. All of these versions are treated at length in chap. 31.

the caption "Revised Version," but actually meaning revision, is the Confraternity of Christian Doctrine edition of the New Testament (1941).

Recension

A recension is the product of critically and systematically revising a text, rather than its translation, although such works may not be called recensions. Some outstanding examples of recension are the Rheims-Douay-Challoner edition (1749/50) of the Rheims-Douay Bible (1582, 1609/10), *The Variorum Edition of the New Testament of Our Lord and Saviour Jesus Christ* (1880), the English Revised Version (1881, 1885), its counterpart, the *American Standard Version* (1901), the *Revised Standard Version* (1945, 1952) and *The New King James Version* (1979, 1980, 1982).

Paraphrase

Paraphrases are free translations or restatements of sentences, passages, or works in an attempt to keep the original sense of a text while expressing its meaning more fully or clearly than could be done by a more literal translation. Such treatments appear quite early and frequently in the history of English Bible translations[4] Among the most popular examples of twentieth-century paraphrases are J. B. Phillips, *The New Testament in Modern English* (1958) and Kenneth N. Taylor, *The Living Bible* (1971). *Good News for Modern Man: The New Testament in Today's English Version* is another form of paraphrase, for those who have English as a second language. Clarence Jordan's colloquial modern translation, *The Cotton Patch Version* (1968-1973), is designed for another level of communication.[5]

Abridgement

An abridgement is actually a selection and condensation of a larger text. The Reader's Digest Association has published *The Reader's Digest Bible: Condensed from the Revised Standard Version* (1982). It is not a paraphrase in the technical sense of the term because in it the actual RSV text is used rather than paraphrased.

Commentary

A commentary is simply the comments on, or explanation of, a text. With regard to the Scripture text, commentaries occur early in the history of Bible transmission. The Midrash (to be discussed later this chapter) is the earliest example of a Bible commentary. In recent times, some translations have tended to become "expanded" or "amplified" into something like commentaries on the biblical text. It is customary for such expanded or amplified

4. See "Appendix: A Short-Title Checklist of English Translations of the Bible."
5. These and other modern speech translations are discussed in chap. 32.

translations to appear in series before they are gathered into their final format. Kenneth S. Wuest, *The New Testament: An Expanded Translation* (1961), and Frances Siewert (ed.) *The Amplified Bible* (1971) are examples of such commentary translations. It is not unusual for translations to appear in commentaries on various books of the Bible. There are a great multitude of Bible commentaries available in many languages. They add valuable insights to verify and vindicate the texts of the Old and New Testaments as they appear in the manuscripts, lectionaries, inscriptions, and so on. It is important to note, however, that the major role in applying manuscript evidence to Scripture comes from versions of the Bible rather than from commentaries.

Distinctions

Ancient, Medieval, and Modern Works Distinguished

In dealing with the works bearing witness to the Bible, it is important to distinguish between their three general categories: ancient, medieval, and modern.[6]

Ancient works. Ancient works containing parts of the Old and/or New Testaments appeared before the period of the church councils began (c. A.D. 350).[7] These items include such works as the Samaritan Pentateuch, the Aramaic Targums, the Talmud, the Midrash, and the LXX. After the apostolic period, there were such works as Aquila's version, Symmachus's revision, Origen's Hexapla, and the Syriac versions.[8]

Medieval contributions. These cover those works containing parts of the Old and/or New Testaments from about 350 to about 1400.[9] Of primary concern in this group is the Vulgate of Jerome (c. 340-420). It was this work that dominated Bible translation and commentary production up to the Reformation period. It was the basis for such works as Caedmon's paraphrases, Bede's *Ecclesiastical History of the English Nation,* and Wycliffe's translation of the Bible. This latter work was the first complete Bible in English, and rounds out the medieval period.[10]

Modern counterparts. Modern counterparts containing parts of the Old and/or New Testaments actually begin with the work of William Tyndale (c. 1492-1536), who translated his version directly from the original languages.

6. See William E. Nix, "Versions, Ancient and Medieval," pp. 1768b-1777a.
7. See P. R. Ackroyd, ed., *The Cambridge History of the Bible,* vol. 1, *From the Beginnings to Jerome*.
8. For the material beginning with Aquila's version see discussion below. Latin versions, including Jerome's Vulgate, will be treated in chap. 29.
9. See G. W. Lampe, ed., *The Cambridge History of the Bible,* vol. 2, *The West from the Fathers to the Reformation*.
10. For a fuller treatment of the English translations of the Bible prior to the Authorized Version see chap. 30 and William E. Nix, "Theological Presuppositions and Sixteenth Century English Bible Translation," pp. 42-50, 117-24.

In fact, it is this version, completed by Myles Coverdale, that begins what may be properly called Protestant Bible translation, for it is at that point that the Latin Vulgate is set aside in favor of the original languages for all except Roman Catholics.[11] Since Tyndale's day, multitudes of renderings have been produced containing all or parts of the Old and/or New Testaments.[12]

Ancient Renderings Discussed

Two important facts about ancient versions merit treatment in the consideration of God's communication to man.

The purpose of the materials indicates their importance. These works were used to help disseminate the message of the autographs to those who were followers of the Lord. They were also used to assist God's people in keeping their religion pure. Therefore, such items as the Samaritan Pentateuch and the Targums were in use before the time of Christ. After the introduction of Christianity into the world, the new proselyting religion used such things as versions and commentaries to meet the needs of the church in its evangelization, expansion, and establishment.

Proximity of the ancient renderings to the autographs. This proximity also indicates their importance. These works take the Bible scholar back to the very threshold of the autographs. The Samaritan Pentateuch, for example, may be from the period of Nehemiah's rebuilding of Jerusalem, and although it is not really a version, it does indicate the need for careful study in tracing the true text. The LXX began to be translated in Alexandria, Egypt during the rule of Ptolemy II Philadelphus (285-246 B.C.). It is sufficient evidence to weaken the higher critical view of the evolutionary canon, even if no other material is considered. Some of the New Testament versions date from the middle of the second century A.D., quite close to the date of John's writings. As a result, the ancient versions, translations, paraphrases, and commentaries warrant consideration by the careful student of Scripture if he desires to rest his text upon the foundation of that material which may be scientifically verified and affirmed.

Delineation of Major Ancient Works

The Samaritan Pentateuch (SP)

The Samaritan Pentateuch[13] is not a version in the strict sense of the word. It is rather a manuscript portion of the text itself. It contains the five books of

11. This in turn helped lead to the decree enunciating the Vulgate as authoritative at the Council of Trent (1545-1563).
12. For expanded treatment of this point, see chaps. 31-32. See also Appendix and S. L. Greenslade, ed., *The Cambridge History of the Bible*, vol. 3, *The West from the Reformation to the Present Day*.
13. See William E. Nix on the Samaritan Pentateuch in "Bible Manuscripts," pp. 249b-250a.

Moses, and is written in a palaeo-Hebrew script, quite similar to that found on the Moabite Stone, the Siloam Inscription, the Lachish Letters, and some of the older biblical manuscripts from Qumran.[14] It was in 1616 that Pietro della Valle first discovered a form of the Samaritan text; however, it was known to such Fathers of the church as Eusebius of Caesarea and Jerome. Its textual tradition is independent of the Masoretic Text, the reasons for which a review of the history of the Samaritans will adequately illustrate.

The roots of the Samaritan race actually can be traced back to the time of David. It was during those years that the northern portion of the kingdom engineered an abortive revolt. After Solomon's death, the two kingdoms were divided, as Jeroboam wrested control of the ten northern tribes from the hands of Solomon's son Rehoboam. During the reign of Omri (c. 880-874 B.C.), a northern king, Samaria was made the capital (1 Kings 16:24), and the term *Samaritan* became applied to the entire kingdom rather than merely to the inhabitants of the city. In 732 B.C. the Assyrian Empire, under Tiglath-pileser III (745-727), conquered the northeast portion of Israel and followed its established policy of deportation of inhabitants and importation of other captive peoples into the area. Under Sargon II, in 721 B.C., the same procedure was followed after the Assyrians had captured the rest of Israel. Not all of the Israelites were deported, and intermarriage was imposed upon those who remained. This method was used as an attempt to guarantee that no revolt would ensue, as there would be an automatic denationalization and commingling of cultures (2 Kings 17:24—18:1). At first the colonists worshiped their own gods, but by or after the time of Judah's return from the Babylonian captivity, they appeared to want to follow Israel's God. However, they were rebuffed by the Jews and, as a result, opposed Israel's restoration (cf. Ezra 4:2-6; Neh. 5:11—6:19). Nevertheless, in about 432 B.C. the daughter of Sanballat was married to the grandson of the high priest Eliashib. This resulted in the expulsion of the couple, and provided the historical incident for the break between the Jews and the Samaritans (cf. Neh. 13:23-31). During the conflict the Jews overstressed the foreign element in the ancestry of the Samaritans, and called them Cutheans after the name of the Middle-Babylonia city, Cuthah, from whence the Assyrians imported the foreign element into Samaria (cf. 2 Kings 17:24, 30).

The Samaritans were still looked upon with scorn during New Testament times (John 4:3-45). They are still a separated group in Palestine; some 250 live in the original area in Nablus and about 50 reside in Tel Aviv. The Samaritan religion as a separate system of worship actually dates from the expulsion of the high priest's grandson, whose name was probably Manasseh,

14. F. F. Bruce, *The Books and the Parchments*, p. 129. See also Gleason L. Archer, Jr., *A Survey of Old Testament Introduction*, p. 44.

21. Samaritan high priest and Samaritan Pentateuch (Howard F. Vos)

in about 432 B.C.[15] At that time a copy of the Torah may have been taken to Samaria and placed in the temple built on Mount Gerizim at Shechem (Nablus), where the rival worship and priesthood were established. The fifth-century date may account for the palaeo-Hebrew script,[16] as well as categorization of books into only two groups: The Law, and what the Samaritans regarded as the noncanonic books.[17] Their adherence to the Torah, as well as their isola-

15. Josephus *Antiquities of the Jews* 9.7; also see 13.9. It should be noted that Josephus misplaces this incident, putting it in the period of Alexander the Great, a century later than Nehemiah's record. He does, however, name the priest, Manasseh, and relates that the temple at Shechem was built for him; he also refers to the Samaritans as Cutheans.
16. However, its script may be the result of a deliberate attempt to give it an archaistic character, as in the case of that manuscript attributed to Abishua, the great-grandson of Aaron. Cf. J. D. Douglas, ed., *The New Bible Dictionary,* p. 1257.
17. See chap. 14; also see R. Laird Harris, *Inspiration and Canonicity of the Bible,* p. 143.

tion from the Jews, has resulted in another textual tradition for the law. In addition, the Samaritan Pentateuch has illustrated the Jewish-Samaritan hostility quite effectively, as it emphasizes the importance of Mount Gerizim instead of Jerusalem, and inserts additional material into the text, for example, after Exodus 20:2-17 and Deuteronomy 5:6-21.

The Samaritan Pentateuch was first published in the Paris Polyglot (1645), and then in the London Polyglot (1657). It was quickly regarded as superior to the Masoretic text; then, after careful study, it was relegated to an inferior status, and has just recently been raised to a higher level of appreciation, though still secondary to the Masoretic Text.[18] The earliest manuscript of the Samaritan Pentateuch dates from the mid-eleventh century, and that is only a fragmentary part of a fourteenth-century parchment, the Abisha scroll.[19] The oldest codex of the Samaritan Pentateuch bears a note regarding its sale in A.D. 1149-50, but it is actually a much older manuscript. Another copy is owned by the New York Public Library dating from about 1232. The merits of this textual tradition may be seen in the fact that its approximately 6,000 variants from the Masoretic Text are relatively few, mainly orthographic, and rather insignificant (see chaps. 21 and 26). It also illustrates the purity of the Masoretic Text, as the latter was governed by much stricter rules than the LXX, with which it agrees against the Masoretic Text in some 1,900 instances.[20] Sir Frederic Kenyon rightly states that when the LXX and the Samaritan Pentateuch agree against the Masoretic Text, "they represent the original reading,"

> but when the *LXX* and the Masoretic Text are opposed, it is possible that, sometimes the one may be right and sometimes the other; but in any case the difference is one of *interpretation,* not of *text*. Then, again, there can be no doubt that the authors of the Septuagint made many actual mistakes of translation.[21]

Because this text tradition covers the best documented portion of the Old Testament, its contributions indicate cultural trends in the Hebrew social setting: the sectarian insertions of the Samaritans, the repetition of commands given by God, trends toward popularizing the Old Testament text, tendencies to modernize antique word forms, and the simplifying of difficult Hebrew sentence constructions.[22]

18. It was highly esteemed by Morinus, who first published the text in 1632; Wilhelm Gesenius condemned it as nearly worthless in 1815; Sir Frederic Kenyon, following Geiger and Kahle, renders it as valuable to the study of textual criticism. See Archer, p. 44.
19. See Bruce, pp. 127-29.
20. Archer, p. 44.
21. Sir Frederic Kenyon, *Our Bible and the Ancient Manuscripts,* pp. 91-92.
22. Cf. Archer, p. 44.

The Aramaic Targums

Origin of Targums. There is evidence that the scribes were making oral paraphrases of the Hebrew Scriptures into the Aramaic vernacular as early as the time of Ezra (Neh. 8:1-8). These paraphrases were not strictly translations, but were actually aids in understanding the archaic language forms of the Torah. The translator or interpreter involved in that work was called a *methurgeman.* The necessity for such helps arose because Hebrew was becoming less and less familiar to the ordinary people as a spoken language. By the close of the last centuries B.C., this gradual process had continued until almost every book in the Old Testament had its oral paraphrase or interpretation (Targum). During the early centuries A.D., these Targums were committed to writing, and an official text came to the fore, since the Hebrew canon, text, and interpretation had become well solidified before the rabbinical scholars of Jamnia (c. A.D. 90), and the expulsion of the Jews from Palestine in A.D. 135. The earliest Targums were apparently written in Palestinian Aramaic during the second century A.D.; however, there is evidence of Aramaic Targums from the pre-Christian period.[23] These early official Targums contained the Law and the Prophets, but the Writings were included in unofficial Targums in later times. It is interesting to note that a pre-Christian Targum of Job was written in Palestinian Aramaic and discovered in Cave XI at Qumran. Cave IV contained a Targum of the Pentateuch. These unofficial Aramaic Targums were superseded by official texts in the second century A.D. The official Palestinian Targums of the Law and Prophets were practically swallowed up by the Babylonian Aramaic Targums of the Law and Prophets during the third century. Targums on the Writings were apparently done on an unofficial basis, and have already been mentioned.

Outstanding Targums. During the third century A.D., there appeared in Babylonia an Aramaic Targum on the Torah. This Targum was possibly a recension of an earlier Palestinian tradition but may have originated in Babylonia. It has been traditionally ascribed to Onkelos (Ongelos), a name probably confused with Aquila.[24] Another Babylonian Aramaic Targum accompanies the Prophets (Former and Latter), and is known as the Targum of Jonathan ben Uzziel. It dates from the fourth century A.D., and is freer and more paraphrastic in its rendering of the text. Both of those Targums were read in the synagogues: Onkelos along with the Torah, which was read in its entirety, and Jonathan along with selections from the Prophets (*haphtaroth,* pl.). Because the Writings were not read in the synagogues, there was no

23. Bruce, pp. 133-45, where these materials are discussed and several quotations of the Targums are presented. Also cf. Harris, pp. 154-59.
24. Aquila is the name of the scholar who made a slavishly literal Greek translation of the Hebrew Old Testament as a substitute for the LXX (discussion below); the confusion of the names was undoubtedly enhanced by the rigid rendering of the text of this Targum, which is itself regarded as a recension by many scholars.

reason to have official Targums for them, although unofficial copies were used by individuals. During the middle of the seventh century A.D. a Targum of the Pentateuch appeared called the Pseudo-Jonathan Targum. It is a mixture of the Onkelos Targum and Midrash materials. The Jerusalem Targum also appeared at about 700, but has survived in fragments only. None of these Targums is important to the textual critic, but they are all rather significant to the study of hermeneutics, as they indicate the manner in which Scripture was interpreted by rabbinical scholars.

The Talmud

Following the first period of Old Testament scribal tradition, the period of the Sopherim (c. 400 B.C.-c. A.D. 200), there appeared a second, the Talmudic period (c. A.D. 100-c. 500), which was followed by the better-known Masoretic tradition (c. 500-c. 950). Ezra worked with the first of these groups, and they were regarded as the Bible custodians until after the time of Christ.[25] Between A.D. 100 and 500, the Talmud (instruction, teaching) grew up as a body of Hebrew civil and canonical law based on the Torah. The Talmud basically represents the opinions and decisions of Jewish teachers from about 300 B.C. to A.D. 500, and it consists of two main divisions: the Mishnah and the Gemara.

Mishnah. The *Mishnah* (repetition, explanation, teaching) was completed at about A.D. 200, and was a digest of all the oral laws from the time of Moses. It was regarded as the Second Law, the Torah being the First Law. This work was written in Hebrew, and it covered traditions as well as explanations of the oral law.

Gemara. The *Gemara* (to complete, accomplish, learn) was written in Aramaic rather than Hebrew, and was basically an expanded commentary on the Mishnah. It was transmitted in two traditions, the Palestinian Gemara (c. A.D. 200), and the larger and more authoritative Babylonian Gemara (c. A.D. 500).

The Midrash

The Midrash (textual study, textual interpretation) was actually a formal doctrinal and homiletical exposition of the Hebrew Scriptures written in Hebrew and Aramaic. Midrashim (plural) were collected into a body of material between 100 B.C. and A.D. 300. Within the Midrash were two major parts: the *Halakah* (procedure), a further expansion of the Torah only, and the *Haggada* (declaration, explanation), being commentaries on the entire Old Testament. These Midrashim differed from the Targums in that the former

25. See Archer, pp. 61-65, for a discussion of the contributions of each of these scribal traditions to Old Testament textual criticism.

were actually commentaries, whereas the latter were paraphrases. The Midrashim contain some of the earliest extant synagogue homilies on the Old Testament, including such things as proverbs and parables.

THE SEPTUAGINT (LXX), OR ALEXANDRIAN VERSION

Just as the Jews had abandoned their native Hebrew tongue for Aramaic in the Near East, so they abandoned the Aramaic in favor of Greek in such Hellenistic centers as Alexandria, Egypt. During the campaigns of Alexander the Great, the Jews were shown considerable favor. In fact, Alexander was sympathetic toward the Jews as a result of their policies toward him in the siege of Tyre (332 B.C.). He is even reported to have traveled to Jerusalem to do homage to their God. As he conquered new lands, he built new cities, which frequently had Jewish inhabitants, and frequently named them Alexandria.

After his great conquests and sudden death, Alexander's empire was divided into several dynasties: Ptolemaic Egypt, the Seleucid dynasty in Asia Minor, and Antigonid Macedonia, as well as several minor kingdoms. It was in Ptolemaic Egypt, named after Ptolemy I Soter, son of Lagus, that many Jews resided, in the city of Alexandria. Ptolemy I was governor of Egypt from 323 to 305, when he became king and reigned until his death in 285. He was succeeded by his son Ptolemy II Philadelphus (285-246 B.C.), who followed the Pharaonic practice of marrying his sister, Arsinoë II.

It was during the reign of Ptolemy Philadelphus that full political and religious rights were granted to the Jews. Egypt also underwent a tremendous cultural and educational program under the patronage of Arsinoë II, spearheaded by the founding of the Museum at Alexandria and the translation of great works into Greek. It was in that period (c. 250-c. 150 B.C.), that the Hebrew Old Testament was being translated into Greek—the first time it had ever been extensively translated. The leaders of Alexandrian Jewry had a standard Greek version produced, known as the LXX,[26] the Greek word for "seventy." It was undoubtedly translated during the third and/or second centuries B.C. and was purported to have been written as early as the time of Ptolemy II in a Letter of Aristeas to Philocartes (c. 130-100 B.C.).[27]

The Letter of Aristeas relates that the librarian at Alexandria persuaded Ptolemy to translate the Torah into Greek for use by Alexandrian Jews. As a

26. It should be noted that the term *Septuagint* applies strictly to the Pentateuch, which was probably the only portion of the Old Testament translated during the time of Ptolemy II Philadelphus. "The Jews might have gone on at a later time to authorize a standard text of the rest of the Septuagint, but ... they lost interest in the Septuagint altogether. With but few exceptions, every manuscript of the Septuagint which has come down to our day was copied and preserved in Christian, not Jewish, circles." Bruce, p. 150.
27. No one seems to date the LXX precisely, and the dates given range from before c. 150 B.C. Bruce, pp. 69-73, 146-62, states the general consensus of opinion as it is reflected in the text.

result, six translators were selected from each of the twelve tribes, and the translation was completed in just seventy-two days. The details of this story are undoubtedly fictitious, but the letter does relate the authentic fact that the LXX was translated for the use of the Greek-speaking Jews of Alexandria.

The Greek Old Testament of the Septuagint differs from the Hebrew canon in the quality of its translation as well as its contents and arrangement. In addition to the twenty-two books of the Hebrew Old Testament, the LXX contained a number of books that were never part of the Hebrew canon (see chap. 15 discussion). Apparently those books were circulated in the Greek-speaking world, but they were never part of the Hebrew canon. The quality of translation in the LXX reflects this situation and provides for several observations. (1) The LXX varies in excellence ranging from slavishly literal renditions of the Torah to free translations in the Writings.[28] (2) The LXX was not designed to have the same purpose as the Hebrew text, being used for public services in the synagogues rather than for scholarly or scribal purposes. (3) The LXX was the product of a pioneer venture in transmitting the Old Testament Scriptures, and an excellent example of such an effort. (4) The LXX was generally loyal to the readings of the original Hebrew text (as was observed in chapter 21), although some have maintained that the translators were not always good Hebrew scholars. The importance of the LXX may be observed in several dimensions. It bridged the religious gap between the Hebrew- and Greek-speaking peoples as it met the needs of Alexandrian Jews. It bridged the historical gap between the Hebrew Old Testament of the Jews and the Greek-speaking Christians who would use the LXX with their New Testament. It set a precedent for missionaries to make translations of the Scriptures into various languages and dialects. It bridges the textual criticism gap in its substantial agreement with the Hebrew Old Testament text (א, A, B, C, etc.). Although the LXX does not measure up to the excellence of the Hebrew Old Testament text, it does indicate the purity of the Hebrew text.

As a result of Jewish criticism during the early centuries of Christianity a reaction set in among the Jews against the Septuagint. That reaction has proved to be helpful to the textual critic, because it produced a new wave of translations and versions of the Old Testament. Some of the new works included the Greek translations known as Aquila's version and Symmachus's revision, and even led to the great work of textual criticism in the mid-third century, the *Hexapla* of Origen. Before proceeding on to those items, it seems advisable to recall that the foregoing ancient translations provide a valuable

28. Sir Frederic Kenyon, *The Text of the Greek Bible,* 3d ed., revised and augmented by A. W. Adams, pp. 16-19. Adams indicates that the text of Job in the original LXX is actually one-sixth shorter than its Hebrew counterpart. There are also large variations in Joshua, 1 Samuel, 1 Kings, Proverbs, Esther, and Jeremiah, as well as lesser variations in other books. The cause of these divergencies is one of the major difficulties of the Septuagint.

witness to the text of the Old Testament. For example, the LXX preserves a textual tradition from the third or second century B.C., while the Samaritan Pentateuchal tradition may date from the fifth century B.C. Although the Septuagint and the Samaritan Pentateuch, together with the Masoretic Text, form three separate textual traditions, when critically evaluated, they provide overwhelming support for the integrity of the Old Testament text. In fact, the two former texts provide some of the closest links to the autographs available to textual scholars, even closer than many Hebrew manuscript copies.

Greek versions of the Old Testament in the Christian era. F. F. Bruce has advanced two basic reasons for the rejection of the Septuagint by Jewish Bible scholars in the first centuries of the church. In the first place, it had been adopted by the Christians as their own version of the Old Testament, and was freely used in the propagation and defense of their faith. Second, about the year A.D. 100 a revised edition of the standard Hebrew text of the Old Testament was established, first the Pentateuch and later the remainder of the Old Testament. It was the end of this process of revision that resulted in the Masoretic Text.[29]

Opposition to the Septuagint found expression in the writings of such a man as Justin Martyr, in his *Dialogue with Trypho the Jew* (chap. 73) and his *First Apology* (chap. 41). Those works, written at about 140, followed the pattern of the New Testament writers in quoting from the LXX rather than the Hebrew text, and gave a basis of accusation by Trypho for not following the Hebrew text, which he regarded as authoritative. Thus, because there was no authority acceptable to both camps, and because Christianity was rapidly emerging from its Judaistic antecedents, the Jewish scholars decided to counteract the trend. As a result, several translations were attempted that would help preserve the Old Testament for future generations.

1. *Aquila's version* (c. 130) was a new translation of the Old Testament into Greek. It was done for Greek-speaking Jews, but not before some interesting events had taken place. Aquila is reported to have been a relative of the Emporer Hadrian. He is said to have moved to Jerusalem from Sinope as a civil servant, and there he was converted to Christianity. He was not able to extricate himself completely from some of his pre-Christian ideas and habits, and he was publicly rebuked by the elders of the church. As a result, he took offense, forsook Christianity, and turned to Judaism. Having become a Jewish proselyte, he studied under the famed Rabbi Aqiba and translated the Old Testament into Greek.

   Although much of that story is probably fictitious, Aquila was undoubtedly a Jewish proselyte from the coast of the Black Sea. He appears to have flourished during the first half of the second century, and he did make a new translation of the Hebrew Old Testament into Greek. He is

29. Bruce, pp. 150-52.

the Aquila wrongly associated with the Targum Onkelos as mentioned earlier in this chapter. His translation (version) was a rigidly slavish one; for although the words were Greek, the thought patterns and sentence structures followed the Hebrew rules of composition. This translation became the official Greek translation of the Scriptures used among the non-Christian Jews. Although it was made in the interest of Judaism, Aquila's version was highly regarded by Christian scholars like Origen and Jerome because of its fidelity to the Hebrew text.[30] Aquila's version has survived only in fragments and quotations.

2. *Theodotion's revision* (c. 180-190) occupies the next place of interest in Greek translations of the Old Testament. The exact place of this work is disputed, but it appears to have been a revision of an earlier Greek version: either of the LXX, possibly of Aquila's, or of another Greek version.[31] Theodotion is reported to have been a native of Ephesus, and either a Jewish proselyte or an Ebionite Christian.[32] His revision was much freer than Aquila's version, and in a few instances his work even replaced some of the older Septuagint renderings among Christians. Daniel, as translated by Theodotion, soon replaced the older LXX version, and even superseded it in Christian catalogs. It is possible that his rendering of Ezra-Nehemiah superseded the older LXX version, as may be seen by comparing it with the apocryphal 1 Esdras, which is a much looser and expanded version.[33]

30. Kenyon, *The Text of the Greek Bible,* p. 19.
31. Authorities are quite divided over this issue, as well as the date of Theodotion's revision. Merrill F. Unger, *Introductory Guide to the Old Testament,* p. 159, says it is a revision of the LXX, and dates it "early in the second century, possibly before Aquila." Archer, p. 42, dates it c. 180 or 190, but offers no solution to the problem of its source, as he writes that Theodotion's work is "a revision of an earlier Greek version, whether *LXX* or of some other is much disputed." He, incidentally, dates Aquila's work earlier. Kenyon, *Our Bible and the Ancient manuscripts,* p. 104, says: "But of recent years the view has been gaining ground that what Theodotion revised was not the Septuagint but another independent version. The reasons for this are that 'Theodotionic' readings are found in the New Testament. . . ." Bruce, p. 153, suggests that Theodotion "seems to have . . . taken an older Greek translation belonging to the pre-Christian era—one, indeed, which appears to lie behind some of the Old Testament quotations in the New Testament, particularly in Revelation—and revised it in accordance with the standard Hebrew text." He further states that the date for this revision is the late second century A.D. H. G. G. Herklots, *How Our Bible Came to Us,* pp. 117-19, 156, tends to agree with Bruce, and even adds that it was Theodotion, not Aquila, who was an Ephesian Jewish convert, and that his translation was "a free revision of the *LXX* rather than an independent translation (after H. B. Swete)." Bruce's position appears to be the most feasible, in that it is comprehensive enough to absorb the essential characteristics of the other views into a common and tenable position.
32. The Ebionites were a Jewish-oriented faction in the early church. They appeared very early as a legalistic group within the church, and may have been the element involved in the disputation with Paul and Barnabas that led to the Jerusalem council in Acts 15.
33. Cf. Kenyon, *Our Bible and the Ancient Manuscripts,* p. 57, and Bruce, p. 153.

3. *Symmachus's revision* (c. 170) seems to have followed Theodotion's in time, as well as theological commitment.[34] Symmachus was either an Ebionite, as Jerome thought, or a Samaritan convert to Judaism, as Epiphanius held. The purpose of Symmachus was to make an idiomatic Greek version and, as a result, he was at the opposite pole to Aquila. He was concerned with the sense of his rendering rather than the letter of the Hebrew. Nevertheless, Symmachus exhibited high standards of accuracy, and influenced later Bible translators, as is seen by Kenyon:

> The special feature of this translation is the literary skill and taste with which the Hebrew phrases of the original are rendered into good and idiomatic Greek. In this respect Symmachus approaches nearer than any of his rivals to the modern conception of a translator's duty; but he had less influence than any of them on the history of the Greek Bible. Curiously enough, he had more influence upon the Latin Bible: for Jerome made considerable use of him in the preparation of the Vulgate.[35]

4. *Origen's Hexapla* (c. 240-50). The work of Old Testament translation led to four Greek textual traditions by the third century A.D.: the Septuagint, and versions by Aquila, Theodotion, and Symmachus. This muddled state of affairs set the stage for the first really outstanding attempt at textual criticism, the *Hexapla* ("sixfold") by Origen of Alexandria (A.D. 185-254). Because of the many divergencies between the existing manuscripts of the LXX, the discrepancies between the Hebrew text and the LXX, and the attempts at revising the Old Testament Greek translations, Origen appears to have settled upon a course that would give the Christian world a satisfactory Greek text of the Old Testament. His work was essentially a recension rather than a version, as he corrected textual corruptions and attempted to unify the Greek text with the Hebrew. Thus his twofold aim was to show the superiority of the various revisions of the Old Testament over the corrupted LXX and to give a comparative view of the correct Hebrew and the divergent LXX. In this he followed the view that the Hebrew Old Testament was a sort of "inerrant transcript" of God's revealed truth to man.

   The arrangement of the *Hexapla* was in six parallel columns. Each column contained the Old Testament in the original Hebrew or a particular version, thus making the manuscript far too bulky to be marketable in ancient times.[36] The six columns were arranged as follows: column one, the Hebrew original; column two, the Hebrew original transliterated into Greek letters; column three, the literal translation of Aquila; column

34. Archer, p. 48, dates Symmachus's revision prior to Theodotion's, but his view tends to counter the mainstream of opinion.
35. Kenyon, *Our Bible and the Ancient Manuscripts,* p. 57.
36. Cf. Herklots, pp. 119-20.

four, the idiomatic revision of Symmachus; column five, Origen's own revision of the LXX; and column six, the Greek revision of Theodotion. In his *Hexapla* of Psalms, Origen added three additional columns, but actually only two of those are different translations. He also made a separate work called the *Tetrapla* ("fourfold"), that is, the *Hexapla* with columns one and two omitted.[37] This tremendous work has not survived the ravages of time, but Eusebius and Pamphilus did publish the fifth column, Origen's translation of the LXX with additions, which is extant in the fourth- or fifth-century Codex Sarravianus (G). This codex contains portions of Genesis through Judges, and is the only Greek edition of any significance preserved. There is a Syriac translation of the *Hexapla* dating from the seventh century, and some manuscripts of it have been preserved.[38]

The accomplishment of the *Hexapla* is observable in what it has discovered and disclosed in matters of textual criticism. Origen had discovered many corruptions, omissions, additions and transpositions in the copies of the Septuagint of his day. Often these discoveries were observed in comparing the various revisions of the Old Testament into Greek, but Origen was primarily concerned with bringing the texts of the LXX and the Hebrew Old Testament into greater conformity. Thus, his attention was primarily focused on the Hebrew text of column one and his personal translation of the LXX in column five. In disclosing the problems uncovered in his work, Origen used an elaborate system of critical markings. Thus the reader would be able to see the corruptions that were corrected, omissions and additions as indicated, and instances where transpositions of words were made in order to agree with the Hebrew text as then settled. When passages occurred in the Septuagint but not in the Hebrew, Origen would indicate it with an obelus (–), a horizontal diacritical stroke. When a passage occurred in the Hebrew but not in the Septuagint, Origen would insert that passage from Theodotion's version and mark its beginning with an asterisk (·⋇· or ⁜). To mark the close of either of these corrections, he would insert a metobelus (⋎).[39] When transposed passages of short length differing from the Hebrew and other versions were observed, he would permit them to remain in their setting, but would mark them with an asterisk and obelus combined (·⋇·– or ⁜–) and use the metobelus at the close. If the transposed passage were

37. Eusebius *Ecclesiastical History* 6.16. Loeb ed., 2:51-53.
38. See Archer, p. 46; Kenyon, *Our Bible and the Ancient Manuscripts,* p. 59; Bruce, p. 156; Herklots, pp. 119-23.
39. Kenyon, *Our Bible and the Ancient Manuscripts,* pp. 58-59; however, Archer, p. 46, indicates that the insertion into the LXX would be from any of the other versions, not just Theodotion's. The various signs are given differently in Herklots, p. 120. There, they are the obelus (– or –– or ÷), the asterisk (*), and the metobelus (: or ⁄· or ⁒).

long, the Hebrew order would be restored in order to gain better conformity with the latter. Although the task was of monumental significance, it is well for the modern textual critic to observe the difference between his own and Origen's objectives, as has been so succinctly stated by Kenyon:

> For Origen's purpose, which was the production of a Greek version corresponding as closely as possible with the Hebrew text as then settled, this procedure was well enough; but for ours, which is the recovery of the original Septuagint text as evidence for what the Hebrew was before the Masoretic text, it was most unfortunate, since there was a natural tendency for his edition to be copied without the critical symbols, and thus for the additions made by him from Theodotion to appear as part of the genuine and original Septuagint.[40]

This unfortunate situation did in fact take place, and the transcribed Septuagint text without the diacritical markings led to the dissemination of a corrupted Greek Old Testament text, rather than the achievement of a Septuagint version in conformity with the Hebrew text of the day.

F. F. Bruce writes, "If Origen's *Hexapla* had survived entire, it would be a treasure beyond price."[41] That is certainly true, as it would have given the standard Hebrew text of the third century A.D., have aided in the disputation over Hebrew pronunciation, and have given information about the Greek versions of the Old Testament in Origen's day. Nevertheless, the entire text has not survived. It was housed in the library at Caesarea until the Saracens conquered and burned the city in 638. The *Hexapla* manuscript was probably destroyed at that time, although the fifth column has survived, largely through the Syriac translation of Bishop Paul of Tella (c. 616), known as the Syro-Hexaplar text, and its subsequent faithful reproduction in an eighth-century copy that is housed in the museum at Milan.

5. *Other recensions of the Septuagint*. Early in the fourth century, Eusebius of Caesarea and his friend Pamphilus published their own editions of Origen's fifth column. Hence, they advanced the version of the LXX that became the standard in many places. In addition to their efforts, two other scholars attempted to revise the Greek text of the Old Testament. The first of those was Hesychius, an Egyptian bishop martyred in 311. His recension is preserved only in the quotations from the text made by church writers in Egypt. As a result, the recovery of the recension of Hesychius is dependent upon quotations of such Egyptians as Cyril of Alexandria (d. 444). The works of Chrysostom (d. 407) and Theodoret (d. c. 457) may be used to recover still another recension of the Old Testa-

40. Kenyon, *Our Bible and the Ancient Manuscripts,* p. 59.
41. Bruce, p. 155.

ment text: the Lucian Recension. Lucian, a resident of Samosata and Antioch, was also martyred in A.D. 311. Thus, by the time of Jerome, as Henry Barclay Swete observes, Christians could read the "Old Testament in the recension of Lucian, if they lived in North Syria, Asia Minor, or Greece; in that of Hesychius, if they belonged to the Delta or the valley of the Nile; in Origen's Hexaplaric edition, if they were residents at Jerusalem or Caesarea."[42]

Summary and Conclusion

The various ancient translations of the Old Testament provide the textual scholar with valuable witnesses to the text. The Septuagint, for example, preserves a textual tradition from the third century B.C., and the Samaritan Pentateuchal tradition may date from the fifth century B.C. These and the Masoretic Text provide three Old Testament textual traditions, which, when critically evaluated, supply an overwhelming support for the integrity of the Old Testament text. The witness of the Samaritan Pentateuch, and especially that of the LXX with its revisions and recensions, is by no means a minor one in the confirmation of that textual integrity.

42. Henry Barclay Swete, *An Introduction to the Old Testament in Greek*, p. 85.

28
Translations Containing Both the Old and New Testament Texts

Syriac Versions of the Old and New Testaments

Among the multitudes in Jerusalem on the day of Pentecost were "Parthians and Medes and Elamites, and residents of Mesopotamia, Judea and Cappadocia, Pontus and Asia, Phrygia and Pamphylia, Egypt and the districts of Libya around Cyrene, and visitors from Rome, both Jews and proselytes, Cretans and Arabians" (Acts 2:9-11). Those individuals would undoubtedly need the Scriptures in their own tongues if they were to be able to study them. For this reason some believe that the Syriac version of the Old Testament dates from the centuries before Christ, whereas others hold that the version was translated during the early Christian centuries. It is probable that the Old and New Testaments stemmed from separate traditions at first, and were later brought together. Therefore, it is best to treat these traditions separately.

The Language and the Early Church

The Syriac (Aramaic) language of the Old Testament, and indeed of the gospels, was comparable to the Koine in Greek and the Vulgar in Latin. It was the common language of the market. Because the Palestinian Jews of our Lord's time undoubtedly spoke Aramaic, the language common to that entire region, it is reasonable to assume that the Jews in nearby Syria also spoke it. In fact, Josephus relates the proselyting work of Jews in the first century in the areas east of ancient Nineveh, near Arbela.[1] This movement of Judaism in the middle of the first century paved the way for the spread of Christianity into Syria. It was at Antioch of Syria, the third-largest city of the Roman Empire, that the followers of Jesus were first called Christians (Acts 11:26).

1. Josephus *Antiquities of the Jews* 20.2, pp. 1ff., tells of the conversion of Helena, queen of Adiabene, and her son Izates to Judaism.

From Antioch Christianity spread into central Asia, India, and even as far as China. The basic language of this branch of Christianity was Syriac, or what F. F. Bruce has called "Christian Aramaic." It was actually a dialect of Aramaic that differed from the Aramaic of the Palestinian Jews who wrote in the Western dialect of that language.

The Syriac Peshitta

Once the church began to move out from Syria in a missionary effort, the need for a version of the Bible in the language of those parts made itself urgently manifest.[2] Thus, contemporary to the formation of the Jewish Targum in Aramaic, the Christians were translating the Bible into a more usable dialect of the same language, although they used a distinctive variation of the Aramaic alphabet.[3] The Syriac Bible corresponding to the Latin Vulgate is known as the Peshitta ("simple"). Although this name dates from the ninth century and is of uncertain origin,[4] the text of the Old Testament Peshitta undoubtedly stems from the period between the mid-second and early third centuries. It appears to have been the work of many hands, and possibly was done in the area at or near Edessa.

The translation of the Old Testament was probably from the Hebrew language, but was later revised in conformity with the LXX. The Syriac Pentateuch resembles the Targum of Onkelos,[5] following the Masoretic Text, but subsequent books demonstrate a rather unsystematic and not too thorough influence from the LXX. Where the Syriac Peshitta follows the Masoretic Text, it gives valuable aid to securing that text, but it is not too reliable as an independent witness to the text of the Old Testament. One important contribution of the Peshitta comes in the study of canonicity, as it omits the apocryphal books of the Alexandrian Canon (see discussion in chap. 15).

The standard Syriac edition of the New Testament is generally believed to stem from a fifth-century revision by Rabbula, the bishop of Edessa (411-35). His revision was actually a recension of earlier Syriac versions that were brought into an approximation of the Greek manuscripts then in use in Constantinople (Byzantium). It, plus the Christian recension of the Syriac Old Testament, has come to be known as the Peshitta. Rabbula ordered that a copy of his recension be placed in every church in his diocese, which led to its widespread circulation during the middle and late fifth century. Hence,

2. The role of Antioch, Syria, is readily seen in such passages as Acts 6:5; 11:26; 13:1; etc.
3. Cf. F. F. Bruce, *The Books and the Parchments,* p. 193; also see Gleason L. Archer, Jr., *A Survey of Old Testament Introduction,* pp. 51-52.
4. Merrill F. Unger, *Introductory Guide to the Old Testament,* p. 168, suggests that the name Peshitta (simple) was presumably used to denote its character in contrast to the complex symbols used in Syro-Hexaplaric version.
5. Paul E. Kahle, *The Cairo Geniza,* p. 273, states that "there can be no doubt that the closest contact exists between the Syriac Pentateuch and the Old Palestinian Targum."

while there are many witnesses for the Peshitta, they are not nearly so authoritative in reclaiming the Bible text as are some earlier Old Syriac witnesses. This fact is largely because of their being brought into conformity with the Byzantine text-type.[6] It is important to note at this point that the Peshitta was "the 'authorized version' of the two main opposed branches of Syriac Christianity, the Nestorians and the Jacobites, indicating that it must have been firmly established by the time of their final cleavage, well before the fifth century."[7]

The Syro-Hexaplaric Version

As has been mentioned in chapter 27, the Syro-Hexaplar text was a Syriac translation of the fifth column of Origen's *Hexapla*. This work was done under the sponsorship of Bishop Paul of Tella in about 616. This work has never actually taken root in the Syrian churches, partly due to its excessively literal rendering of the Greek, in violation of Syriac idiom. The manuscript portions that have been preserved are in the Codex Mediolanensis, and consist of 2 Kings, Isaiah, the Twelve, Lamentations, and the poetical books (except Psalms). It is their literal character that makes the Syro-Hexaplar manuscripts valuable aids in ascertaining the correct text of the *Hexapla,* especially because Origen's text was never published in its entirety, and because it was probably destroyed in the burning of Caesarea by the Muslims in 638. The Pentateuch and the historical books were in existence as late as 1574, but have subsequently disappeared. The text is basically Byzantine, with marked Western influences.

The Diatessaron of Tatian (c. 170)

Tatian was an Assyrian Christian and follower of Justin Martyr. After the death of Justin in Rome (A.D. 165), Tatian was excommunicated for doctrinal abberations (c. 172) and he returned to the East, where he died. During that time his "scissors and paste" harmony of the gospels known as the *Diatessaron* (from the Greek word having a musical meaning, "through the four") began to be circulated in Syria. About the same time, Christianity took root in Edessa, and a notable convert named Bar Daisan began to write learned

6. See chaps. 24-26 for detailed presentation of textual families and their relative merit in terms of textual criticism. At this point, however, it is noted that of the 250 or more manuscripts of the Syriac Peshitta, the earliest date from the fifth century. According to Sir Frederic G. Kenyon, *The Text of the Greek Bible,* p. 58, one biblical manuscript in Syriac at the British Museum is dated A.D. 464. Bruce M. Metzger, *The Early Versions of the New Testament: Their Origin, Transmission and Limitations,* pp. 48-51, lists eleven dated Syrian MSS from the 5th-6th centuries and identifies nearly fifty other Peshitta manuscripts that have been assigned to the sixth century on the basis of palaeographical considerations.
7. Bruce, pp. 194-95. Metzger, *The Early Versions of the New Testament,* pp. 48-9, concurs that the Peshitta version antedates this division.

treatises in his native tongue (Syriac). In addition, another center of early Syrian Christianity arose in Arbela, east of the Tigris. The large concentration of Jews in that area provided impetus for Christian missions in the region, and for the translation of Scripture into Syriac.[8] Tatian's work is known mainly through indirect references,[9] and may have been originally written in Syriac, a language similar to the Aramaic of the New Testament, or more likely it was written in Greek and subsequently translated into Syriac.[10] It was the widespread popularity of the *Diatessaron* that probably caused Rabbula and Theodoret, bishop of Cyrrhus in 423, to abolish its use in the early fifth century. That attitude was undoubtedly based upon the fact that Tatian belonged to the heretical sect of the Encratites, as identified by Eusebius.

> He established his own type of doctrine, telling stories of invisible Aeons, like the followers of Valentinus, and rejecting marriage as corruption and fornication similarly to Marcion and Saturninus. And as his own contribution, denied the salvation of Adam. But a little later a certain man named Severus strengthened the above mentioned heresy, and is the reason why those who have sprung from it obtained the name Severiani from him.... Their former leader Tatian composed in some way a combination and collection of the gospels, and gave this the name of *The Diatessaron,* and this is still extant in some places....[11]

Tatian's work was so popular that Ephraem, a Syrian Father, wrote a commentary on it. Nevertheless, Theodoret had all the copies (about two hundred) of the *Diatessaron* destroyed because he felt the potential danger of their corrupting influence on the Christians who would use Tatian's text. In its place, Theodoret presented another translation of the gospels of the four evangelists. Ephraem's commentary and the *Diatessaron* in Syriac are both lost, but an Armenian translation of the former has survived,[12] as have two Arabic translations of the latter. Hence, while the original *Diatessaron* would bear heavily on New Testament textual criticism, its secondary and tertiary witness merely supports primary materials, as influence is evident from both Eastern and Western texts.

The Old Syriac Manuscripts

The *Diatessaron* was not the only form of the gospels used among the

8. Metzger, *The Early Versions of the New Testament,* pp. 6-8.
9. A fragment of Tatian's *Diatessaron* was found at Dura-Europos. Cf. Bruce, pp. 195-200.
10. Cf. J. Harold Greenlee, *An Introduction to New Testament Textual Criticism,* pp. 48-49; Alexander Souter, *The Text and Canon of the New Testament,* C. S. C. Williams, rev., pp. 50-52; also see Bruce, pp. 196-98; and Sir Frederic G. Kenyon, *Handbook to the Textual Criticism of the New Testament,* pp. 221-26.
11. Eusebius *Ecclesiastical History* 4.29. Loeb ed., 1:397.
12. See Bruce M. Metzger, *The Text of the New Testament,* pp. 91-92, and his "Tatian's *Diatessaron* and a Persian Harmony of the Gospels," in *Chapters in the History of New Testament Textual Criticism,* pp. 97-120, for an extensive treatment of this subject matter.

Syrian churches. Among the scholars, at least, there was a tendency to read the gospels in separate forms. Even before the time of Tatian, there were quotations of the Bible from the Syriac by such writers as Hegesippus, a Jewish scholar turned Christian, during the second century. This Old Syriac text of the gospels, representative of the Western text-type, has survived in two manuscripts: a parchment known as the Curetonian Syriac and a palimpsest manuscript known as the Sinaitic Syriac. These gospels were called "The Gospel of the Separated Ones," indicating that they were separated, not interwoven, and also suggesting that other "harmonies" were in existence. The Curetonian is a fifth-century manuscript named after William Cureton, the man who discovered it in 1858. The Sinaitic is an earlier manuscript, fourth century, although it is sometimes corrupted where the Curetonian manuscript is not. This manuscript was found in 1892 by Mrs. Agnes Smith Lewis and her twin sister, Mrs. Margaret Dunlop Gibson, in the monastery of St. Catherine, where Tischendorf had earlier discovered Codex א . Although there are differences in these manuscripts, they are representatives of the same version of a text that "dates from the close of the second or beginning of the third century."[13] No Old Syriac texts of the remainder of the New Testament have survived, though they have been reconstructed.[14] With this information, it would appear that the Old Syriac is much more valuable in terms of textual reconstruction than any other Syriac versions.

Other Syriac Versions

There are other Syriac versions that require comment, but they are all later versions than those already discussed, and not nearly so significant to the textual critic. In 508 a new Syriac New Testament was completed, which included the books omitted by the Peshitta (2 Peter, 2 John, 3 John, Jude, and Revelation). This version was actually a Syriac revision of the whole Bible by the rural bishop *(chorepiskopos)* Polycarp, under the direction of Zenaia (Philoxenus), Jacobite bishop of Mabbug (Hierapolis), in eastern Syria. Sir Frederic Kenyon states:

> ... [this] version was written in free and idiomatic Syriac, being the most literary in form of all the translations of the New Testament into this language. The Greek text underlying it was that of the great mass of later manuscripts, which (as is abundantly clear from other evidence also) was firmly established as the standard type of text in the Greek-speaking Church at the time when Polycarp prepared this version of the Scriptures for Philoxenus.[15]

13. Metzger, *The Text of the New Testament*, p. 69.
14. Metzger, *The Early Versions of the New Testament*, pp. 36-39. These reconstructions are based on citations of the text found in the writings of the Fathers of the Eastern church.
15. Kenyon, pp. 165-66. However, experts disagree on this point; e.g., Vaganay, Souter, and Vööbus, cf. Greenlee, p. 49 n. 4. Also see Metzger, *The Early Versions of the New Testament*, pp. 63-65.

This text is known as the Philoxenian Syriac version, and it reveals that it was the sixth century before the Syrian church accepted all the books of the New Testament as canonical.

In 616 Thomas of Harkel (Heraclea), also Bishop of Mabbug, reissued the Philoxenian version. He either merely added some marginal notes or thoroughly revised the earlier edition, making it much more literal, a problem much too complex to be handled at this point.[16] This version is known as the Harklean version, although some scholars view it as another edition of the Philoxenian version. Its "apparatus of Acts is the second most important witness to the Western text, being surpassed in this respect only by Codex Bezae."[17] The Old Testament portion of that work was done by Paul of Tella.

A final Syriac text is known as the Palestinian Syriac version. This translation is known mainly from a lectionary of the gospels, as no book of the New Testament exists complete in this version. The text probably dates from the fifth century, and it is in fragmentary form only. The present witness to the text is seen in three eleventh- and twelfth-century lectionaries, and these follow the pattern of the earlier Greek lectionaries.

Coptic Versions

Coptic is the latest form of ancient Egyptian writing. Prior to Christian times, Egyptian writing was done in hieroglyphic, hieratic, and demotic scripts. The Greek language, with seven demotic characters added, became the written mode with the beginning of the Christian era. The name *Coptic* seems to come from the Greek term *Aigyptos,* probably a corrupted form of the Egyptian word for "the house of Ptah." The Arabic derivative was *Kibt,* which gave rise to the European form of the name. This system of writing came to be called Coptic, and the Bible was translated into its several dialects.[18]

Sahidic (Thebaic)

The Coptic dialect of Upper (southern) Egypt was Sahidic. In the region of Thebes, virtually all of the New Testament was translated into Sahidic by the beginning of the fourth century. As early as the third century, portions of the New Testament were translated into this dialect. Manuscripts in this dialect represent the earliest Coptic versions of the New Testament, as may be seen by the fact that Pachomius (c. 292-c. 346), the great organizer of Egyptian

16. See sources mentioned in footnotes 29 and 30 of this chapter for materials pertaining to this matter.
17. Metzger, *The Text of the New Testament,* p. 71.
18. The best treatment of the following materials may be found in Metzger, *The Early Versions of the New Testament,* pp. 99-152; Metzger, *The Text of the New Testament,* pp. 78-81; and H. G. G. Herklots, *How Our Bible Came to Us,* pp. 72-74.

monasticism, required his followers to be diligent in the study of Scripture. Because the Sahidic was so early in Egypt, its evidence to text-type carries considerable weight. Basically, its underlying text is Alexandrian, although the Gospels and Acts follow the Western type. It is thus a representative of a mixed or combined text-type.[19]

Bohairic (Memphic)

In Lower (northern) Egypt, around the Delta, another dialect of Coptic was used along with the Greek. This was in the area of Alexandria, and its centrality in Christian history is reflected by the fact that Bohairic became the basic dialect of the Egyptian church. The Bohairic versions appear somewhat later than the Sahidic, probably due to the continuing widespread use of Greek in the Delta area, and have survived only in late manuscripts. The only early manuscript is the Bodmer papyrus codex of the gospel of John (Papyrus Bodmer III). Although badly mutilated at the beginning, it is in much better condition following John 4; and it casts added light on two textual problems: John 5:3*b*-4 and John 7:53—8:11.[20] "The Greek prototype of the Bohairic version appears to be closely related to the Alexandrian text-type."[21]

Middle Egyptian Dialects

In the region between Thebes and Alexandria is the third area of a Coptic dialect. Fragments of these "Middle Egyptian" dialects, which are classified as Fayumic, Achmimic, and sub-Achmimic,[22] have been discovered. No New Testament book is extant in these dialects, but John is almost complete. One fourth-century papyrus codex in the Fayumic dialect contains John 6:11—5:11, and is closer to the Sahidic than the Bohairic text.[23] Thus, these manuscripts appear to follow the Alexandrian text-type. The Old Testament in both dialects follows the LXX.

Other Versions

Ethiopic Version

The time and circumstances of the planting of the church in Ethiopia are difficult to ascertain. An account in Acts 8:26-39 speaks of the conversion of the Ethiopian chamberlain of the Candace (or queen) of Ethiopia and is

19. See Metzger, *The Early Versions of the New Testament,* pp. 133-37.
20. See chap. 26 for a lengthy discussion of the textual problem of John 7:53—8:11.
21. Ibid., pp. 137-38; Metzger, *The Text of the New Testament,* p. 80.
22. Metzger, *The Early Versions of the New Testament,* pp. 138-41; Greenlee, p. 51.
23. This codex is housed at the University of Michigan, Ann Arbor, and its affinities to the Sahidic are two for every one to the Bohairic. Cf. Elinor M. Husselman, *The Gospel of John in Fayumic Coptic.*

often viewed as bearing on the introduction of Christianity into Ethiopia, but there are conflicting traditions that suggest that the evangelization of Ethiopia was carried out by different apostles, such as Matthew, Bartholomew, or Andrew. Apart from a brief comment by Origen, the first more or less firm literary evidence for the presence of Christianity in Ethiopia comes from the end of the fourth century, and it relates that this evangelization occurred during the time of Constantine the Great (c. 330). Whatever the case, as Christianity moved into Ethopia, a need arose for another translation of the Bible.[24]

Although there is no authoritative statement on the subject, the Old Testament appears to have been translated from the Greek into Ethiopic beginning in the fourth century A.D., with revisions made in light of the Hebrew text. This translation seems to have been completed by the seventh century, at which time the New Testament was translated. The complete translation was probably done by Syrian monks who moved into Ethiopia during the Monophysite Controversy in the fifth and sixth centuries and the rise of Islam in the seventh and eighth centuries. That their influence was great is seen in the fact that this church is Monophysite in the present day.[25] There have been two recensions of the Ethiopic New Testament, "one in the fifth, the other in the twelfth century."[26] The text of the Ethiopic version was later influenced by Coptic and Arabic versions, and may itself have been based on Syriac rather than Greek manuscripts. These manuscripts were undoubtedly of fourth- or fifth-century heritage, and thus reduce the Ethiopic to a minor position in textual study, as they bear the marks of their admixture, although they are basically of Byzantine origin. The Old Testament includes the noncanonical 1 Enoch (1 Enoch 1:9 is quoted in Jude 14-15)[27] and the Book of Jubilees. These books indicate the breadth of the accepted books included in the Ethiopic version, and their secondary character as translations, even though they were revised in accordance with Hebrew manuscripts. There are over one hundred manuscript copies extant, but none are earlier than the thirteenth century, and those are from late sources. Although those little-known manuscripts may deserve more thorough study, it is probable that they will remain neglected because of their late date.

Gothic Version

It is not clear exactly when Christianity penetrated into the Germanic

24. Metzger, *The Early Versions of the New Testament*, pp. 215-23.
25. That the Coptic church exerted a profound influence on its Ethiopic counterpart may be seen from the Coptic influence in later Ethiopic manuscripts.
26. A. T. Robertson, *An Introduction to the Textual Criticism of the New Testament*, p. 129; but Greenlee, p. 52, says it was the fourteenth century.
27. This book is to be distinguished from 2 and 3 Enoch. See Bruce, p. 171. Also see Kenyon, pp. 13-19, for a discussion of the distinctions in the identity of these books as they appear in various textual formats.

tribes in the regions of the Rhine and Danube rivers. It is certain that the area was evangelized prior to the Council at Nicea (325), because Theophilus, bishop of the Goths, was in attendance. The Goths were among the chief Germanic tribes, as their role in the events of the fifth century clearly indicates. In the area of the lower Danube, the Ostrogoths were the first of those tribes to be evangelized. Their second bishop, Ulfilas (311-381), the "Apostle of the Goths," led his converts into the land now known as Bulgaria. There he translated the Greek Bible into Gothic. That enterprise was of great moment, especially if Ulfilas did what is generally attributed to him, namely, create a Gothic alphabet and reduce the spoken language to written form.[28] At any rate, his translation of the Old Testament was a remarkably faithful rendering of the Lucian recension. Although this work was done in the mid-fourth century (c. 350), very little remains of his Old Testament.[29] The books of Samuel and Kings were not translated because the translator believed that those books were "too warlike to be transmitted" to the Gothic tribes. Much more remains of the New Testament translation made by Ulfilas, the earliest known literary monument in the Germanic dialect, but it is not found in a single complete extant manuscript. This translation adheres closely, almost literally, to the Greek text of the Byzantine type, and tells little to the textual critic. The value of the Gothic version is in the fact that it is the earliest literary work in the Germanic group, to which English belongs.[30] There are five fragmentary manuscripts of the Gothic version, the most famous of which is the Codex Argenteus, "the silver codex." It was written on purple vellum in silver and some gold letters. All the other manuscripts in Gothic are palimpsests, except a vellum leaf of a bilingual Gothic-Latin codex. Gothic, like Coptic, is a language whose script was expressly devised for the writing of the Scriptures. All the manuscripts of the Gothic version date from the fifth and sixth centuries A.D., and they provide a severely literal rendition of the gospels in affinity with the Syrian or Antiochian form of text.[31]

Armenian Version

As the Syrian churches carried out their work of evangelization in the early centuries, they contributed to several secondary translations of the Bible. Those secondary translations are so named because of the fact that they were not translated from the original languages but from translations of the originals. One of the foremost is the Armenian, although not everyone holds that it is a translation of a translation. Armenia claims the honor of being the first kingdom to accept Christianity as its official religion. The

28. Metzger, *The Early Versions of the New Testament,* pp. 375-78.
29. According to Archer, p. 52, only Nehemiah 5-7 remains in Codex Argenteus.
30. Bruce, p. 216. Also see discussion in chap. 30.
31. Metzger, *The Early Versions of the New Testament,* pp. 375-94; Metzger, *The Text of the New Testament,* p. 82.

Scriptures were soon translated into that language. There are two basic traditions concerning the origin of the Armenian version. One attributes it to St. Mesrob (d. 439), a soldier turned missionary who created a new alphabet to assist Sahak (Isaac the Great, 390-439) in translating the Bible from the Greek text. The other view claims that Sahak translated it from the Syriac text. Although there is merit in both views, the latter best fits the situation because it stems from the nephew and disciple of Mesrob himself.[32] The earliest Armenian versions were revised prior to the eighth century in accordance with "trustworthy Greek codices" that were brought from Constantinople following the Council at Ephesus (431). This revision gained a dominant position over the Old Armenian by the eighth century, and is still the common Armenian text in use today.[33] It is the revised text that has been preserved, as the oldest manuscripts from the ninth century. Therefore, the Armenian text does not weigh heavily in matters of textual criticism, for its text-type is either Caesarean or Byzantine. This matter has not yet been clearly determined, but the gospels tend toward the Caesarean text.[34] The Armenian Old Testament was first translated in the early fifth century and manifests a marked influence from the Syriac Peshitta, as its rendition of the Hexaplaric recension was revised in accordance with the Peshitta.

Georgian (Iberian) Version

Georgia, the mountainous area between the Black and Caspian seas, north of Armenia, received the Christian message during the fourth century, and had its own Bible translation about the middle of the fifth. The message of Christianity proceeded from Armenia into Georgia, and so did the translation of the Bible.[35] Accordingly, if the Armenian Old Testament were a translation of the LXX or the Syriac Peshitta, and the New Testament were a translation of the Old Syriac, they would themselves be secondary translations, and the Georgian version (translated from the Armenian) would be a tertiary work at best. If the Armenian versions were based on the originals, the Georgian version would still be a secondary translation, that is, a translation of a translation. The great majority of manuscripts of the Georgian Bible indicate that it follows the same textual tradition as the Armenian. Its alphabet, like the Armenian and Gothic, was developed expressly for the purpose of Bible transmission.

32. Metzger, *The Text of the New Testament*, pp. 82-83; also see Bruce, p. 212; Souter, pp. 65-67; Robertson, p. 129, has attributed a Greek translation to Mesrob, and a Syriac translation to Sahak.
33. Greenlee, p. 51.
34. Bruce, p. 212; Metzger, *The Early Versions of the New Testament*, pp. 153-81; Metzger, *The Text of the New Testament*, p. 83; Souter, pp. 65-67.
35. Metzger, *The Early Versions of the New Testament*, pp. 182-214.

Nestorian Versions

When the Nestorians were condemned at the Council at Ephesus (431), their founder, Nestorius (d. c. 451), was placed in a monastery and a compromise brought many of his supporters into the camp of his opponents. The Persian Nestorians broke away, however, and became a separate, schismatic church. They spread into central and even east Asia in the succeeding period, and translated the Scriptures into several languages as they went, for example, the so-called Sogdian versions.[36] Their translations were based upon the Syriac Scriptures rather than the Hebrew and Greek Testaments. There are scant remains of their work, all of which date from the ninth to tenth centuries and later, but this is late and tertiary evidence of the text. The devastating work of Tamerlane, "the Scourge of Asia," almost exterminated the Nestorians toward the close of the fourteenth century.

Arabic Version

Subsequent to the rise of Islam (after the *hejirah,* flight of Muhammad, 622), the Bible was translated into Arabic from the Greek, Syriac, Coptic, Latin, and various combinations of those versions. It is not known who made the first Arabic translation of the Scriptures, and various traditions have assigned the honor to different persons.[37] The earliest of the numerous Arabic translations appears to stem from the Syriac, possibly the Old Syriac, near the time of Islam's emergence as a major force (c. 720). Muhammad (570-632), the founder of Islam, knew of the gospel story through the oral tradition only, and that was based on Syriac sources. One Old Testament in Arabic was the result of a translation by the Jewish scholar Saadia Gaon (c. 930). Other than that, the Old Testament was not standardized in its Arabic translations. In terms of textual criticism, the Arabic manuscripts, which range from the ninth to the thirteenth centuries, offer little, if any, assistance to the textual critic. They are secondary translations, except the Old Testament.

Slavonic Version

In the middle of the ninth century a Moravian empire was formed in east-central Europe. That kingdom espoused Christianity, and its church leaders used Latin in their liturgy. But the natives were not familiar with Latin, and Rostislav, the founder of the kingdom, requested that Slavonic priests be sent to conduct the liturgy in the language of the people. At that time only one native tongue was spoken in the region of eastern Europe, namely Slavonic. In response to Rostislav's request, the Emperor Michael III sent two

36. Metzger, *The Early Versions of the New Testament,* pp. 279-82, identifies Sogdian as a Middle Iranian (Persian) tongue that played in central Asia the same role as Greek played in the ancient world, but on a much smaller scale.
37. Ibid., pp. 257-68, discusses several of these traditions.

monks from Byzantium to Moravia. Those monks were brothers, Methodius and Constantinus. Constantinus changed his name upon entry into the monastery, and is better known by his assumed name, Cyril. The brothers were natives of Thessalonica, and they devised a new alphabet for their work in translating the Scriptures. That alphabet, known as the Cyrillic alphabet and having thirty-six letters, is still used in the Russian, Ukrainian, Serbo-Croatian, and Bulgarian languages.[38] The Glagolithic alphabet, which was superseded by the Cyrillic in the tenth century, is also attributed to Methodius and Cyril, the "Apostles to the Slavs." Shortly after the mid-ninth century, they began translating the gospels into Old Church Slavonic. Their Old Testament was formerly regarded as a translation of the LXX, although recent evidence indicates that it was a translation from the Latin. The New Testament of the Old Church Slavonic version follows the Byzantine text basically, but it has many readings that are of the Western and Caesarean types.[39] Most of the known Slavonic manuscripts are lectionaries, and the first version may itself have been in the form of a lectionary.[40]

Miscellaneous Versions

There are several other translations and versions of the Bible text that need to be mentioned, although their witness is of little or no concern to the recovery of the original text of the New Testament. The Nubian version, for instance, arose with Christianity in the region between Egypt and Ethiopia. Athanasius (d. 373) asserted that he consecrated a certain Marcus as bishop of Philae, where Christians had been driven from Egypt during the time of Diocletian's persecution (302/3). Missionaries were sent into the area on a formal basis during the sixth century. The Nubian version of the Scriptures that has survived has been found in fragmentary form, and its textual affiliations are difficult to ascertain with precision because of the scarcity of the fragments. An examination of the textual variants reveals that the Nubian version agrees with the Textus Receptus against the Westcott Hort text or follows a Western and/or Caesarean tradition.[41] Two Old Persian versions of the gospels are known, but they are translations of a fourteenth-century

38. Thomas Pyles, *The Origins and Development of the English Language*, pp. 98-99, and Albert C. Baugh, *A History of the English Language*, pp. 33 ff, for discussion of this and other related topics.
39. See Metzger, *The Text of the New Testament*, p. 85. Also see Metzger, *Chapters of the New Testament*, pp. 73-96, for a full treatment of the Slavonic version. Metzger, *The Early Versions of the New Testament*, pp. 395-442, relates past and current studies of the Old Church Slavonic to indicate that these texts have little merit for the textual critic because of their late and secondary origins.
40. Greenlee, pp. 53-54.
41. Metzger, *The Early Versions of the New Testament*, pp. 268-74.

version based on the Syrian,[42] and from a later version based on the Greek. This latter work has some affinity to the Caesarean text but is little used in textual criticism.[43] There is an Anglo-Saxon version, with numerous copies, translated from the Latin Vulgate, but those and the Old German versions will be considered in chapter 30. "One fragmentary eighth-century manuscript preserves parts of Matthew in Frankish, a language of west-central Europe, with Frankish and Latin on facing pages."[44] This rounds out the survey of ancient versions and translations containing the Old and New Testaments except for the Latin Vulgate version and its antecedents. That tradition will be the subject of the next chapter.

Summary and Conclusion

The multitude of early versions of the Bible demonstrates not only the universality of Christianity but the antiquity of the biblical text as well. These early versions provide some of the earliest copies of the complete canon of Scripture, and in many cases they outdate the manuscript copies in Greek. The Syrian church, for example, had begun its Peshitta in the second century. Tatian's *Diatessaron* dates back to a time prior to A.D. 170. Soon after that time, in the third century and following, other versions began to appear in Egypt and the area near the Mediterranean Sea. Hence, the early existence of the Ethiopic, Coptic, Sahidic, Bohairic, Gothic, Arabic, and other versions provide ample evidence of the presence of the entire Bible during the second, third, and fourth centuries. These early versions of the Bible text also provide another valuable link in the work of reconstructing the original text of the Scriptures.

42. Metzger, *The Early Versions of the New Testament*, pp. 274-79, discusses the Old Persian version; on pp. 17-19 of the same work, he considers the Persian Diatessaron as the latest Tatianic text to be given attention by biblical scholars, since it was based on a Syriac original.
43. See Metzger's chapter in M. M. Parvis and A. P. Wikgren, eds., *New Testament Manuscript Studies*, pp. 25-68. Also see Metzger, *The Early Versions of the New Testament*, pp. 274-79, and his *The Text of the New Testament*, pp. 85-86.
44. Greenlee, p. 54.

29
Latin Versions of the Old and New Testament Texts

Western Christianity produced only one great translation of the Scriptures during the Middle Ages, the Latin Vulgate, which was destined to reign unchallenged for a thousand years. There were of course some forerunners to Jerome's great Vulgate, which need to be discussed first.

The Forerunners in the Latin Language

The Linguistic Setting in the Roman Empire

Before an accurate picture of the forerunners of the Latin Vulgate version may be traced, it is necessary to note the linguistic setting of the ancient world in general and the Roman Empire in particular.[1] Because the geographic structure played a major role in the linguistic and cultural aspects of life, it will be well to observe the latter by the former.

The Near East. The fortunes of the Near East have been quite varied in terms of language as well as politics and society. There were several languages that were spoken in the area of Palestine and Asia Minor at any given moment in ancient times, but during various periods the official language of the regions under consideration underwent radical shifts. Most of the important languages of the Semitic family have been considered (see chap. 18), but their periods of dominance need to be presented in order to give a sense of perspective to the overall study of Bible transmission. After the Babylonian captivity, in the sixth century B.C., the official language of Palestine became Aramaic. This language was used in the writings of the scribes as early as the time of Ezra (Neh. 8:1-8).[2] It was Aramaic that gave rise to the Targums during the Sopherim period (c. 400 B.C.-c. A.D. 200) and to the Gemara later on in the Talmudic period (c. A.D. 100-500).[3] That Aramaic language was

1. See discussion and chart in chap. 30.
2. See chap. 18.
3. See chap. 27.

commonly spoken in Palestine during the life of Christ and His disciples, and it supplanted Hebrew among the Jews insofar as their religious life was concerned.

After the campaigns of Alexander the Great (335-323 B.C.), the Greek language became the official language within the confines of his conquests. Much of that territory was later incorporated into that part of the Roman Empire bordering on the eastern part of the Mediterranean Sea. Hellenistic Greek prevailed as the official language in the Near East under the Ptolemaic and Seleucid empires in Egypt and Syria, respectively, and even in Palestine during the Hasmonean independence (142-63 B.C.). Beginning with the death of Attalus III (133 B.C.), when the kingdom of Pergamum was bequeathed to Rome, and ending in 63 B.C., when the East was incorporated into the Roman Republic, the Latin language gradually spread as the "military language" in the Near East.

Greece. The various dialects of Hellenic Greek[4] were related to three waves of immigration into the southern part of the Balkan Peninsula during the second millennium B.C.: the Ionian, Achaean, and Dorian. The Ionians were early pushed out and forced to settle across the Aegean Sea.[5] Later, other Greeks immigrated and/or founded colonies in the Near East, North Africa, and even in southern Italy and the islands of the Mediterranean. The Greeks were divided into a series of small states, and their unifying feature was their common language. The Dorians made their dialect well known, but the Attic dialect became the most famous. That Attic dialect came into its own as a result of the one great example of Greek unification, their united effort against the Persians (490-480 B.C.) who were led by Darius I and his son Xerxes.[6] In the fifty years following, the Athenian Empire advanced only to be defeated by the Spartans during the Peloponnesian War (431-404 B.C.). The independent city-states again went their separate ways, only to find Philip of Macedonia (c. 359-336 B.C.) making a bid to reunify them. He was killed, and his young son Alexander (356-323 B.C.) crushed the revolts among the Greek city-states in 335 B.C. With his ascendancy, the Hellenic period shifts into what is commonly called the Hellenistic Age.[7] This age was characterized by the intentional advancement of Greek culture and civilization into the areas conquered by Alexander. The language used in Hellenistic society was derived from blending the various dialects of the Greeks into a

4. *Hellenic* is derived from the word *Hellene,* the name applied to the Greeks by themselves. *Hellene* is derived from the Greek work for Greece, *Hellas*.
5. As they came into contact with the Near Eastern peoples they were called Ionians, and that name was used to refer to all Greeks. Hebrew *Javan* (Gen. 10:2, 4; Isa. 66:19; Ezek. 27:13) is equivalent to Greek *Ion,* the ancestor of the Ionians.
6. Xerxes I, known in the Bible as Ahasuerus (Ezra 4:6; Esther 1:1), reigned over Persia from 486 B.C. to 464 B.C.
7. *Hellenic* is applied to Greek culture of the Classical Age, whereas *Hellenistic* refers to Greek culture as it was carried out from Greece following Alexander the Great.

new "common speech" (*Koinē dialektos*), as the individualistic Greek city-states lost their older differences when they were united under Alexander. The philosopher-teacher of Alexander played a major role in developing this new Koine Greek; he is the well-known Aristotle (384-322 B.C.), who is more noted for his work in politics, zoology, metaphysics, and philosophic method than his linguistic efforts. Although the Koine Greek was an admixture of various dialects, it was based primarily on the Attic.

After the death of Alexander, this new speech became the official language of the eastern Mediterranean. It was this very dialect that was used in the translation of the Septuagint in Alexandria (c. 250-c. 150 B.C.). After the rise of Alexander, his *Koinē dialektos* was the official language of Greece. It remained so even after Rome had made its advances into the Near East and Egypt. Latin was used by military personnel in Greece, and especially after the Battle at Actium (31 B.C.). It was that battle that gained the victory over the forces of Mark Antony and Cleopatra for Octavian. During the years between 31 B.C. and 27 B.C., Octavian was busy consolidating his gains and converting the Roman Republic into the Roman Empire. The Greeks had expended their energies in their independent activity, and were no longer in a role of leadership. Their golden age had turned to silver, and their culture was no longer Hellenic, but Hellenistic.

Italy. During the first century B.C., and the centuries following, all roads truly led to Rome. Here was the center of the greatest empire the West had ever seen. Its rise continued to progress from about the tenth century B.C., before the city itself was founded (c. 753). About 509 B.C., the Tarquin kings were expelled from the city, and the Roman Republic was born. From that point, the chief city in Latium began to extend its nearly three-hundred-square-mile territory along the Tiber River until it and its allies controlled most of the Italian Peninsula (c. 265 B.C.). Hence the language of *Latium* (Latin) became the common speech of the Romans. As the unification of the peninsula was completed, Rome came into conflict with Carthage, an African colony of the Phoenicians, in the Punic Wars (264-146 B.C.). Before that series of wars was half over, Rome was involved in the eastern Mediterranean area in the Illyrian and Macedonian wars (c. 229-148 B.C.). By 148 B.C. Macedonia was a Roman province, and in 133 B.C. (when Attalus III of Pergamum died and left his kingdom to Rome) Rome became involved in the Near East. With these intrusions came the military and commercial language of Rome, Latin, although it never actually became the official language in the East.

In Italy, and especially Rome, the people were thoroughly bilingual, including slaves (often Greeks) and freedmen. The literary language of the upper classes was often Greek, and even Latin literature followed the Greek pattern. The language of the military and the market was Latin, and this was the official language, because it was the native tongue. During the early years of the church, the Christians in Rome were largely Greek-speaking, as demonstrated by such works as *Romans* by the apostle Paul, and *Corinthians* by Clement of Rome. It was later that the Christians in the West took Latin for the language of their writings, and during the late fourth and early fifth centuries A.D., the Germanic tribes used the familiar Latin instead of the more literary Greek. This latter point is easily understood when it is recalled that the Germanic tribes were in more intimate contact with the Roman legions and merchants long before they were with their literature.

Africa. The basic languages of North Africa were Greek and Latin. Greek was in vogue in Egypt under the Ptolemies. It was in Alexandria that the Hebrew Old Testament underwent a Greek translation, and a widespread Greek literature was preserved. Farther to the west, Latin was the basic tongue within the Roman Empire, and this was a result of the military, commercial, and administrative contacts of the Romans beginning as early as the Punic Wars. As the Romans became better entrenched in North Africa, their native tongue became the leading official language of that province. It was this language which Tertullian, who actually wrote in both Greek and Latin, Cyprian, and others used in writing their message to the Christians of the area. Thus, the earliest church within the whole Roman Empire used Greek as its literary language, and only later did Latin literature become necessary and widespread.

The Old Latin Version

Although Latin was the official as well as the market (common) language in the West, Greek retained its position as the literary language of Rome and the West until the third century A.D. By the third century, many Old Latin versions of the Scriptures were already circulating in North Africa and Europe, indicating that local Christians had begun to express a desire to have the Scriptures in Latin as early as the second century. The roots of the Old Latin version(s) are doubtless to be found in the practice of the double reading of Scripture during religious services, first from the Greek text (the Septuagint for the Old Testament), then in the vernacular tongue. The reading would probably be done in more or less brief sections, one after another, just as the Jews were accustomed to provide an Aramaic Targum at the reading of the Hebrew Scriptures. One of the earliest known of these Christian translations was the Old Latin (composed prior to c. A.D. 200). Although information concerning the Old Latin translation is very defective, several observations may be made about it.[8] It was actually a translation from the Septuagint, making it a secondary translation rather than a version, which probably arose in North Africa. It was widely quoted and used in North Africa, and may have been the Old Testament translation quoted by Tertullian (c. 160-c. 220) and Cyprian (c. 220-258). The unrevised apocryphal books of this translation apparently were reluctantly added to Jerome's Vulgate version of the Old Testament. The remainder of the Old Testament fell into disuse after Jerome's translation appeared. Nothing other than citations and fragments remains of the Old Latin text of the Old Testament, and because it was merely a translation of a translation, its value to the textual critic is minimal at best.

The Old Latin version of the New Testament is an entirely different matter, however, for some twenty-seven manuscripts of the gospels have survived, along with seven of Acts, six of the Pauline epistles, as well as fragments of the Catholic epistles and of the book of Revelation.[9] Although no codex of the entire New Testament is extant, the manuscript witnesses date from the fourth to the thirteenth centuries, and thus indicate that the Old Latin version continued to be copied long after it had been displaced by the Vulgate in general use. The fact that the Old Latin version was eventually superseded by the Vulgate ultimately led to a scarcity and impurity of the older text. Nevertheless, the Old Latin sources are of an early date, and represent at least two and possibly three different texts.[10] The African text was that used by Tertullian and Cyprian, the European text is found in the writings of Irenaeus and Novatian, "while the Italian text appears conspicuously in Augustine (A.D. 354-430)."[11] With the above evidence it is easy to see that the African and European texts of the Old Latin appeared before the beginning of the third century. The Italian version, if it was distinct from the Vulgate, probably appeared about two centuries later, but the variants among the manuscripts make a coherent history of the text all but impossible to determine. Perhaps this is a contributing factor to why "present-day scholars prefer to speak of the Old Latin Bible or the pre-Vulgate, though to be strictly accurate they ought to speak of Old Latin versions."[12] Thus the Old Latin versions are among the most valuable evidence pertaining to the condition of the New Testament text from early times. The multiplicity of texts that appeared in the

8. It is probably a mistake to consider the "Itala" as a precursor of the Vulgate; cf. H. S. Miller, *A General Biblical Introduction,* p. 237, whom Merrill F. Unger apparently follows, *Introductory Guide to the Old Testament,* pp. 170-71. It seems better to consider Augustine's reference to the "Itala" version as simply a reference to the Vulgate New Testament. Cf. Sir Frederic G. Kenyon, *Handbook to the Textual Criticism of the New Testament,* pp. 213-16. See also F. F. Bruce, *The Books and the Parchments,* pp. 203-9; Bruce M. Metzger, *The Text of the New Testament,* pp. 72-73; Bruce M. Metzger, *The Early Versions of the New Testament: Their Origin, Transmission and Limitations,* pp. 285-330; Sir Frederic G. Kenyon, *The Text of the Greek Bible,* pp. 145-57.
9. Bruce, p. 203.
10. Sir Frederic G. Kenyon, *Our Bible and the Ancient Manuscripts,* pp. 171-73, discusses this matter at length, as does Metzger, *The Early Versions of the New Testament,* pp. 290-93.
11. Kenyon, *Our Bible and the Ancient Manuscripts,* p. 171. Metzger, *The Early Versions of the New Testament,* p. 293, expresses less certainty about the matter than does Kenyon.
12. Metzger, *The Early Versions of The New Testament,* p. 293.

third and fourth centuries led to an intolerable situation in the late fourth century and, as a result, the bishop of Rome, Damasus (366-384), commissioned Jerome to make a revision of the Old Latin in 382. The most important witness to the African text is the Codex Bobiensis, which represents a free and rough translation of the original, and may stem from a second-century papyrus.[13] That codex is designated k in the critical apparatus of Matthew and Mark. The European text of the Old Latin is best represented by Codex Vercellensis (a) and Codex Veronensis (b), which represent a more polished and literal translation of the original text. The former is reported to have been written by Eusebius of Vercelli (d. 370 or 371), and the latter represents the same text type as that used by Jerome. Both of those codices contain most of the gospels; incidentally, the arrangement in b is Matthew, John, Luke and Mark, whereas a follows the common order.[14]

The Famous Latin Vulgate Version

As was indicated above, a revision of the Scriptures into Latin became necessary during the last half of the fourth century. In A.D. 382, Jerome was commissioned by the Bishop of Rome to revise the Old Latin text.

Author of the Translation

Sophronius Eusebius Hieronymus (c. 340-420), better known as St. Jerome,[15] was born to Christian parents in Stridon, Dalmatia. He was trained in the local school until he went to Rome at the age of twelve. He studied Latin, Greek, and pagan authors for the next eight years, and became a Christian at the age of nineteen. After his baptism by the bishop of Rome, Jerome devoted himself to a life of rigid abstinence and service to the Lord. He spent several years pursuing a semiascetic and later a hermitic life. In so doing, he traveled to the East, southwest of Antioch, where he employed a Jewish rabbi to teach him Hebrew (374-379). He was ordained a presbyter at Antioch, and went to Constantinople where he studied under Gregory Nazianzen. In 382 Damasus, the Bishop of Rome, called Jerome to Rome as his secretary, and commissioned him to undertake a revision of the Latin Bible. Damasus picked Jerome to do this revision because of the latter's qualifications as an outstanding scholar. Jerome probably accepted the task in order to please the bishop, as he knew of the strong opposition his translation would encounter among the less educated.

13. Metzger, *The Text of the New Testament,* p. 73.
14. Metzger, *The Early Versions of the New Testament,* pp. 295-330, 461-64, catalogues and describes the corpus of Old Latin Witnesses in a "Check-list of Old Latin Manuscripts of the New Testament" and its "Addenda."
15. See C. S. C. Williams, "Jerome," in G. W. H. Lampe, ed., *The Cambridge History of the Bible,* vol. 2, *The West from the Fathers to the Reformation,* pp. 80-101.

Date of the Translation

Jerome was commissioned for his task in 382 and began his work immediately.[16] He completed his translation of the Old Testament in 405 and spent the last fifteen years of his life writing, translating, and supervising his monks at Bethlehem. He cared little for the Apocrypha and only reluctantly made a hasty translation of portions of it— Judith, Tobit, the rest of Esther, and the additions to Daniel—before his death. Hence, the Old Latin version of the Apocrypha was only brought into the Vulgate version of the Old Testament in the Middle Ages "over his dead body."

At the request of Damasus, Jerome made a slight revision of the gospels, which he completed in 383. In submitting his work to Damasus, Jerome wrote the following:

> You urge me to revise the old Latin version, and, as it were, to sit in judgment on the copies of the Scriptures which are now scattered throughout the whole world; and, inasmuch as they differ from one another, you would have me decide which of them agree with the Greek original. The labour is one of love, but at the same time both perilous and presumptuous; for in judging others I must be content to be judged by all.... Is there a man, learned or unlearned, who will not, when he takes the volume into his hands, and perceives that what he reads does not suit his settled tastes, break out immediately into violent language, and call me a forger and a profane person for having the audacity to add anything to the ancient books, or to make any changes or corrections therein? Now there are two consoling reflections which enable me to bear the odium—in the first place, the command is given by you who are the supreme bishop; and secondly, even on the showing of those who revile us, readings at variance with the early copies cannot be right.[17]

The Latin text used by Jerome for that revision is not known, but it was probably of the European type, and it was corrected in accordance with a Greek manuscript apparently following the Alexandrian text.

Shortly after he had completed the revision of the gospels, Jerome's patron died (384) and a new bishop was elected. Jerome, who had aspired to the Holy See and had also hastily revised the so-called Roman Psalter, now returned to the East and settled at Bethlehem. Before he left, however, he made an even more cursory revision of the remainder of the New Testament. The exact date of that revision is now known, and some have felt that Jerome did not even do

16. Metzger, *The Early Versions of the New Testament,* pp. 330-62, discusses Jerome and his work, the noteworthy manuscripts of the Vulgate, noteworthy printings of the Vulgate, and problems concerning Jerome's work as a translator. He then provides a translation (from German) of Benifatius Fischer, "Limitations of Latin in Representing Greek," pp. 362-74.
17. Jerome, *The Four Gospels,* "Preface," as cited in Philip Schaff and Henry Wace, eds., *Nicene and Post-Nicene Fathers,* 2d series, 6:487-88.

INCIPIT LIB
SAPIENTIAE

22. *Jerome is supposed to have translated the Vulgate while living in a cave under the present Church of the Nativity in Bethlehem. Commemorating this fact, a statue of Jerome has been erected in the courtyard of the church (Howard F. Vos)*

23. *Alcuin's ninth-century revision of the Vulgate (By permission of the British Library)*

the work.[18] He soon turned his attention to a more careful revision of the Roman Psalter and completed it in in 387. That revision is known as the Gallican Psalter and is the version of Psalms currently employed in the Vulgate version of the Bible. It has also been the version used in Roman Catholic services until recently.[19] This version of the Psalter was actually based on the fifth column of Origen's *Hexapla,* and was thus only a translation, not a version.

As soon as the Psalter was completed, Jerome began a revision of the Septuagint, but that had not been his original objective. While at Bethlehem, Jerome set about perfecting his knowledge of the Hebrew language so he could make a fresh translation of the Old Testament directly from the original language. Whereas his friends and admirers applauded his endeavor, those more remote to him became suspect that he might be Judaizing, and even

18. Metzger, *The Text of the New Testament,* p. 76, mentions De Bruyne, Cavallera, and B. Fischer, but adds that this is not the common view.
19. Bruce, p. 205 n. 2, indicates that the earlier revision of Jerome, the Roman Psalter, is employed by the Catholic church in Rome. In very recent times the vernacular has become the utilized language, though based on the Vulgate.

became outraged that "he should cast doubts on the divine inspiration of the Septuagint."[20] The first portion of the Hebrew text to be translated was Jerome's Hebrew Psalter, based on the Hebrew text then currently in use in Palestine. This translation was never really able to supersede and replace Jerome's earlier Gallican, or even his Roman, Psalter in liturgical use. Jerome persisted in his translation of the Hebrew Old Testament in spite of opposition and even illness. In his many prefaces he would lash out at the opposers of his work for their unreasonableness in the whole matter. Finally, by 405, his Latin translation based upon the Hebrew was completed, but it was not readily received. Nevertheless, his work of revision continued after the completion of his Old Testament translation.

Place of the Translation

Jerome had done his revision of the gospels, the Roman Psalter, and his hurried work on the remainder of the New Testament in Rome. These works were done prior to the election of Damasus's successor, Siricius (384-398), to the Episcopal See at Rome. At that time Jerome left Rome with his brother, a few monks, and his new patroness, Paula, and her daughter Eustochium. He departed from Rome on a pilgrimmage "from Babylon to Jerusalem, that not Nebuchadnezzar, but Jesus, should reign over him."[21] In Bethlehem he presided over a monastery, while Paula governed a convent, from 386 to his death in 420. It was during those years that he studied Hebrew, revised the Roman Psalter, translated the Hebrew Old Testament, began revising his work, and started his translation of the Apocrypha. This latter work was done quite reluctantly, as Jerome had a low regard for the Apocrypha, and it was his successors who inserted the Old Latin version of the Apocrypha into his Vulgate Old Testament.

Purpose of the Translation

Damasus, Bishop of Rome (366-384), demonstrated a keen interest in the Scriptures as well as in scholars whom he befriended and patronized. With that twofold interest in view, it is readily seen that he would be concerned that the diversity of Bible versions, translations, revisions, and recensions by the mid-fourth century demanded a new and authoritative edition of the Scriptures. This situation is especially true in light of the fact that the church in the West had, and has, always demonstrated an attitude of outward conformity that was virtually unknown, and certainly uncommon, in the church of the

20. Philip Schaff, *History of the Christian Church,* 3:974 n. 3, states the terms used, *"Falsarius, sacrilegus, et corruptor Scriptura."*
21. Ibid., p. 212.

East. Several factors demanding a new and authoritative Bible translation may be observed in passing.

Confusion in the Latin texts. Much confusion existed in the Latin texts of the Bible. This diversity in the Latin language alone was a result of the copying and recopying of the Latin texts by independent and unauthorized, or formal and informal, means. A case in point would be Tertullian, who wrote equally well in both Greek and Latin. He would generally quote the African text of the Old Latin version when writing his many treatises, but not infrequently he would make his own on-the-spot translation of the Greek text into Latin. This practice has caused no end of problems to those who have attempted to trace the text underlying the writings of Tertullian and others.

Many translations existed. Many translations of the Scriptures existed. The situation within the Latin language, which was rapidly becoming the official language of the church, was not the only one demanding a new and authoritative text. Take, for example, the Old Testament. In Jerome's time,

> Men read their Old Testament in the recension of Lucian, if they lived in North Syria, Asia Minor, or Greece; in that of Hesychius, if they belonged to the Delta or the valley of the Nile; in Origen's Hexaplaric edition, if they were residents at Jerusalem or Caesarea.[22]

Add to this the two basic Old Latin texts, the African and the European, and it is little wonder that the Bishop of Rome desired a new and authoritative translation upon which the official doctrines of the church could be based.

Heresies and disputes. Multiple heresies and disputes with the Jews were springing up in the Empire. Many of the heretical groups that appeared in the second, third, and fourth centuries—for example, the Marcionites, the Manichaeans, the Montanists—based their doctrines on their own Bible translation and/or canon. The Arian controversy led to the Council at Nicea (325), and the Council at Constantinople (I) (381) was followed by the Council at Ephesus (431), which met just a decade after Jerome's death. The fact that Jerome met with such marked oppostion when he began translating the Hebrew Old Testament supports the view that there were conflicts between the Christians and the Jews. But the most obvious reason for the need of a Hebrew-based Old Testament translation was the error held by many, including Augustine, that the Seputagint was actually the inspired and inerrant Word of God. That view led to the fourth factor demanding a new and authoritative Bible translation.

Need for standard text. Manifold needs in the existing situation demanded a scholarly, authentic, and authoritative standard text of the Christian Scriptures to facilitate the church's missionary and teaching activities. Also, in order to defend the doctrinal position of the conciliar movement there

22. Henry Barclay Swete, *An Introduction to the Old Testament in Greek,* p. 85.

needed to be an authoritative text. The transmission of copies of the Scriptures to the churches in the Empire required that a trustworthy (authentic) text be secured. Nevertheless, although Jerome was eminently qualified for his task, his New Testament revision was not nearly so adequate as was his Old Testament revision, for he was less prone to revise the available texts after the initial reactions to his work on the four gospels.

Reaction to the Translation

When Jerome published his revisions of the four gospels, sharp criticisms were made. But, because the Bishop of Rome had sponsored his work, the opposition was silenced. The fact that Jerome was even less disposed to alter the remainder of the New Testament in his revision indicates that he may have been aware of his patron's imminent death, and he desired that his revision be mild enough to be met with approval by his critics in the event that his benefactor should die. The fact that Jerome left Rome the year after Damasus's death reinforces this view. The Roman Psalter remained the official text in the church at Rome, which indicates where Jerome's translation was first used and that his scholarship was already apparent. The acceptance of his Gallican Psalter in churches outside Rome shows the influence of those who were critical of his earlier work under Damasus.

When Jerome began to study Hebrew at Bethlehem, and when he had translated his Hebrew Psalter, sharp cries of accusation arose against him. He was accused of presumption, making unlawful innovations, and sacrilege. Not being one to take biting criticism without retaliation, Jerome used his prefaces as the tools of his counterattack. His accusations and acid rejoinders merely added fuel to the flame of opposition against his version of the Old Testament. Jerome's work was opposed by many of the most outstanding leaders of the church, including Augustine, who was outspoken against Jerome's Old Testament while wholeheartedly favoring his New Testament revision (after c. 398).

Augustine's position gives a candid recapitulation of what actually happened to the Vulgate Old Testament. During the early years of Jerome's translation of the Old Testament, Augustine (and the large majority of influential leaders in the church) opposed the translation because it was not based on the Septuagint. In fact, Augustine used Jerome's New Testament revision while he urged him to translate the Old Testament from the LXX, which the bishop at Hippo believed to be inspired. Philip Schaff aptly states this point:

> Augustine feared, from the displacement of the Septuagint, which he regarded as apostolically sanctioned, and as inspired, a division between the Greek and Latin church, but yielded afterwards, in part at least, to the correct view of Jerome, and rectified in his Retractions several false translations in his former works. Westcott, in his scholarly article on the Vulgate (in Smith's *Dictionary of the Bible,*

iii, 702), makes the remark: "There are few more touching instances of humility than that of the young Augustine bending himself in entire submission before the contemptuous and impatient reproof of the veteran scholar."[23]

Shortly after the great scholar's death in 420, his Old Testament translation gained a complete victory in the field of Bible translations. Whether this fact is attributed to the sheer weight of the translation alone can only be questioned, as the biting criticism and scathing denunciation of all opponents by Jerome would hardly lend to the acceptance of his greatest endeavor. But, while Jerome's Vulgate was unofficially recognized as the standard text of the Bible throughout the Middle Ages, it was not until the mid-sixteenth century Council of Trent (1545-63) that it was officially placed into that position by the Roman Catholic church. In the interim it was published in parallel columns with other versions as well as by itself. When the Latin tongue became the lingua franca of Europe, the other translations and versions acquiesced and succumbed to the majestic Vulgate.

Results of the Translation

Of primary concern to the modern Bible student is the relative weight of the Latin Vulgate.[24] It is important therefore to consider this version in the light of history. As has been previously demonstrated, the Vulgate New Testament was merely a revision of the Old Latin text, and not too critical a revision at that. In terms of the Apocrypha, the Vulgate is of even less value, as it was simply the Old Latin text attached to Jerome's Old Testament, with minor exceptions. The Old Testament of the Vulgate has a somewhat different character and merit, however, as it was actually a version of the Hebrew text, not a revision or another translation. Thus, the value of the Old Testament is higher than the New. But it was inevitable that the text of the Vulgate would be corrupted in its transmission during the Middle Ages, "sometimes by careless transcription and with copies of the Old Latin"[25] with which it was often published. As a result, several revisions and/or recensions of the Vulgate were made in medieval monasteries, leading to a total of over ten thousand extant Vulgate manuscripts.[26] It is among those manuscripts that the

23. Schaff, p. 975 n. 1.
24. Kenyon, *The Text of the Greek Bible,* pp. 157-66, discusses the Latin Vulgate before categorizing its text into several distinguishable groups or families: the Northumbrian group, the Cassiadorian and non-Cassiadorian groups of Italian mss, an Irish group, and a Spanish group.
25. Metzger, *The Text of the New Testament,* p. 76.
26. See Raphael Loewe, "The Medieval History of the Latin Vulgate," in G. W. H. Lampe, ed., *The Cambridge History of the Bible,* vol. 2, *The West from the Fathers to the Reformation,* pp. 102-54. Also see chap. 26.

greatest amount of "cross-contamination" of textual types is evident.[27]

The above information notwithstanding, the Council of Trent issued a "Decree Concerning the Edition, and the Use, of the Sacred Books," which stated:

> Moreover, the same sacred and holy Synod,—considering that no small utility may accrue to the Church of God, if it be made known which out of all the Latin editions, now in circulation, of the sacred books, is to be held as authentic, —ordains and declares, that the said old and Vulgate edition, which, by the lengthened usage of so many ages, has been approved of in the Church, be, in public lectures, disputations, sermons, and expositions, held as authentic; and that no one is to dare, or presume to reject it under any pretext whatever.[28]

However, it might be asked which editions of the Vulgate should be regarded as the ultimate authority. Thus the Council of Trent decided to have an authentic edition of the Latin Scriptures prepared. The work was committed to a papal commission, but it was unable to overcome the difficulties set before it. Finally Pope Sixtus V published an edition of his own in 1590. That was not the first edition of the printed Vulgate, as it had been printed by Johann Gutenberg in Mainz between 1450 and 1455. In 1590, Pope Sixtus V died, just a few months after publication of his Vulgate edition. The Sixtene edition was quite unpopular among scholars, especially the Jesuits, and it was circulated for only a short time. Gregory XIV (1590-91) succeeded to the papal chair and immediately proceeded to make a drastic revision of the Sixtene text. His sudden death would have ended the revision of the Vulgate text had it not been for the sympathies of Clement VIII (1592-1605). In 1592, Clement VIII recalled all of the remaining copies of the Sixtene edition and continued the revision of its text. In 1604 a new, authentic Vulgate edition of the Bible appeared, known today as the Sixto-Clementine edition. It differed from the Sixtene edition with some 4,900 variants. Since 1907 the Benedictine order has been making a critical revision of the Vulgate Old Testament. The New Testament has been undergoing a critical revision, with apparatus, under the auspices of a group of Anglican scholars at Oxford. This work was begun by Bishop John Wordsworth and Professor H.J. White between 1877 and 1926, and was completed by H.F.D. Sparks in 1954. The most recently published critical edition of the Vulgate was issued in 1969 by the Wurttenbergische Bibelanstadt, under the supervision of both Roman Catholic and Protestant scholars. According to Metzger, "the text is printed *per cola ed commata* according to the ancient manuscripts and without punctuation," so it differs from previously published editions in minor points as well as in many passages.[29]

The consistency of the value of the Vulgate text is rather mixed after the

27. Metzger, *The Text of the New Testament,* p. 76.
28. Schaff, ed., *The Creeds of Christendom,* 2:82.

sixth century, and its overall character is rather faulty. The influence of the Vulgate on the language and thought of Western Christianity has been immense, but its value in textual criticism is not nearly so high. When the text of Jerome is arrived at, by its own textual study, it is valuable in ascertaining rather late manuscript evidence to the Greek and/or Hebrew Text. Jerome's New Testament was a late-fourth-century revision of the Old Latin, and his Old Testament was a late-fourth- or early-fifth-century version of the Hebrew text. The Apocrypha witnesses to the disregard that Jerome had for it, as he only worked on four books (and those were reluctantly done), and the inclusion of it is evidence of the popularity it had in the Roman Catholic church. Only a few voices that supported the Septuagint Old Testament as authoritative and inspired were capable of admitting their error, and acknowledging the accuracy of the Hebrew text underlying Jerome's Vulgate.

Summary and Conclusion

Christianity was born into a Roman world, and it was not long before its Western branch adopted the langauge of that world, Latin. There is evidence that the Old Latin versions of the Bible were in existence prior to A.D. 200. In the third century Latin versions were circulated freely in North Africa. However, it was Jerome's Latin version, the Vulgate, that endured longest, reigning for nearly a thousand years before it was challenged in the sixteenth century. The Vulgate version of the Bible was not only the Bible of the Middle Ages, it also served as the basis for most of the modern Bible translations made prior to the nineteenth century.

29. Metzger, *The Early Versions of the New Testament*, pp. 351-52. Metzger also mentions another enterprise to pursue a new critical edition utilizing Spanish mss. That work was begun in 1933 at the newly established St. Jerome Abbey in Rome. Only portions of the Old Testament have been published to date.

30

The Bible in English

The chain "from God to us" takes on a new dimension at this point, as the general transmission of the text in the original languages and early translations gives way to the particular transmission of the text in the English language. Before this may be traced, however, it is necessary to sketch the background of the English language and the biblical text therein.

The Background of the English Language

The Languages and Nations of the Indo-European Family

Whereas the Old Testament was originally recorded in languages belonging to the Semitic family and the New Testament was written in the Indo-European family (with influence from the Semitic), the Bible was transmitted to the Western world via the Indo-European family. And, just as the Semitic family was subdivided into several divisions, so the Indo-European languages, the languages of the Japhetic peoples of Genesis 10, formed two basic divisions, with their subfamilies (see chart at end of chap.). These divisions are characterized by their dialectic and geographic similarities.

The Eastern Division (satem). The Eastern division of the Indo-European family is observed in the similarities of pronunciation in the satem dialects. Although those similarities may sound strange to the modern ear, they probably stem from a common source. The Indo-European languages that reflect an *s* sibilant in the word for "hundred" are classified as satem dialects. The subdivisions of the satem branch include four basic groups.

1. The Indo-Iranian (Aryan) group includes the Indic and Iranian branches. The Indic branch is reflected in ancient Sanskrit Prakrits as well as modern Hindi, Punjabi, Bengali, Mahrati, and Romany. Iranic includes Old Iranian in two branches: the eastern dialect of Avestan (formerly called Zend) is the language of the Avesta; the western dialect includes Old Persian, Middle Persian, and Modern Persian (Iranian).

2. The Thraco-Phrygian group was trapped in the mountain valley region of Trans-Caucasia, and has Armenian as its representative. Whatever written records may have been extant before Christianity and the Bible were introduced (in the fifth century A.D.), were destroyed, and the earliest records in this language are of the Bible text.

3. The Thraco-Illyrian group settled in the Balkan Peninsula, and is represented by Albanian. The earliest texts in Albanian date from the seventeenth century.

4. The Balto-Slavic group fills in the satem division of the Indo-European languages. This group is distributed over the region around the Baltic Sea and down to the area of Bulgaria and Yugoslavia. It is further divided into the Baltic branch, including Latvian (Lettish), Lithuanian, and Prussian; and the Slavic branch, including Great Russian (Russian), Ukrainian, White Russian (Byelorussian), Polish, Czechoslovak, Serbian (Wendish), Bulgarian, Serbo-Croatian, and Slovenian. The Baltic branch is very old and some of it is even extinct, for example, Prussian was replaced by German in the seventeenth century. On the other hand, no Slavic language was written prior to the ninth century, but Old Church Slavic has much in common with Old Bulgarian. One of the interesting features of the Slavic languages is their use of the Cyrillic alphabet, which was developed especially for the Slavic languages by the monks Cyril and Methodius in the ninth century.[1]

The Western Division (centum). The Western division of the Indo-European family is also observed in the similarities of pronunciation in the centum dialects. Whereas the *s* sibilant is reflected in the satem words for "hundred," the centum dialects reflect either a *c* or *h* sibilant sound. There are, of course, other differences, but these are common characteristics. Just as the satem division has four groups, so has the centum.

1. The Hellenic group has been sketched in chapter 29, and is represented by the various dialects of Greek.

2. The Italic group is represented by several relatively unimportant ancient languages (Oscan, Umbrian, Sabine, Faliscan, and Volscian), and one important one, namely, Latin. The modern representatives are called Romance languages, as they are derived from Latin, the language of the Roman Empire. These languages include such notables as Spanish, French, Italian, Portuguese, Catalan, Rhaeto-Romanic, and Rumanian.

3. The Celtic group is divided into two branches: Continental, represented by Gallic, the language of ancient Gaul, and the Insular, represented by

1. See chap. 28, where the background factors to the development of this alphabet are presented.

the Britannic group of Cornish, Welsh, Breton, and Pictish, and the Gaelic group of Irish, Scots Gaelic, and Manx. Before the beginning of the Christian era, Celtic languages were spoken over the greater part of central and western Europe, and by the latter part of the third century B.C., even in Asia Minor, in the region called for them Galatia. It was to people of that region that the apostle Paul wrote one of his epistles.[2]

4. The Teutonic (Germanic) group is divided into three branches, and is of special interest to the English-speaking individual.
   a. East Teutonic is represented by the Gothic language. Its earliest records date from the fourth century A.D., when Ulfilas (311-381) introduced Christianity to the ancient Germans.[3]
   b. North Teutonic (Scandinavian) is closely related to the Eastern branch. Its earliest records are inscriptions dating from the third century A.D., written in the Rhunic alphabet. Scandinavian is divided into the Old Norse, Icelandic, Norwegian, Swedish, and Danish languages.
   c. West Teutonic is subdivided on the basis of a shift in consonants known as the High German sound shift, which began at about A.D. 600 in south Germany and moved north. The impulse of that consonant shift died out as it reached the lowlands. Thus, the languages to the north are called "Low German," and to the south, "High German."[4] High German is represented by Old High German, Bavarian, Middle High German, Modern Standard German, and Yiddish. Low German includes Old Low Franconian, Old Saxon, and Modern Low German, or *Plattdeutsch*. A third group is Anglo-Frisian, the family of Dutch, Flemish Afrikaans, Frisian, Anglo-Saxon, Middle English, and English.

The Late Development of the English Language

English, in the Anglo-Frisian group, is a sort of tag end dialect of Low German that has developed into a predominant world language. Just how this development took place is not known with certainty, but the most scholarly estimates, based on the available evidence, generally agree with the traditional account as presented by the Venerable Bede (c. 673-735) in his *Ecclesiastical History of the Saxons*.[5] This account begins with the landing of Henga and Horsa and the Germans in A.D. 449. They had been invited by the Britons to help withstand the Picts and Scots. The Celts were the earliest Indo-Europeans to settle in Britain, and their invasion occurred prior to about

2. Thomas Pyles, *The Origins and Development of the English Language*, p. 100.
3. See chap. 28 for a discussion of the spread of Christianity to the Goths.
4. It should be noted that these designations have nothing to do with cultural levels, as "Low German" is *Plattdeutsch*, from the lowlands, whereas "High German" is from the highlands (so to speak), and is the textbook variety.
5. This text was written in Latin, and completed in 731; it was later translated into Old English by Alfred the Great (849-901).

1000 B.C. Their language was the first one recorded in Britain, and their widespread culture was related to that of the Gauls on the Continent. When the Romans expanded their empire under Julius Caesar, they attempted an invasion of Britain (55 B.C.); however, they were not able to conquer it until the reign of the Emperor Claudius (A.D. 43). It was at that time that the Druid religion of the Britons was abolished and the religion of Rome introduced. Between that time and A.D. 410, the year when the last of the Roman armies were officially withdrawn from the island, the Britons underwent a period of Romanization. Their culture and language were affected, and both went into a state of decline after the Roman withdrawal.

When the Romans withdrew, Saxon pirates and the unconquered Picts and Scots, who had been pushed into the northern part of the island during the Roman period, began to make attacks on the Britons. The Britons had relied on the Romans for protection, but the Romans had now been forced to return to protect their tottering empire. As a result, the Britons had to appeal to their "continental cousins" for assistance. Subsequently, the Jutes and the Saxons answered the call, but for a price. The former were very capable warriors, and their contact with the Romans had not made them less savage in battle. They were fully the match for the Picts and the Scots, but they decided to settle in their newly found home. In 447, the *Anglo-Saxon Chronicle* records the founding of the first settlement of Saxons. They settled in the south (Sussex), and later groups settled in the west (Wessex, 495), east (Essex), and central areas north of the Thames River (Middlesex). The Angles followed in 547 and settled in the area north of the Humber River, establishing an Anglican kingdom. All three of those peoples were of Teutonic stock, as were the Britons. They drove their predecessors out of the heartland, into Cornwall, Wales, France, and Brittany. Because the Angles were the predominant group to settle in Britain at this time, the name of the whole country became known as Angle-land (hence, England). Their culture borrowed little or no vocabulary from its predessors, and this at least implies a drastic and sudden conquest. All of this took place prior to the end of the sixth century A.D., before the missionary expedition under a St. Augustine (not the Bishop of Hippo, c. A.D. 400) arrived in England in 597. An account of the landing of that missionary group sent by the first medieval pope (Gregory I, 590-604) is extant in Bede's *Ecclesiastical History*.

But Christianity was introduced to Britain long before 597. It may have been introduced during the late first century or early second century, and was most assuredly there during the third century. There were enough Christians in Britain to send three bishops to the Council (synod) at Arles in 314. Pelagius (c. 370-450), the arch-opponent of Augustine of Hippo and the author of Pelagianism, was from Britain. In fact, St. Patrick (c. 389-461), whose date and place of birth are quite uncertain, was the son of a deacon in the Celtic church, and a grandson to a priest.

Thus, by the time Gregory's missionary force arrived in England, a variety of Christianity was certainly known to the Angles, Saxons, and Jutes. That expedition, however, injected another period of Latinization into the language with its influence on the speech. Nevertheless, the language of the Angles, Saxons, and Jutes, in its various dialects, has come to be known as Old English, Old Saxon, or Anglo-Saxon. Its period of dominance extends from about 450 to about 1100, at which time the influence of the Normans, following their conquest at Hastings in 1066, came to the fore. Prior to the Norman invasion, however, Scandinavians had settled in large numbers in England, as evidenced by the institution of the ancient law they observed and imposed on the northeastern part of England at the Treaty of Wedmore in 878 (called the Danelaw).

The second period, Middle English, extends from about 1100 to about 1500. The language of that period was again influenced by the Scandinavians, as the Normans were actually a transplanted group of sea-roving Northmen from Scandinavia and Denmark. Their exploits during the eighth and ninth centuries made Europe tremble. Some of the great literature in English arose during the Middle English period, including the works of Geoffrey Chaucer (c. 1340-1400). It was during that period that John Wycliffe (c. 1330-84) was associated with the first complete translation of the Bible into English.

The third period, Modern English, had its beginning shortly after Johann Gutenberg's invention of movable type (c. 1454). But it was not related to that invention. Instead, it was related to a "great vowel shift" that took place within the fifteenth century. This event is strictly an English language phenomenon, and it occurred primarily in the south of England. External forces only exerted an influence on the change but did not cause it, as no satisfactory answer has been discovered to explain its cause.[6] Before 1400, there was no indication of the shift in vowel sounds (Middle English), but after 1500, the sounds had completed their shift and Modern English was born. With this background in view, the history of the translations of the Bible into English should be more meaningful.

The Beginnings of the Bible in Old and Middle English (Partial Versions)

Old English Partial Versions (c. 450-c. 1100)

At first only pictures, preaching, poems, and paraphrases were used to communicate the message of Scripture to the Britons. These early transla-

6. It is beyond the province of this study to go into this subject, but further information and discussion may be seen in works similar to and including Pyles, pp. 181-94; Albert C. Baugh, *A History of the English Language*, pp. 287 ff.; Margaret M. Bryant, *Modern English and its Heritage;* and Otto Jesperson, *Growth and Structure of the English Language*.

tions of portions of Scripture were based upon the Old Latin and Vulgate versions of the Bible.[7] None of those translations included the entire Bible, but they do illustrate the way that the Bible entered into the English tongue.[8] Several individuals and their translations made contributions in that direction.[9]

Caedmon (d. c. 680). Caedmon was a laborer at the monastery at Whitby in Yorkshire (Northumbria). His story, recorded in Bede's *Ecclesiastical History* (4. 24), indicates that he was completely ungifted in poetry until one night when he slipped away from a party. He left the party for fear that he would be called upon to sing. That night he dreamed that he was commanded to sing by an angel. When he asked what he should sing, he was told to sing how all things were first created. Hence, he began to sing praises unto God in words he had never before heard:

> Now we must praise the Maker of the Celestial Kingdom, the power and counsel of the Creator, the deeds of the Father of Glory, how he, since he is the Eternal God, was the beginning of all wonders, who first, Omnipotent Guardian of the human kind, made for the sons of men Heaven for their roof, and then the earth.[10]

Other paraphrases and poems sung by Caedmon included the full story of Genesis, the story of Israel's exodus, the incarnation, passion, resurrection, and ascension of the Lord, the coming of the Holy Spirit, the apostles' teaching, and so on.[11] His work became the basis for other poets, writers, and translators, as well as the popularized people's Bible of the day, for his songs were memorized and disseminated throughout the land. F.F. Bruce adds that Caedmon "may very reasonably be credited with the ultimate authorship of a metrical version of the narratives of Genesis, Exodus, and Daniel."[12]

Aldhelm (640-709). Aldhelm made the first straightforward translation of portions of the Bible into English. Aldhelm was the first Bishop of Sherborne in Dorset, southern England, and he translated the Psalter into Old English shortly after A.D. 700.

Egbert (fl. c. 700). Egbert of Northumbria became the Archbishop of York shortly before the death of Bede. He was also the teacher of Alcuin of York, who was later called by Charlemagne to establish a school at the court

7. See Bruce M. Metzger, *The Early Versions of the Bible: Their Origin, Transmission and Limitations,* pp. 443-55, for an in-depth study of these minor Western versions of the Bible text.
8. It should be pointed out at this juncture that Old English (Anglo-Saxon) is so different from Middle and Modern English as to be for all practical purposes a foreign language. But the transition was not radical, and thus there is a close relationship between the Bible in Old, Middle, and Modern English.
9. See "Appendix: A Short-Title Checklist of English Translations of the Bible."
10. Caedmon, as cited by H.W. Hoare, *The Evolution of the English Bible,* p. 27.
11. Bede *Ecclesiastical History of the English Nation* 4.24.
12. F.F. Bruce, *The English Bible: A History of Translations,* p. 3.

of Aachen (Aix-la-Chapelle). Egbert was the first to translate the gospels into English (c. 705).

The Venerable Bede (674-735). The Venerable Bede was one of the greatest scholars of all Europe, and undoubtedly the greatest in England. He was situated at Jarrow-on-the-Tyne in Northumbria, where he wrote his ecclesiastical history and other works. He also translated the fourth gospel, probably to supplement the other three, which were done by Egbert.[13] He was able to finish translating the gospel of John in the very hour of his death. Tradition relates that he was suffering much in his final days, but that he compelled his scribe to take dictation until the very last verse was translated. Then, he is reported to have chanted a "Gloria" as he passed on to the great Master.

Alfred the Great (849-901). Alfred the Great was king of England and a scholar of first rank. It was during his reign that the Danelaw was established under the Treaty of Wedmore (878), with only two basic stipulations: Christian baptism and loyalty to the king. Along with his translation of Bede's *Ecclesiastical History* from Latin into Anglo-Saxon, Alfred translated the Ten Commandments, extracts from Exodus 21-23, Acts 15:23-29, and a negative form of the Golden Rule. It was a largely a result of his efforts that the religious life of Britain, which had nearly become extinct, experienced a revival.

Aldred (fl. c. 950). Aldred introduced a new element in the history of the English Bible, as he wrote an interlinear "gloss" in the Northumbrian dialect between the lines of a late-seventh-century Latin copy of the gospels. The Latin copy was the work of Eadfrid, Bishop of Lindisfarne (698-721) and from that individual the interlinear work of Aldred receives its name, the Lindisfarne Gospels. About a generation later, an Irish scribe, Mac Regol, made another Anglo-Saxon gloss known as the Rushworth Gospels.[14]

Aelfric (c. 950-c. 1020). Alefric, abbot of Eynsham, Oxfordshire (Wessex), translated portions of the first seven books of the Old Testament from the Latin, in addition to other Old Testament portions, which he cited in his homilies. Before his time, the Wessex Gospels had also been translated into the West Saxon dialect. The Wessex Gospels constitute the first extant independent Old English version of the gospels.[15]

13. Whether the actual translation by Egbert is extant is a moot question; but the inference is that he only did three of the gospels, as Bede corresponded with him during the translation process, and it is doubtful that he would retranslate a gospel with other books still untranslated.
14. The Rushworth Gospels are almost transcriptions of the Lindisfarne Gospels, except that the gospel of Matthew is in the Mercian dialect rather than the Northumbrian.
15. See Metzger, *The Early Versions of the New Testament,* pp. 448-52, for a discussion of the relationship of extant West Saxon gospel manuscripts to the original ms (now lost).

Middle English Partial Versions (c. 1100-c. 1400)

A dispute over the throne of Edward the Confessor (1042-1066) erupted after his death. It was between Harold, the eldest son and successor to Godwin, the adviser of Edward, and William, the duke of Normandy and second cousin to the late king. At the Battle of Hastings (1066), William defeated Harold, who was slain in the battle, and became king. That ended the Saxon period of domination in Britain and began the period of domination by the Northmen, rather than a time of their mere influence. The Norman Conquest brought a tremendous Norman-French influence into the language of the people, and after a time the language itself was transformed into Middle English. In this period, several other partial translations of the Scriptures were made, as well as some complete versions toward the end of the period.[16]

Orm, or Ormin (fl. c. 1200). Orm was an Augustinian monk who wrote a poetical paraphrase of the gospels and Acts, which was accompanied by a commentary. This work, called the *Ormulum,* is preserved in only one manuscript, possibly the autograph, of some 20,000 lines. Although the vocabulary is purely Teutonic, the cadence and syntax show evidence of Norman influence. Orm states his own justification of his version as he writes, "If any one wants to know why I have done this deed, I have done it so that all young Christian folk may depend upon the Gospel only, and may follow with all their might its holy teaching, in thought, in word and deed."[17]

William of Shoreham. William of Shoreham has often been credited with producing the first prose translation of a Bible portion into a southern dialect of English (c. 1320). Prior to the fourteenth century no complete book of Scripture had been literally translated into English. Although the Psalter ascribed to Shoreham was translated in the dialect of the West Midlands from the Vulgate, William is known to have written his poetry in Kentish. Thus, the actual author of one of the literal translations of a Bible book into English is still unknown.

Richard Rolle. "The Hermit of Hampole," Richard Rolle was responsible for the second of these literal translations into English. He lived near Doncaster, Yorkshire, and made his literal translations into the North English dialect from the Latin Vulgate (c. 1320-1340). This literal translation of the Psalter was widely circulated, but even more important is the fact that it reflects the history of the English Bible to the time of John Wycliffe, who was born about 1320.

16. See Appendix.
17. As cited in Hoare, p. 40, with the note that the author (Hoare) has rendered "his words in modern English."

The Bible in Complete Versions in Middle and Early Modern English

Whereas there were no complete Bibles in the English language prior to the fourteenth century, there were several indications that such an enterprise would be forthcoming.[18] Among those indications were the attempts at translating the Psalter literally, the wide circulation of those early translations, the fact that the language of the rulers and the ruled was rapidly becoming fused, the recently completed Crusades, the rebirth of learning, and, perhaps the most important, the conflict between the leading princes of the church, which resulted in the "Babylonish Captivity" (1309-1377). During that period, the papal court was moved from Rome to Avignon and back to Rome.

John Wycliffe (c. 1320-84)

"The Morning Star of the Reformation," John Wycliffe was a contemporary of the "Babylonish Captivity," Geoffrey Chaucer, and John of Gaunt. In his recoil from the spiritual apathy and moral degeneracy of the clergy, Wycliffe was thrust into the limelight as an opponent to the papacy.

> The readiest key to Wycliffe's career is to be found in the conviction,—a conviction which grew deeper as life went on,— that the Papal claims are incompatible with what he felt to be the moral truth of things, incompatible with his instinct of patriotism, and finally, with the paramount authority of the inspired Book which was his spiritual Great Charter.[19]

He seems to have become one of the king's chaplains about 1366, and became a doctor of theology in 1372, before being sent to France in 1374 to negotiate peace and meet with papal authorities in the matter of filling ecclesiastical appointments in England. Upon his return to England he began to speak as a religious reformer and issued nineteen articles in 1377, which resulted in the issuance of five papal bulls against him. In 1382 he denied the doctrine of transubstantiation and was relieved of his teaching duties at Oxford, but he was permitted to retire to his parsonage at Lutterworth, where he died on December 31, 1384, in communion with the church.

Wycliffe cast aside his dry scholastic Latin to appeal to the English people at large in their common language. That appeal was primarily through the Lollards, an order of itinerant preachers, "poor priests," who went throughout the countryside preaching, reading, and teaching the English Bible.

Toward the close of the fourteenth century the great Wycliffite translations of the Bible were made. The New Testament (1380) and Old Testament (1388)[20] translations associated with him formed a new epoch in the history of the

18. See Appendix.
19. Hoare, p. 71. For further study see William E. Nix, "Theological Presuppositions and Sixteenth Century English Bible Translations."

24. *A page from the Wycliffe Bible (By permission of the British Library)*

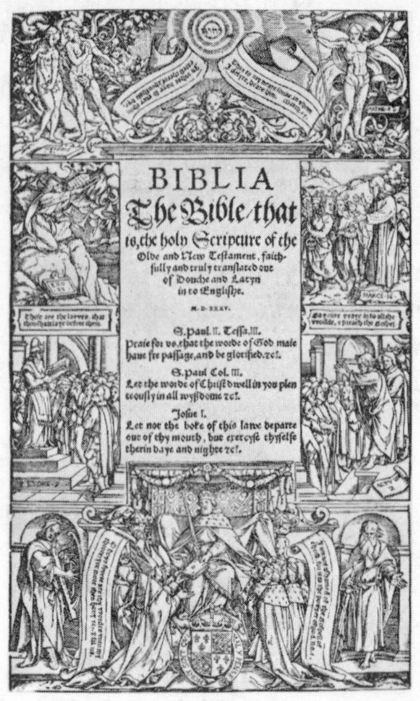

BIBLIA
The Bible, that
is, the holy Scripture of the
Olde and New Testament, faithfully and truly translated out
of Douche and Latyn
in to Englishe.
M.D.XXXV.

S. paul. II. Tessa. III.
Praie for vs, that the worde of God maie
haue fre passage, and be glorified. &c.

S. paul Col. III.
Let the worde of Christ dwell in you plen
teously in all wysdome &c.

Josue I.
Let not the boke of this lawe departe
out of thy mouth, but exercyse thyselfe
therin daye and nighte &c.

25. *Title page of the Coverdale translation, the first printed English Bible (By permission of the British Library)*

Bible in England. They were translated from contemporary manuscripts of the Latin Vulgate, with the probability that the translator(s) followed the principles of translation set forth in *The English Hexapla,* which makes the following observation:

> In translating from the Vulgate, Wycliffe has most faithfully adhered to that version; he seems to have adopted Hampole's principle: In this work y seke no straunge englishe, bot esieste and communeste, and siche that is moost luche to the latyne, so that thei that knoweth not the latyne by the englishe may come to many latyne words.[21]

20. See Appendix. The actual date of this translation is unknown. The original New Testament was completed prior to Wycliffe's death in 1382, but extant manuscript copies reflect the Old Testament by Nicholas Hereford, and the work of John Purvey was completed some time after Wycliffe's death. For extended treatment of this subject see Margaret T. Hills, *A Ready-Reference History of the English Bible,* p. 4; Henry Hargreaves, "The Wycliffite Versions," in G.W.H. Lampe, ed., *The Cambridge History of the Bible,* vol. 2, *The West from the Fathers to the Reformation,* pp. 387-415; Jack P. Lewis, *The English Bible from the KJV to the NIV: A History and an Evaluation,* pp. 17-34.
21. *The English Hexapla in Parallel Columns,* p. 8, col. 2.

He adhered to this principle to such an extent that "the earlier Wycliffite version is an extremely literal rendering of the Latin original. Latin constructions and Latin word-order are preserved even where they conflict with the English idiom."[22] Although this Wycliffite version is attributed to John Wycliffe, it must be noted that the work was completed after his death by Nicholas of Hereford. The translation was based on poor Latin manuscripts, and was circulated by the Lollards, who were the followers of Wycliffe and the anticlerical party in the church.

John Purvey (c. 1354-1428)

John Purvey, who had served as Wycliffe's secretary, is credited with a revision of the earlier Wycliffite translation at about 1395. This work replaced many of the Latinate constructions by the native English idiom, as well as removing the prefaces of Jerome in favor of an extensive prologue. The result of this revision was a weakening of papal influence over the English people, as this revision tended to drift away from the liturgical Latin of the church. This work, known as the Later Wycliffite version, was published prior to the invention of Johann Gutenberg, which had a dampening effect on the spread of these particular vernacular versions. Nevertheless, the first complete English Bible was published, revised, and in circulation prior to the work of John Hus (c. 1369-1415) in Bohemia. It was the close identity with the work of Hus that resulted in the exhumation of Wycliffe's body; it was burned and the ashes were scattered on the River Swift in 1428, still a generation before Gutenberg's invention.

William Tyndale (c. 1492-1536)

William Tyndale came onto the English scene at one of the most opportune moments in history. In the wake of the Renaissance, he brought with him one of the major contributions to the transmission of the English Bible. This contribution was the first printed edition of any part of the English Bible, although not the first complete Bible printed in the English language. Coverdale laid claim to that honor in 1535.

The transformation of England, and all of Europe for that matter, followed the Renaissance and the features accompanying it: the rise of nationalism, the spirit of exploration and discovery, and the literary revival. The resurgence of the classics followed the fall of Constantinople in 1453; then, Johann Gutenberg (1396-1468) invented movable type for the printing press, the Mazarin Bible was published in 1456, and cheap paper was introduced into Europe. In 1458 Greek began to be studied publicly at the University of Paris, the first Greek grammar appeared in 1476, and the first Greek lexicon was published

22. Bruce, p. 15.

in 1492. The first Hebrew Bible was published in 1488, the first Hebrew grammar in 1503, and a Hebrew lexicon followed in 1506. Over eighty editions of the Latin Bible appeared in Europe before 1500, only a generation after the new printing method was introduced into England by William Caxton (1476). The situation in Europe has been aptly stated by Basil Hall, as he writes,

> There was a *preparatio evangelico* in the first quarter of the sixteenth century, for it was then, and not before, that there appeared in combination the achievements of the humanist scholar-printers; the fruits of intensive study in grammar and syntax of all three languages; and the energy provided by the economic development and regional patriotism of the cities where *bonae litterae* flourished—Basle, Wittenberg, Zurich, Paris, Strassburg, Geneva.[23]

But an English printed version of the Bible was yet to come. The galling knowledge that vernacular versions were circulating, sometimes with the consent of the church, in many European countries merely stiffened the determination of Christians in England for an English Bible. A scholarly man was needed for the enterprise of fashioning the Hebrew and Greek originals into a fitting English idiom, as no mere rendering of the Vulgate would suffice.

William Tyndale was the man who could do what was wanted, for he was "a man of sufficient scholarship to work from Hebrew and Greek, with genius to fashion a fitting English idiom and faith and courage to persist whatever it cost him."[24] Before Tyndale finished his revision work, he became involved in a dispute wherein a man charged that Englishmen were "better without God's Law than without the Pope's." He replied with his now famous statement, "I defy the Pope and all his laws; if God spares my life, ere many years I will cause a boy that driveth the plough shall know more of the Scriptures than thou dost."

After his unsuccessful attempts to do his translations in England, he sailed for the Continent in 1524. Further difficulties ensued, and he finally had his New Testament printed in Cologne toward the end of February 1526. This was the first such achievement to be accomplished, and it was followed by a translation of the Pentateuch, at Marburg (1530), and Jonah, from Antwerp (1531). Tyndale worked under constant threat of being exposed. Lutheran and Wycliffite influence was clearly observable in his work, and his version had to be smuggled into England. Once it was there it was greeted with sharp opposition by Cuthbert Tunstall, Bishop of London, who purchased copies of it to be burned at St. Paul's Cross. Sir Thomas More issued a *Dialogue* in

23. Basil Hall, "Biblical Scholarship: Editions and Commentary," in S.L. Greenslade, ed., *The Cambridge History of the Bible*, vol. 3, *The West from the Reformation to the Present Day*, p. 38.
24. S.L. Greenslade, "English Versions of the Bible," ibid., p. 141.

which he attacked Tyndale's version as belonging to the same "pestilent sect" as Martin Luther's translation. Nevertheless, the first English version of the Pentateuch, Jonah, and the New Testament was published and began circulating in England.

In 1534 Tyndale published a revision of Genesis. It was at that time that he "diligently corrected" his New Testament, as he rigorously objected to a revised edition of his 1526 text that was published by George Joye in 1534. About that same time, the Catholic lord chancellor Sir Thomas More was removed from office, sent to the Tower of London, and executed in 1535. More, who was succeeded by Thomas Cromwell as lord chancellor, successfully spearheaded Henry VIII's Reformation movement between 1534 and 1540, when he too fell from royal favor. Shortly after the completion of his revision, Tyndale was kidnapped, conveyed out of Antwerp, imprisoned in the fortress at Vilvorde in Flanders where he continued his translation of the Old Testament (Proverbs, the Prophets, etc.) before he was found guilty of heresy in August 1536. He was then "degraded from his priestly office, handed over to the secular power for execution, which was carried out on October 6 ... crying thus at the stake with the fervent zeal and a loud voice: 'Lord, open the King of England's eyes.' "[25]

Tyndale's version of the New Testament provided the basis for all the successive revisions between his day and ours. The King James Version is practically a fifth revision of Tyndale's revision; and where it departs from his, the revision committee of 1881, 1885, and 1901 return to it with regularity.[26]

Miles Coverdale (1488-1569)

Paralleling the death prayer of Tyndale, much was happening to bring an answer to his request, including more versions "by the Protestants, fresh proposals from the conservatives, royal proclamations, and the publication of the first complete English Bible."[27] The key individual in the publication of this first complete English Bible in printed form was Miles Coverdale, Tyndale's assistant and proofreader at Antwerp in 1534. Although he did not translate directly from the Hebrew and Greek, he was

> ... lowly and faithfully following his interpreters, five in number, according to the *Dedication to the King*. They were the Vulgate, Pagnini's Latin version of 1528 (very literal in rendering the Old Testament), Luther's German, the Zurich Bible in 1531 and 1534 editions, and Tyndale, or, if Tyndale was not counted; Erasmus's Latin version.[28]

25. Bruce, p. 52.
26. See Appendix.
27. Greenslade, p. 147.
28. Ibid., p. 148.

His translation was basically Tyndale's version revised in the light of the German versions, and not noticeably improved thereby.[29] He introduced chapter summaries, separated the Apocrypha from the other Old Testament books (a precedent generally followed by English Protestant Bibles ever since), and introduced some new expressions into the text. Although the Coverdale Bible, first published in 1535, was reprinted twice in 1537, once in 1550, and once again in 1553, the true successor to the first edition was the Great Bible of 1539. That may be because Anne Boleyn favored Coverdale's Bible, and her execution in 1536 probably brought disfavor upon his work.

Thomas Matthew (c. 1500-1555)

Thomas Matthew was the pen name of John Rogers, the first martyr of the Marian Persecution. He too had been an assistant to Tyndale, and merely combined the Tyndale and Coverdale Old Testaments with the 1535 revision of Tyndale's New Testament to make another version. He would not associate his name with the work that was done by others, but he used his pen name and added copious notes and references to his edition. He borrowed heavily from the French versions of Lefèvre (1534) and Olivétan (1535), as well as Martin Bucer's Latin Psalter with its marginal notes.[30] Matthew secured the consent of the crown for his 1537 version.

Thus, within one year of Tyndale's death at Vilvorde, two of his assistants had secured separate licenses for the publication of their printed English Bibles. With these two licensed Bibles, the widespread circulation of the Scriptures in English was inevitable. But Coverdale's Bible was not based on the original languages, thus alienating the scholars in the church, and Matthew's Bible offended the conservatives in the church because of its notes and its origin. Hence, a new revision was necessary.

Richard Taverner (1505-1575)

Richard Taverner, a layman who knew Greek quite well, used his talent to revise Matthew's Bible in 1539. He improved the translation, especially in more accurately rendering the Greek article. But, this revision was soon followed by another revision of Matthew's Bible, known as the Great Bible, under the leadership of Miles Coverdale and with the approval of Thomas Cranmer (1489-1556), the first Protestant Archbishop of Canterbury, and Thomas Cromwell (c. 1485-1540), Protestant lord chancellor under Henry VIII (1509-1547). The Great Bible soon eclipsed Taverner's work, and the latter has had little influence on subsequent English Bible translations.

29. Bruce, p. 52.
30. See chap. 7 discussion as well as Constantin Hopf, *Martin Bucer and the English Reformation* (Oxford: Oxford U., 1946), pp. 213-17.

The Great Bible (1539)

The Great Bible was done under the direction of Coverdale, with the approval of Cranmer and Cromwell. It received its name because of its size, and was offered as a means of easing the tense situation stemming from John Rogers's work, which brought about the fact that "Royal injunctions of November 1538 forbade printing or importation of English Bibles with notes or prologues unless authorized by the king."[31] The Great Bible was authorized for use in the churches in 1538, but it was not able to solve the problem either, as it was actually a revision of Rogers's revision of Tyndale's Bible, so far as Tyndale's version went. Not only was the Great Bible not a version, nor a revision of a version, but it had the apocryphal books removed from the remainder of the Old Testament and had the title Hagiographa (holy writings) attached to them, and the bishops of the church were still predominantly Roman Catholic. Thus, when the second edition of the Great Bible appeared (1540), it had a preface by Cranmer (hence, Cranmer's Bible) that was included in all subsequent editions of the Great Bible. One interesting feature of that preface is the note at the bottom of the page that reads, "This is the Byble apoynted to the use of the churches." Five other editions of this Bible followed in 1540 and 1541, and even the edicts of Henry VIII in 1543, which forbade anyone of any "estate, condition, or degree . . . to receive, have, take, or keep, Tyndale's or Coverdale's New Testament,"[32] were not sufficient to keep the Great Bible from maintaining its prominent position in the churches. Thus, when Henry VIII died on January 28, 1547, the Great Bible was still appointed to read in the Church of England. Edward VI (1547-1553) ascended to the throne and the Great Bible was reprinted twice, in 1549 and 1553. It was this Bible that was the authoritative text of *The Booke of the Common Prayer and Administration of the Sacraments,* published in 1549 and 1552. The prestige of the Great Bible was able to withstand the onslaughts of the brief but violent reign of Mary Tudor (1553-1558), as the order of 1538 was not revoked.

The Geneva Bible (1557, 1560)

The Geneva Bible[33] was produced during the reign of Mary Tudor. When persecution in England resulted in the death of such men as John Rogers and Thomas Cranmer, others fled to the Continent, including Miles Coverdale. That faith is strengthened in persecution is among the commonest lessons of history, yet those lessons are rarely learned. Thus, while England was offering persecution, Geneva was offering refuge, and there John Knox was lead-

31. Greenslade, p. 151 n. 1, makes reference to Alfred W. Pollard, *Records of the English Bible*.
32. Bruce, p. 79.
33. See Lewis Lupton, *A History of the Geneva Bible*.

ing a group of Protestant exiles in the preparation of an English version of the Bible to meet their religious needs. In 1557 they produced an edition of the New Testament, which was merely a stopgap measure. It is interesting to note:

> The New Testament of 1557 was the work principally of William Whittingham, later Dean of Durham, who took as his basic text not the Great Bible but Tyndale, perhaps in Jugge's edition of 1552, and revised it "by the most approved Greek examples and conference of translations in other tongues."[34]

The Geneva Bible was in several respects an improvement on previous English versions. Geddes MacGregor identifies four significant contributions that led making the English Bible more popular with the people:

> First, in the Old Testament it followed the Hebrew more closely than its predecessors had done. Secondly, though it followed customary practice of the day in providing notes to the text, its notes were comparatively free of the controversial violence that was the fashion of the age. Thirdly, the use of a smaller (quarto) page ... made it an easier book to handle, while plain Roman type made it more legible than Bibles printed in Gothic letter.... Fourthly—and perhaps the most striking feature of all—the plan of division into verses ... was used for the first time for the whole English Bible.[35]

In addition, the Geneva Bible introduced italicized words into the text where English idiom required additional words, and the latest textual evidence was utilized, including the *editio regia* of Stephanus (1550) with its collection of variants, and Beza's Latin version of 1556. The Old Testament and a revised translation of the New Testament were completed by 1560, and the Geneva Bible began its long and eventful history. It went through at least 140 editions prior to 1644, and retained its popularity against the Bishops' Bible (1568) and the first generation of the King James Version (1611). Although the notes were too Calvinistic for Elizabeth I (1558-1603) and James I (1603-1625) they were much milder than those of Tyndale. The Puritans in England used this Bible extensively, and its influence permeated the pages of Shakespeare as well as the households of English-speaking Protestants. Even the address from "The Translators to the Reader," which is prefaced to the King James Version of 1611, took its quotations of Scripture from the Geneva Bible.[36] Still another innovation made by the translators of the Geneva Bible exhibited itself in that "the distinguishing method of the Geneva Committee had been a system of careful and methodical collaboration, as contrasted with the isolated labours of the pioneers of translation."[37]

34. Greenslade, p. 156.
35. Geddes MacGregor, *The Bible in the Making*, p. 133.
36. Bruce, p. 92.
37. Hoare, p. 227.

The Bishops' Bible (1568)

The Bishops' Bible was a revision of the Great Bible, as the immediate success of the Geneva Bible among the common people and the Puritans made it impossible for the Anglican Church leaders to continue using the Great Bible in the churches. Their revision was called the Bishops' Bible, because most of the translators were bishops, and their work was "a compromise—a dignified and 'safe' version for public reading, a sign that the bishops were not unmindful of their responsibilities, in scholarship an improvement upon the Great Bible, less radical than Geneva but willing to learn from it."[38] The scholars involved were better equipped in Hebrew and Greek, and many of their innovations were carried over into the Rheims-Douay and the King James Versions.

Had the Bishops' Bible appeared prior to 1557, it would have been the best translation to date. However, even with the strong support given by the Convocation of Canterbury in 1571, it could not overcome its insurmountable disadvantage of being introduced after there had already been a better translation in circulation, the Geneva Bible. And although the "Bishops' Bible was that generally found in churches from 1568 to 1611, the Geneva Bible was still the home Bible, and no copies of the Bishops' Bible were printed after 1602 [sic]."[39] Although the Bishops' Bible was not a work of high merit in itself, it was the official basis for the revision of 1611.

Summary and Conclusion

Although the English language is only a sort of tag-end dialect of Low German, it has nevertheless become the most significant vehicle of the biblical text in modern times. From Caedmon's paraphrases (late seventh century) to the first complete book of the Bible (Psalms) in Shoreham's day (fourteenth century), then to the pioneer works of Wycliffe, Tyndale, and the publication of the first complete English Bible under the direction of Miles Coverdale (1535), and on to the Great Bible and the Geneva Bible, which soon followed, there proceeded a continual parade of translations that linked their Latin predecessors to the monumental King James Version and its English successors. In a real sense, then, the long chain of transmission "from God" has been brought "to us" in the English-speaking world by the events recorded in this chapter.

38. Greenslade, p. 160.
39. See Appendix and Margaret T. Hills, *A Ready-Reference History of the English Bible,* p. 19. The date here should be 1606 instead of 1602, cf. Hoare, Bruce, Greenslade, Nix, et al.

A Chart of the Major Indo-European Languages, Part 1

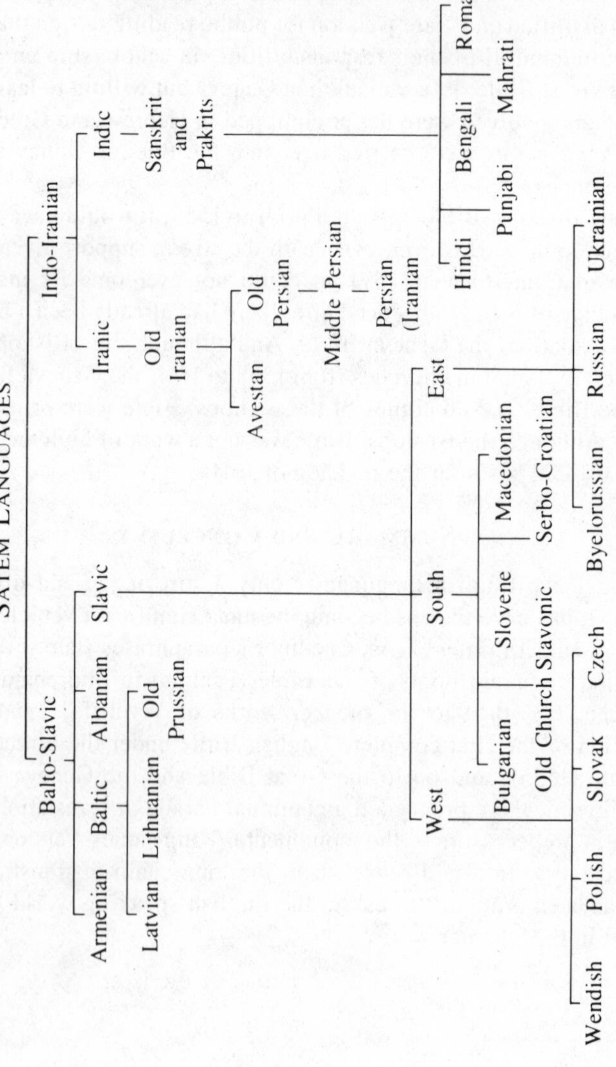

A Chart of the Major Indo-European Languages, Part 2

Centum Languages

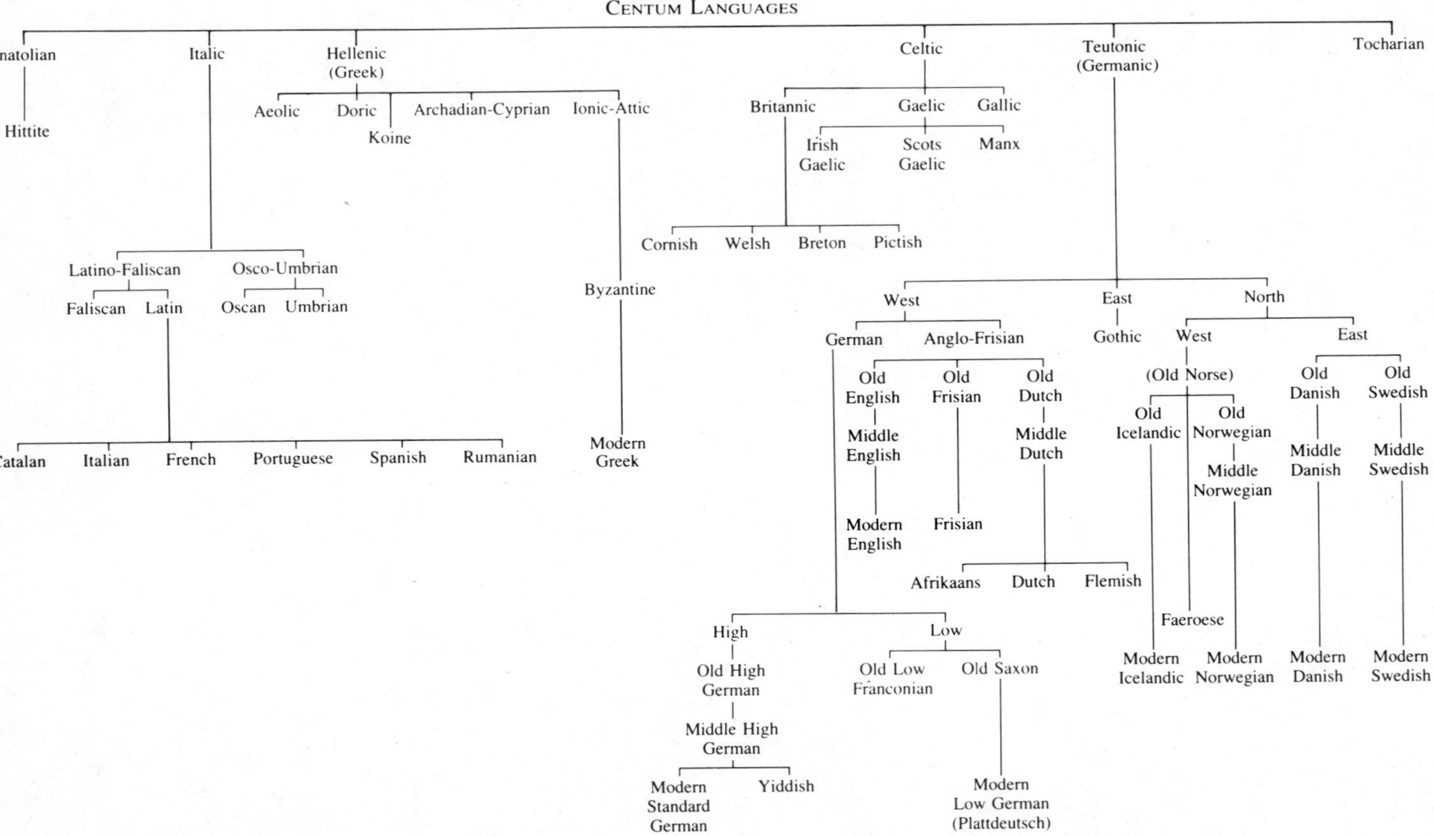

31
Modern English Versions and Translations of Scripture

The English Bible for Roman Catholics

While the Protestants were busy making vernacular translations of the Bible for use in England, their Roman Catholic counterparts were experiencing a similar desire. After the death of Mary Tudor, Elizabeth I (1558-1603) ascended to the throne, and the Roman Catholic exiles of her reign undertook a task similar to that of the Protestant exiles at Geneva during her predecessor's reign.

The Rheims-Douay (Rhemes-Douay) Version (1589, 1609/10)

During the first decade of Elizabeth's reign, a group of English Roman Catholics moved to and settled in Spanish Flanders, easily accessible to England and under Roman Catholic rulers. While there they founded the English College at Douay (1568), for the training of priests and the maintenance of their Catholic faith. William Allen (1532-94), Oxford canon under Mary Tudor, led in the founding of the college and its move to Rheims in France (1578) when political troubles arose. At Rheims the English College came under the direction of another Oxford scholar, Richard Bristow (1538-81), who had gone to Douay in 1569. Meanwhile, Allen was called to Rome, where he founded another English College and was later made a cardinal. In 1593 the college at Rheims returned to Douay.

In a letter written to a professor at the college in Douay in 1578, Allen expressed the feeling of the Roman hierarchy toward an English translation of the Vulgate, as he wrote,

> Catholics educated in the academies and schools have hardly any knowledge of the Scriptures except in Latin. When they are preaching to the unlearned and are obliged on the spur of the moment to translate some passage into the vernacular, they often do it inaccurately and with unpleasant hesitation because either there is no vernacular version of the words, or it does not occur to them at the moment.

> Our adversaries, however, have at their finger tips from some heretical version all those passages of Scripture which seem to make for them, and by a certain deceptive adaptation and alteration of the second words produce the effect of appearing to say nothing but what comes from the Bible. This evil might be remedied if we too had some Catholic version of the Bible, for all the English versions are most corrupt.... If his Holiness shall judge it expedient, we ouselves will endeavor to have the Bible faithfully, purely and genuinely translated according to the edition approved by the Church, for we already have men most fitted for the work.[1]

Only four years later the translation that he had projected was completed by Gregory Martin (d. 1582). That Oxford scholar received his M.A. in 1564. He then renounced Protestantism and went to Douay to study, becoming lecturer in Hebrew and Holy Scripture in 1570. In 1578 he first began to translate the Old Testament, usually doing about two chapters a day over three and a half years. Just before his death the New Testament was published, with many notes. Those notes were the work of Bristow and Allen. Another Protestant-turned-Catholic who had a part in the publication of the Rheims New Testament (1582) was William Reynolds, but his role in the project is uncertain.

Whereas the Rheims translation of the New Testament was designed to act as an antidote to the existing Protestant versions in English, it had some serious defects. In the first place, it was a poor rendition of the English language. It was based on the Latin Vulgate, and as such was actually a translation of a translation. Again, the principles of translation explained in the preface indicate that the translators guarded themselves "against the idea that the Scriptures should always be in our mother tongue, or that they ought, or were ordained by God, to be read indifferently by all."[2] In addition, the Rheims New Testament was vitiated by its self-imposed limitation of being avowedly polemic in nature, a purpose often clearly stated in its copious notes. The New Testament was republished in 1600, but that time from Douay, as the political climate reversed itself and the English College moved back to its place of origin in 1593. The new edition was published under Thomas Worthington, another Oxford scholar, alumnus of the college at Douay and recipient of a D.D. from the Jesuit University of Trier in 1588. Worthington became the third president of the college at Douay in 1599, and was himself active in mission work.

Meanwhile the Old Testament, which had actually been translated before the New, was delayed in its publication. The reason for the delay was actually twofold: primarily, there was a lack of funds available to finance the project;

1. *Letters and Memorials of Cardinal Allen,* with introduction by T.F. Knox, pp. 64f., as cited by Geddes MacGregor, *The Bible in the Making,* pp. 248-49.
2. William E. Nix, "Theological Presuppositions and Sixteenth Century English Bible Translations," pp. 120-21. Also see Clyde L. Manschreck, *A History of Christianity,* 2:131(a)-139(b).

then there was the contributory fact that between 1582 and 1609 there were several new editions of the Vulgate text that needed to be taken into consideration by the translators and revisers. At length the Douay Old Testament was published (1609/10), but it was greeted with criticisms similar to those made of the two editions of the New Testament. It followed the Latin Vulgate exclusively, introduced excessive Latinisms into the text (especially the Psalms), followed the principle of guarding against the idea of translating the Scriptures into the vernacular, and added polemical notes to the translation (although not so extensive as in the New Testament). Because the Old Latin and Vulgate versions generally contained the Old Testament Apocrypha, the Douay translation followed the example and placed them within the Old Testament.[3] Actually there were only seven full books added to the other thirty-nine: Judith, Tobit, Wisdom of Solomon, Ecclesiasticus, Baruch (with the Epistle of Jeremiah attached), 1 Maccabees, and 2 Maccabees. In addition to those full books, four parts of books were added to the English translation: added to Daniel were the portions about Bel and the Dragon, the Song of the Three Hebrew Children, and Susanna; and Esther was expanded.

The Old Testament translation was begun by Martin and probably completed by Allen and Bristow, although little exact evidence is available to determine that matter with certainty, and the notes were apparently furnished by Worthington. "The version had been based on the unofficial Louvain Vulgate (1547, ed. Henten), but was 'conformed to the most perfect Latin edition,' the Sixtine-Clementine of 1592."[4] The annotations were basically designed to bring the interpretation of the text into harmony with the decrees of the Council of Trent (1546-1563). The Translation was uniform throughout, including the over-literal Latinizations.

Whereas the New Testament was reprinted in 1600, 1621, and 1633, it was not until 1635 that the second edition of the Old Testament was published. The New Testament had been in circulation long enough to have an important influence on the translators of the King James Version, as may be seen in the reentry of several ecclesiastical terms, the increased number of Latinisms and so on. The King James Version of the Old Testament, however, was probably set for printing by the time the Douay Old Testament was published, and the lack of its influence on the King James Version is manifest. Nonetheless, with a Protestant queen on the throne, and then a Protestant king, the Rheims-Douay Bible had little possibility of succeeding the Protestant Bibles in the religious life in England. The paucity of reprint editions has led some to observe that in contrast to the Protestants, the Catholics should have

3. See discussion of the Old Latin and Vulgate versions in chap. 29; see chap. 15 for the treatment of the Old Testament Apocrypha.
4. See Appendix and S.L. Greenslade, "English Versions of the Bible 1525-1611," in Greenslade, ed., *The Cambridge History of the Bible,* vol. 3, *The West from the Reformation to the Present Day,* p. 163.

"no fear that the few available copies would be found in the hand of every husbandman."[5]

The Rheims-Douay-Challoner Version (1749/50)

Although several reissues of the Rheims-Douay appeared after 1635, it was not until 1749/50 that Richard Challoner, Bishop of London, published the second revised edition. This publication was little short of a new translation. In the meantime, a New Testament translation based on the Latin Vulgate appeared in Dublin (1718) as the work of Cornelius Nary. In 1730 Robert Whitham, president of the college at Douay, published a revision of the Rheims New Testament. In 1738 a fifth edition of the Rheims New Testament was published, with some revisions generally attributed to Challoner, who had been associated with Whitman at Douay.[6] Challoner published his revision of the Douay Old Testament in 1750 and 1763, and his revised Rheims New Testament in 1749, 1750, 1752, 1763, and 1772. Since that time, further revisions of the Rheims-Douay Bible have been made, but they are practically all based on the Challoner revision of 1749-50.[7] Therefore, the verdict of Father Hugh Pope, in his *English Versions of the Bible* (1952) still stands, namely, "English-speaking Catholics the world over owe Dr. Challoner an immense debt of gratitude, for he provided them for the first time with a portable, cheap, and readable version which in spite of a few inevitable defects has stood the test of two hundred years of use.[8]

The Confraternity of Christian Doctrine Version (1941)

Although the Confraternity edition of the New Testament was not the first English translation of the Catholic Bible in the United States, it is the official one. The first Catholic Bible published in the United States (1790) was a large quarto edition of the Douay Old Testament, with admixtures of several of the Challoner revisions and the third Rheims-Challoner revision of 1752. That Bible was actually "the first *quarto* Bible of any kind *in English* to be published in the United States."[9] Francis Patrick Kenrick then made a new revision of the Rheims-Douay-Challoner Bible in six volumes (1849-60), although he claimed that it was "translated from the Latin Vulgate, diligently compared with the Hebrew and Greek."[10] After that time other editions appeared on both sides of the Atlantic.

In 1936 a new revision of the Rheims-Challoner New Testament was begun

5. Ibid., p. 163.
6. Whereas the 1738 Rheims New Testament is called the "fifth edition," it should be noted that the fourth edition was the 1633 issue, not the 1730 edition of Whitman.
7. See Appendix. For a fuller development of this topic see MacGregor, pp. 256-62.
8. Cf. citation in Greenslade, p. 357.
9. See Appendix and MacGregor, p. 258.
10. Ibid., p. 269.

under the auspices of the Episcopal Committee of the Confraternity of Christian Doctrine. A committee of the twenty-eight scholars of the Catholic Biblical Association began the revision under the direction of Edward P. Arbez. Although the Vulgate text was still used as its basis, the new translation took advantage of the most recent developments in biblical scholarship. It removed many of the archaic expressions of the Rheims-Challoner version, incorporated paragraphs, used American spelling and removed many of the prolific notes of its forbears. The Confraternity New Testament was published by the St. Anthony Guild Press in 1941, and became widely used by English-speaking Catholics around the world as a by-product of the Second World War (1939-1945).

In 1943 Pope Pius XII published the papal encyclical *Divino Afflante Spiritu,* in which he indicated that translations of the Bible could be based on the original Hebrew and Greek texts rather than only on the Latin Vulgate. That was a major shift in Roman Catholic policy, but it was not able to be achieved because of World War II. After wartime restrictions were lifted, the Confraternity began to produce a new version of the Old Testament based on the original texts. In the meantime a Roman Catholic edition of the *Revised Standard Version* (1946, 1952) was published in 1965, while the Old Testament was being produced in installments: Genesis-Ruth (1952), Job-Sirach [Ecclesiasticus] (1955), Isaia-Malachia (1961), and Samuel-Maccabees (1967).[11] The translation of the Old Testament was completed by 1969, and the Episcopal Commitee whose work was under the chairmanship of Louis F. Hartman and was based on the Greek text, turned its attention to the New Testament. It was published in 1970 as the New American Bible.[12] In 1966 Roman Catholic scholars also joined members of the Revised Standard Version Committee to produce the ecumenical *Common Bible* (1973) and the *New Oxford Annotated Bible* (1977).[13]

The Ronald A. Knox Translation (1944, 1948)

Just as the Confraternity Version is the official American edition of the Roman Catholic Bible, the Knox Version is the official Catholic Bible in Great Britain. After the papal encyclical of 1943, a new edition of the Latin Vulgate was published (1945). That Vulgate text was not the basis of Monsignor Knox's New Testament translation (1944). In 1948 Knox's Old Testament was published, but that was based on the new Vulgate, actually a revision of

11. See Appendix and Hills, p. 29.
12. See discussion below on the *Revised Standard Version,* the *Common Bible,* and the *New Oxford Annotated Bible.* Also see Appendix and Sakae Kubo and Walter F. Specht, *So Many Versions? Twentieth-century English Versions of the Bible,* pp. 54-60.
13. See Appendix; Kubo and Specht, pp. 213-21; Lloyd R. Bailey, ed., *The Word of God: A Guide to English Versions of the Bible,* pp. 139-51; and Jack P. Lewis, *The English Bible from the KJV to the NIV: A History and Evaluation,* pp. 215-28.

the 1592 Sixto-Clementine Vulgate. In 1955 hierarchical approval was given to Knox's translation, some sixteen years after the English hierarchy had asked the convert to Roman Catholicism to undertake the work (1939). It should be pointed out at this juncture that the Confraternity edition of the Roman Catholic Bible in English is based on older and more reliable Latin texts, and on original texts throughout most of the Old Testament. Hence, the Confraternity Version is based on a much firmer foundation than Knox's. Both of those are superseded by the *Revised Standard Version Catholic Bible,* the *Common Bible,* and the *New Oxford Annotated Bible.*

The English Bible for Protestants

Turning now to the Protestant versions of the Bible in English,[14] it becomes quite apparent that the diversity and multiplicity of translations that appeared during the early Reformation period began to take on a more unified front as the various groups used the same translations. Thus when James VI of Scotland became James I of England (1603-1625), he summoned a conference of churchmen and theologians to discuss things "amiss in the Church." It was at this conference that the wheels were set in motion for the most influential single translation of the English Bible that the Protestants were to produce.

King James ("Authorized") Version (1611)

In January 1604, James I called the Hampton Court Conference in response to the Millenary Petition, which had been presented to him while he was traveling from Edinburgh to London. The Millenary Petition, so called because it contained about a thousand signatures, set forth the grievances of the Puritan party in the English church. The Puritans were a force to be reckoned with in James's new domain, and James was obliged to hear their petitions. Although James, who regarded himself above all religious parties and principles, treated the Puritans with rudeness at the conference, it was there that John Reynolds, the Puritan president of Corpus Christi College, Oxford, raised the question of the advisability and desirability of having an authorized version of the English Bible that would be acceptable to all parties in the church. James I voiced his wholehearted support of such a venture, as it gave him the opportunity to act as peacemaker in his newly acquired realm. It also provided him with the occasion to replace the two most popular versions of the English Bible: the Bishops' Bible, used in the churches, and the Geneva Bible, the home Bible that he regarded as the worst of the existing transla-

14. See Appendix; Luther A. Weigle, "English Versions Since 1611," in S.L. Greenslade, ed., *The Cambridge History of the Bible,* 3:361-82; F.F. Bruce, *The English Bible: A History of Translations;* Bailey; Lewis; and Kubo and Specht.

tions. This was due largely to his distaste for the accessories that accompanied the translation rather than the translation itself. James had been brought up to believe that kings were appointed by God and had a divine right to rule their people. As a result, his view of "no bishop no king" led him to call for a version "which would embody the best in the existing versions and which could be read both in the public services of the Church and in homes by private individuals."[15]

The first order of business was to select a committee of revisers, a precedent established by the translators of the Geneva Bible.[16] That was done, and six companies were assigned, totaling fifty-four men, though only forty-seven actually did the work of revision.[17] Two companies met at Cambridge to revise 1 Chronicles through Ecclesiastes, and the Apocrypha; at Oxford two other companies met to revise Isaiah through Malachi, the four gospels, Acts, and the Apocalypse; and the two remaining companies met at Westminster, where they revised Genesis through 2 Kings and Romans through Jude. Each company was given a set of instructions, which included the English translations to be used when they agreed better with the text than the Bishops' Bible: Tyndale's, Matthew's, Coverdale's, Whitchurche's, Geneva.[18] Using the Bishops' Bible as the basis for the revision, the committees retained many old ecclesiastical words, undoubtedly the influence of the Rheims New Testament, which had recently been published. No marginal notes were affixed, except for the explanation of the Hebrew and Greek words that would require them. Many Latinisms were reintroduced, but the Geneva Bible influenced the precision of expression and contributed to the clarity of the revision. Frequently the new revision departed from Tyndale's version, as did the Great Bible, only to have the revisers of 1881 and 1885 return to the earlier rendering.

Strictly speaking, the so-called Authorized Version (KJV) was never authorized. That tradition seems to rest merely upon a printer's claim on the title page that contained the clause from earlier Bibles, "Appointed to be read in Churches."[19] It replaced the Bishops' Bible in public use, as the latter was last printed in 1606 and no other large, folio-size Bible was printed after 1611. In competition among the laymen of England, the King James Version ran headlong into the popular Geneva Bible of the Puritans, but the grandeur of its translation ultimately swept all opposition aside. Nevertheless, there is one fact that has often been overlooked by the adherents to the King James

15. Kenneth Scott Latourette, *A History of Christianity,* p. 817.
16. Nix, pp. 122 ff.; also see chap. 30.
17. See Hills, pp. 21-22; MacGregor, pp. 164-78; F.F. Bruce, *The English Bible: A History of Translations,* pp. 96-112; H.W. Hoare, *The Evolution of the English Bible,* pp. 241-70; et al.
18. Hoare, pp. 252-54, lists fifteen rules; number fourteen is cited here. Whitchurche's translation was the 1549 folio edition of the Great Bible.
19. Lewis, p. 35.

Version, namely, the King James Version is not really a version at all. Even the original title page of 1611 indicates that it is a translation, as it reads,

> THE HOLY BIBLE, Conteyning the Old Testament, and the New:
> *Newly Translated out of* the Originall Tongues:
> and with the former Translations diligently compared and revised,
> by his Majesties speciall Commandement.
>
> Appointed to be read in Churches.
>
> IMPRINTED at London by Robert Barker,
> Printer to the Kings most Excellent Maiestie
> Anno Dom. 1611
> Cum Privilegio.[20]

There is no evidence that any formal appointment as to the King James Version's liturgical use by either the king, Parliament, Privy Council, or Convocation was actually made. Actually, this Bible was the third "Authorized Bible" rather than "The Authorized Bible." It should be kept in mind that "authorized" was used as a synonym for "recognized by various churches as accepted for use in public worship."[21] The actual purpose of the translators of the King James Version was set forth in a lengthy preface written by Myles Smith. In it he illustrates how the translation being done by the six committees actually rested on the immediate predecessors rather than being a new translation from the original tongues. In following that reasoning, the message from "the translators to the Reader" indicates their purpose:

> But it is high time to issue them, and to shew in briefe what was proposed to our selues, and what course we held in this our perusall and suruay of the Bible. Truly (good Christian Reader) wee neuer thought from the beginning, that we should needs to make a new Translation, nor yet to make a bad one a good one, (for then the imputation of Sixtus had bene true in some sort, that our people had bene fed with gall of Dragons in stead of wine, with whey in stead of milke:) but to make a good one better, or out of many good ones one principall good one, not iustly to be excepted against; that hath bene our indeauour, that our marke.[22]

The King James Version text was based on little if any of the superior texts of the twelfth to the fifteenth centuries, as it followed the 1516 and 1522 editions of Erasmus' Greek text, including the interpolation of 1 John 5:7.[23]

The reasons for the gradual but overwhelming success of the King James

20. *The Holy Bible, an Exact Reprint Page for Page of the Authorized Version Published in the Year MDCXI.*
21. Edgar J. Goodspeed, "The Versions of the New Testament," *Tools for Bible Study,* Palmer H. Kelly and Donald G. Miller, eds. (Richmond: Knox, 1956), p. 118.
22. Myles Smith, "The Translators to the Reader," *The Holy Bible, an Exact Reprint Page.*
23. See the discussion in chaps. 21, 22, 25, and 26.

Version have been well stated by several writers and may be briefly summarized as follows:[24]

1. the personal qualifications of the revisers, who were the choice scholars and linguists of their day as well as men of profound and unaffected piety
2. the almost universal sense of the work as a national effort, supported wholeheartedly by the king, and with the full concurrence and approval of both church and state
3. the availability and accessibility of the results of nearly a century of diligent and unintermittent labor in the field of biblical study, beginning with Tyndale and Purvey rather than Wycliffe, and their efforts to "make a good translation better"
4. the congeniality of the religious climate of the day with the sympathies and enthusiasm of the translators, as the predominant interest of their age was theology and religion
5. the organized system of cooperative work that followed the precedent of the Geneva translators, although it may have been improved, resulted in a unity of tone in the King James Version that surpassed all its predecessors
6. the literary atmosphere of the late sixteenth and early seventeenth centuries paralleled the lofty sense of style and artistic touch of the translators

The publishers added their contribution to the success of the King James Version by ceasing the publication of the Bishops' Bible in 1606, and by issuing the King James Version in the same format as the Geneva Bible. Nevertheless, the quality of the work needs no commendation at this late date. Although Jack P. Lewis asserts that "those who feel they can escape the problem of translations by retreating into the citadel of the KJV have a zeal for God not in accord with knowledge,"[25] it reigns supreme as the "intrinsically" authorized version of English-speaking Protestantism. That, following on the thousand-year reign of the Latin Vulgate, is surely a notable achievement.

Three editions of the King James Version appeared during its first year of publication. Those folio editions (16 by 10½ inches) were succeeded by quarto and octavo editions in 1612. As the early editions continued to be published, many various readings and misspellings appeared, some of which are quite humorous: for example, in 1631 the word "not" was omitted from the seventh of the Ten Commandments, hence, it was called the "Wicked Bible"; the 1717 edition printed at Oxford was called the "Vinegar Bible" because of

24. After Hoare, pp. 257-70.
25. Lewis, p. 67.

the chapter heading of Luke 20, which reads "vinegar" instead of "vineyard"; in 1795 the Oxford edition misspelled "filled" (writing "killed") in Mark 7:27, and was called the "Murderers' Bible." In the course of time, the spelling of the earliest editions of the King James Version was modernized and modified. In 1701 the dates of Archbishop Ussher were inserted into the margin at the insistence of Bishop Lloyd and have remained there since. This item has resulted in much inappropriate and unfair criticism of Christians, as well as argument and discussion by them, for it is that system of dates that marks creation at 4004 B.C.

During the reign of Charles I (1625-1649) the Long Parliament (1640-1660) set up a commission to consider revising the King James Version or producing a new translation, but nothing further was done in the matter. Only minor revisions of the King James Version actually took place, but they were begun quite early and were well scattered over a long period of time; for example, in 1629 and 1638, then the efforts of Long Parliament in 1653, again in 1701, and finally by Dr. Paris of Cambridge in 1762, and by Dr. Blayney of Oxford in 1769. In the latter two revisions,

> efforts were made to "correct and harmonize its spelling, and to rid it of some antique words like 'sith.' " Some points escaped these professors, but Blayney's edition has remained the standard form of the version ever since unto this day. His edition probably differs from that of 1611 in at least 75,000 details.[26]

The English Revised Version (1881, 1885)

Antecedents to the revision of 1881-1885. All of the revisions of the King James Version mentioned above were made without ecclesiastical or royal authority. In fact, no "official" revision of the King James Version was forthcoming for over one hundred years after the revision of Dr. Blayney (1769). Many of the revisions were ill-advised, such as Ussher's chronology, and the exclusion of the apocryphal books that brought a penalty of imprisonment decreed by the Archbishop of Canterbury, George Abbott, shortly thereafter. There were, however, some excellent revisions made in an "unofficial" manner, as in the case of an anonymous edition of *The Holy Bible Containing the Authorized Version of the Old and New Testaments, with Many Emendations*. The preface of that work states:

> The history of the English Bible records the great alarm that has always been excited by attempts to improve the translation, or to correct its acknowledged defects; and never did these apprehensions exist in a greater degree than when our present version was issued: but the result has proved groundless; for nothing, perhaps, has contributed more to establish the truth of revelation, or to refute the sophistry of scepticism, than these corrections.[27]

26. Goodspeed, pp. 117-18.

The author states further:

> Since the publication of the authorized version, scholars of pre-eminent piety and profound learning, of untiring industry, and inflexible integrity, have expended more time and talent on the Bible than any other book in existence; and their combined labours have brought it nearer to a state of perfection than any ancient work. And, surely, if this blessed volume, . . . be the most precious boon conferred on the heirs of immortality; if it be the common property of all the children of Adam, . . . as well for such as are of comparatively feeble attainments, as for those of powerful intellect, and of cultivated minds; it should be presented to the church and to the world with the results of those labours which have shed so much light on its obscure and difficult passages; light—which has hitherto been scattered through publication so numerous, rare, or costly, as to be inaccessible to the great mass of mankind.[28]

In his "unofficial" revision of the King James Version (published in 1841), the author mentions his use of manuscripts that were not available in 1611.[29]

With the advances in nineteenth-century scholarship, the accumulation of earlier and better manuscript materials, the archaelogical discoveries in the ancient world in general, and the actual changes in English society and its literary style, the revision of the King James Version on a more "official" basis was mandatory. Even before the "official" revision took place, a group of outstanding scholars published *The Variorum Edition of the New Testament of Our Lord and Saviour Jesus Christ* (1880). That work was edited by R.L. Clark, Alfred Goodwin, and W. Sanday, and was translated from the original Greek with diligent comparison and revision in light of former translations "by his majesty's special command."[30] The Variorum Bible was merely a revision of the King James in light of the various readings from the best authorities. The variations appeared in the notes and margin, and were "designed not merely to correct some of the more important mistranslations, but to supply the means of estimating the authority by which the proposed corrections are supported."[31] Thus, although following in the tradition of the Tyndale, Coverdale, Great, Geneva, Bishops', and various editions of the King James Version, the Variorum Bible prepared the way for the English Revised Version, which was published in 1881 and 1885, and which had access to the renderings and critical apparatus of the Variorum Bible.

27. *The Holy Bible Containing the Authorized Version of the Old and New Testaments, with Many Emendations,* p. iv.
28. Ibid., p. v.
29. See chap. 20 on the discoveries and contents of the New Testament manuscripts. One of the manuscripts used by this author was "the *Codex Vaticanus* and other rare and valuable manuscripts in the Vatican library at Rome." Ibid., p. ix. Also see Appendix.
30. Cf. title page of the *The Variorum Edition of the New Testament of Our Lord and Saviour Jesus Christ.*
31. Ibid., Editors' Preface.

Actual Revision of the King James Version. The desire for a full revision of the King James Version (Authorized Version) was so widespread among Protestant scholars after the mid-nineteenth century that a Convocation of the Province of Canterbury was called in 1870 for the proposal of a revision of the text where the Hebrew and Greek texts have been inaccurately or wrongly translated. Samuel Wilberforce, bishop of Winchester, made the resolution to revise the New Testament, and Bishop Ollivant enlarged it to include the Old Testament. Two companies were appointed, originally having twenty-four members each, but later including some sixty-five revisers of various denominations. The actual process of revision was begun in 1871, and in 1872 a group of American scholars was asked to join the work.[32]

The general principles of procedure for the revisers were as follows:

1. To introduce as few alterations as possible into the Text of the Authorized Version consistently with faithfulness.
2. To limit, as far as possible, the expression of such alterations to the language of the Authorized and earlier English versions.
3. Each Company to go twice over the portion to be revised, once provisionally, the second time finally, and on principles of voting as hereinafter is provided.
4. That the Text to be adopted be that for which the evidence is decidedly preponderating; and that when the Text so adopted differs from that from which the Authorized Version was made, the alteration be indicated in the margin.
5. To make or retain no change in the Text on the second final revision by each company, except *two-thirds* of those present approve of the same, but on the first revision to decide by simple majorities.
6. In every case of proposed alteration that may have given rise to discussion, to defer the voting thereupon till the next Meeting, whensoever the same shall be required by one-third of those present at the Meeting, such intended vote to be announced in the notice of the next Meeting.
7. To revise the headings of the chapters, pages, paragraphs, italics, and punctuation.
8. To refer, on the part of each Company, when considered desirable, to Divines, Scholars, and Literary men, whether at home or abroad, for their opinions.[33]

Oxford and Cambridge university presses absorbed the costs for the translation, with the proviso that they would have exclusive copyrights to the finished product. After six years the first revision was completed, and another two-and-one-half years were spent in consideration of the suggestions of the American committee. Finally, on May 17, 1881, the *English Revised Version of the New Testament* was published in paragraph form. In less than a year after publication nearly three million copies were sold in England and Amer-

32. Hills, pp. 25-26, names the English and American committee members.
33. Bruce, p. 137.

ica, with 365,000 copies sold in New York and 110,000 in Philadelphia. Most of those were sold in the first few weeks.

The English Revised Version (RV or ERV) appeared in the United States in New York and Philadelphia on May 20, 1881, and on May 22 the entire New Testament was published in the *Chicago Times* and the *Chicago Tribune*. The response to the RV was generally disappointing, as the old familiar phrases were often replaced by new ones, and old words were removed in favor of new ones. The paragraph arrangement satisfied those who tended to dislike the verse arrangement of the King James Version verses, but they were not satisfied with the "minor changes" in the English. Although the text was much more accurate, it would take several generations for acceptance of the altered words and rhythms. In 1885 the Old Testament was published, the Apocrypha appeared in 1896 (1898 in the United States), and the entire Bible was published in 1898.

The American Standard Version (1901)

Some of the renderings of the English Revised Version were not completely favored by the American revision committee, but they had agreed to give for fourteen years "no sanction to the publication of any other editions of the Revised Version than those issued by the University Presses of England."[34] But in 1901 *The American Standard Edition of the Revised Version (American Standard Version,* ASV), was published. The title indicates that several "unauthorized" editions of the Revised Version had been published in the United States and that was indeed true. Further revisions were made in the *American Standard Version,* namely, some antiquated terms were replaced by more modern ones, for example, "Jehovah" instead of "Lord," and "Holy Spirit" replaced "Holy Ghost." The paragraph structures were revised and shortened, and short page headings were added. The version slowly won its way into American churches, and copies were imported into England, as many favored the Americanisms in the *American Standard Version*. Although the *American Standard Version* lacks the beauty of the King James Version, its more accurate readings made it acceptable for teachers and students alike. In 1929 the copyright passed to the International Council of Religious Education, and that group later revised its text again. The ASV, based on the English Revised Version of 1881, 1885, "was the work of many hands and of several generations. The foundation was laid by William Tyndale."[35]

The Revised Standard Version (1946, 1952)

Half a century after the English Revised Version was published, the

34. See Appendix; Hills, p. 27; also see Lewis, pp. 69-106.
35. Preface, *The Revised Version of the New Testament*.

International Council of Religious Education expressed its desire to utilize the great advances in biblical scholarship.[36] The Westcott-Hort text of the New Testament, the basis underlying the English and American Revised Versions, had been modified sharply by the light cast upon it by papyrus discoveries, older manuscripts coming to light, and so on. In addition, the literary style and taste of English had continued to change, and a new revision was considered necessary. Hence in 1937 the International Council authorized a committee to proceed with a revision that would

> embody the best results of modern scholarship as to the meaning of the Scriptures, and express this meaning in English diction which is designed for use in public and private worship and preserves those qualities which have given to the King James Version a supreme place in English literature.[37]

The revision committee consisted of some twenty-two outstanding scholars who were to follow the meaning of the *American Standard Version* in the elegance of the King James Version, and change the readings only if two-thirds of the committee agreed.[38] It uses simpler, more current forms of pronouns such as "you" and "yours," except in reference to God, and more direct word order. *The Revised Standard Version: The New Testament* (RSV) was published in 1946, delayed because of World War II, the Old Testament in 1952, and the Apocrypha in 1957. A second edition of the *Revised Standard Version* New Testament was published in 1977.

The publication of the *Revised Standard Version* was launched with a grand publicity campaign, and certain reactions were sure to be set in motion. Whereas the *American Standard Version* was charged with over-literalization of the Old Testament, the *Revised Standard Version* was criticized for going to the opposite extreme; for example the blurring of traditional "Messianic" passages, such as the substitution of "young woman" for the traditional "virgin" of Isaiah 7:14, raised sharp cries of criticism. The criticisms of the New Testament were not nearly so vitriolic, but they were sharp enough. In fact, F.F. Bruce indicates that

> when the whole Bible was published in 1952, the criticism which greeted it from some quarters was remarkably reminiscent of criticism voiced in earlier days against the Greek Septuagint and the Latin Vulgate, against the versions of Luther and Tyndale, against the AV and RV.[39]

All the criticism notwithstanding, the *Revised Standard Version* has provided

36. See Appendix. Kubo and Specht, pp. 45-60; Lewis, pp. 107-28; and Bruce M. Metzger, "The Revised Standard Version," in Bailey, pp. 28-44.
37. Preface, *The Revised Standard Version*.
38. Hills, pp. 27-28.
39. Bruce, p. 195.

the English-speaking church with an up-to-date revision of the Scripture text based on the "critical text." As Jack Lewis sees it, "The publication of the RSV marked both the end of one era and the opening of another in the effort to communicate God's Word to the English reader. For many its publication marked the end of the age in which 'The Bible' meant the KJV. The RSV opened the era of the multiple translations flooding today's market, all competing with each other."[40] In addition, the RSV has been used as the basis for ecumenical Bible translations, but that is a matter to be treated in chapter 32.

The New English Bible (1961, 1970)

Not satisfied that the *Revised Standard Version* was a continuation of the long-established tradition of the earlier English versions, the General Assembly of the Church of Scotland met in 1946 to consider a completely new translation.[41] A joint committee was appointed in 1947, and three panels were chosen: for the Old Testament, New Testament, and Apocrypha. C.H. Dodd was appointed chairman of the New Testament panel, and in 1949, director of the whole translation.[42] In March 1960, the New Testament portion was accepted by the committe; and it was published in 1961. The principles of the translation were set forth in a memorandum by Dodd:

> It is to be genuinely English in idiom, such as will not awaken a sense of strangeness or remoteness. Ideally, we aim at a "timeless" English, avoiding equally both archaisms and transient modernisms. The version should be plain enough to convey its meaning to any reasonably intelligent person (so far as verbal expression goes), yet not bald or pedestrian. It should not aim at preserving "hallowed" associations; it should aim at conveying a sense of reality. It should be as accurate as may be without pedantry. It is to be hoped that, at least occasionally, it may produce arresting and memorable readings. It should have sufficient dignity to be read aloud.... We should like to produce a translation which may receive general recognition as an authoritative second version alongside the A.V. for certain public purposes as well as for private reading, and above all a translation which may in some measure remove a real barrier between a large proportion of our fellow-countrymen and the truth of the Holy Scriptures.[43]

On March 16, 1970, *The New English Bible* (NEB), including a second edition of the New Testament, was published by Oxford and Cambridge University Presses, which underwrote the translation project and hold its copy-

40. Lewis, pp. 127-28.
41. See Roger A. Bullard, "The New English Bible," in Bailey, pp. 45-62; Lewis, pp. 129-63; Kubo and Specht, pp. 198-212.
42. Bruce, pp. 225-26, gives the names and details of the members of the committee.
43. As cited by T.H. Robinson, "A New Translation of the English Bible," *The Bible Translator* 2 (Oct. 1951): 168.

right. This was the first translation to break completely with the King James tradition, and it has enjoyed widespread publication, selling over seven million copies of the entire Bible within the first twelve years. The approach to the text is one of the distinctives of the *New English Bible*. The basic text for the Old Testament translation is R. Kittel's *Biblia Hebraica* (BHK; see chap. 21), with some conjectural emendations, and a heavier reliance on the Dead Sea Scrolls as against the Masoretic Text than any previous version of the English Bible. In the revised edition of the New Testament, the *New English Bible* has made more than four hundred changes, and it has brought some of its readings into harmony with the renderings of its Old Testament translation. In all, some of the NEB changes are more accurate than those that have appeared in the KJV, RV, ASV, or RSV, as the translation is very readable and in many cases ambiguities are clarified. The beauty of its English has brought praise to the NEB, but it has not gained as much favor in the United States as it has in Great Britain. Some critics believe it has gone "metric," charging that the rearrangement of verses in the NEB (more than one hundred textual displacements occur in the Old Testament alone) has no textual basis. Some of its "Anglicisms" sound strange to the American ear (e.g. "cudgels" for "staves" [KJV] or "clubs" [RSV] in Matt. 26:47, and "put to rout" instead of "scattered" in Luke 1:51, as well as "mealtub" for "bushel" in Matt. 5:15). The overruling principle of "intelligibility" rather than "literalness" of meaning certainly indicates the influence of contemporary theology on the translation via its translators, but that has been the case with all of its English forebears.

Summary and Conclusion

Protestants were not alone in the production of English translations of the Bible. Their enterprise was paralleled by a Roman Catholic thirst for the same. This Roman Catholic desire culminated in the publication of the Rheims-Douay Bible (1582, 1609), the Challoner revision (1740/50), the Confraternity of Christian Doctrine edition in America (1941), and the version of Monsignor Ronald A. Knox in England (1944, 1948). Although the Rheims-Douay was published by the Roman Catholic church almost two years before the Protestants published the King James Version (1611), the latter was destined to take precedence over the former in both popularity and style. After almost three hundred years the first attempt at an official replacement for the King James Version resulted in the production of the English Revised Version (1881, 1885) and the *American Standard Version* (1901). Following that have come the attempts of the *Revised Standard Version* (1946, 1952) and the *New English Bible* (1961, 1970) to update the translation. However, despite those official revisions, the King James Version, with all its archaism, remains one of the most widely circulated books in the world today.

32
Modern Speech Versions and Translations of Scripture

One of the strongest evidences of the universality of the Bible is the multiplicity of translations and the variety of languages into which it has been translated. According to figures from the British and Foreign Bible Society, the entire Bible has been translated into more than two hundred languages, and biblical portions into over a thousand languages and dialects.[1] A sample selection of these will serve to illustrate this final link in the chain of transmission that connects the Hebrew and Greek autographs to the languages of the twentieth century.

Foreign Language Versions and Translations

After the invention of movable type in printing and the rise of the Reformation in the first part of the sixteenth century, the first group of Bible translations in the vernacular were printed.

Latin Versions in the Reformation Period

On the very eve of the Reformation the Roman Catholic church was producing translations of the Bible into Latin. Among those Latin versions were the works of Desiderius Erasmus (1466-1536) in 1516, Santi Pagninus (1466-1541) in 1528, Cardinal Cajetan (1469-1534) in 1530, and Arius Montanus (1527-1598) in 1571. Meanwhile, the early Protestants were busy publishing their own Latin versions of the Bible. Noteworthy in that area are the works of Sebastian Münster (1489-1552) in 1543/44, Théodore de Bèze (1519-1605) in 1556/57, and Tremellius (1510-1580) who worked with Junius

1. The British and Foreign Bible Society alone has translated Bible portions into some 782 languages in recent times. For a complete listing of those see *Historical Catalogue of the Printed Editions of Holy Scripture in the Library of the British and Foreign Bible Society*, compiled by T. H. Darlow and H. F. Moule.

to produce the last Latin version of the Old Testament by Protestants to receive widespread fame (1575-1579).[2]

German Versions in the Reformation Period

Prior to the fifteenth century there were some 230 manuscript copies of the Bible in German. After that time 128 more were made. The first printed German version of the Bible appeared in 1466, and eighteen others were published before 1521. In 1521/22 Martin Luther published his German version of the New Testament. It was the most common version to circulate in Germany, as Luther took every precaution to see that his work became the official German version. That was especially true after he completed his Old Testament translation in 1534. By the year 1580 there were seventy-two editions of the German New Testament and thirty-eight of the Old. The multiplication of German versions has continued to the present.[3]

French Versions in the Reformation Period

After the twelfth century, several French translations of the Latin Vulgate were made in manuscript form. Unlike the German and English counterparts, there is no authorized version of the French Bible. The first printed edition of a French Bible appeared in Lyons in 1477/78, and a better edition appeared in Paris in 1487. It was not until the translation of the Vulgate by the humanist Catholic Jacques Lefèvre d'Etaples was published at Paris in 1523-1530 that an important French version came into being. By 1535 the first important Protestant version was published. That was the work of Pierre Robert Olivétan, John Calvin's cousin. His French version was published at Serriéres, with the Waldenses agreeing to contribute to the cost. In 1540 a second edition was published, and in 1545 and 1551 John Calvin revised this first Protestant version of the French Bible.

Dutch Versions of the Bible

Before the Reformation, Dutch translations of the Bible tended to be incomplete and were based on earlier metrical paraphrases and translations. With the change in climate following the Reformation came an increased interest in Bible translation in the vernacular. Roman Catholics published Dutch translations of the Bible based on Erasmus's Latin text in 1516. In 1522 another translation began to be published in parts; in 1523 the New Testament

2. For a fuller treatment of this subject see S. L. Greenslade, ed., *The Cambridge History of the Bible,* vol. 3, *The West From the Reformation to the Present Day,* pp. 38-93.
3. Space would not permit listing the more recent translations in even the major foreign languages. The British and Foreign Bible Society has compiled three volumes (1,849 pp.) with some 10,000 entries of Bibles published in 628 languages between 1400 and the early 1900s in its *Historical Catalogue of the Printed Editions of Holy Scripture*.

was finished, and the Old Testament followed in 1527. Other Roman Catholic editions were published in 1539 and 1548. Meanwhile, Protestants began publishing their own translations of the Bible into Dutch. In 1525 a Dutch translation of Luther's New Testament appeared in Antwerp, and his Old Testament was translated and published in 1526. It was not until 1637 that a Dutch version based on the original texts and authorized by the States General was published. That work was revised in 1866-1897.

Italian Versions of the Bible

From the fourteenth century onward, devotional paraphrases of Scripture in Italian were published. The first vernacular version of the New Testament was not published until 1530, by a layman suspected of heresy, Antonio Brucioli (c. 1495-1566). In 1531 he published the Psalms, and the remainder of the Old Testament in 1532. The latter work appears to have drawn heavily on Santi Pagnini's interlinear version of 1528. In 1538 the first complete Italian Bible to receive papal sanction was published by Santi Marmochini. It claims to have been based on the Greek and Hebrew, but it was undoubtedly based on an existing version. Protestants did not actually publish an Italian version until 1607, when Giovanni Diodati (1576-1649) published the first edition of his Bible in Geneva. The second edition appeared in 1641, with enlarged notes and introductions and a revised text. It too was published in Geneva. This work is of very high quality and was later circulated by the British and Foreign Bible Society. It remained the basic Protestant version of the Italian Bible into the present century.

Spanish Versions of the Bible

The first printed Index of the Spanish Inquisition (Toledo, 1551) prohibited the use of vernacular versions of the Bible in Spain. Thus, Roman Catholics did not actually have a Spanish Bible with papal sanction until Pius VI authorized A. Martini's Italian translation, and Anselmo Petite's Spanish New Testament (1785) was permitted by the Inquisition's Index of 1790. Until that time, verse translations and "outlaw" versions were used. Protestants provided some of those items as early as 1543, when the New Testament in Spanish was published by Francis of Emzinas in Antwerp. In 1553 a literal Spanish translation of the Old Testament was published by the Jewish press at Ferrara. In 1569 the first complete translation of the Bible into Spanish was published at Basle. This translation included the Apocrypha and was reissued at Frankfurt in 1602 and 1622. The Spanish Bible, the work of Cassiodoro de Reyna revised in 1602 by Cipriano de Valera, is still a basic edition, and it has been the basis of many Spanish Protestant Bibles published by the British and Foreign Bible Society since 1861.

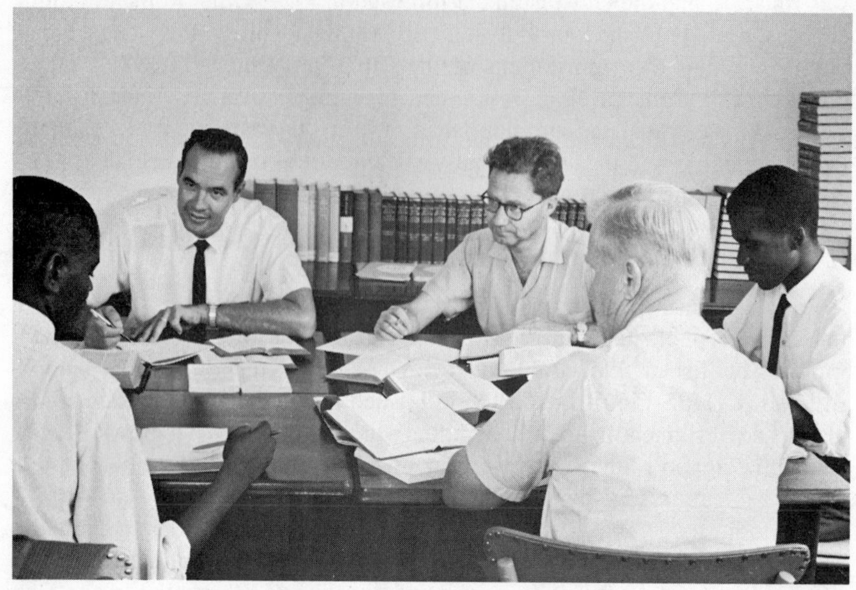

26. A group of participants in the Zambia Translators Institute studying problems of the Chibemba translation (American Bible Society Library)

Other Versions and Translations of the Bible

In addition to the above languages into which the Bible has been translated, there are over eight hundred other modern languages into which portions of the Bible have been translated.[4] But some of the major translations and versions are worthy of note.

Portuguese. A Roman Catholic Missionary turned Protestant, Fereira d'Almeida published his New Testament translation in 1681, and it went into a second edition in 1712. He began an Old Testament translation, which was completed by others in 1751. Roman Catholics did not produce a Portuguese Bible until 1784.

Danish. The earliest Danish translation was a fourteenth- or fifteenth-century manuscript now housed in Copenhagen. In 1524 the first printed New Testament was published in Leipsig by J.D. Michaelis. The first complete Bible appeared in 1550.

Norwegian. Until 1814 the Danish version was used in Norway. Then a revision of the 1647 edition was begun in 1842 and finally completed in 1890.

Swedish. In 1523 Sweden and Denmark separated, and in 1526 a Swedish

4. MacGregor, *The Bible in the Making*, pp. 331-83, has an excellent summary of the editions, languages, Bibles, New Testaments, and portions of Scripture based on the records of the British and Foreign Bible Society.

New Testament based on Luther's 1522 German edition was published. In 1541 a complete Bible was translated into Swedish, based on Luther's 1534 edition.

Polish. There were many early partial versions in Polish, but the first complete New Testament was published in 1551 at Königsberg. This work was translated by Jan Seklucjan and was based on the Greek and Latin texts. The whole Bible, translated from the Vulgate at Kraków, was published in 1561.

Russian. Acts and the Pauline and general epistles were published in 1554 from Moscow. The publishers were forced to flee to Lithuania, and in 1584 the whole Bible was published in Slavonic from there. This Bible is known as the Ostrog Bible, and it was revised in 1751, almost forty years after Peter the Great (1672-1725) ordered it (1712). It was not until about 1815/18 that the first Russian New Testament was actually published.

Hungarian. Manuscript fragments from the tenth through the fifteenth centuries have been discovered. After several antecedents, the Visoly Bible 1589/90 was published based on Greek and Hebrew manuscripts. That occurred over a hundred years after the printing press was introduced into Hungary (1473).

Bohemian. Many portions of the Scriptures appeared in Bohemia between the tenth and fifteenth centuries. During the fourteenth century John Hus (1373-1415) was actively involved in placing the Scriptures into the vernacular, as were the United Brethren, who published the New Testament in 1518.

Icelandic. The New Testament translation of Oddur Gottskalksson was completed in 1539/40. It was based on the Vulgate and corrected by Luther's German Bible. In 1584 the Gudgrand Bible was translated into Icelandic from the German and Vulgate versions.

Far Eastern translations and versions. These began to appear after William Carey went to India. Between 1793 and 1834 more than thirty-four Asian languages had translations of portions of the Scriptures. Among those was the work of Robert Morrison, who began his Chinese New Testament in 1809 and completed it in 1814.

The above survey is only a sample selection, as indicated in Geddes MacGregor's "Appendix III."[5] Yet, even his work is provincial, in that it follows the British and Foreign Bible Society. S.L. Greenslade attempts to trace the history of the Bible in the West from the Reformation period to the present day.[6] His work is also limited, but it is only a portion of a projected work. One other older work is that by Robert Kilgour, in which the author attempts to trace the total picture of Scripture translations.[7] This work is out of date, having been written in 1939. The work of such organizations as the Wycliffe

5. Ibid.
6. Greenslade, pp. 38-39.
7. R. Kilgour, *The Bible Throughout the World: A Survey of Scripture Translations*.

Bible Translators makes it difficult to keep abreast with the widening scope of Bible translations.[8] But the basic direction of the present discussion is the English Bible, and to that subject the study returns.

Modern English Translations and Versions

Besides the major versions of the English Bible discussed in chapters 30-31, there are numerous independent translations of the Bible or the New Testament, called "modern speech translations."[9]

Roman Catholic Translations and Versions

The initial attitude of the Roman Catholic church toward publishing the Scriptures for laymen was far from enthusiastic. The British and Foreign Bible Society was founded in 1804, and sixty years later Pope Pius IX in his famous *Syllabus of Errors*—once thought to be infallible, though now discounted by Roman Catholic theologians—condemned Bible societies as "pests." However, as early as 1813 a group of enthusiastic churchmen, including some Roman Catholics, founded the Roman Catholic Bible Society. The enterprise evoked the ire of Bishop Milner, who objected to the society's publication of the Rheims-Douay Version without notes. Another Roman Catholic bishop, William Poynter, accepted the presidency of the organization, and it published an improved edition of the Rheims-Douay Version in 1815.

Meanwhile, a host of editions of the Bible for use by Roman Catholics appeared, including *Coyne's Bible* (1811), *Haydock's Bible* (1811-1814), the *Newcastle New Testament* (1812), *Syer's Bible* (1813-14), *MacNamara's Bible* (1813-14), *Bregan's New Testament* (1814), and *Gibson's Bible* (1816-17).[10] In 1836 John Lingard of England published (anonymously) a lively Roman Catholic translation of the Bible that regularly replaced "do pennance" with "repent," an innovation that the Confraternity edition was to pick up a century later (1936), instead of following the Rheims-Douay. In the United States, a Roman Catholic scholar, Francis Patrick Kenrick, pioneered a translation of the entire Bible, which was published in sections between 1849 and 1860. Like that of most of his Roman Catholic precursors, his work is best described as "a revised and corrected edition of the Douay Version."[11] Many

8. Cf. such works on their efforts as Ethel Emily Wallis and Mary Angela Bennett, *Two Thousand Tongues to Go*.
9. See Appendix for the items discussed from this point. Further reading on the English Bible will be found in Brooke Foss Westcott, *History of the English Bible,* and Hugh Pope, *English Versions of the Bible*. Also see Sakae Kubo and Walter F. Specht, *So Many Versions? Twentieth-Century English Versions of the Bible;* Lloyd R. Bailey, ed., *The Word of God: A Guide to English Versions of the Bible;* Jack P. Lewis, *The English Bible: A History and Evaluation*.
10. Listed by MacGregor, p. 266.
11. Ibid., p. 269.

other versions of the Bible continued to pour forth, but few of them were notable, except as they perpetuated old errors or created new ones. In 1901, however, a remarkable version of the gospels appeared by a Dominican father. Francis A. Spencer completed his New Testament before his death in 1913, and it was eventually published in New York in 1937 by C. J. Callan and J. McHugh.

The *Layman's New Testament,* first published in London in 1928, was designed as a Bible for zealous Roman Catholic apologists in squelching "Hyde Park hecklers." That work simply set forth the Challoner text on the left page and provided ammunition for the militant laymen to fire at the skeptics on the right. The *Westminster Version* was a more scholarly attempt at translation. Cuthbert Lattey, a Jesuit scholar, began it between 1913 and 1918. Contributions came from both sides of the Atlantic until parts of the Old Testament were published in 1934, but it is still incomplete. By 1935 the New Testament was completed, and a shorter edition was published in 1948.

A fully "Americanized" edition of the New Testament was published in the United States in 1941. The widely known Confraternity edition surpassed all previous versions for its innovations. It was arranged in paragraph form, was rendered into modern speech, and the text was accompanied by notes. Monsignor Ronald Knox undertook a translation of the Bible;[12] the New Testament was completed in 1944, the Old Testament in 1948. Although Knox was an Oxford scholar and literary wit, he incorporated few changes into his translation, which has been officially sanctioned by the church. A much more independent translation was made in America by James A. Kleist and Joseph L. Lilly in 1954, under the title *The New Testament Rendered from the Original Greek with Explanatory Notes.* More recently these translations have been superseded by the New American Bible (1970).

One of the most significant recent translations by Roman Catholic scholars is the *Jerusalem Bible*[13] (1966), produced under the direction of the Dominican scholar Père Roland de Vaux. As the title page admits, "the English text of the Bible itself, though translated from the ancient texts, owes a large debt to the work of the many scholars who collaborated to produce *La Bible de Jerusalem*...." In fact, the introduction and notes of this Bible are taken, without substantial variation, directly from the French edition published by Les Editions du Cerf, Paris (1961). Those very extensive notes represent the work of the "liberal" wing of Catholic biblical scholars. Characteristic of the translation is the use of "Yahweh" for the usual "Lord" in the Old Testament. Its translation is basically literal, although it avoids the King James style and attempts to use a "contemporary" English. As a result of criticism

12. *The Holy Bible: A Translation from the Latin Vulgate in the Light of the Hebrew and Greek Originals,* John Knox, trans.
13. See Bruce Vawter, "The Jersalem Bible," in Bailey, pp. 98-112; Kubo and Specht, pp. 154-61; Lewis, pp. 199-214.

of the first edition, a different approach was taken when the editors published *The New Jerusalem Bible* (1985). Although it is a translation based on the 1973 French revised translation of *La Bible de Jerusalem,* "the translation has been made directly from the Hebrew, Greek or Aramaic."[14] Nevertheless, its achievement is inferior to that of the New American Bible (1970).

Jewish Translations and Versions

Although Jews have attempted to preserve the study of Scripture in its "sacred" language (Hebrew), it has been their experience, like that of the Roman Catholics with the Latin,[15] that that is not always possible. The very existence of the Greek Septuagint (LXX) bears a witness to the fact that as early as the third century B.C. the Jews found it necessary to translate their sacred Scriptures into another language. Conditions under which Jews lived during the Middle Ages were not conducive to such scholarship. Nevertheless, by about 1400, Jewish translations of the Old Testament began to appear in various languages. But it was not until some four centuries later that English versions of the Old Testament were published by the Jews. In 1789, the year of the French Revolution, a version of the Pentateuch by Isaac Delgado appeared, claiming to be an emendation of the King James Version. That work was dedicated to Dr. Barrington, Bishop of Salisbury. In 1839, Salid Neuman published a similar work. Between 1851 and 1856 Rabbi Abraham Benisch produced a complete Bible for English-speaking Jewry, which was published in 1861. One final attempt to amend the King James Version for use by Jews was made by Michael Friedlander in 1884.

Isaac Leeser made a version of the Hebrew Bible in 1853. This long-time favorite in British and American synagogues shows a more marked departure from the King James Version than the other attempts. Before the close of the century, however, the inadequacy of Leeser's work was felt in the United States, as Anglo-Jewry had increased in size. Thus, in 1892, at its second biennial convention, the Jewish Publication Society decided to revise Leeser's version thoroughly. As the work proceeded under the direction of Dr. Marcus Jastrow, it became obvious that an entirely new translation would result. After considerable time and reorganization, the Jewish Publication Society's version of the Hebrew Bible was published in English (1917). It was a translation that tended to favor the renditions of the *American Standard Version* instead of those of the King James Version.

In 1962 the Jewish Publication Society began publishing *The New Jewish Version of the Old Testament.*[16] The first installment of that new translation

14. General Editor's Foreword, *The New Jerusalem Bible,* p. v.
15. Not only have Roman Catholics found it necessary to translate the Latin Scriptures into local language, but, in a historic stride, Vatican Council II approved the use of the local language for the Mass in 1965.
16. See Keith R. Crim, "The New Jewish Version," in Bailey, pp. 63-73; Kubo and Specht, pp. 117-43.

was *The Torah: A New Translation of the Holy Scriptures according to the Masoretic Text*. The *New Jewish Version* (NJV) is not a revision of the Jewish Version of 1917 nor any other Jewish or Christian version. Instead, it is a completely fresh translation from the traditional Hebrew text in living, up-to-date, highly readable English. According to its preface, its purpose is "to improve substantially on earlier versions in rendering both the shades of meaning of words and expressions and the force of grammatical forms and constructions." That improvement was sought with the help of "neglected insight of ancient and medieval Jewish scholarship and partly by utilizing the new knowledge of the . . . Near East." The three branches of Judaism (Conservative, Reform, and Orthodox) were represented by three learned rabbis—Max Arzt, Bernard J. Bamberger, and Harry Freedman, respectively—and three eminent Hebraists were selected as editors: Harry M. Orlinsky, H. L. Ginsberg, and Ephraim A. Speiser.

Following Ginsberg's death in 1965, *The Five Migilloth and Jonah* were published (1969) in good, contemporary English. In 1973 a second edition of *The Torah* was issued, as was a separate *Book of Isaiah*. Those were followed by the publication of the *Book of Jeremiah* in 1974. *The Prophets* was released in 1974, including a revised and corrected form of Jonah. The third section of the Old Testament, *Kethuvim,* was published as *The Writings* in 1982, although *Psalms* (1972) and *Job* (1980) had already appeared separately. In all of those sections, there is very little departure from the traditional Masoretic Text of the Old Testament.

In September 1985, the Jewish Publication Society published its one-volume work entitled *TANAKH: A New Translation of THE HOLY SCRIPTURES According to the Traditional Hebrew Text*. This complete Jewish Bible is a collaborative effort representing the three largest branches of organized Judaism in America. Not since the third century B.C. Septuagint translation has a broadly-based committee of Jewish scholars produced a major translation.[17] Thus, a quarter century of careful planning and diligent effort has resulted in a new version of the Hebrew Old Testament in modern English. The *TANAKH* (NJV) is a monument to careful and responsible scholarship.

Protestant Translations and Versions

In keeping with their Reformation principle of "private interpretation," Protestants have produced a greater multiplicity of private translations of the Bible than have Roman Catholics.[18] Some of the earliest attempts at private translations grew out of the discovery of better manuscripts. None of the

17. *TANAKH: A New Translation of THE HOLY SCRIPTURES According to the Traditional Hebrew Text*.
18. See Appendix. Unless otherwise noted, this section follows the treatment found in the excellent work of F. F. Bruce, *The English Bible: A History of Translations*, pp. 127ff.

great manuscripts had been discovered when the King James Version was translated except Codex Bezae (D), and it was used very little in that version.

Eighteenth- and nineteenth-century translations and versions. In 1702 Daniel Whitby edited a *Paraphrase and Commentary on the New Testament,* which included explanations and expansions of the King James Version with a postmillennial emphasis. Edward Wells followed with a revised text of the King James Version, which he called *The Common Translation Corrected* (1718-1724). A few years later, Daniel Mace published (anonymously) a critical Greek text of the New Testament with a corrected KJV text alongside. In 1745 William Whiston, best known today for his translations of Josephus, published his *Primitive New Testament*. He leaned heavily on a Western text, and particularly on Codex Bezae, in the gospels and Acts. Other eighteenth-century translations continued to make alterations of the King James Version; for example, John Wesley's edition contained some 12,000 changes in all. Edward Harwood's *Liberal Translation of the New Testament: Being an attempt to translate the Sacred Writings with the same Freedom, Spirit, and Elegance, with which other English Translations from the Greek Classics have lately been executed* (1768), aroused little more than literary curiosity. In 1808 Charles Thompson, one of the founding fathers of the United States, published an English translation of the Old Testament from the Greek Septuagint,[19] and another translation from the LXX was produced by Lancelot Brenton in 1844.[20] Samuel Sharpe, a Unitarian scholar, issued his *New Testament, translated from the Greek of J. J. Griesbach* in 1840 and the Old Testament in 1865. Meanwhile, Robert Young, best known for his analytical concordance, published his *Literal Translation of the Bible* (1863) in order "to put the English reader as far as possible on a level with the reader of the Hebrew and Greek texts."[21] Dean Alford, who also published a famous Greek New Testament, issued a revision of the King James Version in 1869. His hope had been to provide a work that would serve only as an "interim report" until an authoritative revision could replace it. This was fulfilled in 1881 and 1885 when the English Revised Version appeared.

On the eve of the publication of the English Revised Version, John Nelson Darby, the leader of the "Plymouth Brethren," published his *New Translation of the Bible* (1871, 1890). That translation was equipped with a full critical apparatus of variant readings, but it "falls short in regard to English style."[22] Another fairly literal translation was Joseph Bryant Rotherham's *The Emphasized Bible* (1872; Old Testament, 1897-1902). The first two editions were based on Tregelles's text, whereas the third followed Westcott and Hort. That version was one of the first to render the ineffable name of God in the Old

19. This work, *The Septuagint Bible,* has been reprinted by Falcon Wing Press.
20. This translation was reprinted by Bagster, *The Septuagint Version of the Old Testament*.
21. Bruce, pp. 127ff.
22. Ibid., p. 132.

Testament as Yahweh. Thomas Newberry's *The Englishman's Bible,* edited in the 1890s, contained the text of the King James Version arranged by means of dots, dashes, and other notes to aid the English reader instead of actually being a new version.

There were other nineteenth-century translations of portions of the Bible that were included in commentaries. One of the best known examples of such a work was *The Life and Epistles of St. Paul* by W. J. Conybeare and J. S. Howson (1864). Their example, as well as others, has led F. F. Bruce to remind the Bible student that "it must be borne in mind that much excellent Bible translation is to be found, down to the present day, embedded in commentaries on various books of the Bible."[23]

Twentieth-century translations and versions. The great profusion of modern speech translations did not occur until the twentieth century for a number of reasons. First of all, the great biblical manuscripts that prompted such attempts at translation were not discovered until the late nineteenth century. Although the committees of the English Revised Version (1881, 1885) and the *American Standard Version* (1901) incorporated the findings of those newly discovered manuscripts into their texts, the public was not entirely satisfied with their translations. Then too there was the discovery of the nonliterary papyri which had shown the New Testament to be written in the colloquial (Koine) language of the first century.[24] This not only prompted a desire to reproduce the New Testament into a similar colloquial, modern speech translation, but the papyri cast new light on the meanings of words, and they needed a fuller expression and clarification in their English translation. Arthur S. Way, a classical scholar, published his translation, *The Letters of St. Paul,* in 1901. *The Twentieth Century New Testament: A New Translation into Modern English Made from the Original Greek* (based on the text of Westcott and Hort) appeared in 1902 in three volumes. It was appropriately named, but strangely conceived, as it was not until about fifty years later[25] that the identity of the twenty pastors and laymen (none were linguists or textual critics) who had produced this work was revealed. Their desire was to "mediate the word of God in a plainer English idiom."[26] It is a remarkable fact that as nonexperts they were so successful in their endeavor. As Kenneth W. Clark has observed, "Somewhere along the line, some transforming miracle seems to have occurred. We are forced to conclude that their devotion to their task has made them better scholars than they were at first."[27]

23. Ibid., p. 134.
24. See chap. 23 discussion. It was not until 1895 that Adolf Deissmann drew attention to the papyri.
25. Kenneth W. Clark disclosed the real translators from their secretarial records deposited in the John Rylands Library, Manchester. See his article, "The Making of the Twentieth Century New Testament," *Bulletin of the John Rylands Library* (1955).
26. Ibid., p. 66.
27. Ibid., p. 81.

Richard Francis Weymouth, a consultee of the *Twentieth Century New Testament,* translated his own version of the New Testament. It was published posthumously in 1903 and was based on his own critical Greek text, *The Resultant Greek Testament*. Weymouth's New Testament was thoroughly revised in 1924 by James A. Robertson of Aberdeen.[28] Weymouth himself had envisioned his effort as a "succinct and compressed running commentary (not doctrinal) to be used side by side with its elder compeers the AV and RV."

Perhaps the most pretentious translation of the twentieth century was Ferrar Fenton's *The Holy Bible in Modern English, containing the complete sacred scriptures of the Old and New Testament, translated into English direct from the original Hebrew, Chaldee and Greek* (1895, Old Testament, 1903). In the preface to the 1910 edition, the author states, "I contend that I am the only man who has ever applied real mental and literary criticism to the Sacred Scriptures." As F. F. Bruce adroitly observes, "On this the best comment is perhaps that of Proverbs 27:2, in Ferrar Fenton's own translation: 'Let a stranger praise you, not your mouth, another, and not your own lips.' "[29] Unique features of the translation include the following: the King James Version "Lord" was translated "The Life" or "The ever-Living"; Old Testament names were retransliterated (e.g., Elisha to Alisha), the order of books in the Old Testament followed the Hebrew Bible, and the gospel of John was placed first in the New Testament. The work as a whole was forceful and unique, but not too significant.

Another of the early twentieth-century translations was that of Oxford scholar James Moffatt, *The New Testament: A New Translation* (1913) and *The Old Testament: A New Translation* (1924). Later the entire work appeared in a single volume as *A New Translation of the Bible* (1928). That translation, which at times reflects a Scottish tone, was characterized by freedom of style and idiom. It was based primarily on von Soden's Greek text. Moffatt was more expert in the New Testament than the Old, as is evident in his translation, where his liberal theology was not concealed (cf. John 1:1: "*Logos* was divine"). He also regularly translated the name of God in the Old Testament as "The Eternal" rather than "Lord" (KJV) or "Jehovah" (ASV).

The American counterpart to Moffatt was *The Complete Bible: An American Translation* (1927). Edgard J. Goodspeed, in the first installment, which appeared in 1923, pointed out that "for American readers . . . who have had to depend so long upon versions made in Great Britain, there is room for a New Testament free from expressions which, however familiar in England or Scotland, are strange in American ears."[30] The translation was made with dignity

28. In this revision the rendering "life of the ages" (which reflected the unorthodox views on eternal life) was corrrected to read "eternal life."
29. Bruce, p. 162.
30. Edgar J. Goodspeed, "Preface," *The Complete Bible: An American Translation*.

and readability and had a minimum of "Americanisms." In 1938 he completed his translation of the Apocrypha.

G. W. Wade's *The Documents of the New Testament* (1934) "is a fresh translation of the New Testament documents, arranged in what the translator believed to be their chronological order."[31] The translation was expanded by means of italicized words, which were added for the purpose of clarification. *The Concordant Version of the Sacred Scriptures* (1926 and following years) was based on the principle that "every word in the original should have its own English equivalent." Despite this mechanical word-for-word translation, and the tacit assumption that Hebrew was the original and pure language of the human race, the attempt reflects a dedicated effort. In 1937 Charles B. Williams, an American Greek scholar, issued *The New Testament in the Language of the People*. In it the author aimed to convey the exact shade of meaning of the Greek verb tenses. Although some scholars take issue with particular renderings,[32] Williams did accomplish his goal, but not always in "the language of the people." His renderings were sometimes unique (cf. Heb. 12:2: "who instead of the joy") and often powerful (cf. 2 Cor. 4:9: "always getting a knock-down, but never a knockout"). *St. Paul from the Trenches* by Gerald Warre Cornish, a Cambridge graduate, was published posthumously in 1937. He died in action during World War I (1916), and among his possessions was a muddy but legible copy of 1 and 2 Corinthians and part of Ephesians. It was an expanded-type translation. Archbishop W. C. Wand produced *The New Testament Letters* (1943) in an attempt, as he put it, "to put the Epistles into the kind of language a Bishop might use in writing a monthly letter for his diocesan magazine." The result reflects a somewhat ecclesiastical and formal style of the cleric.

The Basic English Bible (1940-1949) was an attempt by a committee (S. H. Hooke, chairman), using only one thousand "basic" English words to convey all the biblical truth. Considering the vocabulary limitations, the authors did produce a text of marked simplicity while retaining much of the variety of the original Greek. Another simplified form of English, called "plain English," was comprised of fifteen hundred "fundamental and common words that make up ordinary English speech."[33] *The New Testament: A New Translation in Plain English* (1952) was the work of Charles Kingsley Williams, who, with the underlying Greek text of Souter, and a broader vocabulary than "basic" English by some 160 or 170 words—including more verbs—achieved a more expressive translation than did *The Basic English Bible*.

The Berkeley Version in Modern English:[34] *New Testament* (1945), *Old Testament* (1959), has been described as "a more conservative counterpart to

31. Bruce, p. 173.
32. Based on the *Interim Report on Vocabulary Selection* (London, 1936).
33. Bruce, p. 220.
34. See Kubo and Specht, pp. 89-97.

the RSV."[35] The New Testament was translated and the Old Testament edited by a staff of twenty under the chairmanship of Gerrit Verkuyl of Berkeley, California. In that version there is an attempt to render the messianic prophecies of the Old Testament more clearly than in prior versions. In addition, the desire is to be less interpretive than Moffatt, more cultured in language than Goodspeed, more American than Weymouth, and freer from the King James Version than the *Revised Standard Version*. Divine persons are addressed as "Thou," "Thy (Thine)," and "Thee," and God's words are set off with quotation marks because the whole Bible is considered to be the Word of God. Some inconsistencies and inaccuracies occur,[36] particularly in the Old Testament, but the effort is praiseworthy as a whole. A revised edition entitled the *Modern Language Bible* (1969) was published by Zondervan Publishing House, which had obtained the publication rights to *The Berkeley Version*.

One of the most popular of all the modern speech translations has been that of J. B. Phillips,[37] whose *Letters to Young Churches* (1947) was followed by *The Gospels in Modern English* (1952), *The Young Church in Action* (1955), *The Book of Revelation* (1957), and finally the one-volume edition of the completed *New Testament in Modern English* (1958). It was published again as a revised edition in 1960 and as *The New Testament in Modern English: A Wholly New Book* (1972). In 1973 M. Collins published a second revised edition of Phillips's *The New Testament*. J. B. Phillips also worked on a paraphrase of the Old Testament. He completed only *The Four Prophets: Amos, Hosea, Isaiah, and Malachi* (1963), which appeared in a revised edition in 1973. The translation by Phillips was more properly a paraphrase, a "meaning-for-meaning" translation rather than a "word-for-word" translation. The former involves more interpretation than the latter, and that may be regarded as the only real weakness in Phillips's effort. Nevertheless, the strength and freshness of the translation have recaptured in a unique manner the spirit and heart of the first-century writers for twentieth-century readers.

In 1961 Olaf M. Norlie, an American Lutheran scholar, published *The Simplified New Testament in Plain English—For Today's Readers*, along with *The Psalms for Today: A New Translation in Current English*, by R. K. Harrison. A short time later Norlie presented *The Children's Simplified New Testament* (1962). According to the preface, the *Simplified New Testament* is "a new translation from the original Greek designed to make the language of the New Testament more interesting and intelligible, especially for today's young people." The author attempted to make the translation "readable" and "meaningful" in its appeal "to teen-agers, young people and young adults, for whom it will make the rough places plain." That objective was accomplished in a remarkable way, for when the Jesus People Movement rose during the

35. Bruce, pp. 222-23.
36. Ibid.
37. See Kubo and Specht, pp. 69-88.

1970s, Norlie's *Simplified New Testament* became their mainstay, and it was reissued as *One Way: The Jesus People New Testament* (1972).

Using the King James Version as a foundation, Jay P. Green began paraphrasing the Bible for use by young people during the 1960s and 1970s. He published *The Children's "King James" Bible* (1960), but it was not the edition of 1611. He used a more recent text as the basis for his paraphrase. He then published *The Children's Old Testament with Stories* (1962) and a *Teen-Age Version of the Holy Bible* (1962). Green then produced *The King James II New Testament* (1970) and *The Holy Bible: King James II* (1971) before turning his hand to an *Interlinear Greek-English New Testament* (1976). His work in making the Bible intelligible to children and young people reflects an ages-long desire to popularize and paraphrase the Bible for use by those who do not have high degrees of learning and expertise.

One of the most successful attempts to popularize the Bible in recent years has been the work of Kenneth N. Taylor in *The Living Bible* (1971).[38] He began publishing this paraphrase of the Bible as *Living Letters: The Paraphrased Epistles* in 1962, and he set forth his purpose in the preface. He wrote, "This book is a paraphrase of the New Testament letters. Its purpose is to say as exactly as possible what Paul, James, Peter, John, and Jude meant, and to say it simply, expanding where necessary for a clear understanding by the modern reader." Taylor recognized the implicit danger of the paraphrastic method of translating, as he added, "whenever the author's exact words are not translated from the Greek there is the possibility that the translator, however honest, may be giving the English reader something that the original writer did not mean to say." However true this statement may be, he also acknowledged that "the theological lodestar in this book has been a rigid evangelical position."

Instead of using the King James Version as the basis for his paraphrase, Taylor used the *American Standard Version* (1901) as the basis for his enterprise. That means that the underlying Greek text for *The Living Bible* (LB) is the Critical Text rather than the Received Text, but Taylor does not remain consistent to the text of the *American Standard Bible,* and he provides no indications when he departs from it. Nevertheless, following his *Living Letters,* Taylor produced *Living Prophecies* (1965), *Living Gospels and Acts* (1966), *Living Letters,* revised edition (1966), *Living Psalms and Proverbs* (1967), *The Living New Testament* (1967), *Living Lessons of Life and Love* (1968), *Living Books of Moses* (1969), and *Living History of Israel* (1970) all in the same style before releasing the completed work as *The Living Bible* in 1971. For the most part, it is a simplified, easy-to-follow rendering in effective and idiomatic, present-day English. At times imaginative details are provided that

38. See James D. Smart, "The Living Bible," in Bailey, pp. 134-51; Lewis, pp. 237-60; Kubo and Specht, pp. 231-42.

have no textual basis, and at other times it does less than justice to what the original says. On other occasions, Taylor departs from his initial purpose when he assumes the role of commentator and interprets or reinterprets passages in ways that may not be true to the intent of the original. Taylor's *The Living Bible* meets a genuine communication need because this paraphrase, like Norlie's translation, was extremely popular with young people and adults alike during the 1970s and since.

Another addition to the long list of modern speech translations by an individual is F. F. Bruce, *The Letters of Paul: An Expanded Paraphrase* (1965). It is designed, according to the author, "to make the course of Paul's argument as clear as possible." Bruce confesses frankly of his work, "Well, this one *is* a paraphrase," which according to his own acknowledgement is often an interpretation rather than a mere translation. Paul's epistles are arranged chronologically, Galatians through 2 Timothy, rather than topically. The translation itself is a kind of amplified version of the English Revised Version (1881), which Bruce considers the most accurate translation of the Greek text ever made. The English Revised Version is printed in parallel for comparison. Although there is much merit in his paraphrase, such as its better precision than Phillips's *Letters to Young Churches,* it lacks the popular punch of Taylor's *Living Letters*.

Taking the cue from John Beekman and John Callow, *Translating the Word of God,* who emphasized the two important components of language—form and meaning—a well-known Christian counselsor, Jay E. Adams, published *The New Testament in Everyday English* (1979). In it he attempted to find a "middle road between wooden literalness and too much freedom with the text." Although it tends to drift toward the freedom side of the road, that translation is another in the long tradition to communicate the Bible meaningfully in the modern age. Julian G. Anderson, a retired professor of classical and biblical Greek and Lutheran pastor and writer of Bible study materials, published *A New Accurate Translation of the Greek New Testament into simple Everyday American English* (1984), which is accompanied by notes and illustrations for study. This translation purports to correct many inaccuracies "where the King James Version and all its direct revisions—RV, ASV, RSV, NIV—translate the Greek incorrectly." In addition Anderson attacks the "decided preference for long words, including many that only the pastor and professors understand" in the King James Version and its children. This leads him to try "to get rid of all such big technical words, and use short, simple English words, so that the average Bible reader with a minimum education, and school children can understand what God has to say." In order to accomplish his task, Anderson has "taken the long Greek sentences apart and rearranged the clauses and phrases into short, clear English sentences we use in our everyday conversation." The textual basis appears to be that of the United Bible Societies, third edition. His notes do not mention the manuscript evidence, but he does make judgments based on that textual evidence.

In an attempt to reach more limited audiences, some colloquial translations have been produced in the twentieth century. Carl F. Burke published *God is for Real, Man: Interpretations of Bible Passages and Stories as Told by Some of God's Bad Tempered Angels with Busted Halos to Carl F. Burke* (1966). Burke was chaplain of Erie County Jail, Buffalo, New York. His work is a free retelling of portions of the Bible by inmates rather than an actual translation. One of the best translations for a more limited audience is the colloquial New Testament by Clarence Jordan, *The Cotton Patch Version* (1968-1973).[39] It was done for a local Southern dialect, particularly from the area around Atlanta. Local place names are substituted for biblical names, and other modern equivalents are also employed. Everything becomes vividly close to the reader in that approach, which names local cities, automobiles, and so on. The author's intention is to give the reader a greater sense of participation by stripping away the fancy language, artifical piety, and other barriers. The Southern dialect comes through best in conversational sections, but it is rather inconsistent in narrative passages. Another effort in that regard is a three-volume work by Andrew Edington called *The Word Made Flesh* (1975).[40] It does not purport to be accurate, but it is a down-to-earth, pungent, colloquial paraphrase of the Bible. Finally, there is the joint effort of Dick Williams and Frank Shaw, *The Gospels in Scouse* (1966, revised 1977).[41] The translation follows J. M. Thompson's edition of the synoptic gospels, and it is rendered in the dialect of Liverpool, England.

The American Bible Society publication of *Good News for Modern Man: The New Testament in Today's English* (1966), directed by Robert G. Bratcher, is yet another modern speech translation. A second edition of it was published in 1967, and a third in 1968, with work on the Old Testament being released periodically until it was completed in 1975 and published as *Today's English Version: Good News Bible* (1976).[42] According to its brief preface, the *Good News* New Testament, also known as GNB or TEV, "does not conform to traditional vocabulary or style, but seeks to express the meaning of the Greek text in words and forms accepted as standard by people everywhere who employ English as a means of communication." It attempts to avoid outdated and technical words and present the Bible in a kind of newspaper English. The New Testament translation is based on the Greek text prepared by the international committee of scholars sponsored by the United Bible Societies (1966). Broad sponsorship of both the Greek text and the translation insured

39. See Kubo and Specht, pp. 329-34.
40. Ibid., pp. 330-33.
41. Ibid., pp. 333-34.
42. See W. F. Stinespring, "Today's English Version (Good News Bible)," in Bailey, pp. 113-33; Kubo and Specht, pp. 171-97; Lewis, pp. 261-91. The publisher prefers to call it the *Good News Bible* rather than *Today's English Version*.

the success of the translation in advance of its publication. In general, the New Testament seems to read more smoothly and be more accurate than its Old Testament counterpart. When the translators had difficulty with the textual reading, they would occasionally insert footnotes to indicate "Hebrew unclear," "Aramaic has two additional words," "some manuscripts do not have," "some manuscripts add verse," and so on. The reader is well advised to read all those footnotes, for they indicate that the Hebrew and Greek Bible is not simple and easy to read after all, and that is especially true in places where the manuscripts are ambiguous or unclear.

In a quite different vein is *The New World Translation of the Greek Scriptures,* which was issued in 1950, with a corrected edition in 1951, and *The New World Translation of the Hebrew Scriptures,* which appeared periodically in five sections between 1953 and 1960. *The New World Translation* of the Holy Scriptures was published by the Watchtower Bible and Tract Society of the Jehovah's Witnesses.[43] It was not well done, for it was revised in 1961, a second revision was published in 1970, and a third revised edition made its appearance in 1971. Having decided to depart from their former allegiance to the King James Version, the translators used the Westcott-Hort text and many other sources to make their new translation. Some of their translations reflect the distinctive theological interpretations of the Jehovah's Witnesses (e.g., "the word was a god," John 1:1; and "grave" for "hell" throughout), others are colloquial (e.g., "Excuse me, Jehovah," Ex. 4:10), and some few are doctrinally suggestive (e.g., "a jealous God" is one "exacting exclusive devotion"). In 1953, when Bruce M. Metzger wrote his classic critique of the Jehovah's Witnesses, he mentioned that the footnotes in the New World translation of the New Testament frequently cite Benjamin W. Wilson, *The Emphatic Diaglott* (1864), which is a rather wooden interlinear translation using J. J. Greisbach's New Testament text of 1806. Wilson's so-called *Diaglott,* with its uninformed but confident assertions about the Greek meanings, was an ancestor to the New World Translation.[44] H. H. Rowley was so distressed by *The New World Translation* that he wrote a review of it entitled "How Not to Translate the Bible."[45]

When the Watchtower Bible and Tract Society published its new version, *The Bible in Living English* (1972),[46] it was thought to be merely a revision of its earlier *New World Translation*. However, that was not the case. Instead, it published an entirely new translation by Steven T. Byington (1868-1957). Byington was a member of a Congregational church that later merged with another to form the United Church of Ballard Vale, Massachusetts. He had

43. See Lewis, pp. 229-35; Kubo and Specht, pp. 98-110.
44. Bruce M. Metzger, "The Jehovah's Witnesses and Jesus Christ: A Biblical and Theological Appraisal," pp. 65-85.
45. H. H. Rowley, "How Not to Translate the Bible," pp. 41-42.
46. Kubo and Specht, pp. 110-16.

received a degree in classics from the University of Vermont before attending Union Theological Seminary for a year and Oberlin for another half year studying biblical languages. After Byington's death, the Watchtower Bible and Tract Society of Pennsylvania obtained the copyright to his translation and published it as their own in 1972. The translator sought to put the Bible into living, present-day English. There are some strange characteristics about his translation of the pronouns addressed to God. He used "you" in the Old Testament but "thou" in the New. The reason he gave for that change is that people in New Testament times felt toward God nearly the same way as modern men do, but Old Testament people did not have such feelings as to require a special pronoun. One feature that did attract the Jehovah's Witnesses to Byington's translation was his rendering of the name of God as "Jehovah." Although the translation has some interesting renderings, there are too many peculiar, erroneous, and awkward translations for it to be considered an acceptable translation.

The Authentic New Testament (1955/56) was an attempt by a well-known Jewish scholar, Hugh J. Schonfield, to approach the New Testament documents "as if they had recently been recovered from a cave in Palestine or from beneath the sands of Egypt, and had never been previously given to the public." His work, which is of good quality, attempts to reconstruct the "authentic" New Testament Jewish atmosphere for Gentile readers. It was presented in 1955 in a subscriber's edition, and the general edition was published in 1956. Without textual warrant, Schonfield excises an important phrase verifying the resurrection of Christ, "most of whom remain until now" (1 Cor. 15:6). *The Authentic New Testament* was published in a revised edition in 1962. Schonfield, as Jewish historian of Christian beginnings, then wrote a novel entitled *The Passover Plot* (1966) before editing and publishing "A Radical Translation and Reinterpretation" of *The Original New Testament* (1985).[47]

George M. Lamsa translated *The Holy Bible from Ancient Eastern Manuscripts* (1957) from the Peshitta, the "authorized" Bible of the church of the East. His rendition of the gospels (1933), the whole New Testament (1939), and the Psalms (1940) were published earlier, with the complete work reaching the public in 1957. Lamsa's claim that his work is produced from original Aramaic sources is generally questioned, because the Peshitta is not to be identified with the "original Aramaic." The use of the Aramaic textual tradition has provided some interesting materials for comparison, because the New Testament translation is based on a fifth-century manuscript (the Mortimer-McCawler ms), housed in the Ambrosian Library in Milan, Italy. This manuscript contains many interesting variant readings. In Matthew 19:24, for example, it reads, "It is easier for a rope [*gamla,* the same Aramaic word

47. Hugh J. Schoenfield, *The Original New Testament.*

as 'camel'] to go through the eye of a needle." In Matthew 27:46 the manuscript records, "My God, My God, for this I was spared!"

Interpretive translations are an important development in biblical scholarship during the twentieth century. Kenneth S. Wuest provides an example of that enterprise in his *Expanded Translation of the New Testament,*[48] issued in parts (1956-1960) before it was published as a unit in 1961. Wuest endeavored to do for all the parts of speech what Charles B. Williams had done for the Greek verb. Approaching his project from a conservative theological position, the professor of Greek at Moody Bible Institute tried to indicate philological and theological nuances with greater precision. Because his translation, based on a limited number of sources, was intended for study, its stylistic inferiority need not be pressed. The trait of "expanded" translations is that they permit the translator to be more interpretive than do other forms, perhaps because the translator must sometimes "read into" the text before the interpretation is "read out" of it.

Another interpretive effort is *The New Testament: A New Translation by William Barclay* (1969). Barclay published his New Testament in two installments as *Gospels and Acts* (1968) and *Letters and the Revelation* (1969). A one-volume paperpack edition was published in 1980. Barclay was long known for his popularization of scholarly research in readable prose. In that activity he used the United Bible Society Greek text as the basis for his translation, although he departed from it in some instances. In his first volume, Barclay added a chapter "On Translating the New Testament." He added two appendixes to the second volume. In the first of those he treats various New Testament words taken from the King James Version, followed by the Greek original. The second contains "Notes on Passages," in which he lists those passages he has expanded in the text. These expanded treatments are printed in italics in the translation. One of Barclay's objectives was "to try to make the New Testament intelligible to the man who is not a technical scholar." Another aim was "to make a translation which did not need a commentary to explain it." That approach involves the use of paraphrase in the translation, according to Barclay. The most serious objection to Barclay's New Testament is that his interpretive comments are "highly personal and sometimes even idiosyncratic translation." Another criticism is that the total impression of Barclay's translation is that it is "a perplexing mixture of the new with the traditional, the technical with the non-technical."[49]

In an attempt to avoid the pitfals of personal, subjective, and idiosyncratic translations arising from one-person efforts, group involvement in Bible translation provides an avenue where one individual is checked by others. This was in view when *The Amplified Bible* (1965)[50] was produced by the Lockman

48. Kubo and Specht, pp. 327-29.
49. Ibid., pp. 162-70.
50. Ibid., pp. 144-53.

Foundation of La Habra, California. A committee working under the direction of Frances Siewert produced *The Amplified New Testament* (1958). This expanded translation shows an even more marked tendency to "add to" the biblical text while "expanding" upon it than did Wuest's translation. Based upon the critical text, the editors attempt to give a full expression to the various shades of thought and meaning of the original text by the use of brackets, dashes, and italics. As F. F. Bruce has observed, "The work includes several features of a commentary as well as a translation." More recently *The Amplified Old Testament* (1962, 1964) was produced in the same style and was combined into a single-volume edition in 1965. An analysis of its text indicates that some of the amplifications are unnecessary, for they add nothing because the text is clear without them. At times there are unjustifiable amplifications that are not derived from the text. On other occasions, there are additions that are completely redundant, because in most instances one English word is sufficient to carry the meaning of the original. Perhaps the tedious style is necessary, because a word is repeated with the same or similar amplifications by the use of brackets, dashes, and italics. On the other hand, there are also some noticeable lacks of amplification. *The Amplified Bible* is in reality a mini-commentary. Some applaud it, whereas others are critical. In the last analysis, however, it does purport to be "free from private interpretation" and "independent of denominational prejudice." In this regard, *The Amplified Bible* falls short of its claims. Apart from the amplification, the translation has little merit. It would be far better to take a faithful translation, such as the *American Standard Version,* and use a good commentary as it is needed. There is all too much danger that the ordinary person may assume "that the interpretations and amplifications are part of God's revelation. Scripture is quite capable of being understood, and the Holy Spirit is still present."[51]

About the same time it was producing *The Amplified Bible,* the Lockman Foundation moved in another direction in its efforts to revise the *American Standard Version* (1901) as the *New American Standard Bible* (1963, 1967).[52] The gospel of John had been published in 1960, and the gospels had appeared in 1962, before the New Testament was released in 1963. In the preface the committee writes, "It has been the purpose of the Editorial Board to present the modern reader a revision of the American Standard Version in clear contemporary language," because the *American Standard Version* was a standard, monumental product, internationally conceived and universally endorsed as a trustworthy translation. The stated goals of the *New American Standard Bible* (NASB) translators are three: accuracy of translation, clarity of English, and adequacy of notes. The New Testament translation is based on the

51. Ibid., p. 153.
52. See Barclay M. Newman, Jr., "The New American Standard Bible," in Bailey, pp. 74-97; Lewis, pp. 165-97; Kubo and Specht, pp. 222-30.

twenty-third edition of the Nestle Greek text, and that differs in a number of places from the text underlying the *American Standard Version*. On occasion, however, the *New American Standard Bible* translators followed the *American Standard Version* as against the Nestle text, as in the case of printing the long ending to the gospel of Mark (16:9-20).[53] Although the translation is printed in a paragraph format, it does not follow a paragraph sense. Instead, each verse is set into an individual paragraph, following the long-standing tradition of the King James Version. The English style is made difficult because of the long sentence structure, heavy grammatical arrangements, ecclesiastical "in group" language, and occasional ambiguities and arbitrary shifts in language level. However, the NASB is to date the best relatively literal translation done by a committee of conservative scholars.

Publication of *The Holy Bible, New International Version* (1973, 1978)[54] was the culmination of a process that began in the 1950s. After years of dissatisfaction with existing translations, a group of biblical scholars decided to formalize its efforts and to undertake a new translation project in 1965. The project received new impetus in 1967 when the New York International Bible Society agreed to support it financially. Although a number of modern-speech versions had appeared since the project was first conceived, there was still a distinctive place for a new translation suitable for private reading as well as public worship. After the New Testament was published as *The Great News* (1973), the name of the translation was changed to *The New International Version* (NIV). More than one hundred biblical scholars from various English-speaking countries were engaged in the project, with a fifteen-member general committee making the final editorial decisions. Work on the Old Testament proceeded, and trial volumes were released for *Isaiah and Daniel* (1976) and *Proverbs and Ecclesiastes* (1977). The Old Testament was issued in 1978, and the completed Bible was published in 1978.

According to the preface, the Greek text is "an eclectic one" based on "accepted principles of New Testament textual criticism" in consultation with "the best current printed texts of the Greek New Testament."[55] It is difficult to determine exactly what is meant by the term *eclectic*. In general it means that the *New International Version* follows the modern critical Greek texts, such as Nestle-Aland/United Bible Society (NU-Text), but not always. Sometimes the *New International Version* is not consistent in its rendition of ambiguous passages in the Greek text, and that has resulted in some awkward expressions. In addition, it is inconsistent in translating expressions of time, money, measure, and distance.

The *New International Version* follows current practice in replacing the

53. See discussion on texts in chaps. 25 and 26.
54. See Robert G. Bratcher, "The New International Version," in Bailey, pp. 152-67; Lewis, pp. 293-328; Kubo and Specht, pp. 243-72.
55. See discussion in chaps. 25 and 26.

obsolete "thou," "thee," "thy," and "thine" with appropriate forms of "you," even when Jesus or the Father is addressed. Unfortunately, the long-standing tradition of using italics for words not found in the Hebrew and Greek texts has been discontinued in the NIV. When the complete Bible was published in 1978, a collation of the two editions of the New Testament reveal nearly three hundred changes. These changes tend to be directed toward more literal renderings, more traditional readings, and more conformation to the Old Testament wording. In the Old Testament, the translators followed the standard Masoretic Text for the Hebrew and Aramaic text as published in the latest edition of Kittel's *Biblia Hebraica,*[56] although some renderings disagree with the Masoretic text in favor of the Dead Sea Scrolls, Septuagint, Syriac, and Vulgate, which were consulted and sometimes chosen in preference to the Masoretic Text reading.

Few translations since the King James Version of 1611 have been as systematically done as the *New International Version*. The translators sought to produce a version that would be characterized by accuracy, clarity, and literary quality. They sought a middle-of-the-road version in which a high degree of "formal correspondence" is combined with renderings that are "dynamically equivalent." The *New International Version* is a new translation (version) made directly from the originals, and it is not a revision of any of the historic English versions. Nevertheless, the translators "sought to preserve some measure of continuity with the long tradition of translating the Scriptures into English." The traditional and modern are intermingled throughout the *New International Version*. One reviewer hopes "that at long last the *New International Version* will once and for all lay to final rest the still widespread belief that the King James Version is the original Word of God and that any translation that differs from it is a perversion, a devil's masterpiece produced by people with a low view of Scripture."[57] Although this hope is too optimistic, the NIV is an example of contemporary evangelical scholarship.

In the meantime, the champions of the King James Version have not been idle about Bible translation during the twentieth century. After all, nearly one third of American readers still used it. The King James Version had been revised numerous times in the 375 years since it made its appearance in 1611. The fruit of their labors is the *Holy Bible, The New King James Version* (1979, 1980, 1982).[58] In the mid-1970s Thomas Nelson Publishers, successor to the firm that had first published the *American Standard Version* (1901) and the *Revised Standard Version* (1952), summoned leading clergymen and lay Christians who discussed and decided to revise sensitively the King James Version. From the outset their purpose was "to apply the best knowledge—of ancient

56. See discussion in chaps. 21 and 26 regarding the BHK and BHS text.
57. Bratcher, p. 165.
58. See Lewis, pp. 329-62; Kubo and Specht, pp. 273-307.

Hebrew and Greek, 17th century English, and contemporary English—to polish with sensitivity the archaisms and vocabulary of the 1611 (King James) Version, so as to preserve and enhance its originally intended beauty and content." Over 130 scholars from a broad spectrum of the Christian church were commissioned to work on the revision. Their efforts were directed toward several specific goals. They sought to preserve the true meaning of the words of the King James Version in view of changes in word meanings since 1611. The revisers endeavored to protect the theological terminology of the King James Version. Their aim was to improve the understanding of verb forms and verb endings by bringing them into conformity with twentieth-century usage. Punctuation and grammar have been updated to help in the understanding of the text. In addition, they capitalized pronouns that refer to God and added quotation marks, common features in the twentieth century that were not practiced in 1611.

The producers of *The New King James Version* (NKJV) used the Old Testament text of the *Biblïa Hebraica Stutgardensia* (1967/1977), frequently compared with the Bomberg edition (1524-1525), and consultation with the Septuagint (Greek) and Latin Vulgate, as has been the case with most twentieth-century translators. With the New Testament, however, they pursued an altogether different course. They seem convinced that New Testament textual criticism has followed a wrong path over the past century. This means that they prefer a different textual basis from nearly all translations that have been made since the English Revised Version (1881).[59] As a result, *The New King James Version,* like its classic predecessor, is based on the Textus Receptus. This is a critical matter, as may be seen from the Introduction to the new revision, even though the revisers are not necessarily convinced that the Textus Receptus is the best Greek text available. To buttress their position, the revisers identify their textual basis as the "Traditional Text" or "Majority Text" (M-Text).[60] They identify the Textus Receptus and the Majority Text as coming from the same textual tradition, but indicate that the Textus Receptus is a somewhat late and corrupted form of the Majority Text, or Traditional Text. Their principle of deriving the Majority Text reading is the persuasion "that the best guide to a precise Greek text is the close concensus of the majority of Greek manuscripts."

In order to show where the Majority Text differs from the Critical Text, which is identified as the Nestle-Aland/United Bible Societies' Text (NU-Text), they have presented textual information "in a unique provision in the

59. See David Otis Fuller, ed., *Which Bible?* The first edition of this collection of essays was published in 1970. Also see David Otis Fuller, *True or False?, the Westcott-Hort Theory Examined*. Also see the discussions in chaps. 22, 25, and 26.

60. Following the publication of the NKJV, a Majority-Text edition Greek text was published by Zane C. Hodges and Arthur L. Farstad, eds., *The Greek New Testament, According to the Majority Text*. It has also appeared in a secnd edition consisting of correcting typographical errors and summarizing the detailed introduction.

history of the English Bible." They have identified the Critical Text variations as "NU-Text" and points of variation in the Majority Text from the Traditional Text as "M-Text." This is a most significant and helpful contribution. The preference of the Textus Receptus (TR) over the Majority Text (M-Text) reading in many instances is a matter of accommodation, bringing clarity to the Textus Receptus that hardly delights advocates of the Majority Text or the NU-Text. The inclusion of the NU-Text readings in the footnotes, on the other hand, may not bring joy to the proponents of the Textus Receptus or the Majority Text.

Supporters of *The New King James Version* will rejoice that it has preserved, to a large extent, an eloquence of style that is not apparent in other twentieth-century translations. Others will be distressed that the NKJV has not gone far enough in modernizing the King James Version, especially if they are convinced that a version is no better than the original text on which it is based and that a modern critical Greek text based on the ancient manuscripts is to be preferred to the Textus Receptus. The editorial decision to follow the King James Version in making every verse a separate paragraph is not as helpful to the modern reader. Nevertheless, the diligent efforts by the revisers of *The New King James Version* to produce an English Bible that retains as much of the classic King James Version as possible while at the same time bringing its English up-to-date has been achieved to a great degree.

For those who preferred using the *Revised Standard Version* of the Bible, a new rendition of that work was also published as *The Reader's Digest Bible, Condensed from the Revised Standard Version Old and New Testaments* (1982).[61] That work was based on the 1971 revision of the *Revised Standard Version* text done under the authority of the Division of Education of the National Council of Churches in the U.S.A., which holds the copyright. The Reader's Digest Association commissioned the "condensation, not abridgment," of the *Revised Standard Version* under the direction of Bruce M. Metzger, who served as general editor in its production. The *Reader's Digest Bible* (RDB) editors distinguished their effort from the numerous abridgments published in the past. They define *condensation* as a "reduction [of the Bible] principally through line-by-line, word-by-word diminution, as well as through deletion of selected blocks of text." That is to be distinguished from an *abridgment,* which "means reduction of length by elimination of entire sections of text and, in the case of the Bible, often whole books as well." According to its preface, "*The Reader's Digest Bible* offers the general reader a more direct means of becoming intimately acquainted with the *whole* body of the Scriptures. It can be read more rapidly and with swifter comprehension, for instruction even for pure heart-lifting enjoyment."

Chapter and verse divisions have been removed, although each book has a

61. See Kubo and Specht, pp. 308-25.

short introduction in this eight-hundred-page condensation (including index), which reduces the Old Testament text by about fifty percent and the New Testament by about twenty-five percent. Some of the deletions involve nonessential words. This includes words that are repetitious, words multiplied for rhetorical effect, and those words that have a reduced relevance for modern readers. In the Old Testament, which is about forty percent poetry, only Psalms, the Song of Solomon, Exodus 15, and Judges 15 are set in poetic form. The rest of the poetic passages are printed in prose. In addition to the line-by-line condensations, blocks of material are deleted. Nearly six full chapters of Genesis are cut, along with ten from Leviticus, at least twelve from 1 Chronicles; seventy of the Psalms are completely eliminated, thirteen chapters are deleted from Isaiah, and the last five chapters of Daniel are removed. Geneological lists have been deleted in the Old Testament as well as those in Matthew 1:1-14 and Luke 3:23-38, even though they were extremely important in Israelite history (the basis for their tribal system) and the Christian church (the lineage of Jesus Christ). In addition, some of the materials have been transposed, and a large body of materials common to the synoptic gospels has been eliminated (only about half of Luke and about 28 percent of Matthew are unique to those gospel accounts), with Mark being the basic text for the condensation. *The Reader's Digest Bible* has made some stylistic improvements over the *Revised Standard Version,* and that includes some alterations in word order. In all, the RDB has made significant improvements in condensing and communicating the text of the Bible to the modern reader, even though the editors have truncated the full canon of Scripture.

When comparing it with other modern versions of the Bible, one must ask whether *The Reader's Digest Bible* even has a place among them. The editors state that it is designed to supplement, not replace, the complete and uncondensed text of the Bible. Nevertheless it raises concerns about the implied unimportance of the omitted portions. For the individual who approaches the Bible to read it for the first time, even in one of the historic versions, the task may seem overwhelming. Even in its modern speech translations, the Bible is often forboding in its format. Moreover, it seems that the Bible is not used as a guide for living even among those who regularly attend church. In addition, there are vast numbers of people who do not read the Bible at all. The *Reader's Digest* condensation of the RDB was designed for a specific audience that is not greatly affected by the numerous Bible translations and versions that are already in place—whether they be college students, young people who need an introduction to the complexities of Bible times, or adults who simply wish to read the spiritual heart of the greatest book mankind possesses.

Ecumenical Translations and Versions

With the great profusion of Protestant, Roman Catholic, Jewish, and personal Bibles being published in the twentieth century, it was inevitable that in an "ecumenical age" some attempts at producing ecumenical Bibles would be attempted. The first attempt of a joint committee to produce a common Bible was *The Anchor Bible,* published in a series under the general editorship of William F. Albright and David Noel Freedman. Their endeavor claimed to be "a project of international and interfaith scope: Protestant, Catholic, and Jewish scholars from many countries contribute individual volumes." The Anchor Bible series is "an effort to make available all the significant historical and linguistic knowledge which bears on the interpretation of the biblical record." Truly it is a monumental task, being produced in separate volumes by different scholars, and its overall unity has varied greatly as a result of this diversity.

Other attempts at producing an ecumenical Bible may be associated with the publication of the *Revised Standard Version* (1946, 1952). As one writer asserts, "The publication of the RSV marked both the end of one era and the opening of another in the effort to communicate God's Word to the English reader. For many its publication marked the end of the age in which 'The Bible' meant the KJV. The RSV opened the era of the multiple translations flooding today's market, all competing with each other."[62]

The *Revised Standard Version* was used as the basis for *The Revised Standard Version, Catholic Edition* (1965, 1966). The New Testament portion was prepared by the Catholic Biblical Association of Great Britain with the approval of the Standard Bible Committee. Its minimal changes from the *Revised Standard Version,* about twenty-four in number and listed in an appendix, centered on the underlying Greek text and some different translations of the Greek text. Those changes included translating "Jesus' brothers" as "Jesus' brethren" (Matt. 12:46, 48), "divorce her [Mary]" (Matt. 1:19), adding "and fasting" (Mark 9:29), and reintroducing the long ending to Mark (16:9-20) as well as the passage on the woman taken in adultery (John 7:53-8:11). The *Revised Standard Version, Catholic Edition* of the entire Bible was published in 1966, with no changes being made in the text of the Old Testament, although all parts of what Protestants call the Apocrypha, except 1 and 2 Esdras and the Prayer of Manasseh, were included as integral parts of the canon. The RSV Bible Committee continued its work of revising the text of the *Revised Standard Version* as it seemed advisable, and in 1971 a revised New Testament was published, although its actual second edition did not appear until 1977. The Old Testament is currently being revised, with publication anticipated for the mid-1980s.

While continuing its work of revision, the RSV Bible Committee has become even more international and ecumenical. In addition to American and Canadian Protestants, the committee received into its ranks six Roman Catholic scholars (1969) from Great Britain and Canada, as well as a representa-

62. Lewis, pp. 127-28.

tive from the Greek Orthodox Church (1972). In the interest of ecumenism the committee published the *Common Bible: The Holy Bible; Revised Standard Version, containing the Old and New Testament with Apocryphal/Deuterocanonical Books* (1973). The Apocryphal/Deuterocanonical Books are divided into two groups in the *Common Bible*: those accepted by Roman Catholics as canonical are grouped together, and those not regarded as canonical are together in another grouping. The position of the various Christian bodies with respect to the Apocrypha is set forth in the preface. The *Common Bible* did not include 3 Maccabees, which is recognized by the Orthodox churches (Greek, Russian, Ukrainian, Bulgarian, and Armenian). Psalm 151 and 4 Macabees are included as an appendix to the Old Testament because both are included in the Greek Bible. When that work was completed, Oxford University Press published the *Expanded Edition of the New Oxford Annotated Bible* (1977), edited by Herbert G. May and Bruce G. Metzger, and it included a translation of those three documents.[63]

Conclusion

Even a cursory glance at the seemingly endless procession of modern translations and versions of the Bible in English provides sufficient evidence to indicate that the twentieth century, as no century before it in human history, possesses the greatest profusion and proliferation of translations of the Bible. With that great diversity and multiplicity of translations, individual, corporate, denominational, and ecumenical, there comes to this century, as to no century before it, a greater responsibility to understand and to communicate the "whole counsel of God" contained in this inspired Book.

63. Kubo and Specht, pp. 213-21.

General Conclusion

The general purpose of this book has been twofold: historical and theological. Historically and critically, it has been an attempt to answer the question as to whether the Bible of the twentieth century, based as it is on the critical Hebrew and Greek texts, is a faithful reproduction of the books produced by its original authors. The answer is by now obvious, and it is this: No book from antiquity comes to the modern world with greater evidence for its authenticity than does the Bible. Both the kind and the amount of evidence that supports the fidelity of the present critical text are greater than for any other book from the ancient world.

Directly related to this historical conclusion is a theological one. For if there is overwhelming evidence that the biblical documents are genuine and authentic—that they stem from alleged periods and authors—then one must face seriously their persistent claim to divine inspiration. When these claims are thoroughly examined and honestly faced, one can but conclude that the Bible as a whole claims to be the Word of God, and the evidence confirms that claim.

Along with the question as to *whether* the books of the Bible are divinely inspired, it has been necessary to address the kindred question as to *which* books of the Bible are inspired, that is, the question of canonicity. One statement will suffice as a summary for both this and the foregoing question. The sixty-six books of the Protestant Bible known today are the entire and complete canon of inspired Scripture, handed down through the centuries without substantial change or any doctrinal variation.

Appendix

A Short-Title Checklist of English Translations of the Bible

(Chronologically Arranged)

Date	Contents	Person or Group / Short-Title (Comment)
7th cent.	Portions	Caedmon / paraphrases of OT and NT portions
c. 700	Psalter	[Aldhelm] / trans. of Psalter (Saxon characters)
c. 705	Gospels	Egbert / trans. of the Synoptic Gospels
8th cent.	Gospels	Bede / trans. of Gospel of John
9th cent.	Gospels	Cynewulf / poetic account of Christ's Passion
9th cent.	Psalter	Anon. / Vespasian Psalter gloss over Latin
c. 875	Portions	Alfred the Great / OT portions translated
c. 900	Psalter	Alfred the Great? / portions of the Paris Psalter
c. 950	Gospels	Aldred / interlinear gloss, Lindisfarne Gospels
c. 975	Gospels	Farman, Owun / gloss of Rushworth Gospels
c. 1000	Heptateuch	Aelfric / West Saxon trans. of Genesis-Judges
c. 1000	Gospels	Aelfric / West Saxon portions of Gospels-Acts
c. 1000	Gospels	[Corpus Christi MS] / West Saxon Gospels
11th cent.	Gospels	[Cambridge MS] / West Saxon Gospels
11th cent.	Gospels	[Bodleian MS] / West Saxon Gospels
11th cent.	Gospels	[Brit. Museum Cotton MS] / West Saxon Gospels
12th cent.	Gospels	[Brit. Museum Royal MS] / West Saxon Gospels
12-13 cent.	Gospels	[Bodleian Hatton MS] / West Saxon Gospels
12th cent.	Psalter	Anon. / Canterbury (Eadwine) glosses of Latin
12th cent.	Psalter	Anon. / Benedictine Office with Paris Psalter
12 cent.	Psalter	Anon. / Anglo-Norman Psalter (A)
12th cent.	Psalter	Anon. / Anglo-Norman Psalter (B)
12th cent.	Portions	Anon. / Anglo-Norman prose books of Kings
c. 1200	Gospels	Orm (Ormulum) / poetic paraph. of gospels-Acts
13th cent.	Psalter	Anon. / additional versions of the Psalter
13th cent.	Gospels	Anon. / several Passion narratives
13th cent.	Gospels	Robert of Greatham / trans. of the Sunday Gospels
c. 1250	Portions	Anon. / paraphrases of Genesis and Exodus
c. 1300	Bible	Anon. / Cursor Mundi paraphrase of Bible story
c. 1300	Psalter	Anon. / Surtees Psalter (from Paris Psalter)

c. 1320	Psalter	William of Shoreham? / literal trans. of Psalter
c. 1325	Psalter	R. Rolle / English Psalter (literal trans.; 30 MSS)
14th cent.	Acts	Anon. / Latin-English—Acts
14th cent.	Epistles	Anon. (Wycliffe?) / Acts, Pauline, Gen. Epistles
c. 1340	Apocalypse	Anon. / Anglo-Norman Apocalypse (80+ MSS)
c. 1340	Psalter	Anon. / West Midland Psalter (English-Latin)
14th cent.	Epistles	Anon. / (Lat.-Eng.) Mark, Luke, Pauline Epistles
14th cent.	Gospels	Anon. / Latin-English—Matthew
c. 1360	Bible	Anon. / various Anglo-Norman MSS
14th cent.	Epistles	Anon. [Wycliffite] / Acts, Pauline, Gen. Epistles
14th cent.	Gospels	Wycliffe? / Acts and the Gospels
c. 1380	NT	J. Wycliffe / NT trans. (early Wycliffe)
c. 1384	Bible	[N. Hereford] / Wycliffite OT (35 MSS)
c. 1387	Bible	[John of Trevisa?] / trans. of the Bible
c. 1388	OT	J. Wycliffe / OT trans. (early Wycliffe)
c. 1390	Gospels	[J. Purvey] / glossed Gospels
c. 1395	Portions	Anon. / Job, Psalms, Major Prophets
c. 1395	Bible	J. Purvey / Wycliffite rev. (later Wycliffe: 140 MSS)
c. 1400	Gospels	Anon. / Gospel harmonies passages (many MSS)
c. 1400	Gospels	Anon. / Passion narratives (numerous MSS)
c. 1400	Gospels	Anon. / Gospel readings (numerous MSS)
c. 1400	Portions	Anon. / Matthew, Acts, Epistles (crude trans.)
c. 1400	Epistles	Anon. / Latin-English Pauline epistles
1410	Gospels	Nicholas Love / Mirrour (Gospel paraphrases)
15th cent.	Portions	Anon. / Old Testament metrical paraphrases
15th cent.	Portions	Littlehales / Prymer (Lay Peoples Prayer-Book)
15th cent.	Portions	Littlehales / Prymer (Lay Folks Prayer Book)
1483	Portions	W. Caxton / Golden Legend (1st printed in Eng.)
1486	Gospels	N. Love / Mirror of the Life of Christ (printed)
c. 1495	Portions	[J. Wotton] / Speculum Christiani (Decalogue)
1496	Portions	Anon. / Dives and Pauper (Decalogue)
1500	Portions	Betson / Ryght profytable treatyse (Lord's Prayer)
c. 1520	Bible	M. Nisbet / (Purvey's) Wycliffite ver. into Scots
1521	Portions	Wynkyn de Worde / The Myrrour of the Chyrche
1525	Portions	[W. Tyndale] / NT in Englysshe (with glosses)
1525	NT	W. Tyndale / NT in Englysshe (first printed)
1526	NT	W. Tyndale / NT in Englyshe (first known)
1526	NT	W. Tyndale / NT (1st Eng. trans. of Greek NT)
1526	Portions	W. Bonde / The Pylgrimage of Perfection
1527	Portions	Anon. / Book of Hours (Eng. title, 1523 ed.)

1529	Portions	Anon. / Primer (Book of Hours; 1st pub. Eng. ed.)
1530	Pentateuch	W. Tyndale / Pentateuch
1530	Psalms	G. Joye / trans. of Bucer's Latin Psalms
1531	Prophets	G. Joye / Isaiah (trans.)
1531	Prophets	W. Tyndale / Jonah (trans.)
1532	Portions	W. Tyndale / NT (omits several epistles)
1534[1]	NT	W. Tyndale / NT diligently corrected
1534	Psalms	G. Joye / Psalms trans.
1534	Prophets	G. Joye / Jeremiah (trans.)
1534	Psalms	[M. Coverdale] / Campensis Lat. Psalms (paraph.)
1534	Genesis	W. Tyndale / revision of Gen.
1534	NT	G. Joye / revision of Tyndale's NT
1534	NT	W. Tyndale / Tyndale's NT revision
1535	NT	W. Tyndale / NT yet once agayne (last Tyndale rev.)
1535	Portions	M. Coverdale / Psalmes with Eccles. (reprint)
1535	Wisdom	[G. Joye?] / Prov. and Eccles. (trans.)
1535	NT	M. Coverdale / revised Tyndale NT (1535 ed.)
1535	Bible	M. Coverdale / Bible (revision of Tyndale)
1536	NT	W. Tyndale / NT corrected (1st NT printed in Eng.)
1536	NT	M. Coverdale / Tyndale NT (revised)
1537	Bible	T. Matthew [J. Rogers] / Tyndale-Coverdale (rev.)
1537	Bible	M. Coverdale / revised and printed by Nicolson
1537	Wisdom	M. Coverdale / the books of Solomon
1538	NT	M. Coverdale / NT (1st ed. Lat.-Eng.)
1538	NT	J. Hollybushe / NT (2d Coverdale Lat.-Eng. ed.)
1538	Bible	T. Matthew [John Rogers] / Matthew Bible (rev.)
1539	NT	R. Taverner / Matthew NT (revision)
1539	Bible	[M. Coverdale] / Great Bible (Tyndale-Coverdale-Matthew)
1539	Bible	R. Taverner / Matthew Bible (revision)
1540	Bible	T. Cranmer / Great Bible (2d ed., "Authorized")
1540	Psalter	(M. Coverdale) / Psalter . . . Psalms (Lat.-Eng.)
1540	NT	Anon. / trans. of Lat. NT of Erasmus
c. 1540	NT	Anon. / NT trans.
1540	Bible	Great Bible (3d ed.) / (at least 22 eds. by 1564)

1. The first edition of Tyndale's New Testament definitely known was completed in 1525 and probably printed in 1526 before a revised edition was published by George Joye in 1534. Tyndale vigorously objected to Joye's tampering with his translation and this issued the "diligently corrected" edition that was the basis of some forty subsequent editions of Tyndale's New Testament.

1541	Bible	T. Cuthber and H. Nicholas / Bible trans.
1541	Bible	Great Bible (4th ed.)
1541	Bible	Great Bible (5th ed.)
1541	Bible	Great Bible (6th ed.)
1541	Bible	Great Bible (7th ed.)
[1545]	Portions	J. Fisher / Psalms in 1545 Royal Prayer Book
1546	Portions	Great Bible / Eng. Gospels and Epistles
1547	Bible	Great Bible (8th ed.) / (accession of Edward VI)
1548	NT	(W. Tyndale) / NT Lat. and Eng. (2d ed.)
1548f.	NT	[N. Udall] / NT paraphrase of Erasmus
1548	NT	E. Becke and W. Seres / NT (Tyndale revised)
1548	NT	[R. Jugge] / NT (revision of Tyndale)
1549	Bible	Anon. / Matthew 1537 ed. with alterations
1549	Portions	E. Becke and W. Seres / Bible: Joshua . . . Job
1549	Bible	Great Bible (9th ed.)
1549	NT	W. Tyndale / NT of the Last Trans.
1549	NT	[W. Tyndale] / NT Latin and English (3d ed.)
1549	NT	M. Coverdale / NT Diligently Translated (rev. ed.)
1550	Portions	E. Becke and W. Seres / Bible: Psalter . . . Song
1550	Prophets	E. Becke and W. Seres / Bible: Isaiah . . . Malachi
1550	NT	[W. Tyndale] / NT in Eng. . . Erasmus in Lat. (4th ed.)
1550	Bible	Great Bible (10th ed.)
1550	Bible	M. Coverdale / Bible (repr. by Froschauer)
1551	Bible	Anon. / Matthew (or Taverner) rev.
1551	Bible	E. Becke and W. Seres / Bible: Gen. . . . Deut.
1551	Bible	E. Becke and W. Seres / The Bible (Taverner rev.)
1552	Bible	R. Jugge / NT (Tyndale revised)
1553	Bible	Great Bible (11th ed.)
1553	Bible	M. Coverdale / Whole Byble (last normal ed.)
1553	NT	[W. Whittingham] / NT (accession of Mary I)
1553	NT	[R. Jugge] / NT (rev. 1548 ed.)
1556	NT	[R. Jugge] / NT (another ed.)
[1557][2]	NT	W. Whittingham / NT (English Hexapla)
1557	Psalms	[A. Gilby?] / Psalms (pre-Genevan version)
1558	Bible	[Whittingham] / Bible (accession of Elizabeth I)
1559	Psalms	W. Whittingham / Psalms (rev. of 1557 Psalmes)

2. In 1557 the first pocket New Testament that gained wide circulation was published.

1560[3]	Bible	W. Whittingham / Geneva Bible (multiple texts)
1561	NT	Anon. / translated from the Greek text
1561	NT	[R. Jugge] / NT (another ed.)
1562	Bible	M. Parker / Great Bible (12th ed.)
1562	Psalms	T. Starnhold et al. / Whole Booke of Psalms
1565	NT	M. Parker / NT trans.
1566?	NT	[R. Jugge] / NT (40th and last ed. of Tyndale)
1566	Bible	M. Parker / Great Bible (13th ed.)
1568[4]	Bible	[M. Parker] / Holie Bible (Bishops' Great Bible)
1569	Bible	[J. Cawood] / Great Bible (last ed.)
1569	Bible	[M. Parker] / Holie Bible (2d ed. Bishops' Bible)
1570	Bible	Geneva Bible / (2d quarto ed., title dates vary)
1571	Gospels	[M. Parker] / Gospels (Anglo-Saxon, editio princeps)
1572	Bible	Bishops' Bible (NT revised, 2d folio ed.)
1572	Bible	Geneva Bible / (rev. Great-Bishops' Psalters)
1573?	Bible	Bishops' Bible (2d quarto ed.)
1574	Bible	Bishops' Bible (3d folio ed.)
1575	Bible	Geneva Bible (NT rev. 1st ed. printed in England)
1576	NT	L. Thomson / NT from Beza Latin (1st Geneva rev.)
1577	Bible	Geneva Bible / (first octavo issue)
1578	Bible	Geneva Bible (first large folio ed.)
1579	Bible	Geneva Bible (first Bible printed in Scotland)
1579	Bible	Geneva Bible (first quarto ed.)
1579	Bible	Geneva Bible (apparently the 2d octavo ed.)
1579?	Psalter	Great Bible / The Psalter of the Psalms of David
1581	Bible	Geneva Bible / (3d octavo ed.; also called 1st ed.)
1582	NT	[W. Allen et al.] / NT (Rheims editio princeps)
1584	Bible	Bishops' Bible (apparently the last quarto ed.)
1585	Bible	Geneva Bible / edition with parallel Psalters
1587	Bible	Geneva Bible / (first Thomson NT; Roman type)
1589	NT	W. Fulke / Rheims-Bishops' NT (parallel columns)
1591	Bible	Geneva Bible/(1st Eng. Bible printed at Cambridge)
1592	Apocalypse	M.F. Junius/Apocalypse (commentary in Lat.-Eng.)
1594	Apocalypse	M.F. Junius / Revelation of Saint John the Apostle

3. The Geneva Bible, 1560, went through 120 editions before 1611, 140 editions prior to 1644, and 180 editions altogether.
4. In 1571 the Convocation of the Province of Canterbury ordered that copies of this edition should be placed in every cathedral, and as far as possible in every church (making it the "second" Authorized Version). The Bishops' Bible was published in about nineteen editions over a period of thirty-four years, with the last edition coming in 1602; the New Testament continued to be published until 1633, in about nineteen editions.

1595	Bible	F. Junius / Geneva Bible (revisions in Apocalypse)
1596	Prophets	[H. Broughton] / Dan.... Chaldie Visions ...Heb.
1596	Apocalypse	Fr. Dv. Ion / The Apocalypse
1599	Bible	Geneva Bible / (with Thomson NT; Junius Rev.)
1600	Bible	Geneva Bible / (differs from former octavo eds.)
1600	NT	T. Worthington / Rheims NT (2d ed.)
1601	NT	W. Fulke/Rheims-Bishops' NT (parallel cols. 2d ed.)
1602	Bible	Bishops' Bible (last ed. of entire Bishops' Bible)
1602	Bible	Geneva Bible / (1st Geneva-Thomson-Junius ed.)
1609	OT	R. Bristow / Rheims-Douay OT (editio princeps)
1610	NT	R. Bristow / Rheims-Douay NT (1609; 2 vols.)
1610	Bible	Geneva Bible / (2d ed. printed in Scotland)
1611[5]	Bible	T. Bilson and M. Smith / KJV (editio princeps)
1611	Bible	KJV / ([AV] earliest separate ed.)
1612	Bible	KJV / (revisions; earliest quarto in Roman type)
1612	Bible	KJV / (earliest octavo edition in Roman type)
1612	Psalms	H. A[insworth] / Psalmes: ... Prose and Metre
1612	NT	KJV / (earliest quarto ed. of the KJV NT)
1613	Bible	KJV / (2d folio edition, revisions)
1613	Bible	KJV / (true 1613 folio ed.; smaller type)
1613	Bible	KJV / (first black-letter quarto ed.)
1616	Bible	KJV / (first extensive revision; 1st small folio ed.)
1616	Bible	KJV / (distinct 3d folio ed.)
1616	Bible	R. Barker / Geneva Bible reprint
1616f.	Bible	H. Ainsworth / English trans. from Amsterdam
1617	Bible	KJV / (earliest duodecimo edition)
1617	NT	W. Fulke / Rheims-Bishops' NT (3d ed. parallel)
1618	NT	T. Cartwright / Confutation of the Rheims NT
1618	Bible	Geneva Bible / (from Continent after ban)
1621	NT	Rheims / NT (3d ed.; first pocket ed.)
1627[6]	Portions	H. Ainsworth / Pentateuch, Psalms, Canticles
1628	NT	KJV / (first KJV NT printed in Scotland)
1628	Psalms	Geneva Bible / Whole Booke ... Prose ... Meettre
1629	Bible	KJV [revision] / (1st ed. to exclude Apocrypha)
1629	Bible	KJV [revision] / (1st ed. printed at Cambridge)

5. Many hundreds of editions and revisions of the King James Version (Authorized Version) were made between 1611 and 1881, when the English Revised Version of the New Testament was published.
6. Henry Ainsworth was a Hebrew scholar whose rendition was too literal to be good English, but his Psalter came with the Plymouth Pilgrims to America.

1631	Bible	KJV [revision] / "Wicked Bible" (suppressed)
1631	Psalms	[W. Alexander] / Psalmes of David
1633	Bible	KJV / (first KJV printed in Scotland)
1633	NT	Rheims / New Testament (4th ed.)
1633	NT	Bishops' Bible / NT (last ed. published)
1633	NT	W. Fulke/Rheims-Bishops' NT (parallel cols; 4th ed.)
1634	Bible	KJV / (4th distinct folio ed.)
1635	Bible	Rheims-Douay Bible / (2d ed.)
1638	Bible	KJV / (duodecimo ed. printed in Holland; many errors)
1638	Bible	T. Goad, S. Ward et al. / Cambridge (corrected)
1642	Bible	KJV / (printed in Holland with Geneva Notes)
1643	Portions	Geneva Bible / The Souldiers Pocket Bible
1644[7]	Bible	Geneva Bible / (last ed. published)
1646	Bible	W. Bentley / KJV (with "dangerous errors")
1647	Bible	J. Canne / The Holy Bible (fully cross-referenced)
1649	Bible	KJV / (printed in England with Geneva Notes)
c. 1650	Bible	KJV / six eds. printed in England (many errors)
1653[8]	NT	H. Hammond / NT paraphrase and annotations
1657	Bible	T. Haak / translated from the Dutch Bible of 1637
1659	NT	H. Hammond / NT (2d ed., corrected)
1660	Bible	KJV / (marginal references added)
1662	Portions	J. Lightfoot / Hugh Broughton's portions of OT
1666	Wisdom	[H. Danvers] / Solomon's Proverbs
1668	Gospels	S. Cradock / Harmony of the Four Evangelists
1671	NT	H. Hammond / NT (3d ed., enlarged)
1672	Acts	S. Cradock / Apostolic History (Acts paraphrased)
1672	Bible	KJV / (printed in Holland with Geneva Notes)
1675	Bible	KJV / (first English Bible printed at Oxford)
1675	Epistles	Anon. [Oxford scholars] / Epistles (paraphrase)
1679	Bible	KJV / (Oxford 2d ed.; earliest with marginal dates)
1679	Bible	KJV / (printed in England; Geneva Notes; chron.)
1683	Bible	A. Scatterwood / (rev. KJV; no longer extant)
1683	Bible	KJV / (printed in Holland with Geneva Notes)
1683	NT	S. Clark [Clarke?] / NT

7. The Geneva Bible had already lost ground to the King James Version: there were 182 printings of the King James Version and only 15 for the Geneva Bible.
8. Henry Hammond's paraphrase went through numerous editions until its final edition in four volumes (1845). It was the first example for the era of "paraphrases" in modern English Bible translations.

1685	NT	R. Baxter / A Paraphrase on the NT
1690	Bible	S. Clark / Holy Bible ... Annotations
1690	Bible	[W. Lloyd?] / Welsh Bible (Bishop Lloyd's Bible?)
1695	NT	R. Baxter / A Paraphrase on the NT (2d ed.)
1696	Apocalypse	S. Cradock / Brief and Plain Expos and paraph.... Rev.
1698	NT	H. Hammond / Paraphrase and Annotations (6th ed.)
1700	Psalms	C. Caryll / Psalmes of David (Vulgate; several eds.)
1701	NT	R. Baxter / Paraphrase on the NT (3d ed., corrected)
1701	Bible	W. Lloyd / KJV (Lloyd's ed.? Ussher chronology)
1701	NT	S. Clarke / KJV paraphrase inserts (2 vols.)
1702	NT	D. Whitby / NT Paraph. and Commentary (2 vols.)
1705	Epistles	J. Fell/paraphrase of Epistles (3d ed. of 1675 work)
1708	Bible	KJV / printed in England with Geneva Notes
1710	Bible	C. Mather / Biblia Americana: Sacred Scrip. (MS)
1710	NT	D. Whitby / Paraphrase and Commentary (rev. ed.)
1711f.	NT	E. Wells / Greek-English NT (with Paraphrase)
1714	Bible	KJV / (1st extant Bible printed in Ireland)
1714	Wisdom	S. Perkins / Solomon's Proverbs (Danvers and Lat.)
1715	Bible	KJV / printed in England with Geneva Notes
1717f.	Bible	T. Pyle / KJV paraphrase inserts for the NT
1718	NT	C. Nary / NT translated from Lat.
1719f.	NT	R. Russell / NT, with moral relections (4 vols.)
1722	NT	F. Fox / NT ... notes
1724	OT	E. Wells / Common Trans. corrected
1724[9]	NT	Anon. [Daniel Mace] / NT in Greek and English
1724	Bible	Harris / Bible (for those with weak memories)
1725f.	NT	S. Clarke and T. Pyle / KJV NT paraphrase inserts
1726	NT	[De Beausobre and Lenfant] / New Version ... NT
1727	Wisdom	S. (Patrick) / Books of Job...Song.
1729[10]	NT	Anon. [Daniel Mace] / NT in Greek and Eng.
1730	NT	W. Webster/NT...trans. Lat., French, Simon (2 vols.)
1730	NT	R. Witham / Annotations...NT (Vulgate; 2 vols.)
1731	NT	[Wycliffe] / NT (1378) (1st printed ed.)
1733	NT	R. Witham / Annotations...NT (Vulgate; rev. ed.)

9. At least seventy "private" versions, not counting Roman Catholic ones, appeared between 1611 and 1881. Of those, only a few are represented here.

10. This anonymously published New Testament translation was the work of Daniel Mace, a Presbyterian minister, although it has been erroneously attributed to William Mace, a lecturer at Civil Law. The error has been perpetuated in the Catalogue of the British Museum, Cotton's *Editions of the English Bible,* and even such reliable scholars as Luther Weigle and Hugh Pope have reproduced the error.

1735	NT	S. Clarke, T. Pyle / Scrip. Preservative (paraph.)
1736	Bible	S. Smith / Complete History (Family Bible)
1736	NT	J. Lindsay / NT. . .compared with original Greek
1737	NT	J. Lindsay / The NT. . .compared (another ed.)
1737	NT	Anon. / NT (school ed., Scotland)
1737	Apocalypse	M. Lowman / Paraphrase and Notes on Rev.
1738	Bible	R. Challoner/Rheims-Douay-Bible (5th ed. of NT)
1739f.	NT	P. Doddridge / Family Expositor, (paraph.; 6 vols.)
1739f.	NT	J. Guyse / Practical Expositor (paraphrase; 3 vols.)
1740	NT	R. Witham / Rheims NT (3d ed.)
1741	Gospels	D. Scott / New Version of St. Matthew's Gospel
1743	NT	J. Marchant / Exposition (mistranslations rectified)
1745	NT	W. Whiston / Whiston's Primitive NT
1745	NT	P. Doddridge / NT paraphrase (revision)
1745	Apocalypse	M. Lowman / Paraphrase ... Rev. (2d ed.)
1746	Bible	S. Humphreys / Sacred Books (OT and NT)
1749	NT	R. Challoner / Rheims NT (slight revision, 2 vols.)
1749	Gospels	J. Heylyn / An Interpretation of the Four Gospels
1750[11]	Bible	R. Challoner / Rheims-Douay-Challoner Bible
1750	NT	R. Challoner / Rheims NT (2d slight rev.)
1750	OT	R. Challoner / Douay OT (1st rev. in 4 vols.)
1752	NT	R. Challoner / Rheims NT (3d rev., major)
1755	NT	J. Wesley / NT (rev. utilizing Greek text)
1755	NT	J. Newberry / The NT Adapted to Children
1759	Bible	R. Goadby / Illustration ... Holy Scrip. (6th ed.)
1760	NT	S. Clarke / NT trans. (KJV revision?)
1760	NT	D. Whitby / Paraphrase and Commentary (7th ed. rev.)
1761	Gospels	[Mr. Mortimer] / Divers Portions (gospels-Acts)
1761	NT	J. Guyse / Practical Expositor (2d ed. corrected)
1761	Epistles	J. Heylyn / Interpretation ... Acts ... Epistles
1762	Bible	Paris and Trehold / KJV (Cambridge "Standard")
1762	Bible	F. Fawkes / The Complete Family Bible
1763	Bible	KJV / (Cambridge; Baskerville's magnum opus ed.)
1763	Bible	R. Challoner / Rheims-Douay-Challoner Bible (rev.)
1764	Bible	A. Purver / New and Literal Trans. (Quaker's Bible)
1764	Bible	Rheims-Douay-Challoner / OT (2d ed.), NT (4th ed.)

11. The subsequent editions of the Rheims-Douay-Challoner (R-D-C) Bible have been based on this 1749/50 revision by Richard Challoner.

1764	NT	R. Wynne / NT carefully collated (trans.)
1765	NT	P. Dodderidge [S. Palmer] / New Trans. NT (rev.)
1766	NT	Anon. / Family Testament (child's ed.)
1768	NT	E. Harwood / Liberal Trans. of the NT
1769	Bible	B. Belayney / KJV (Oxford "Standard")
1770	Bible	Mr. Osterveld / Holy Bible ... translated (SPCK)
1770	NT	J. Worsley / NT, or New Covenant
1771	Wisdom	T. Scott / Book of Job, in Eng. Verse
1772	NT	Rheims-Douay-Challoner / NT (5th rev., 1749 ed.)
1773	Bible	H. Southwell [R. Sanders] / Universal Family Bible
1773	Portions	J. Bate / Literal trans. (Gen. to 2 Kings)
1773	Apocalypse	M. Lowman / Paraphrase ... on Revelation (3d ed.)
1774	NT	J. Ashton / Christian Expositor NT
1774	Bible	A. Fortescu / The Holy Family Bible
1774	Bible	Bailey / Heb. and Eng. Bible (corrections)
1775	NT	J. Guyse / Practical Expositor ... paraphrase (3d ed.)
1776	Gospels	Anon. / Liberal and Minute Inspection ... Gospel
1777	NT	KJV / (Phila.; earliest NT printed in America)
1778	Bible	J. Brown / Self-Interpreting Bible (many eds.)
1778	Bible	J. Fellows / The Bible in Verse (4 vols.)
1779	Prophets	R. Lowth / Isaiah, A New Trans. (many reprints)
1779	Prophets	R. Lowth / Isaiah, A New Trans. (2d ed.)
1782	Bible	KJV / Holy Bible (earliest ed. printed in America)
1783	NT	B. MacMahon / NT (4th ed.; Challoner NT revised)
1784	Bible	Anon. / The Hieroglyphic Bible (several eds.)
1785	Pentateuch	A. Alexander / First [-Fifth] Book of Moses
1785	Prophets	W. Newcome / KJV (rev. of the minor prophets)
1788	Portion	W. Newcome / KJV (rev. of Ezekiel)
1788	Bible	H. Doddridge / Christian's New Family Bible (Amer.)
1789	Pentateuch	I. Delgado / New Eng. Trans. (KJV Pentateuch rev.)
1789	Gospels	G. Campbell / Four Gospels (trans. from Greek)
1790	Bible	Rheims-Douay-Challoner / (1763; 1st Amer. ed.)
1790	NT	W. Gilpin / Exposition of NT (modern speech)
1790	NT	Anon. / NT with Alterations
1790	Psalms	S. Street / A New Literal Version ... Psalms
1791	Bible	B. MacMahon / Holy Bible (5th ed.; Challoner rev.)
1791	NT	J. Wesley / NT Explanatory Notes (1st Amer. ed.)
1791	NT	G. Wakefield / Trans. of the NT (Unitarian)
1792f.	Bible	A. Geddes / The Holy Bible

1793	Bible	T. Priestly / New Evangelical Family Bible
1794	OT	W. Roberts/Authorized Version (corrections)
1794	Bible	B. MacMahon / Holy Bible (6th ed.; Challoner rev.)
1794	Bible	J. Butler / Christian's New Universal Family Bible
1794	Bible	Rheims-Douay-Challoner / (6th rev. of 1749 ed .)
1795	Epistles	J. Macknight / The Epistles
1795	NT	S. Clarke, T. Pyles / Scripture Preservative (2d ed.)
1795	NT	T. Haweis / A Trans. of the NT (2 vols.)
1795	NT	G. Wakefield / Trans. of NT (improvements)
1796	NT	W. Newcome / KJV (rev. of NT pub. in 1800)
1796	Gospels	G. Campbell/The Four Gospels (trans. from Greek)
1797	NT	J. Guyse / Practical Expositor (paraphrase, 5th ed.)
1798	NT	N. Scarlett / Trans. of the NT from Greek
1799	Bible	[J. M. Ray or D. McRae] / A Revised Trans.
1800	Bible	M. Talbot / An Analysis of the Holy Bible
1800	Gospels	W. Newcome / Harmony of the Gospels (Eng.)
1801	Gospels	R. Darling / The Four Gospels, a poetic version
1802	Bible	[J. Reeves] / Holy Bible (Reeve's Bible; in 10 vols.)
1803	Bible	R. Tomlinson / The AV, with a new trans.
1803	Bible	B. MacMahon / Holy Bible (7th ed., Challoner rev.)
1805	Wisdom	J. Stock / The Books of Job
1805	Bible	Douay-Rheims-Challoner / (1st Amer. ed.; 5th Dublin ed.)
1806	Bible	G. Eyre and A. Strahan / KJV (rev. with authority)
1806	Bible	Brit. and For. Bible Soc. / KJV (1st with Soc. name)
1807	NT	Palmer / Fam. Expositor Abr. . . . Doddridge (Amer.)
1807	Portions	E. Evanson / NT According to Luke, Paul and John
1807	Apocalypse	M. Lowman / Paraphrase . . . Rev. (4th ed.)
1807	Bible	J. Canne [Ind, d.1677?] / Holy Bible (Canne's Notes)
1807	Gospels	S. Henshall / Gothic Gospel of Saint Matthew
1808	Bible	Thomson / Holy Bible, OT (Septuagint, 4 vols.)
1808	NT	[T. Belsham, Unitarian] / Improved Ver. (Newcome)
1808	Bible	Thomas Scott / Holy Bible (1st Amer. ed.)
1810	Bible	B. MacMahon / Holy Bible (8th ed., Challoner rev.)
1810	Epistles	J. Macknight / New Literal Trans. (1st Amer. ed.)
1812	NT	[J. Worswick] / NT, Rheims-Challoner (newly rev.)
1812	NT	[W. Williams] / Modern Trans. of NT
1812	Gospels	G. Campbell / Four Gospels, a new trans.
1813[12]	Bible	G. Woodfall / reprint of 1806 Eyre and Strahan

12. Standard edition, Protestant Episcopal Church of America.

1813	Gospels	A. Bradford [Unitarian] / Evang. History . . . Acts
1813	NT	J. McDonald / NT (2d Amer. from Cambridge ed.)
1814	Bible	Comm. Educ. Ireland / Extracts (KJV and R-D-C)
1815	Bible	J. M. Ray / Holy Bible (KJV; rev. and improved)
1815	NT	[T. Rigby] / NT (rev. 1749 Rheims-Challoner)
1815	NT	S. Payson / NT, carefully examined and corrected
1816	NT	J. McDonald / NT (2d Amer. rev. and corrected)
1816	NT	W. Thompson / NT trans. from Greek (literal)
1816	Bible	[S. Bagster] / Eng. Polyglott (many editions)
1816	Bible	P. Walsh / Rheims-Douay (rev. begun 1813; Troy)
1816	Epistles	J. Macknight / New Lit.Trans. (new ed., 6 vols.)
1817	Bible	B. Boothroyd / New Fam. Bible (impr. KJV)
1818	Bible	J. Bellamy / The Holy Bible, newly trans.
1818	Pentateuch	S. Clapham / Pentateuch (explication of phraseology)
1818[13]	NT	Campbell, Macknight, Doddridge / Sacred Writings
1819	Bible	C. Wellbeloved / Holy Bible (new trans.)
1819	NT	T. Belsham / Unitarian ver. (5th ed. of 1808)
1819	Epistles	Philalethes [J. Jones] / [Sev.] Epistles (new ver.)
1820?	Epistles	W. Heberden / Literal trans. . . . Apost. Eps. . . . Rev.
1822	Bible	R-D-C / Troy (Dublin 5th ed.; see 1816 ed.)
1822	NT	Israel Alger, Jr. / Pronouncing Testament (Amer.)
1823	NT	A. Kneeland [Universalist] / NT (Greek-Eng.)
1823	NT	A. Kneeland [Universalist] / NT (Eng. only)
1823	Bible	J. Christie / The Holy Bible
1823	NT	[Anon.] / Trans. . . . from the Vulgate
1824	Bible	B. Boothroyd / New Family Bible (Improved)
1824	NT	[J. H. Wilkins] / The NT (rev. ed.)
1824	NT	E. Jones / NT Interlinear MS Trans.
1824	Bible	Rheims-Douay / Holy Bible (Troy's 5th Dublin ed.)
1825	NT	[W. Carpenter] / Scientia Biblica (Eng. Vulgate)
1825	Bible	I. Alger, Jr. / Pronouncing Bible (many eds.)
1825	Bible	T. Williams / Cottage Bible and Family Expositor
1825	Wisdom	G. Hunt / Job (trans. from Heb.)
1825	NT	G. Townsend / NT (chron. and historical order)
1826	NT	Alexander Campbell / Sacred Writing (Campbell, Macknight, Doddridge, 1818; Amer.)
1827	NT	[A. Greaves] / Gospel of God's Anointed
1827	Bible	Greenfield / Comprehensive Bible (var. readings)

13. This Campbell, Macknight, Doddridge (C-M-D) version, first issued in 1818, continued to be published by Alexander Campbell.

1827	Wisdom	G. R. Noyes [Unitarian] / Job (Amended Ver.)
1828	NT	[J.G. Palfrey (Unitarian)] / NT Common Vers.)
1828	Bible	W. Alexander / The Holy Bible
1828	Bible	Quaker's / Holy Bible (unsuitable passages italics)
1828	NT	A. Campbell / Sacred Writings, 2d ed.
1830	NT	[J. Palfrey—Unitarian] / NT (Common Vers., rev.)
1830	NT	[J. Palfrey—Unitarian] / NT (Common Vers., 3d ed.)
1830	Portions	Keseph / Genesis-2 Kings [Job] (preface signed)
1830	Prophets	J. Jones / The Prophet Isaiah (trans. Heb.)
1831	Bible	[S. Bagster] / Biblia Polyglotta (eight lang., 1 vol.)
1831	Bible	[S. Bagster] / English Vers. of the Polyglott Bible
1832	NT	A. Campbell / Family Testament (rev. and enl.)
1832	NT	S. Bagster / (Polymicrian Testament) NT
1833	NT	A. Campbell / Sacred Writings (3d pocket ed.)
1833	NT	R. Dickinson / New and Corrected Vers.
1833	Bible	KJV / (exact repr. of first-ed. King James 1611)
1833	Bible	N. Webster / Holy Bible (rev. of KJV; Amer.)
1833	NT	W. Paton / Village Testament (2 vols. in 1)
1833f.	Bible	Patton [T. Williams] / Cottage Bible Fam. Expos.
1834	Bible	R. Davenport / The Right-Aim School Bible
1835	NT	A. Campbell / Sacred Writings, 4th ed.
1835	NT	A. Macknight / New Literal Trans. (new ed.)
1835	NT	[J. Caldecott?] / Holy Writings, First Christians
1836	Gospels	J. Lingard / Catholic trans. of Gospels from Greek
1836	NT	[G. Penn] / Book of the New Covenant
1836	NT	J.A. Cummings / NT (4th ed., rev. and impr.)
1837	Prophets	G. R. Noyes [Unitarian] / New Trans. [of] Prophets
1837	NT	R. Dickenson / Productions: Evangelists-Apostles
1837	Bible	[E. Swedenborg] / Holy Bible (Swedenborgian)
1837	Epistles	E. Barlee / A Free and Explanatory Ver.
1838	NT	[G. Penn] / Book of the New Covenant (Supplement)
1838	NT	Amer. and For. Bible Soc. / NT (1833 Oxford KJV)
1839	OT	S. Neuman / Pentateuch (Eng., rev. trans. of KJV)
1839	NT	N. Webster / NT, 2d ed.
1839	NT	A. Campbell / Sacred Writings (6th ed.)
1840[14]	Bible	Amer. Bible Soc. / Holy Bible (ABS instituted)
1840	Bible	Sharpe [Unitarian] / Holy Bible (Greisbach NT)
1840	NT	N. Webster / New Testament (3d ed.)

14. The American Bible Society (ABS) originated in 1816.

[1840]	Gospels	T. Jefferson / Life and Morals of Jesus of Nazareth
1840	NT	G. Knight / The Orthoepic NT (pronunciation)
1840	NT	[E. Taylor] / Rev. from the AV ... by a Layman
1840	NT	[Matthew] / Irishman's Friend (three-version NT)
1840	OT	F. Barham / Heb. and Eng. Holy Bible (diglott ed.)
1841	Bible	J.T. Conquest / AV (Twenty Thousand Emendations)
1841	Portions	A. Jenour / Books of the OT: Vol II: Job
1841	NT	[S. Bagster] / Eng. Hexapla (reprinted 1844, 1846)
1841	Bible	Webster / Common Vers. (OT, 2d ed.; NT, 4th ed.)
1842f.	NT	[F. Parker] / A Literal Trans.
1842	Bible	Several scholars / Eng. Ver. (rev. and amended)
1843	NT	J. Etheridge / Horae Aramaicae (NT, Peschito)
1843f.	Bible	[Harper] / Illuminated Bible (issued 1846)
1844	OT	L. Brenton / Vatican Septuagint translated
1844	Bible	[S. Bagster] / Eng. Version of Polyglott Bible
1844	Bible	Sharpe [Unitarian] / Bible (2d ed., Griesbach NT)
1844	Bible	T.J. Hussey / AV (with a rev. vers.)
1845	Wisdom	T. Preston / Book of Solomon (Heb., Lat., Eng.)
1845	Prophets	J. M'Farlan / The Prophecies of Ezekiel
1845f.	Pentateuch	I. Leeser / Law of God (Torah: Heb.-Eng., 5 vols.)
1846	Gospels	J.W. Etheridge / Four Gospels, from Peshitto Syriac
1846	Psalms	J. Jebb / Literal Trans. of the Book of Psalms
1846	Wisdom	G. R. Noyes [Unitarian] / New Trans. (Wisdom)
1846?	Bible	[S. Bagster, J.P. Lippincott] / Comprehensive Bible
1847	Bible	C. Roger / Collation of the Sacred Scriptures
1848	Epistles	H. Heinfetter / Literal Trans. Romans.
1848	NT	J. Morgan / NT ... Trans. ... Into Pure Eng.
1848	NT	A. Komstock / NT in Komstok's Purfekt Alfabet
1848	Bible	M. Budinger / Way of Faith (Abr. trans. from Ger.)
1849	Gospels	F.P. Kenrick [R-D-C] / Gospels, rev. (Amer.)
1849	Portions	J.W. Etheridge / Acts ... Rev. from Peshitto
1849	NT	[Whiting, Adventist] / Good News of Our Lord
1850	NT	Amer. Bible Soc. / NT (first "Standard Edition")
1850	Bible	F. Barham / The Bible Revised (KJV)
1850	NT	Amer. Bible Union / Commonly Received Ver.
1850	NT	J. McMahon [Rheims-Challoner] / (pictorial ed.)
1850	NT	S.H. Cone, W.H. Wycoff / Commonly Received Ver.
1850	NT	Anon. / Spiritual Ver. (dictated by the Spirit)
1851	NT	J. Murdock / NT (Literal trans. from Syriac Peshitto)

1851	Bible	ABS / Bible, corrected (standard KJV text)
1851	Epistles	F.P. Kenrick [R-D-C] Acts-Apoc. (Amer. rev.)
1851	Epistles	J. Turnbull / Romans (original trans.)
1851	Epistles	H. Heinfetter / Literal Trans.... Epistles of Paul
1852	NT	H. Woodruff / Exposition of the NT (idiomatic)
1852	Pentateuch	J.J-W. Jervis / Genesis, Elucidated, a New Trans.
1852f.	NT	J. Taylor / The Emphatic NT
1852f.	NT	Amer. Bible Union / Common Eng. Vers. (in parts)
1853	OT	I. Leeser / (The OT) Masoretic Text (MT)
1853	NT	I. Cobbin / NT Designed for the Study of Youth
1853	Bible	B. Boothroyd / New Family Bible, Improved
1854	Epistles	H. Heinfetter (F. Parker) / Literal (Gen. Ep. Rev.)
1854	Epistles	J. Turnbull / Epistles of Paul (an original trans.)
1855	Gospels	A. Norton / Trans. of the Gospels (Unitarian)
1855	Bible	Amer. Bible Soc. / Holy Bible (new ABS text)
1855	NT	L. Bruderz / Nu Testament, otorized, Fonetik Spelin
1856	Bible	Sharpe [Unitarian] / Bible (3d ed., Griesbach (NT)
1856	Bible	ABS / Bible, "revised text" (Great Primer)
1857	Bible	ABS / Bible, Pica Ref. Oct. (new standard)
1857?	Portions	F.P. Kenrick [R-D-C] / Psalms-Cant. (Amer.)
1857	Wisdom	T.J. Conant / Job (KJV, Hebrew, ABU, rev. vers.)
1857	Portions	T.S. Green / NT (part 1, Matt. and Rom.)
1857	Gospels	Henry Alford et al. / AV Gospel of John (rev.)
1857	NT	F.P. Kenrick / [Rheims-Challoner] / NT (rev.)
1857	Gospels	J.B. Barrow et al. [Five Clergymen] / John (2d ed.)
1858	OT	A. Vance / AV of OT, Harmonized, Revised
1858	NT	L.A. Sawyer [Unitarian] / NT, trans.... Greek
1858	Epistles	Five Clergyman / Romans (AV, Newly Rev. Ver.)
1858	Epistles	Five Clergyman / Corinthians (AV, Newly Rev. Ver.)
1859	Bible	Sharpe [Unitarian] / Bible (4th ed., Griesbach NT)
1859	Gospels	W.G. Cookesley / Revised Trans. NT: Matt.
1859	Portions	F.P. Kenrick / [Rheims-Douay-Challoner] / Job, Prophets (Amer.)
1859	NT	J.N. Darby / The NT, a trans.
1860	Bible	E.B. Pusey / The Holy Bible with Commentary
1860	NT	L.A. Sawyer [Unitarian] / NT (rev. and improved)
1860	Pentateuch	F.P. Kenrick [R-D-C] / Pentateuch
1861	OT	A. Benisch / Jewish School and Family Bible
1861	OT	L.A. Sawyer [Unitarian] / The Old Testament

1861[15]	NT	Tenn. Bible Soc. and SBC / (Civil War NT)
1861	Epistles	Four Clergymen / Epistles: Gal.-Col. (see 1858)
[1861]	NT	L. Thorn / NT Rev. and Corrected by the Spirits
[1861]	NT	Giles / NT trans. word for word
1861f.	NT	W. H. Kelly / Lectures and Expositions (new trans.)
1862	Bible	L.A. Sawyer [Unitarian] / Holy Bible
1862	NT	Amer. Bible Union / Common English Vers. (2d ed.)
1862	Bible	Sharpe [Unitarian] / Bible (5th ed., Griesbach NT)
1862	OT	C. Wellbeloved et al. / Holy Scripture Old Cov.
1862	NT	H. Highton / A Rev. Trans. of the NT
1862	NT	F.P. Kenrick / NT trans. from the Vulgate
1862f.	NT	Amer. Bible Union / NT Common English Vers.
1863	Bible	R. Young / Holy Bible (literal and idiomatic trans.)
1863	Psalms	W. Kay / The Psalms, trans. from the Heb.
1863	Prophets	J. Bellamy / The Book of Daniel, Trans.
1863	Bible	R. Young / The Holy Bible, Literal trans. (rev.)
1863	NT	[Frederick Parker] / Literal trans. of NT (6th ed.)
1863	Gospels	G.W. Brameld / The Holy Gospels
1863	NT	Anon. / NT Proper Names Divided and Accented
1864	Bible	Amer. Bible Union / KJV rev. ("immersion" vers.)
1864	Wisdom	J.M. Rodwell / Job, Translated from Heb.
1864	NT	B. Wilson / Emphatic Diaglott (several eds.)
1864	Prophets	L. Sawyer [Unitarian] / Daniel, Apocryphal Adds.
1864	NT	H. Heinfetter [F. Parker] / Eng. Vers. (Vatican MS)
1864	NT	H.T. Anderson / NT, Trans. from Greek (several eds.)
1864	NT	T.S. Green / Twofold NT (1857, part 1)
1864	Epistles	Conybeare and Howson / Life and Ep. of Paul
1865	Bible	Amer. Bible Union / KJV (2d rev.)
1865	OT	I. Leeser / OT, Masoretic Text (MT) (rev. ed.)
1865	OT	Sharpe [Unitarian] / The Heb. Scriptures
1865	NT	T.S. Green / Twofold NT (parallel cols.)
1866	Pentateuch	Amer. Bible Union / Gen., Common Vers. (corrected)
1866	NT	Amer. Bible Union / NT, Common Vers. (corrected)
1866	NT	H.T. Anderson / NT, rev.
1867	Bible	J. Smith, Jr. / KJV (trans. and corrected)
1868	NT	J.B. Rotherham / NT (Gospel of Matthew)
1868	NT	Anon. / NT Narrative (trans. according to Vulgate)

15. The Tennessee Bible Society and the Southern Baptist Convention (SBC) prepared this NT for use during the Civil War.

1868	Prophets	G. Noyes [Unitarian] / New Trans. (3d ed.)
1868f.	Bible	F. Gotch and G. Jacob / Bible (AV, emend.)
1868	Wisdom	G. Noyes [Unitarian] / New Trans. (4th ed.)
1869	Psalms	C. Carter / Psalms (trans. from the Heb.)
1869	NT	G. R. Noyes [Unitarian] / NT (trans. Tischendorf)
1869	NT	H. Alford [Five Clergymen] / AV (newly rev.)
1869	NT	R. Ainslie / NT (trans. Tischendorf)
1869	Gospels	N. S. Folsom / Four Gospels (trans. Tischendorf)
c. 1870	Bible	Anon. / Children's Bible (AV; reissued 1871, 79)
1870	Gospels	G. Brameld / Gospels (spurious pass. expunged)
1870	Bible	Sharpe [Unitarian] / Bible (6th ed., Griesbach NT)
1870	Wisdom	Francis Barham / The Writings of Solomon
[1870]	OT	Anon. / Septuagint with Eng. Trans.
1870	Bible	F. Gotch and G. Jacob / Holy Bible (another ed.)
1870	NT	T. Newberry / NT with Analysis
1870	NT	Anon. / A Critical English NT
1870	NT	J. Bowes / NT ("from the purest Greek")
1871	NT	J.N. Darby / NT, a new trans. (2d ed.)
1871	OT	Sharpe [Unitarian] / Heb. Scriptures (2d ed.)
1871	NT	Anon. / A Critical English NT (2d ed.)
1871	Wisdom	F. Barham / Job (newly trans. from the original)
1871	Psalms	Barham and Hare / Psalms (from Heb., Syriac)
1871	Bible	R.D. Hitchcock / Hitchcock's Holy Bible
1871?[16]	NT	J. Woodford / NT Trans. (Eng. Rev. Company)
1872	NT	J.B. Rotherham / NT, newly trans.
1872	Bible	A.J. Holman / Holman Bible (first ed.)
1872?	Gospels	Alexander Bell / The Four Gospels ... Acts
1873f.	Bible	P. Wichsteed / Bible for Young People (Dutch)
1873	Bible	F. Scrivener / Cambridge Paragraph (KJV rev.)
1873	Bible	W. Rogers / School and Children's Bible (shortened)
1873	Gospels	R. Hunt / Universal Syllabic Gospel: St. John
1874f.	Bible	F. Oakley, T. Law [R-D-C-] / Bible (rev., 2 vols.)
1875	NT	S. Davidson / NT (trans. Tischendorf)
1875	NT	Anon. / NT (trans. Tischendorf)
1875	NT	J.B. McClellan / NT, A New Trans.
1875	NT	S. Davidson / NT trans.
1875?	Bible	R. Challoner / The Holy Bible (Council of Trent)

16. This NT translation was adopted by the English Revision Company as the basis for the RV (ERV) published in 1881.

1876	OT	Sharpe [Unitarian] / Heb. Scriptures (3d ed.)
1876	Bible	J. E. Smith / Holy Bible Trans. Literally
1877	Bible	[J. Gurney et al.] / Rev. Eng. Bible (KJV; rev.)
1877	Bible	Anon. / Rev. Eng. Bible
1877	NT	J. A. Richter / NT, rev. and corrected
1877	NT	Anon. / Englishman's Greek NT (new ed. in 1946)
1878	NT	J.B. Rotherham / NT (2d ed., rev.; 12 eds.)
1878f.	Bible	P.H. Wicksteed / Bible for Learners (Dutch; 3 vols.)
1879	Bible	P.H. Wicksteed / Bible for Young People (new ed.)
1879	Psalms	J.P. Gell / The Psalms from the Heb.
1879	Wisdom	J. Medley / Job, trans. from the Heb. text
1880	Bible	S. Sharpe [Unitarian] / Holy Bible (Auth. Eng. Vers.)
1880	Bible	H. Gollancz / The Holy Bible, rev.
1880	NT	R.L. Clark et al. / Variorum Edition of NT
1881	Bible	Sharpe [Unitarian] / Bible (7th ed.; Griesbach NT)
1881	NT	S. Williams / NT ("immersion" ver.)
1881	Gospels	W.B. Crickmer / Greek Testament Englished
1881	NT	Brit. Rev. Com. / Eng. Rev. Ver. (RV; 10 vols.)
1881	NT	Amer. Rev. Com. / Rev. Ver. (Amer. Edition)
1881	NT	Amer. Rev. Com. / Rev. Ver. (Amer. Rev.; ASV)
1881	NT	E. Leigh / The Sinai and Comparative NT
1881	NT	M. Williams / NT New Rev. Ver. (KJV), (parallel)
1881	NT	[H. Weston et al.] / New RV (Americanized)
1881	NT	Amer. Tract Society / NT, 1881 (numerous eds.)
1881	NT	(J. James) / Sacred Writings (C-M-D, 3d ed. rev.)
1882	NT	AV and RV / Parallel NT (comparative)
1882	NT	C. Hebert / NT Scriptures (from Greek, 1611)
1883	NT	C. Tischendorf / Good News (Codex Siniaticus)
1883	NT	C. Jackson / NT (Greek with apostolic refs.)
1883f.	OT	J.N. Darby / "Holy Scriptures" ... OT (parts 1-4)
1884	Psalms	T.K. Cheyne / Psalms trans.
1884	Psalms	R. Brinkerhoff / Praise-Songs of Israel, ... Psalms
1884	Epistles	F. Fenton / St. Paul's Epistles in Modern Eng.
1884	Bible	T. Newberry / Englishman's Bible (several eds.)
1884	OT	M. Friedlander / Jewish Family Bible (Eng. trans.)
1884f.	NT	J.W. Hanson / The New Covenant (2 vols.)
1885	OT	Brit. Rev. Com. / RV: OT (4 vols.)
1885	Bible	Brit. Rev. Committee / RV (5 vols.)
1885	Bible	J.N. Darby / Holy Scriptures (French, Ger.) 4 parts)

1885	OT	H. Spurrell / OT trans. from Hebrew
1885	Bible	AV and RV / Bible (AV, RV, parallel cols.)
1885	NT	Amer. Bible Union / NT, Improved
1885	NT	W.D. Willard / Teachings and Acts of Jesus
c. 1886	Epistles	F. Fenton / The Epistles of St. Paul (2d ed.)
1887	Bible	T. Newberry / Holy Bible
1887	Bible	R. Young / Young's Literal Trans. rev.
1887	Gospels	W.W. Skeat / The Gospels (Old English gospels)
1887	NT	[G. Penn] / Book of the New Covenant (3d ed.)
1888	Gospels	E. Bolton / The Four Gospels . . . Modern Eng.
1890	Bible	J.N. Darby / Holy Scriptures (a new Trans.)
1890	Epistles	F. Fenton / St. Paul's Epistles (3d ed.)
1891	Acts	[C. Tischendorf] / Apostles (Codex Siniaticus)
1891	Bible	Amer. Bible Union / Holy Bible (KJV, 3d rev.)
1891	NT	Amer. Bible Union / NT ("immersion" ed.)
1891	NT	L.A. Sawyer [Unitarian] / The Bible: Analyzed
1891	Bible	A.J. Holman / Pronouncing Bible (KJV and ERV)
1891	Pentateuch	F.W. Grant et al. / Numerical Bible (Pentateuch)
1894	Bible	Brit. Rev. Com. / ERV (One vol.; marginal refs.)
1894	Gospels	A.S. Lewis / The Four Gospels (from Syriac)
1894	Epistles	F. Fenton / Epistles of St. Paul (4th ed.)
1894	Portions	F. Grant et al. / Numerical Bible (Cov. Hist.)
1895f.	Bible	R.G. Moulton / Modern Reader's Bible (22 vols.)
1895	Pentateuch	Anon. / Woman's Bible (Part I: Gen. . . . Deut.)
1896	NT	F. Fenton / NT Trans. (Greek into current Eng.)
1896	Psalms	F.W. Grant et al. / Numerical Bible (Psalms)
1896f.	Bible	P.H. Wicksteed / The Bible for Learners (new ed.)
1896f.	Bible	(C.G. Montefiore) / Bible for Home Reading (KJV)
1897	Bible	F.W. Grant et al. / Numerical Bible (Gospels, Rev.)
1897	NT	R.D. Weekes / New Dispensation, (NT trans. Greek)
1897	NT	G.R. Berry / Interlinear Greek-Eng. NT
1897	NT	H.E. Morrow / NT Emphasized
1897	NT	J.B. Rotherham / Emphasized NT (3d ed.)
1897	Gospels	F.S. Ballentine / Good News (Mod. Amer. Dress)
1898	Bible	Amer. Bible Soc. / Holy Bible (chron. omitted)
1898	Bible	Amer. Rev. Com. / Holy Bible (RV, 1881-85)
1898	Bible	A.J. Holman / Holy Bible (Linear Parallel Ed.)
1898	Portions	Anon. / Woman's Bible (part 2, Josh. to Rev.)
1898	Wisdom	F. Fenton / Book of Job (Heb. into Eng.)

1898	Psalter	S.R. Driver / Parallel Psalter (Prayer-Book, new)
1898f.	Bible	F. Saunders, C. Kent et al. / Messages of the Bible
1898	Pentateuch	Anon. / Twentieth Century (Part 1, five hist. books)
1898	Gospels	F.A. Spencer / Four Gospels (trans. from Lat.)
1898	NT	G.W. Horner / Coptic Version: Gospels (2 vols.)
1898	Bible	R. Young / Young's Literal Trans. (new rev.)
1898f.	Bible	Anon. / The Polychrome Bible
1899	Bible	H.H. Furnes et al. / Sacred Books (new Eng. trans.)
1899	NT	Anon. / NT . . . Color (first red-letter)
1899	Bible	[J. Gibbons] / Holy Bible (Vulgate; a new ed.)
1900	Bible	P.H. Wicksteed / Learner's Bible (2 vol. ed.)
1900	Epistles	Anon. / Twentieth Century NT (part 2, epistles)
1900	Epistles	H. Hayman / Epistles of the NT
1900	Epistles	F. Fenton / Epistles of St. Paul (6th ed.)
1900	Hexateuch	J.E. Carpenter / Hexateuch according to the RV
1900?	NT	F. Fenton / NT in Modern Eng. (rev.)
1901f.	OT	F. Fenton / Bible in Modern Eng. (4 vols.)
1901	Bible	Amer. Rev. Com. / RV (Standard Ed. / ASV)
1901	Gospels	F.A. Spencer / Four Gospels (Lat.-Syriac)
1901	Epistles	Anon. / Twentieth Century NT (part 3)
1901	Epistles	F.W. Grant et al. / Numerical Bible (Acts-2 Cor.)
1901	NT	W.W. Smith / NT in Braid Scots
1901	NT	F.S. Ballentine / The Modern American Bible
1901	NT	J. Moffatt / Historical NT
1901	Epistles	A.S. Way / Letters of St. Paul
1901	Bible	H.N. Jones / Young People's Bible
1902	Bible	Anonymous / Twentieth Century NT (3 vols.)
1902	OT	J. Rotherham / Emphasized OT (3 vols.)
1902	Bible	J. Rotherham / Emphasized Bible (4 vols.)
1902?	NT	W.B. Godbey / NT
1902	NT	[G.W. Moon] / "Revised English" NT (AV)
1903	Bible	F. Fenton / Holy Bible in Modern Eng.
1903	NT	R.F. Weymouth and E. Hampden-Cook / NT
1903	Epistles	F.W. Grant et al. / Numerical Bible (Heb.-Rev.)
1903	Psalms	Jewish Pub. Soc. [K. Kohler] / Psalms
1904f.	Bible	The Century Bible (based on RV, 1885)
1904	Bible	Twentieth Century NT (1-vol. ed. rev.)
1904	OT	S.F. Pells / Old Covenant (new ed.; Thomson's)
1904	NT	R.F. Weymouth / NT in Modern Speech (2d ed.)

1904	NT	Anon. / Corrected Eng. NT (KJV)
1904	NT	S. Lloyd / [Lloyd's] Corrected NT
1904	NT	A.S. Worrell / NT Rev. and Trans.
1904	OT	I. Leeser / OT from the MT (5th ed.)
1904	Gospels	R. D'Onston / Patristic Gospels
1904	Gospels	T. Jefferson / Life and Morals of Jesus of Nazareth
1904f.	Gospels	E.S. Buchanan / Lat. Gospels (2d cent. trans.)
1905?	Bible	Anon. / Red Letter Holy Bible (Prophetic OT)
1905?	NT	Amer. Bible Soc. / New Covenant Called the NT
1905	Bible	Anon. / English Bible (KJV, rev.)
1905	Bible	J.W. Genders / Holy Bible for Daily Reading
1905	NT	S. Lloyd et al. / Corrected English NT
1906	NT	A.S. Way / Letters of St. Paul (rev. ed.)
1906	Bible	F. Fenton / Complete Bible (modern Eng.; 4th ed.)
1906	Epistles	H.L. Forster / St. John's Gospel, Epistles, Rev.
1906	NT	T.M. Lindsay / NT of Our Lord and Savior (KJV)
1906	Psalms	[Swedenborgian] / Psalms (new U.S. trans.)
1907	OT	R.B. Taylor / Ancient Heb. Literature (KJV, 4 vols.)
1907	Gospels	A. Bourne / Fourfold Portrait...Heavenly King
1907	NT	T.M. Lindsay / NT of Our Lord (rev.; several eds.)
1907	Bible	R.G. Moulton / Modern Reader's Bible (1-vol. ed.)
1908	Bible	Sharpe / Holy Bible (8th ed.; Griesbach NT)
1908	Epistles	W.G. Rutherford / Paul's Epistles (Thess. and Cor.)
1908	Bible	J.W. Genders / Holy Bible for Daily Reading
1908	Bible	F. Thompson / Marginal Chain-Reference (KJV)
1909	Bible	Anon. / Bible in Modern English
1909	NT	F.S. Ballentine / Modern Amer. Bible (rev. ed.)
1909	NT	R.F. Weymouth / NT in Modern Speech (3d ed.)
1909	Bible	C.I. Scofield / Scofield Ref. Bible (KJV)
1910	Bible	F. Fenton / Holy Bible in Modern English (5th ed.)
1910	NT	S. Weaver / NT (mod. historical and literary form)
1910	Gospels	F.W. Cunard / First Judgment of Christians
1911	Bible	Amer. Scholars / 1911 Bible (Tercentenary Bible)
1911	Bible	Eminent Scholars / 1911 Tercentenary ... Bible
1911	Psalter	W.A. Wright / Hexaplar Psalter
1911f.	NT	F.J. Firth / Comparison Bible (Amer. Protestant and Roman Catholic versions)
1912	Bible	Amer. Baptist Pub. Soc. / Holy Bible (improved)
1912	Bible	J. Smith, Jr. / The Holy Scriptures (17th ed.)

1912?	OT	I. Leeser / OT from MT (new form; 4 vols.)
1912	Pentateuch	[Swedenborgians] / Genesis (new trans.; U.S.)
1913	Bible	Amer. Baptist Pub. Soc. / Bible (Improved Ed.)
1913	NT	Edward Clarke / AV (corrected)
1913	NT	J. Moffatt / New Trans. in Modern Speech
1913f.	NT	[Cuthbert Lattey] / Westminster Version
1914	NT	I. Panin / Numeric NT
1914	NT	E.E. Cunnington / New Covenant (rev. 1611 KJV)
1914	Bible	J.A. Murray / The War Bible of the Moment
1914	Gospels	E.S. Buchanan / Four Gospels from the Lat. Text
1915	Portions	N. Holm [Christian Scientist] / Runner's Bible
[1916]	Bible	E.W. Bullinger / Companion Bible
1916	Psalms	J. McFadyen / Psalms in Modern Speech, Rhythmic
1916	OT	A. Harkavy / Twenty-Four Books (Heb.-Eng.; rev.)
1917f.	Wisdom	McFadyen / Wisdom Books (Lam.-Song of Sol.)
1917	OT	Jewish Pub. Soc. / Holy Scriptures (MT)
1917	NT	J. Moffatt / NT in Modern Speech (rev.)
1917	Bible	C.I. Scofield / Scofield Ref. Bible (new and impr.)
1917	NT	J.R. Lauritzen / NT (trans. of Luther's German)
1918	Prophets	J.E. McFadyen / Isaiah in Modern Speech
1918f.	NT	C. F. Kent / Shorter Bible: NT
1918	NT	H.T. Anderson / NT, fresh trans. (Siniaticus)
1919	Prophets	J.E. McFadyen / Jer. in Modern Speech
1919f.	Bible	[A.E. Knoch] / Concordant Version
[1919]	Bible	F. Sanders and C. Kent / Messages of Bible
1920	Epistles	[G. Horner] / Coptic Bible: Epistles of Paul (2 vols.)
1921	Gospels	T.W. Pym / Mark's Account ("Common Speech")
1921	OT	C.F. Kent et al. / Shorter Bible: OT
1922	Acts	[G.W. Horner] / Coptic Version: Acts
1922	NT	[F.S.] Ballentine / Plainer Bible for Plain People
1922f.	NT	Anon. / Student's NT Compilation
1923	NT	E.J. Goodspeed / NT: An American Trans.
1923	Gospels	A.T. Robertson / Trans. of Luke's Gospel
1923	NT	W.G. Ballantine / Riverside NT
1923	Psalms	W.M. Furneaux / Psalms (rev. version)
1924	Apocalypse	[G.W. Horner] / Coptic Version: The Revelation
1924	NT	S.W. Green et al. / [Weymouth's] NT in Modern Speech (rev.)
1924	NT	H.B. Montgomery / Centenary Trans. (2 vols.)
1924	Portions	J. Moffatt / OT: A New Trans. (vol. 1, Gen.-Esth.)

1924	NT	Amer. Labor Determinative Rev. Com. / New Cov.
1924	NT	Dubois H. Loux / New Covenant
1925	Psalms	E.H. Askwith / Psalms Books IV and V
1925	Portions	J. Moffatt / OT: A New Trans. (vol. 2, Job-Mal.)
1925	NT	A. Overbury / People's New Cov. (metaphysical)
1925	Portions	H.A. Gherman and C.F. Kent / Children's Bible
1926	Psalms	J.M.P. Smith / Psalms
1926	Bible	[A.E. Knoch] / Concordant Version (rev. ed.)
1926	Bible	J. Moffatt / New Trans. of the Bible (3 vols.)
1926	NT	E.E. Cunnington / Western NT (KJV rev.)
1927	Bible	J.P. Smith, E.J. Goodspeed / Bible (Amer. trans.)
1927	OT	C.G. Kent / Student's OT (logically and chron. arr.)
1927	OT	Smith, Meek et al. / OT: An Amer. Trans.
1927	NT	G. N. Le Fevre / The Christian's Bible: NT
1928	Bible	J. Moffatt / New Trans. in Modern Speech
1928	OT	E. Czarnomska / Authentic Literature of Israel
1928	NT	Anon. / Layr. en's NT (London, 1928)
1928	Psalms	W.W. Martin / Psalms Complete (in 3 books)
1928	Gospels	J.W. Potter [Spiritualist] / Good Message (Matt.)
1929	Wisdom	W.W. Martin / Job in Two Versions
1929	NT	S.F. Pells / New Covenant (new ed., Thomson's Bible)
1929	Psalms	H.H. Gowen / Psalms (new transcription and trans.)
1929	NT	J. Robertson / [Weymouth's] NT Mod. Speech (3d ed.)
1929	NT	George W. Woff / NT in Blank Verse (KJV)
1929	Bible	F.C. Thompson / Chain-Ref. Bible (2d rev. ed.)
1930	Gospels	H. Loux / Mark: . . . Work, Pay, Rest
1930	NT	E.E. Cunnington / New Covenant (AV, 1611, rev. ed.)
1931	Bible	J.M.P. Smith et al. / The Bible (Amer. trans., vol. 1)
1931	Psalms	Frank H. Wales / Psalms, a revised trans.
1931	Bible	(A.E. Knoch) / Concordant Bible (Internatl. ed.; rev.)
1931	Prophets	F.W. Grant et al. / Numerical Bible: Ezekiel
1932	Bible	Amer. Bible Soc. / Holy Bible (ASV, new ed.)
1932	NT	A.E. Overbury / People's New Covenant, rev.
1932	Portions	[F.S.] Ballentine / Our God and Godhealth
1932	Bible	Amer. Bible Soc. / Holy Bible (new ed.)
1932	Gospels	James A. Kleist / Memoirs of St. Peter, . . . Mark
1933	Acts	[K. Lake] / Beginnings of Christianity (part 1, Acts)
1933	Gospels	G.M. Lamsa / Four Gospels, from the Aramaic
1933	Gospels	C.C. Torrey / Four Gospels, a New Trans.
1933	Bible	Smith-Goodspeed / Short Bible (Amer. trans.)

1934	NT	W.G. Ballantine / Riverside NT (rev.)
1934	NT	G.W. Wade / Documents of the NT
1934	Gospels	T.G. Royds / Epistles and Gospels
1934	Bible	F.C. Thompson / New Chain-Ref. Bible (3d ed.)
1934	OT	Anon. / Books of the OT in Colloquial English
1934f.	Portions	C. Lattey et al. / Westminster Version (OT books)
1935	Bible	J. Moffatt / New Trans. (rev. and final ed.)
1935	Bible	Smith-Goodspeed / Bible (Amer. trans., NT, rev.)
1935	NT	C. Lattey / Westminster Version . . . Scriptures
1935	NT	Ivan Panin / Numeric NT (2d ed.)
1935	NT	E.E. Cunnington / The Western NT (rev. ed.)
1935	Bible	Latter Day Saints / Holy Bible (specially bound)
1936	Bible	E.S. Bates / The Bible . . . Living Literature
1936	OT	A. Harkavy / Holy Scriptures
1937	NT	J. Gerber / NT (trans. and explanation)
1937	NT	C.B. Williams / NT in the Language of the People
1937	Wisdom	E.D. Dimnent / Job (Epic Ver. in Eng.)
1937	Psalms	G. O'Neill / Psalms and Canticles (new Eng. trans.)
1937	NT	W.W. Martin / NT critically reconstructed (2 vols.)
1937	NT	C.J. Callan and J. McHugh / [F.A. Spencer's] NT
1937	Epistles	G.W. Cornish [posthumous] / Paul from the Trenches
1938	Bible	B. Hall / Living Bible (Whole Bible in Fewest Words)
1938	NT	R.M. Wilson / Book of Books (trans. of NT)
1938	Psalms	M. Buttenweiser / Psalms (chronologically treated)
1938	NT	E.L. Clementson / NT (a trans.)
1938	NT	R.M. Wilson / Book of Books (trans. of NT complete)
1939	Portions	Z.H. Copp / Book of Life. Vol. 1, Interwoven
1939	Psalms	W.O.E. Osterley / Psalms (trans., text-critical notes)
1940	Gospels	J.A. Dakes / Christ Jesus: The Original Story
1940	NT	S.H. Hooke et al. / NT in Basic Eng.
1940	NT	G. M. Lamsa / Modern NT from Aramaic
1940	Gospels	M. L. Matheson / St. Mark in Current English
1940	Prophets	W.W. Martin / Isaian Prophecies
1940	Prophets	W.W. Martin / Jeremian-Ezekiel Prophecies
1941	Bible	J. Sterling / Bible for Today (based on KJV)
1941	NT	Episcopal Com. / Confraternity NT (R-D-C rev.)
1941	Gospels	H. Beevor / Christ's Chronicle
1941	Genesis	W.W. Martin / Gen. Complete
1941	Prophets	W.W. Martin / Twelve Minor Prophets, Complete
1943	Gospels	E.E. Stringfellow / Gospels, a trans.: Vol. I

1943	Gospels	O.M. Norlie / Gospel of John in Modern Eng.
1944	NT	R.A. Knox / NT, from the Vulgate
1944	Psalms	C.J. Callan / Psalms (trans. from the Lat. Psalter)
1944	NT	F. Fenton / NT in Modern Eng. (2d ed.)
1944	Bible	Concordant Pub. Concern / Concordant Bible
1944	Epistles	J.W.C. Wand / NT Letters (paraphrased)
1944	Bible	Latter Day Saints / Inspired Ver. (J. Smith, rev.)
1945	NT	G. Verkuyl / NT: Berkeley Ver.
1945	NT	E.E. Stringfellow / NT (vol. 2, Acts-Rev.)
1946	NT	E.J. Goodspeed / NT: American Trans. (21st ed.)

1946	NT	Int'l. Coun. Rel. Ed. / NT (RSV)
1946	NT	R.C.H. Lenski/Interpretation NT (12 vols., 1931-46)
1946	OT	Anon. / OT (American Trans.)
1946	NT	Anon. / Englishman's Greek NT (new ed.)
1947	Psalms	B.D. Eerdmans / Heb. Books of Psalms
1947	NT	G. Swann / NT . . . from Greek
1947	Epistles	J.B. Phillips / Letters to Young Churches (epistles)
1948	NT	T.F. and R.E. Ford / Letchworth Ver. (mod. Eng.—TR)
1948	OT	R.A. Knox / OT from Vulgate
1948	NT	C. Lattey / Westminster Ver. NT (smaller ed.)

1948	Bible	E.S. English et al. / Pilgrim Bible (KJV abr.)
1949	Gospels	A.G. Alexander / Interpretation NT (vol. 1, gospels)
1949	NT	S.H. Hooke et al. / Basic Bible in Basic Eng.
1949	OT	R.A. Knox / OT translated from Vulgate (new ed.)
1949	Psalms	E. A. Leslie / Psalms, trans. and interpreted
1950	Bible	R.B. Chamberlain et al. / Dartmouth Bible (abr.)
1950	OT	R.A. Knox / OT trans. from Vulgate (2 vols.)
1950	NT	Watchtower / NT (New World trans.)
1950	Psalms	E. Orlinger / Psalms and Canticles (Confraternity)
1950	Bible	S.H. Hooke et al. / The Basic Bible (rev. ed.)

1950	NT	A.B. Traina / NT: Sacred Name Ver.
1950	NT	C.B. Williams / NT (slightly rev. ed.)
1951	NT	Auth. Bible Soc. [C.B. Pershall] / NT (Authentic Ver.)
1951	NT	Watchtower / NT (New World trans., rev.)
1951	NT	O.M. Norlie / NT in Modern English
1951	Gospels	E. Vernon / Gospel of St. Mark . . . Simple Eng.
1952	OT	Soncino Press / Soncino Books of the Bible (indiv.)
1952	NT	C. Kingsley Williams / NT in Plain Eng.
1952	Portions	Conf. on Chr. Doc. / Holy Bible (vol. 1, Gen.-Ruth)
1952	Gospels	J.B. Phillips / Gospels

1952	OT	Int'l. Coun. Rel. Ed. / OT (RSV, 2 vols.)
1952	Gospels	E.V. Reiu / Four Gospels (Penguin Bible)
1952	Bible	Int'l. Coun. Rel. Ed. / Holy Bible: RSV
1953	OT	M. Friedlander / Heb. Bible with Eng. (reissue)
1953	NT	W. Hendriksen / NT Commentary
1953	Bible	Conf. / Holy Bible (Catholic Action ed.)
1953	Portions	Watchtower / New World Trans. (vol. 1, Gen.-Ruth)
1954	NT	G.A. Moore / NT (new, independent, individual trans.)
1954	NT	J.A. Kleist and J.L. Lilly / NT
1954	Psalms	E.J. Kissane / Psalms (trans. from Hebrew, 2 vols.)
1954	Psalms	J.A. Kleist and T.J. Lynam / Psalms in Rhythmic Prose
1954	Gospels	Lockman / Self Explaining Gospel (John)
1954	Bible	Epis. Com. / New Cath. Holy Bible (R-D-C; Conf.)
1955	OT	Jewish Pub. Soc. / Holy Scriptures (MT, new ed.)
1955	NT	W. Barclay / Daily Study Bible
1955	Wisdom	Conf. of Chr. Doc. / Holy Bible (vol. 3, Sapiential)
1955	Bible	Anon. / Modern Family Bible (AV with changes)
1955	Acts	J.B. Phillips / Young Church in Action (Acts)
1955	Bible	M. Nicholson / Compact Bible (abr. text)
1955	Psalms	M.P. Ryan / The Psalms: Fides trans.
1955	Portions	Watchtower / New World Trans. (vol. 2, Sam.-Esther)
1955	NT	H.J. Schonfield / Authentic NT (sub. edition)
1955	Bible	R.A. Knox / Holy Bible, trans. from Lat. Vulgate
1955	Epistles	A. Cressman / Paul's Letter to the Romans
1955	NT	P.G. Parker / Clarified NT
1956	NT	J.A. Kleist and J.L. Lilly / NT (rev.)
1956	NT	H.J. Schonfield / Authentic NT (gen. ed.)
1956	Gospels	K. Wuest / Gospels: An Expanded Trans.
1956	Bible	R.A. Knox / Holy Bible ... Lat. Vulgate (2d ed.)
1956	Epistles	F.C. Laubach / Inspired Letters in Clearest Eng.
1956	NT	R. Cox / NT Narrative (abridged NT)
1957	Apocalypse	J.B. Phillips / Book of Revelation
1957	Wisdom	Watchtower / New World Trans. (vol. 3, Job-S. Sol.)
1957	Bible	G. M. Lamsa / Holy Bible, from the Peschitta
1957	OT	Jewish Pub. Soc. / Holy Scriptures (MT)
1957	Epistles	J.B. Phillips / Letters to Young Churches (correct. ed.)
1957	Bible	R.A. Knox / Holy Bible (School ed.)
1957	Bible	Concordant Pubs. / Concordant Ver.: Int'l. Ed. (rev.)
1958	Gospels	J.B. Phillips / Gospels (corrected ed.)
1958	Prophets	Watchtower / New World Trans. (vol. 4, Isa.-Lam.)

1958	Gospels	L. Meissner / NT Gospels
1958	NT	J.B. Phillips / NT in Modern English
1958	NT	Lockman [F. Siewert] / Amplified NT
1958	NT	J.L. Tomanek / NT of Our Lord and Savior Jesus Christ
1958f.	NT	Anon. / Greek-Eng. Diglot
1958	Epistles	K. Wuest / Expanded Trans.: Acts-Eph.
1958	Epistles	J.T. Hudson / Pauline Epistles
1959	Bible	G. Verkuyl / Holy Bible: Berkeley Version
1959	Gospels	A. Cressman / Mark: Simplified for Liberians
1959	Epistles	K. Wuest / Expanded Trans.: Phil.-Rev.
1960	NT	V.T. Roth / Critical and Emphatic Paraphrase
1960	Bible	Watchtower / New World Trans.
1960	Gospels	A. Cressman / Mark: Simplified English (2d ed.)
1960	Bible	R.A. Knox / Holy Bible School Ed. (some rev.)
1960	Prophets	Watchtower / New World Trans. (vol. 5, Ezek.-Mal.)
1960	NT	J.P. Green / Children's "King James" (not 1611 KJV)
1960	NT	J.B. Phillips / NT in Modern English (rev.)
1960	Bible	Int'l. Coun. Rel. Ed. / RSV (corrections)
1960	Gospels	Lockman/Gospel John, New Am. Stand. Bible (NASB)
1961	NT	Moody Press / Twentieth Century NT (new ed.)
1961	NT	K. Wuest / NT (expanded trans.)
1961	NT	Joint Committee / New Testament New English Bible
1961	NT	F.S. Noli / NT of Our Lord and Savior
1961	Prophets	Conf. of Chr. Doc. / Holy Bible (vol. 4: Prophetic)
1961	Psalms	Watchtower [Byington] / Bible in Living Eng.
1961	Portions	O.M. Norlie / Simplified NT, Psalms
1961	Bible	Anon. / Bible in Basic Eng.
1961	Bible	Watchtower / The New World Trans. (1 vol., rev.)
1962	Gospels	A. Cressman / John: Simplified Eng.
1962	Gospels	Lockman / Gospel of John (NASB, 2d ed.)
1962	Gospels	Lockman / Gospels (NASB)
1962	Bible	J.P. Green / Children's OT with Stories (KJV text)
1962	Bible	J.P. Green / Teen-Age Ver. of the Holy Bible
1962	Bible	J.P. Green / Modern KJV of the Holy Bible
1962	Pentateuch	Jewish Pub. Soc. / The Torah (MT)
1962	Prophets	Lockman [F. Siewert] / Amp. OT (part 2, Job-Mal.)
1962f.	Epistles	K. N. Taylor / Living Letters: Paraphrased Epistles
1962	NT	Lockman / NT (NASB)
1962	NT	O.M. Norlie / Children's Simplified NT
1962	NT	H.J. Schonfield / Authentic NT (rev. ed.)

1963	NT	W.F. Beck / NT in the Lang. of Today
1963	Psalms	J. Gelineau / Psalms: A New Trans.
1963	Bible	A.B. Traina / Holy Name Bible (rev. ed.)
1963	Prophets	J.B. Phillips / Four Prophets
1963	NT	Lockman / NT (NASB, text ed.)
1963	NT	C.K. Williams / NT in Plain English (Amer. ed.)
1963	NT	V.T. Roth / Critical and Emphatic Paraph. (rev. ed.)
1964	Bible	W. F. Albright and D.N. Freedman / Anchor Bible
1964	Psalms	G. Hadas / Psalms for the Modern Reader
1964	OT	Lockman [F. Seiwert] / Ampl. OT (Part 1, Gen.-Est.)
1964	NT	Lockman / NT (NASB, 2d ed. rev.)
1964	NT	Lockman / NT (NASB, 3d ed. rev.)
1964	NT	W.F. Beck / NT in the Language of Today (rev.)
1964	Gospels	Amer. Bible Soc. [R. Bratcher] / Right Time, Mark's Story
1965	Epistles	F.F. Bruce / Expanded Paraphrase . . . Epistles of Paul
1965	NT	Catholic Biblical Assoc. / NT (RSV)
1965	Bible	Lockman [F. Seiwert] / Amplified Bible (1 volume)
1965	Epistles	Conf. of Chr. Doc. / Lectionary on Roman Missal
1965	Bible	H.S. Hooke et al. / Bible in Basic Eng.
1965f.	Prophets	K. Taylor / Living Prophecies (Minor Prophets, Dan., Rev.)
1966	Bible	Alexander Jones / Jerusalem Bible
1966[17]	NT	Amer. Bible Soc. / Good News for Modern Man
1966	Bible	Liturgical Press / Bible in Simplified Eng.
1966	Epistles	K. Taylor / Living Letters (rev.)
1966	Gospels	C.F. Burke / God Is for Real, Man
1966	Bible	J.P. Green / The Living Scriptures (new trans., (KJV)
1966	Gospels	K.N. Taylor / Living Gospels and Acts
1966	NT	C.B. Williams / NT in the Lang. of the People (rev.)
1966	Bible	Catholic Biblical Assoc. / Bible (Catholic, RSV)
1967	Bible	Anon. / Holy Scriptures (new trans.)
1967	NT	D.J. Klingensmith / NT
1967	OT	Lockman / OT (NASB)
1967	Portions	K. Taylor / Living Psalms, Proverbs, Major Proph.
1967	NT	K. Taylor / Living NT (paraphrase)
1967	Gospels	M. Grunberg / West-Saxon Gospels (critical ed.)

17. *Today's English Version: Good News Bible* appeared in parts until it was completed in 1976. Since its completion, the publisher prefers to call it the *Good News Bible* (GNB) rather than *Today's English Version* (TEV), although both designations are used.

1967	Portions	A.T. Dale / New World: Heart of the NT in plain Eng.
1967	Gospels	D. Williams and F. Shaw / Gospels in Scouse
1967	Bible	G. Linday / Rhyming Bible
1967	NT	ABS [Bratcher] / Good News (TEV, 2d ed.)
1967	Portions	Conf. of Chr. Doc. / Holy Bible (vol. 2, Sam.-Macc.)
1967	Bible	E.S. English et al. / New Scofield Ref. Bible
1968	Wisdom	K. Taylor / Living Lessons of Life and Love
1968	NT	Good News for Modern Man (rev.)
1968	Epistles	C. Jordan / Cotton Patch Version (Paul's Epistles)
1968	Psalms	R.S. Hanson / Psalms in Modern Speech (3 vols.)
1968	NT	Miss. Dispens. Bible Res. / Sacred Name NT
1968	NT	A. Marshall / Interlinear Greek-Eng. NT (rev. ed.)
1968	Gospels	W. Barclay / NT (vol. 1, Gospels-Acts)
1969	Epistles	W. Barclay / NT (vol. 2, Letters and Rev.)
1969	Portions	Jewish Pub. Soc. / Five Megilloth and Jonah (MT)
1969	Bible	Modern Lang. Bible (New Berkeley Ver. (rev. ed.)
1969	Pentateuch	K. Taylor / Living Books of Moses
1969	NT	Conf. of Chr. Doc. / NT (trans. from Greek)
1969	Gospels	C. Jordan / Cotton Patch Ver. (Luke and Acts)
1969	NT	A. Cressman / Good News for the World
1969	NT	G. H. Ledyard / New Life Testament (KJV)
1969	NT	G. H. Ledyard / The Children's NT (KJV)
1969	Gospels	NY Bible Soc. [E.H. Palmer] / Gospel [of] John
1969	NT	Watchtower / Kingdom Interlinear Trans. of the Greek
1969	Bible	G. Verkuyl / Modern Lang. Bible (New Berkeley Ver.)
1970	Gospels	C. Jordan / Cotton Patch Ver. (Matthew and John)
1970	NT	[J.P. Green] / King James II NT
1970	NT	Miss. Disp. Bible Res. / Sacred Name Bible
1970	Bible	Joint Committee / New Eng. Bible (rev. NT)
1970	Bible	Cath. Biblical Assoc. of Amer. / New Amer. Bible
1970	Gospels	Kevin Condon / Mercier NT (part 1, gospels)
1970	Portions	K. Taylor / Living History of Israel
1970	NT	Anon. / NT in Worldwide Eng.
1970	NT	Anon. / NT Judean and Authorized
1970	Psalms	ABS [Bratcher] / Psalms for Mod. Man (TEV)
1971	Wisdom	Amer. Bible Soc. [Bratcher] / Job (TEV)
1971	Bible	Lockman / NASB
1971	Prophets	Amer. Bible Soc. / Amos (New Int'l. Bible)
1971	Bible	Int'l. Coun. Rel. Ed. / NT (RSV, 2d ed.)

1971	Bible	[J.P. Green] / The Holy Bible: King James II
1971	Epistles	B. Blackwelder / Letters from Paul (exeg.)
1971	Bible	K. Taylor / The Living Bible (paraphrase)
1972	Wisdom	Amer. Bible Soc. [Bratcher] / Wisdom (TEV)
1972	NT	Lockman / NT (NASB, Soul-winner's ed.)
1972	Bible	Lockman / NASB (text ed.)
1972	NT	Compass / One Way: Jesus People NT (Norlie 1951)
1972	Bible	Watchtower [S.T. Byington] / Bible in Living Eng.
1972	NT	J.B. Phillips / NT in Mod. Eng. (a "wholly new book")
1972	Psalms	Jewish Pub. Soc. / Psalms (rev. ed., MT)
1973	Pentateuch	Jewish Pub. Soc. / Torah (2d rev. ed.)
1973	Prophets	Jewish Pub. Soc. / Isa. (MT)
1973	NT	Brit. and For. Bible Soc. / Translator's NT
1973	NT	C. Estes / NT
1973	Bible	Int'l. Rev. Com. / Com. Bible (Ecumenical, RSV)
1973	NT	NY Int'l. Bible Soc. / NT: New Int'l. Version (NIV)
1973	Bible	A. Edwards and S. Steen / Child's Bible (color)
1973	Prophets	J.B. Phillips / Four Prophets (rev. ed.)
1973	Epistles	C. Jordan / Cotton Patch Ver. (Heb., Gen. Ep.)
1973	NT	MDBR / Original Sacred Name Bible (3d ed.)
1973	NT	Anon. / Translator's NT
1973	Psalms	Lydia Gysi / Psalms (explanatory trans.)
1973	NT	Brit. and For. Bible Soc. / Translator's NT
1973	NT	C. Estes / Better Version of the NT
1973	NT	M. Collins / Phillips' NT (mod. Eng. 2d rev. ed.)
1974	NT	D.J. Klingensmith / NT in Everyday Eng.
1974	Prophets	Jewish Pub. Soc. / Jeremiah (MT)
1974	Prophets	Jewish Pub. Soc. / Prophets: Nevi'im (MT)
1975	Gospels	A. Edington / Word Made Flesh (paraphrased)
1976	Pentateuch	Nutt / Train Up a Child (Part 1, Gen.; paraphrase)
1976	Bible	Philip Birnbaum / Concise Jewish Bible
1976	Bible	ABS / Good News Bible (GEB; TEV)
1976	Bible	J.P. Green / Interlinear Hebrew-Greek-English
1976	Bible	W.F. Beck / Holy Bible in the Lang. of Today
1976	NT	G.H. Ledyard / New Life Testament
1976	NT	R.O. Yaeger / Renaissance NT
1976	Gospels	R. Cox / Gospel Jesus (The Story in Mod. Eng.)
1977	Gospels	Williams and Shaw / Gospels in Scouse (rev. ed.)
1977	Wisdom	M. Falk / Song of Songs (Bible Love Poems)

1977	Psalms	N. de Lange / Psalms (trans. from Heb.)
1977	Gospels	Brit. and For. Bible Soc. / The Four Gospels
1977	Psalms	David L. Frost / Psalms, A Trans. for Worship
1977	NT	Jay E. Adams / Christian Counselor's NT
1977	Bible	A.H. Johsmann / Holy Bible for Children
1977	Bible	Int'l. Rev. Com. / New Oxford Annotated Bible
1977	NT	Int'l. Rev. Com. / RSV: NT (2d ed.)
1978	Bible	Anon. / Holy Name Bible (Brandywine, Md., ed.)
1978	Bible	NY Int'l. Bible Soc. / Holy Bible: NIV
1978	NT	Anon. / NT (Eng. Ver. for the Deaf)
1979	NT	Nelson / NT New King James Version (NKJV)
1979	Gospels	R. Lattimore / The Four Gospels and Revelation
1979	Psalms	B. Zerr / The Psalms: A Trans.
1979	NT	J.E. Adams / NT in Everyday English
1979	Epistles	R. Paul Caudill / Ephesians
1979	Portions	J.M. Sasson / Ruth: A New Trans.
1979	Wisdom	S. Mitchell / Into the Whirlwind (a trans. of Job)
1982	Portions	Jewish Pub. Soc. / Writings, Kethubim (MT)
1982	Bible	Nelson / Holy Bible: NKJV
1982	Bible	Nelson / Holy Bible: Rev. Auth. Ver. (NKJV)
1982	Bible	Metzger / Reader's Digest Bible (Condensed RSV)
1982	Epistles	R. Lattimore / Acts and Letters of the Apostles
1983	Bible	Cath. Bible Assoc. of Amer./New Amer. Bible (NAB)
1983	Portions	Int'l. Coun. Rel. Ed. / Inclusive Lect.
1984	NT	J.G. Anderson / New Accurate Trans.
1984	Portions	Int'l. Coun. Rel. Ed. / Inclusive Lect. (rev. ed.)
1985	NT	H.J. Schonfield / Original NT
1985	OT	Jewish Pub. Soc. / TANAKH (New trans., MT)
1985	Bible	[Doubleday] / New Jerusalem Bible

Glossary

ACCOMMODATION THEORY—The view of the German rationalists and others that Christ and the apostles accommodated their teaching to the current (but false) Jewish traditions about authorship, inspiration, and so forth, of the Old Testament without thereby either asserting or approving those beliefs.

AMANUENSIS—A scribal secretary or one employed to take dictation.

ANTILEGOMENA—Literally, the books "spoken against," that is, the books of the New Testament canon whose inspiration has been disputed, usually meaning Hebrews, James, 2 Peter, 2 and 3 John, Jude, and Revelation.

ANTINOMIANISM—Literally "without (or against) law," it designates the ethical position that there are no binding moral laws; all is relative or situational.

APOCALYPSE—The English transliteration of the Greek word *apocalypsis* (revelation), this term used as the title for the last book of the Bible in English Roman Catholic versions.

APOCALYPTIC LITERATURE—A designation sometimes applied to the pseudepigraphal books because their contents are largely "revelations" and "visions"; it is also used to describe the canonical books of Ezekiel, Daniel, Zechariah, and Revelation.

APOCRYPHA—The Protestant designation for the fourteen or fifteen books of doubtful authenticity and authority that are not found in the Hebrew Old Testament but are in manuscripts of the LXX; most of these books were declared canonical by the Roman Catholic church at the Council of Trent in 1546, and they call these books deuterocanonical (second canon).

APOSTOLICITY—In the narrow sense, it refers to that which comes directly from an apostle; but in a broader sense, it may refer to teaching produced under apostolic authority, whether by apostolic *authorship* or by apostolic *teaching* through a prophetic ministry.

AUTHENTICITY—A word describing the truthfulness of the contents of a given text or composition; it is sometimes incorrectly used interchangeably with *genuineness* (see below).

AUTOGRAPHS or AUTOGRAPHA—Sometimes inaccurately defined as the original writings from the hand of an apostle or prophet, these are, more precisely, writings produced under the authority of an apostle or prophet, whether or not through a scribe or in several editions.

CANONICITY—The character of a biblical book that marks it as a part of the canon of Scripture, namely, the divine inspiration and authority that designate a book as part of the rule or standard of faith and practice.

CODEX—A manuscript in book form, that is, with sheets bound together rather than in the form of a roll or scroll.

COLOPHON—Literally "finishing touch," that is, a literary device used at the end of a book sometimes connecting it with a following book.

CONSERVATIVE—The theological position that affirms the basic doctrines of Christianity as the virgin birth, the deity of Christ, the substitutionary atonement, the resurrection of Christ, and the divine inspiration of the Bible. In this sense, conservative is used interchangeably with fundamental, evangelical and orthodox, and it is to be contrasted with liberal, or modernist.

COVENANT—An agreement or compact between two parties, such as the Mosaic Covenant.

CREDIBILITY—As applied to the Scriptures, it is their right to be believed and received as the truth of God.

CRITICAL TEXT—An edited text of the Bible that attempts, by critical comparison and evaluation of all of the manuscript evidence, to approximate most closely what was in the autographs; the Westcott and Hort text of the Greek New Testament is an example of a critical text.

CURSIVE MANUSCRIPTS—Usually the equivalent of minuscule or small-lettered manuscripts written in a "running hand," hence "cursive"; it is akin to handwriting rather than printing.

DECALOGUE—Literally, "ten words," that is, the Ten Commandments as recorded in Exodus 20 or Deuteronomy 5.

DEISM—The belief that there is a Creator who operates in His creation only through natural law that He has ordained from the beginning and who never intervenes in the world by miracles; hence, it is antisupernaturalistic in outlook.

DEMYTHOLOGY—A modern critical method of biblical interpretation espoused by Rudolph Bultmann and others that attempts to divest biblical stories of the *religious myth* of their day in order to arrive at their "*real message,*" and to see through the *historical* to their *supra-historical* truth; hence, this view does not accept the historicity and inerrancy of the Bible.

DESTRUCTIVE CRITICISM—A term used by conservative theologians to describe the harmful result of certain liberal or negative forms of higher criticism of the Bible (see below).

DOCETISM—An early Christian heresy which affirmed the deity but denied the humanity of Christ.

ECLECTIC—A view composed of various teachings drawn from different sources.

EXISTENTIALISM—Religious existentialism holds, among other things, that revelation is not *propositional* but that it is *personal*. That is, it is not found in objective statements but only in a subjective and personal encounter with God.

FATHERS OF THE CHURCH—The writing theologians and teachers of the first seven or eight centuries of the Christian church, usually, the great bishops and leaders noted for sound judgment and holy living, whose writings preserve the doctrines, history, and traditions of the early church.

FIDEISM—From the Latin *fides* ("faith"), it designates the view that faith alone, without evidence or reason, is a sufficient ground or support for holding a view.

FOLIO—A book made of full-sized leaves or sheets, each folded once to form four pages (twelve by nineteen inches, scale of American Library Association), or a book of the largest size.

FORMER PROPHETS—Designation for the first subdivision of the second section of the present Hebrew Scriptures known as the Prophets, including Joshua, Judges, 1 and 2 Samuel, and 1 and 2 Kings.

GENUINENESS—The character of a composition that guarantees its alleged authorship; genuineness is sometimes popularly used interchangeably with authenticity, which properly concerns the truthfulness of the contents of a composition or text.

GERMAN RATIONALISM—A movement among eighteenth and nineteenth century German biblical scholars that, while attempting to defend Christianity on rational grounds, actually undercut the authority and inerrancy of the Scriptures, and subsequently the other fundamental doctrines arising therefrom. Destructive (negative) higher criticism and the "accommodation theory" are two examples of the teachings of this movement.

GNOSTIC—From the Greek *gnosis* ("knowledge"), it denotes the religious movement prominent in the second century. A.D. that believed it had special knowledge. Beliefs included the denial of Christ's deity and the affirmation that matter is evil, which encouraged asceticism.

GRAPHĒ—The Greek word for "writings" (Scriptures), which are inspired of God, according to 2 Timothy 3:16.

HAGIOGRAPHA—The English equivalent of the Greek word for "holy writings," which designates the same section of the Old Testament canon as does the Hebrew *Kethuvim* (see below). In the Middle Ages this term was applied to writings about the saints and saints' lives. This latter sense is not in view throughout the present work.

HEXAPLA—A manuscript with six parallel columns arranged for comparative and critical study, such as Origen's *Hexapla* that contained various Hebrew and Greek translations of the Old Testament.

HEXATEUCH—The first six books of the Old Testament, namely, the Pentateuch plus Joshua.

HIGHER CRITICISM—The scholarly discipline dealing with the genuineness of the text including questions of authorship, date of composition, destination, and so forth. It is often called "historical criticism," but in its more radical expressions it has been labeled "destructive criticism" or "negative criticism."

HOMOLOGOUMENA—Literally, "to speak the same," that is, those books of the New Testament that have been universally acclaimed as canonical, or all of the twenty-seven books of the New Testament except the Antilegomena (see above).

ILLUMINATION—The process by which God enlightens a person's mind so that he understands the significance of the objective disclosure of God (revelation) for his life subjectively.

INERRANCY—Meaning "without error" and referring to the complete accuracy of Scripture, including the historical and scientific parts.

INFALLIBLE—Literally, "not fallible or breakable"; it refers to the divine character of Scripture that necessitates its truthfulness (cf. John 10:35).

INSPIRATION—Meaning literally "God-breathed" (from 2 Tim. 3:16), and referring to the divinely authoritative writings of Holy Scripture, which God produced without destroying the individual styles of the writers.

KETHUVIM—The English equivalent for this Hebrew word is "Writings"; the title of the third division of the Hebrew Old Testament.

KOINĒ GREEK—The common trade language, the "language of the market place" of the first-century Western world; the New Testament was originally written in Koinē Greek.

LATTER PROPHETS—The second subdivision of the Hebrew Prophets, including all of the prophets after 2 Kings, which is the second division of the present Hebrew Bible.

LECTIONARIES—Early church service books containing selected Scripture readings usually from the gospels and sometimes from Acts or the epistles.

LIBERAL—The theological position that denies many of the fundamental doctrines of historic Christianity, such as the deity of Christ, the inspiration of the Bible. It denies that the Bible *is* the Word of God but believes that it merely *contains* the Word of God.

LITERAL TRANSLATION—A word-for-word translation from one language to another as opposed to an idiomatic, thought-for-thought translation or paraphrase.

LOWER CRITICISM—The scholarly discipline dealing with the authenticity of the biblical text and that seeks to discover the original words of the autographs. It is also called "textual criticism."

LXX—Symbol for the Septuagint, meaning "The Seventy," which is the Greek translation of the Old Testament alleged to have been translated by some seventy scribes at Alexandria, Egypt, at about 250-150 B.C.

MAJUSCULE— See "Uncial."

MANUSCRIPT—A handwritten literary composition rather than a printed copy.

MASORETES—Jewish textual scribes of the fifth through ninth centuries A.D. who standardized the Hebrew text of the Old Testament, which is therefore called the Masoretic Text.

MEGILLOTH—The transliteration into English of the Hebrew word meaning "rolls"; it is used to designate the Five Rolls, the group of books from the third division of the Hebrew canon (the Writings) that were read at the festal ceremonies.

MINUSCULE MANUSCRIPT—A manuscript written in rather small letters, commonly in a cursive or free-flowing hand.

NEVI'IM—The transliteration into English of the Hebrew word for "prophets"; it designates the second division of the Hebrew Old Testament (the Prophets).

NEO-ORTHODOXY—A modern theological view that, while reacting against liberalism, never quite returned to the orthodox position on the verbal inspiration of the Scriptures; it asserts that the Bible becomes the Word of God when it speaks to an individual personally. In itself the Bible is only a witness to the Word of God (Who is Christ).

NEO-PLATONIC—The pantheistic philosophy stemming from the third-century mystic Plotinus who studied with the church Father Origen under Ammonius Saccas.

OSTRACA—Broken pieces of pottery used as writing material by poorer classes who could not afford parchment or papyrus.

PALIMPSEST—A manuscript that has been "rubbed again," erased for reuse as a rescriptus (see below).

PANDECT—From Greek, *pandektos* ("all receiving"). A manuscript containing the entire Bible, both Old and New Testaments.

PAPYRUS (papyri)—A kind of ancient paper or writing material made from the pith of a plant by that name, which grew in the marshes of Egypt.

PARATACTIC—Literally "placing side by side" or the device of placing clauses of phrases one after another without subordinating connectives (see chap. 23).

PARCHMENT—An ancient writing material usually prepared from goat or sheep skin.

PENTATEUCH—Literally, a fivefold book; used specifically with reference to the first five books of the Old Testament.

PIETISM—A religious movement in late seventeenth-century Germany stressing the subjective and experiential personal aspects of Christianity. This movement often tended to neglect the theological and technical side of Christian truth, and consequently opened the door for skepticism, rationalism, and other such movements.

PLENARY INSPIRATION—The doctrine that the inspiration and divine authority of the Bible are full and complete, meaning that they extend (equally) to every part of the Scriptures.

POLYGLOT—Literally, "many tongues." A multiple-columned edition of a particular writing or composition, usually containing the original and various other versions or translations in the several columns for means of comparison.

PROGRESSIVE REVELATION—The view that the divine disclosure of doctrine did not come in a single deposit, but that at divers times in its historical development later revelation added to former disclosures.

PSEUDEPIGRAPHA—A word meaning "false writings" and used to designate those spurious and unauthentic books of the late centuries B.C. and early centuries A.D. These books contain religious folklore and have never been considered canonical by the Christian church.

QUARTO—Literally, "one quarter," referring to manuscripts or books having four leaves (eight pages) to the sheet, that is 9½ by 12 inches (scale of American Library Association).

RECENSION—The systematic and critical revision of a text or composition.

RESCRIPTUS—A manuscript that has been rewritten over lettering that had been erased; it is a palimpsest that has been rescripted.

REVELATION—An objective disclosure of truth by God, and used in contrast to interpretation, which is the subjective understanding of a revelation.

REVISION—A text or composition that has been reviewed and has undergone some necessary changes or corrections.

SEPTUAGINT—Literally, "The Seventy"; the Greek translation of the Old Testament allegedly done by some seventy scribes in Alexandria, Egypt, at about 250-150 B.C. and symbolized LXX.

SOPHERIM—Literally "scribes." They were Jewish scholars who worked between the fifth and third centuries B.C. to standardize and preserve the Hebrew text.

TANAKH—An acronym for "Torah, Nevi'im, and Kethuvim," used as the title for the Jewish Publication Society translation of the Old Testament, also called the New Jewish Version (NJV).

TANNAIM—Literally "repeaters" or "teachers." These Jewish scribes succeeded the Zugoth and labored between the first century A.D. to around A.D. 200. Their work can be found in the Midrash ("textual interpretation"), which was later divided into Mishnah ("repetitions") and Gemara ("the matter to be learned").

TESTAMENT—Loosely the equivalent of "covenant," but technically a testament does not require a two-way agreement, as it needs only the action of the testator with or without the assent of the heir (see Heb. 9:15-22).

TEXTUAL CRITICISM—Synonymous with "lower criticism" (see above).

TEXTUS RECEPTUS—The Greek text presumed to underlie the Authorized Version of 1611 (King James Version). This text is basically that of Erasmus and Stephen's third edition (1550). It was named the Received Text in the introduction of the Elzevir Brothers' second edition (1633). It is based on few early manuscripts and is opposed by Westcott, Hort, and all those who accept a "Critical Text" (C.T.; see above).

THEOPNEUSTOS—The English equivalent of this Greek word is "inspiration," which literally means "God-breathed" (see 2 Tim. 3:16).

TORAH—The English transliteration of the Hebrew word for "law"; it often refers to the first five books of the Old Testament.

TRANSLATION—The rendering of a composition or piece of literature from one language to another, as contrasted with a version, which is a translation from the original language of a manuscript into another language.

TRANSLITERATION—A letter-for-letter transposition of a word from one language to another.

TRANSMISSION—The process by which the biblical manuscripts have been copied and recopied down through the ages; it deals with the history of the text from the autographs to the present printed Hebrew and Greek Testaments.

UNCIAL MANUSCRIPT (or majuscule)—Literally, "inch high," referring to a manuscript written in formally printed large letters similar in size to capital letters.

VELLUM—A fine quality writing material in ancient times, usually prepared from calf or antelope skin.

VERBAL INSPIRATION—The doctrine holding that the very words of the Bible are vested with divine authority and not merely the thoughts or ideas.

VERSION—A literary composition that has been translated from its original language into another tongue.

VULGATE—Literally, "common" or "usual"; generally the designation for the Latin translation of the Bible made by Jerome in the fourth century A.D.

ZUGOTH—Literally, "pairs" of textual scholars who worked during the second and first centuries B.C. They were succeeded by the Tannaim (see above).

Bibliography

Bibles

Aland, Kurt, Matthew Black, Carlo M. Martini, Bruce M. Metzger, and Allen Wikgren, eds. *The Greek New Testament*. 3d ed. New York: United Bible Societies, 1975.

Alford, Henry. *The Greek New Testament*. 5th ed. London: Rivingtons, 1871.

Clarke, R. L., Alfred Goodwin, and W. Sanday, eds. *The Variorum Edition of the New Testament of Our Lord and Saviour Jesus Christ*. London: Eyre & Spottiswoode, 1881.

Criswell, W. A., ed. *The Criswell Study Bible*. Nashville: Thomas Nelson, 1979.

The English Hexapla, exhibiting the six important English translations of the New Testament Scriptures, Wyclif, M.CCC.XXXIX.; Tyndale, M.D.XXXIV.; Cranmer, M.D.XXXIX.; Genevan, M.D.LVII.; Anglo-Rhemish, M.D.LXXXII.; Authorised, M.DC.XI.; the original Greek text after Scholz, with the various readings of the textus receptus and the principal Constantinopolitan and Alexandrine manuscripts, and a complete collation of Scholz's text with Griesbach's edition of M.DCCC.V.; preceded by a history of English translations and translators .... London: S. Bagster and Sons, 1841.

Ellinger, K[arl], and W[ilhelm] Rudolph, eds. *Biblia Hebraica Stuttgartensia*. 2d ed., W. Rudolph and H. P. Rüger. Stuttgart: Deutsche Bibelstiftung, 1967-1977, 1983; Editio minor, 1984.

Fischer, Bonifatio, Iohanne Gribomont, H. F. D. Sparks, and W. Theile, eds. *Biblia Sacra: Iuxta Vulgatam Versionem*. Editio tertia emendata. Stuttgart: Deutsche Bibelgesellschaft, 1983; Editio minor, 1984.

Goodspeed, Edgar J. *The Complete Bible: An American Translation*. Chicago: U. of Chicago, 1923.

Hodges, Zane C., and Arthur L. Farstad, eds. *The Greek New Testament, According to the Majority Text*. Nashville: Thomas Nelson, 1982. 2d ed., 1985.

The Holy Bible Containing the Authorized Version of the Old and New Testaments with Many Emendations. London: Bartlett, 1841.

The Holy Bible, an Exact Reprint Page for Page of the Authorized Version Published in the Year MDCXI. Oxford: Oxford U., 1833.

The Holy Bible. Authorized Version. New York: Oxford U. Press, n.d.

———. English Revised Version. Cambridge U. Press, 1881, 1885.

———. Newly edited by the American Revision Committee. New York: Nelson, 1901.

———. *Revised Standard Version*. New York: Nelson, 1945, 1952.

Holy Bible, The New King James Version: Containing the Old and New Testament. Nashville: Thomas Nelson, 1979, 1980, 1982.

The Holy Bible: New International Version, Containing the Old and the New Testament. Grand Rapids: Zondervan, for New York International Bible Society, 1973, 1978.

The Holy Scriptures According to the Masoretic Text. Philadelphia: Jewish Publishing Society of America, 1917.

International Children's Version, New Testament. Fort Worth, Tex.: Sweet, 1983.

Jefferson, Thomas. *The Life and Morals of Jesus of Nazareth*. Cleveland: World, 1940. This is the so-called *Jefferson Bible*.

The Jerusalem Bible. Garden City, N.Y.: Doubleday, 1966.

Kittel, Rudolf, and Paul E. Kahle, eds. *The Bible According to the Masoretic Text*.

———. *Biblia Hebraica*. 7th ed. Stuttgart: Deutsche Bibelstiflung, 1951.

Knox, John, trans. *The Holy Bible: A Translation from the Latin Vulgate in the Light of the Hebrew and Greek Originals*. New York: Sheed & Ward, 1948.

Metzger, Bruce M., gen. ed. *The Reader's Digest Bible: Condensed from the Revised Standard Version Old and New Testaments*. Pleasantville, N.Y.: Reader's Digest, 1982.

Nestle, Eberhard, ed. *Novum Testamentum Graece, cum apparatu*. 26th ed. New York: American Bible Societies, 1979.

The New American Bible: Translated from the Original Languages with Critical Use of All the Ancient Sources, by Members of the Catholic Biblical Association of America. Nashville: Thomas Nelson, 1983.

New American Standard Bible. Chicago: Moody, for the Lockman Foundation, 1960, 1962, 1963, 1968, 1971, 1972, 1973, 1975, 1977.

The New English Bible, with the Apocrypha. Oxford U. and Cambridge U., 1961, 1970.

The New Jerusalem Bible. Garden City, N.Y. : Doubleday, 1985.

Rahlfs, Alfred, ed. *Septuaginta: Id est Vetus Testamentum graece iuxta LXX interpretes*. Editio minor (Duo volumina in uno). Stuttgart: Deutsche Bibelstiftung, 1935.

Robertson, Archibald T. *A Harmony of the Gospels for Students*. Nashville: Broadman, 1922.

The Septuagint Version of The Old Testament. London: S. Bagster, n.d.

TANAKH: A New Translation of THE HOLY SCRIPTURES According to the Traditional Hebrew Text. Philadelphia: The Jewish Publication Society, 1985.

Thomas, Robert L., and Stanley N. Gundry, eds. *A Harmony of the Gospels, With Explanations and Essays: Using the Text of the New American Standard Bible*. Chicago: Moody, 1978.

Westcott, Brooke Foss, and Fenton John Anthony Hort, eds. *The New Testament in the Original Greek*. 2d ed. New York: Macmillan, 1928.

The Word New Century Version, New Testament. Fort Worth, Tex.: Sweet, 1984.

Wuest, Kenneth S. *Wuest's Expanded Translation of the Greek New Testament*. Grand Rapids: Eerdmans, 1961.

Young, Robert. *Young's Literal Translation of the Holy Bible*. 3d ed. Grand Rapids: Baker, 1898. Reprint. Grand Rapids: Baker, 1956.

Sources

Allen, Cardinal. *Letters and Memorials of Cardinal Allen*. Introduction by T. F. Knox. London, 1882.

Ambrose. *Letters*. Translated and edited by S. L. Greenslade. In *Library of Christian Classics, Early Latin Theology,* vol. 5, edited by John Baillie, John T. McNeill, and Henry P. Van Dusen. Philadelphia: Westminster, 1956.

St. Anselm, Basic Writings: Proslogium, Monologium, Gaunilon's: On Behalf of the Fool, Cur Deus Homo. Translated by S. W. Deane. 2d ed. LaSalle, Ill. 1962.

———. *Truth, Freedom, and Evil: Three Philosophical Dialogues*. Edited and translated by Jasper Hopkins and Herbert Richardson. New York: Harper & Row, 1967.

Apocrypha. Revised Standard Version of the Old Testament. New York: Thomas Nelson, 1957.

The Apostolic Fathers. 2 vols. Loeb Classical Library Series. Edited by Kirsopp Lake. New York: Putnam, 1930.

Aquinas, Thomas. *Summa Theologiae*. Edited by Thomas Gilby. New York: McGraw-Hill, 1964.

Arminius, Jacobus. *The Writings of James Arminius*. 3 vols. Translated from the Latin by James Nichols and W. R. Bagnall. Grand Rapids: Baker, 1956.

Astruc, Jean. *Conjectures sur les memoires origineaux dont il paroit que Moyse s'est servi pour composer le livre de la Genese*. Brussels (Paris): 1753.

Athanasius. *Letters*. Translated by Archibald Robertson. In *Nicene and Post-Nicene Fathers,* vol. 4, 2d series, edited by Philip Schaff and Henry Wace. Grand Rapids: Eerdmans, 1953.

Augustine, Aurelius. *The City of God*. Translated by Marcus Dods, introduction by Thomas Merton. New York: Random House, 1949.

———. *Enchiridion*. Edited by Philip Schaff. In *Nicene and Post-Nicene Fathers,* vol. 3, 1st series. Grand Rapids: Eerdmans, 1956.

———. *Expositions on the Book of Psalms*. Translated by A. Cleveland Coxe. In *Nicene and Post-Nicene Fathers,* vol. 8, 2d series, edited by Philip Schaff and Henry Wace. Grand Rapids: Eerdmans, 1956.

———. *Harmony of the Gospels*. In *Nicene and Post-Nicene Fathers,* vol. 6, 1st series, edited by Philip Schaff. Grand Rapids: Eerdmans, 1956.

———. *Letters*. In *Nicene and Post-Nicene Fathers,* vol. 1, 1st series, edited by Philip Schaff. Grand Rapids: Eerdmans, 1956.

———. *On Christian Doctrine*. Translated by J. F. Shaw. In *Nicene and Post-Nicene Fathers,* vol. 2, 1st series, edited by Philip Schaff. Grand Rapids: Eerdmans, 1956.

Ayer, Joseph Cullen. *A Source Book for Ancient Church History.* New York: Scribner's, 1913.

Bachmann, E. Theodore, ed. *Luther's Works.* Vol. 35, *Word and Sacrament.* Philadelphia: Muhlenberg, 1960.

Bacon, Francis. *Advancement of Learning; Novum Organum; New Atlantis.* In *Great Books of the Western World,* vol. 30, edited by Robert Maynard Hutchins, Mortimer J. Adler, et al. Chicago: Encyclopedia Britannica, 1952.

Baillie, John, John T. McNeill, and Henry P. Van Dusen, eds. *The Library of Christian Classics.* 26 vols. Philadelphia: Westminster, 1953-69.

Bede, Venerable. *Ecclesiastical History of the English Nation.* Cambridge: Cambridge U., 1881.

Bettenson, Henry, ed. *Documents of the Christian Church.* 2d ed. London: Oxford U., 1963.

———, ed. and trans. *The Early Christian Fathers: A Selection from the writings of the Fathers from St. Clement of Rome to St. Athanasius.* London: Oxford U., 1956.

———, ed. and trans. *The Later Christian Fathers: A Selection from the writings of the Fathers from St. Cyril of Jerusalem to St. Leo the Great.* London: Oxford U., 1970.

Calvin, John. *Commentary on the Harmony of the Evangelists.* Calvin Translation Society.

———. *Institutes of the Christian Religion.* 2 vols. Edited by John T. McNeill. Translated by Ford Lewis Battles. In *Library of Christian Classics,* vols. 20-21, edited by John Baillie, John T. McNeill, and Henry P. Van Dusen. Philadelphia: Westminster, 1960.

———. *Treatises Against the Anabaptists and Against the Libertines: Translation, Introduction, and Notes.* Edited and translated by Benjamin Wirt Farley. Grand Rapids: Baker, 1982.

Calvin's Commentaries. Vols. 1-12, edited by David W. Torrance and Thomas F. Torrance. Grand Rapids: Eerdmans, 1972.

Charles, Robert Henry, ed. *The Apocrypha and Pseudepigraphia of the Old Testament.* 2 vols. Oxford: Clarendon, 1913.

Clarke, Adam. *Miscellaneous Works.* 13 vols. London: T. Tegg, 1839-1845.

Clement of Alexandria. *Stromata.* Edited by Alexander Roberts and James Donaldson. In *Ante-Nicene Fathers,* vol. 2. Grand Rapids: Eerdmans, 1951.

Cyprian. "Epistle About Cornelius and Novatian." Edited by Alexander Roberts and James Donaldson. In *Ante-Nicene Fathers,* vol. 5. Grand Rapids: Eerdmans, 1957.

———. *The Unity of the Catholic Church.* Translated and edited by S. L. Greenslade. In *Library of Christian Classics,* vol. 5, *Early Latin Theology,* edited by John Baillie, John T. McNeill, and Henry P. Van Dusen. Philadelphia: Westminster, 1956.

Cyril of Jerusalem. *Catechetical Lectures*. Revised translation by Edwin H. Gifford. In *Nicene and Post-Nicene Fathers,* vol. 7, 2d series, edited by Philip Schaff and Henry Wace. Grand Rapids: Eerdmans, 1956.

Dagg, John Leadley. *The Evidences of Christianity.* Macon, Ga.: J. W. Burke, 1869.

Darwin, Charles. [On] *The Origin of Species by Means of Natural Selection*. In *Great Books of the Western World,* vol. 49, edited by Robert Maynard Hutchins, Mortimer Adler, et al. Chicago: Encyclopedia Britannica, 1952; reprint of the 2d ed. published in 1860.

Dead Sea Manual of Discipline. Translated by P. Wernberg-Moller. Grand Rapids: Eerdmans, 1957.

The Dead Sea Scrolls in English. Translated by Geza Vermes. New York: Heritage, 1962.

Descartes, René. *Discourse on Method; Meditations on First Philosophy.* Translated by Elizabeth S. Haldane and G. R. T. Ross. In *Great Books of the Western World,* vol. 31, edited by Robert Maynard Hutchins, Mortimer Adler, et al. Chicago: Encyclopedia Britannica, 1952.

Doctrinal Standards of the Christian Reformed Church. Grand Rapids: Publication Committee of the Christian Reformed Church, 1962.

DuPont-Sommer, Andre. *The Essene Writings from Qumran*. Translated by G. Vermes. Cleveland: World, 1962.

Eusebius. *Ecclesiastical History.* 2 vols. Loeb Classical Library Series. Kirsopp Lake, ed. Vol. 1 translated by Kirsopp Lake, 1926. Vol. 2 translated by J. E. L. Oulton, 1932. London: Heinemann.

Flannery, Austin P., ed. *Documents of Vatican II*. New rev. ed. Grand Rapids: Eerdmans, 1975, 1984.

Galileo. *Le Opere Di Galileo Galilei*. Firenze: G. Barbera Editore, 1965.

Gaussen, L[ouis]. *Theopneustia: The Bible, Its Divine Origin and Entire Inspiration, Deduced from Internal Evidence and the Testimonies of Nature, History, and Science*. Translated from the French by David D. Scott. Edinburgh: 1841. Reprint. Grand Rapids: Baker, 1971.

Geisler, Norman L., ed. *Decide for Yourself: How History Reviews the Bible*. Grand Rapids: Zondervan, 1982.

The Glorious Koran. An explanatory translation by Mohammed Marmaduke Pickthall. New York: New American Library, 1953.

Gregory the Great. *The Commentary of Job*. Translated and edited by George McCracken. In *Library of Christian Classics,* vol. 9, *Early Medieval Theology,* edited by John Baillie, John T. McNeill, and Henry P. Van Dusen. Philadelphia: Westminster, 1957.

Hegel, G.W.F. *Encyclopedia of Philosophy.* Translated by Gustav Emil Mueller, New York: Philosophical Library, 1959.

———. *Werke*. Edited by Era Molderhauer and Karl Markus Michel. Frankfurt: Suhrkamp, 1970.

Heidel, Alexander. *The Babylonian Genesis*. 2d ed. Chicago: U. of Chicago, 1954.

Hennecke, Edgar, and Wilhelm Schneemelcher, eds. *New Testament Apocrypha*. 2 vols. Philadelphia: Westminster, 1963, 1965.

Hippolytus. *Contra Noetum,* as cited in Westcott, *An Introduction to the Study of the Gospels,* 7th ed. London: Macmillan, 1888.

———. *De AntiChristo,* as cited in Westcott, *An Introduction to the Study of the Gospels,* 7th ed. London: Macmillan, 1888.

Hobbes, Thomas. *Leviathan, Or Matter, Form, and Power of a Commonwealth Ecclesiastical and Civil*. In *Great Books of the Western World,* vol. 23, edited by Robert Maynard Hutchins, Mortimer Adler, et al. Chicago: Encyclopedia Britannica, 1952.

Holtzmann, Heinrich Julius, *Einleitug in das Neue Testament*. Tübingen, 1885.

The Humble Advice of the Assembly of Divines, Now by Authority of Parliament, Sitting at Westminster, Concerning A Confession of Faith: With Questions and Texts of Scripture Annexed. London: 1647. Commonly known as *The Westminster Confession,* it was accompanied by *A Larger Catechism* (1647) and *A Shorter Catechism* (1647).

Hume, David. *An Enquiry Concerning Human Understanding*. Edited with an introduction by Charles H. Hendel. Indianapolis: Bobbs-Merrill, 1955.

Husselman, Elinor M. *The Gospel of John in Fayumic Coptic*. (P. Mich. inv. 3521.) Ann Arbor: U. of Michigan, 1962.

International Council on Bible Inerrancy. *The Chicago Statement on Biblical Inerrancy.* Oakland, Calif.: International Council on Biblical Inerrancy, 1978.

Irenaeus. *Against Heresies*. In *Library of Christian Classics,* vol. 3, *Christology of the Later Fathers*. Translated and edited by Edward Rochie Hardy. Philadelphia: Westminster, 1953.

James, Montague Rhodes. *The Apocryphal New Testament*. Oxford: Clarendon, 1955.

Jerome. *Commentary on Matthew* and *Epist. 120 to Hedibia*. In *New Testament Apocrypha,* vol. 2, edited by Edgar Hennecke and Wilhelm Schneemelcher. Philadelphia: Westminster, 1963, 1965.

———. *The Four Gospels*. Edited by Philip Schaff and Henry Wace. In *Nicene and Post-Nicene Fathers,* vol. 6, 2d series. Grand Rapids: Eerdmans, 1954.

———. *Letters*. Translated and edited by S. L. Greenslade. Philadelphia: Westminster, 1956. In *Library of Christian Classics,* vol. 5, *Early Latin Theology,* edited by John Baillie, John T. McNeill, and Henry P. Van Dusen.

———. Vol. 6, *Nicene and Post-Nicene Fathers,* 2d series, edited by Philip Schaff and Henry Wace. Grand Rapids: Eerdmans, 1952.

———. *Lives of Illustrious Men*. Edited by Philip Schaff and Henry Wace. In *Nicene and Post-Nicene Fathers,* vol. 3, 2d series, Grand Rapids: Eerdmans, 1952.

Josephus, Flavius. *The Life and Works of Flavius Josephus*. Translated by William Whiston. Philadelphia: Winston, 1936.

Justin Martyr. *Apology.* In *Ante-Nicene Fathers,* vol. 1, edited by Alexander Roberts and James Donaldson. Grand Rapids: Eerdmans, 1952.

———. *Justin's Hortatory Oration to the Greeks*. Edited by Alexander Roberts and James Donaldson. In *The Ante-Nicene Fathers,* vol. 1. Grand Rapids: Eerdmans, 1952.

Kahle, Paul E. *The Cairo Geniza*. 2d ed. Oxford: Oxford U., 1959.

Kant, Immanuel. *Religion Within the Limits of Reason Alone*. Translated with an introduction by Theodore M. Greene and Hoyt H. Hudson. New York: Harper & Row, 1960.

Kierkegaard. Søren. *Concluding Unscientific Postscript*. Translated by David F. Swenson and Walter Lowrie. Princeton: Princeton U., 1941, 1963.

———. *Johannes Climacus, Philosophical Fragments: Or A Fragment of Philosophy.* Translation and introduction by David F. Swenson. Princeton: Princeton U., 1936.

Lactantius. *On the Deaths of the Persecutors,* 12-13, as printed in J. Stevenson, ed., *A New Eusebius: Documents illustrative of the history of the Church to A.D. 337*. London: SPCK, 1957.

Leith, John H., ed. *Creeds of the Churches*. Rev. ed. Atlanta: John Knox, 1973.

The Living Talmud. Selected and translated by Judah Goldin. Chicago: U. of Chicago, 1957.

The London Confession of 1644. In Oklahoma *Baptist Messenger* 58, no. 32 (August 1969): 3-8.

Lumpkin, William L. *The Baptist Confessionof Faith*. Rev. ed. Chicago: Judson, 1959.

Luther, Martin. *Luther's Works*. Edited by E. Theodore Bachmann. Philadelphia: Muhlenberg, 1960.

Manschreck, Clyde L., ed. *A History of Christianity.* Vol. 2, *Readings in the History of the Church from the Reformation to the Present*. Englewood Cliffs, N.J.: Prentice-Hall, 1964.

The Manual of Discipline. Translated by P. Wernberg-Moller. Grand Rapids: Eerdmans, 1972.

Marx, Karl. *Zur Kritik der politischen Oekonomie* [Critique of Political Economy]. Berlin, 1859.

The Massorah. 4 vols. Compiled from manuscripts by C. D. Ginsberg. London: British & Foreign Bible Society, 1926.

The Mishnah. Translated by Herbert Danby. Oxford: Oxford U., 1933. Reprint. 1958, 1983.

The New Hampshire Declaration of Faith. As published in Oklahoma *Baptist Messenger* 58, no. 32 (August 1969): 9-12.

Origen. *Commentary on Matthew.* Edited by Alexander Roberts and James Donaldson. In *The Ante-Nicene Fathers,* vol. 4, Grand Rapids: Eerdmans, 1952.

———. *De Principiis*. Edited by Philip Schaff. In *Ante-Nicene Fathers,* vol. 4. Grand Rapids: Eerdmans, n.d.

Paulus, Heinrich. *Exegetisches Handbuch über die drei ersten Evangelien*. 3 vols. 1830-1833.

———. *Leben Jesu als Grundlage einer reinen Geschichte des Urchristenthums*. 2 vols. 1828.

Petry, Ray C., and Clyde L. Manschreck, eds. *A History of Christianity. Vol 1: Readings in the History of the Early and Medieval Church*. 2 vols. Englewood Cliffs, N.J.: Prentice-Hall, 1962.

The Philadelphia Confession of Faith. 6th ed. [as printed by Benjamin Franklin]. Philadelphia: Baptist Association, 1743.

Philo. Vol 9. Translated by F. H. Colson. Cambridge, Mass.: Harvard U., 1941.

Polycarp. *Philippians*. Edited by Alexander Roberts and James Donaldson. In *The Ante-Nicene Fathers,* vol. 1. Grand Rapids: Eerdmans, 1952.

Rees, Thomas. *The Racovian Catechism, with Notes and Illustrations, translated from the Latin: to which is prefixed A Sketch of the history of Unitarianism in Poland and Adjacent Countries*. London: Longman, Hurst, Rees, Orme, and Brown, 1818. Reprint. Lexington, Ky.: American Theological Library Association, 1962.

Roberts, Alexander, and James Donaldson, eds. *The Ante-Nicene Fathers*. 10 vols. 1884-86. Reprint. Grand Rapids: Eerdmans, 1956.

Rodkinson, Michael L. *The Babylonian Talmud*. 1916.

Schaff, Philip, ed. *The Creeds of Christendom*. 3 vols. 6th ed. Revised and enlarged. New York: Harper, 1919.

Schaff, Philip, and Henry Wace, eds. *Ante-Nicene Fathers*. vols. 1 and 4. Grand Rapids: Eerdmans, 1952.

Schaff, Philip, ed. *Nicene and Post-Nicene Fathers*. 14 vols. 1st series. 1886-94. Reprint. Grand Rapids: Eerdmans, 1952.

Schaff, Philip, and Henry Wace, eds. *Nicene and Post-Nicene Fathers*. 12 vols. 2d series. 1890-95. Reprint. Grand Rapids: Eerdmans, 1952.

The Schleitheim Confession of Faith. Edited by John C. Wenger. *Mennonite Quarterly Review* 19 (October 1945): 247-53.

The Seven Ecumenical Councils. Translated by Henry R. Percival. In *Nicene and Post-Nicene Fathers*. Edited by Philip Schaff and Henry Wace. Vol. 14, 2d series. Grand Rapids: Eerdmans, 1952.

Simons, Menno. *The Complete Writings*. Translated by Leonard Verduin, edited by John C. Wenger. Including "A Brief Biography" by Harold Bender. Scottdale, Pa.: Herald, 1956.

———. "On the Ban: Questions and Answers," *Spiritual and Anabaptist Writers: Documents Illustrative of the Radical Reformation*. Edited by George H. Williams and Angel M. Mergal. In *The Library of Christian Classics,* edited by John Baillie, John T. McNeill, and Henry P. Van Dusen. Philadelphia: Westminster, 1957.

Spener, Phillips J. *Pia Desideria*. Philadelphia: Fortress Press, 1964; Paperback ed., 1974.

Spinoza, Benedict De. *The Chief Works of Benedict De Spinoza*. Vol. 1, *Introduction, Tractatus Theologico-Politicus, Tractatus Politicus*. London: George Bell, 1883.

Stevenson, J., ed. *Creeds, Councils, and Controversies: Documents illustrative of the history of the Church A.D. 337-461*. London: SPCK, 1966.

———. *A New Eusebius: documents illustrative of the history of the Church to A.D. 337*. London: SPCK, 1957.

Stuart, Moses. *Critical History and Defence of the Old Testament Canon*. London: Tegg, 1849.

Tertullian. *On the Apparel of Women*. Edited by Alexander Roberts and James Donaldson. In *Ante-Nicene Fathers,* vol. 4, Grand Rapids: Eerdmans, 1951.

———. *On Exhortation to Chastity.* Edited by Alexander Roberts and James Donaldson. In *Ante-Nicene Fathers,* vol. 4. Grand Rapids: Eerdmans, 1951.

Turretin, Francis. *The Doctrine of Scripture: Locus 2 of Institutio theologiae elencticae*. Edited and translated by John W. Beardslee III. Grand Rapids: Baker, 1981. The *Institutio theologiae elencticae,* in 3 volumes was published with a collection of *Disputationes* as *Opera,* 4 vols. Utrecht and Amsterdam: Jacobum a Poolsum, 1688, 1734; Edinburgh, 1847.

Watson, Richard. *The Works of Richard Watson*. 12 vols. London: John Mason, 1834-1837.

Wellhausen, Julius. *Die Geschichte Israels*. 1878. Translated into English in 1883. Its 2d ed. was published as *Prolegomena zur Geschichte Israels,* 2 vols., 1883.

———. *Die Komposition des Hexateuchs und der historischen Bücher des Alten Testaments*. 1885.

Wenger, John C. "The Schleitheim Confession of Faith." *Mennonite Quarterly Review* 19 (October 1945): 247-53.

Wesley, John. *The Works of John Wesley.* London: Wesleyan Conference Office, 1872. Reprint. Grand Rapids: Zondervan.

Wycliffe, John. *Wyclif—English Sermons*. Edited by Herbert Winn. London: Oxford U., 1929.

References

Aland, Kurt. *Bericht der Stiftung zur Forderung der neutestamentlichen Textforschung für die Jahre 1972 bis 1974*. Munster: 1974, 9-16.

———. *Bericht der Stiftung zur Forderung der neutestamentlichen Textforschung für die Jahre 1975 und 1976*. Munster: 1977, 10-12.

———. *Kurzgefaßte Liste der griechischen Handschriften des Neuen Testaments*. Berlin: 1963.

———. *Materialien zur neutestamentlichen Handschriften*. Berlin, 1969, 1-37.

Aland, Kurt, and Barbara Aland. *Der Text des Neuen Testaments: Einführung in die wissenschaftlichen Ausgaben sowie in Theorie und Praxis der modernen Textkritik*. Deutsch Bibelgesellenschaft, 1982.

Anderson, Christopher. Annals of the English Bible. 2 vols. London 1945.

Bauer, Walter. *Griechisch-Deutsches Worterbuch zu den Schriften des Neuen Testaments und der übrigen urchristlichen Literatur.* 4th rev. and augmented ed., 1952. Translated by William F. Arndt and F. Wilbur Gingrich, *A Greek-English Lexicon of the New Testament and Other Early Christian Literature*. Chicago: U. of Chicago, 1957. 2d rev. ed., 1979.

Blaiklock, E.M., and R.K. Harrison, eds. *The New International Dictionary of Biblical Archeology.* Grand Rapids: Zondervan, 1983.

British Museum (Library) Catalogue of Printed Books, 1968-1975.

Brown, Colin, ed. *The New International Dictionary of New Testament Theology.* 3 vols. Translated from Lothar Coenen, Eríchh Beyreuther,, and Hans Beitenhard, eds. *Theologisches Begriffslexikon zum Neuen Testament* (1967-71). Grand Rapids: Zondervan, 1975-78.

The Catholic Encyclopedia. 16 vols., including index vol. New York: Appleton, 1907-14. Supplements, 1921 and 1954.

The Catholic Encyclopedia for School and Home. 13 vols. Grolier, 1965.

Cotton, Henry. *Editions of the Bible and Parts Thereof in English, From the Year MDV to MDCCL.* London: Oxford U., 1852.

Cross, F. L., and E. A. Livingstone, eds. *The Oxford Dictionary of the Christian Church*. 2d ed. London: Oxford U., 1974.

Douglas, J. D., ed. *The New Bible Dictionary.* Grand Rapids: Eerdmans, 1962.

———, ed. *The New International Dictionary of the Christian Church*. Rev. ed. Grand Rapids: Zondervan, 1978.

Edwards, Tryon. *A Dictionary of Thoughts*. Detroit: Dickerson, 1904.

Ellicott, Charles John, ed. *Ellicott's Commentary of the Whole Bible*. 8 vols. Introduction by Stanley Leaves. Grand Rapids: Zondervan, 1954.

Elwell, Walter A., ed. *Evangelical Dictionary of Theology.* Grand Rapids: Baker, 1984.

Englishman's Greek Concordance. 9th ed. London: S. Bagster, 1903.

Gaebelein, Frank E., gen. ed. *The Expositor's Bible Commentary.* 12 vols. Grand Rapids: Zondervan, 1979ff.

Gore, Philip Babcock, ed. *Webster's Third International Dictionary.* Springfield, Mass.: Merriam, 1961.

Hammond, N. G. L., and H. H. Scullard, eds. *The Oxford Classical Dictionary.* 2d ed. Oxford: Clarendon, 1970.

Harrison, Everett F., ed. *Baker's Dictionary of Theology.* Grand Rapids: Baker, 1960.

Hastings, James, ed. *A Dictionary of the Bible*. 4 vols, plus one extra volume. New York: Scribner's, 1909.

Hastings, James, et al., eds. *Encyclopedia of Religion and Ethics*. 13 vols. New York: Scribner's, 1908-26.

Herbert, A. S. *Historical Catalogue of Printed Editions of the English Bible, 1525-1961: Revised and Expanded from the Edition of T. H. Darlow and H. F. Moule, 1903*. London: British and Foreign Bible Society; New York: American Bible Society, 1968.

Hills, Margaret T. *A Ready-Reference History of the English Bible*. Rev. ed. New York: American Bible Society, 1962.

———. *A Ready-Reference History of the English Bible*. Revised by Elizabeth Eisenhart. New York: American Bible Society and the New York Public Library, 1971.

———, ed. *The English Bible in America: A Bibliography of Editions of the Bible and the New Testament Published in America, 1777-1957*. New York: American Bible Society and New York Public Library, 1961.

Historical Catalogue of the Printed Editions of Holy Scripture in the Library of the British and Foreign Bible Society. 2 vols. Compiled by T. H. Darlow and H. F. Moule. London: 1903. Reprint. New York: Kraus, 1963.

The Jewish Encyclopedia. Singer, I., ed. 12 vols. New York: Funk & Wagnalls, 1904. Reprint. Ktav, 1964.

Keil, C. [Karl] F., and Franz Delitzsch. *Commentary on the Old Testament*. 25 vols. Translated by James Martin et al. Grand Rapids: Eerdmans, many reprints.

Kittel, Gerhard, ed. *Theological Dictionary of the New Testament*. Translated and edited by Geoffrey W. Bromily. Grand Rapids: Eerdmans, 1964-76.

Kraeling, Emil G., ed. *The Rand-McNally Bible Atlas*. New York: Rand-McNally, 1956.

Lange, John Peter. *Commentary on the Holy Scriptures: Critical, Doctrinal and Homiletical*. 24 vols. in 12. Translated from the German and edited with additions by Philip Schaff. Grand Rapids: Zondervan, 1960.

Lewis, John. *A Complete History of Several Translations of the Holy Bible and New Testament into English*. "Appendix: A List of Various Editions of the Bible and Parts Thereof in English: 1526-1800." This is a continuation of Archbishop William Newcome's *A Historical View of English Bible Translations*. London: no publisher; 1818.

Loescher, Lefferts A., ed. *The Twentieth-Century Encyclopedia of Religious Knowledge*. 15 vols. Grand Rapids: Baker, 1955.

Moulton, J. H. *A Grammar of New Testament Greek*. Vol. 1, *Prolegomena*. Edinburgh: T. & T. Clark, 1908. Reprint. 1949.

Moulton, J. H., and W. F. Howard. *A Grammar of New Testament Greek*. Vol. 2, *Accidence and Word-Formation, with an Appendix on Semiticisms*. Edinburgh: T. & T. Clark, 1919-29.

Moulton, J. H., and G[eorge] Milligan. *The Vocabulary of the Greek Testament Illustrated from the Papyri and Other Non-Literary Sources*. Grand Rapids: Eerdmans, 1914-30.

Murray, James Augustus Henry, et al. *A New English Dictionary on Historical Grounds*. 10 vols. in 13. Oxford: Clarendon Press, 1888-1923.

The New Catholic Encyclopedia. 15 vols. and index. New York: McGraw-Hill, 1967.

Nicoll, W. Robertson, ed. *The Expositor's Greek New Testament*. 5 vols. 1887ff. Reprint. Grand Rapids: Eerdman's, 1951.

Orr, James, ed. *International Standard Bible Encyclopedia*. Rev. ed., 5 vols. Grand Rapids: Eerdmans, 1943.

Pfeiffer, Charles F., Howard F. Vos, and John Rea. *Wycliffe Bible Encyclopedia*. 2 vols. Chicago: Moody, 1975.

Pope, Hugh. *English Versions of the Bible*. Revised and Amplified by Sebastian Bullough. New York: B. Herder Book Co., 1952. Reprint. Westport, Conn.: Greenwood, 1972.

Strong, Augustus H. *Systematic Theology*. 3 vols. in one. Grand Rapids: Revell, 1907.

Thayer, Joseph Henry. *A Greek-English Lexicon of the New Testament*. New York: American Book Company, 1889.

Thomas, Robert L., gen. ed. *New American Standard Exhaustive Concordance of the Bible*. Nashville: Holman, 1981.

Thompson, Edward Maunde. *A Handbook of Greek and Latin Paleography*. Chicago: Argonaut Publishers, 1966.

Yust, Walter, ed. *Encyclopedia Britannica*. Chicago: Encyclopedia Britannica, 1954.

Articles, Chapters, and Theses

Albright, William F. "A Biblical Fragment from the Maccabean Age: The Nash Papyrus." *Journal of Biblical Literature* 56 (1937): 145-76.

———. "The Elimination of King So." *Bulletin of the American Schools of Oriental Research* 171 (October 1963).

———. "Recent Discoveries in Palestine and the Gospel of St. John." In *The Background of the New Testament and Its Eschatology,* edited by William D. Davies and D. Daube. Cambridge: Cambridge U.

———. "Toward a More Conservative View." *Christianity Today,* 18 January 1963, p. 3 (359).

Allison, Leon M. "The Doctrine of Scripture in the Theology of John Calvin and Francis Turretin." Th.M. thesis, Princeton Theological Seminary, 1958.

Bahnsen, Greg L. "The Inerrancy of the Autographia." In Norman L. Geisler, ed., *Inerrancy.* Grand Rapids: Zondervan, 1980.

Bainton, Roland H. "The Bible in the Reformation." In S.L. Greenslade, ed., *The Cambridge History of the Bible*. Vol. 3, *The West from the Reformation to the Present Day.* Cambridge: Cambridge U., 1963.

Baridon, Michel. "Lumieres et Enlightenment Faux parallele ou vrai mouvement philosophique?" *Dix-huitieme siecle* 10 (1978): 45-69.

Beck, W. David. "Agnosticism: Kant." In Norman L. Geisler, ed., *Biblical Errancy: An Analysis of Its Philosophical Roots*. Grand Rapids: Zondervan, 1981.

"Biblical Inspiration and Interpretation." *Review and Expositor* [Thematic issue] (Spring 1974).

Biggs, Robert. "The Ebla Tablets: An Interim Perspective." *Biblical Archaeologist* 43, no. 2 (Spring 1980): 76-86.

Birdsall, J.N. "The New Testament Text." In P.R. Ackroyd, ed., *The Cambridge History of the Bible*. Vol. 1, *From the Beginnings to Jerome*. Cambridge: Cambridge U., 1970.

Bock, Darrell L. "Textual Criticism Notes." Dallas: Dallas Theological Seminary, 1984.

Carnell, Edward John. "The Problem of Religious Authority." *His* magazine, February 1950.

Carter, J. E. "American Baptist Confessions of Faith: A Review of Confessions of Faith Adopted by Major Baptist Bodies in the United States." In *The Lord's Free People in a Free Land: Essays in Baptist History in Honor of Robert A. Baker,* edited by Willliam R. Estep. Fort Worth, Tex.: Southwestern Baptist Theological Seminary, 1976.

Clark, Gordon H. "Bultmann's Historiography." In Carl F. H. Henry, ed., *Jesus of Nazareth: Saviour and Lord*. Grand Rapids: Eerdmans, 1966.

Clark, Kenneth W. "The Making of the Twentieth Century New Testament." *Bulletin of the John Rylands Library* (1955).

Colwell, E. C., and Gordon Fee. "A Critique of N. W. Pickering's *The Identity of the New Testament Text:* A Review Article." *Westminster Theological Journal* 41 (1979).

———. "Modern Textual Criticism and the Revival of the Textus Receptus." *Journal of the Evangelical Theological Society* 21 (1978).

———. "Modern Textual Criticism and the Majority Text: A Rejoinder." *Journal of the Evangelical Theological Society* 21 (1978).

———. "Scribal Habits in Early Papyri: A Study of the Corruption of the Text." *The Bible in Modern Scholarship,* pp. 370-89.

Corduan, Winfred. "Hegelian Themes in Contemporary Theology." *Journal of the Evangelical Theological Society* 22, no. 4 (December 1979).

Cross, F. M. "The Contribution of the Qumran Discoveries to the Study of the Biblical Text. *Israel Exploration Journal* 16 (1966): 81-95.

Cross, Frank Moore, Jr. "New Directions in Dead Sea Scroll Research." *Bible Review* 1:2 (Summer 1985): 12-25; 1:3 (Fall 1985): 26-35.

Culver, Robert D. "The Old Testament as Messianic Prophecy." *Bulletin of the Evangelical Theological Society* 7, no. 3 (1964).

Dagg, John Leadly. "The Inspiration of Bible." *The Evidences of Christianity.* Macon, Ga.: J. W. Burke & Co., 1869.

Dahood, Mitchell. "Afterward: Ebla, Ugarit, and the Bible." In Giovanni Pettinato, *The Archives at Ebla: An Empire Inscribed in Clay.* Garden City, N.Y.: Doubleday, 1981.

Dyck, Cornelius J. "Ebla Update" articles in *Biblical Archaeology Review,* 1977ff.

Estep, W. R. "Balthasar Hubmaier: Martyr Without Honor." *Baptist History and Heritage* 13, no. 2 (April 1978): 5-10.

Fee, Gordan D. "The Textual Criticism of the New Testament." In Frank E. Gabelein, gen. ed., *The Expositor's Bible Commentary.* Vol. 1, *Introductory Articles: General, Old Testament, New Testament*. Grand Rapids: Zondervan, 1979.

Field, Clyde W. "The Myth of NIV Superiority: Unanswered Critique of NIV's Abuse of the Critical Greek Text of the Gospel of John." Cape May, N.J.: tract published by the author at Shelton College, 1984.

Ford, Lewis. "Biblical Recital and Process Philosophy." *Interpretation* 26, no. 2 (April 1972).

Foster, Lewis. "The Earliest Collection of Paul's Epistles." *Bulletin of the Evangelical Theological Society* 10, no. 1 (Winter 1967).

Gelb, Ignace J. "Thoughts About Ebla: A Preliminary Evaluation, March 1977." *Syro-Mesopotamian Studies* 1, no. 1 (May 1977): 1-30.

Geisler, Norman L. "Bible Manuscripts." In Charles F. Pfeiffer, Howard F. Vos, and John Rea, eds., *Wycliffe Bible Encyclopedia*. 2 vols. Chicago: Moody, 1975.

———. "The Extent of the Old Testament Canon." In Gerald F. Hawthorne, ed., *Current Issues in Biblical and Patristic Interpretation*. Grand Rapids: Eerdmans, 1975.

———. "Inerrancy and Free Will: A Reply to the Brothers Basinger." *The Evangelical Quarterly* 57, no. 4 (October 1985): 349-53.

———. "Meaning and Purpose: The Cart and the Horse." *Grace Theological Journal* (1984).

Gerstner, John H. "Jonathan Edwards and the Bible." *Tenth: An Evangelical Quarterly* 9, no. 4 (October 1979).

———. "The View of the Bible Held by the Church: Calvin and the Western Divines." In Norman L. Geisler, ed., *Inerrancy.* Grand Rapids: Zondervan, 1980.

Goedicke, Hans. "The End of 'So,' King of Egypt." *Bulletin of the American Schools of Oriental Research* 171 (October 1963).

Goshen-Gottstein, Moshe. "Biblical Manuscripts in the United States." *Textus* 3 (1962).

Grounds, Vernon. "Postulate of Paradox." *Bulletin of the Evangelical Theological Society* 7, no. 1 (1964).

Guthrie, Donald. "The Historical and Literary Criticism of the New Testament." In Frank E. Gaebelein, ed., *The Expositor's Bible Commentary.* Vol. 1, *Introductory Articles: General, Old Testament, New Testament.* Grand Rapids: Zondervan, 1979.

Habermas, Gary R. "Skepticism: Hume." In Norman L. Geisler, ed., *Biblical Errancy: An Analysis of Its Philosophical Roots.* Grand Rapids: Zondervan, 1981.

Hargreaves, Henry. "The Wycliffe Versions," in "The Vernacular Scriptures." G.W. H. Lampe, ed., *The Cambridge History of the Bible.* Vol. 2, *The West from the Fathers to the Reformation.* Cambridge: Cambridge U., 1969.

Harris, R. Laird. "Was the Law and the Prophets Two-Thirds of the Old Testament Canon?" *Bulletin of the Evangelical Theological Society* 9, no. 4 (Fall 1966).

Harrison, Everett F. *"Gemeindetheologie:* The Bane of Gospel Criticism." In Carl F. Henry, ed., *Jesus of Nazareth: Saviour and Lord.* Grand Rapids: Eerdmans, 1966.

Harrison, R. K. "Historical and Literary Criticism of the Old Testament." In Frank E. Gaebelein, ed., *The Expositor's Bible Commentary.* Vol. 1, *Introductory Articles: General, Old Testament, New Testament.* Grand Rapids: Zondervan, 1979.

Hatch, W.H.P. "The Origin and Meaning of the Term 'Uncial.'" *Classical Philology* 30 (1935).

Henry, Carl F. H. "Cross-currents in Contemporary Theology." In Carl F. H. Henry, ed., *Jesus of Nazareth: Saviour and Lord.* Grand Rapids: Eerdmans, 1966.

Hills, Russell Paul. "A Brief Introduction to New Testament Textual Criticism Containing a Defense of the Majority Text." Ph.D. dissertation, California Graduate School, 1985.

Hodges, Zane C. "The Critical Text and the Alexandrian Family in Revelation." *Bibliotheca Sacra* 119 (1962): 129-38.

———. "A Defense of the Majority-Text, A Revised Edition of a Paper Originally Called 'Introduction to the Textus Receptus,' with Mathematical Formulations by David M. Hodges." Classroom notes, Dallas Theological Seminary, n.d.

———. "The Ecclesiastical Text of Revelation—Does It Exist?" *Bibliotheca Sacra* 125 (1962):335-45.

———. "Form-Criticism and the Resurrection Accounts." *Bibliotheca Sacra* 124 (1967): 339-48.

———. "Modern Textual Criticism and the Majority Text: A Response." *Journal of the Evangelical Theological Society* 21 (1978).

———. "Modern Textual Criticism and the Majority Text: A Surrejoinder." *Journal of the Evangelical Theological Society* 21 (1978).

———. "The Text of *Aleph* in the Apocalypse." Th.M. thesis, Dallas Theological Seminary, 1958.

———."The Woman Taken in Adultery (John 7:53-8:11): The Text." *Bibliotheca Sacra* 163 (1979):318-32.

Holmes, Michael W. "The 'Majority text debate': new form of an old issue." *Themelios* 8.2 (January 1983):13-19.

Hoskier, H. G. "Evan. 157 (Rome Vat. Urb. 2)." *Journal of Theological Studies* 14 (1913).

Jastrow, Robert. "A Scientist Caught Between Two Faiths." *Christianity Today,* 6 August 1982.

Kantzer, Kenneth S. "Calvin and the Holy Scriptures." In John F. Walvoord, ed., *Inspiration and Interpretation*. Grand Rapids: Eerdmans, 1957.

———. "Redaction Criticism: Is It Worth the Risk?" *Christianity Today,* 18 October 1985, pp. 55-66.

Kaufmann, Walter A. "The Hegel Myth and Its Method." *Philosophical Review* 60 (1951):459-86.

Kilpatrick, G.D. "An Eclectic Study of the Text of Acts." In J.N. Birdsall and R.W. Thomson, eds., Biblical and Patristic Studies in Memory of C.R. Casey. Freiburg: 1963.

———. "The Greek New Testament Text of Today and the Textus Receptus." In H. Anderson and W. Barclay, eds., *The New Testament in Historical and Contemporary Perspective: Essays in Memory of G.H.C. MacGregor.* Oxford: Oxford U., 1965.

King, Marchant A. "Notes on the Bodmer Manuscript of Jude and 1 and 2 Peter." *Bibliotheca Sacra* 121, no. 481 (1964).

———. "The Text of I Peter in Papyrus 72." *Journal of Biblical Literature* 90 (September 1961).

Korsmeyer, Jerry. "A Resonance Model for Revelation." *Process Studies* (1976).

Leonard, R. C. "The Origin of Canonicity in the Old Testament." Ph.D. dissertation, Boston University, 1972.

Lewis, John. "Appendix: A List of Various Editions of the Bible and Parts Thereof in English, 1526-1800." *A Complete History of Several Translations of the Holy Bible and New Testament into English*. London, 1818.

Lods, Adolphe. "Astruc et la critique biblique de son temps." *Revue d'histoire et de philosophie religieuses* (1924): 123-27.

Loomer, Bernard. "A Response to David R. Griffin." *Encounter* 36, no. 4 (Autumn 1975).

Lyon, Robert W. "Re-examination of Codex Ephraemi Rescriptus." *New Testament Studies* 5 (1959).

Mallard, William. "John Wycliffe and the Tradition of Biblical Authority." *Church History* 30 (1961): 50-60.

Marshall, I. Howard. "Jesus in the Gospels." In Frank E. Gabelein, ed., *Expositor's Bible Commentary.* Vol. 1, *Introductory Articles: General, Old Testament, New Testament.* Grand Rapids: Zondervan, 1979.

Martin, Ralph P. "The New Quest of the Historical Jesus." In Carl F. H. Henry, ed., *Jesus of Nazareth: Saviour and Lord.* Grand Rapids: Eerdmans, 1966, 23-45.

McCarter, P. Kyle. "The Early Diffusion of the Alphabet." *Biblical Archaeologist* 37, no. 3 (September 1974): 54-58.

McGonigal, Terence P. " 'Every Scripture Is Inspired': An Exegesis of 2 Timothy 3:16-17," *Studia Biblica et Theologica* 8 (April 1978): 53-64.

Metzger, Bruce M. "The Jehovah's Witnesses and Jesus Christ: A Biblical and Theological Appraisal." *Theology Today* 10 (April 1953).

Merrill, Eugene. "Ebla and Biblical Historical Inerrancy." *Bibliotheca Sacra* 140, no. 560 (October 1983): 302-21.

Millard, A. R. "The Practice of Writing in Ancient Israel." *Biblical Archaeologist* 35, no. 4 (December 1972): 98-111.

Montgomery, John Warwick. "Lessons from Luther on the Inerrancy of Holy Writ." In John Warwick Montgomery, ed., *God's Inerrant Word: An International Symposium on the Trustworthiness of Scripture.* Minneapolis: Bethany Fellowship, 1973.

Moo, Douglas J. "Gospel Origins: A Reply to J.W. Wenham." *Trinity Journal* [new series] 2, no. 1 (1981):24-36.

Mueller, Gustav E. "The Legend of 'Thesis-Antithesis-Synthesis.' " *Journal of the History of Ideas* 19, no. 3 (June 1958): 411-14.

Nettles, Tom J. "Baptists and Scripture." In *Inerrancy and the Church,* edited by John D. Hannah. Chicago: Moody, 1984.

Nicole, Roger R. Introduction to Archibald A. Hodge and Benjamin B. Warfield, *Inspiration.* Grand Rapids: Presbyterian Board of Publication, 1881; reprint by Baker, 1979.

Nix, William E. "The Doctrine of Inspiration Since the Reformation." *Journal of the Evangelical Theological Society* 25, no. 4 (December 1982):443-54.

———. "The Doctrine of Inspiration Since the Reformation, Part II: Changing Climates of Opinion." *Journal of the Evangelical Theological Society* 27, no. 4 (December 1984):439-57.

———. "Joshua," "Judges," "1 Chronicles," "2 Chronicles." In *The Criswell Study Bible,* edited by W.A. Criswell. Nashville: Thomas Nelson, 1979.

———. "Theological Presuppositions and Sixteenth-Century English Bible Translations." *Bibliotheca Sacra* 124, no. 493 (January-March 1967): 42-50; 124, no. 494 (April-June 1967): 117-24.

———. "Versions, Ancient and Medieval." In *Wycliffe Bible Encyclopedia,* edited by Charles F. Pfeiffer, Howard F. Vos, and John Rea. Chicago: Moody, 1975.

Ogden, Shubert. "The Authority of Scripture for Theology." *Interpretation* 30, no. 3 (July 1976).

———. "On Revelation." In John Deschner et al., eds, *Our Common History as Christians: Essays in Honor of Albert C. Outler.* New York: Oxford U., 1975.

Packer, J.I. "Calvin's View of Scripture." In John Warwick Montgomery, ed., *God's Inerrant Word: An International Symposium on the Trustworthiness of Scripture*. Minneapolis: Bethany Fellowship, 1973.

———. "On the Adequacy of Human Language." In Norman L. Geisler, ed., *Inerrancy.* Grand Rapids: Zondervan, 1980.

Payne, J. Barton. "The Validity of Numbers in Chronicles." *Bulletin of the Near East Archaeological Society.* New series. 11 (1978):5-58.

Pei, Mario A. "The World's Chief Languages." In *Encyclopedia Britannica,* 4th ed., 1954.

Phillips, Timothy R. "The Argument for Inerrancy: An Analysis," *Journal of the American Scientific Affiliation* 31 (January 1979): 80-88.

Pickering, Wilbur N. "An Evaluation of the Contribution of John William Burgon to New Testament Textual Criticism." Th.M. thesis, Dallas Theological Seminary, 1968. An edited form of this thesis appeared in David Otis Fuller, ed., *True or False?* Grand Rapids: International Publications, 1973.

———. " 'Queen Anne. . .' and All That: A Response." *Journal of the Evangelical Theological Society* 21 (1978).

Rowley, H. H. "How Not to Translate the Bible." *Expository Times* 65 (November 1953).

———. "The Interpretation of the Song of Songs." *Journal of Theological Studies* 38 (1937).

Ste. Croix, E.M. de. "Aspects of the 'Great' Persecution." *Harvard Theological Review* 47 (1954).

Sandeen, Ernest. "The Princeton Theology: One Source of Biblical Literalism in American Protestantism." *Church History* 31 (September 1962).

Schipper, Reiner. "Paul and the Computer." *Christianity Today,* 4 December 1964.

Silva, Moises. "Ned B. Stonehouse and Redaction Criticism, Part I: The Witness of the Synoptic Witnesses to Christ." *The Westminster Journal* 40 (1977/78): 77-88.

———. "Ned B. Stonehouse and Redaction Criticism, Part II: The Historicity of the Synoptic Tradition." *The Westminster Journal* 40 (1977/78): 281-303.

Skehan, Patrick W. "Exodus in the Samaritan Recension from Qumran." *Journal of Biblical Literature* (1955).

Skilton, John Hamilton. "The Translation of the New Testament into English, 1881-1950: Studies in Language and Style." 2 vols. Ph.D. dissertation, University of Pennsylvania, 1961.

Sparks, H.F.D. "Jerome as Biblical Scholar." In P.R. Ackroyd and C.F. Evans, eds., *The Cambridge History of the Bible*. Vol. 1, *From the Beginnings to Jerome*. Cambridge: Cambridge U., 1970.

Streeter, B. H. "Codices 157, 1071, and the Caesarean Text." *Quantualacumque, Studies Presented to Kirsopp Lake* (1937).

Taylor, Richard A. "Queen Anne Resurrected? A Review Article." *Journal of the Evangelical Theological Society* 20 (1977).

———. "'Queen Anne' Revisited: A Rejoinder." *Journal of the Evangelical Theological Society* 21 (1978).

Thomas, Robert L. "An Investigation of the Agreements Between Matthew and Luke Against Mark." *Journal of the Evangelical Theological Society* 19 (1976): 103-12.

Thomas, Robert L., and Stanley N. Gundry. "Form Criticism." In Robert L. Thomas and Stanley N. Gundry, eds., *A Harmony of the Gospels with Explanations and Essays: Using the Text of the New American Standard Bible*. Chicago: Moody, 1978; San Francisco: Harper & Row, 1985.

———. "Redaction Criticism." In Robert L. Thomas and Stanley N. Gundry, eds., *A Harmony of the Gospels with Explanations and Essays: Using the Text of the New American Standard Bible*. Chicago: Moody, 1978; San Francisco: Harper & Row, 1985.

———. "Source Criticism." In Robert L. Thomas and Stanley N. Gundry, eds., *A Harmony of the Gospels with Explanations and Essays: Using the Text of the New American Standard Bible*. Chicago: Moody, 1978; San Francisco: Harper & Row, 1985.

Trever, J. C. "The Discovery of the Scrolls." *Biblical Archaeologist* 11 (September 1948).

Van der Valk, M. "Observations on Mark 16:9-20 in Relation to St. Mark's Gospel." *Humanitas* (1958).

Waltke, Bruce K. "The Textual Criticism of the Old Testament." In Frank E. Gabelein, ed., *The Expositor's Bible Commentary.* Vol. 1, *Introductory Articles: General, Old Testament, New Testament*. Grand Rapids: Zondervan, 1979.

Ware, Kallistos. "A Note on Theology in the Christian East: The Eighteenth to Twentieth Centuries. In *A History of Christian Doctrine: In Succession to the Earlier Work of G.P. Fisher Publisher in the International Theological Library Series,* edited by Hubert Cunliffe-Jones, assisted by Benjamin Drewery. Philadelphia: Fortress, 1978.

Wenham, Gordon. "1. History and the Old Testament." In Collin Brown, ed., *History, Criticism and Faith: Four Exploratory Studies*. Downers Grove, Ill.: InterVarsity, 1976.

Wenham, John W. "Gospel Origins." *Trinity Journal* [old series] 7 (1978): 112-34.

———. "Gospel Origins: A Rejoinder." *Trinity Journal* [new series] 2, no. 1 (1981): 37-39.

Wikgren, Allen P. "Papyri, Biblical and Early Christian." In *The Twentieth Century Encyclopedia of Religious Knowledge*. Vol. K-Z, edited by Lefferts A. Loetscher.

Wiles, M.F. "Theodore of Mopsuestia as Representative of the Antiochene School." In P.R. Ackroyd and C.F. Evans, eds., *The Cambridge History of the Bible*. Vol. 1, *From the Beginnings to Jerome*. Cambridge: Cambridge U., 1970.

Wilson, Robert Dick. "Scientific Biblical Criticism." *Princeton Theological Review* 17 (1919): 190-240.

Wiseman, D.J. "Archeology and the Old Testament." In Frank E. Gabelein, ed., *The Expositor's Bible Commentary.* Vol. 1, *Introductory Articles General, Old Testament, New Testament*. Grand Rapids: Zondervan, 1979.

Witmer, John A. "The Biblical Evidence for the Verbal-Plenary Inspiration of the Bible." *Bibliotheca Sacra* 121, no. 483 (1964).

Woodbridge, John D. "Biblical Authority: Towards an Evaluation of the Rogers McKim Proposal." Review article, *Trinity Journal* [n.s.] 1, no. 2 (Fall 1980).

———. "The 'Great Manuscript Chase,' the Eucharistic Controversy and Richard Simon." Paper read at the thirtieth annual meeting of the Evangelical Theological Society, December 27-29, 1978.

———. "Recent Interpretations of Biblical Authority." *Bibliotheca Sacra* 142, nos. 565-68 (1985): 3-15, 99-113, 195-208, 292-305.

Yamauchi, Edwin M. "Unearthing Ebla's Ancient Secrets." *Christianity Today,* May 1981, pp. 18-21.

———. "The Word from Nag Hammadi." *Christianity Today,* 13 January 1978.

Young, Edward J. "The Authority of the Old Testament." In *The Infallible Word,* edited by Ned B. Stonehouse and Paul Wooley. Philadelphia: Presbyterian Guardian, 1946.

Books

Abraham, William J. *Divine Revelation and the Limits of Historical Criticism*. Oxford: Oxford U., 1982.

Achtemeier, Paul J. *The Inspiration of Scripture: Problems and Proposals*. Philadelphia: Westminster, 1980.

Ackroyd, P. R., ed. *The Cambridge History of the Bible*. Vol. 1, *From the Beginnings to Jerome*. Cambridge: Cambridge U., 1970.

Ahlstrom, Sidney E., ed. *Theology in America: The Major Protestant Voices from Puritanism to Neo-Orthodoxy.* Indianapolis: Bobbs-Merrill, 1967.

Albright, William F. *Archeology of Palestine*. Baltimore: Penguin, 1960.

———. *Archaeology and the Religion of Israel*. Baltimore: Johns Hopkins, 1953.

———. *From the Stone Age to Christianity.* 2d ed. Garden City, N.Y.: Doubleday, 1957.

———. *Recent Discoveries in Bible Lands*. New York: Funk & Wagnalls, 1956.

Allegro, John M. *The Treasure of the Copper Scroll*. 2d rev. ed. Garden City, N.Y.: Doubleday, 1965.

Anchor, Robert. *The Enlightenment Tradition*. New York: Harper & Row, 1967. Reprinted and updated, Berkeley, Calif.: U. of California, 1979.

Anderson, Charles C. *Critical Quests of Jesus*. Grand Rapids: Eerdmans, 1969.

Anderson, H., and W. Barclay, eds. *The New Testament in Historical and Contemporary Perspective: Essays in Honor of G.H.C. MacGregor.* Oxford: Oxford U., 1965.

Andrews, Herbert T. *An Introduction to the Apocryphal Books of the Old and New Testaments*. Revised and edited by Charles F. Pfeiffer. Grand Rapids: Baker, 1964.

Angus, Joseph. *The Bible Handbook*. Revised by Samuel G. Green. Grand Rapids: Zondervan, 1952.

Archer, Gleason L., Jr. *Encyclopedia of Bible Difficulties*. Grand Rapids: Zondervan, 1982.

———. *A Survey of Old Testament Introduction*. Rev. ed. Chicago: Moody, 1974.

Arndt, W. *Bible Difficulties: An Examination of Passages of the Bible Alleged to be Irreconcilable with Inspiration*. St. Louis: Concordia, 1971.

———. *Does the Bible Contradict Itself? A Discussion of Alleged Contradictions in the Bible*. 5th ed. rev. St. Louis: Concordia, 1955.

Babcox, Neil. *A Search for Charismatic Reality.* Portland: Multnomah, 1985.

Bailey, Lloyd R., ed. *The Word of God: A Guide to English Versions of the Bible*. Atlanta: John Knox, 1982.

Baillie, Donald MacPherson. *God Was in Christ*. New York: Scribner's, 1948.

Baillie, John. *The Idea of Revelation in Recent Thought*. New York: Columbia U., 1956.

Barnstone, Willis, ed. *The Other Bible*. San Francisco: Harper & Row, 1984.

Baron, S. W., and J. L. Blau. *Judaism: Postbiblical and Talmudic Period*. The Library of Liberal Arts 135. Indianapolis: Bobbs-Merrill, 1954.

Barr, James. *Fundamentalism*. Philadelphia: Westminster, 1977, 1978.

———. *Holy Scripture*. Philadelphia: Westminster, 1983.

———. *The Scope and Authority of the Bible*. Philadelphia: Westminster, 1980.

Barth, Karl. *Church Dogmatics*. 13 vols. Translated by G. T. Thompson, T. F. Torrence, G. W. Bromily, et al. Naperville: Allenson, 1936-69.

———. *Church Dogmatics*. Vol. 1, *The Doctrine of the Word of God*. Translated by G. W. Bromiley, Harold Knight, and G. T. Thompson. Edinburgh: T & T Clark, 1956.

———. *The Doctrine of the Word of God,* 2d half-vol. Edited by G. W. Bromily and T. F. Torrence. New York: Scribner's, 1956.

———. *The Epistle to the Romans*. English translation. New York: Oxford U., 1933.

———. *Evangelical Theology: An Introduction*. New York: Holt, Rinehart, and Winston, 1965.

Barthelemy, D., and J. T. Milik. *Discoveries in the Judaean Desert*. London: Oxford U., 1955ff.

Baugh, Albert C. *A History of the English Language*. 2d ed. New York: Appleton-Century-Crofts, 1957.

Bavinck, Herman. *Our Reasonable Faith*. Translated by Henry Zylstra. Grand Rapids: Eerdmans, 1956.

Beardslee, John W. III. *Reformed Dogmatics: J. Wollebuis, G. Voetius, F. Turretin*. New York: Oxford U., 1965. Reprint. Grand Rapids: Baker, 1977.

Beckwith, Roger. *The Old Testament Canon of the New Testament Church and Its Background in Early Judaism*. Grand Rapids: Eerdmans, 1986.

Beegle, Dewey M. *The Inspiration of Scripture*. Philadelphia: Westminster, 1963.

———. *Scripture, Tradition and Infallibility.* Ann Arbor, Mich.: Pettengill, 1979.

Beekman, John, and John Callow. *Translating the Word of God*. Grand Rapids: Zondervan, 1974.

Bell, Richard. *Introduction to the Qu'ran*. Edinburgh: Edinburgh U., 1953.

Berkhof, Louis. *The History of Christian Doctrines*. Grand Rapids: Eerdmans, 1937.

Berkouwer, G. C. *Holy Scripture*. Translated by Jack Rogers. Grand Rapids: Eerdmans, 1975.

Bermant, Chaim, and Michael Weitzman. *Ebla: An Archaeological Enigma*. London: Weidenfeld and Nicholson, 1979.

Bewer, Julius A. *The Literature of the Old Testament in Its Historical Development*. Records of Civilization: Sources and Studies. New York, 1922; 2d ed, 1933.

Birdsall, J. N., and R.W. Thomson, eds. *Biblical and Patristic Studies in Memory of C.R. Casey.* Freiburg: 1963.

Bloesch, Donald G. *Essentials of Evangelical Theology.* Vol. 1, *God, Authority, and Salvation*. San Francisco: Harper & Row, 1978.

Boer, Harry R. *Above the Battle? The Bible and Its Critics*. Grand Rapids: Eerdmans, 1975, 1976, 1977.

Boice, James Montgomery, ed. *The Foundation of Biblical Authority.* Grand Rapids: Zondervan, 1978.

Bornkamm, Günther. *Jesus of Nazareth*. Translated by I. and F. McLuskey with J.M. Robinson. New York: Harper & Row, 1960.

Bornkamm, Gunther, G. Barth, and H.J. Held. *Tradition and Interpretation in Matthew.* Translated by P. Scott. London: SCM, 1963.

Briggs, Charles Augustus. *The Higher Criticism of the Hexateuch.* 1893.

Brinton, Crane. *Ideas and Men: The Story of Western Thought.* 2d ed. Englewood Cliffs, N.J.: Prentice-Hall, 1963.

Bromily, Geoffrey W. *Historical Theology: An Introduction.* Grand Rapids: Eerdmans, 1978.

Brown, Colin. *Philosophy & the Christian Faith: A Historical Sketch from the Middle Ages to the Present Day.* Downers Grove, Ill.: InterVarsity, 1968.

———. ed. *History, Criticism and Faith: Four Exploratory Studies.* Downers Grove, Ill.: InterVarsity, 1976.

Brown, Delwin, Ralph E. James, Jr., and Gene Reeves, eds. *Process Philosophy and Christian Thought.* Indianapolis: Bobbs-Merrill, 1971.

Brownlee, William Hugh. *The Meaning of the Qumran Scrolls for the Bible.* New York: Oxford U., 1964.

Bruce, F. F. *The Books and the Parchments.* Rev. ed. Westwood, N.J.: Revell, 1963.

———. *The English Bible: A History of Translations.* 3d ed. New York: Oxford U., 1978.

———. *The New Testament Documents: Are They Reliable?* Grand Rapids: Eerdmans, 1965.

———. *Second Thoughts on the Dead Sea Scrolls.* Grand Rapids: Eerdmans, 1956.

Bruce, F. F., and Edmund Kidley Simpson. *Commentary on the Epistles to the Ephesians and Colossians.* Grand Rapids: Eerdmans, 1957.

Brunner, Emil. *The Christian Doctrine of God.* Translated by Olive Wyon. London: Lutterworth, 1949.

———. *The Word of God and Modern Man.* Translated by David Cairns. Richmond: John Knox, 1964.

———. *The Mediator.* Translated by Olive Wyon. Philadelphia: Westminster, 1947.

———. *Revelation and Reason.* Translated by Olive Wyon. Philadelphia: Westminster, 1946.

Brunner, Heinrich Emil. *Theology of Crisis.* New York: Scribner's, 1929.

Bryant, Margaret M. *Modern English and Its Heritage.* New York: Macmillan, 1948.

Buhl, Franz, P.W. *The Canon and Text of the Old Testament.* Edinburgh: T. & T. Clark, 1892.

Bultmann, Rudolf [Rudolph Karl]. *History of the Synoptic Tradition.* Translated by J. Marsh. New York: Harper & Row, 1963.

———. *Jesus Christ and Mythology.* New York: Scribner's, 1958.

———. *Theology of the New Testament.* 2 vols. Translated by K. Grobel. London: SPCK, 1952-55.

Bultmann, Rudolf, and Karl Kundsin. *Form Criticism: Two Essays on New Testament Research*. Translated by Frederick C. Grabt. New York: Willett, Clark & Co., 1934.

Burgon, John W. *The Last Twelve Verses of the Gospel According to St. Mark*. Marshallton, Del.: Sovereign Grace, 1959.

Burkill, T. A. *The Evolution of Christian Thought*. Ithaca, N.Y.: Cornell U., 1970.

Burrows, Millar. *The Dead Sea Scrolls*. New York: Viking, 1955.

———. *More Light on the Dead Sea Scrolls*. New York: Viking, 1958.

———. *What Mean These Stones?* New Haven, Conn.: American Schools of Oriental Research, 1941.

Burtchaell, James Tustead. *Catholic Theories of Inspiration Since 1810*. Cambridge: Cambridge U., 1960.

Burtner, Robert W., and Robert E. Chiles. *A Compend of Wesley's Theology*. Nashville: Abingdon, 1954.

Bush, L. Russ, and Tom J. Nettles. *Baptists and the Bible*. Chicago: Moody, 1980.

Butterfield, Herbert. *The Origins of Modern Science*. Rev. ed. New York: Macmillan, 1957.

Campenhausen, Henry von. *The Foundation of the Christian Bible*. Translated by J.A. Baker. Philadelphia: Fortress, 1972.

Carnell, Edward John. *The Case for Orthodox Theology*. Philadelphia: Westminster, 1959.

Carroll, B. H. *The Inspiration of the Bible*. Compiled and edited by J. B. Cranfill. Reprint of 1930 edition with introduction and notes by Paige Patterson. Nashville: Nelson, 1980.

Carson, D. A. *The King James Version Debate: A Plea for Realism*. Grand Rapids: Baker, 1979.

———. *Redaction Criticism: The Nature of an Interpretive Tool*. Carol Stream, Ill.: Christianity Today Institute, 1985.

Cassirer, Ernst. *The Philosophy of the Enlightenment*. Boston: Beacon, 1964; reprint of 1951 translation by Fritz C. A. Koelln and James P. Pettegrove. *Die Philosophie der Aufklärung*. Tübingen: 1932.

Chase, Mary Ellen. *Life and Language in the Old Testament*. New York: Norton, 1955.

Cheyne, T. K. *Aids to the Devout Study of Criticism*. 1892.

Childs, Brevard S. *Introduction to the Old Testament as Scripture*. Philadelphia: Fortress, 1979.

———. *Introduction to the New Testament as Canon*. Philadelphia: Fortress, 1984.

Christiansen, Michael J. *C. S. Lewis on Scripture: His Thoughts on the Nature of Biblical Inspiration, the Role of Revelation and the Question of Inerrancy*. Waco, Tex.: Word, 1979.

Clark, Gordon, H., et al. *Can I Trust My Bible?* Chicago: Moody, 1963.

———. *God's Hammer: The Bible and Its Critics*. Jefferson, Md.: Trinity Foundation, 1982.

Clark, H. W. *History of English Nonconformity from Wyclif to the Close of the Nineteenth Century.* 2 vols. 1911.

Coates, George W., and O. Long Burke, eds. *Canon and Authority: Essays in Old Testament Religion and Theology.* Philadelphia: Fortress, 1977.

Collett, Sidney. *All About the Bible.* Westwood, N.J.: Revell, 1959.

Conzelmann, Hans. *The Theology of Luke.* Translated by G. Buswell. London: SCM, 1959.

Copleston, Frederick. *A History of Philosophy.* Vol. 5, *Modern Philosophy: The British Philosophers, Part I, Hobbes to Paley.* Garden City, N.Y.: Doubleday, Image, 1959.

Coss, Thurman L. *Secrets from the Caves.* Nashville: Abingdon, 1963.

Cross, Frank Moore, Jr. *The Ancient Library of Qumran and Modern Biblical Studies.* Garden City, N.Y.: Doubleday, 1958.

Cullmann, Oscar. *The Christology of the New Testament.* London: SCM, 1959.

Cumont, Franz. *Textes et Monuments figures relatifs aux Mysteres de Mithra.* 2 vols. Bruxelles: 1896, 1899; English translation by T. J. McCormick. London: 1903.

Cunliffe-Jones, Hubert, ed. *A History of Christian Doctrine: In Succession to the Earlier Work of G. P. Fisher Published in the International Theological Library Series.* Assisted by Benjamin Drewery. Philadelphia: Fortress, 1980.

Davidson, Samuel. *Introduction to the Old Testament.* London: 1862.

———. *The Hebrew Text of the Old Testament.* London: 1856.

———. *The Canon of the Bible.* 2d ed. London: 1877.

Davies, William D., and D. Daube, eds. *The Background of the New Testament and Its Eschatology.* Cambridge: Cambridge U., 1956.

Davis, G. T. B. *Bible Prophecies Fulfilled Today.* Philadelphia: Million Testaments Campaigns, 1955.

Davis, Stephen T. *The Debate About the Bible: Inerrancy Versus Infallibility.* Philadelphia: Westminster, 1977.

Dāwūd, Ibn Abi. *Materials for the History of the Text of the Qur'an.* Edited by Arthur Jeffrey. Leiden: Brill, 1937.

Deissmann, Gustav Adolf. *Light from the Ancient East.* Translated by L. R. M. Strachan. New York: Harper, 1923.

Delumeau, Jean. *Le catholicisme entre Luther et Voltaire,* 1971. Published in the series *Nouvelle Clio—Clio.* Translated into English by Jeremy Moiser as *Catholicism Between Luther and Voltaire: A New View of the Counter-Reformation.* London: Burns & Oates, 1977.

Demarest, Bruce. *General Revelation: Historical Views and Contemporary Issues.* Grand Rapids: Zondervan, 1983.

Deschner, John, et al., eds. *Our Common History as Christians: Essays in Honor of Albert C. Outler.* New York: Oxford U., 1975.

Devreese, Robert. *Introduction a l'etude des manuscrits grecs.* Paris: 1954.

Dewey, John. *The Influence of Darwin on Philosophy & Other Essays*. New York: Holt, 1910. Reprint. Magnolia, Mass.: Peter Smith, n.d.

DeWolf, L. Harold. *The Case for Theology in Liberal Perspective*. Philadelphia: Westminster, 1959.

Dibelius, Martin. *From Tradition to Gospel*. Translated by B. L. Woolf, 2d ed., from the 1919 German edition. London: Nicholson & Watson, 1934.

Dietrich, Karl. *Untersuchen zur Geschichte der grieschischen Sprache von der hellenistichen Zeit bis zum 10. Jahrhundert nach Christus (Researches on the History of the Greek Language from the Hellenistic Period to the Tenth Century* A.D.*)*. Leipzig: Teubner, 1898.

Dodd, C. H. *The Authority of the Bible*. London: 1928.

———. *The Bible To-Day*. Cambridge: Cambridge U., 1968.

Draper, James T., Jr. *Authority: The Critical Issue for Southern Baptists*. Old Tappan, N.J.: Revell, 1984.

Driver, Samuel R. *Introduction to the Literature of the Old Testament*. Edinburgh, 1891.

Dyck, Cornelius J., ed. *An Introduction to Mennonite History: A Popular History of the Anabaptists and the Mennonites*. Scottdale, Pa.: Herald, 1967.

Eissfeldt, Otto. *The Old Testament: An Introduction*. New York: Harper & Row, 1965.

Elliot, J. K. *The Greek Text of the Epistles to Timothy and Titus*. Salt Lake City: U. of Utah, 1968.

Enslin, Morton S. *Christian Beginnings*. New York: Harper, 1938.

Epp, E. J. *The Theological Tendency of Codex Bezae Cantabrigiensis*. Cambridge: Cambridge U., 1966.

Erickson, Millard J. *Christian Theology*. 3 vols. Grand Rapids: Baker, 1983-85.

Estep, W. R. *The Anabaptist Story*. Rev. ed. Nashville: Broadman, 1963.

Evans, William. *The Great Doctrines of the Bible*. Chicago: Moody, 1949.

Ewert, David. *From Ancient Tablets to Modern Translations: A General Introduction to the Bible*. Grand Rapids: Zondervan, 1983.

Farmer, William F. *The Last Twelve Verses of Mark*. London: Cambridge U., 1974.

Farmer, William R. *The Synoptic Problem*. New York: Macmillan, 1964.

Ferm, Robert O. *The Psychology of Christian Conversion*. Westwood, N.J.: Revell, 1959.

Finegan, Jack. *Light from the Ancient Past*. 2d ed. Princeton, N.J.: Princeton U., 1959.

Fosdick, Harry Emerson. *A Guide to Understanding the Bible*. New York: Harper & Brothers, 1938.

———. *A Great Time to Be Alive*. New York: Harper & Brothers, 1944.

———. *Modern Use of the Bible*. New York: Association, 1926.

Francke, Hermann. *A Guide to the Reading and Study of the Holy Scriptures*. Philadelphia: David Hogan, 1823.

Free, Joseph P. *Archeology and Bible History*. 5th ed. rev. Wheaton, Ill.: Scripture Press, 1956.

Frend, W. H. C. *Martyrdom and Persecution in the Early Church*. Oxford: Oxford U.; New York: New York U., 1967.

Fuchs, Ernst. *Studies on the Historical Jesus*. London: SCM, 1964.

Fuller, David Otis, ed. *True or False? The Westcott-Hort Textual Theory Examined*. Grand Rapids: Grand Rapids International Publications, 1973.

———, ed. *Which Bible?* 5th ed. Grand Rapids: Grand Rapids International Publications, 1975.

Gaebelein, Frank E., gen. ed. *The Expositor's Bible Commentary.* 12 vols. Vol. 1, *Introductory Articles: General, Old Testament, New Testament*. Grand Rapids: Zondervan, 1979.

Gasque, W. Ward, and William Sanford LaSor, eds. *Scripture, Tradition, and Interpretation*. Grand Rapids: Eerdmans, 1978.

Gay, Peter. *The Enlightenment: An Interpretation*. 2 vols. New York: Vintage Books, 1966-1969.

———. *The Party of Humanity: Essays in the French Enlightenment*. New York: W. W. Norton, 1971.

———. *Voltaire's Politics: The Poet and Realist*. New York: Vintage, 1971.

Geisler, Norman L. *Biblical Errancy: An Analysis of Its Philosophical Roots*. Grand Rapids: Zondervan, 1981.

———. *Christ: the Theme of the Bible*. Chicago: Moody, 1968.

———. *Christian Apologetics*. Grand Rapids: Baker, 1976.

———. *Inerrancy.* Grand Rapids: Zondervan, 1980.

———. *Miracles and Modern Thought*. Grand Rapids: Zondervan, 1982.

———. *Summit II: Hermeneutics*. Oakland, Calif., International Conference on Biblical Inerrancy, 1983.

Gladstone, W. E. *The Impregnable Rock of Holy Scripture*. London: George Newnes, 1899.

Glassman, Eugene H. *The Translation Debate, What Makes a Bible Translation Good?* Downers Grove, Ill.: InterVarsity, 1981.

Gleuck, Nelson. *Rivers in the Desert: A History of the Negev.* New York: Farrar, Strauss & Cudahy, 1959.

Glickman, S. Craig. *A Song for Lovers*. Downers Grove, Ill.: InterVarsity, 1976.

Gonzalez, Justo L. *A History of Christian Thought*. Vol. 3, *From the Reformation to the Twentieth Century.* Nashville: Abingdon, 1975.

Gooch, George Peabody. *History and Historians in the Nineteenth Century.* New York: Longmans, Green & Co., 1913.

Gore, C. *The Incarnation of the Son of God*. 1891.

Grant, Robert M. *The Secret Sayings of Jesus*. Garden City, N.Y.: Doubleday, 1960.

Green, William H. *General Introduction to the Old Testament: The Canon*. New York: Scribner's, 1899.

Greenlee, J. Harold. *An Introduction to New Testament Textual Criticism*. Grand Rapids: Eerdmans, 1964.

Greenslade, S. L., ed. *The Cambridge History of the Bible*. Vol. 3, *The West from the Reformation to the Present Day.* Cambridge: Cambridge U., 1963.

Gregory, Caspar Rene. *Canon and Text of the New Testament*. Edinburgh: T. & T. Clark, 1907. Reprint. New York: Scribner's, 1912.

Griffith-Thomas, W. H. *The Principles of Theology: Introduction to the Thirty-Nine Articles*. 5th ed. Grand Rapids: Baker, 1880. Reprint, 1977.

Gundry, Robert. *Matthew: A Commentary on His Literary and Theological Art*. Grand Rapids: Eerdmans, 1982.

Guthrie, Donald. *New Testament Introduction: The Gospels and Acts*. London: Tyndale, 1965.

———. *New Testament Introduction: Hebrews to Revelation*. Downers Grove, Ill.: InterVarsity, 1966.

Hackett, Stuart Cornelius. *The Resurrection of Theism*. 2d ed. Grand Rapids: Baker, 1982.

Haenchen, Ernst. *Acts of the Apostles*. Translated by B. Noble and G. Shinn; revised by R. McL. Wilson. Philadelphia: Westminster, 1971.

Haley, John W. *An Examination of the Alleged Discrepancies of the Bible*. Grand Rapids: Baker, 1951.

Hall, A. R. *The Scientific Revolution 1500-1800: The Formation of the Modern Scientific Attitude*. 2d ed. Boston: Beacon, 1966.

Haller, William. *The Rise of Puritanism*. New York: Columbia U., 1938. Reprint. New York: Harper Torchbook, 1957.

Hannah, John D., ed. *Inerrancy and the Church*. Chicago: Moody, 1984.

Harnack, Adolf. *What Is Christianity?* Translated by Thomas Bailey Saunders. New York: Putnam, 1901.

Harris, R. Laird. *Inspiration and Canonicity of the Bible*. Grand Rapids: Zondervan, 1957.

Harrison, Everett F. *Introduction to the New Testament*. Grand Rapids: Eerdmans, 1964.

Harrison, R. K. *Introduction to the Old Testament*. Grand Rapids: Eerdmans, 1969.

Harrison, R. K., B. K. Waltke, D. Guthrie, and G. D. Fee. *Biblical Criticism: Historical, Literary and Textual*. Grand Rapids: Zondervan, 1978.

Hasel, Gerhard. *New Testament Theology: Basic Issues in the Current Debate*. Grand Rapids: Eerdmans, 1978.

———. *Old Testament Theology: Basic Issues in the Current Debate*. 3d ed., rev. and updated. Grand Rapids: Eerdmans, 1972, 1982.

Hawthorne, Gerald F., ed. *Current Issues in Biblical and Patristic Interpretation*. Grand Rapids: Eerdmans, 1975.

Hazard, Paul. *The European Mind, 1680-1715*. Translated by J. L. May. Cleveland: Meridian, 1963.

———. *European Thought in the Eighteenth Century: From Montesquieu to Lessing*. Translated by J. L. May. Cleveland: Meridian, 1963.

Hefley, James C. *The Truth in Crisis: The Controversy in the Southern Baptist Convention*. Dallas: Criterion, 1986.

Henry, Carl F. H. *God, Revelation and Authority.* Vol. 2, *God Who Speaks and Shows: Fifteen Theses, Part One*. Waco, Tex.: Word, 1976.

———. *God, Revelation and Authority.* Vol. 3, *God Who Speaks and Shows: Fifteen Theses, Part Two*. Waco, Tex.: Word, 1979.

———. *God, Revelation and Authority.* Vol. 4, *God Who Speaks and Shows: Fifteen Theses, Part Three*. Waco, Tex.: Word, 1979.

———, ed. *Jesus of Nazareth: Saviour and Lord*. Grand Rapids: Eerdmans, 1966.

———. *Revelation and the Bible*. Grand Rapids: Baker, 1958.

Herklots, Hugh G. G. *How Our Bible Came to Us*. New York: Oxford U., 1954.

Hills, Edward F. *The King James Version Defended!* Des Moines: Christian Research, 1956.

Hoare, H. W. *The Evolution of the English Bible*. 2d ed. London: Murray, 1902.

Hodge, Archibald A., and Benjamin B. Warfield. *Inspiration*. Philadelphia: Presbyterian Board of Publication, 1881. Reprint. Grand Rapids: Baker, 1979. Roger R. Nicole has supplied or written an introduction and several appendixes for this reprint, which had been published earlier as an article in *Presbyterian Review* 2 (April 1881): 225-60.

Hodge, Charles. *Systematic Theology.* 3 vols. New York: Scribner's 1872; reprint. Grand Rapids: Eerdmans, 1940.

Hoehner, Harold W. *Chronological Aspects of the Life of Christ*. Grand Rapids: Zondervan, 1978.

Hopf, Constantin. *Martin Bucer and the English Reformation*. Oxford: Basil Blackwell, 1946.

Hordern, William. *The Case for a New Reformation Theology.* Philadelphia: Westminster, 1959.

Horne, Thomas. *An Introduction to the Critical Study and Knowledge of the Holy Scriptures*. 8th ed. London: 1856.

Howie, Robert, ed. *The Westminster Doctrine Anent Holy Scripture: Tractates by A. A. Hodge and Warfield, with Notes on Recent Discussions*. Glasgow: Bryce, 1891.

Jauncey, James H. *Science Returns to God*. Grand Rapids: Zondervan, 1961.

Jeremias, Joachim. *Unknown Sayings of Jesus*. 2d ed. London: SPCK, 1957. Reprint. Naperville, Ill.: Allenson, 1964.

Jespersen, Otto. *Growth and Structure of the English Language*. 9th ed. Garden City, N.Y.: Doubleday, 1955.

Jewitt, Paul K. *Man As Male and Female*. Grand Rapids: Eerdmans, 1975.

Johnston, Robert K. *The Use of the Bible in Theology.* Atlanta: John Knox, 1985.

Jones, A. H. M. *Constantine and the Conversion of Europe*. New York: Macmillan, 1948.

Kantzer, Kenneth S., and Stanley N. Gundry, eds. *Perspectives on Evangelical Theology.* Grand Rapids: Baker, 1979.

Käsemann, Ernst. *Essays on New Testament Themes.* Translated by W. J. Montague. Naperville: Abingdon, 1985.

Kaufmann, Walter A. *Hegel: A Reinterpretation.* Garden City, N.Y.: Doubleday, 1965.

Kelly, J. N. D. *Early Christian Doctrines.* San Francisco: Harper & Row, 1978.

Kelly, Palmer H., and Donald G. Miller, eds. *Tools for Bible Study.* Richmond: John Knox, 1956.

Kelsey, David H. *The Uses of Scripture in Recent Theology.* Philadelphia: Fortress, 1975.

Kenny, Anthony. *The Five Ways: St. Thomas Aquinas' Proof of God's Existence.* New York: Schocken, 1969.

Kenyon, Sir Frederic G. *Archaeology in the Holy Land.* New York: W. Norton, 1979.

———. *The Bible and Archaeology.* New York: Harper, 1940.

———. *Handbook to the Textual Criticism of the New Testament.* 2d ed. Grand Rapids: Eerdmans, 1912.

———. *Our Bible and the Ancient Manuscripts.* 4th ed., revised by A. W. Adams. New York: Harper, 1958.

———. *The Text of the Greek Bible.* 3d ed., revised and augmented by A. W. Adams. London: Gerald Duckworth, 1975.

Khayyám, Omar. *Rubaiyat.* Translated by Edward FitzGerald. New York: Black, 1942.

Kikawada, Isaac M., and Arthur Quinn. *Before Abraham Was: The Unity of Genesis I-II.* Nashville: Abingdon, 1985.

Kilby, Clyde S. *The Christian World of C. S. Lewis.* Grand Rapids: Eerdmans, 1964.

Kilgour, R. *The Bible Throughout the World: A Survey of Scripture Translations.* London: World Dominion, 1939.

Kistemaker, Simon. *The Gospels in Current Study.* Grand Rapids: Baker, 1972.

Klein, R.W. *Textual Criticism of the Old Testament.* Philadelphia: Fortress, 1977.

Kline, Meredith G. *The Structure of Biblical Authority.* 2d ed. Grand Rapids: Eerdmans, 1972.

Knappen, M. M. *Tudor Puritanism: A Chapter in the History of Idealism.* Chicago: U. of Chicago, 1939.

Kramer, Samuel Noah. *History Begins at Sumer.* New York: Doubleday, 1959.

Krentz, Edgar. *The Historical-Critical Method.* Philadelphia: Fortress, 1975.

Kubo, Sakae, and Walter F. Specht. *So Many Versions?: Twentieth Century English Versions of the Bible.* Revised and enlarged ed. Grand Rapids: Zondervan, 1983.

Lampe, G. W. H., ed. *The Cambridge History of the Bible.* Vol. 2, *The West from the Fathers to the Reformation.* Cambridge: Cambridge U., 1969.

Larson, Mildred. *A Manual for Problem Solving in Bible Translation*. Grand Rapids: Zondervan, 1975.
Latourette, Kenneth Scott. *A History of Christianity.* New York: Harper, 1953.
Leach, Charles. *Our Bible: How We Got It*. Chicago: Moody, 1897.
Leiman, Sid Z. *The Canonization of Hebrew Scripture: The Talmudic and Midrashic Evidence*. Hamdon: Conn.: Transactions of the Connecticut Academy of Arts and Sciences, Archon Books, 1976.
———, ed. *The Canon and Masorah of the Hebrew Bible: An Introductory Reader.* New York: KTAV, 1974.
Leupold, Herbert Carl. *Exposition of Ecclesiastes*. Columbus, Ohio: Wartburg, 1952.
Levi, Peter. *The English Bible: 1534-1859*. Grand Rapids: Eerdmans, 1974.
Lewis, C. S. *Christian Reflections*. Grand Rapids: Eerdmans, 1967.
———. *Miracles*. New York: Macmillan, 1947.
———. *Reflections on the Psalms*. New York: Harcourt, Brace, 1958.
Lewis, Gordon R., and Bruce Demarest, eds. *Challenges to Inerrancy: A Theological Response*. Chicago: Moody, 1984.
Lewis, Jack P. *The English Bible from KJV to NIV: A History and Evaluation*. Grand Rapids: Baker, 1982.
Lightfoot, J. B. *Saint Paul's Epistles to the Colossians and to Philemon*. Grand Rapids: Zondervan, 1965.
Lightfoot, Neil R. *How We Got the Bible*. Grand Rapids: Baker, 1963.
Lindsell, Harold. *The Battle for the Bible*. Grand Rapids: Zondervan, 1976.
———. *The Bible in the Balance*. Grand Rapids: Zondervan, 1979.
Loetscher, Lefferts A. *The Broadening Church: A Study of Theological Issues in the Presbyterian Church Since 1869*. Philadelphia: U. of Pennsylvania, 1954.
Lohse, Eduard. *The Formation of the New Testament*. Translated from the 3d German ed. by Eugene Boring. Nashville: Abingdon, 1981.
Longnecker, Richard N., and Merrill C. Tenney, eds. *New Dimensions in New Testament Study.* Grand Rapids: Zondervan, 1974.
Lupton, Lewis. *A History of the Geneva Bible*. 7 vols. London: Olive Tree, 1970f.
MacGregor, Geddes. *The Bible in the Making*. Philadelphia: Lippencott, 1959.
Machen, J. Gresham. *Christianity and Liberalism*. Grand Rapids: Eerdmans, 1956.
Macquarrie, John. *Principles of Christian Theology.* New York: Scribner's, 1966.
Maier, Gerhard. *The End of the Historical-Critical Method*. Translated by Edwin W. Leverenz and Rudolph F. Norden. St. Louis: Concordia, 1974.
Manley, G. T., ed. *The New Bible Handbook*. 3d ed. London: InterVarsity, 1950.
Mansoor, Menahem. *The Dead Sea Scrolls*. Grand Rapids: Eerdmans, 1964.
Mackwardt, Albert. *Introduction to the English Language*. New York: Oxford U., 1942.
Marshall, I. Howard. *Biblical Inspiration*. Grand Rapids: Eerdmans, 1983.
———. *I Believe in the Historical Jesus*. Grand Rapids: Eerdmans, 1977.

———. *The Gospel of Luke: A Commentary on the Greek Text*. New International Greek Testament Commentary. Grand Rapids: Eerdmans, 1978.

———. *Luke: Historian and Theologian*. Grand Rapids: Zondervan, 1970.

———. *The Origins of New Testament Christology*. Downers Grove: InterVarsity, 1976.

Marxen, Willi, *Mark the Evangelist*. Translated by R. A. Harrisville. Nashville: Abingdon, 1969.

Matthiae, Paolo. *Ebla: An Empire Rediscovered*. Translated by Christopher Holme. Garden City, N.Y.: Doubleday, 1981.

McDonald, H. D. *Theories of Revelation: An Historical Study, 1700-1960*. 2 vols. in 1. Grand Rapids: Baker, Twin Books Series, 1979.

McDowell, Josh. *Evidence That Demands a Verdict*. San Bernardino: Campus Crusade/Here's Life, 1972, 1985.

McKim, Donald K., ed. *The Authoritative Word: Essays on the Nature of Scripture*. Grand Rapids: Eerdmans, 1983.

Metzger, Bruce M. *Chapters in the History of New Testament Textual Criticism*. Grand Rapids: Eerdmans, 1963.

———. *The Early Versions of the New Testament: Their Origins, Transmission and Limitations*. Oxford: Clarendon, 1977.

———. *An Introduction to the Apocrypha*. New York: Oxford U., 1957.

———. *Lessons from Luke in the Greek Gospel Lectionary*. Chicago: 1944.

———. *Manuscripts of the Greek Bible: An Introduction to Greek Paleography*. New York: Oxford U., 1981.

———. *The Text of the New Testament: Its Transmission, Corruption, and Restoration*. New York: Oxford U., 1964.

———. *A Textual Commentary on the Greek New Testament: A Companion Volume to the United Bible Societies' Greek New Testament (third edition)*. London; New York; United Bible Societies, 1975.

Miller, H. S. *A General Biblical Introduction*. 7th ed. rev. Houghton, N.Y.: Word-Bearer, 1952.

Moltmann, Jurgen. *Theology of Hope: On the Ground and Implications of a Christian Eschatology*. London: SCM, 1967.

Montgomery, John Warwick. *God's Inerrant Word: An International Symposium on the Trustworthiness of Scripture*. Minneapolis: Bethany Fellowship, 1973.

———. *The Suicide of Christian Theology*. Minneapolis: Bethany Fellowship, 1970.

Moody, Dale. *The Word of Truth: A Summary of Christian Doctrine Based on Biblical Revelation*. Grand Rapids: Eerdmans, 1981.

Morris, Leon. *I Believe in Revelation*. Grand Rapids: Eerdmans, 1976.

Morton. A. Q., and James McLeman. *Christianity in the Computer Age*. New York: Harper & Row, 1964.

Mould, Elmer W. K. *Essentials of Bible History*. Revised ed. New York: Ronald, 1951.

Moule, C. F. D. *The Birth of the New Testament.* 3d ed., rev. and rewritten [1st U.S. ed.]. San Francisco: Harper & Row, 1982.

Mullins, Edgar Young. *The Christian Religion in Its Doctrinal Expression.* Philadelphia: Judson, 1917.

Murray, John. *Calvin on Scripture and Divine Sovereignty.* Grand Rapids: Baker, 1960. Reprint of Articles from *Torch and Trumpet.*

Nash, Ronald. *The New Evangelicalism.* Grand Rapids: Zondervan, 1963.

———. *The Word of God and the Mind of Man.* Grand Rapids: Zondervan, 1982.

Nestle, Eberhard. *Introduction to the Textual Criticism of the Greek New Testament.* New York: G. P. Putnam's Sons, 1901.

Nicole, Roger R., and J. Ramsey Michaels, eds. *Inerrancy and Common Sense.* Grand Rapids: Baker, 1980.

Nix, William E. "Inerrancy: Theological Issue of the Hour?" Otterbourne, Manitoba: Winnipeg Theological Seminary Lectureship Series, 1980.

Oesterly, W. O. E., and Theodore H. Robinson. *An Introduction to the Books of the Old Testament.* London: Society for Promoting Christian Knowledge, 1934.

Orlinsky, Harry M. *Ancient Israel.* Rev. ed. Ithaca N.Y.: Cornell U., 1960.

Orr, James. *The Problem of the Old Testament.* London: Nisbet, 1906.

———. *Revelation and Inspiration.* Grand Rapids: Eerdmans, 1952.

Ottley, R. L. *The Doctrine of the Incarnation.* 1896.

Otto, Rudolph. *The Idea of the Holy.* Translated by John Harvey. Oxford: Oxford U., 1967.

Pack, Roger A. *The Greek and Latin Literary Texts from Greco-Roman Egypt.* Ann Arbor: 1952.

Packer, J. I. *Beyond the Battle for the Bible.* Westchester, Ill.: Cornerstone, 1980.

———. *"Fundamentalism" and the Word of God.* Grand Rapids: Eerdmans, 1958.

———. *God Has Spoken.* Downers Grove, Ill.: InterVarsity, 1979.

———. *God Speaks to Man.* London: Hodder and Stoughton, 1965.

Palmer, R. R., and Joel Colton. *A History of the Modern World.* 5th ed. New York: Alfred A. Knopf, 1978.

Pannenberg, Wolfhart, ed. *Revelation as History: A Proposal for a more open, less authoritarian view of an important theological concept.* Translated from the German by David Granskow. London: Collier-Macmillan, 1968.

Parvis, M. M., and A. P. Wikgren, eds. *New Testament Manuscript Studies.* Chicago: U. of Chicago, 1950.

Payne, J. Barton. *Encyclopedia of Biblical Prophecy.* London: Hodder and Stoughton, 1973.

Pei, Mario A. *The World's Chief Languages.* 4th ed. New York: Vanni, 1955.

Perrin, Norman. *The New Testament, An Introduction: Proclamation and Parenesis, Myth and History.* New York: Harcourt, Brace Jovanovich, 1974.

Peters, F. E. *The Harvest of Hellenism.* New York: Simon and Schuster, 1971.

Pettinato, Giovanni. *The Archives at Ebla: An Empire Inscribed in Clay.* New York: Doubleday, 1981.

Pfeiffer, Robert H. *History of New Testament Times with an Introduction to the Apocrypha*. New York: Harper & Row, 1949.

———. *Introduction to the Old Testament*. Rev. ed. New York: Harper & Brothers, 1948.

Pickering, Hy. *One Thousand Wonderful Things About the Bible*. London: Pickering & Inglis, n.d.

Pickering, Wilbur N. *The Identity of the New Testament Text*. Rev. ed. Nashville: Thomas Nelson, 1977, 1980.

Pinnock, Clark. *The Scripture Principle*. San Francisco: Harper & Row, 1984.

Plummer, Alfred. *International Critical Commentary: II Corinthians*. New York: Scribner's, 1915.

Pollard, Alfred W. *Records of the English Bible*. London: Oxford U., 1911.

Pope, Hugh. *English Versions of the Bible*. St. Louis: Herder, 1952. Revised and amplified by Sebastian Bullough. Westport, Conn.: Greenwood, 1972.

Popkin, Richard H. *The History of Scepticism from Erasmus to Descartes*. New York: Harper Torchbook, 1964.

Preus, Robert D. *Inspiration of Scripture*. Edinburgh: Oliver & Boyd, 1955.

Pyles, Thomas. *Origins and Development of the English Language*. 2d ed. New York: Harcourt, Brace Jovanovich, 1971.

Radmacher, Earl D., ed. *Can We Trust the Bible?* Wheaton, Ill.: Tyndale House, 1979.

Radmacher, Earl D., and Robert D. Preus. *Hermeneutics, Inerrancy, and the Bible*. Grand Rapids: Zondervan, 1984.

Ramm, Bernard. *After Fundamentalism: The Future of Evangelical Theology.* San Francisco: Harper & Row, 1983.

———. *Protestant Biblical Interpretation*. Rev. ed. Boston: Wilde, 1956.

———. *Protestant Biblical Interpretation: A Textbook of Hermeneutics*. 3d rev. ed. Grand Rapids: Baker, 1970.

Ramsay, W. M. *St. Paul the Traveller and the Roman Citizen*. 3d ed. Grand Rapids: Baker, 1949.

Randall, John Herman, Jr. *The Making of the Modern Mind: A Survey of the Intellectual Background of the Present Age*. Rev. ed. New York: Columbia U., 1926, 1940.

Reu, M. *Luther and the Scriptures*. Columbus, Ohio: Wartburg, 1944. Reissued with correction to notes in *The Springfielder.* Springfield, Ill.: Concordia Theological Seminary, August 1960.

Rice, John R. *Our God-Breathed Book—The Bible*. Murfreesboro, Tenn.: Sword of the Lord Publishers, 1969.

———. *Twelve Tremendous Themes*. Wheaton, Ill.: Sword of the Lord, 1943.

Ridderbos, Herman. *Studies in Scripture and Its Authority.* Grand Rapids: Eerdmans, 1978.

Roberts, B[leddyn] J. *The Old Testament Text and Versions*. Cardiff: U. of Wales, 1951.

Robertson, Archibald T. *An Introduction to the Textual Criticism of the New Testament*. Nashville: Broadman, 1925.

Robinson, G. L. *Where Did We Get Our Bible?* New York: Doubleday, Doran, 1928.

Robinson, John A. T. *Redating the New Testament*. Philadelphia: Westminster, 1976.

Rodkinson, Michael L. *Babylonian Talmud*. Boston: Talmud Society, 1918.

Rogers, Jack B., ed. *Biblical Authority*. Waco, Tex.: Word, 1978.

Rogers, Jack B., and Donald K. McKim. *The Authority and Interpretation of the Bible: An Historical Approach*. San Francisco: Harper & Row, 1979.

Ryle, Herbert Edward. *The Canon of the Old Testament: An Essay on the Gradual Growth and Formation of the Hebrew Canon of Scripture*. 2d ed. London: Macmillan, 1892, 1895.

Ryrie, Charles C. *Biblical Theology of the New Testament*. Chicago: Moody, 1959.

Sanday, W. *Inspiration: Eight Lectures on the Early History and Origin of the Doctrine of Biblical Inspiration*. 5th impression. London: Longmans, Green, 1903.

———. *The Oracles of God*. 1891.

Sandeen, Ernest. *The Origins of Fundamentalism: Toward a Historical Interpretation*. Philadelphia: Fortress, 1968.

———. *The Roots of Fundamentalism: British and American Millenarianism, 1800-1930*. Chicago: U. of Chicago, 1970. Reprint. Grand Rapids: Baker, 1978.

Sanders, E. P. *The Tendencies of the Synoptic Tradition*. Cambridge: Cambridge U., 1969.

Sanders, James A. *Torah and Canon*. Philadelphia: Fortress, 1972.

Saphir, Adolph. *Christ and the Scriptures*. Kilmarnock, Scotland: Ritchie, n.d.

Saucy, Robert L. *The Bible: Breathed from God*. Wheaton, Ill.: Victor, 1978.

Sauer, Erich. *The Dawn of World Redemption*. Translated by G. H. Land. London: Paternoster, 1951.

———. *The Triumph of the Crucified*. Translated by G. H. Lang. London: Paternoster, 1951.

Schaeffer, Francis. *Escape from Reason*. Downers Grove, Ill.: InterVarsity, 1968.

Schaff, Philip. *Companion to the Greek Testament and the English Version*. 3d ed., rev. New York: Harper, 1883.

———. *History of the Apostolic Church; with a general introduction to church history*. New York: Charles Scribner, 1867.

———. *History of the Christian Church*. 7 vols. 5th ed., rev. New York: Scribner, 1910.

Schleiermacher, Friedrich D. E. *The Christian Faith*. Translated by H. R. Mackintosh and J. S. Stewart. Edinburgh: T. & T. Clark, 1928.

Schonfield, High J. *The Original New Testament*. San Francisco: Harper & Row, 1985.

Schultz, Samuel J., *The Old Testament Speaks*. 3d ed. New York: Harper & Row, 1980.

Schweitzer, Albert. *The Quest for the Historical Jesus*. Translated by W. Montgomery. New York: Macmillan, 1910.

Scrivener, F. H. A. *A Plain Introduction to the Criticism of the New Testament*. 2 vols. 4th ed. Edited by Edward Miller. London: Bell, 1894.

Scroggie, W. Graham. *Know Your Bible*. 2 vols. London: Pickering & Inglis, n.d.

Sherwin-White, A. N. *Roman Society and Roman Law in the New Testament*. Oxford: Clarendon, 1963.

A Short Explanation of Dr. Martin Luther's Small Catechism: A Handbook of Christian Doctrine. Rev. ed. St. Louis: Concordia, 1965.

Smith, William Robertson. *The Old Testament and the Jewish Church*. Edinburgh and London, 1881; 2d ed., 1892; 3d ed., 1926.

Souter, Alexander. *The Text and Canon of the New Testament*. London: Duckworth, 1913. Reprint. Edited by C. S. C. Williams. Naperville, Ill.: Allenson, 1954.

Sproul, R. C. *Explaining Inerrancy: A Commentary.* Oakland, Calif.: International Council on Biblical Inerrancy, 1980.

Stonehouse, Ned B. *The Witness of Matthew and Mark to Christ*. 2d 1ed. Grand Rapids: Eerdmans, 1958.

Stonehouse, Ned B., and Paul Wooley, eds. *The Infallible Word*. Philadelphia: Presbyterian Guardian, 1946.

Streeter, B. H. *The Four Gospels: A Study of Origins*. London: Macmillan, 1936.

Stromberg, Roland N. *An Intellectual History of Modern Europe*. New York: Appleton-Century-Crofts, 1966.

Sturz, Harry A. *The Byzantine Text-Type and New Testament Textual Criticism*. Nashville: Thomas Nelson, 1984.

Sundberg, Albert C., Jr. *The Old Testament of the New Testament Church*. Cambridge, Mass.: Harvard University Studies XX, Harvard U., 1964.

Swete, Henry Barclay. *An Introduction to the Old Testament in Greek*. 2d ed. Cambridge: Cambridge U., 1902.

Tenney, Merril C., ed. *The Bible: The Living Word of Revelation*. Grand Rapids: Zondervan, 1968.

———. *New Testament Survey.* Rev. ed. Grand Rapids: Eerdmans, 1961.

———, ed. *The Word for This Century.* New York: Oxford U., 1960.

Terry, Milton S. *Biblical Hermeneutics*. Grand Rapids: Zondervan, 1950.

Thielicke, Helmut. *The Evangelical Faith*. Vol. 1, *Prolegomena: The Relation of Theology to Modern Thought-Forms*. Grand Rapids: Eerdmans, 1974.

Thomas, Robert L., and Stanley N. Gundry, eds. *A Harmony of the Gospels with Explanations and Essays: Using the Text of the New American Standard Bible*. Chicago: Moody, 1978; San Francisco: Harper & Row, 1985.

Thomas, W. H. Griffith. *Christianity Is Christ*. Chicago: Moody, 1965.

Thorndike, Lynn. *A History of Magic and Experimental Science*. 8 vols. New York: Columbia U., 1923-1958.

Torrey, C. C. *The Apocalyptic Literature: A Brief Introduction*. New Haven: Yale U., 1945. Reprint. Hamden, Conn.: Archon, 1963.

———. *The Four Gospels*. New York: Harper, 1933.

Unger, Merrill F. *Archeology and the New Testament*. Grand Rapids: Zondervan, 1962.

———. *Archaeology and the Old Testament*. Grand Rapids: Zondervan, 1954.

———. *Commentary on Zechariah*. Grand Rapids: Zondervan, 1963.

———. *Introductory Guide to the Old Testament*. 2d ed. Grand Rapids: Zondervan, 1956.

Van Bruggen, Jakob. *The Ancient Text of the New Testament*. Translated by C. Kleijn. Winnipeg, Canada: Premier, 1976.

Van Loon, Henrik W. *The Story of the Bible*. Garden City, N.Y.: Garden City, 1941.

Vawter, Bruce. *Biblical Inspiration*. Philadelphia: Westminster, 1972.

Voobus, Arthur. *Early Versions of the New Testament*. Stockholm: Estonian Theological Society in Exile, 1954.

Wade, Ira. *The Intellectual Origins of the French Enlightenment*. Princeton, N.J.: Princeton U., 1971.

Walker, Williston. *A History of the Christian Church*. 3d ed. rev. by Robert T. Handy. New York: Scribner's, 1970.

Wallis, Ethel Emily, and Mary Angela Bennett. *Two Thousand Tongues to Go*. New York: Harper, 1959.

Walvoord, John F., ed. *Inspiration and Interpretation*. Grand Rapids: Eerdmans, 1957.

Warfield, Benjamin B. *The Inspiration and Authority of the Bible*. Philadelphia: Presbyterian & Reformed, 1948.

———. *An Introduction to the Textual Criticism of the New Testament*. London: 1886.

———. *Syllabus on the Special Introduction to the Catholic Epistles*.

Wenham, John W. *Christ and the Bible*. Downers Grove, Ill: InterVarsity, 1973.

Westcott, Brooke Foss. *The Bible in the Church*. 2d ed. New York: Macmillan, 1887.

———. *A General Survey of the History of the Canon of the New Testament*. 6th ed. New York: Macmillan, 1889. Reprint. Grand Rapids: Baker, 1980. Note Appendix D, "The Chief Catalogues of the Books of the Bible During the First Eight Centuries," especially item XIV, which is an extract from *The Festive Letters of Athanasius,* translated from the Syriac by the Rev. H. Burgess.

———. *History of the English Bible*. New York: Macmillan, 1905.

———. *An Introduction to the Study of the Gospels*. 7th ed. London: Macmillan, 1888.

Wikgren, Allen P. *The Text, Canon and Principal Versions of the Bible, an Extract from the Twentieth Century Encyclopedia of Religious Knowledge*. Grand Rapids: Baker, 1955.

Wildeboer, Gerrit. *The Origin of the Canon of the Old Testament*. London: Luzac, 1895.

Williams, C. S. C. *Alterations to the Text of the Synoptic Gospels and Acts*. Oxford: Basil Blackwell, 1951.

Williams, Charles B. *Interim Report on Vocabulary Selection*. London: 1936.

Williams, George Huntston. *The Radical Reformation*. Philadelphia: Westminster, 1962.

Wilson, Clifford A. *Rocks, Relics and Biblical Reliability*. Grand Rapids: Zondervan; Probe Ministries International, 1977.

Wilson, Robert Dick. *A Scientific Investigation of the Old Testament*. Chicago: Moody, 1959.

Winer, George Benedict. *A Grammar of the Idiom of the New Testament Greek*. 8th English ed. Translated by W. F. Moulton, from 2d ed. Edinburgh: T. & T. Clark, 1877.

Wolfson, Harry Austryn. *Philo: Foundations of Religious Philosophy in Judaism, Christianity, and Islam*. Vol 2. Cambridge, Mass.: Harvard U., 1962.

Woodbridge, John D. *Biblical Authority: A Critique of the Rogers/McKim Proposal*. Grand Rapids: Zondervan, 1982.

Wright, G. E., ed. *The Bible and the Ancient Near East*. Garden City, N.Y.: Doubleday, 1961.

Würthwein, Ernst. *The Text of the Old Testament*. Translated by P. R. Ackroyd. New York: Macmillan, 1957.

———. *The Text of the Old Testament: An Introduction to the Biblia Hebraica*. Translated by Erroll F. Rhodes. Grand Rapids: Eerdmans, 1979.

Young, Edward J. *An Introduction to the Old Testament*. Grand Rapids: Eerdmans, 1958.

———. *My Servants the Prophets*. Grand Rapids: Eerdmans, 1952.

Zeitlin, Solomon. *The Dead Sea Scrolls and Modern Scholarship*. Philadelphia: Dropsie College, 1956.

Index of Subjects

B

D

M

N

T

Index of Persons

H

I

J

K

M

N

S

Index of Scripture

Moody Press, a ministry of the Moody Bible Institute, is designed for education, evangelization, and edification. If we may assist you in knowing more about Christ and the Christian life, please write us without obligation: Moody Press, c/o MLM, Chicago, Illinois 60610.